T0213574

Lecture Notes in Computer Science 9720

Commenced Publication in 1973
Founding and Former Series Editors:
Gerhard Goos, Juris Hartmanis, and Jan van Leeuwen

Editorial Board

More information about this series at http://www.springer.com/series/7408

Simon Devitt · Ivan Lanese (Eds.)

Reversible Computation

8th International Conference, RC 2016
Bologna, Italy, July 7–8, 2016
Proceedings

 Springer

Editors
Simon Devitt
National Institute of Informatics
Tokyo
Japan

Ivan Lanese
University of Bologna/Inria
Bologna
Italy

ISSN 0302-9743   ISSN 1611-3349 (electronic)
Lecture Notes in Computer Science
ISBN 978-3-319-40577-3   ISBN 978-3-319-40578-0 (eBook)
DOI 10.1007/978-3-319-40578-0

Library of Congress Control Number: 2016941301

LNCS Sublibrary: SL2 – Programming and Software Engineering

Printed on acid-free paper

This Springer imprint is published by Springer Nature
The registered company is Springer International Publishing AG Switzerland

Preface

This volume contains the papers presented at RC 2016, the 8th Conference on Reversible Computation, held during July 7–8, 2016, in Bologna (Italy), hosted by the Computer Science Department of the University of Bologna.

The Conference on Reversible Computation brings together researchers from computer science, mathematics, engineering, and physics to discuss new developments and directions for future research in the emerging area of reversible computation. This includes, e.g., reversible formal models, reversible programming languages, reversible circuits, and quantum computing.

The conference received 38 submissions by authors from 22 countries. All papers were reviewed by at least three members of the Program Committee. After careful deliberations, the Program Committee selected 23 papers for presentation. In addition to these papers, this volume contains the abstracts of the two invited talks: "DEMONIC Programming: A Computational Language for Single-Particle Equilibrium Thermodynamics, and Its Formal Semantics" by Samson Abramsky (University of Oxford, UK) and "Classical Problems to Make Quantum Computing a Reality" by Adam Whiteside (University of Melbourne, Australia and Google).

The conference would not have been possible without the enthusiasm of the members of the Program Committee; their professionalism and their helpfulness were exemplary. For the work of the Program Committee and the compilation of the proceedings, the EasyChair system was employed, which was extermely useful. Finally, we would like to thank all the authors for their submissions, their willingness to continue improving their papers, and their presentations!

April 2016

Ivan Lanese
Simon Devitt

Organization

Program Committee

Michael Bremner	University of Technology, Sydney, Australia
Andrew Cross	IBM T.J. Watson Research Center, USA
Simon Devitt	NII, Japan
Gerhard Dueck	University of New Brunswick, Canada
Simon Gay	University of Glasgow, UK
Robert Glück	University of Copenhagen, Denmark
Jarkko Kari	University of Turku, Finland
Ivan Lanese	University of Bologna, Italy and Inria, France
Michael Miller	University of Victoria, Canada
Alexandru Paler	University of Passau, Germany
Markus Schordan	Lawrence Livermore National Laboratory, USA
Ulrik Schultz	University of Southern Denmark, Denmark
Peter Selinger	Dalhousie University, Canada
Indranil Sengupta	Indian Institute of Technology, Kharagpur, India
Mathias Soeken	University of Bremen, Germany
Jean-Bernard Stefani	Inria, France
Irek Ulidowski	University of Leicester, UK
Benoît Valiron	CentraleSupélec, France
Rodney Van Meter	Keio University, Japan
Robert Wille	University of Bremen, Germany
Tetsuo Yokoyama	Nanzan University, Japan

Additional Reviewers

Axelsen, Holger Bock	Mezzina, Claudio Antares
Cristescu, Ioana	Mogensen, Torben Ægidius
De Vos, Alexis	Oppelstrup, Tomas
Giachino, Elena	Phillips, Iain
Kaarsgaard, Robin	Quaglia, Francesco
Klimov, Andrei	Thomsen, Michael Kirkedal

Abstracts of Invited Talks

Classical Problems to Make Quantum Computing a Reality

Adam C. Whiteside[1,2], Austin G. Fowler[2,1]

[1]Centre for Quantum Computation and Communication Technology,
School of Physics, The University of Melbourne,Victoria, 3010, Australia
[2]Google Inc., Santa Barbara, CA 93117, USA
(Dated: April 15, 2016)

Recent experiments have shown exciting progress toward creating reliable quantum bits (qubits) that will make up tomorrow's quantum computers. While experiments and engineers continue to make the physical side a reality, computer scientists and software engineers will be essential to getting the most out of such expensive hardware. An entire stack of classical software must be developed, requiring creative solutions to a broad range of problems. We provide an introduction to quantum computing and an overview of the problems left to face in an effort to inspire more research in these important areas.

DEMONIC Programming: A Computational Language for Single-particle Equilibrium Thermodynamics, and its Formal Semantics

Samson Abramsky[1] and Dominic Horsman[2]

[1]Department of Computer Science, University of Oxford, Wolfson Building,
Parks Road, Oxford, OX1 3QD, UK
samson.abramsky@cs.ox.ac.uk
[2]Joint Quantum Centre Durham-Newcastle, Durham University,
Department of Physics, Rochester Building, Science Laboratories,
South Road, Durham DH1 3LE, UK
dominic.horsman@durham.ac.uk

Abstract. Maxwell's Demon, 'a being whose faculties are so sharpened that he can follow every molecule in its course', has been the centre of much debate about his abilities to violate the second law of thermodynamics. Landauer's hypothesis, that the Demon must erase its memory and incur a thermodynamic cost, has become the standard response to Maxwell's dilemma, and its implications for the thermodynamics of computation reach into many areas of quantum and classical computing. It remains, however, still a hypothesis.

Debate over the existence of an erasure cost for information has often centred around simple toy models of a single particle in a box. Despite their simplicity, the ability of these systems to accurately represent thermodynamics (specifically to satisfy the second law) and whether or not they display Landauer Erasure, has been a matter of ongoing argument. The recent Norton-Ladyman controversy is one such example.

In this paper we give a computational language for formal reasoning about thermodynamic systems. We formalise the basic single-particle operations as statements in the language, and then show that the second law must be satisfied by any composition of these basic operations. This is done by finding a computational invariant of the system. We show, furthermore, that this invariant requires an erasure cost to exist within the system, equal to $kT \ln 2$ for a bit of information: Landauer Erasure becomes a theorem of the formal system. The Norton-Ladyman controversy can therefore be resolved in a rigorous fashion, and moreover the formalism we introduce gives a set of reasoning tools for further analysis of Landauer erasure, which are provably consistent with the second law of thermodynamics.

Contents

Quantum Computing

Quantum Programming

Circuit Theory

Syntheses

Process Calculi

Rigid Families for the Reversible π-Calculus

Ioana Cristescu[1]([✉]), Jean Krivine[2], and Daniele Varacca[3]

[1] Harvard Medical School, Boston, USA
ioana_cristescu@hms.harvard.edu
[2] IRIF - Équipe PPS - Université Paris Diderot, Paris, France
jean.krivine@pps.univ-paris-diderot.fr
[3] LACL - Université Paris Est - Créteil, Créteil, France
daniele.varacca@u-pec.fr

Abstract. Rigid families, a causal model for concurrency based on configuration structures, can interpret CCS and the π-calculus. However, it is also a causal model suited for reversible calculi. In this paper we use rigid families to give a denotational representation to the reversible π-calculus. The reversible π-calculus defines a causal semantics for the π-calculus as well. We discuss the difference in the two causal representations, in rigid families and in the reversible π-calculus.

Reversible calculi allow one to backtrack computation events as long as the causal order between events is respected: one cannot undo the cause before the effect. Moreover, in reversible operational semantics [1–3] backtracking is also *maximally concurrent*: any forward execution is a valid backward path.

In this paper we are interested in an extensional or non-interleaving representation of reversible calculi and in particular the reversible π-calculus [4]. In configuration structures [5], one uses sets of events, called *configurations*, to represent reachable states of computations. The extensional behaviour of a process is represented as a domain the elements of which are configurations ordered by set inclusion. It is noteworthy that such non-interleaving models are implicitly reversible as the inclusion between configurations dictates the allowed forward and backward transitions.

Rigid families [6,7] is a non interleaving model that is close to configuration structures. In this model, configurations are additionally equipped with a partial order on events, called *precedence*, that is a *temporal* relation between computation events that is made during the run of a process. When two events are not ordered by precedence one can see them as having occurred either simultaneously or in such a way that no common clock can be used to compare them. More traditional causality and concurrency relations are derivable from precedence.

Though there have been several non interleaving models proposed for process algebra, one may argue that rigid families is the most suited formalism to study causal semantics of the π-calculus [7] where two notions of causality coexist. A first type of causality, induced by the prefix operator, is called *structural*.

This work was partly supported by the ANR-11-INSE-0007 REVER and by the ICT COST Action IC1405.

S. Devitt and I. Lanese (Eds.): RC 2016, LNCS 9720, pp. 3–19, 2016.
DOI: 10.1007/978-3-319-40578-0_1

The second type of causality is *contextual* and induced by the mechanism of scope extrusion. We illustrate these two notions with some examples.

The process $\bar{b}\langle a\rangle.a(d)$ is an example for structural causality: the communication on channel b occurs always before the one on channel a. The same situation, this time due to contextual causality, occurs in $\nu a(\bar{b}\langle a\rangle \mid a(d))$, where one cannot use channel a to communicate with the environment as a is private. However, a can be sent on channel b. The output of a private name a to the context is traditionally called *scope extrusion*, and we say that the event that sends a on channel b is an *extruder* of a. Once the context receives a it can use it for future communications. However, contextual causality can also be *disjunctive*. In the following process $\nu a(\bar{b}\langle a\rangle \mid \bar{c}\langle a\rangle \mid a(d))$ the name is a is private but there are two possible extruders of a: one on channel b and the other on channel c. Only one of the two is responsible for the sending of a to the context, but there are executions in which we cannot tell which of the two is the cause. In the trace

$$\nu a(\bar{b}\langle a\rangle \mid \bar{c}\langle a\rangle \mid a(d)) \xrightarrow{\bar{b}\langle a\rangle} \xrightarrow{\bar{c}\langle a\rangle} \xrightarrow{a} 0$$

either the output on channel b or the one on channel c is the cause. If the execution backtracks the communication on b, while b is the cause, we are reaching an inconsistent state, where the cause is undone before the effect. Thus, detecting which extruder is the cause of the communication on channel a is important for a correct backtracking mechanism.

Rigid families can express both structural and contextual causality and disambiguate examples as the one above. It was therefore postulated (see Ref. [4]) that in addition of being a suitable causal model for the classical π-calculus, rigid families should naturally represent reversible computations of the π-calculus [4]. This is what this paper investigates.

Outline. This paper is as self contained as space permits although familiarity with the π-calculus [8] is assumed. In Sect. 1 we briefly introduce the reversible π-calculus. In Sect. 2 we recall how rigid families are defined and, following Ref. [4], show how one can interpret the π-calculus. In Sect. 3 we present the first contribution of this paper, which is the interpretation of *reversible* π-processes in terms of rigid families. Both the reversible π-calculus and the rigid families provide a causal semantics for the π-calculus. In Sect. 4 we compare the two. The second contribution of the paper is presented Sect. 5, where we show an operational correspondence between reversible π processes and their encoding in rigid families. We conclude with Sect. 6.

1   The Reversible π-calculus

In this section we give a brief summary of the syntax and the semantics of the reversible π-calculus. We let the reader refer to Ref. [4] for more details.

Rπ processes use memories, added on top of simple π processes to record past computations. Every entry in a memory, called an event, can be used to backtrack. We use the same notations as in Ref. [4]. Denote I the set of event identifiers, with a distinguished symbol $* \in \mathsf{I}$. Let i, j, k range over elements of I and Δ, Γ range over subsets of I. Terms are built according to the following grammar:

$$
\begin{aligned}
P, Q &:: = 0 \parallel \pi.P \parallel (P \mid Q) \parallel \nu a(P) && (\pi \text{ processes}) \\
R, S &:: = 0 \parallel m \rhd P \parallel (R \mid S) \parallel \nu a_\Gamma(R) && (\text{R}\pi \text{ processes}) \\
m &:: = \emptyset \parallel \curlyvee.m \parallel e.m && (\text{memory stacks}) \\
e &:: = \langle i, k, \alpha \rangle && (\text{memory events}) \\
\alpha &:: = \overline{b}\langle a \rangle \parallel b[*/c] \parallel b[a/c] && (\text{event labels})
\end{aligned}
$$

where $\pi :: = b(c) \mid \overline{b}\langle a \rangle \mid \tau$ denotes π prefixes.

We store two types of information in the memory. The first is a fork symbol $\curlyvee$, which distributes memory stacks whenever processes are forking. Secondly, events are stored in the memory as triplets of the form $\langle i, k, \alpha \rangle$. For any event $e = \langle i, k, \alpha \rangle$, we say that $i \in \mathsf{I} - \{*\}$ is the *identifier* of e, $k \in \mathsf{I}$ is the identifier of its *contextual cause* and α its *label*. The label of an event is similar to π prefixes, except that we also store the substitution in case of a synchronisation.

For all events $e = \langle i, k, \alpha \rangle$, we define $id(e) = i$, $c(e) = k$ and $\ell(e) = \alpha$.

Some syntactically correct processes are not correct semantically. Henceforth we only consider semantically correct, reachable processes.

Definition 1 (Relations on events [4, Definition 2.2]). *Let R be a process, we define the following relations on events of R.*

- *Structural causal relation: $e' \sqsubset_R e$ if there exists $m \in R$ such that $m = m_2.e.m_1.e'.m_0$ for some (possibly empty) m_2, m_1, m_0. Structural causality is propagated by synchronisations, thus we use $\sqsubset_R^*$ to denote the transitive closure of $\sqsubset_R$.*
- *Contextual causal relation: $e' \ll_R e$ if $c(e) = id(e')$.*
- *Instantiation relation: $e' \leadsto_R e$ if $e' \sqsubset_R e$ and $\ell(e') = b[a/c]$, for some name a, b, c and c is in subject position in $\ell(e)$. Furthermore for all memories m, we write $\mathsf{inst}_m(c) = i$ if there is an event of the form $\langle i, k, b[a/c] \rangle$ in m that instantiates c. Note that there is at most one such event in m. If no such event exists in m we write $\mathsf{inst}_m(c) = *$.*

For any events $e \in R$ and $e' \in R$ such that $id(e) = i$ and $id(e') = j$, we use the overloaded notations $i \sqsubset_R j$ or $i \ll_R j$, if e and e' are in the corresponding relation. Define in a similar manner $i \leadsto_R j$ iff $e \leadsto_R e'$ for $id(e) = i$, $id(e') = j$ and $\star \leadsto_R j$, for any $j \in \mathsf{I}$.

Definition 2 (Structural congruence [4, Section 2-A]). *Structural congruence on monitored processes is the smallest equivalence relation generated by the following rules:*

$$\frac{P \equiv Q}{m \triangleright P \equiv m \triangleright Q} \qquad (\pi \text{ congruence})$$

$$m \triangleright (P|Q) \equiv (\curlyvee.m \triangleright P | \curlyvee.m \triangleright Q) \qquad (\text{distribution memory})$$

$$m \triangleright \nu a(P) \equiv_m \nu a_\emptyset(m \triangleright P) \text{ with } a \notin m \qquad (\text{scope of restriction})$$

The third rule in the definition above rewrites π-calculus restrictions into
Rπ restrictions. An Rπ restriction is indexed by a set $\Gamma \subset \mathsf{I}$ (initially empty)
and behaves as a classical restriction only when $\Gamma = \emptyset$. It will be used to keep
track of past variable scope whenever $\Gamma \neq \emptyset$.

Definition 3 (Bound, free and liberated names [4, Section 2-A]). *Free
and liberated names are defined inductively on the structure of processes ($f(a)$
denotes either* $\mathrm{fn}(a)$ *or* $\mathrm{lib}(a)$ *whenever the distinction is irrelevant):*

$$
\begin{aligned}
f(\nu a_\emptyset R) &= f(R) - \{a\} & (\Gamma \neq \emptyset)\ f(\nu a_\Gamma R) &= f(R) \cup \{a\} \\
f(R \mid S) &= f(R) \cup f(S) & \mathrm{fn}(\bar{b}\langle a\rangle.P) &= \mathrm{fn}(P) \cup \{a, b\} \\
\mathrm{fn}(m \triangleright P) &= \mathrm{nm}(m) \cup \mathrm{fn}(P) & \mathrm{lib}(m \triangleright P) &= \emptyset \\
\mathrm{fn}(b(a).P) &= \{b\} \cup (\mathrm{fn}(P) - \{a\})
\end{aligned}
$$

with $\mathrm{nm}(m)$ *being all the names occurring in the memory* m. *All liberated names
are free. As usual, names which are not free in* R *are called bound.*

1.1 Name Substitution

In the late LTS of the π-calculus substitutions are applied only upon synchronisation. However, in the case of reversible processes, we do not apply a substitution
directly on the process as it can lead to cases where the backtracking is ambigu-
ous. Instead we use *explicit* substitutions: the substitutions are recorded in the
memory and are applied only when needed. Therefore, after a synchronisation
we *update* the memory in order to store the new substitution. A process communicating on a liberated channel, has to make an assumption on the identity of
the event that made the channel public (via an *extrusion*), called its *contextual
cause*. The initial assumption can be made more precise while more structure of
the process is revealed by the LTS, thus we also need to update the contextual
cause.

Definition 4 (Memory updates [4, Definition 2.1]). *The synchronisation
update, denoted by* $R_{[a/c]@i}$, *replaces the partial substitution* $[\star/c]$ *with the complete substitution* $[a/c]$ *at the event identified by* $i \in \mathcal{I} - \{\star\}$, *it is defined as:*

$$
\begin{aligned}
(R \mid S)_{[a/c]@i} &= R_{[a/c]@i} \mid S_{[a/c]@i} \\
(\nu a'_\Gamma R)_{[a/c]@i} &= \nu a'_\Gamma (R_{[a/c]@i}) \\
(\langle i, \_, b[\star/c]\rangle.m \triangleright P)_{[a/c]@i} &= \langle i, \_, b[a/c]\rangle.m \triangleright P \\
(m \triangleright P)_{[a/c]@i} &= m \triangleright P \quad \text{otherwise}
\end{aligned}
$$

The contextual cause update, denoted by $R_{[k/k']@i}$ *proceeds similarly but substi-
tutes the old cause* k' *for a new one:*

$$\begin{aligned}
(R \mid S)_{[k/k']@i} &= R_{[k/k']@i} \mid S_{[k/k']@i} \\
(\nu a_\Gamma R)_{[k/k']@i} &= \nu a_\Gamma(R_{[k/k']@i}) \\
(\langle i, k', \_ \rangle.m \rhd P)_{[k/k']@i} &= \langle i, k, \_ \rangle.m \rhd P \\
(m \rhd P)_{[k/k']@i} &= m \rhd P \quad otherwise
\end{aligned}$$

The substitutions on a variable are applied only when a process uses it for a communication. The *public name* is thus a name on which all the substitutions were applied.

Definition 5 (Public label [4, Definition 2.3]). *For all process of the form* $m \rhd \pi.P$ *let* $m[\pi]$ *be the* public label *of* π. *It is defined by lexicographical induction on the pair* (π,m):

$$\begin{aligned}
\emptyset[a] &= a & m[b(c)] &= m[b](c) \\
m[\overline{b}\langle a \rangle] &= \overline{m[b]}\langle m[a] \rangle & (\langle i, k, b[c/a] \rangle.m)[a] &= c \\
(\langle i, k, b[\star/a] \rangle.m)[a] &= a & (\Upsilon.m)[a] &= m[a] \\
(e.m)[a] &= m[a] \ otherwise
\end{aligned}$$

We recall the following notations from Ref. [4]: we write $m \in R$ if there exists a context $C[\bullet]$ such that $R = C[m \rhd P]$. Similarly we write $e \in R$ when there is $m \in R$ such that $m = m_1.e.m_0$ for some (possibly empty) m_1 and m_0. Finally for all $i \in \mathsf{I}$ we write $i \in R$ if there exists $e \in R$ such that $id(e) = i$ or $c(e) = i$.

1.2 The LTS

The label ζ of a transition $t : R \xrightarrow{\zeta} S$ is a quadruple of the form $(i, j, k) : \alpha$ where $i \in \mathcal{I} - \{*\}$ is the *identifier* of t, $j \in \mathcal{I}$ is the instantiator of i and $k \in \mathcal{I}$ is the contextual cause of i. The labels α are built on the following grammar:

$$\alpha ::= b(c) \| \overline{b}\langle a \rangle \| \overline{b}(\nu a_\Gamma)$$

where $\overline{b}(\nu a_\Gamma)$ corresponds to the bound output of the π-calculus, whenever $\Gamma = \emptyset$, and otherwise corresponds to a free output, decorated with a set of event identifiers. We extend the subj and obj functions from the π-calculus in a straightforward manner in order to include labels $\overline{b}(\nu a_\Gamma)$.

The labelled transition system of $\mathrm{R}\pi$ can be divided into positive rules, presented in Fig. 1, and negative rules, derived from the positive ones by simply inverting the rules and keeping the side conditions invariant. We denote $\xrightarrow{\zeta}$ the *positive* transitions and $\xrightarrow{\zeta^-}$ the *backward* ones. The notation $i =_* j$, for $i, j \in I$, stands for $* \in \{i, j\}$ or $i = j$.

Note that the complete positive LTS contains also the symmetrical rules for the COM+, CLOSE+ and PAR+ rules with respect to the $\mid$ operator.

2 Rigid Families for the π-Calculus

In this section we introduce the rigid families [9] and recall how they can be used as a model for the π-calculus [7]. We first introduce unlabelled rigid families, and then, using the set of labels of the π-calculus, we define the labelled rigid families.

$$\text{In+} \frac{i \notin m \quad j = \text{inst}_m(b)}{m \rhd b(c).P \xrightarrow{(i,j,*):m[b(c)]} \langle i, *, b[\star/c] \rangle.m \rhd P}$$

$$\text{Out+} \frac{i \notin m \quad j = \text{inst}_m(b)}{m \rhd \overline{b}\langle a \rangle.P \xrightarrow{(i,j,*):m[\overline{b}\langle a \rangle]} \langle i, *, \overline{b}\langle a \rangle \rangle.m \rhd P}$$

$$\text{Open+} \frac{R \xrightarrow{(i,j,k):\alpha} R' \quad \alpha = \overline{b}\langle a \rangle \vee \alpha = \overline{b}\langle \nu a_{\Gamma'} \rangle}{\nu a_\Gamma R \xrightarrow{(i,j,k):\overline{b}\langle \nu a_\Gamma \rangle} \nu a_{\Gamma+i} R'} \qquad \text{New+} \frac{R \xrightarrow{\varsigma} R'}{\nu a_\Gamma R \xrightarrow{\varsigma} \nu a_\Gamma R'} a \notin \varsigma$$

$$\text{Cause ref+} \frac{R \xrightarrow{(i,j,k):\alpha} R' \quad a \in subj(\alpha) \quad either k = k'}{\nu a_\Gamma R \xrightarrow{(i,j,k'):\alpha} \nu a_\Gamma R'_{[k'/k]@i}} or \exists k' \in \Gamma, k \rightsquigarrow_R k'$$

$$\text{Com+} \frac{R \xrightarrow{(i,j,k):\overline{b}\langle a \rangle} R' \quad S \xrightarrow{(i,j',k'):b(c)} S' \quad k =_* j'}{R \mid S \xrightarrow{(i,*,*):\tau} R' \mid S'_{[a/c]@i}} k' =_* j$$

$$\text{Close+} \frac{R \xrightarrow{(i,j,k):\overline{b}\langle \nu a_\Gamma \rangle} R' \quad S \xrightarrow{(i,j',k'):b(c)} S' \quad k =_* j'}{R \mid S \xrightarrow{(i,*,*):\tau} \nu a_\Gamma(R' \mid S'_{[a/c]@i})} k' =_* j \; with \; a \notin \text{fn}(S) \; whenever \; \Gamma = \emptyset$$

$$\text{Par+} \frac{R \xrightarrow{(i,j,k):\alpha} R'}{R \mid S \xrightarrow{(i,j,k):\alpha} R' \mid S} \text{bn}(\alpha) \cap \text{fn}(S) = \emptyset, i \notin S \qquad \text{Mem+} \frac{R \equiv_m S \xrightarrow{\varsigma} S' \equiv_m R'}{R \xrightarrow{\varsigma} R'}$$

Fig. 1. The positive rules of the LTS

2.1 The Unlabelled Rigid Families

A set equipped with a partial order is denoted x, with $|x|$ the underlying set and $e \leq_x e'$ whenever $(e, e') \in x$. The partial orders are called *precedences*, and they represent temporal ordering between the events.

Definition 6 (Rigid families [7, Definitions 1 and 2]).

– Rigid inclusion *of partial orders* $x \preceq y$ *is defined iff the following hold:*

$$|x| \subseteq |y| \; and \; \begin{cases} \forall e, e' \in x : e \leq_x e' \iff e \leq_y e' \\ \forall e \in y, \forall e' \in x, e \leq_y e' \implies e \in x \end{cases}$$

– *A* rigid family $\mathcal{F} = (E, C)$ *is a set of events E and a non-empty family C of partial orders, called* configurations*, such that* $\forall x \in C, |x| \in \mathcal{P}(E)$ *and C is downward closed w.r.t. rigid inclusion:* $\forall y \preceq x, y \in C$.
– *A* rigid morphism *on rigid families* $f : (E, C) \to (E', C')$ *is a partial function on events* $f : E \rightharpoonup E'$ *that is* local injective:

$$for \; all \; x \in C, e, e' \in x, f(e) = f(e') \implies e = e'$$

and that extends to a (total) function on configurations:

$$f(x) = x' \; iff \; \begin{cases} |x'| = \{f(e) \mid e \in x\} \\ e \leq_x e' \iff f(e) \leq_{x'} f(e') \end{cases}$$

Rigid families and their morphisms form a category. Next, let us define some operations on rigid families. In the following $E^\star = E \cup \{\star\}$.

Definition 7 (Operations on rigid families [7, Definition 6]).

1. **Product.** *Let $\star$ denote undefined for a partial function. Define $(E,C) = (E_1, C_1) \times (E_2, C_2)$ where $E = E_1 \times_\star E_2$ is the product in the category of sets and partial functions with the projections $\sigma_1 : E \to E_1^\star$, $\sigma_2 : E \to E_2^\star$. Define the projections $\pi_1 : (E,C) \to (E_1, C_1)$, $\pi_2 : (E,C) \to (E_2, C_2)$ such that $\pi_1(e) = \sigma_1(e)$ and $\pi_2(e) = \sigma_2(e)$ and the collection of configurations $x \in C$ such that the following hold:*
   (a) x is a partial order with $|x| \in \mathcal{P}(E)$;
   (b) $\pi_1(x) \in C_1$ and $\pi_2(x) \in C_2$;
   (c) $\forall e, e' \in x$, if $\pi_1(e) = \pi_1(e') \neq \star$ or $\pi_2(e) = \pi_2(e') \neq \star$ then $e = e'$.
   (d) $\forall e, e' \in |x|$, $e <_x e' \iff \pi_1(e) <_{\pi_1(x)} \pi_1(e')$ and $\pi_2(e) <_{\pi_2(x)} \pi_2(e')$, where $\pi_i(e)$ defined.
   (e) $\forall y \preceq x$ we have that $\pi_1(y) \in C_1$ and $\pi_2(y) \in C_2$.
2. **Restriction.** *Define the restriction of an upward closed set of configurations $X \subseteq C$ as $(E,C) \upharpoonright X = (\cup C', C')$ with $C' = C \setminus X$. We equip the operation with a projection $\pi : (E,C) \upharpoonright X \to (E,C)$ such that π is the identity on events.*
3. **Prefix.** *Define $e.(E,C) = (e \cup E, C' \cup \emptyset)$, for $e \notin E$ where*

$$x' \in C' \iff x' = (\{e <_{x'} e' \mid \forall e' \in x\} \cup x) \text{ for some } x \in C.$$

Let $\pi : e.(E,C) \to (E,C)$ the projection such that $\pi(e)$ is undefined and π is the identity on the rest of the events.

Causality and concurrency. Precedence is a partial order that is local to a configuration, but one may also define a global (partial) order as follows.

Definition 8 (Causality [7, Definition 3]). *Let $e, e' \in E$ for (E,C) a rigid family. Define $e' < e$ if there exists $x \in C$ such that $e, e' \in x$ and for every $y \in C$, if $e, e' \in y$ then $e' <_y e$.*

We can generalise Definition 8 to define *disjoint* causality: i.e. an event e_1 is caused by either e_2 or e_3.

Definition 9 (Disjoint causality [7, Definition 4]). *Let (E,C) a rigid family and $e \in E$, $X \subset E$ such that $e \notin X$. Then X is a disjoint causal set for e, denoted $X < e$ iff the following hold:*

1. **disjointness** $\forall e' \in X$, $\exists x \in C$ such that $e' <_x e$ and $\forall e'' \in X \setminus e'$, $e'' \not<_x e$.
2. **completeness** $\forall x \in C$, $e \in x \implies \exists e' \in X$ such that $e' <_x e$;

In particular $e' < e$ whenever $\{e'\} < e$.

Definition 10 (Concurrency [7, Definition 5]). *Let (E,C) a rigid family and $e, e' \in E$. Define $e \lozenge e' \iff \exists x \in C$, $e, e' \in x$ such that $e' \not<_x e$ and $e \not<_x e'$.*

Example 1. Consider as an example the rigid family in the left of Fig. 2 corresponding to the product of $(\emptyset \prec \{e_1\})$ and $(\emptyset \prec \{e_2\})$. We have that $e_1 \lozenge e_2$ thanks to the configuration $\{e_1, e_2\}$.

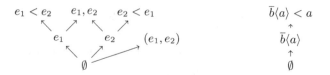

Fig. 2. Examples of rigid families

2.2 The Labelled Rigid Families for the π-Calculus

Definition 11 (Labelled rigid families [7, Definition 7]). *A labelled rigid family $\mathcal{F} = (E, C, \ell, \mathsf{P})$ is a rigid family equipped with a distinguished set of names P (the private names of $\mathcal{F}$) and a labelling function $\ell : E \to L$, where L is the set of labels.*

As in Rπ we apply the substitutions only when needed. Let Σ be the set of all name substitutions. Consider the function $\sigma_x : x \to \Sigma$ that returns a set of substitutions in x. We can then apply the substitutions to the label of e.

Definition 12 (Substitution [7, Definition 13]). *We define σ_x by induction on the partial order in x:*

$$\sigma_\emptyset = \emptyset$$
$$\sigma_x = \sigma_{x \backslash e} \ \textit{if} \ \ell(e) \neq (d(a), \overline{b}\langle a' \rangle)$$
$$\sigma_{x \backslash e} \cup \{a'/a\} \ \textit{if} \ \ell(e) = (d(a), \overline{b}\langle a' \rangle) \ \textit{and} \ \{a''/a'\} \notin \sigma_{x \backslash e}$$
$$\sigma_{x \backslash e} \cup \{a''/a\} \ \textit{if} \ \ell(e) = (d(a), \overline{b}\langle a' \rangle) \ \textit{and} \ \{a''/a'\} \in \sigma_{x \backslash e}$$

Define $\ell_x(e) = \ell(e)\sigma_x$, where

$$\big(d(a)\big)\sigma_x = \begin{array}{l} d'(a) \ \textit{if} \ \{d'/d\} \in \sigma_x \\ d(a) \ \textit{otherwise} \end{array} \qquad \big(\overline{b}\langle a \rangle\big)\sigma_x = \begin{array}{l} \overline{b'}\langle a' \rangle \ \textit{if} \ \{b'/b\}, \{a'/a\} \in \sigma_x \\ \overline{b}\langle a' \rangle \ \textit{if} \ \{a'/a\} \in \sigma_x \\ \overline{b'}\langle a \rangle \ \textit{if} \ \{b'/b\} \in \sigma_x \end{array}$$
$$\big((\alpha, \beta)\big)\sigma_x = \big((\alpha)\sigma_x, (\beta)\sigma_x\big) \qquad \overline{b}\langle a \rangle \ \textit{otherwise}$$

The label $\ell_x(e)$ is the *public label* of an event, similar to the public label in Rπ.

The product of rigid families, as in other models for concurrency [10,11], creates all pairs of events that respects the constraints imposed by the morphisms. Labels are then used to detect and remove the events that do not correspond to events in the parallel composition of processes. We do not give here the formal definition of an allowed label[1]. Intuitively, disallowed labels cannot occur during a run of the encoded process. We then extend the operations of Definition 7 in order to take labels into account.

---

[1] The reader can refer to the appendix or to [7] for the formal definition.

Definition 13 (Dynamic label [7, Definition 17]). *Define the dynamic label of an event as* $\widehat{\ell_x}(e) = \ell_x(e)$ *if* $\ell_x(e)$ *is allowed and* $\bot$ *otherwise.*

Definition 14 (Operations on labelled rigid families [7, Definition 10]).

1. **Restriction of a name.** *Let a be a free name. Then* $(E, C, \ell, \mathsf{P}) \upharpoonright a = (E, C, \ell, \mathsf{P} \cup \{a\}) \upharpoonright X$, *where* $x \in X$ *iff* $\exists e \in x$ *such that* $\widehat{\ell_x}(e) = \bot$.
2. **Prefix.** *Define* $\alpha.(E, C, \ell, \mathsf{P}) = (E', C', \ell', \mathsf{P})$ *where, for some* $e \notin E$, $e.(E, C) = (E', C')$ *and* $\ell'(e) = \alpha$ *and* $\ell'(e') = \ell(e')$ *for* $e' \neq e$.
3. **Product.** *Let* $(E, C) = (E_1, C_1) \times (E_2, C_2)$ *be the product and* π_1, π_2 *the projections* $\pi_i : (E, C) \to (E_i, C_i)$. *Then*

$$(E_1, C_1, \ell_1, \mathsf{P}_1) \times (E_2, C_2, \ell_2, \mathsf{P}_2) = (E, C, \ell, \mathsf{P}_1 \cup \mathsf{P}_2)$$

where $\ell(e) = \begin{cases} \ell_i(\pi_i(e)) & \text{if } \pi_{3-i}(e) = \star \\ (\ell_1(\pi_1(e)), \ell_2(\pi_2(e))) & \text{otherwise} \end{cases}$

4. **Parallel composition.** *Define*

$$(E_1, C_1, \ell_1, \mathsf{P}_1) \mid (E_2, C_2, \ell_2, \mathsf{P}_2) = ((E_1, C_1, \ell_1, \mathsf{P}_1) \times (E_2, C_2, \ell_2, \mathsf{P}_2)) \upharpoonright X$$

where $x \in X$ *iff* $\exists e \in x$ *such that* $\widehat{\ell_x}(e) = \bot$.

A rigid family $\mathcal{F}$ is *sound* iff $\forall x \in \mathcal{F}, \forall e \in x, \widehat{\ell_x}(e) \neq \bot$. All operations defined above preserve the class of sound rigid families. The interpretation of a π process as a rigid family is defined by induction on the structure of a term:

$$\llbracket \alpha.P \rrbracket = \alpha.\llbracket P \rrbracket \quad \llbracket P \mid Q \rrbracket = \llbracket P \rrbracket \| \llbracket Q \rrbracket \quad \llbracket \nu a(P) \rrbracket = \llbracket P \rrbracket \upharpoonright a \quad \llbracket 0 \rrbracket = \mathbf{0}$$

One can then show that the encoding is correct by showing that there is an *operational correspondence* between π-processes and their encoding in rigid families. This consists in introducing an LTS defined on rigid families and then establishing a bisimulation between P and $\llbracket P \rrbracket$.

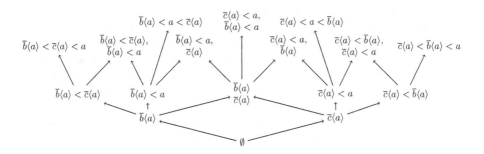

Fig. 3. $\nu a(\overline{b}\langle a \rangle \mid \overline{c}\langle a \rangle \mid a)$ in rigid families

Example 2. Consider first the encoding of the process $\bar{b}\langle a\rangle.a$ depicted in the right of Fig. 2, where events are replaced by their labels. We have that $\{\bar{b}\langle a\rangle\}$ is the (only) causal set for a, that is $\bar{b}\langle a\rangle < a$. Moreover, the process $\nu a(\bar{b}\langle a\rangle \mid a)$ has the same interpretation as $\bar{b}\langle a\rangle.a$.

Let us now consider the process $\nu a(\bar{b}\langle a\rangle \mid \bar{c}\langle a\rangle \mid a)$ with its encoding in rigid families presented in Fig. 3. The disjoint causal set for the event labelled a consists of the events labelled $\bar{b}\langle a\rangle$ and $\bar{c}\langle a\rangle$, that is $\{\bar{b}\langle a\rangle, \bar{c}\langle a\rangle\} < a$.

3   Encoding the Reversible π-Calculus

In this section we present our first contribution, which consists in interpreting reversible π-processes in rigid families. We use a similar encoding to the one proposed in Ref. [12] for the encoding of reversible CCS in configuration structures. However, there are notable differences due to name substitution and the extrusion of private names, mechanisms specific to the π-calculus.

The interpretation of a reversible process R consists in a tuple $(\mathcal{F}, x)$, where $x \in \mathcal{F}$ is a configuration, called the *address* of R in $\mathcal{F}$. The tuple $(\mathcal{F}, x)$ can mimick the computations of R: for every forward transition $R \xrightarrow{(i,j,k):\alpha} S$ there exists a configuration $y \in \mathcal{F}$ such that $y = x \cup \{e\}$ and $\ell_y(e) = \alpha$. Similarly, for a backward transition $R \xrightarrow{(i,j,k):\alpha^-} S$, there exists $y \in \mathcal{F}$ such that $x = y \cup \{e\}$ and $\ell_y(e) = \alpha$. The new configuration y is then the address of S inside the same rigid family $\mathcal{F}$.

The configuration $x = \emptyset$ of a rigid family $\mathcal{F}$ corresponds to the initial state of a computation, that is a process with an empty memory. A reversible process R can backtrack all events in its memory until the process with an empty memory is reached. We call this process the *origin* of R and denote it O_R. We apply an *erase* function on O_R, denoted ε, which consists in simply removing the empty memory from the structure of the process. Thus one obtains a π process, which is then encoded in a rigid family using the operations in Definition 14.

In order to interpret a reversible process R one has first to backtrack R to its origin and encode $\varepsilon(O_R)$ in a rigid family $\mathcal{F}$. The encoding of R is then defined by induction on a (forward) trace $\sigma : O_R \longrightarrow^* R$. The address of the origin is the empty set in $\mathcal{F}$ and every transition in σ is mimicked by a transition inside the same rigid family $\mathcal{F}$. We denote the interpretation of R as $[\![R]\!]_\sigma = (\mathcal{F}, x)$. The configuration x is thus the address of R, which corresponds to the computational state of R, in the sense that they agree on all possible future and past computations.

In the memory of a reversible process we also encode causal relation between events (see Definition 1). We want to ensure that we have the same causal information in the address of the process. For example, consider the origin process $P = \bar{a}\langle d\rangle.\bar{b}\langle c\rangle.Q \mid \bar{b}\langle c\rangle.Q$ and the trace $\emptyset \triangleright P \xrightarrow{(i',*,*):\bar{a}\langle d\rangle} R' \xrightarrow{(i,*,*):\bar{b}\langle c\rangle} R$, where we know, by inspecting the memory of R whether $i <_R i'$ or not. We keep track of causality in the rigid family by defining a label and order-preserving bijection between events in R and events in the address of R. The bijection is augmented whenever R does a forward computation and reduced when R backtracks.

Definition 15 (Encoding an Rπ process in rigid families).

$$[\![R]\!]_\sigma = (\mathcal{F}, \mathrm{ad}_\mathcal{F}(\emptyset, \emptyset, O_R \longrightarrow^\star R)) \text{ where } \mathcal{F} = [\![\varepsilon(O_R)]\!], \sigma : O_R \longrightarrow^\star R \text{ and}$$

$$\mathrm{ad}_\mathcal{F}(x_1, f, R_1 \xrightarrow{(i,j,k):\alpha} R_2 \longrightarrow^\star R_3) = \mathrm{ad}_\mathcal{F}(x_2, f \cup \{e \leftrightarrow i\}, R_2 \longrightarrow^\star R_3)$$

$$where \begin{cases} (a) & \exists x_2 \in \mathcal{F}, x_1 \prec x_2 \text{ and } |x_2| = |x_1| \cup \{e\} \\ (b) & \ell_{x_2}(e) = \alpha \\ (c) & [\![\varepsilon(R_2)]\!] = (\mathcal{F} \setminus x_2) \\ (d) & \forall l \in \mathsf{I}(R_2), l <_{R_2} i \text{ and } l \neq k \iff f(l) <_{x_2} e \\ (e) & f(k) <_{x_2} e \end{cases}$$

$$\mathrm{ad}_\mathcal{F}(x, f, R_2 \longrightarrow^\star R_3) = x \text{ if } R_2 = R_3$$

In the definition above we denote $\mathrm{ad}_\mathcal{F}(x, f, R \longrightarrow^\star S)$ a function that computes the address of S, given $\mathcal{F}$ a rigid family, with $x \in \mathcal{F}$ and f a label and order-preserving bijection between events in R and events in x. It also takes as input a trace from R to S. We initially call the function on the empty set of $\mathcal{F}$ and with an empty bijection, that is $\mathrm{ad}_\mathcal{F}(\emptyset, \emptyset, O_R \longrightarrow^\star R)$, and proceed by induction on the trace $\sigma : O_R \longrightarrow^\star R$.

In computing the next address there are several constraints that have to be met, described informally above. Consider the transition $R_1 \xrightarrow{(i,j,k):\alpha} R_2$ and let x_1 be the address of R_1 in $\mathcal{F}$. Then x_2 is the address of R_2 if x_1 can be extended to x_2 (condition a) with an event e that has the corresponding label (condition b) and causal relations in x_2 (conditions d and e). Condition c ensures that R_2 and x_2 agree on future computations.

Remark 1 (Auto-concurrency). The encoding looks for a configuration that has the same past and the same future as the process. It might not always be the case that such a configuration is unique. For instance in the process $a \mid a$ one cannot choose between the two identical singleton configurations. Such processes exhibit *auto-concurrency* [13] and for simplicity we do not consider them in this paper.

Lemma 1 (Soundness of the encoding). *Let R be an Rπ process, O_R its origin and $\sigma : O_R \longrightarrow^\star R$ a trace. Denote $\mathcal{F} = [\![\varepsilon(O_R)]\!]$ the encoding of O_R. There exists $x \in \mathcal{F}$ such that $[\![R]\!]_\sigma = (\mathcal{F}, x)$.*

Proof (Sketch). We use the correspondence between the π-calculus and Rπ from Ref. [4]. Also we have to define an LTS on rigid families and use the correspondence between the π-calculus and rigid families from Ref. [7]. We can then proceed by induction on the trace.

Lemma 1 shows that the encoding is correct: a configuration corresponding to the computational state of a reversible process always exists. The encoding is parametric on the trace. Given a trace from the origin of a process R that leads to R there exists a unique[2] configuration that corresponds to R. However the configuration corresponding to R should be the same for any trace $O_R \longrightarrow^* R$. This is required by the notion of backtracking used in reversible operational semantics: any forward execution is a valid backward path.

Lemma 2. *Let R a process. There exists $x \in [\![\varepsilon(O_R)]\!]$ a configuration such that for all $\sigma : O_R \longrightarrow^* R$ one has $[\![R]\!]_\sigma = x$.*

Proof. It follows from configurations being uniquely identified by the order on the events, by their labels and by their "future".

4   Causality

In Sect. 3 we presented the encoding of an $R\pi$ term in rigid families. Then in Sect. 5 we will see that we can establish a (weak form) of operational correspondence between $R\pi$ processes and their interpretation in rigid families. Usually, the operational correspondence consists in establishing a bisimulation relation between a process and its encoding. However we cannot show this (strong form of) correspondence as a reversible π process and its interpretation in rigid families are not bisimilar. This is due, intuitively, to the fact that in rigid families all temporal orderings are explicit, not just the causal ones. In this section we make this intuition more concrete, by discussing the difference in the causality relations induced in $R\pi$ and in rigid families.

We say that a configuration x in $\mathcal{F}$ is a *temporal* order if for two events $e, e' \in x$ such that $e <_x e'$, $\exists y \in \mathcal{F}$ with $e \Diamond_y e'$. On the other hand, it is a *causal* order if whenever $e, e' \in x$ such that $e <_x e'$, $\nexists y \in \mathcal{F}$ with $e \Diamond_y e'$.

Example 3. Consider the process $P = \overline{a}\langle d \rangle \mid \overline{b}\langle c \rangle$ with its encoding $[\![P]\!]$ depicted in Fig. 4, where events are replaced by labels. The configurations $\{\overline{a}\langle d \rangle < \overline{b}\langle c \rangle\}$ and $\{\overline{b}\langle c \rangle < \overline{a}\langle d \rangle\}$ are temporal, while $\{\overline{a}\langle d \rangle, \overline{b}\langle c \rangle\}$ is causal. There is no back-and-forth bisimulation between P and $[\![P]\!]$. In a temporal configuration (for instance $\{\overline{a}\langle d \rangle < \overline{b}\langle c \rangle\}$) backtracking can only follow the exact order of the forward execution.

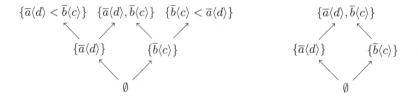

Fig. 4. $\overline{a}\langle d \rangle \mid \overline{b}\langle c \rangle$ in rigid families vs. the LTS of $\overline{a}\langle d \rangle \mid \overline{b}\langle c \rangle$ in RCCS

---

[2] From Remark 1.

The causal configurations capture the structural causality induced by a term. Thus one should consider only the orders that are causal and ignore the ones that are temporal. We can define an operator, applied on a rigid familiy that removes the temporal configurations. This step is not compositional, however.

Lemma 3 (Maximal concurrency). *Let $\mathcal{F}$ a rigid family. $\{\mathcal{F}\}$ is obtained by removing all temporal configurations in $\mathcal{F}$:*

$$\{\mathcal{F}\} = \mathcal{F} \upharpoonright X \; where$$
$$x \in X \iff \forall e, e' \in x \; if \; e <_x e' \; then \; \forall Y \subseteq E \; with \; Y < e, e' \notin Y.$$

Proof. We show that the set X defined above is upward closed. The rest follows from the restriction operator in Definition 7. X is upward closed follows from the rigid inclusion between sets.

Remark 2 (Maximal and minimal concurrent versions of a rigid family). $\{[\![P]\!]\}$ preserves all causal configurations and removes all temporal ones. Let us define an opposite operation that removes causal configurations. Denote $\{\{[\![P]\!]\}\}$ the rigid family $[\![P]\!] \upharpoonright X$, where

$$x \in X \iff \exists e, e' \in x, e \diamondsuit_x e'.$$

The rigid family $\{\{[\![P]\!]\}\}$ contains all temporal configurations in $[\![P]\!]$. It follows from a property on rigid families [7] which states that whenever two events are concurrent in a configuration, there exist two temporal configurations that orders the two events.

Considering only forward transitions, one can establish bisimulations between $\{\{[\![P]\!]\}\}$ and either $\{[\![P]\!]\}$ or $[\![P]\!]$. Intuitively, the only difference between the three encodings consists in the backtracking mechanism, and thus the three are bisimilar for the forward computations.

However, rigid families cannot capture the contextual causality as it is defined in Rπ.

Example 4. Consider $P = \nu a(\bar{b}\langle a \rangle.a \mid \bar{c}\langle a \rangle)$ a process with a private name a. The event labelled $\bar{b}\langle a \rangle$ is both a contextual and a structural cause for the input on a. The encoding of P is shown in Fig. 5. Denote with e, e', e'' three events such that $\ell(e) = \bar{b}\langle a \rangle$, $\ell(e') = \bar{c}\langle a \rangle$ and $\ell(e'') = a$. The only causal set for event e'' is the singleton $X = \{e\} < e''$. The set $Y = \{e, e'\}$ is not disjoint and it is not a causal set for e''. Lemma 3 applied on this structure yields the rigid family at the right in Fig. 6.

In Rπ however, there exists a trace where e'' chooses e' as contextual cause. In such a trace it is not possible then to reverse neither e or e'' before e. The LTS of P is depicted in the left of Fig. 6 and indeed, it contains an additional configuration corresponding to the case where e' is a contextual cause.

Note that the encoding of $\nu a(\bar{b}\langle a \rangle.a \mid \bar{c}\langle a \rangle)$ is isomorphic to the encoding of $\bar{b}\langle a \rangle.a \mid \bar{c}\langle a \rangle$. It suggest that in order to capture the causality in Rπ, one needs an ad-hoc condition on rigid families that takes into account labels and private names.

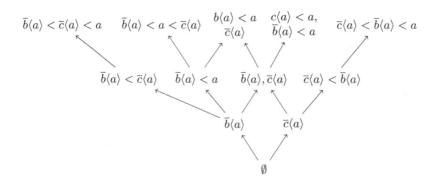

Fig. 5. $[\![\nu a(\overline{b}\langle a\rangle.a \mid \overline{c}\langle a\rangle)]\!] \cong [\![(\overline{b}\langle a\rangle.a \mid \overline{c}\langle a\rangle)]\!]$

$R\pi$ and rigid families both induce causal semantics for the π-calculus. Both integrate reversibility and account for a contextual cause in the case of scope extrusion. Which one is better?

The causal relation in rigid families is coarser than the one in $R\pi$ but it is sufficient for the correctness criteria for reversibility mentioned in the introduction, which consists in *causal consistency* and *maximal concurrency*. These correctness criteria do not require to explicitly choose a contextual cause when a structural one is available. In rigid families, as all temporal orders are explicit, there are configurations where an event is preceded by several contextual causes. It is however not a global relation and it is up to the context to materialise it (i.e. to transform precedence into structural causality).

The contextual causality induced in $R\pi$ satisfies the correctness criteria of reversibility as well. Moreover it also captures the information flow. The contextual cause of an event always precedes the event due to a structural link *in the context*. It is the scope extrusion mechanism that guarantees that such a

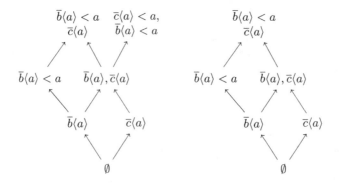

Fig. 6. The LTS in $R\pi$ of $\nu a(\overline{b}\langle a\rangle.a \mid \overline{c}\langle a\rangle)$ and $\{[\![\nu a(\overline{b}\langle a\rangle.a \mid \overline{c}\langle a\rangle)]\!]\}$

structural causality exists in the context. In the process $P = \nu a(\overline{b}\langle a\rangle.a \mid \overline{c}\langle a\rangle)$ of Example 4 if the contextual cause of a is $\overline{c}\langle a\rangle$, then a possible reduction context is $C[\cdot] = c(d).\overline{d}$. Thus the synchronisation on channel c structurally precedes the one on channel a. This type of causality requires one to inspect the labels and track the information flow of a name, which is possible in the syntactic setting of Rπ but it is a contrived relation in rigid families.

5 Operational Correspondence Between Rπ and Rigid Families

We have seen in the example above that we do not have a bisimulation between R and $\llbracket R \rrbracket$. Instead we show Theorem 1 where we only consider transitions on rigid families where both the source and the target of the transitions are interpretations of processes. Let us first define a reversible LTS on rigid families.

Definition 16 (Reversible LTS in rigid families). *Define* $(\mathcal{F}, x_1) \xrightarrow{\ell(e)} (\mathcal{F}, x_2)$ *for* $x_1 \prec x_2$ *and* $|x_2| = |x_1| \cup \{e\}$. *Similarly,* $(\mathcal{F}, x_2) \xrightarrow{\ell(e)^-} (\mathcal{F}, x_1)$. *For* $x_1,\ x_2$ *above, one can write* $x_1 \xrightarrow{e} x_2$ *and* $x_2 \xrightarrow{e^-} x_1$.

Theorem 1 (Operational correspondence between an Rπ process R and its image in rigid families). *Let* R *a process and* $\llbracket R \rrbracket = (\mathcal{F}, x)$ *its interpretation.*

1. *$\forall \alpha,\ S$ and $i, j, k \in \mathsf{I}$ such that $R \xrightarrow{(i,j,k):\alpha} S$ then $\llbracket R \rrbracket \xrightarrow{\alpha} \llbracket S \rrbracket$;*
2. *$\forall \alpha,\ S$ and $i, j, k \in \mathsf{I}$ such that $R \xrightarrow{(i,j,k):\alpha^-} S$ then $\llbracket R \rrbracket \xrightarrow{\alpha^-} \llbracket S \rrbracket$;*
3. *$\forall e \in E,\ (\mathcal{F}, x) \xrightarrow{\ell(e)} (\mathcal{F}, y)$ such that $\exists S$ with $(\mathcal{F}, y) = \llbracket S \rrbracket$ then for some $i, j, k \in \mathsf{I},\ R \xrightarrow{(i,j,k):\alpha} S$;*
4. *$\forall e \in E,\ (\mathcal{F}, x) \xrightarrow{\ell(e)^-} (\mathcal{F}, y)$ such that $\exists S$ with $(\mathcal{F}, y) = \llbracket S \rrbracket$ then for some $i, j, k \in \mathsf{I},\ R \xrightarrow{(i,j,k):\alpha^-} S$ and $\llbracket S \rrbracket = (\mathcal{F}, y)$.*

Proof (Sketch).

1. As $R \xrightarrow{(i,j,k):\alpha} S$, $O_R = O_S$ and there exists a trace $O_R \longrightarrow^\star R \xrightarrow{(i,j,k):\alpha} S$. We have that $\llbracket S \rrbracket = (\mathcal{F}, x_s)$, where $x_s = \mathrm{ad}_{\mathcal{F}}(\emptyset, f_\emptyset, O_R \longrightarrow^\star S) = \mathrm{ad}_{\mathcal{F}}(\emptyset, f_\emptyset, O_R \longrightarrow^\star R \xrightarrow{i:\alpha} S)$ and $x_R \prec x_S$, $x_R \setminus x_S = \{e\}$, $\ell(e) = \alpha$ by Lemma 1. As $\llbracket R \rrbracket = (\mathcal{F}, x_R)$ it follows that $(\mathcal{F}, x_R) \xrightarrow{\alpha} (\mathcal{F}, x_S)$.
2. Consider the transition $(\mathcal{F}, x) \xrightarrow{e} (\mathcal{F}, y)$ with $y \in \mathcal{F}$, $|y| = |x| \cup \{e\}$ and $x \prec y$. We have that $\llbracket \varepsilon(R) \rrbracket = \mathcal{F} \setminus x$ and $\{e\}$ is a configuration in $\llbracket \varepsilon(R) \rrbracket$. Then $\llbracket \varepsilon(R) \rrbracket \xrightarrow{e} \llbracket \varepsilon(R) \rrbracket \setminus \{e\} \implies \varepsilon(R) \xrightarrow{\ell(e)} P$ and $\llbracket P \rrbracket \cong \llbracket \varepsilon(R) \rrbracket \setminus \{e\}$ which follows from the correspondence between the π-calculus and the rigid families. It implies that $\exists i, j, k.R \xrightarrow{(i,j,k):\ell(e)} S$ and $\varepsilon(S) = P$ using the correspondence between the π-calculus and Rπ. From Definition 15, the encoding of R in

rigid families uses a bijection $f_R : I(R) \leftrightarrow x$. We extend the bijection to $f = f_R \cup \{e \leftrightarrow i\}$. We have that there exists S and $i, j, k \in I(S)$ such that $R \xrightarrow{(i,j,k):\ell(e)} S$. First we show that for all $i' \in I(R)$ if $f(i') \leq e$ then either $i' <_s i$ or $i' = k$. Secondly we show that we can derive $R \xrightarrow{(i,j,k):\ell(e)} S$ for k such that if $\exists e' \in y, e' <_y e$ and $e' \not< e$ then $f(k) = e'$. Lastly we show that for such an S we have that $[\![S]\!] = (\mathcal{F}, y)$.

6   Conclusion

In this paper we propose a denotational model for the reversible π-calculus, consisting of (i) interpretating the reversible π-calculus in rigid families and (ii) establishing an operational correspondance. Rigid families can be viewed as a causal model for process calculi. Similarly, the reversible π-calculus defines a causal semantics for the π-calculus. We compare the two causal models and show that there are subtle differences between the two, due to intuitively, the syntactic nature of causality in the reversible π-calculus.

Configuration structures and rigid families are causal models of process algebra and are thus natural fit for *causal consistent* reversibility. *Out-of-order* reversibility [14] on the other hand, cannot be interpreted in such denotational models.

References

1. Danos, V., Krivine, J.: Reversible communicating systems. In: Gardner, P., Yoshida, N. (eds.) CONCUR 2004. LNCS, vol. 3170, pp. 292–307. Springer, Heidelberg (2004)
2. Phillips, I., Ulidowski, I.: Reversibility and models for concurrency. Electron. Notes Theor. Comput. Sci. **192**, 93–108 (2007)
3. Lanese, I., Mezzina, C.A., Stefani, J.-B.: Reversing higher-order Pi. In: Gastin, P., Laroussinie, F. (eds.) CONCUR 2010. LNCS, vol. 6269, pp. 478–493. Springer, Heidelberg (2010)
4. Cristescu, I., Krivine, J., Varacca, D.: A compositional semantics for the reversible π-calculus. Proc. LICS **2013**, 388–397 (2013)
5. van Glabbeek, R.J., Plotkin, G.D.: Configuration structures. Proc. LICS **1995**, 199–209 (1995)
6. Castellan, S., Hayman, J., Lasson, M., Winskel, G.: Strategies as concurrent processes. In: Proceedings of the MFPS XXX, ENTCS, vol. 308, pp. 87–107 (2014)
7. Cristescu, I.D., Krivine, J., Varacca, D.: Rigid families for CCS and the π-calculus. In: Leucker, M., Rueda, C., Valencia, F.D. (eds.) ICTAC 2015. LNCS, vol. 9399, pp. 223–240. Springer, Heidelberg (2015)
8. Milner, R.: Communicating and Mobile Systems: The π-Calculus. Cambridge University Press, New York (1999)
9. Hayman, J., Winskel, G.: Event structure semantics for security protocols. Submitted for Publication (2013)
10. Crafa, S., Varacca, D., Yoshida, N.: Event structure semantics of parallel extrusion in the Pi-calculus. In: Birkedal, L. (ed.) FOSSACS 2012 and ETAPS 2012. LNCS, vol. 7213, pp. 225–239. Springer, Heidelberg (2012)

11. Winskel, G.: Event structure semantics for CCS and related languages. In: Nielsen, M., Schmidt, E.M. (eds.) Automata, Languages and Programming. LNCS, vol. 140, pp. 561–576. Springer, Heidelberg (1982)
12. Aubert, C., Cristescu, I.: Reversible barbed congruence on configuration structures. In: Proceedings of the ICE 2015, EPTCS, vol. 189, pp. 68–85 (2015)
13. van Glabbeek, R.J., Goltz, U.: Refinement of actions and equivalence notions for concurrent systems. Acta Inf. **37**(4/5), 229–327 (2001)
14. Phillips, I., Ulidowski, I., Yuen, S.: A reversible process calculus and the modelling of the ERK signalling pathway. In: Glück, R., Yokoyama, T. (eds.) RC 2012. LNCS, vol. 7581, pp. 218–232. Springer, Heidelberg (2013)

A Calculus for Local Reversibility

Stefan Kuhn$^{(\boxtimes)}$ and Irek Ulidowski

Department of Computer Science, University of Leicester, Leicester LE1 7RH, UK
{shk12,iu3}@le.ac.uk

Abstract. We introduce a process calculus with a new prefixing operator that allows us to model locally controlled reversibility. Actions can be undone spontaneously, as in other reversible process calculi, or as pairs of concerted actions, where performing a weak action forces undoing of another action. The new operator in its full generality allows us to model out-of-causal order computation, where effects are undone before their causes are undone, which goes beyond what typical reversible calculi can express. However, the core calculus, with a restricted form of the new operator, is well behaved as it satisfied causal consistency. We demonstrate the usefulness of the calculus by modelling the hydration of formaldehyde in water into methanediol, an industrially important reaction, where the creation and breaking of some bonds are examples of locally controlled out-of-causal order computation.

Keywords: Reversible process calculi · Local reversibility · Modelling of chemical reactions

1 Introduction

There are many different computation tasks which involve undoing of previously performed steps or actions. Consider a computation where the action a causes the action b, written $a < b$, and where the action c occurs independently of a and b. There are three executions of this computation that preserve *causality*, namely abc, acb and cab. We note that a always comes before b. There are several conceptually different ways of undoing these actions [18]. *Backtracking* is undoing in precisely the reverse order in which they happened. So, undo b undo c undo a is a backtrack of the execution acb. *Reversing* is a more general form of undoing: here actions can be undone in any order provided causality is preserved (meaning that causes cannot be undone before effects). For example, undo c undo b undo a is a reversal of acb for the events a, b and c above.

In biochemistry, however, there are networks of reactions where actions are undone seemingly *out of causal order*. The creation and breaking of molecular bonds between the proteins involved in the ERK signalling pathway is a good example of this phenomenon [16]. Let us assume for simplicity that the creation of molecular bonds is represented by actions a, b, c where, as above, $a < b$ and c is independent of a and b. In the ERK pathway, the molecular bonds are broken in the following order: undo a, undo b, undo c, which seems to undo

© Springer International Publishing Switzerland 2016
S. Devitt and I. Lanese (Eds.): RC 2016, LNCS 9720, pp. 20–35, 2016.
DOI: 10.1007/978-3-319-40578-0_2

the cause a before the effect b. The first process calculus for the out-of-causal order reversible computation was proposed in [16], where the calculus CCSK [13] which is extended with an *execution control mechanism* for managing the pattern and the direction of computation. The control mechanism is external to the processes it controls, and it can have a global scope. Out-of-causal order computation was also studied in [14,15]. Other reversible process calculi were proposed in [3–5,8–10,12,13].

We introduced informally a novel and purely local in character mechanism for undoing of computation in a short paper [7]. Here, we build a process calculus around this mechanism and give it operational semantics. We then discuss various properties that hold in the calculus. Most importantly, we show that out-of-causal order computation can be modelled in the calculus. Hence, in general, the *causal consistency* property [4] does not hold. There are reachable states that can only be arrived at by a mixture of forward and reverse steps. However, we argue that causal consistency holds in a restricted version of our calculus, thus the full calculus is in effect a "conceptual" extension of a causally consistent reversible process calculus. The benefits of the calculus are shown by modelling hydration of formaldehyde in water. The molecules of formaldehyde and water are modelled as compositions of carbon, oxygen and hydrogen atoms. When composed in parallel, the molecules react and the reactions are represented by sequences of transitions of *concerted actions*. We are able to represent different forms of reversibility, including out-of-causal-order reversibility, and computation can proceed in any directions without external control.

The novel features of our calculus are introduced via an example of catalytic reaction. Consider two molecules A and B that are only able to bond if assisted by the catalyst C. We assume $A \overset{def}{=} (a;p).A'$, $B \overset{def}{=} (b,p).B'$ and $C \overset{def}{=} (a,b).C'$. We use a new prefix operator $(s;p).P$ where s is a sequence of actions or executed actions and p is a *weak* action. Initially the actions in s,p take place, and then we compute with P. The three molecules can bond by performing synchronously the matching actions according to the function $\gamma(a,a) = c$, $\gamma(b,b) = d$ and $\gamma(p,p) = q$, producing thus new actions c,d and q. A weak action p can be left out resulting in the prefix $(s;p).P$ (as in B and C above). Actions in s can take place in any order, and p can happen if all actions in s have already taken place. Once p takes place, one of the executed actions in s must be undone immediately: this is our new mechanism for triggering reverse computation. We shall model these two almost simultaneous events as a transition of concerted actions. This is a simple but realistic representation of the mechanism of covalent bonding, the most common type of chemical bonds between atoms, hence our calculus is called a *Calculus of Covalent Bonding*.

Returning to our example, we represent the system of molecules A, B and C as $((a;p).A' \mid (b,p).B' \mid (a,b).C') \setminus \{a,b,p\}$, where ' $\mid$ ' is the parallel composition and '$\setminus$' the restriction as in CCS and ACP [1,11]. We note that A and B cannot interact initially since $\gamma(a,b)$ is not defined. But they can both interact with C:

$$(a;p).A' \mid (b,p).B' \mid (a,b).C' \xrightarrow{c[1]} (a[1];p).A' \mid (b,p).B' \mid (a[1],b).C' \xrightarrow{d[2]}$$
$$(a[1];p).A' \mid (b[2],p).B' \mid (a[1],b[2]).C'$$

where 1 and 2 are communication keys [13] indicating which pairs of actions created bonds. Molecules A and B can now do p synchronously, producing action q. This causes immediately the breaking of the bond c, which means undoing of actions a in A and C, leaving A and B bonded. We model such pairs of events by pairs of concerted actions:

$$(a[1]; p).A' \mid (b[2], p).B' \mid (a[1], b[2]).C'$$
$$\xrightarrow{\{q[3], \underline{c}[1]\}} (a; p[3]).A' \mid (b[2], p[3]).B' \mid (a, b[2]).C'$$

The bond 3 on weak actions p is unstable and thus gets *promoted* to a stable stronger bond on a and p. Finally, the catalyst dissolves the bond with B:

$$(a; p[3]).A' \mid (b[2], p[3]).B' \mid (a, b[2]).C' \Rightarrow (a[3]; p).A' \mid (b[2], p[3]).B' \mid (a, b[2]).C'$$
$$\xrightarrow{\underline{d}[2]} (a[3]; p).A' \mid (b, p[3]).B' \mid (a, b).C'$$

We note that A and B are now bonded although the synchronisation function did not allow it to happen initially. The main consequence of this is that the bond between $a[3]$ and $p[3]$ is *irreversible*, namely it cannot be undone. Looking at the pattern of doing and undoing of bonds we obtain $c[1]d[2]q[3]\underline{c}[1]\underline{d}[2]$. Since creation of bonds c and d causes the bond q, we have here an example of out-of-causal order computation.

Biochemical reactions can also be modelled, for example, with the kappa calculus [6]. Various calculi have also been employed to model biochemical processes (e.g. [2,5]), where the focus was on the modelling the reaction rates in complex networks and their interdependence. On the other hand, the question of how the behaviour of a network emerges out of the behaviour of its components has not been often addressed. An attempt at a structural modelling was [13], where global controllers were used to drive reactions forwards and in reverse. In contrast the calculus introduced in this paper has no global control and the behaviour of a biochemical network emerges from its components.

2   A Calculus of Covalent Bonding

We define the set of (forward) action labels $\mathcal{A}$ which is ranged over by a, b, c, d, e. We partition $\mathcal{A}$ into the set of *strong actions*, written as $\mathcal{SA}$, and the set of *weak actions* $\mathcal{WA}$. Reverse action labels belong to $\underline{\mathcal{A}}$, with typical members $\underline{a}, \underline{b}, \underline{c}, \underline{d}, \underline{e}$, and represent undoing of actions. The set $\mathcal{P}(\mathcal{A} \cup \underline{\mathcal{A}})$ is ranged over by L.

Let $\mathcal{K}$ be an infinite set of *communication keys* (or *keys* for short), ranged over by k, l, m, n. The Cartesian product $\mathcal{A} \times \mathcal{K}$, denoted by $\mathcal{AK}$, represents past actions, which are written as $a[k]$ for $a \in \mathcal{A}$ and $k \in \mathcal{K}$. Correspondingly, we have the set $\underline{\mathcal{AK}}$ that represents undoing of past actions. We use α, β to identify actions which are either from $\mathcal{A}$ or $\mathcal{AK}$. It will be useful to consider sequences of actions or past actions, namely the elements of $(\mathcal{A} \cup \mathcal{AK})^*$, which are ranged over by s, s' and sequences of purely past actions, namely the elements of $\mathcal{AK}^*$, which are ranged over by t, t'. The empty sequence is denoted by ϵ and $\alpha : s$ is the sequence with the head α and the tail s.

We shall also use two sets of auxiliary action labels, namely the set $(\mathcal{A}) = \{(a) \mid a \in \mathcal{A}\}$, and its product with the set of keys, namely $(\mathcal{A})\mathcal{K}$.

We now define a Calculus of Covalent Bonding, or CCB for short. The syntax is given below, where $f : \mathcal{A} \rightarrow \mathcal{A}$. We have a set of process identifiers (constants) $\mathcal{PI}$, with typical elements S, T, which contains the deadlocked process $\mathbf{0}$. The set of CCB closed terms is denoted by Proc. We shall refer to closed terms as processes, and let P, Q, R to range over processes. Each process identifier S has a defining equation $S \stackrel{def}{=} P$.

$$P ::= S \mid (s; b).P \mid P \mid Q \mid P \backslash L \mid P[f]$$

We have a prefixing operator $(s; b).P$, where s is a non-empty sequence of actions or past actions. The actions in s, which have not happened yet, can happen in any order. The action b is a weak action in $\mathcal{WA}$ and it can only happen after all actions in s have taken place. Performing b then forces undoing one of the past actions in s (using the concert rule in Fig. 4). The action after the ; in $(s; b).P$ can be omitted, in which case the prefixing is simply $(s).P$, and is the prefixing in [16]. In this form, one of the actions in s may be a weak action from $\mathcal{WA}$. If s is a single element sequence, then the action is a strong action in $\mathcal{SA}$ and the prefixing operator is the prefixing of CCS [11]. We often omit trailing $\mathbf{0}$s so, for example, $(s).\mathbf{0}$ is written as (s). All actions in s in $(s; b).P$ are strong actions (in $\mathcal{SA}$).

$P \mid Q$ represents processes P and Q which can perform actions or reverse actions on their own, or which can interact with each other according to a communication function γ (much like in ACP [1]). Or, they can perform a pair of the so-called *concerted actions*, which is the new feature of our calculus. We also have the usual restriction (encapsulation) operator $\backslash L$, where L is a set of labels, and the relabelling operator $[f]$.

The forward and reverse SOS rules for CCB are in Figs. 2, 3, 4 and 5, where the rules in Figs. 2 and 3 are influenced by [13]. Since we do not use the relabelling operator in the systems modelled in this paper, we omit all SOS rules for $[f]$. Note that the reverse rules in Fig. 3 are simply the symmetric versions of the corresponding forward rules.

We use two predicates, $\mathsf{std}(P) : \mathcal{P}(\mathsf{Proc})$ and $\mathsf{fsh}[m](P) : \mathcal{P}(\mathcal{K} \times \mathsf{Proc})$ in our SOS rules. They are defined in Fig. 1. Two further auxiliary functions, $\mathsf{k}(i) : (\mathcal{A} \cup \mathcal{A}\mathcal{K})^* \rightarrow \mathcal{P}(\mathcal{K})$ and $\mathsf{keys}(P) : \mathsf{Proc} \rightarrow \mathcal{P}(\mathcal{K})$, are also used. The function $\mathsf{k}()$ is defined as follows: $\mathsf{k}(\epsilon) = \emptyset$; $\mathsf{k}(\alpha : s) = \{l\} \cup \mathsf{k}(s)$ if $\alpha = a[l], a \in \mathcal{A}, l \in \mathcal{K}$; and $\mathsf{k}(\alpha : s) = \mathsf{k}(s)$ if $\alpha \in \mathcal{A}$. The function $\mathsf{keys}()$ is defined as $\mathsf{keys}(\mathbf{0}) = \emptyset$; $\mathsf{keys}(S) = \mathsf{keys}(P)$ if $S \stackrel{def}{=} P$; $\mathsf{keys}((s; b).P) = \mathsf{k}(s) \cup \mathsf{k}(b) \cup \mathsf{keys}(P)$; $\mathsf{keys}(P \mid Q) = \mathsf{keys}(P) \cup \mathsf{keys}(Q)$; and $\mathsf{keys}(P \backslash L) = \mathsf{keys}(P)$. Informally $\mathsf{keys}(P)$ associates with each P the set of its keys. A process P is standard, written $\mathsf{std}(P)$, if it contains no past actions. A key n is fresh in Q, written $\mathsf{fsh}[n](Q)$, if n is not used in Q. We extend the notion of fresh keys to the sequences of actions and past actions s and t via the function $\mathsf{k}()$.

$$\frac{}{\mathsf{std}(0)} \qquad \frac{\mathsf{std}(P)}{\mathsf{std}(S)} \; S \overset{def}{=} P \qquad \frac{\mathsf{k}(s) = \emptyset \quad \mathsf{std}(P)}{\mathsf{std}((s;b).P)} \qquad \frac{\mathsf{std}(P) \quad \mathsf{std}(Q)}{\mathsf{std}(P \mid Q)} \qquad \frac{\mathsf{std}(P)}{\mathsf{std}(P \setminus L)}$$

$$\frac{}{\mathsf{fsh}[m](0)} \qquad \frac{\mathsf{fsh}[m](P)}{\mathsf{fsh}[m](S)} \; S \overset{def}{=} P \qquad \frac{m \notin \mathsf{k}(s) \; m \neq n \; \mathsf{fsh}[m](P)}{\mathsf{fsh}[m]((s;b[n]).P)} \qquad \frac{m \notin \mathsf{k}(s) \quad \mathsf{fsh}[m](P)}{\mathsf{fsh}[m]((s;b).P)}$$

$$\frac{\mathsf{fsh}[m](P) \quad \mathsf{fsh}[m](Q)}{\mathsf{fsh}[m](P \mid Q)} \qquad \frac{\mathsf{fsh}[m](P)}{\mathsf{fsh}[m](P \setminus L)}$$

Fig. 1. Predicates std and fsh

$$\text{act1} \; \frac{\mathsf{std}(X) \quad \mathsf{fsh}[k](s)}{(s,a;b).X \xrightarrow{a[k]} (s,a[k];b).X} \qquad \qquad \text{act2} \; \frac{X \xrightarrow{a[k]} X' \quad \mathsf{fsh}[k](t)}{(t;b).X \xrightarrow{a[k]} (t;b).X'}$$

$$\text{par} \; \frac{X \xrightarrow{a[k]} X' \quad \mathsf{fsh}[k](Y)}{X \mid Y \xrightarrow{a[k]} X' \mid Y} \qquad \qquad \text{com} \; \frac{X \xrightarrow{a[k]} X' \quad Y \xrightarrow{b[k]} Y'}{X \mid Y \xrightarrow{c[k]} X' \mid Y'} \; \gamma(a,b) = c$$

$$\text{res} \; \frac{X \xrightarrow{a[k]} X'}{X \setminus L \xrightarrow{a[k]} X' \setminus L} \; a \notin L \qquad \qquad \text{con} \; \frac{X \xrightarrow{a[k]} X' \quad S \overset{def}{=} X}{S \xrightarrow{a[k]} X'}$$

Fig. 2. Forward SOS rules

The semantics of CCB is given by the labelled transition system (lts),

$$(\mathsf{Proc}, L, \rightarrow : \subseteq \mathsf{Proc} \times L \times \mathsf{Proc})$$

where the set of action labels L is $\mathcal{AK} \cup \underline{\mathcal{AK}} \cup (\mathcal{AK} \times \underline{\mathcal{AK}})$: it contains the pairs of concerted actions $\mathcal{AK} \times \underline{\mathcal{AK}}$ (see Fig. 4) as well as actions and past actions. The transition relation $\rightarrow$ is the least relation defined by our SOS rules and reduction rules in Definition 2.

Figure 4 contains the rule concert that defines when a pair of concerted actions takes place. We also have two auxiliary rules aux1 and aux2 which define the auxiliary transition relations needed in the concert rule. Note that aux1 and aux2 define transitions with the auxiliary labels $(b)[k]$ for all $(b) \in \mathcal{A}$ and $k \in \mathcal{K}$. Overall, transitions are labelled with $a[k] \in \mathcal{AK}$, or with $\underline{b}[l] \in \underline{\mathcal{AK}}$, or with concerted pairs $\{a[k], \underline{b}[l]\}$. Note that the concert rule uses *lookahead* [17].

We also need a reduction relation to define *promotion* of actions. First we define *free names* of processes.

Definition 1. Function fn, with $\mathsf{fn} : \mathsf{Proc} \rightarrow \mathcal{P}(\mathcal{K})$, is defined as follows: $\mathsf{fn}(0) = \emptyset$, $\mathsf{fn}(S) = \mathsf{fn}(P)$ if $S \overset{def}{=} P$, $\mathsf{fn}((\alpha : s; b).P) = \{\alpha\} \cup \mathsf{fn}(s; b).P)$, $\mathsf{fn}((a; b).P) = \{a, b\} \cup \mathsf{fn}(P)$, $\mathsf{fn}(P \mid Q) = \mathsf{fn}(P) \cup \mathsf{fn}(Q)$ and $\mathsf{fn}(P \setminus L) = \mathsf{fn}(P) \setminus L$.

Definition 2. The reduction relation $\Rightarrow$ is the smallest reflexive and transitive binary relation that satisfies the following rules: (red1) $P \mid Q \Rightarrow Q \mid P$,

$$\text{rev act1} \quad \frac{\text{std}(X) \quad \text{fsh}[k](s)}{(s, a[k]; b).X \xrightarrow{a[k]} (s, a; b).X} \qquad \text{rev act2} \quad \frac{X \xrightarrow{a[k]} X' \quad \text{fsh}[k](t)}{(t; b).X \xrightarrow{a[k]} (t; b).X'}$$

$$\text{rev par} \quad \frac{X \xrightarrow{a[k]} X' \quad \text{fsh}[k](Y)}{X \mid Y \xrightarrow{a[k]} X' \mid Y} \qquad \text{rev com} \quad \frac{X \xrightarrow{a[k]} X' \quad Y \xrightarrow{b[k]} Y'}{X \mid Y \xrightarrow{c[k]} X' \mid Y'} \; \gamma(a, b) = c$$

$$\text{rev res} \quad \frac{X \xrightarrow{a[k]} X'}{X \backslash L \xrightarrow{a[k]} X' \backslash L} \; a \notin L \qquad \text{rev con} \quad \frac{X \xrightarrow{a[k]} X'}{X \xrightarrow{a[k]} S} \; S \stackrel{def}{=} X'$$

Fig. 3. Reverse SOS rules

$$\text{aux1} \quad \frac{\text{std}(X) \quad \text{fsh}[k](t)}{(t; b).X \xrightarrow{(b)[k]} (t; b[k]).X} \qquad \text{aux2} \quad \frac{X \xrightarrow{(b)[k]} X' \quad \text{fsh}[k](t)}{(t; a).X \xrightarrow{(b)[k]} (t; a).X'}$$

$$\text{concert} \quad \frac{X \xrightarrow{(a)[k]} X' \quad X' \xrightarrow{b[l]} X'' \quad Y \xrightarrow{a[k]} Y' \quad Y' \xrightarrow{d[l]} Y''}{X \mid Y \xrightarrow{\{e[k], \underline{f}[l]\}} X'' \mid Y''}$$

$$\text{concert act} \quad \frac{X \xrightarrow{\{a[k], \underline{b}[l]\}} X' \quad \text{fsh}[k](t)}{(t; a).X \xrightarrow{\{a[k], \underline{b}[l]\}} (t; a).X'}$$

$$\text{concert par} \quad \frac{X \xrightarrow{\{a[k], \underline{b}[l]\}} X' \quad \text{fsh}[k](Y)}{X \mid Y \xrightarrow{\{a[k], \underline{b}[l]\}} X' \mid Y} \qquad \text{concert res} \quad \frac{X \xrightarrow{\{a[k], \underline{b}[l]\}} X'}{X \backslash L \xrightarrow{\{a[k], \underline{b}[l]\}} X' \backslash L}$$

Fig. 4. SOS rules for concerted transitions. Rule concert applies if 1. α is c or (c) and $\gamma(a, c) = e$ for some $c \in \mathcal{A}$, and 2. $\gamma(b, d) = f$. Rule concert res applies if $a, \underline{b} \notin L \cup (L)$.

(red2) $P \mid (Q \mid R) \Rightarrow (P \mid Q) \mid R$, (red3) $(P \mid Q) \mid R \Rightarrow P \mid (Q \mid R)$, (red4) $P \mid \mathbf{0} \Rightarrow P$, (red5) $(P \mid Q)\backslash L \Rightarrow P\backslash L \mid Q$ if $\text{fn}(Q) \cap L = \emptyset$, (red6) $P\backslash L \mid Q \Rightarrow (P \mid Q)\backslash L$ if $\text{fn}(Q) \cap L = \emptyset$, (red7) $(s; b).P\backslash(s'; b).P$ if s' is a permutation of s, (prom) $(a : t; b[k]) \Rightarrow (a[k] : t; b)$ if $a \in \mathcal{SA}, b \in \mathcal{WA}$, (move) $(a : b[k] : s) \Rightarrow (a[k] : b : s)$ if $a \in \mathcal{SA}, b \in \mathcal{WA}$, where $t \in \mathcal{AK}^*$ and $s \in (\mathcal{A} \cup \mathcal{AK})^*$.

We have two promotion rules in Definition 2. The rule prom promotes a weak bond to a strong bond. Since weak bonds are only temporary they get replaced by bonds on strong actions as soon as these become available. In more detail, after a bond is created on the weak action b another bond is broken at the same location involving a strong action, here a. This pair of concerted actions $\{b[k], a[l]\}$, for some l, results in $(a : t; b[k])$, which is subjected immediately to bond promotion from a weak b to a strong a, giving us $(a[k] : t; b)$. Now weak b can bond again. We have another rule move which promotes correspondingly a weak bond b to a strong a. In order to model what happens in chemical reactions more faithfully, we assume that prom and move are used as soon as they becomes applicable. We also have the usual structural congruence rules (sc and rev sc)

$$\text{sc} \quad \frac{X \Rightarrow^* Y \quad Y \xrightarrow{\mu} Y' \quad Y' \Rightarrow^* X'}{X \xrightarrow{\mu} X'} \qquad \text{rev sc} \quad \frac{X \Rightarrow^* Y \quad Y \xrightarrow{\mu} Y' \quad Y' \Rightarrow^* X'}{X \xrightarrow{\mu} X'}$$

Fig. 5. Structural congruence rules

in Fig. 5, where $\mu \in \mathcal{AK} \cup \underline{\mathcal{AK}} \cup (\mathcal{AK} \times \underline{\mathcal{AK}})$, which combine potentially several reductions (including prom reductions) with transitions.

Definition 3. A process P is *consistent* if $\mathsf{std}(P)$ or $Q \rightarrow^* P$ for some process Q such that $\mathsf{std}(Q)$.

Example 1. Consider the process $(a; b) \mid a \mid b$ with $\gamma(a, a) = c$ and $\gamma(b, b) = d$. After the initial synchronisation of actions a, which produces the transition $c[1]$, we have a transition with a pair of concerted actions by rule concert in Fig. 4

$$(a[1]; b) \mid a[1] \mid b \xrightarrow{\{d[2], \underline{c}[1]\}} (a; b[2]) \mid a \mid b[2]$$

since $(a[1]; b) \xrightarrow{(b[2])} (a[1]; b[2]) \xrightarrow{a[1]} (a; b[2])$ and $a[1] \mid b \xrightarrow{b[2]} a[1] \mid b[2] \xrightarrow{a[1]} a \mid b[2]$.

Example 2. Consider $(a[1]; b) \mid (a[1]; b) \mid e$ with $\gamma(a, a) = c$ and $\gamma(b, b) = d$. We clearly have the following pair of concerted actions

$$(a[1]; b) \mid (a[1]; b) \mid e \xrightarrow{\{d[2], \underline{c}[1]\}} (a; b[2]) \mid (a; b[2]) \mid e.$$

There are processes with weak actions that can potentially communicate but there are no concerted actions due to our SOS rules:

Example 3. Consider $(a[1]; b) \mid (e[2]; b) \mid (a[1], e[2])$ with $\gamma(a, a) = c$ and $\gamma(b, b) = d$. It cannot perform any concerted actions: Although $(a[1]; b) \xrightarrow{(b)[l]} \xrightarrow{a[1]} (a; b[l])$, for any l different from 1 and 2, but $(e[2]; b) \mid (a[1], e[2])$ cannot perform the $(b[l])$ transition since there are no SOS rules for parallel composition and auxiliary actions (b). This forces us to treat $(a[1]; b)$ and $(e[2]; b)$ as X and Y in the concert rule, respectively, and we notice that we cannot undo a communication on a or e.

Example 4. The transition $(a[1]; b) \mid a[1] \mid b \xrightarrow{\{d[2], \underline{c}[1]\}} (a; b[2]) \mid a \mid b[2]$ from Example 1 is followed by the application of the reduction rule prom that moves the bond 2 from the weak b to the strong a:

$$(a; b[2]) \mid a \mid b[2] \Rightarrow (a[2]; b) \mid a \mid b[2]$$

As a result, we can bond on the weak b again and, importantly, the $a[2]$ to $b[2]$ bond is irreversible as $\gamma(a, b)$ is undefined. Note that reaching this bond by computing forwards alone is not possible.

3   Properties of CCB

In this section we establish some properties of the lts for CCB. We start by showing the expected properties of keys, namely that when an action takes place it uses a fresh key, and when a past action is undone its key is removed from the resulting process. We also show that the reverse part of the transition relation inverts the forward part.

Proposition 1. *Let P be consistent. Then*

1. *If $P \xrightarrow{a[k]} Q$ then $k \notin \mathsf{keys}(P)$ and $\mathsf{keys}(Q) = \mathsf{keys}(P) \cup \{k\}$ for all Q.*
2. *If $P \xrightarrow{a[k]} Q$ then $k \in \mathsf{keys}(P)$ and $\mathsf{keys}(Q) = \mathsf{keys}(P) \setminus \{k\}$ for all Q.*
3. *$P \xrightarrow{a[k]} P'$ if and only if $P' \xrightarrow{a[k]} P$ for all P'.*

Next, we introduce some notation. We define a new transition relation $\longmapsto$ by $P \stackrel{a[k]}{\longmapsto} Q$ if $P \xrightarrow{a[k]} Q$ or $P \xrightarrow{a[k]} Q$. Process P is called the *source* and Q the *target* of $P \stackrel{a[k]}{\longmapsto} Q$. We will use $t, t', t_1, \ldots$ to denote transitions, for example $t : P \stackrel{a[k]}{\longmapsto} Q$. Two $\longmapsto$ transitions are *coinitial* if they have the same source, and they are *cofinal* if their targets are identical.

We define when two transitions are concurrent.

Definition 4. *Two coinitial transitions $P \stackrel{a[k]}{\longmapsto} P'$ and $P \stackrel{b[l]}{\longmapsto} P''$ are* concurrent *if and only if there exists $M \neq P$ such that $P' \stackrel{b[l]}{\longmapsto} M$ and $P'' \stackrel{a[k]}{\longmapsto} M$.*

Note that two concurrent transitions are coinitial and, together with the two transitions (with the target M) required by Definition 4, they form a "diamond" structure with the nodes P, P', P'' and M.

When transitions in Definition 4 are forward, we may not be able to complete the diamond as the following example shows. In such case, we say that the transitions are in *conflict*. Consider $P \stackrel{def}{=} (a).\mathbf{0} \mid (b).\mathbf{0} \mid (b).\mathbf{0}$ with $\gamma(a, b) = c$. The two coinitial transitions below are in conflict:

$$(a).\mathbf{0} \mid (b).\mathbf{0} \mid (b).\mathbf{0} \xrightarrow{c[1]} (a[1]).\mathbf{0} \mid (b[1]).\mathbf{0} \mid (b).\mathbf{0}$$
$$(a).\mathbf{0} \mid (b).\mathbf{0} \mid (b).\mathbf{0} \xrightarrow{c[2]} (a[2]).\mathbf{0} \mid (b).\mathbf{0} \mid (b[2]).\mathbf{0}$$

However, coinitial reverse transitions are concurrent:

Proposition 2 (Reverse Diamond). *Let P be a consistent process and let $t' : P \xrightarrow{a[k]} P'$ and $t'' : P \xrightarrow{b[l]} P''$ with $l \neq k$. Then t' and t'' are concurrent.*

Coinitial forward transitions are concurrent if they result in cofinal computations:

Proposition 3 (Forward Diamond). *If P is a consistent process and $t_1 \equiv P \xrightarrow{a[k]} P'$, $t_2 \equiv P \xrightarrow{b[l]} P''$, with $l \neq k$, and $P' \to^* T$ and $P'' \to^* T$, for some T, then there is M such that $P' \xrightarrow{b[l]} M$, $P'' \xrightarrow{a[k]} M$ and $M \to^* T$.*

$$act_f \; \frac{}{(a:s).X \xrightarrow{a}_f (s).X}
\qquad\qquad
par_f \; \frac{X \xrightarrow{a}_f X'}{X \mid Y \xrightarrow{a}_f X' \mid Y}$$

$$com_f \; \frac{X \xrightarrow{a}_f X' \quad Y \xrightarrow{b}_f Y'}{X \mid Y \xrightarrow{c}_f X' \mid Y'} \; \gamma(a,b)=c
\qquad
es_f \; \frac{X \xrightarrow{a}_f X'}{X\backslash L \xrightarrow{a}_f X'\backslash L} \; a \notin L$$

$$con_f \; \frac{X \xrightarrow{a}_f X'}{S \xrightarrow{a}_f X'} \; S \overset{def}{=} X
\qquad
sc \; \frac{X \Rightarrow^* Y \quad Y \xrightarrow{a}_f Y' \quad Y' \Rightarrow^* X'}{X \xrightarrow{a}_f X'}$$

Fig. 6. Syntax and SOS rules for CCB$_f$.

3.1   CCB Without Weak Actions

We now discuss the main properties of the sub-calculus of CCB that uses the simplified form of prefixing $(s).P$: namely without a weak action b following ; in $(s;b).P$. We call this calculus CCB$_s$. Its SOS rules are as for CCB except that the rules in Fig. 4 do not apply as there are no weak actions. We shall also consider the forward-only version of CCB$_s$ called CCB$_f$. The syntax of CCB$_f$ is $P ::= S \mid (s).P \mid P \mid Q \mid P\backslash L$ and the SOS rules are given in Fig. 6 (relabelling is not included); we also have the reduction rules from Definition 2 which, together with rules in Fig. 6, generate the transition relation $\rightarrow_f$ for CCB$_f$. Note that we do not record past actions (act_f rule); hence CCB$_f$ is similar to the core of ACP. We note that CCB$_s$ is different from CCSK [12,13] as it uses multiset prefixing and ACP-like communication.

We show firstly that $\rightarrow$ for CCB$_s$ is essentially conservative over $\rightarrow_f$. A process of CCB$_s$ is converted to a CCB$_f$ process by "pruning" past actions:

Definition 5. The pruning map $\pi : \text{Proc}_{CCB_s} \rightarrow \text{Proc}_{CCB_f}$ is defined as follows, where $t \in \mathcal{AK}^*$ and $s \in \mathcal{A}^*$:
$$\pi(\mathbf{0}) = \mathbf{0} \qquad\qquad \pi((s,t).P) = (s).\pi(P) \quad \pi((t).P) = \pi(P)$$
$$\pi(P \mid Q) = \pi(P) \mid \pi(Q) \quad \pi(P \backslash L) = \pi(P) \backslash L \quad \pi(S) = \pi(P) \text{ if } S \overset{def}{=} P$$

Theorem 1 (Conservation). Let $P \in \text{Proc}_{CCB_s}$.

1. If $P \xrightarrow{\mu[k]} Q$ then $\pi(P) \xrightarrow{\mu}_f \pi(Q)$.

2. If $\pi(P) \xrightarrow{\mu}_f Q$, then for any $k \in \mathcal{K}\backslash\text{keys}(P)$ there is Q' such that $P \xrightarrow{\mu[k]} Q'$ and $\pi(Q') = Q$.

We now consider the causal consistency property [4] in CCB$_s$. We define when a set of keys is a cause for another key:

Definition 6. The set of causes of a key k in P is defined as follows:
$$cau(\mathbf{0}, k) = \emptyset \qquad cau(P \mid Q, k) = cau(P,k) \cup cau(Q,k)$$
$$cau((s).P, k) = k(s) \cup cau(P,k) \text{ if } k \in \text{keys}(P) \qquad cau((\mu[k]{:}s).P, k) = \emptyset$$
$$cau((s).P, k) = \emptyset \text{ if } k \notin \text{keys}(P) \qquad cau(S) = cau(P) \text{ if } S \overset{def}{=} P$$
$$cau(P\backslash L, k) = cau(P,k)$$

If one of two coinitial transitions is forward and the other reverse, either they are concurrent or the forward transition depends causally on the reverse one. The following result holds in the full calculus CCB:

Proposition 4. If $t_1 \equiv P \xrightarrow{\mu[k]} P'$ and $t_2 \equiv P \xrightarrow{\nu[l]} P''$, then either t_1 and t_2 are concurrent or $k \in cau(P'', l)$.

We introduce a trace: a sequence of pairwise composable forward and reverse transitions over CCB_s. Traces are ranged over by $\sigma, \sigma', \sigma_1, \ldots$. Two transitions are composable if the target of the first transition is the source of the second transition. The composition of transitions is denoted by ';'. We denote the reverse transition corresponding to a forward transition t (and the forward transition corresponding to a reverse transition t) as $t^\bullet$. Similarly to denoting reverse transitions by $^\bullet$, we denote the reverse trace of σ as $\sigma^\bullet$. The empty trace with the source P is written as ϵ_P. We can now define causal equivalence between traces.

Definition 7. *Causally equivalent* traces are defined by the least equivalence relation $\asymp$ which is closed under composition and obeys the following rules, where t_1 is $P \xrightarrow{a[k]} Q$, t_2 is $P \xrightarrow{b[l]} R$, d_1 is $Q \xrightarrow{b[l]} S$ and d_2 is $R \xrightarrow{a[k]} S$:

$$t_1; d_1 \asymp t_2; d_2 \qquad t; t^\bullet \asymp \epsilon_{source(t)} \qquad t^\bullet; t \asymp \epsilon_{target(t)}$$

The first rule in Definition 7 states that the concurrent transitions t_1 and t_2 are causally independent, hence they can happen in any order. The trace $t_1; d_1$ forms a diamond with $t_2; d_2$, so the traces are causally equivalent. The remaining rules state that doing a transition and its reverse version is the same as doing nothing.

The next two results are needed to prove causal consistency for CCB_s; they follow closely [4]. The first states that any computation has a causally equivalent version in which we first compute in reverse for a while and then we only compute forwards. The second result says that a trace which has a forward-only coinitial and cofinal and causally equivalent trace can always be shortened to a forward-only trace. Then, we have the second important result for CCB_s.

Proposition 5 (Rearrangement). *If σ is a trace then there exist forward traces σ_1 and σ_2 such that $\sigma \asymp \sigma_1^\bullet; \sigma_2$.*

Proposition 6 (Shortening). *If σ_1 and σ_2 are coinitial and cofinal traces, with σ_2 forward, then there exists a forward trace σ_1' of length at most that of σ_1 such that $\sigma_1' \asymp \sigma_2$.*

Theorem 2 (Causal consistency). *Let σ_1 and σ_2 be traces. Then $\sigma_1 \asymp \sigma_2$ if and only if σ_1 and σ_2 are coinitial and cofinal.*

One of the consequences of causal consistency for sub-calculus CCB_s concerns reachability: any state that can be reached from a standard process during an arbitrary computation can be reached by computing forwards alone. This property is not valid in the full calculus CCB as can be seen in the Introduction and in Example 4. The next section explores some properties of concerted transitions.

3.2 Concerted Transitions

The properties of keys corresponding to those in parts 1 and 2 of Proposition 1 hold also for the concerted transitions in CCB.

Proposition 7. *Let P be consistent. If $P \xrightarrow{\{\mu[k],\underline{\nu}[l]\}} Q$ then $k \notin \mathrm{keys}(P)$, $l \in \mathrm{keys}(P)$ and $\mathrm{keys}(Q) = \mathrm{keys}(P) \cup \{k\} \setminus \{l\}$ for all Q.*

The property corresponding to part 3 of Proposition 1, namely $P \xrightarrow{\{\mu[k],\underline{\nu}[l]\}}$ P' if and only if $P' \xrightarrow{\{\underline{\nu}[l],\mu[k]\}} P$ does not hold in general but only in certain circumstances. Consider $(a[k]; b).Q \mid R$ and c, d such that $\gamma(a,c) = d = \gamma(b,c)$ with $R \xrightarrow{c[l]} R'$ and $R' \xrightarrow{c[k]} R''$. We obtain, by concert and prom rules,

$$(a[k]; b).Q \mid R \xrightarrow{\{\underline{d}[l],\underline{d}[k]\}} (a; b[l]).Q \mid R'' \Rightarrow (a[l]; b).Q \mid R''$$

Since $R'' \xrightarrow{c[k]} R' \xrightarrow{c[l]} R$, we get, again by concert and prom rules

$$(a[l]; b).Q \mid R'' \xrightarrow{\{\underline{d}[k],\underline{d}[l]\}} (a; b[l]).Q \mid R \Rightarrow (a[k]; b).Q \mid R$$

This gives us the following result:

Proposition 8. *Consider $(a[k]; b).Q$ for any Q and c, d such that $\gamma(a,c) = d = \gamma(b,c)$. There exist R, S and l such that $(a[k]; b).Q \mid R \xrightarrow{\{\underline{d}[l],\underline{d}[k]\}} S$ if and only if $S \xrightarrow{\{\underline{d}[k],\underline{d}[l]\}} (a[k]; b).Q \mid R$.*

4 The Hydration of Formaldehyde in Water

In this section we model the hydration of formaldehyde in an aqueous solution. Formaldehyde is a good preservative and is well known for its use in preserving specimen samples. It also serves as an important building block in many industrial processes and is therefore produced in large quantities. The reaction is shown in Fig. 7: two water molecules and formaldehyde are on the left and the resulting compound, methanediol, and one molecule of water is on the right. Note that the carbon atom is not shown in line with a common convention. It resides at the point where the lines from the oxygen and the hydrogens meet.

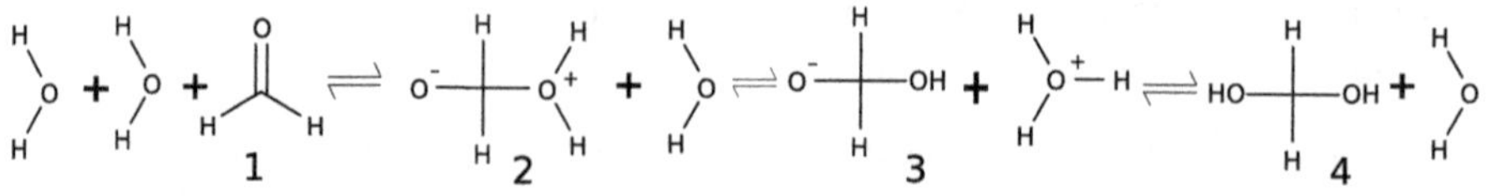

Fig. 7. The most common path through hydration of formaldehyde

The carbon in the formaldehyde has a positive partial charge and the oxygen in the water is attracted by the carbon and forms a bond to the carbon. This bond is formed out of the electrons of one of the lone pairs of the oxygen. Since the carbon cannot have more than four bonds this reaction is compensated by the double bond in the formaldehyde becoming a single bond and the electrons from the double bond forming a lone pair on the oxygen (which now has three lone pairs). These movements are concerted, namely they happen together without a stable intermediate state and cannot be separated. The resulting intermediate (denoted by 2 in Fig. 7) has one oxygen which is negatively charged, whereas the other oxygen is positively charged. The intermediate 2 abstracts one of the hydrogens to the positively charged oxygen. This leads to the intermediate 3 and a H_3O molecule, a water with and additional hydrogen and a positively charged oxygen. One of these hydrogens can be re-donated to the negatively charged oxygen. We then get the final products: methanediol and a molecule of water.

4.1   The Most Common Path Through the Reaction

We shall represent the formaldehyde molecule and the two water molecules as appropriate compositions of hydrogen, oxygen and carbon. We use our general prefixing operator, noting that O has no weak action:

$$H \stackrel{def}{=} (h; p).H' \qquad O \stackrel{def}{=} (o, o, n).O' \qquad C \stackrel{def}{=} (c, c, c, c; p).C'$$

Carbon has four strong actions c, representing the potential for four covalent bonds, and a weak action p, standing for a positive partial charge. The oxygen is modelled as a flexible element with up to 3 bonds. The action n represents the potential for a negative partial charge. The hydrogen has one strong bond h and one weak bond p. We employ subscripts to denote individual copies of actions and atoms. The synchronisation function is defined as follows: $\gamma(c_i, h_j) = c_i h_j$ for $i \in \{1, \ldots, 4\}$ and $j \in \{1, \ldots, 6\}$; $\gamma(c_i, n) = c_i n$ for $i \in \{1, \ldots, 4\}$; $\gamma(h_i, n) = h_i n$ and $\gamma(h_i, o_j) = h_i o_j$ for $i, j \in \{1, \ldots, 6\}$; and $\gamma(n, p) = np$.

The three molecules of the reaction are placed in parallel: $CH_2O \mid H_2O \mid H_2O$. Each molecule is a parallel composition of its atoms, and we use restriction to force the atoms to bond together (and in some cases to stay bonded). We also restrict actions n, p so that they can only happen together. The reaction starts from the following initial configuration, where keys $1, \ldots, 8$ specify the bonds existing initially among the atoms of formaldehyde and the two waters.

$$((c_1[1], c_2[2], c_3[3], c_4[4]; p).C' \mid (h_1[1]; p).H_1' \mid (h_2[2]; p).H_2' \mid (o_1[3], o_2[4], n).O_1'$$
$$\mid (h_3[5]; p).H_3' \mid (h_4[6]; p).H_4' \mid (o_3[5], o_4[6], n).O_2'$$
$$\mid (h_5[7]; p).H_5' \mid (h_6[8]; p).H_6' \mid (o_5[7], o_6[8], n).O_3') \setminus L$$

We have grouped all restricted actions at the outer-most level and L is $\{c_1, c_2, c_3, c_4, h_1, h_2, h_3, h_4, h_5, h_6, o_1, o_2, o_3, o_4, o_5, o_6, n, p, \underline{c_1 h_1}, \underline{c_2 h_2}\}$. Apart from the restrictions of the appropriate versions of the c_i, o_j and h_k actions, we also restrict $\underline{c_i h_i}$ for $i \in \{1, 2\}$. It prevents breaking any of the bonds between C_1 and its hydrogens H_1, H_2. This serves two purposes. Firstly, it makes sure that once we have done the p action of the carbon, we will break one of the bonds between the carbon and the oxygen. This is justified since in reality it is one of the oxygen bonds which is broken. Secondly, it also prevents O_2 or O_3 from abstracting H_1 or H_2 from the carbon.

We now model the reactions in Fig. 7. The first step is the n, p reaction between C_1 and O_2 or O_3. There are other n, p reactions that are allowed by our model: we describe them in Sect. 4.2. We assume that O_2 bonds with C_1 with key 9, followed immediately by breaking of the bond 3 or 4. Note that breaking of 1 or 2 is not possible because of the restriction on breaking $c_1 h_1$ and $c_2 h_2$. Without a loss of generality we break bond 4. These two partial reactions give us a concerted transition: we create the bond $np[9]$ and break the bond $\underline{c_4 o_2}[4]$:

$$\xrightarrow{\{np[9], \underline{c_4 o_2}[4]\}} ((c_1[1], c_2[2], c_3[3], c_4; p[9]).C' \mid (h_1[1]; p).H_1' \mid (h_2[2]; p).H_2' \mid$$
$$(o_1[3], o_2, n).O_1' \mid (h_3[5]; p).H_3' \mid (h_4[6]; p).H_4' \mid (o_3[5], o_4[6], n[9]).O_2'$$
$$\mid (h_5[7]; p).H_5' \mid (h_6[8]; p).H_6' \mid (o_5[7], o_6[8], n).O_3') \setminus L$$

Next, we promote the bond 9 of the carbon on a weak p to a stronger bond on c_4, which has become available. Using prom in Definition 2 we obtain

$$\Rightarrow ((c_1[1], c_2[2], c_3[3], c_4[9]; p).C' \mid (h_1[1]; p).H_1' \mid (h_2[2]; p).H_2' \mid (o_1[3], o_2, n).O_1'$$
$$\mid (h_3[5]; p).H_3' \mid (h_4[6]; p).H_4' \mid (o_3[5], o_4[6], n[9]).O_2'$$
$$\mid (h_5[7]; p).H_5' \mid (h_6[8]; p).H_6' \mid (o_5[7], o_6[8], n).O_3') \setminus L$$

We note that O_1 is now negatively charged (it has only one bond), but we do not need to consider it to get our desired result. The next step is to form a bond between O_3 and either H_3 or H_4. We bond with H_3 with key 10 and break the bond 5, producing a pair of concerted actions. We then promote a weak bond 9 on n in O_2 using rule move from Definition 2 to a strong bond on o_3 which has become available. Also, we promote a weak bond 10 in H_3 to a strong bond on h_3, and, by the structural congruence rule in Fig. 5, we derive the transition

$$\xrightarrow{\{np[10], \underline{h_3 o_3}[5]\}} ((c_1[1], c_2[2], c_3[3], c_4[9]; p).C' \mid (h_1[1]; p).H_1' \mid (h_2[2]; p).H_2' \mid$$
$$(o_1[3], o_2, n).O_1' \mid (h_3[10]; p).H_3' \mid (h_4[6]; p).H_4' \mid (o_3[9], o_4[6], n).O_2'$$
$$\mid (h_5[7]; p).H_5' \mid (h_6[8]; p).H_6' \mid (o_5[7], o_6[8], n[10]).O_3') \setminus L.$$

The next step is a proton transfer from O_3 to O_1. We transfer H_5, but we could have used H_6 or H_3 since they all have the p action ready. Performing the transfer of H_5 from O_3 to O_1 (and breaking the bond 7), we obtain

$$\xrightarrow{\{np[11], \underline{h_5 o_5}[7]\}} ((c_1[1], c_2[2], c_3[3], c_4[9]; p).C' \mid (h_1[1]; p).H_1' \mid (h_2[2]; p).H_2' \mid$$
$$(o_1[3], o_2, n[11]).O_1' \mid (h_3[10]; p).H_3' \mid (h_4[6]; p).H_4' \mid (o_3[9], o_4[6], n).O_2'$$
$$\mid (h_5; p[11]).H_5' \mid (h_6[8]; p).H_6' \mid (o_5, o_6[8], n[10]).O_3') \setminus L$$

and promoting the bond 10 in O_3 by the rule move and the bond 11 in H_5 by rule prom we obtain the final products of the reaction:

$$((c_1[1], c_2[2], c_3[3], c_4[9]; p).C' \mid (h_1[1]; p).H_1' \mid (h_2[2]; p).H_2' \mid (o_1[3], o_2[11], n).O_1'$$
$$\mid (h_3[10]; p).H_3' \mid (h_4[6]; p).H_4' \mid (o_3[9], o_4[6], n).O_2'$$
$$\mid (h_5[11]; p).H_5' \mid (h_6[8]; p).H_6' \mid (o_5[10], o_6[8], n).O_3') \setminus L$$

We have methanediol $CH_2(OH)_2$ and a molecule of water (oxygen O_3 plus hydrogens H_6 and H_3). Note that the n, p actions are ready again and all the existing bonds are on strong actions. So we can now reverse the reaction by getting O_3 to abstract a hydrogen from H_4 or H_5.

Finally, let us inspect the bonds with keys 4, 5 and 7 which are broken during this sequence of reactions. These bonds were formed prior to the reaction starting. They are broken as a result of application of our new general prefixing operator. This operator, in conjunction with the driving forces of the partial charges, guides the reaction without relying on any sort of global memory or global control. This is one the main advantages of our approach.

4.2   Other Paths Through the Reaction

There are two other less common ways in which the hydration of formaldehyde in water can happen. They require an additional molecule of water. The three paths through the reaction are shown in Fig. 8, now with three waters. The path in Fig. 7 is from FA | W | W | W via i2 | W | W and i3 | H_3O | W where FA stands for formaldehyde, W is water, i2 and i3 are the intermediates 2 and 3 in Fig. 7 and MD is methanediol. The other two paths start with an interaction of two water molecules which involves a hydrogen transfer and which leads to FA | W | HO | H_3O. The reaction now branches: either the HO interacts with the

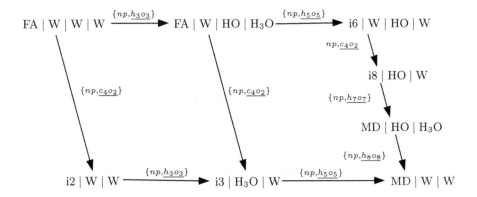

Fig. 8. Three paths through hydration of formaldehyde. Communication keys in concerted transitions are omitted for clarity. The intermediates i6 and i8 are CH_2O^+H and $COH_3O^+H_2$ respectively.

formaldehyde, which takes us to i3 | H_3O | W and then we follow the remainder of the main path, or we can go via a more complicated sequence of reactions. The H_3O interacts with the formaldehyde, then a water molecule attaches and finally an interaction with HO brings us to the final state. As we can see all the reactions but one are driven by concerted actions.

We note that in this example the rates of the individual reactions, and the overall rates achieved through the various paths, vary because of the change of energy in the products compared to the reactants. We have decided not to model rates at this stage but rather to concentrate on obtaining all possible valid reactions. We also do not consider spatial arrangement of molecules.

5   Conclusion

We have introduced a reversible process calculus CCB with a novel prefixing operator which is inspired by the mechanism of covalent bonding that allows us to model locally controlled reversibility. We have given the calculus operational semantics. The new operator permits us to perform pairs of concerted actions, where the first element of the pair is a creation of a (weak) bond and the second element is breaking one of the existing bonds. Moreover, our prefixing provides a purely local control of computation; there is no need for an extensive memory or global control. We have shown that the sub-calculus CCB_s satisfies conservation and causal consistency, and the full calculus satisfies several diamond properties. CCB is more expressive than other reversible calculi as it can also model out-of-causal order computation. We have shown that biochemical reactions with covalent bonding can be represented naturally and faithfully thanks to our new prefixing operator and concerted actions transitions.

Acknowledgements. The authors acknowledge partial support of COST Action IC1405 on Reversible Computation - extending horizons of computing.

References

1. Baeten, J.C.M., Weijland, W.P.: Process Algebra. Cambridge Tracts in Theoretical Computer Science, vol. 18. Cambridge University Press, Cambridge (1990)
2. Cardelli, L., Laneve, C.: Reversible structures. In: 9th International Conference on Computational Methods in Systems Biology, pp. 131–140. ACM (2011)
3. Cristescu, I., Krivine, J., Varacca, D.: A compositional semantics for the reversible pi-calculus. In: Proceedings of LICS 2013, pp. 388–397. IEEE, Computer Society (2013)
4. Danos, V., Krivine, J.: Reversible communicating systems. In: Gardner, P., Yoshida, N. (eds.) CONCUR 2004. LNCS, vol. 3170, pp. 292–307. Springer, Heidelberg (2004)
5. Danos, V., Krivine, J.: Formal molecular biology done in CCS-R. In: Proceedings of the 1st Workshop on Concurrent Models in Molecular Biology BioConcur 2003, ENTCS, vol. 180, pp. 31–49 (2007)

6. Danos, V., Laneve, C.: Formal molecular biology. Theoret. Comput. Sci. **325**(1), 69–110 (2004)
7. Kuhn, S., Ulidowski, I.: Towards modelling of local reversibility. In: Krivine, J., Stefani, J.-B. (eds.) Reversible Computation. LNCS, vol. 9138, pp. 279–284. Springer, Heidelberg (2015)
8. Lanese, I., Mezzina, C.A., Schmitt, A., Stefani, J.-B.: Controlling reversibility in higher-order pi. In: Katoen, J.-P., König, B. (eds.) CONCUR 2011. LNCS, vol. 6901, pp. 297–311. Springer, Heidelberg (2011)
9. Lanese, I., Mezzina, C.A., Stefani, J.-B.: Reversing higher-order pi. In: Gastin, P., Laroussinie, F. (eds.) CONCUR 2010. LNCS, vol. 6269, pp. 478–493. Springer, Heidelberg (2010)
10. Lanese, I., Mezzina, C.A., Stefani, J.-B.: Controlled reversibility and compensations. In: Glück, R., Yokoyama, T. (eds.) RC 2012. LNCS, vol. 7581, pp. 233–240. Springer, Heidelberg (2013)
11. Milner, R.: A Calculus for Communicating Systems. LNCS, vol. 92. Springer, Heidelberg (1980)
12. Phillips, I., Ulidowski, I.: Reversing algebraic process calculi. In: Aceto, L., Ingólfsdóttir, A. (eds.) FOSSACS 2006. LNCS, vol. 3921, pp. 246–260. Springer, Heidelberg (2006)
13. Phillips, I.C.C., Ulidowski, I.: Reversing algebraic process calculi. J. Log. Algebraic Program. **73**, 70–96 (2007)
14. Phillips, I., Ulidowski, I.: Reversibility and asymmetric conflict in event structures. In: D'Argenio, P.R., Melgratti, H. (eds.) CONCUR 2013 – Concurrency Theory. LNCS, vol. 8052, pp. 303–318. Springer, Heidelberg (2013)
15. Phillips, I., Ulidowski, I., Yuen, S.: Modelling of bonding with processes and events. In: Dueck, G.W., Miller, D.M. (eds.) RC 2013. LNCS, vol. 7948, pp. 141–154. Springer, Heidelberg (2013)
16. Phillips, I., Ulidowski, I., Yuen, S.: A reversible process calculus and the modelling of the ERK signalling pathway. In: Glück, R., Yokoyama, T. (eds.) RC 2012. LNCS, vol. 7581, pp. 218–232. Springer, Heidelberg (2013)
17. Ulidowski, I.: Equivalences on observable processes. In: Proceedings of LICS 1992, pp. 148–159. IEEE, Computer Science Press (1992)
18. Ulidowski, I., Phillips, I., Yuen, S.: Concurrency and reversibility. In: Yamashita, S., Minato, S. (eds.) RC 2014. LNCS, vol. 8507, pp. 1–14. Springer, Heidelberg (2014)

Static VS Dynamic Reversibility in CCS

Doriana Medić and Claudio Antares Mezzina[(⊠)]

IMT School for Advanced Studies Lucca, Lucca, Italy
{doriana.medic,claudio.mezzina}@imtlucca.it

Abstract. The notion of reversible computing is attracting interest because of its applications in diverse fields, in particular the study of programming abstractions for fault tolerant systems. Reversible CCS (RCCS), proposed by Danos and Krivine, enacts reversibility by means of memory stacks. Ulidowski and Phillips proposed a general method to reverse a process calculus given in a particular SOS format, by exploiting the idea of making all the operators of a calculus static. CCSK is then derived from CCS with this method. In this paper we show that RCCS is at least as expressive as CCSK.

1 Introduction

The interest in reversibility dates back to the 60's, with Landauer [6] observing that only irreversible computations need to consume energy, fostering application of reversible computing in scenarios of low-energy computing. Landauer's principle has only been shown empirically in 2012 [1]. Nowadays reversible computing is attracting interests because of its applications in diverse fields: biological modelling [10], since many biochemical reactions are by nature reversible; program debugging and testing [4], allowing during debugging time to bring the program state back to a certain execution point in which certain conditions are met [8]; and parallel discrete event simulations [9]. Of particular interest is the application of reversible computation notions to the study of programming abstractions for dependable systems. Several techniques used to build dependable systems such as transactions, system-recovery schemes and checkpoint-rollback protocols, rely in one way or another on some forms of undo. The ability to undo any single action provides us with an ideal setting to study, revisit, or imagine alternatives to standard techniques for building dependable systems and to debug them. Indeed distributed reversible actions can be seen as defeasible partial agreements: the building blocks for different transactional models and recovery techniques. Good examples on how reversibility in CCS and Higher-Order π can be used to model transactional models are respectively [3,7].

The first reversible variant of CCS, called RCCS, was introduced by Danos and Krivine [2]. In RCCS each process is monitored by a *memory*, that serves as stack of past actions. Memories are considered as unique process identifiers, and in order to preserve this uniqueness along a parallel composition, a structural

---

Research partly supported by the EU COST Action IC1405.

S. Devitt and I. Lanese (Eds.): RC 2016, LNCS 9720, pp. 36–51, 2016.
DOI: 10.1007/978-3-319-40578-0_3

$$P, Q ::= \mathbf{0} \mid a.P \mid \overline{a}.P \mid \tau.P \mid (P \parallel Q) \mid \sum \alpha_i.P \mid P \backslash A$$

Fig. 1. CCS syntax

law permits to obtain unique memories though a parallel composition. A general method for reversing process calculi, given in a particular SOS format, has been proposed by Phillips and Ulidowski in [11]. The main idea of this approach is the use of communication keys to uniquely identify communications, and to make *static* each operator of the calculus. By applying this method to CCS, CCSK is obtained. Since in CCSK the history is directly annotated in the process itself, there is no need of splitting history through a parallel composition. We call this kind of recording histories as *static* reversibility; while we call the one used by RCCS as *dynamic*, since each thread is endowed with its own history. Hence a natural question arises: are these two reversible calculi equivalent? In this paper we start answering to this question by showing that RCCS is at least as expressive as CCSK. We do it by means of an encoding and show its correctness by means of strong back and forth bisimulaiton.

The rest of the paper is organized as follows: Sect. 2 starts with a brief recall to the syntax of CCS. In Sect. 2.1 will present RCCS with its syntax and semantics. Section 2.2 will be about CCSK and its semantics. In Sect. 3 we will present our encoding function from CCSK to RCCS and prove our main result. In Sect. 4 we will sketch an encoding of RCCS into CCKS and discuss about the difficulties it takes to prove its correctness. Section 5 concludes the paper with a discussion of the future work.

2   CCS and Its Reversible Variants

In this section we briefly present the syntax of CCS [8], and then we show the two reversible extensions of it, namely RCCS [2] and CCSK [11].

Let $\mathcal{A}$ the set of actions such that $a \in \mathcal{A}$, and $\overline{\mathcal{A}}$ the set of co-actions such that $\overline{\mathcal{A}} = \{\overline{a} \mid a \in \mathcal{A}\}$. We let μ, λ and their decorated versions to range over the set $\mathtt{Act} = \mathcal{A} \cup \overline{\mathcal{A}}$, while we let α, β and their decorated versions to range over the set $\mathtt{Act}_\tau = \mathtt{Act} \cup \{\tau\}$, where τ is the *silent* action.

The syntax of CCS is given in Fig. 1. $\mathbf{0}$ represents the idle process. A prefix (or action) can be an input a, an output $\overline{a}$ and the silent action τ. $P \parallel Q$ represents the parallel composition of processes P and Q, while $\sum \alpha_i.P$ represents the guarded choice. Some actions in a process P can be restricted, and this is represented by the process $P \backslash A$, where A is the set of restricted actions. The set $\mathcal{P}$ denotes the set of all possible CCS processes.

2.1   Reversible CCS

One of approaches to make CCS reversible is to add a memory to each process. A memory then will be recording every action and communication that the

(CCS Processes)	$P, Q ::= \mathbf{0} \mid a.P \mid \bar{a}.P \mid \tau.P \mid (P \parallel Q) \mid \sum \alpha_i.P_i \mid P \backslash A$
(RCCS Processes)	$R, S ::= m \triangleright P \mid (R \parallel S) \mid R \backslash A$
(Memories)	$m ::= \langle \rangle \mid \langle i, \alpha, P \rangle \cdot m \mid \langle \uparrow \rangle \cdot m$

Fig. 2. RCCS syntax

process will undergo. Syntax of RCCS is given in Fig. 2. As we can see, RCCS processes are built on top of CCS processes. A term of the form $m \triangleright P$, is called *monitored* process, where m represents a memory carrying the information that this process will need in case it wants to backtrack, and P is a standard CCS process. Two monitored process R and S can be composed in parallel $S \parallel R$, and some actions of a monitored process R can be restricted via $R \backslash A$. *Memories* are organised as stacks of events, with the top of the memory representing the very last action of the monitored process. $\langle \rangle$ represent the empty memory; $\langle i, \alpha, Q \rangle$ represent an action event meaning that the monitored process did the action α identified by i and its "context" was Q; while $\langle \uparrow \rangle$ represents a splitting event. When there is no ambiguity, we will omit the trailing event $\langle \rangle$ in memories.

We assume the existence of a infinite denumerable set of action *identifiers* (sometimes called keys) $\mathcal{K}$ such that $\mathcal{K} \cap \mathsf{Act} = \emptyset$. Let $\mathsf{ActK} = \mathsf{Act} \times \mathcal{K}$ the set of pairs formed by an action μ and an identifier i. In the same way we define $\mathsf{ActK}_\tau = \mathsf{Act}_\tau \times \mathcal{K}$. The operational semantics of RCCS is defined as a labelled transition system (LTS), $(\mathcal{P}_R, \to \cup \leadsto, \mathsf{ActK}_\tau)$ where $\mathcal{P}_R$ is the set of RCCS (monitored) processes, $\to \subseteq \mathcal{P}_R \times \mathsf{ActK}_\tau \times \mathcal{P}_R$ and $\leadsto \subseteq \mathcal{P}_R \times \mathsf{ActK}_\tau \times \mathcal{P}_R$. Relations $\to$ and $\leadsto$ are the smallest reduction relations induced by respectively rules in Figs. 4 and 5. Both reduction relations exploit the structural congruence $\equiv$ relation, which is the smallest congruence, on processes and monitored processes, containing the abelian monoid laws for choice (that is *commutativity*, *associativity* and $\mathbf{0}$ as the identity element) and the rules of Fig. 3.

Remark 1. In its first incarnation [2] RCCS used events of this form $\langle n_*, \alpha, Q \rangle$, $\langle 1 \rangle$ and $\langle 2 \rangle$, where: n_* is n in case the process synchonized with a process monitored by memory n or $*$ is case of partial synchronization. Events $\langle 1 \rangle$ and $\langle 2 \rangle$ were used to split a process along a parallel composition according to the following rule:

$$m \triangleright (P \parallel Q) \equiv ((\langle 1 \rangle \cdot m \triangleright P \parallel \langle 2 \rangle \cdot m \triangleright Q)$$

The version we are using, appeared in [5], simplifies the handling of memories and makes the splitting through the parallel composition commutative. However they are conceptually the same, and we have chosen this version since it simplifies some technicalities when dealing with the proof of our main Theorem.

Identifiers of RCCS are similar to communication keys of CCSK. They are defined as follows:

$$(\textsc{Split}) \quad m \triangleright (P \parallel Q) \equiv (\langle \uparrow \rangle \cdot m \triangleright P \parallel \langle \uparrow \rangle \cdot m \triangleright Q)$$
$$(\textsc{Res}) \quad m \triangleright P \backslash A \equiv (m \triangleright P) \backslash A$$

Fig. 3. RCCS structural laws

Definition 1 (Memory Identifiers). *The set of identifiers of a memory m, written* $\mathtt{id}(m)$, *is inductively defined as follows:*

$$\mathtt{id}(\langle \uparrow \rangle \cdot m) = \mathtt{id}(m) \qquad \mathtt{id}(\langle i, \alpha, Q \rangle \cdot m) = \{i\} \cup \mathtt{id}(m)$$

Definition 2. *A identifier i belongs to a memory m, written $i \in m$, if $i \in \mathtt{id}(m)$.*

Definition 3 (Process Identifiers). *The set of identifiers of a process R, written* $\mathtt{id}(R)$, *is inductively defined as follows:*

$$\mathtt{id}(\alpha.P) = \mathtt{id}(\mathbf{0}) = \emptyset \qquad \mathtt{id}(m \triangleright P) = \mathtt{id}(m)$$
$$\mathtt{id}(R \backslash A) = \mathtt{id}(R) \qquad \mathtt{id}(R \parallel S) = \mathtt{id}(R) \cup \mathtt{id}(S)$$

Definition 4. *A identifier i belongs to a process R, written $i \in R$, if $i \in \mathtt{id}(R)$.*

$$(\text{R-ACT}) \; \frac{i \notin m}{m \triangleright \alpha.P + Q \to_\alpha^i \langle i, \alpha, Q \rangle \cdot m \triangleright P} \qquad (\text{R-PAR}) \; \frac{R \to_\alpha^i R' \quad i \notin S}{R \parallel S \to_\alpha^i R' \parallel S}$$

$$(\text{R-SYN}) \; \frac{R \to_\alpha^i R' \quad S \to_{\bar\alpha}^i S'}{R \parallel S \to_\tau^i R' \parallel S'} \qquad (\text{R-RES}) \; \frac{R \to_\alpha^i R' \quad \alpha \notin A \cup \bar A}{R \backslash A \to_\alpha^i R' \backslash A}$$

$$(\text{R-EQUIV}) \; \frac{R \equiv R \quad R' \to_\alpha^i S' \quad S' \equiv S}{R \to_\alpha^i S}$$

Fig. 4. RCCS forward semantics

Let us now comment on the forward rules of Fig. 4. Rule R-ACT allows a monitored process to perform a forward action. As we can see, this action is bound with a particular fresh identifier i. Moreover, the part of the process which has not contributed to the action, that is Q, is stored on top of the memory along with the action and the identifier. Rule R-PAR propagates an action along a parallel composition, with the condition that the identifier of the action is not used by other processes. This check guarantees that all the identifiers are unique. Rule R-SYN allows two processes in parallel to syncrhonize. To do so, they have to match both the action and the identifier. Rule R-RES deals with restriction

$$(\text{R-ACT}^\bullet) \; \frac{i \notin m}{\langle i, a, Q \rangle \cdot m \rhd P \leadsto^i_\alpha m \rhd \alpha.P + Q} \qquad (\text{R-PAR}^\bullet) \; \frac{R \leadsto^i_\alpha R' \quad i \notin S}{R \parallel S \leadsto^i_\alpha R' \parallel S}$$

$$(\text{R-SYN}^\bullet) \; \frac{R \leadsto^i_\alpha R' \quad S \leadsto^i_{\bar\alpha} S'}{R \parallel S \leadsto^i_\tau R' \parallel S'} \qquad (\text{R-RES}^\bullet) \; \frac{R \leadsto^i_\alpha R' \quad \alpha \notin A \cup \bar A}{R \backslash A \leadsto^i_\alpha R' \backslash A}$$

$$\text{R-EQUIV}^\bullet \; \frac{R \equiv R' \quad R' \leadsto^i_\alpha S' \quad S' \equiv S}{R \leadsto^i_\alpha S}$$

Fig. 5. RCCS backward semantics

in the normal way, while rule R-EQUIV brings structural equivalence into the reduction relation.

Backward rules are reported in Fig. 5. For each of forward rule there exists an opposite backward one. Rule R-ACT$^\bullet$ allows a monitored process to revert its last action. To do so, the event on top of the memory is taken and the information contained in it is used to build back the previous form of the process, that is the prefix and the process that was composed with the + operator. Rule R-PAR$^\bullet$ allows a reversible action to be propagated through a parallel composition, only when the identifier of the action does not belong to monitored processes in parallel. This check is crucial to avoid partial undo of some synchronizations. The remaining rules are similar to the forward ones.

Definition 5 (Reachable Process). *A RCCS process R is reachable if it can be derived from an initial process $\langle \rangle \rhd P$, by using rules of* Figs. 4 and 5.

Lemma 1. *For any transition $m \rhd \alpha.P + Q \to^i_\alpha \langle i, \alpha, Q \rangle \cdot m \rhd P$ we can derive the following transitions:*

- $\langle j, \beta, Q_1 \rangle \cdot m \rhd \alpha.P + Q \to^i_\alpha \langle i, \alpha, Q \rangle \cdot \langle j, \beta, Q_1 \rangle \cdot m \rhd P$, *for $i \neq j$*

- $\langle \uparrow \rangle \cdot m \rhd \alpha.P + Q \to^i_\alpha \langle i, \alpha, Q \rangle \cdot \langle \uparrow \rangle \cdot m \rhd P$

and its opposite:

Lemma 2. *For any transition $\langle i, \alpha, Q \rangle \cdot m \rhd P \leadsto^i_\alpha \langle \rangle \rhd \alpha.P + Q$, we can derive the following transitions:*

- $\langle i, \alpha, Q \rangle \cdot \langle j, \beta, Q_1 \rangle \cdot m \rhd P \leadsto^i_\alpha \langle j, \beta, Q_1 \rangle \cdot m \rhd \alpha.P + Q$, *for $i \neq j$*

- $\langle i, \alpha, Q \rangle \cdot \langle \uparrow \rangle \cdot m \rhd P \leadsto^i_\alpha \langle \uparrow \rangle \cdot m \rhd \alpha.P + Q$

An easy induction on the structure of terms provides us with a kind of normal form for RCCS processes (by convention $\prod_{i \in I} R_i = \mathbf{0}$ if $I = \emptyset$):

Lemma 3. (Normal Form). *For any RCCS reachable process R we have that*

$$R \equiv (\prod_{i \in I} (m_i \rhd \alpha_i.P_i + Q_i) \backslash A_i) \backslash B$$

2.2   CCS with Communication Keys

The main idea behind this approach is to directly record the actions inside a process and to make all the operator of CCS static. In this way there is no need of using an external memory, since all the information are syntactically presents inside a term. Syntax of CCSK is given in Fig. 6. The only difference with respect to CCS processes is that prefixes now can be annotated with an identifiers.

$$
\begin{array}{ll}
\text{(CCS Processes)} & P, Q ::= \mathbf{0} \mid a.P \mid \bar{a}.P \mid \tau.P \mid (P \parallel Q) \mid \sum \alpha_i.P_i \mid P\backslash A \\
\text{(CCSK Processes)} & X, Y ::= P \mid \alpha[i].X \mid X + Y \mid (X \parallel Y) \mid X\backslash A
\end{array}
$$

Fig. 6. CCSK syntax

Definition 6 (Process Keys). *The set of keys of a process X, written $\mathtt{key}(X)$, is inductively defined as follows:*

$$
\begin{array}{ll}
\mathtt{key}(\alpha.P) = \mathtt{key}(\mathbf{0}) = \emptyset & \mathtt{key}(\alpha[i].X) = \{i\} \cup \mathtt{key}(X) \\
\mathtt{key}(X \parallel Y) = \mathtt{key}(X) \cup \mathtt{key}(Y) & \mathtt{key}(X + Y) = \mathtt{key}(X) \cup \mathtt{key}(Y) \\
\mathtt{key}(X\backslash A) = \mathtt{key}(X)
\end{array}
$$

Definition 7. *A key i is fresh in a process X, written $\mathtt{fresh}(i, X)$ if $i \notin \mathtt{key}(X)$.*

Definition of keys in CCSK correspond to the definition of identifiers in RCCS. The operational semantics of CCSK is defined as a labelled transition system (LTS), $(\mathcal{P}_K, \rightarrow \cup \rightsquigarrow, \mathtt{ActK}_\tau)$ where $\mathcal{P}_K$ is the set of CCSK processes, $\rightarrow \subseteq \mathcal{P}_R \times \mathtt{ActK}_\tau \times \mathcal{P}_R$ and $\rightsquigarrow \subseteq \mathcal{P}_R \times \mathtt{ActK}_\tau \times \mathcal{P}_R$. Relations $\rightarrow$ and $\rightsquigarrow$ are the smallest reduction relations induced by respectively rules in Figs. 7 and 8. Differently from RCCS, CCSK does not exploit any structural congruence.

Remark 2. In the following when in proofs, rules and so on we use P instead of X we just indicate that the process P has no labelled actions, as P being a CCS process. An alternative is to use predicate $\mathtt{std}(X)$ as in [11].

Rules for forward transitions are given in Fig. 7. Rule K-ACT1 deals with prefixed processes $\alpha.P$. It just transforms a prefix into a label but differently from the normal CCS rule for prefix, it generates a fresh new key i which is bound to the action α becoming $\alpha[i]$. As we can note the prefix is not discarded after the reduction. Rule K-ACT2 inductively allows a prefixed process $\alpha[i].X$ to execute if X can execute. The actions that X can do are forced to use keys different from i. Rules K-PLUS-L and K-PLUS-R deal with the + operator. Let us note that these rule do not discard the context, that is part of the process which has not contributed to the action. In more detail, if the process $P+Q$ does an action, say $\alpha[i]$, and becomes X then the process becomes $X+Q$. In this way the information about $+Q$ is preserved. Moreover since Q is a standard process

$$(\text{K-ACT1}) \; \frac{}{\alpha.P \xrightarrow{\alpha[i]} \alpha[i].P} \qquad\qquad (\text{K-ACT2}) \; \frac{X \xrightarrow{\beta[j]} X' \quad i \neq j}{\alpha[i].X \xrightarrow{\beta[j]} \alpha[i].X'}$$

$$(\text{K-PLUS-L}) \; \frac{X \xrightarrow{\alpha[i]} X'}{X + P \xrightarrow{\alpha[i]} X' + P} \qquad (\text{K-PLUS-R}) \; \frac{Y \xrightarrow{\alpha[i]} Y'}{P + Y \xrightarrow{\alpha[i]} P + Y'}$$

$$(\text{K-PAR-L}) \; \frac{X \xrightarrow{\alpha[i]} X' \quad \texttt{fresh}(i,Y)}{X \parallel Y \xrightarrow{\alpha[i]} X' \parallel Y} \qquad (\text{K-PAR-R}) \; \frac{Y \xrightarrow{\alpha[i]} Y' \quad \texttt{fresh}(i,X)}{X \parallel Y \xrightarrow{\alpha[i]} X \parallel Y'}$$

$$(\text{K-SYN}) \; \frac{X \xrightarrow{\alpha[i]} X' \quad Y \xrightarrow{\bar{\alpha}[i]} Y' \quad a \neq \tau}{X \parallel Y \xrightarrow{\tau[i]} X' \parallel Y'} \qquad (\text{K-RES}) \; \frac{X \xrightarrow{\alpha[i]} X' \quad \alpha \notin A \cup \bar{A}}{X \backslash A \xrightarrow{\alpha[i]} X' \backslash A}$$

Fig. 7. CCSK forward semantics

then it will never executes even if it is present in the process $X + Q$. So we can say that $+Q$ is just a decoration of X. Let us note that in order to apply one of the plus rule one of the two processes has to be a CCS process P (e.g. not containing labelled prefixes), meaning that it is impossible for two non standard process to both execute if composed by the choice operator. Rules K-PAR-L and K-PAR-R propagate an action $\alpha[i]$ through a parallel composition, provided that the key i is not used by the other processes in parallel (use of $\texttt{fresh}(\cdot)$ predicate in the premises). Rule K-SYN allows two processes in parallel to syncrhonize. To do so, they have to match both the action and the identifier. Rule K-RES deals with restriction in the canonical (CCS) way. Backward rules are the exact opposite of the forward ones.

Definition 8 (Reachable Process). *A CCSK process X is reachable if it can be derived from an CCS process P, by using rules of* Figs. 7 and 8.

Property 1 (Plus Form). If X is a reachable process, and $X = Y + Q$, then

$$Y = P_1 + \ldots + (Y_1 \parallel \ldots \parallel Y_m) + P_j + \ldots + P_n$$

for some α, m, n and with P_i not having top level $+$.

Proof. By induction on the length of the derivation that led an initial process to X and by case analysis on the last applied rule.

3   Encoding CCSK in RCCS

We now adapt the concept of *bisimulation* [12] to work in a reversible setting and with two different semantics. To this aim, we indicate with $\rightarrow_{s_i}$ the forward relation of the s_i semantics, and with $\rightsquigarrow_{s_i}$ the backward one. Moreover, we indicate with $\mathcal{P}_{s_i}$ the set of processes of semantics s_i and with $\mathcal{L}_{s_i}$ the set of labels produced by semantics s_i.

$$(\text{K-ACT1}^\bullet) \; \frac{}{\alpha[i].P \xrightsquigarrow{\alpha[i]} \alpha.P} \qquad\qquad (\text{K-ACT2}^\bullet) \; \frac{X \xrightsquigarrow{\beta[j]} X' \qquad i \neq j}{\alpha[i].X \xrightsquigarrow{\beta[j]} \alpha[i].X'}$$

$$(\text{K-PLUS-L}^\bullet) \; \frac{X \xrightsquigarrow{\alpha[i]} X'}{X + P \xrightsquigarrow{\alpha[i]} X' + P} \qquad\qquad (\text{K-PLUS-R}^\bullet) \; \frac{Y \xrightsquigarrow{\alpha[i]} Y'}{P + Y \xrightsquigarrow{\alpha[i]} P + Y'}$$

$$(\text{K-PAR-L}^\bullet) \; \frac{X \xrightsquigarrow{\alpha[i]} X' \qquad \mathbf{fresh}(i, Y)}{X \parallel Y \xrightsquigarrow{\alpha[i]} X' \parallel Y} \qquad (\text{K-PAR-R}^\bullet) \; \frac{Y \xrightsquigarrow{\alpha[i]} Y' \qquad \mathbf{fresh}(i, X)}{X \parallel Y \xrightsquigarrow{\alpha[i]} X \parallel Y'}$$

$$(\text{K-SYN}^\bullet) \; \frac{X \xrightsquigarrow{\alpha[i]} X' \; Y \xrightsquigarrow{\bar{\alpha}[i]} Y' \; \alpha \neq \tau}{X \parallel Y \xrightsquigarrow{\tau[i]} X' \parallel Y'} \qquad (\text{K-RES}^\bullet) \; \frac{X \xrightsquigarrow{\alpha[i]} X' \qquad \alpha \notin A \cup \bar{A}}{X \backslash A \xrightsquigarrow{\alpha[i]} X' \backslash A}$$

Fig. 8. CCSK backward semantics

Definition 9 (Back and Forth Bisimulation). *Given a bijective function* $\gamma : \mathcal{L}_{s_1} \to \mathcal{L}_{s_2}$, *a relation* $_{s_1}\mathcal{R}_{s_2} \subseteq \mathcal{P}_{s_1} \times \mathcal{P}_{s_2}$ *is a strong back and forth simulation if whenever* $P_{s_1}\mathcal{R}_{s_2}R$:

- $P \xrightarrow{\alpha[i]}_{s_1} Q$ *implies* $R \xrightarrow{\gamma(\alpha[i])}_{s_2} S$ *with* $Q_{s_1}\mathcal{R}_{s_2}S$
  $P \xrightsquigarrow{\alpha[i]}_{s_1} Q$ *implies* $R \xrightsquigarrow{\gamma(\alpha[i])}_{s_2} S$ *with* $Q_{s_1}\mathcal{R}_{s_2}S$
-

A relation $_{s_1}\mathcal{R}_{s_2} \subseteq \mathcal{P}_{s_1} \times \mathcal{P}_{s_2}$ *is called strong back and forth bisimulation if* $_{s_1}\mathcal{R}_{s_2}$ *and* $(_{s_1}\mathcal{R}_{s_2})^{-1}$ *are strong back and forth simulations. We call strong bisimilarity and note* $_{s_1}\sim_{s_2}$ *the largest bisimulation with respect to semantics* s_1 *and* s_2.

This definition when instantiated with a single semantics, that is $s_1 = s_2$ and γ being the *identity*, is similar to the definition of *forward-reverse* bisimulation used in [11], with the only difference is that our definition does not take into account predicates. Moreover, when instantiated with CCSK semantics, the two notions coincide.

In this section we will show how CCSK can be encoded in RCCS. We will use the same notation like before. P stands for processes from CCS and X for CCSK processes. Let $\mathcal{P}_K$ and $\mathcal{P}_R$ the set of processes from CCSK and RCCS, respectively, and $\mathcal{M}$ is the set of all the memories derivable by productions in Fig. 2. The encoding function $[\![\cdot]\!] : \mathcal{P}_K \times \mathcal{M} \times \mathcal{P} \to \mathcal{P}_R$, is inductively defined as follows:

$$\begin{aligned}
[\![P, m, \mathbf{0}]\!] &= m \triangleright P \\
[\![X + P, m, Q]\!] &= [\![X, m, P + Q]\!] \\
[\![P + X, m, Q]\!] &= [\![X, m, Q + P]\!]
\end{aligned}$$

$$\llbracket \alpha[i].X, m, P \rrbracket \;=\; \llbracket X, \langle i, \alpha, P\rangle \cdot m, \mathbf{0}\rrbracket$$
$$\llbracket X\backslash A, m, P \rrbracket \;=\; \llbracket X, m, P\rrbracket\backslash A$$
$$\llbracket X \parallel Y, m, P \rrbracket \;=\; \llbracket X, \langle\uparrow\rangle \cdot m, P\rrbracket \parallel \llbracket Y, \langle\uparrow\rangle \cdot m, P\rrbracket$$

Let us comment it. The main difference between RCCS and CCSK is on the way they keep track of the history. In RCCS all the information is local to each monitored process, while in CCSK the information is spread along the structure of a process. Moreover, a CCSK process may correspond to several monitored processes, since in CCSK there is no need of splitting memories through a parallel composition. So the encoding has to inductively drill the structure of a CCSK process X, in order to build the final memory of the process and to find the plus context of each labelled action $\alpha[i]$ present inside X. To this aim, the encoding takes two additional parameters: a memory m and a CCS process P. The parallel and the restriction of CCSK operator are mapped to the corresponding operators of RCCS. Let us note that in the parallel case, the memory m is split into two $\langle\uparrow\rangle \cdot m$. The encoding of a process $\alpha[i].X$ with memory m and context Q is the encoding of process X where the memory stack is augmented of the event $\langle i, \alpha, Q\rangle$. In this case the action $\alpha[i]$ disappears from the process as it goes inside the memory m. The encoding of a process $P + X$ is the encoding of X where its context is the sum composition of its previous context and P. Finally, the encoding of a normal CCS process P is just its monitored version, with memory m representing its history. Since the context parameter is used for past actions, in the case of normal process P, we impose this parameter to be $\mathbf{0}$. In order to understand how the encoding works let us consider the following example. Let $X = (a + b) + c[i].(d[h] \parallel P)$ then

$$\llbracket X, \langle\rangle, \mathbf{0}\rrbracket = \llbracket c[i].(d[h] \parallel P), \langle\rangle, a + b\rrbracket = \llbracket d[h] \parallel P, \langle i, c, a + b\rangle \cdot \langle\rangle, \mathbf{0}\rrbracket =$$
$$\llbracket d[h], \langle\uparrow\rangle \cdot \langle i, c, a + b\rangle \cdot \langle\rangle, \mathbf{0}\rrbracket \parallel \llbracket P, \langle\uparrow\rangle \cdot \langle i, c, a + b\rangle \cdot \langle\rangle, \mathbf{0}\rrbracket =$$
$$\llbracket \mathbf{0}, \langle h, d, \mathbf{0}\rangle \cdot \langle\uparrow\rangle \cdot \langle i, c, a + b\rangle \cdot \langle\rangle, \mathbf{0}\rrbracket \parallel \langle\uparrow\rangle \cdot \langle i, c, a + b\rangle \cdot \langle\rangle \triangleright P =$$
$$\langle h, d, \mathbf{0}\rangle \cdot \langle\uparrow\rangle \cdot \langle i, c, a + b\rangle \cdot \langle\rangle \triangleright \mathbf{0} \parallel \langle\uparrow\rangle \cdot \langle i, c, a + b\rangle \cdot \langle\rangle \triangleright P$$

Before stating our main Theorem, we need some lemmata about operational correspondence.

Lemma 4 (Forward Correspondence). *For all transitions $X \xrightarrow{\alpha[i]} X'$ in CCSK, with $R = \llbracket X, \langle\rangle, \mathbf{0}\rrbracket$, there exists a corresponding RCCS transition such that $R \to_\alpha^i R'$ with $\llbracket X', \langle\rangle, \mathbf{0}\rrbracket = R'$.*

Proof. By induction on the derivation $X \xrightarrow{\alpha[i]} X'$ and by case analysis on the last applied rule. We show the relevant cases:

K-ACT2: We have $\alpha[i].X \xrightarrow{\beta[j]} \alpha[i].X'$ with $X \xrightarrow{\beta[j]} X'$. Be $R = \llbracket X, \langle\rangle, \mathbf{0}\rrbracket$, by Lemma 3 we know that: $R \equiv (\prod_{i\in I}(m_i \triangleright \alpha_i.P_i + Q_i)\backslash A_i)\backslash B$.

By applying inductive hypothesis we have that $\llbracket X, \langle\rangle, \mathbf{0}\rrbracket \to_\beta^j \llbracket X', \langle\rangle, \mathbf{0}\rrbracket$, that is $R \to_\beta^j R'$ with $R' = \llbracket X', \langle\rangle, \mathbf{0}\rrbracket$. Now we to distinguish two cases: either β

is a single action or it has been produced by a synchonization. In the first case we have then that there exists an index $h \in I$ such that $\alpha_h = \beta$, and then

$$[\![X, \langle\rangle, \mathbf{0}]\!] \equiv (\prod_{i \in I} (m_i \triangleright \alpha_i.P_i + Q_i)\backslash A_i)\backslash B \rightarrow^j_\beta$$

$$(\prod_{i \in I\backslash h} (m_i \triangleright \alpha_i.P_i + Q_i)\backslash A_i \parallel (\langle j, \beta, Q_h\rangle \cdot m_h \triangleright P_h)\backslash A_h)\backslash B \equiv [\![X', \langle\rangle, \mathbf{0}]\!]$$

Moreover, by definition of encoding we have that

$$[\![\alpha[i].X, \langle\rangle, \mathbf{0}]\!] = [\![X, \langle i, \alpha, \mathbf{0}\rangle \cdot \langle\rangle, \mathbf{0}]\!]$$

and by using Lemma 1 we can mimic the same transition with an augmented memory: $[\![X, \langle i, \alpha, \mathbf{0}\rangle \cdot \langle\rangle, \mathbf{0}]\!] \rightarrow^j_\beta [\![X', \langle i, \alpha, \mathbf{0}\rangle \cdot \langle\rangle, \mathbf{0}]\!]$ as desired. The synchronisation case is similar.

K-PLUS-L: We have $X = Y + P \xrightarrow{\alpha[i]} Y' + P$. By Property 1, we have that:

$$Y = P_1 + \ldots + (Y_1 \parallel \ldots \parallel Y_m) + P_j + \ldots + P_n$$

Let $T = \sum_{i \in n\backslash l} P_i$, by applying the encoding we have that

$$[\![Y + P, \langle\rangle, \mathbf{0}]\!] = [\![(Y_1 \parallel \ldots \parallel Y_m), \langle\rangle, P + T]\!]$$

$$[\![Y, \langle\rangle, \mathbf{0}]\!] = [\![(Y_1 \parallel \ldots \parallel Y_m), \langle\rangle, T]\!]$$

By Lemma 3 we know that: $[\![Y + P, \langle\rangle]\!] \equiv (\prod_{l \in I} (m_l \triangleright \alpha_l.P_l + Q_l)\backslash A_l)\backslash B$

This implies that there exists a subset $J \subseteq I$ on indexes such that memories in J share the action $\langle k, \beta, T\rangle$, with $T = \sum_{i \in n\backslash l} P_i$, such that:

$$[\![Y, \langle\rangle, \mathbf{0}]\!] \equiv (\prod_{l \in I\backslash J} (m_l \triangleright \alpha_l.P_l + Q_l)\backslash A_l \parallel$$

$$\prod_{h \in J} (m_h \cdot \langle k, \beta, T\rangle \triangleright \alpha_h.P_h + Q_h)\backslash A_h)\backslash B$$

$$[\![Y + P, \langle\rangle, \mathbf{0}]\!] \equiv (\prod_{l \in I\backslash J} (m_l \triangleright \alpha_l.P_l + Q_l)\backslash A_l \parallel$$

$$\prod_{h \in J} (m_h \cdot \langle k, \beta, T + P\rangle \triangleright \alpha_h.P_h + Q_h)\backslash A_h)\backslash B$$

By hypothesis we have that $Y \xrightarrow{\alpha[i]} Y'$ and by inductive hypothesis we have that $[\![Y, \langle\rangle, \mathbf{0}]\!] \rightarrow^i_\alpha [\![Y', \langle\rangle, \mathbf{0}]\!]$, but then also $[\![Y + P, \langle\rangle, \mathbf{0}]\!] \rightarrow^i_\alpha [\![Y', \langle\rangle, P]\!] = [\![Y' + P, \langle\rangle, \mathbf{0}]\!]$, as desired. ∎

Lemma 5 (Backward Correspondance). *For all transitions $X \overset{\alpha[i]}{\rightsquigarrow} X'$ in CCSK, with $R = [\![X, \langle\rangle, \mathbf{0}]\!]$, there exists a corresponding transition $R \rightsquigarrow^i_\alpha R'$ in RCCS with $[\![X', \langle\rangle, \mathbf{0}]\!] = R'$.*

Proof. By induction on the derivation $X \xrightarrow{\alpha[i]} X'$ and by case analysis on the last applied rule. The proof follows the lines of the one of Lemma 4.

With the previous two lemmata we have proved that if we have a couple of processes $(X, R) = (X, [\![X, \langle\rangle, \mathbf{0}]\!])$ where X is reachable, and if process X does an action α in CCSK, then process R does the same action in RCCS. Obtained process $R' = [\![X', \langle\rangle, \mathbf{0}]\!]$ is still encoding of process X'. Now we have to show the opposite direction.

Lemma 6 (Forward Completeness). *For any CCSK process X and RCCS process R, such that $R = [\![X, \langle\rangle, \mathbf{0}]\!]$, if $R \rightarrow^i_\alpha R'$ in RCCS, then there exists a corresponding transition $X \xrightarrow{\alpha[i]} X'$ in CCSK, with $R' = [\![X', \langle\rangle, \mathbf{0}]\!]$.*

Proof. By structural induction on X. We have two main cases, whether $X = P$ or not. We will show just the most significant cases.

In first case we observe form of the processes $X = P$, where P is (standard) CCS process. We then do an induction of the form of P. If $P = \alpha.P_1$: we have that $R = [\![\alpha.P_1, \langle\rangle, \mathbf{0}]\!]$ and by applying encoding

$$[\![\alpha.P_1, \langle\rangle, \mathbf{0}]\!] = \langle\rangle \triangleright \alpha.P_1.$$

Then, by using R-ACT we get $\langle\rangle \triangleright \alpha.P_1 \rightarrow^i_\alpha \langle i, \alpha, \mathbf{0}\rangle \cdot \langle\rangle \triangleright P_1$, where $\langle i, \alpha, \mathbf{0}\rangle \cdot \langle\rangle \triangleright P_1 = [\![\alpha[i].P_1, \langle\rangle, \mathbf{0}]\!] = R'$.
In CCSK process $\alpha.P_1$, can do the same action α by applying the rule K-ACT1 and we get

$$\alpha.P_1 \xrightarrow{\alpha[i]} \alpha[i].P_1 \text{ where } X' = \alpha[i].P_1 \text{ as we desired.}$$

In the second case we observe form of the processes X, when he have a structure of CCSK process and it is not standard process. We consider the significant cases:

$X = \alpha[i].Y$: we have that $R = [\![\alpha[i].Y, \langle\rangle, \mathbf{0}]\!]$. By Lemma 3 we know that:

$$[\![Y, \langle\rangle, \mathbf{0}]\!] \equiv (\prod_{l \in I}(m_l \triangleright \alpha_l.P_l + Q_l)\backslash A_l)\backslash B$$

Now we know that there exists some subset $H \subseteq I$ such that all processes from that subset share the very first action α . For some $t \in H$ such that $\alpha_t = \beta$ we have:

$$[\![Y, \langle\rangle, \mathbf{0}]\!] \equiv (\prod_{l \in I\backslash H}(m_l \triangleright \alpha_l.P_l + Q_l)\backslash A_l \parallel \prod_{h \in H\backslash t}(m'_h \cdot \langle i, \alpha, \mathbf{0}\rangle \triangleright \alpha_h.P_h + Q_h)\backslash A_h \parallel$$

$$(m'_t \cdot \langle i, \alpha, \mathbf{0}\rangle \triangleright \beta.P_t + Q_t)\backslash B \rightarrow^j_\beta$$

$$(\prod_{l \in I\backslash H}(m_l \triangleright \alpha_l.P_l + Q_l)\backslash A_l \parallel \prod_{h \in H\backslash t}(m'_h \cdot \langle i, \alpha, \mathbf{0}\rangle \triangleright \alpha_h.P_h + Q_h)\backslash A_h \parallel$$

$$\langle j, \beta, Q_t\rangle \cdot m'_t \cdot \langle i, \alpha, \mathbf{0}\rangle \triangleright P_t\backslash A_t)\backslash B \equiv [\![Y', \langle\rangle, \mathbf{0}]\!]$$

By definition of encoding we have that $[\![\alpha[i].Y, \langle\rangle, \mathbf{0}]\!] = [\![Y, \langle i, \alpha, \mathbf{0}\rangle \cdot \langle\rangle, \mathbf{0}]\!]$ and using Lemma 1 we can mimic the same transition:

$$[\![Y, \langle i, \alpha, \mathbf{0}\rangle \cdot \langle\rangle, \mathbf{0}]\!] \rightarrow_\beta^j [\![Y', \langle i, \alpha, \mathbf{0}\rangle \cdot \langle\rangle, \mathbf{0}]\!]$$

By inductive hypothesis we have that $Y \xrightarrow{\beta[j]} Y'$ and using rule K-ACT2 we get:

$$\alpha[i].Y \xrightarrow{\beta[j]} \alpha[i].Y' \quad \text{as desired.}$$

$X = Y_1 \parallel Y_2$ We have that $R = [\![Y_1 \parallel Y_2, \langle\rangle, \mathbf{0}]\!]$ and by applying encoding

$$[\![Y_1 \parallel Y_2, \langle\rangle, \mathbf{0}]\!] = [\![Y_1, \langle\uparrow\rangle \cdot \langle\rangle, \mathbf{0}]\!] \parallel [\![Y_2, \langle\uparrow\rangle \cdot \langle\rangle, \mathbf{0}]\!]$$

Now, we distinguish three cases: if first branch of parallel composition do action α, or the second one, or α is syncrhonization action. If $R_1 = [\![Y_1, \langle\rangle, \mathbf{0}]\!]$ in first case we have that in R_1 exists an index $h \in I$ such that $\alpha_h = \alpha$ and then by Lemma 3, we get

$$R_1 \equiv (\prod_{l \in I}(m_l \triangleright \alpha_l.P_l + Q_l)\backslash A_l)\backslash B \rightarrow_\alpha^i$$

$$(\prod_{l \in I\backslash h}(m_l \triangleright \alpha_l.P_l + Q_l)\backslash A_l \parallel (\langle i, \alpha, Q_h\rangle \cdot m_h \triangleright P_h)\backslash A_h)\backslash B \equiv R_1'$$

By Lemma 1 we have: $[\![Y_1, \langle\uparrow\rangle \cdot \langle\rangle, \mathbf{0}]\!] \rightarrow_\alpha^i [\![Y_1', \langle\uparrow\rangle \cdot \langle\rangle, \mathbf{0}]\!]$
Using rule R-PAR we get

$$[\![Y_1, \langle\uparrow\rangle \cdot \langle\rangle, \mathbf{0}]\!] \parallel [\![Y_2, \langle\uparrow\rangle \cdot \langle\rangle, \mathbf{0}]\!] \rightarrow_\alpha^i [\![Y_1', \langle\uparrow\rangle \cdot \langle\rangle, \mathbf{0}]\!] \parallel [\![Y_2, \langle\uparrow\rangle \cdot \langle\rangle, \mathbf{0}]\!]$$

where $[\![Y_1', \langle\uparrow\rangle \cdot \langle\rangle, \mathbf{0}]\!] \parallel [\![Y_2, \langle\uparrow\rangle \cdot \langle\rangle, \mathbf{0}]\!] = [\![Y_1' \parallel Y_2, \langle\rangle, \mathbf{0}]\!] = R'$. By inductive hypothesis we have that also $Y_1 \xrightarrow{\alpha[i]} Y_1'$ and by using rule K-PAR-L, we get: $Y_1 \parallel Y_2 \xrightarrow{\alpha[i]} Y_1' \parallel Y_2$ as desired. The remaining cases are similar.

$X = Y + P$: By Property 1 we have that:

$$Y = P_1 + \ldots + (Y_1 \parallel \ldots \parallel Y_m) + P_j + \ldots + P_n$$

In the same way, like in Lemma 4 we define processes congruent to processes $[\![Y + P, \langle\rangle, \mathbf{0}]\!]$ and $[\![Y, \langle\rangle, \mathbf{0}]\!]$.

Now we know that there exists some $t \in J$ such that $\alpha_t = \alpha$ and we have

$$(\prod_{l \in I\backslash J}(m_l \triangleright \alpha_l.P_l + Q_l)\backslash A_l \parallel \prod_{h \in J}(m_h \cdot \langle k, \beta, T\rangle \triangleright \alpha_h.P_h + Q_h)\backslash A_h \parallel$$

$$(m_t \cdot \langle h, \beta, T\rangle \triangleright \alpha.P_t + Q_t)\backslash A_t)\backslash B \rightarrow_\alpha^i$$

$$(\prod_{l \in I\backslash J}(m_l \triangleright \alpha_l.P_l + Q_l)\backslash A_l \parallel \prod_{h \in J}(m_h \cdot \langle k, \beta, T\rangle \triangleright \alpha_h.P_h + Q_h)\backslash A_h \parallel$$

$$(\langle i, \alpha, Q_t\rangle \cdot m_t \cdot \langle k, \beta, T\rangle \triangleright P_t)\backslash A_t)\backslash B$$

Then we also have $[\![Y + P, \langle\rangle, \mathbf{0}]\!] \rightarrow^i_\alpha [\![Y', \langle\rangle, P]\!] = [\![Y' + P, \langle\rangle, \mathbf{0}]\!]$. By applying the inductive hypothesis we also have $X \xrightarrow{\alpha[i]} X'$ and by rule K-PLUS-L, we get $X + P \xrightarrow{\alpha[i]} X' + P$ as desired.   ∎

Lemma 7 (Backward Completeness). *For any CCSK process X and RCCS process R, such that $R = [\![X, \langle\rangle, \mathbf{0}]\!]$, if $R \rightsquigarrow^i_\alpha R'$ in RCCS, then there exists a corresponding transition $X \xrightarrow{\alpha[i]} X'$ in CCSK, with $R' = [\![X', \langle\rangle, \mathbf{0}]\!]$.*

Proof. By structural induction on X.

We now can state our main result:

Theorem 1 (Operational Correspondance). *For any CCS process P, $P \sim [\![P, \langle\rangle, \mathbf{0}]\!]$.*

Proof. We just need to show that the relation

$$\mathcal{R} = \{(X, [\![X, \langle\rangle, \mathbf{0}]\!]) \text{ with } X \text{ CCSK reachable }\}$$

is a strong back and forth bisimulation.

If X does a forward transition, $X \xrightarrow{\alpha[i]} Y$ by Lemma 4 we have also that $[\![X, \langle\rangle, \mathbf{0}]\!] \rightarrow^\alpha_i [\![Y, \langle\rangle, \mathbf{0}]\!]$, with $(Y, [\![Y, \langle\rangle, \mathbf{0}]\!]) \in \mathcal{R}$. If the transition is a backward one we apply the Lemma 5.

If $R = [\![X, \langle\rangle, \mathbf{0}]\!]$ does a forward transition, $R \rightarrow^i_\alpha S$ then by Lemma 6 we also have that $X \xrightarrow{\alpha[i]} Y$ with $S = [\![Y, \langle\rangle, \mathbf{0}]\!]$, and we have that $(Y, [\![Y, \langle\rangle, \mathbf{0}]\!]) \in \mathcal{R}$. If the transition is a backward one we apply the Lemma 7.   ∎

4   Encoding RCCS in CCSK

In this section we just give the encoding of RCCS into CCSK and discuss how it works, without showing its correctness.

The main difference between RCCS and CCSK is that in RCCS via structural congruence is possible to split a parallel composition of processes sharing the same memory into a parallel composition of different monitored processes. This allows the single monitored processes to continue independently their computation. In CCSK there is no need of splitting rule, as its reversibility is *static*. Then it is the case that different RCCS processes may correspond to a single CCSK process. In order to better understand this main issues, let us consider the following RCCS process:

$$R = \langle j, \beta, P_1\rangle \cdot \langle\uparrow\rangle \cdot \langle i, \alpha, Q\rangle \cdot \langle\rangle \triangleright P_1 \parallel \langle\uparrow\rangle \cdot \langle i, \alpha, Q\rangle \cdot \langle\rangle \triangleright \gamma.P_2$$

derived from the initial process $\langle\rangle \triangleright \alpha.(\beta.P_1 \parallel \gamma.P_2) + Q$. Now the corresponding CCSK process is the following one:

$$\alpha[i].(\beta[j].P_1 \parallel \gamma.P_2) + Q$$

So the encoding has to be able, while encoding monitored processes, to collect partially encoded processes sharing the same memory. In the example before, the encoding has to join together processes $\beta[j].P_1$ and $\gamma.P_2$ and put them in the context $\alpha[i].[\bullet] + Q$. It is clear that such encoding cannot be compositional as it has to reason on the whole process while reconstructing back the history of monitored processes up to a split $\langle\uparrow\rangle$, then somehow apply the structural law SPLIT in order to marge partially encoded processes and then to continue the encoding of the obtained parallel composition under the common memory. This is why the encoding of a RCCS reachable process R is defined as $\delta((\!|R|\!))$, where function $(\!|\cdot|\!)$ is inductively defined as follows

$$(\!|R \parallel S|\!) = (\!|R|\!) \parallel (\!|S|\!) \qquad\qquad (\!|\langle\rangle, X|\!) = X$$

$$(\!|R\backslash A|\!) = (\!|R|\!)\backslash A \qquad\qquad (\!|\langle i, \alpha, Q\rangle \cdot m, X|\!) = (\!|m, \alpha[i].X + Q|\!)$$

$$(\!|m \triangleright P|\!) = (\!|m, P|\!) \qquad\qquad (\!|\langle\uparrow\rangle \cdot m, X|\!) = \{\!\langle\uparrow\rangle \cdot m, X\}$$

As we can see, the encoding of a monitored process $(\!|m, P|\!)$ proceed as long as in m there are events of the form $\langle i, \alpha, Q\rangle$ and *freezes* when it encounters a memory m on top of which there is a split event $\langle\uparrow\rangle \cdot m$, and the act of this freezing produces a partially encoded process of the form $\{\!\langle\uparrow\rangle \cdot m, X\}$.

Function $\delta(\cdot)$, which is in charge of fusing two partially encoded CCSK processes sharing the same memory, is defined as follows:

$$\delta\left(\prod\{\!\langle\uparrow\rangle \cdot m_l, X_l\} \parallel \prod\{\!\langle\uparrow\rangle \cdot m_t, X_t\} \parallel \prod\{\!\langle\uparrow\rangle \cdot m_z, X_z\}\right) \quad =$$

$$\delta\left(\prod(\!|m_l, X_l \parallel X_t|\!) \parallel \prod\{\!\langle\uparrow\rangle \cdot m_z, X_z\}\right) \quad \text{if } \forall l \in L\, \exists t \in T \text{ s.t } m_l = m_t$$

$$\delta(X) = X$$

Let us note that when the δ only stops when an entire CCSK process has been derived, otherwise it applies again the encoding $(\!|\cdot|\!)$ on the fused processes.

The following example shows how the entire mechanism work:

$$R = \langle i, \alpha, T\rangle \cdot \langle\uparrow\rangle \cdot \langle\uparrow\rangle \cdot \langle j, \beta, \mathbf{0}\rangle \triangleright P_1 \parallel \langle\uparrow\rangle \cdot \langle\uparrow\rangle \cdot \langle j, \beta, \mathbf{0}\rangle \triangleright P_2 \parallel \langle\uparrow\rangle \cdot \langle j, \beta, \mathbf{0}\rangle \triangleright P_3$$

$$(\!|R|\!) = \delta\left((\!|\langle i, \alpha, T\rangle \cdot \langle\uparrow\rangle \cdot \langle\uparrow\rangle \cdot \langle j, \beta, \mathbf{0}\rangle, P_1|\!) \parallel (\!|\langle\uparrow\rangle \cdot \langle\uparrow\rangle \cdot \langle j, \beta, \mathbf{0}\rangle, P_2|\!) \parallel (\!|\langle\uparrow\rangle \cdot \langle j, \beta, \mathbf{0}\rangle, P_3|\!)\right)$$

$$= \delta\left((\!|\langle\uparrow\rangle \cdot \langle\uparrow\rangle \cdot \langle j, \beta, \mathbf{0}\rangle, \alpha[i].P_1 + T|\!) \parallel (\!|\langle\uparrow\rangle \cdot \langle\uparrow\rangle \cdot \langle j, \beta, \mathbf{0}\rangle, P_2|\!) \parallel (\!|\langle\uparrow\rangle \cdot \langle j, \beta, \mathbf{0}\rangle, P_3|\!)\right)$$

$$= \delta\left(\{\!\langle\uparrow\rangle \cdot \langle\uparrow\rangle \cdot \langle j, \beta, \mathbf{0}\rangle, \alpha[i].P_1 + T\} \parallel \{\!\langle\uparrow\rangle \cdot \langle\uparrow\rangle \cdot \langle j, \beta, \mathbf{0}\rangle, P_2\} \parallel (\!|\langle\uparrow\rangle \cdot \langle j, \beta, \mathbf{0}\rangle, P_3|\!)\right)$$

$$= \delta\left((\!|\langle\uparrow\rangle \cdot \langle j, \beta, \mathbf{0}\rangle, (\alpha[i].P_1 + T \parallel P_2)|\!) \parallel (\!|\langle\uparrow\rangle \cdot \langle j, \beta, \mathbf{0}\rangle, P_3|\!)\right)$$

$$= \delta\left(\{\!\langle\uparrow\rangle \cdot \langle j, \beta, \mathbf{0}\rangle, (\alpha[i].P_1 + T \parallel P_2)\} \parallel \{\!\langle\uparrow\rangle \cdot \langle j, \beta, \mathbf{0}\rangle, P_3\}\right)$$

$$= \delta\left((\!|\langle j, \beta, \mathbf{0}\rangle, (\alpha[i].P_1 + T \parallel P_2) \parallel P_3|\!)\right)$$

$$= \delta\left((\!|\langle\rangle, \beta[j].((\alpha[i].P_1 + T \parallel P_2) \parallel P_3)|\!)\right)$$

$$= \beta[j].((\alpha[i].P_1 + T \parallel P_2) \parallel P_3)$$

5   Conclusions and Future Work

The first reversible variant of CCS, called RCCS, was introduced by Danos and Krivine [2]. In RCCS each process is monitored by a *memory*, that serves as stack of past actions. Memories are considered as unique process identifiers, and in order to preserve this uniqueness along a parallel composition, a structural law permits to obtain unique memories though a parallel composition. A general method for reversing process calculi, given in a particular SOS format, has been proposed by Phillips and Ulidowski in [11]. The main idea of this approach is the use of communication keys to uniquely identify communications, and to make *static* each operator of the calculus. By applying this method to CCS, CCSK is obtained. Since in CCKS the history is directly annotated in the process itself, there is no need of splitting history through a parallel composition. We call this kind of recording histories as *static* reversibility; while we call the one used by RCCS as *dynamic*, since each thread is endowed with its own history. In order to show that these two methods are similar, e.g. two reversible CCS derived by them are strongly bisimilar, we have provided and encoding from a CCSK process to possibly several RCCS monitored processes. Then we have showed that a CCSK term and its encoding in RCCS are strongly back and forth bisimilar. We then sketched a possible encoding from RCCS to CCSK and discussed the difficulties behind it, mostly due to the fact that multiple split monitored process may correspond to a single CCSK process. We leave as future work showing the correctness of this encoding. Once this will be proven, then we can state that the two calculi (and their underling semantics) are equivalent, and will allow us to bring to CCSK some results about causally consistency already proven for RCCS.

We leave as future work showing that back and forth bisimulation is a congruence. Moreover, another interesting result would be to show that the two calculi are fully abstract, e.g. that two bisimilar CCSK terms are translated into two bisimimilar RCCS terms.

References

1. Berut, A., Arakelyan, A., Petrosyan, A., Ciliberto, S., Dillenschneider, R., Lutz, E.: Experimental verification of Landauer' s principle linking information, thermodynamics. Nature **483**(7388), 187–189 (2012)
2. Danos, V., Krivine, J.: Reversible communicating systems. In: Gardner, P., Yoshida, N. (eds.) CONCUR 2004. LNCS, vol. 3170, pp. 292–307. Springer, Heidelberg (2004)
3. Danos, V., Krivine, J.: Transactions in RCCS. In: Abadi, M., de Alfaro, L. (eds.) CONCUR 2005. LNCS, vol. 3653, pp. 398–412. Springer, Heidelberg (2005)
4. Giachino, E., Lanese, I., Mezzina, C.A.: Causal-consistent reversible debugging. In: Gnesi, S., Rensink, A. (eds.) FASE 2014 (ETAPS). LNCS, vol. 8411, pp. 370–384. Springer, Heidelberg (2014)
5. Krivine, J.: A verification technique for reversible process algebra. In: Glück, R., Yokoyama, T. (eds.) RC 2012. LNCS, vol. 7581, pp. 204–217. Springer, Heidelberg (2013)
6. Landauer, R.: Irreversibility and heat generation in the computing process. IBM J. Res. Dev. **5**, 183–191 (1961)
7. Lanese, I., Lienhardt, M., Mezzina, C.A., Schmitt, A., Stefani, J.-B.: Concurrent flexible reversibility. In: Felleisen, M., Gardner, P. (eds.) ESOP 2013. LNCS, vol. 7792, pp. 370–390. Springer, Heidelberg (2013)

8. Milner, R.: A Calculus of Communicating Systems. LNCS, vol. 92. Springer, Heidelberg (1980)
9. Perumalla, K.S., Park, A.J.: Reverse computation for rollback-based fault tolerance in large parallel systems - evaluating the potential gains and systems effects. Cluster Comput. **17**(2), 303–313 (2014)
10. Phillips, I., Ulidowski, I., Yuen, S.: A reversible process calculus and the modelling of the ERK signalling pathway. In: Glück, R., Yokoyama, T. (eds.) RC 2012. LNCS, vol. 7581, pp. 218–232. Springer, Heidelberg (2013)
11. Phillips, I.C.C., Ulidowski, I.: Reversing algebraic process calculi. J. Log. Algebr. Program. **73**(1–2), 70–96 (2007)
12. Sangiorgi, D., Walker, D.: The Pi-Calculus - A Theory of Mobile Processes. Cambridge University Press, Cambridge (2001)

Reversing Single Sessions

Francesco Tiezzi[1(✉)] and Nobuko Yoshida[2]

[1] University of Camerino, Camerino, Italy
francesco.tiezzi@unicam.it
[2] Imperial College London, London, UK
n.yoshida@imperial.ac.uk

Abstract. Session-based communication has gained a widespread acceptance in practice as a means for developing safe communicating systems via structured interactions. In this paper, we investigate how these structured interactions are affected by reversibility, which provides a computational model allowing executed interactions to be undone. In particular, we provide a systematic study of the integration of different notions of reversibility in both binary and multiparty single sessions. The considered forms of reversibility are: one for completely reversing a given session with one backward step, and another for also restoring any intermediate state of the session with either one backward step or multiple ones. We analyse the costs of reversing a session in all these different settings. Our results show that extending binary single sessions to multiparty ones does not affect the reversibility machinery and its costs.

1 Introduction

In modern ICT systems, the role of communication is more and more crucial. This calls for a communication-centric programming style supporting safe and consistent composition of protocols. In this regard, in the last decade, primitives and related type theories supporting structured interactions, namely *sessions*, among system participants have been extensively studied (see, e.g., [5,10,11,18,22]).

Another key aspect of ICT systems concerns their reliability. Recently, *reversibility* has been put forward as a convenient support for programming reliable systems. In fact, it allows a system that has reached an undesired state to undo, in automatic fashion, previously performed actions. Again, foundational studies of mechanisms for reversing action executions have been carried out (see, e.g., [4,6–9,13,14,19]).

In this paper, we investigate how the benefits of reversibility can be brought to structured communication and, hence, how reversibility and sessions affect

This research has been partially founded by EPSRC EP/K011715/1, EP/K034413/1 and EP/L00058X/1, EU FP7 FETOpenX Upscale, MIUR PRIN Project CINA (2010LHT4KM), and the COST Actions BETTY (IC1201) and Reversible computation (IC1405).

S. Devitt and I. Lanese (Eds.): RC 2016, LNCS 9720, pp. 52–69, 2016.
DOI: 10.1007/978-3-319-40578-0_4

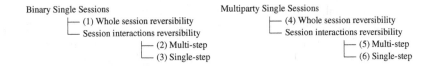

Fig. 1. Sessions and reversibility: considered combinations

each other. We concentrate on the primitives and mechanisms required to incorporate different notions of reversibility into two forms of session, and we analyse the costs of reversing a session in these different settings. To study the interplay between reversibility and sessions we rely on a uniform foundational framework, based on π-calculus [17].

Specifically, we focus on a simplified form of session, called *single*, in which the parties that have created a session can only continue to interact along that single session. This setting permits to consider a simpler theoretical framework than the one with the usual notion of session, called here *multiple*, where parties can interleave interactions performed along different sessions. This allows us to focus on the basic, key aspects of our investigation. Although single sessions are simpler, they are still largely used in practice, and differently from multiple sessions (see, e.g., [2,20]) their effect to reversibility is not studied yet in the literature.

Concerning the parties involved in the sessions, we take into account both *binary* and *multiparty* sessions, which involve two or multiple parties, respectively. For each kind of session, we investigate the use of two forms of reversibility: *(i)* *whole session* reversibility, where a single backward step reverses completely the given session, thus directly restoring its initialisation state; and *(ii)* *session interactions* reversibility, where any intermediate state of the session can be restored, either in a *(ii.a)* *multi-step* or a *(ii.b)* *single-step* fashion. Figure 1 sums up the different combinations of sessions and reversibility we consider.

We exemplify the reversible approaches throughout the paper by resorting to a typical business protocol example, drawn from [11]. In case of binary session (Fig. 2(a)), the protocol involves a Buyer willing to buy a book from a Seller.

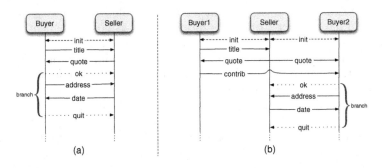

Fig. 2. Single session protocols: Buyer-Seller (a) and Two-Buyers-Seller (b)

Buyer sends the book title to Seller, which replies with a quote. If Buyer is satisfied by the quote, then he sends his address and Seller sends back the delivery date; otherwise Buyer quits the conversation. In the multiparty case (Fig. 2(b)), the above protocol is refined by considering two buyers, Buyer1 and Buyer2, that wish to buy an expensive book from Seller by combining their money. Buyer1 sends the title of the book to Seller, which sends the quote to both Buyer1 and Buyer2. Then, Buyer1 tells Buyer2 how much he is willing to contribute. Buyer2 evaluates how much he has to pay and either accepts, and exchanges the shipping information, or terminates the session. In these scenarios, reversibility can be entered into the game to deal with errors that may occur during the interactions, or to make the protocols more flexible by enabling negotiation via re-iteration of some interactions. For example, a buyer, rather than only accepting or rejecting a quote, can ask the seller for a new quote by simply reverting the interaction where the current quote has been communicated. Similarly, Buyer2 can negotiate the division of the quote with Buyer1. Other possibilities allow the buyers to partially undo the current session, in order to take a different branch along the same session, or even start a new session with (possibly) another seller.

The contribution of this paper is twofold. Firstly, we show for each kind of session discussed above a suitable machinery that permits extending the corresponding non-reversible calculus in order to become reversible. Secondly, we compare the different cases, i.e. (1)–(6) in Fig. 1, by means of their costs for reverting a session, given in

	Binary			Multiparty		
	(1)	(2)	(3)	(4)	(5)	(6)
# backward steps	1	n	1	1	n	1
# memory items	1	n	n	1	n	n

n: number of interactions along the session to be reversed

Fig. 3. Costs of reversing single sessions

terms of number of backward steps and occupancy of the data structures used to store the computation history (which is a necessary information to reverse the effects of session interactions). Our results about reversibility costs are summarised in Fig. 3. It is worth noticing that linearity of sessions permits to achieve costs that are at most linear. Moreover, despite in case of complex interactions the multiparty approach provides a programming style more natural than the binary one, binary and multiparty sessions have the same reversibility costs. We discuss at the end of the paper how our work can extend to multiple sessions, which require a much heavier machinery for reversibility with respect to single ones, and have higher costs. This means that it is not convenient to use in the single session setting the same reversible machineries already developed for calculi with multiple sessions, which further motivates our investigation.

The practical benefit of our systematic study is that it supplies a support to system designers for a conscious selection of the combination of session notion and reversibility mechanism that is best suited to their specific needs.

Summary of the rest of the paper. Section 2 provides background notions on binary and multiparty session-based variants of π-calculus. Section 3 shows how reversibility can be incorporated in single binary sessions and what is its cost, while Sect. 4 focusses on multiparty ones. Section 5 concludes by reviewing strictly related work and by touching upon directions for future work. We refer to the companion technical report [21] for further background material and proofs of results.

2   Background on Session-Based π-calculi

In this section, we give the basic definitions concerning two variants of the π-calculus, enriched with primitives for managing binary and multiparty sessions, respectively.

Binary session calculus. The syntax definition of the binary session π-calculus [22] relies on the following base sets: *variables* (ranged over by x), storing values; *shared channels* (ranged over by a), used to initiate sessions; *session channels* (ranged over by s), consisting on pairs of *endpoints* (ranged over by s, $\bar{s}$) used by the two parties to exchange values within an established session; *labels* (ranged over by l), used to select and offer branching choices; and *process variables* (ranged over by X), used for recursion. Letter u denotes *shared identifiers*, i.e. shared channels and variables together; letter k denotes *session identifiers*, i.e. session endpoints and variables together; letter c denotes *channels*, i.e. session channels and shared channels together. *Values*, including booleans, integers, shared channels and session endpoints, are ranged over by v.

Processes (ranged over by P) and *expressions* (ranged over by e and defined by means of a generic expression operator op representing standard operators on Boolean and integer values) are given by the grammar in Fig. 4.

$P ::=$	Processes
$\quad \bar{u}(x).P \mid u(x).P \mid k!\langle e \rangle.P \mid k?(x).P$	request, accept ,output, input
$\quad \mid k \triangleleft l.P \mid k \triangleright \{l_1 : P_1, \ldots, l_n : P_n\} \mid \mathbf{0} \mid P_1 \mid P_2$	selection, branching, inact, parallel
$\quad \mid (\nu c)\,P \mid \text{if } e \text{ then } P_1 \text{ else } P_2 \mid X \mid \mu X.P$	choice, restriction, recursion
$e ::= v \mid \text{op}(e_1, \ldots, e_n)$	Expressions

Fig. 4. Binary session calculus: syntax

$$\bar{a}(x_1).P_1 \mid a(x_2).P_2 \rightarrow (\nu s)(P_1[\bar{s}/x_1] \mid P_2[s/x_2]) \quad s, \bar{s} \notin \text{fse}(P_1, P_2) \qquad \text{[CON]}$$

$$\bar{k}!\langle e \rangle.P_1 \mid k?(x).P_2 \rightarrow P_1 \mid P_2[v/x] \qquad (k = s \text{ or } k = \bar{s}),\ e \downarrow v \qquad \text{[COM]}$$

$$\bar{k} \triangleleft l_i.P \mid k \triangleright \{l_1 : P_1, \ldots, l_n : P_n\} \rightarrow P \mid P_i \qquad (k = s \text{ or } k = \bar{s}),\ 1 \leq i \leq n\ \text{[LAB]}$$

$$\text{if } e \text{ then } P_1 \text{ else } P_2 \rightarrow P_1 \qquad e \downarrow \text{true} \qquad \text{[IF1]}$$

$$\text{if } e \text{ then } P_1 \text{ else } P_2 \rightarrow P_2 \qquad e \downarrow \text{false} \qquad \text{[IF2]}$$

$$\frac{P_1 \rightarrow P_1'}{P_1 \mid P_2 \rightarrow P_1' \mid P_2}\ \text{[PAR]} \qquad \frac{P \rightarrow P'}{(\nu c)P \rightarrow (\nu c)P'}\ \text{[RES]} \qquad \frac{P_1 \equiv P_1' \rightarrow P_2' \equiv P_2}{P_1 \rightarrow P_2}\ \text{[STR]}$$

Fig. 5. Binary session calculus: reduction relation

The operational semantics of the calculus is given in terms of a structural congruence and of a reduction relation, and is only defined for *closed* terms, i.e. terms without free variables. The *structural congruence*, written ≡, is standard (see [21]). The *reduction relation*, written →, is the smallest relation on closed processes generated by the rules in Fig. 5. We resort to the auxiliary function · ↓ for evaluating closed expressions: $e ↓ v$ says that expression e evaluates to value v. Notationally, for P a process, $\mathrm{fv}(P)$ denotes the set of free variables in P, and $\mathrm{fse}(P)$ the set of free session endpoints. We comment on salient points. A new session is established when two parallel processes synchronise via a shared channel a; this results on the generation of a fresh (private) session channel whose endpoints are assigned to the two session parties (rule [Con]). Along a session, the two parties can exchange values (for data- and channel-passing, rule [Com]) and labels (for branching selection, rule [Lab]). The other rules are standard and state that: conditional choice evolves according to the evaluation of the expression argument (rules [If1] and [If2]); if a part of a larger process evolves, the whole process evolves accordingly (rules [Par] and [Res]); and structural congruent processes have the same reductions (rule [Str]).

The syntax of *sorts* (ranged over by S) and *types* (ranged over by α, β) used in the *binary session type discipline* is defined in Fig. 6. The type $![S].\alpha$ represents the behaviour of first outputting a value of sort S, then performing the actions prescribed by type α; type $![\beta].\alpha$ represents a similar behaviour, which starts with session output (*delegation*) instead; types $?[S].\alpha$ and $?[\beta].\alpha$ are the dual ones, receiving values instead of sending. Type $\oplus[l_1 : \alpha_1, \ldots, l_n : \alpha_n]$ represents the behaviour which would select one of l_i and then behaves as α_i, according to the selected l_i (internal choice). Type $\&[l_1 : \alpha_1, \ldots, l_n : \alpha_n]$ describes a branching behaviour: it waits with n options, and behave as type α_i if the i-th action is selected (external choice). Type end represents inaction, acting as the unit of sequential composition. Type $\mu t.\alpha$ denotes a recursive behaviour, representing

$S ::=$					**Sorts**
	bool $\mid$	int $\mid$	$\langle\alpha\rangle$		boolean, integer, shared channel
$\alpha ::=$					**Types**
	$![S].\alpha \mid$	$![\beta].\alpha \mid$	$?[S].\alpha \mid$	$?[\beta].\alpha$	output, input
$\mid$	$\oplus[l_1 : \alpha_1,\ldots,l_n : \alpha_n] \mid$		$\&[l_1 : \alpha_1,\ldots,l_n : \alpha_n]$		selection, branching
$\mid$	end $\mid$	$t \mid$	$\mu t.\alpha$		end, recursion

Fig. 6. Binary session calculus: sorts and types

$P ::=$				**Processes**
	$\bar{u}[\mathbf{p}](x).P \mid$	$u[\mathbf{p}](x).P \mid$	$k[\mathbf{p}]!\langle e\rangle.P \mid \quad k[\mathbf{p}]?(x).P$	request, accept, output, input
$\mid$	$k[\mathbf{p}] \triangleleft l.P \mid$	$k[\mathbf{p}] \triangleright \{l_1:P_1,\ldots,l_n:P_n\} \mid$	$\mathbf{0} \mid \quad P_1 \mid P_2$	selection, branching, inact, par.
$\mid$	if e then P else $Q \mid$	$(\nu c)\,P \mid$	$X \mid \quad \mu X.P$	choice, restriction, recursion

Fig. 7. Multiparty session calculus: syntax

the behaviour that starts by doing α and, when variable t is encountered, recurs to α again.

Typing judgements are of the form $\Theta; \Gamma \vdash P \rhd \Delta$, where Θ, Γ and Δ, called *basis*, *sorting* and *typing* respectively, are finite partial maps from shared identifiers to sorts, from session identifiers to types, and from process variables to typings, respectively Intuitively, the judgement $\Theta; \Gamma \vdash P \rhd \Delta$ stands for "under the environment $\Theta; \Gamma$, process P has typing Δ". The axioms and rules defining the typing system are standard (see [21]).

Example 1 (Buyer-Seller protocol). We show how the protocol in Fig. 2(a) is rendered in the variant of π-calculus with binary sessions. The behaviour of Buyer is described by the following process:

$$Buyer \triangleq \bar{a}(x).\, x!\langle \text{"}The\ Divine\ Comedy\text{"}\rangle.\, x?(x_{quote}).$$
$$\textbf{if}\ x_{quote} \leq 20\ \textbf{then}\ x \lhd l_{ok}.\, x!\langle addr()\rangle.\, x?(x_{date}).\, P\ \textbf{else}\ x \lhd l_{quit}.\, \mathbf{0}$$

This Buyer is interested in buying the Divine Comedy and is willing to pay not more than 20 euros. The Seller participant instead is rendered as follows:

$$Seller \triangleq a(z).\, z?(z_{title}).\, z!\langle quote(z_{title})\rangle.\, z \rhd \{l_{ok} : z?(z_{addr}).\, z!\langle date()\rangle.\, Q\, ,\, l_{quit} : \mathbf{0}\}$$

Note that $addr()$, $quote()$ and $date()$ are used to get a buyer address, a quote for a given book, and the delivery date, respectively. The overall specification is *Buyer | Seller*.

Multiparty session calculus. The base sets for the synchronous multiparty session calculus [12] are the same of the binary case, except for *session endpoints*, which now are denoted by $s[\mathsf{p}]$, with $\mathsf{p,q}$ ranging over *roles* (represented as natural numbers). Thus, *session identifiers* k now range over session endpoints $s[\mathsf{p}]$ or variables x.

The syntax of the calculus is defined by the grammar in Fig. 7, where expressions e are defined as in the binary case (with values that extends to multiparty session endpoints). Primitive $\bar{u}[\mathsf{p}](x).P$ initiates a new session through identifier u on the other multiple participants, each one of the form $u[\mathsf{q}](x).P_{\mathsf{q}}$ where $1 \leq \mathsf{q} \leq \mathsf{p} - 1$. Variable x will be substituted with the session endpoint used for the interactions inside the established session. Primitive $k[\mathsf{p}]!\langle e\rangle.P$ denotes the intention of sending a value to role p; similarly, process $k[\mathsf{p}]?(x).P$ denotes the intention of receiving a value from role p. Selection and branching behave in a similar way.

As usual the operational semantics is given in terms of a structural congruence and of a reduction relation. The rules defining the structural congruence are the same ones used for the binary calculus where the rule for the scope extension of session channels takes into account the new form of session endpoints. The *reduction relation* $\rightarrow$, instead, is the smallest relation on closed processes generated by the rules [IF1], [IF2], [PAR], [RES] and [STR] in Fig. 5, and the additional rules in Fig. 8. We comment on salient points. Rule [M-CON] synchronously initiates a session by requiring all session endpoints be present for a synchronous reduction, where each role p creates a session endpoint $s[\mathsf{p}]$ on a fresh session

$$\bar{a}[n](x).P_n \mid \prod_{i=\{1,..,n-1\}} a[i](x).P_i \quad\to\quad \qquad s \notin \text{fse}(P_i) \text{ with } i = \{1,..,n\} \quad [\text{M-Con}]$$
$$(\nu s)(P_n[s[n]/x] \mid \prod_{i=\{1,...,n-1\}} P_i[s[i]/x])$$

$$s[\mathsf{p}][\mathsf{q}]!\langle e\rangle.P \mid s[\mathsf{q}][\mathsf{p}]?(x).Q \quad\to\quad P \mid Q[v/x] \qquad\qquad e \downarrow v \quad [\text{M-Com}]$$

$$s[\mathsf{p}][\mathsf{q}] \triangleleft l_i.P \mid s[\mathsf{q}][\mathsf{p}] \triangleright \{l_1 : P_1,\ldots,l_n : P_n\} \quad\to\quad P \mid P_i \qquad 1 \le i \le n \quad [\text{M-Lab}]$$

Fig. 8. Multiparty session calculus: reduction relation (excerpt of rules)

channel s. The participant with the maximum role $(\bar{a}[n](x).P_n)$ is responsible for requesting a session initiation. Rule [M-Com] defines how a party with role p sends a value to the receiving party with role q. Selection and branching are defined in a similar way (rule [M-Lab]).

The type discipline of this synchronous multiparty session calculus is simpler than the asynchronous one in [11], but it is much more elaborate than the binary case, as it considers global and local types. Therefore, due to lack of space, we relegate the definitions of types, as well as the rules of the corresponding type system, to the companion technical report [21] and refer the interested reader to [12] for a detailed account.

Example 2 (Two-Buyers-Seller protocol). We show how the protocol in Fig. 2(b) is rendered in the variant of π-calculus with the multiparty sessions. The behaviour of Buyer1 and Buyer2 are described by the following processes:

$$Buyer1 \triangleq \bar{a}[3](x).\, x[1]!\langle \text{``}The\ Divine\ Comedy\text{''}\rangle.\, x[1]?(x_{quote}).\, x[2]!\langle split(x_{quote})\rangle.\, P_1$$
$$Buyer2 \triangleq a[2](y).\, y[1]?(y_{quote}).\, y[3]?(y_{contrib}).\, \textsf{if}\ \ y_{quote} - y_{contrib} \le 10$$
$$\textsf{then}\ \ y[1] \triangleleft l_{ok}.\, y[1]!\langle addr()\rangle.\, y[1]?(y_{date}).\, P_2\ \ \textsf{else}\ \ y[1] \triangleleft l_{quit}.\, \mathbf{0}$$

Now, Buyer1 divides the quote by means of the $split()$ function. The Seller process is similar to the binary case, but for the form of session endpoints:

$$Seller \triangleq a[1](z).\, z[3]?(z_{title}).\, z[2]!\langle quote(z_{title})\rangle.\, z[3]!\langle lastQuote(z_{title})\rangle.$$
$$z[2] \triangleright \{l_{ok} : z[2]?(z_{addr}).\, z[2]!\langle date()\rangle.P_3\, ,\ l_{quit} : \mathbf{0}\}$$

where $lastQuote()$ simply returns the last quote computed for a given book.

3 Reversibility of Single Binary Sessions

This section formally introduces the notion of single session, and illustrates constructs, mechanisms and costs to support the reversibility in the binary cases.

3.1 Single Sessions

In the single sessions setting, when two processes start a session their continuations only interact along this single session. Thus, neither delegation (i.e., passing of session endpoints) nor initialisation of new sessions (also after the session closure) is allowed. As clarified below, the exclusive use of single sessions

$$
\begin{array}{lll}
P & ::= & \textbf{Reversible processes} \\
 & \quad \dots \quad | \quad \langle s : m \rangle \blacktriangleright P & \pi\text{-calculus processes, single session} \\
m & ::= & \textbf{Memory stacks} \\
 & \quad P \quad | \quad P \cdot m & \text{bottom element, push}
\end{array}
$$

Fig. 9. Reversible extension

is imposed to processes by means of a specific type system, thus avoiding the use of syntactical constraints.

Reversibility is incorporated in a process calculus typically by adding memory devices to store information about the computation history, which otherwise would be lost during computations. In all single session cases, i.e. (1)-(6) in Fig. 1, we will extend the syntax of (binary/multiparty) session-based π-calculus as shown in Fig. 9. The term $\langle s : m \rangle \blacktriangleright P$ represents a *single session* along the channel s with associated memory m and code P. A *memory* m is a (non-empty) stack of processes, each one corresponding to a state of the session (the bottom element corresponds to the term that initialised the session). The term $\langle s : m \rangle \blacktriangleright P$ is a binder, i.e. it binds session channel s in P. In this respect, it acts similarly to operator $(\nu s)P$, but the scope of $\langle s : m \rangle \blacktriangleright P$ cannot be extended.

In the obtained reversible calculi, terms can perform, besides standard *forward computations*, also *backward computations* that undo the effect of the former ones.

We compare approaches (1)-(6) with respect to the *cost* of reverting a session in the worst case, i.e. the cost of completely reverting a session. The cost is given in terms of *(i)* the *number of backward reductions* $(\mathcal{C}_{br})$, necessary to complete the rollback, and *(ii)* *memory occupancy* $(\mathcal{C}_{mo})$, i.e. the number of element in the memory stack of the session when the rollback starts. The two kinds of cost depend on the *length* of the considered session, given by the number of (forward) steps performed along the session.

3.2   Binary Session Reversibility

Not all processes allowed by the syntax presented above corresponds to meaningful processes in the reversible single sessions setting. Indeed, on the one hand, the syntax allows terms violating the single sessions limitation. On the other hand, in a general term of the calculus the history stored in its memories may not be consistent with the computation that has taken place.

We address the above issues by only considering a class of well-formed processes, called *reachable* processes. In the definition of this class of processes, to ensure the use of single sessions only, as in [11] we resort to the notion of *simple* process.

Definition 1 (Simple process). *A process is* simple *if (i) it is generated by the grammar in Fig. 4 and (ii) it is typable with a type derivation using prefix* *rules where the session typings in the premise and the conclusion are restricted to at most a singleton*[1].

The point (i) of the above definition states that a simple process has no memory, while point (ii) states that each prefixed subterm in a simple process uses only a single session.

The following properties clarify the notion of simple process.

Property 1. In a simple process, delegation is disallowed.

Proof. The proof proceeds by contradiction and straightforwardly follows from Definition 1 (see [21]).

Property 2. In a simple process, subordinate sessions (i.e., new sessions initialised within the single session) are disallowed.

Proof. The proof proceeds by contradiction (see [21]).

We explain the meaning of subordinate session used in Property 2 by means of an example. Let us consider the process $a(x).b(y).x!\langle 1 \rangle.P$ with $y \in \text{fv}(P)$, which initialises a (subordinate) session using channel b within a session previously initialised using channel a. This process is not simple, because typing it requires to type the (sub)process $b(y).x!\langle 1 \rangle.P$ under typing $x :![\text{int}].\alpha$, which is not empty as required by Definition 1.

Now, to ensure history consistency, as in [6] we only consider *reachable* processes, i.e. processes obtained by means of forward reductions from simple processes.

Definition 2. (Reachable processes). *The set of* reachable *processes, for the case (i) in Fig. 1 with $i \in \{1, 2, 3\}$, is the closure under relation $\twoheadrightarrow_{(i)}$ (see below) of the set of simple processes.*

We clarify this notion by means of an example. The process stored in the memory of term $\langle s : (\bar{a}(x).x!\langle 1 \rangle \mid a(y).y?(z))) \rangle \blacktriangleright (\bar{s}!\langle 2 \rangle \mid s?(z))$ is not consistent with the related session process, because there is no way to generate the term $(\bar{s}!\langle 2 \rangle \mid s?(z))$ from the stored process (in fact, in the session process, the value sent along the endpoint $\bar{s}$ should be 1 instead of 2).

We now present the semantics of the reversibility machinery in the three binary cases. As usual, the operational semantics is given in terms of a structural congruence and a reduction relation[2]. For all three cases, the laws defining the

---

[1] Using the standard typing system for the binary session π-calculus (see [21, Figure 13]), point (ii) boils down to: Δ of rules [REQ], [ACC], [SEND], [RCV], [SEL] and [BR] are empty; neither [THR] nor [CAT] is used; $\Delta \cdot \Delta'$ in [CONC] contains at most a singleton; and Δ of the remaining rules contain at most a singleton.

[2] We use a reduction semantics with respect to a labelled one because the former is simpler (e.g., it does not require to deal with scope extension of names) and, hence, is preferable when the labelled semantics is not needed (e.g., here we are not interested in labelled bisimulations). Moreover, works about session-based π-calculus use a reduction semantics, as well as many reversible calculi (e.g., [4, 14, 16]).

$$\text{if } e \text{ then } P_1 \text{ else } P_2 \; \twoheadrightarrow_{(i)} \; P_1 \qquad e \downarrow \text{true} \qquad [\text{FW-IF1}]$$

$$\text{if } e \text{ then } P_1 \text{ else } P_2 \; \twoheadrightarrow_{(i)} \; P_2 \qquad e \downarrow \text{false} \qquad [\text{FW-IF2}]$$

$$\frac{P_1 \; \twoheadrightarrow_{(i)} \; P_1'}{P_1 \mid P_2 \; \twoheadrightarrow_{(i)} \; P_1' \mid P_2} \; [\text{FW-PAR}] \qquad \frac{P \; \twoheadrightarrow_{(i)} \; P'}{(\nu c)P \; \twoheadrightarrow_{(i)} \; (\nu c)P'} \; [\text{FW-RES}]$$

$$\frac{P \equiv P' \; \twoheadrightarrow_{(i)} \; Q' \equiv Q}{P \; \twoheadrightarrow_{(i)} \; Q} \; [\text{FW-STR}]$$

Fig. 10. Single sessions: shared forward and backward rules (for $i \in \{1..6\}$); rules [Bw-Par], [Bw-Res], [Bw-Str] are omitted (they are like the forward rules where $\rightsquigarrow_{(i)}$ replaces $\twoheadrightarrow_{(i)}$)

structural congruence are the same of the binary session calculus. Instead, the *reduction* relations for the cases (1)–(3), written $\longmapsto_{(i)}$ with i $\in \{1, 2, 3\}$, are given as the union of the corresponding *forward reduction* relations $\twoheadrightarrow_{(i)}$ and *backward reduction* relations $\rightsquigarrow_{(i)}$, which are defined by different sets of rules in the three cases. Notably, the rules in Fig. 10, whose meaning is straightforward, are shared between the three cases.

The semantics is only defined for closed, reachable terms, where now the definition of *closed* term extends to session endpoints, in the sense that all occurrences of session endpoints s and $\bar{s}$ have to be bound by a single session term $\langle s : m \rangle \blacktriangleright \cdot$. This latter requirement is needed for ensuring that every running session in the considered process can be reverted; for example, in the reachable process $(\bar{s}!\langle 1 \rangle \mid s?(x) \mid Q)$ there is a running session s that cannot be reverted because no computation history information (i.e., no memory stack) is available for it. We discuss below the additional definitions for the operational semantics of the three binary cases.

(1) Whole session reversibility. In this case the reversibility machinery of the calculus permits to undo only whole sessions. The forward rules additional to those in Fig. 10 are as follows:

$$P \; \twoheadrightarrow_{(1)} \; \langle s : P \rangle \blacktriangleright (P_1[\bar{s}/x] \mid P_2[s/y]) \qquad P = (\bar{a}(x).P_1 \mid a(y).P_2) \quad [\text{Fw(1)-Con}]$$

$$\frac{P \; \rightarrow \; P'}{\langle s : m \rangle \blacktriangleright P \; \twoheadrightarrow_{(1)} \; \langle s : m \rangle \blacktriangleright P'} \; [\text{Fw(1)-Mem}]$$

Rule [Fw(1)-Con] initiates a single session s with the initialisation term P stored in the memory stack. As usual the two session endpoints $\bar{s}$ and s replace the corresponding variables x and y in the two continuations P_1 and P_2 (within the scope of the single session construct). Notably, there is no need of using the restriction operator, because in the single session setting the session endpoints cannot be communicated outside the session, i.e., delegation is disallowed (Property 1). Moreover, differently from the non-reversible case (see rule [Con] in Fig. 5), there is also no need of requiring the session endpoints s and $\bar{s}$ to be fresh in the session code (i.e., in P_1 and P_2), because of the notion of closed process given in this section. Rule [Fw(1)-Mem] simply states that a process

within the scope of a single session evolves with a forward reduction according
to its evolution with a standard reduction (defined in Fig. 5).

The only additional backward rule is the following one:

$$\langle s : P \rangle \blacktriangleright Q \rightsquigarrow_{(1)} P \qquad [\text{Bw}(1)]$$

This rule permits to rollback the whole session conversation in every moment
during its execution. In particular, the term that initialised the session is restored
with a single backward reduction step. Notably, the fact that scope extension is
not allowed for the operator $\langle \cdot : \cdot \rangle \blacktriangleright \cdot$ ensures that the process Q in $[\text{Bw}(1)]$
does not contain processes not belonging to session s, i.e. unwanted deletions are
prevented. It is also worth noticing that the rollback of session s does not involve
other sessions, as no subordinate sessions can be active in Q (Property 2).

(2) Multi-step. In this case a session can be reversed either partially or totally.
When the rollback starts, it proceeds step-by-step and can terminate in any intermediate state of the session, as well as in the initialisation state. The additional
forward rules are:

$$P \twoheadrightarrow_{(2)} \langle s : P \rangle \blacktriangleright (P_1[\bar{s}/x] \mid P_2[s/y]) \qquad P = (\bar{a}(x).P_1 \mid a(y).P_2) \quad [\text{Fw}(2)\text{-Con}]$$

$$\frac{P \rightarrow P'}{\langle s : m \rangle \blacktriangleright P \twoheadrightarrow_{(2)} \langle s : P \cdot m \rangle \blacktriangleright P'} \quad [\text{Fw}(2)\text{-Mem}]$$

Differently from the case (1), here it is necessary to keep track in the memory
stack of each (forward) interaction that has taken place in the session. Therefore,
the forward rule $[\text{Fw}(2)\text{-Mem}]$ pushes the process P, representing the state
before the transition, into the stack.

The backward reduction relation is defined by the following additional rules:

$$\langle s : P \rangle \blacktriangleright Q \rightsquigarrow_{(2)} P \quad [\text{Bw}(2)\text{-1}] \qquad \langle s : P \cdot m \rangle \blacktriangleright Q \rightsquigarrow_{(2)} \langle s : m \rangle \blacktriangleright P \quad [\text{Bw}(2)\text{-2}]$$

Rule $[\text{Bw}(2)\text{-1}]$ is like to $[\text{Bw}(1)]$, but here it can be used only when the memory stack contains just one element. The single session is removed because its
initialisation state is restored. Rule $[\text{Bw}(2)\text{-2}]$, instead, permits undoing an intermediate state Q, by simply replacing it with the previous intermediate state P.
In this case, since after the reduction the stack is not empty, the single session
construct is not removed.

(3) Single-step. This is similar to the previous case, but the rollback (also of
intermediate states) is always performed in a single step. The forward reduction
relation is defined by the same rules of case (2), where $\twoheadrightarrow_{(3)}$ replaces $\twoheadrightarrow_{(2)}$, while
the backward one is defined by the following additional rules:

$$\langle s : P \rangle \blacktriangleright Q \rightsquigarrow_{(3)} P \qquad [\text{Bw}(3)\text{-1}] \qquad \langle s : P \cdot m \rangle \blacktriangleright Q \rightsquigarrow_{(3)} \langle s : m \rangle \blacktriangleright P \qquad [\text{Bw}(3)\text{-2}]$$
$$\langle s : m \cdot P \rangle \blacktriangleright Q \rightsquigarrow_{(3)} P \quad [\text{Bw}(3)\text{-3}] \qquad \langle s : m' \cdot P \cdot m \rangle \blacktriangleright Q \rightsquigarrow_{(3)} \langle s : m \rangle \blacktriangleright P \quad [\text{Bw}(3)\text{-4}]$$

Rules $[\text{Bw}(3)\text{-1}]$ and $[\text{Bw}(3)\text{-2}]$ are like $[\text{Bw}(2)\text{-1}]$ and $[\text{Bw}(2)\text{-2}]$, respectively.
In particular, rule $[\text{Bw}(3)\text{-2}]$ is still used to replace the current state by the
previous one. In addition to this, now rule $[\text{Bw}(3)\text{-4}]$ permits to replace the
current state Q also by an intermediate state P of the session computation; this

is done in a single step. Notice that all interactions that took place after the one produced by P (i.e., the states stored in m') are erased when P is restored, while the previous interactions (i.e., the states stored in m) are kept. Notice also that the selection of the past state to restore is non-deterministic. A real-world reversible language instead should provide specific primitives and mechanisms to control reversibility (see discussion on Sect. 5); anyway the controlled selection of the past states does not affect the reversibility costs, hence this aspect is out-of-scope for this paper and left for future investigations. Rule [Bw(3)-3] permits to directly undo the whole session from an intermediate state.

Results. The cost of reverting a session in setting (1), in terms of both backward reductions ($\mathcal{C}_{br}$) and memory occupancy ($\mathcal{C}_{mo}$), is *constant* w.r.t. the session length. In case (2), instead, the costs are linear in the length of the session (recall that we consider the worst case, where the session is completely reversed). Finally, in setting (3) the cost is constant in terms of backward reductions, and linear in terms of memory occupancy.

Theorem 1. *Let n be the length of a session, the costs of reverting it are: case (1) $\mathcal{C}_{br} = \mathcal{C}_{mo} = 1$; case (2) $\mathcal{C}_{br} = \mathcal{C}_{mo} = n$; case (3) $\mathcal{C}_{br} = 1$ and $\mathcal{C}_{mo} = n$.*

Proof. The proof of case (1) is straightforward, while proofs of cases (2) and (3) proceed by induction on n (see [21]). ∎

The following result shows that single binary sessions of cases (2) and (3) enjoy a standard property of reversible calculi (Loop lemma, see [7]): backward reductions are the inverse of the forward ones and vice versa.

Lemma 1 (Loop lemma). *Let $P = \langle s : m \rangle \blacktriangleright Q$ and $P' = \langle s : m' \rangle \blacktriangleright Q'$ be two reachable processes in setting (i), with $i \in \{2, 3\}$. $P \rightarrow_{(i)} P'$ if and only if $P' \rightsquigarrow_{(i)} P$.*

Proof. The proof for the *if* (resp. *only if*) part is by induction on the derivation of the forward (resp. backward) reduction (see [21]). ∎

Notably, case (1) does not enjoy this lemma because backward reductions do not allow to restore intermediate states of sessions.

We conclude the section with an example showing the three approaches at work on the Buyer-Seller protocol.

Example 3. (Reversible Buyer-Seller protocol). Let us consider a reversible scenario concerning the Buyer-Seller protocol specified in Example 1, where there are two sellers and a buyer.

In case (1), the system evolves as follows:

$$Seller_1 \mid Seller_2 \mid Buyer$$
$$\rightarrow_{(1)} Seller_1 \mid \langle s : Seller_2 \mid Buyer \rangle \blacktriangleright (s?(z_{title}).P_s \mid \bar{s}!\langle v_{title} \rangle.P_b)$$
$$\rightarrow^*_{(1)} Seller_1 \mid \langle s : Seller_2 \mid Buyer \rangle \blacktriangleright (Q[\ldots] \mid P[\ldots, v_{date}/x_{date}]) = R$$

where v_{title} stands for *"The Divine Comedy"*. After these interactions between *Buyer* and *Seller$_2$*, the buyer has received a delivery date from the seller. In the unfortunate case that this date is not suitable for the buyer, the session can be reversed as follows:

$$R \rightsquigarrow_{(1)} Seller_1 \mid Seller_2 \mid Buyer$$

Now, *Buyer* can start a new session with *Seller$_2$* as well as with *Seller$_1$*.

In case (2), the parties can reach the same state as follows:

$$Seller_1 \mid Seller_2 \mid Buyer \rightarrow^*_{(2)} Seller_1 \mid \langle s : m \rangle \blacktriangleright (Q[\ldots] \mid P[\ldots, v_{date}/x_{date}]) = R'$$

where m is $R_{date} \cdot R_{addr} \cdot R_{ok} \cdot R_{if} \cdot R_{quote} \cdot R_{title}$, with R_i denoting the process generating the interaction i. In this case, the buyer can undo only the last two session interactions as follows:

$$R' \rightsquigarrow_{(2)} Seller_1 \mid \langle s : m' \rangle \blacktriangleright R_{date} \rightsquigarrow_{(2)} Seller_1 \mid \langle s : m'' \rangle \blacktriangleright R_{addr}$$

with $m' = R_{addr} \cdot m''$ and $m'' = R_{ok} \cdot R_{if} \cdot R_{quote} \cdot R_{title}$. Now, the buyer can possibly send a different address to the seller in order to get a more suitable date (as we assume $addr()$ and $date()$ be two non-deterministic functions abstracting the interaction with buyer and seller backends).

Finally, in case (3), the system can reach again the state R', but this time the session can be also partially reversed by means of a single backward step:

$$R' \rightsquigarrow_{(3)} Seller_1 \mid \langle s : m'' \rangle \blacktriangleright R_{addr}$$

4 Reversibility of Single Multiparty Sessions

For the same motivations of the binary case, we do not consider all processes allowed by the syntax of the reversible multiparty single-session calculus, obtained by extending the grammar in Fig. 7 with the single sessions construct in Fig. 9. Again, we consider only reachable processes, whose definition relies on the notion of simple process.

Definition 3. (Multiparty simple process). *A multiparty process is* simple *if (i) it is generated by the grammar in Fig. 7 and (ii) it is typable with a type derivation using the prefix rules where the session typings in the premise and the conclusion are restricted to at most a singleton*[3].

Definition 4. (Multiparty reachable processes). *The set of* reachable *processes, for the case (i) in Fig. 1 with $i \in \{4, 5, 6\}$, is the closure under relation* $\rightarrow_{(i)}$ *(see below) of the set of multiparty simple processes.*

---

[3] Using the typing system for the synchronous multiparty session π-calculus (see [21], Figure 15]), point (ii) boils down to: Δ of rules [MREQ], [MACC], [SEND], [RECV], [SEL] and [BRA] are empty; neither [DELEG] nor [SRECV] is used; $\Delta \cdot \Delta'$ in [CONC] contains at most a singleton; and Δ of the remaining rules contain at most a single-ton.

We now present the semantics of the three multiparty cases. For the definition of the reduction relations we still rely on the shared rules in Fig. 10.

(4) Whole session reversibility. In case the reversibility machinery only permits to undo a whole session, the forward reduction relation is defined by these additional rules:

$$P \twoheadrightarrow_{(4)} \langle s : P \rangle \blacktriangleright (P_n[s[n]/x] \mid \prod_{i=\{1,..,n-1\}} P_i[s[i]/x]) \qquad [\text{Fw}(4)\text{-M-Con}]$$
$$P = (\bar{a}[n](x).P_n \mid \prod_{i=\{1,..,n-1\}} a[i](x).P_i)$$

$$\frac{P \rightarrow P'}{\langle s : m \rangle \blacktriangleright P \twoheadrightarrow_{(4)} \langle s : m \rangle \blacktriangleright P'} \quad [\text{Fw}(4)\text{-Mem}]$$

The meaning of these rules is similar to that of $[\text{Fw}(1)\text{-Con}]$ and $[\text{Fw}(1)\text{-Mem}]$, with the only difference that the initialised single session is multiparty.

The backward reduction relation is given by the same rules of case (1), of course defined for relation $\rightsquigarrow_{(4)}$ instead of $\rightsquigarrow_{(1)}$.

(5) Multi-step. When sessions can be reversed also partially, in a step-by-step fashion, the additional forward rules are as follows:

$$P \twoheadrightarrow_{(5)} \langle s : P \rangle \blacktriangleright (P_n[s[n]/x] \mid \prod_{i=\{1,..,n-1\}} P_i[s[i]/x]) \qquad [\text{Fw}(5)\text{-M-Con}]$$
$$P = (\bar{a}[n](x).P_n \mid \prod_{i=\{1,..,n-1\}} a[i](x).P_i)$$

$$\frac{P \rightarrow P'}{\langle s : m \rangle \blacktriangleright P \twoheadrightarrow_{(5)} \langle s : P \cdot m \rangle \blacktriangleright P'} \quad [\text{Fw}(5)\text{-Mem}]$$

These rules are the natural extension of the corresponding rules of the binary version, i.e. case (2). Their meaning, indeed, is the same.

The backward reduction relation in setting (5) is given by the same rules of case (2) where relation $\rightsquigarrow_{(2)}$ is replaced by $\rightsquigarrow_{(5)}$.

It is worth noticing that, by Definitions 3 and 4, concurrent interactions along the same session are prevented (by the type discipline in [12], which forces a linear use of session channels). Therefore, there is no need here to use a more complex reversible machinery (as in [20]) for enabling a causal-consistent form of session reversibility.

(6) Single-step. As in the corresponding binary session setting, here the forward reduction relation is defined by the same rules of the multi-step case, i.e. case (5), where $\twoheadrightarrow_{(6)}$ replaces $\twoheadrightarrow_{(5)}$. Instead, the backward reduction relation is defined by the same rules of case (3), where $\rightsquigarrow_{(6)}$ replaces $\rightsquigarrow_{(3)}$.

Results. The cost of reverting a session in setting (4) is constant, while it is linear in the length of the session in case (5). In setting (6), instead, the cost is constant in terms of backward reductions, and linear in terms of memory occupancy.

Theorem 2. *Let n be the length of a session, the costs of reverting it are: case (4) $C_{br} = C_{mo} = 1$; case (5) $C_{br} = C_{mo} = n$; case (6) $C_{br} = 1$ and $C_{mo} = n$.*

Proof. The proof of case (4) is a trivial adaptation of the proof of case (1) in Theorem 1, while proofs of cases (5) and (6) proceed by induction on n (see [21]).

In all multiparty approaches, cases (4)-(6), the backward computations have the same semantics of the corresponding binary approaches, cases (1)-(3), respectively. An important consequence of this fact is that the cost of reverting a session in a multiparty case is the same of the corresponding binary case. In other words, we can claim that *extending binary sessions to multiparty ones, in the single session setting, does not affect the machinery for the reversibility and its costs.*

As in the binary case, also the multiparty sessions of cases (5) and (6) enjoy the Loop lemma.

Lemma 2. (Loop lemma). *Let $P = \langle s : m \rangle \blacktriangleright Q$ and $P' = \langle s : m' \rangle \blacktriangleright Q'$ be two reachable processes in setting (i), with $i \in \{5, 6\}$. $P \twoheadrightarrow_{(i)} P'$ if and only if $P' \rightsquigarrow_{(i)} P$.*

Proof. The proof for the *if* (resp. *only if*) part is by induction on the derivation of the forward (resp. backward) reduction (see [21]).

We conclude by showing the three multiparty approaches at work on the Two-Buyers-Seller protocol.

Example 4. (Reversible Two-Buyers-Seller protocol). We consider a reversible scenario of the Two-Buyers-Seller session protocol specified in Example 2.

In case (4), the system can evolve as follows:

$$Buyer_1 \mid Buyer_2 \mid Seller$$
$$\twoheadrightarrow_{(4)} \langle s : Buyer_1 \mid Buyer_2 \mid Seller \rangle \blacktriangleright$$
$$(s[3][1]!\langle v_{title}\rangle. s[3][1]?(x_{quote}). P_{b1} \mid s[2][1]?(y_{quote}). P_{b2}$$
$$\mid s[1][3]?(z_{title}). s[1][2]!\langle quote(z_{title})\rangle. s[1][3]!\langle lastQuote(z_{title})\rangle. P_s)$$
$$\twoheadrightarrow_{(4)}^{*} \langle s : Buyer_1 \mid Buyer_2 \mid Seller \rangle \blacktriangleright$$
$$(P_{b1}[v_{quote}/x_{quote}] \mid P_{b2}[v_{quote}/y_{quote}] \mid P_{b1}[v_{title}/x_{title}]) \quad = \quad R$$

These interactions lead to a state where both buyers have received the seller's quote for the requested book. Now, if one of the two buyers is not satisfied with the proposed quote, he can immediately stop the session execution and reverse it with a single step:

$$R \rightsquigarrow_{(4)} Buyer_1 \mid Buyer_2 \mid Seller$$

In case (5), instead, the protocol execution can lead to a similar state, say R', with the difference that the session memory m keeps track of the traversed states, i.e. m is $R_{quote2} \cdot R_{quote1} \cdot R_{title}$. In this case, the unsatisfied buyer can enact a sort of negotiation by undoing the last two session interactions:

$$R' \rightsquigarrow_{(5)} \langle s : R_{quote1} \cdot R_{title} \rangle \blacktriangleright R_{quote2} \rightsquigarrow_{(5)} \langle s : R_{title} \rangle \blacktriangleright R_{quote1}$$

From the state R_{quote1} the seller can compute again the quote for the requested book.

Finally, in case (6), the system can reach again the state R' and, likewise case (3), the session can be partially reversed by means of a single backward step:

$$R' \rightsquigarrow_{(6)} \langle s : R_{title} \rangle \blacktriangleright R_{quote1}$$

5   Concluding Remarks

This work falls within a large body of research that aims at studying at foundational level the integration of reversibility in concurrent and distributed systems. In particular, reversible variants of well-established process calculi, such as CCS and π-calculus, have been proposed as *untyped* formalisms for studying reversibility mechanisms in these systems. Relevant works along this line of research have been surveyed in [15]. Among them, we would like to mention the works that are closely related to ours, as they have been source of inspiration: RCCS [7], from which we borrow the use of memory stacks for keeping track of computation history; $R\pi$ [6], from which we borrow the notion of reachable process (see Definition 2); $R\mu Oz$ [16], which analyses reversibility costs in terms of space overhead; and $\rho\pi$ [14], from which we borrow the use of a reversible reduction semantics (which is motivated by the fact that a labelled semantics would complicate our theoretical framework). However, all works mentioned above only focus on causal-consistent reversibility mechanisms for untyped concurrent systems, without taking into account how they may impact on linearity-based structured interactions, which is indeed our aim. Moreover, none of the above work provides a systematic study of the different forms of reversibility we consider, namely whole session, multi-step and single-step, and of their costs.

The works with the aim closest to ours are [2] and [20]. The former paper studies session reversibility on a formalism based on session behaviours [1], which is a sort of sub-language of CCS with a checkpoint-based backtracking mechanism. The commonality with our work is the use of a one-size memory for each behaviour, which records indeed only the behaviour prefixed by the lastly traversed checkpoint. This resembles the one-size memories that we use in cases (1) and (4), with the difference that our checkpoints correspond to the initialisation states of sessions. On the other hand, session behaviours provide a formalism much simpler than session-based π-calculus, as e.g. message passing is not even considered. Differently from our work, [2] does not consider different solutions for enabling alternative forms of reversibility and does not provide a study of session reversibility complexity. The latter paper introduces $ReS\pi$, a reversible variant of the π-calculus with binary multiple sessions. $ReS\pi$ embeds a multi-step form of reversibility and, rather than using a single stack memory per session, it uses a graph-like data structure and unique thread identifiers. Each element of this structure is devoted to record data concerning a single event, corresponding to the taking place of a communication action, a choice or a thread forking. Thread identifiers are used as links among memory elements, in order to form a structure for conveniently keeping track of the causal dependences among the session interactions. These dependences are crucial in the multiple session setting, where computations have to be undone in a *causal-consistent* fashion [3,7], that is independent concurrent interactions can be undone in an order different from that of the forward computation. Differently from the present work, which considers both binary and multiparty session types, [20] only focusses on the binary version. In addition, it does not address any cost issues about reversible sessions.

We plan to study the cost of reversing multiple sessions, where interactions along different sessions can be interleaved. By looking at $ReS\pi$, we can see that passing from single sessions to multiple ones has significant impacts: firstly, in terms of complexity of the memory structure, and secondly in terms of costs. In the multiple case, reverting a session corresponds to revert a concurrent computation in a causal-consistent way, which requires to revert all interactions performed along other sessions that have a casual dependence with the interactions of the session to be reverted. This means that, in general, the cost is not defined only in terms of the length of the considered session, but it must include also the cost of reverting the depending interactions of other sessions.

Another future direction that we plan to consider for our study concerns how the use of primitives and mechanisms to *control* reversibility (see, e.g., [13]) affect our results. In a controlled approach for session reversibility, backward steps would not be always enabled, but they would be triggered by specific rollback actions.

Moreover, we intend to extend our analysis on memory cost. In fact, the approach used in this work is *coarse-grained*, as it is based on the number of elements of the stacks rather than on the amount of memory necessary for storing such elements. A fine-grained view is indeed not necessary for the purpose of this work, as we just want to compare the different combinations of session and reversibility approaches and, in particular, to distinguish the whole session reversibility with respect to the other cases, and we want to show that single-step interaction reversibility and multi-step ones require memory with the same number of elements. Nevertheless, a fine-grained analysis on memory cost and an investigation of more compact representations of computation history would be interesting extensions of this work.

Finally, the enactment of reversibility is currently based on the information stored in the syntactical terms representing the involved processes. We plan to investigate the use of type information to enact and manage reversibility.

References

1. Barbanera, F., de'Liguoro, U.: Sub-behaviour relations for session-based client/server systems. Math. Struct. Comput. Sci. **25**(6), 1339–1381 (2015)
2. Barbanera, F., Dezani-Ciancaglini, M., de'Liguoro, U.: Compliance for reversible client/server interactions. In: BEAT, vol. 162, EPTCS, pp. 35–42 (2014)
3. Berry, G., Lévy, J.-J.: Minimal and optimal computations of recursive programs. J. ACM **26**(1), 148–175 (1979)
4. Cardelli, L., Laneve, C.: Reversible structures. In: CMSB, pp. 131–140. ACM (2011)

5. Coppo, M., Dezani-Ciancaglini, M., Yoshida, N.: Asynchronous session types and progress for object oriented languages. In: Bonsangue, M.M., Johnsen, E.B. (eds.) FMOODS 2007. LNCS, vol. 4468, pp. 1–31. Springer, Heidelberg (2007)
6. Cristescu, I., Krivine, J., Varacca, D.: A compositional semantics for the reversible p-calculus. In: LICS, pp. 388–397. IEEE (2013)
7. Danos, V., Krivine, J.: Reversible communicating systems. In: Gardner, P., Yoshida, N. (eds.) CONCUR 2004. LNCS, vol. 3170, pp. 292–307. Springer, Heidelberg (2004)
8. Danos, V., Krivine, J.: Transactions in RCCS. In: Abadi, M., de Alfaro, L. (eds.) CONCUR 2005. LNCS, vol. 3653, pp. 398–412. Springer, Heidelberg (2005)
9. Danos, V., Krivine, J.: formal molecular biology done in CCS-R. Electr. Notes. Theor. Comput. Sci. **180**(3), 31–49 (2007)
10. Honda, K., Vasconcelos, V.T., Kubo, M.: Language primitives and type discipline for structured communication-based programming. In: Hankin, C. (ed.) ESOP 1998. LNCS, vol. 1381, pp. 122–138. Springer, Heidelberg (1998)
11. Honda, K., Yoshida, N., Carbone, M.: Multiparty asynchronous session types. J. ACM (2015, to appear). http://mrg.doc.ic.ac.uk. An extended abstract appeared in the Proc. of POPL 2008
12. Kouzapas, D., Yoshida, N.: Globally governed session semantics. Log. Methods Comput. Sci. **10**(4), 1–45 (2014)
13. Lanese, I., Mezzina, C.A., Schmitt, A., Stefani, J.-B.: Controlling reversibility in higher-order pi. In: Katoen, J.-P., König, B. (eds.) CONCUR 2011. LNCS, vol. 6901, pp. 297–311. Springer, Heidelberg (2011)
14. Lanese, I., Mezzina, C.A., Stefani, J.-B.: Reversing higher-order pi. In: Gastin, P., Laroussinie, F. (eds.) CONCUR 2010. LNCS, vol. 6269, pp. 478–493. Springer, Heidelberg (2010)
15. Lanese, I., Mezzina, C.A., Tiezzi, F.: Causal-consistent reversibility. Bull. EATCS **114**, 121–139 (2014)
16. Lienhardt, M., Lanese, I., Mezzina, C.A., Stefani, J.-B.: A reversible abstract machine and its space overhead. In: Giese, H., Rosu, G. (eds.) FORTE 2012 and FMOODS 2012. LNCS, vol. 7273, pp. 1–17. Springer, Heidelberg (2012)
17. Milner, R., Parrow, J., Walker, D.: A calculus of mobile processes I and II. Inf. Comput. **100**(1), 1–40 (1992). pp. 41–77
18. Mostrous, D., Yoshida, N.: Session typing and asynchronous subtyping for the higher-order π-calculus. Inf. Comput. **241**, 227–263 (2015)
19. Phillips, I., Ulidowski, I.: Reversing algebraic process calculi. J. Log. Algebr. Program. **73**(1–2), 70–96 (2007)
20. Tiezzi, F., Yoshida, N.: Reversible session-based pi-calculus. J. Log. Algebr. Methods Program. **84**(5), 684–707 (2015)
21. Tiezzi, F., Yoshida, N.: Reversing single sessions. CoRR (2015). abs/1510.07253
22. Yoshida, N., Vasconcelos, V.T.: Language primitives and type discipline for structured communication-based programming revisited: two systems for higher-order session communication. Electr. Notes Theor. Comp. Sci. **171**(4), 73–93 (2007)

Reversible Models

Reversible Causal Graph Dynamics

Pablo Arrighi[1], Simon Martiel[2]($\boxtimes$), and Simon Perdrix[3]

[1] Aix-Marseille University, LIF, F-13288 Marseille Cedex 9, France
pablo.arrighi@univ-amu.fr
[2] University Nice Sophia Antipolis, I3S, 06900 Sophia Antipolis, France
martiel@i3s.unice.fr
[3] CNRS, LORIA, Inria Project Team CARTE, University de Lorraine, Nancy, France
simon.perdrix@loria.fr

Abstract. Causal Graph Dynamics extend Cellular Automata to arbitrary, bounded-degree, time-varying graphs. The whole graph evolves in discrete time steps, and this global evolution is required to have a number of physics-like symmetries: shift-invariance (it acts everywhere the same) and causality (information has a bounded speed of propagation). We study a further physics-like symmetry, namely reversibility. We extend a fundamental result on reversible cellular automata by proving that the inverse of a causal graph dynamics is a causal graph dynamics. We also address the question of the evolution of the structure of the graphs under reversible causal graph dynamics, showing that any reversible causal graph dynamics preserves the size of all but a finite number of graphs.

Keywords: Bijective · Invertible · Cayley graphs · Hedlund · Reversible cellular automata

1 Introduction

Cellular Automata (CA) consist in a $\mathbb{Z}^n$ grid of identical cells, each of which may take a state among a finite set Σ. Thus the configurations are in $\Sigma^{\mathbb{Z}^n}$. The state of each cell at time $t + 1$ is given by applying a fixed local rule f to the cell and its neighbours, synchronously and homogeneously across space. CA constitute the most established model of computation that accounts for euclidean space. They are widely used to model spatially distributed computation (self-replicating machines, synchronization problems...), as well as a great variety of multi-agents phenomena (traffic jams, demographics...). But their origin lies in Physics, where they are commonly used to model waves or particles. Since small scale physics is understood to be reversible, it was natural to endow them with this further, physics-like symmetry: reversibility. The study of Reversible CA (RCA) was further motivated by the promise of lower energy consumption in reversible computation. RCA have turned out to have a beautiful mathematical theory, which relies on topological and algebraic characterizations in order to prove that the inverse of a CA is a CA [12].

© Springer International Publishing Switzerland 2016
S. Devitt and I. Lanese (Eds.): RC 2016, LNCS 9720, pp. 73–88, 2016.
DOI: 10.1007/978-3-319-40578-0_5

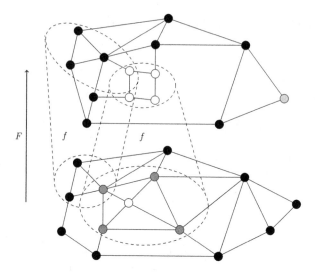

Fig. 1. *Informal illustration of causal graph dynamics.* The entire graph evolves into another according to a global function F. But this evolution is causal (information propagates at a bounded speed) and homogeneous (same causes lead to same effects). This has been shown to be equivalent to applying a local function f to every subdisk of the input graphs, leading to small output graphs whose union makes up the output graph. In this paper, we take the global approach as the starting point, in order to prove that the inverse has the same properties.

Causal Graph Dynamics (CGD) [1,2], on the other hand, deal with a twofold extension of CA. First, the underlying grid is extended to being an arbitrary – possibly infinite – bounded-degree graph G. Informally, this means that each vertex of the graph may take a state among a finite set Σ, so a configuration is an element of $\Sigma^{V(G)}$, and the edges of the graph stand for the locality of the evolution: the next state of a vertex depends only on the states of the vertices which are at distance at most k, i.e. in a disk of radius k, for some fixed integer k. Second, the graph itself is allowed to evolve over time. Informally, this means having configurations in a set composed of the union of $\Sigma^{V(G)}$ for all possible bounded-degree G: $\bigcup_G \Sigma^{V(G)}$. This has led to a model where the local rule f is applied synchronously and homogeneously on every possible subdisk of the input graph, thereby producing small patches of the output graphs, whose union constitutes the output graph. Figure 1 illustrates the concept of these CA over graphs.

CGD are motivated by the countless situations in which some agents interact with their neighbours, leading to a global dynamics in which the notion of who is next to whom also varies in time (e.g. agents become physically connected, get to exchange contact details, move around...). Indeed, several existing models (of physical systems, computer processes, biochemical agents, economical agents, social networks...) feature such neighbour-to-neighbour interactions with time-varying neighbourhood, thereby generalizing CA for their specific sake (e.g. self-reproduction as [22], discrete general relativity à la Regge calculus [19], etc.).

CGD provide a theoretical framework for these models. Some graph rewriting models, such as Amalgamated Graph Transformations [5], Parallel Graph Transformations [8,20,21], and Synchronized Hyperedge Replacement systems [9] also work out rigorous ways to apply a local rewriting rule synchronously throughout a graph, albeit with a different, category-theory-based perspective. In particular the topological approach we follow and the reversibility question that we address have not been considered in these works.

Indeed, this paper studies CGD in the reversible regime. From a theoretical Computer Science perspective, the point is therefore to generalize RCA theory to arbitrary, bounded-degree, time-varying graphs. Apart from particular examples given by [11,16], we are not aware of other extensions of RCA in full generality. From this perspective, our main result is the proof that the inverse of a CGD is also a CGD. This is a non-trivial problem, for instance [13] implies that the radius of the inverse is unbounded: there is no computable function h such that for any reversible CDG of radius r, its inverse has a radius smaller than $h(r)$. Moreover the fact that the graph is time-varying brings up new challenges.

From a mathematical perspective, questions related to the bijectivity of CA over certain classes of graphs (more specifically, whether pre-injectivity implies surjectivity for Cayley graphs generated by certain groups [10]) have received quite some attention. This paper on the other hand provides a context in which to study "bijectivity upon time-varying graphs". In particular, is it the case that bijectivity will necessarily rigidify space (i.e. force the conservation of each vertex)? We prove that any reversible evolution preserves the number of vertices of all but a finite number of graphs.

From a theoretical physics perspective, the question whether the reversibility of small scale physics (quantum mechanics, micro-mechanical), can be reconciled with the time-varying topology of large scale physics (relativity), is a topic of debate and constant investigation. This paper provides a toy, discrete, classical model where reversibility and time-varying topology coexist and interact. But ultimately, this deep question would need to be addressed in a quantum mechanical setting. Indeed, just like RCA were precursors of Quantum CA, this work seeks to pave the way for Quantum CGD.

2   Pointed Graph Modulo, Paths, and Operations

Pointed graph modulo. There are two main approaches to CA. The one with a local rule, usually denoted f, is the constructive one, but CA can also be defined in a more topological way as being exactly the shift-invariant continuous functions from $\Sigma^{\mathbb{Z}^n}$ to itself, with respect to a certain metric. Through a compactness argument, the two approaches are equivalent. This topological approach carries through to CA over graphs. But for this purpose, one has to make the set of graphs into an appropriate compact metric space, which can only be done for certain pointed graphs modulo isomorphism – referred to as generalized Cayley graphs in [2]. This is worth the trouble, as the topological characterization is one of the crucial ingredients to prove that the inverse of a CGD is a CGD.

Basically, the pointed graphs modulo isomorphism (or pointed graphs modulo, for short) are the usual, connected, undirected, possibly infinite, bounded-degree graphs, but with a few added twists:

- Each vertex has *ports* in a finite set π. A vertex and its port are written $u{:}a$.
- An *edge* is an unordered pair $\{u : a, v : b\}$. i.e. edges are between ports of vertices, rather than vertices themselves, à la [6]. Because the port of a vertex can only appear in one edge, the degree of the graphs is bounded by $|\pi|$, which is crucial for compactness. We shall consider connected graphs only.
- The graphs are rooted i.e., there is a privileged pointed vertex playing the role of an origin, so that any vertex can be referred to relative to the origin, via a sequence of ports that lead to it.
- The graphs are considered modulo isomorphism, so that only the relative position of the vertices can matter.
- The vertices and edges are given labels taken in finite sets Σ and Δ, so that they may carry an internal state just like the cells of a cellular automaton.
- The labelling functions are partial, so that we may express our partial knowledge about part of a graph. For instance it is common that a local function may yield a vertex, its internal state, its neighbours, and yet have no opinion about the internal state of those neighbours.

The set of all pointed graphs modulo (see Fig. 2(c)) of ports π, vertex labels Σ and edge labels Δ is denoted $X_{\Sigma,\Delta,\pi}$. A thorough formalization of pointed graphs modulo can be found in [2]. For the sake of this paper, Fig. 2 summarizes the construction of pointed graphs modulo from pointed graphs whose vertex names are dropped.

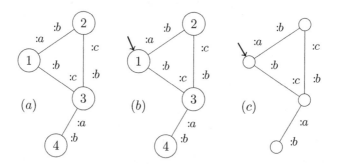

Fig. 2. *The different types of graphs.* (a) A graph G. (b) A pointed graph $(G, 1)$. (c) A pointed graph modulo isomorphism. These are anonymous: vertices have no names and can only be distinguished using the graph structure.

Paths and vertices. Since we are considering pointed graphs modulo isomorphism, vertices no longer have a unique identifier, which may seem impractical when it comes to designating a vertex. Two elements come to our rescue. First, these graphs are pointed, thereby providing an origin. Second, the vertices are

connected through ports, so that each vertex can tell between its different neighbours. It follows that any vertex of the graph can be designated by a sequence of
ports in $(\pi^2)^*$ that lead from the origin to this vertex. The origin is designated
by ε. For instance, say two vertices designated by a path u and a path v, respectively. Suppose there is an edge $e = \{u : a, v : b\}$. Then, v can be designated by
the path $u.ab$, where "." stands for the word concatenation. A thorough formalization of pointed graphs modulo paths and naming conventions can be found
in [2]. Given a pointed graph modulo $X \in \mathfrak{X}_{\Sigma, \Delta, \pi}$, we write $v \in X$ instead of
$v \in V(X)$.

Operations. Given a pointed graph modulo X, X^r denotes the subdisk of radius
r around the pointer. The pointer of X can be moved along a path u, leading to
$Y = X_u$. The pointer can be moved back where it was before, leading to $X = Y_{\overline{u}}$,
where $\overline{u}$ denotes the reverse of path u. We use the notation X_u^r for $(X_u)^r$ i.e., first
the pointer is moved along u, then the subdisk of radius r is taken. A thorough
formalization of pointed graph modulo operations can be found in [2]. For the
sake of this paper, Fig. 3 illustrates the operations.

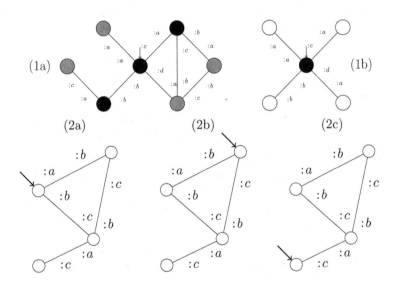

Fig. 3. *Operations over pointed graphs modulo.* (1a) shows a pointed graph modulo X.
(1b) shows X^0, the result of taking the *subdisk of radius* 0. In general the neighbours of
radius r are just those vertices which can be reached in r steps starting from the origin,
whereas the disk of radius r, written X^r, is the subgraph induced by the neighbours
of radius $r + 1$, but with the labellings restricted to the neighbours of radius r and the
edges between them. This restriction of the labelling partial function is the reason why
some vertices have gone blank in (1b). (2a) shows pointed graph modulo X. (2b) X_{ab}
shows the pointed graph modulo X *shifted* by ab. (2c) shows $X_{bc.ac}$ the pointed graph
modulo X *shifted* by $bc.ac$, which also corresponds to the graph X_{ab} *shifted* by $cb.ac$.
Shifting this last graph by $\overline{cb.ac} = ca.bc$ produces the graph (2b) again.

3   Causal Graph Dynamics and Invertibility

We will now recall the definition of CGD. We provide a topological definition in terms of shift-invariant continuous functions, rather than a constructive definition based on a local rule f applied synchronously across space (Fig. 1). The two were proved equivalent in [2].

A crucial point in the topological characterization of CGD is the correspondence between the vertices of a pointed graph modulo X, and those of its image $F(X)$. Indeed, on the one hand it is important to know that a given vertex $u \in X$ has become $u' \in F(X)$, e.g. in order to express shift-invariance $F(X_u) = F(X)_{u'}$, or to express continuity. But on the other hand since u' is named relative to the vertex ε of $F(X)$, its determination requires some knowledge of $F(X)$. Hence the need of establishing a relation between vertices of X and vertices of $F(X)$.

The following analogy provides a useful way of tackling this issue. Say that we were able to place a white stone on the vertex $u \in X$ that we wish to follow across evolution F. Later, by observing that the white stone is found at $u' \in F(X)$, we would be able to conclude that u has become u'. This way of grasping the correspondence between an image vertex and its antecedent vertex is a local, operational notion of an observer moving across the dynamics.

Definition 1 (Dynamics). *A dynamics $(F, R_\bullet)$ is given by*

- *a function $F \colon \mathfrak{X}_{\Sigma, \Delta, \pi} \to \mathfrak{X}_{\Sigma, \Delta, \pi}$;*
- *a map $R_\bullet$, with $R_\bullet \colon X \mapsto R_X$ and $R_X \colon V(X) \to V(F(X))$.*

For all X, the function R_X can be pointwise extended to sets of vertices i.e., $R_X \colon \mathcal{P}(V(X)) \to \mathcal{P}(V(F(X)))$ maps S to $R_X(S) = \{R_X(u) \mid u \in S\}$.

The intuition is that R_X indicates which vertices $\{u', v', \ldots\} = R_X(\{u, v, \ldots\}) \subseteq V(F(X))$ will end up being marked as a consequence of $\{u, v, \ldots\} \subseteq V(X)$ being marked. Now, clearly, the set $\{(X, S) \mid X \in \mathfrak{X}_{\Sigma, \Delta, \pi}, S \subseteq V(X)\}$ is isomorphic to $\mathfrak{X}_{\Sigma', \Delta, \pi}$ with $\Sigma' = \Sigma \times \{0, 1\}$. Hence, we can define the function F' that maps $(X, S) \cong X' \in \mathfrak{X}_{\Sigma', \Delta, \pi}$ to $(F(X), R_X(S)) \cong F'(X') \in \mathfrak{X}_{\Sigma', \Delta, \pi}$, and think of a dynamics as just this function $F' \colon \mathfrak{X}_{\Sigma', \Delta, \pi} \to \mathfrak{X}_{\Sigma', \Delta, \pi}$.

Definition 2 (Continuity). *A dynamics $(F, R_\bullet)$ is said to be* continuous *if for any X and any $m \geq 0$, there exists $n \geq 0$ such that for every Y, $X^n = Y^n$ implies both*

- *$F(X)^m = F(Y)^m$.*
- *$dom\, R_X^m \subseteq V(X^n)$, $dom\, R_Y^m \subseteq V(Y^n)$, and $R_X^m = R_Y^m$.*

where R_X^m denotes the partial map obtained as the restriction of R_X to the codomain $F(X)^m$, using the natural inclusion of $F(X)^m$ into $F(X)$.

In the $F' \colon \mathfrak{X}_{\Sigma', \Delta, \pi} \to \mathfrak{X}_{\Sigma', \Delta, \pi}$ formalism, the two above conditions are equivalent to just one: F' continuous.

Definition 3 (Shift-invariance). *A dynamics $(F, R_\bullet)$ is said to be* shift-invariant *if for every X, $u \in X$, and $v \in X_u$,*

- $F(X_u) = F(X)_{R_X(u)}$
- $R_X(u.v) = R_X(u).R_{X_u}(v)$.

The second condition expresses the shift-invariance of $R_\bullet$ itself. Notice that $R_X(\varepsilon) = R_X(\varepsilon).R_X(\varepsilon)$; hence $R_X(\varepsilon) = \varepsilon$.

Definition 4 (Boundedness). *A dynamics $(F, R_\bullet)$ is said to be bounded if there exists a bound b such that for any X and any $w' \in F(X)$, there exist $u' \in \operatorname{im} R_X$ and $v' \in F(X)_{u'}^b$, such that $w' = u'.v'$.*

The following is the topological definition of CGD:

Definition 5 (Causal graph dynamics). *A CGD is a shift-invariant, continuous, bounded dynamics.*

Inflating grid. An example of causal graph dynamics is the inflating grid dynamics illustrated in Fig. 4. In the inflating grid dynamics each vertex gives birth to four distinct vertices, such that the structure of the initial graph is preserved, but inflated. The graph has maximal degree 4, and the set of ports is $\pi = \{a, b, c, d\}$, vertices are labelled black or white.

For this dynamics, the $R_\bullet$ operator is defined as follows:

$$R_X(u_0.u_1.\ldots.u_n) = R(u_0).R(u_1).\ldots.R(u_n)$$

where R is the function acting on letters in π^2 described in the following tables. Figure 5 gives a visual example of the same operator for a precise graph.

$u \in \pi^2$	$R(u)$	$u \in \pi^2$	$R(u)$
aa	aa.db	ca	ca.ca
ab	ab.db.ac	cb	ca.cb.db
ac	ac.ac	cc	ca.cc.db.ac
ad	ad.bd	cd	ca.cd.ac
ba	bd.ba.db	da	da
bb	bd.bb.db.ac	db	db.db
bc	bd.bc.ac	dc	dc.db.ac
bd	bd.bd	dd	dd.ac

Invertibility is imposed in the most general and natural fashion.

Definition 6 (Invertible dynamics). *A dynamics $(F, R_\bullet)$ is said to be invertible if F is a bijection from $\mathcal{X}_{\Sigma,\Delta,\pi}$ to itself.*

Moving head. Figure 6 is an example of invertible CGD. In this example, a vertex, representing the head of an automaton, is moving along a line graph, representing a tape. The line graph is built using ab−edges, while the head is attached using either a cc−edge if it is traveling forward along the ab−edges, or dd−edges if it is traveling backwards. The transformation can be completed into a bijection over the entire set of graphs with $\pi = \{a, b, c, d\}$. It then accounts for several heads, etc. The resulting transformation is continuous, as the moving heads travel at speed one along the tape, and shift-invariant as it is possible to build a $R_\bullet$ operator verifying the right commutation properties.

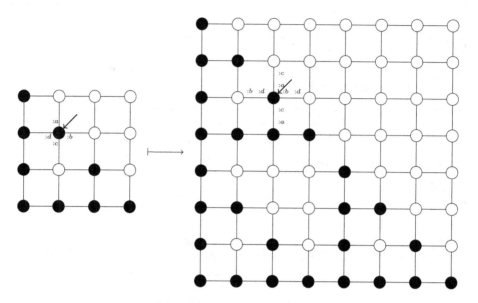

Fig. 4. *The inflating grid dynamics. The inflating grid dynamics.* Each vertex splits into 4 vertices. The structure of the grid is preserved. For this precise graph, all edges are connected to ports as stipulated on the pointed vertex (port $:a$ on top, $:b$ on the right, $:c$ on the bottom and $:d$ on the left).

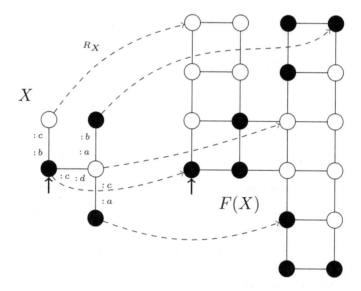

Fig. 5. $R_\bullet$ *operator for the inflating grid dynamics.* To each original vertex of a graph X, R_X associates a vertex of $F(X)$ within the square of four it creates. More precisely, it is mapped to that of the four vertices whose ports a and d get out of the square.

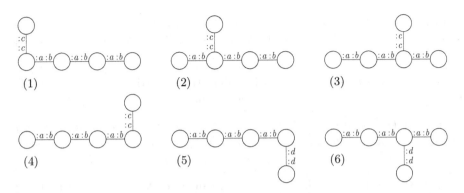

Fig. 6. *Moving head dynamics.* In this example, a moving head is running along a "tape" formed by a linear graph of ab edges. When reaching the end of the line, the head starts moving backwards and changes the ports on its attaching edge to dd. (1) to (6) represent 6 consecutive configurations.

4   Invertibility and Almost-Vertex-Preservingness

Recall that, in general, CGD are allowed to transform the graph, not only by changing internal states and edges, but also by creating or deleting vertices. Since invertibility imposes information-conservation, one may wonder whether invertible CGD are still allowed to create or delete vertices. They are, as shown by Fig. 7. One notices, however, that the RHS of this example features shift-equivalent vertices:

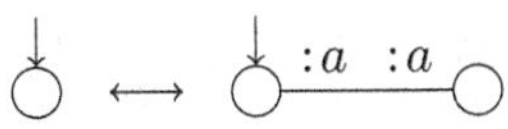

Fig. 7. The *turtle dynamics* has the two above pointed graphs modulo to oscillate between one another. The two vertices of the RHS are shift-equivalent, i.e. pointing the graph upon one or the other does not change the graph.

Definition 7 (Shift-equivalent vertices). *Let* $X \in \mathcal{X}_{\Sigma,\Delta,\pi}$ *and let* $u, v \in X$. *We say that* u *and* v *are shift-equivalent, denoted* $u \approx v$, *if* $X_u = X_v$. *A graph is called* asymmetric *if it has only trivial (i.e. of size one) shift-equivalence classes.*

One can show that all the shift-equivalence classes of a pointed graph modulo have the same size. Intuitively, given two shift-equivalent vertices u, v and a third vertex w, since there is a path from u to w, moving from v along the same path leads to a vertex equivalent to w.

Lemma 1 (Shift-equivalence classes isometry). *Let $X \in \mathfrak{X}_{\Sigma,\Delta,\pi}$ be a graph. If $C_1 \subseteq V(X)$ and $C_2 \subseteq V(X)$ are two shift-equivalence classes of X, then $|C_1| = |C_2|$.*

Moreover, we can show that creation or deletion of vertices by invertible CGD must respect the shift-symmetries of the graph.

Lemma 2 (Invertible CGD preserves shift-equivalence classes). *Let $(F, R_\bullet)$ be a shift-invariant dynamics over $\mathfrak{X}_{\Sigma,\Delta,\pi}$, such that F is a bijection. Then for any X and any $u, v \in X$, $u \approx v$ if and only if $R_X(u) \approx R_X(v)$.*

Shift-symmetry is fragile however, and can be destroyed by adding a few vertices to a graph:

Definition 8 (Primal extension). *Given a finite graph $X \in \mathfrak{X}_{\Sigma,\Delta,\pi}$ where $|\pi| > 1$ such that X has k shift-equivalence classes of size n with $k, n \neq 1$, we obtain a primal extension $^\square X$ by either:*

- *Choosing a vertex v having a free port (i.e. v has a port $i \in \pi$ such that $v : i$ does not appear in any edge): connect $p - kn$ new vertices in a line to this free port, where p is the smallest prime number greater than $kn + 2$,*
- *Or choosing a vertex v such that v is part of a cycle. Remove an edge from this cycle, and do the same construction as above.*

Lemma 3 (Properties of primal extensions). *Any primal extension $^\square X$ is asymmetric.*

Using this fact, one can show that the cases of node creation and deletion in invertible CGD are all of finitary nature, i.e. they can no longer happen for large enough graphs. Indeed, by supposing a big enough graph X whose size is changed through the application of an invertible CGD, and then looking at what would happen to its primal extension $^\square X$, we can show that this would contradict continuity. We obtain:

Theorem 1 (Invertible implies almost-vertex-preserving). *Let $(F, R_\bullet)$ be a CGD over $\mathfrak{X}_{\Sigma,\Delta,\pi}$, such that F is a bijection. Then there exists a bound p, such that for any graph X, if $|X| > p$ then R_X is bijective.*

Proof outline. Let us consider a graph X, as big as we need, such that R_X is not a bijection. If R_X is non injective, there exist two vertices u, v identified by R_X. We can show that we can apply the primal extension to any of the furthers points of X, to obtain an asymmetric graph Y, such that by continuity of $R_\bullet$ the vertices u, v are still identified, and yet they are not shift-equivalent, which contradicts Lemma 2. If R_X is not surjective, some u of $F(X)$ is not reached. Using the continuity of $R_\bullet$, We again apply the primal extension to any of the furthest points of $F(X)$ can construct an asymmetric graph Y such that u of Y is not reached, which contradicts the bijectivity of F.

5   Reversible Causal Graph Dynamics

A CGD $(F, R_\bullet)$ is said reversible if it is invertible *and* its inverse is a CGD itself:

Definition 9 (Reversible). *A CGD* $(F, R_\bullet)$ *is* reversible *if there exists* $S_\bullet$ *such that* $(F^{-1}, S_\bullet)$ *is a CGD.*

Theorem 1 shows that CGD are almost vertex-preserving. Notice that vertex-preservingness guarantees that the inverse of a shift-invariant dynamics is a shift-invariant dynamics.

Lemma 4. *If* $(F, R_\bullet)$ *is an invertible, shift-invariant dynamics such that for all* X, R_X *is a bijection, then* $(F^{-1}, S_\bullet)$ *is a shift-invariant dynamics, with* $S_Y = (R_{F^{-1}(Y)})^{-1}$.

We are now ready to prove our main result which is that the inverse of a causal graph dynamics is a causal graph dynamics:

Theorem 2 (Invertible implies reversible). *If* $(F, R_\bullet)$ *is an invertible CGD, then* $(F, R_\bullet)$ *is reversible.*

Proof Outline. Continuity of F^{-1} is directly given by the continuity of F together with the compactness of $\mathcal{X}_{\Sigma, \Delta, \pi}$. Its boundedness derives either from the bijectivity of R_X for $|X| > p$ or from the finiteness of X when $|X| \le p$. Regarding the construction of $S_\bullet$ such that $(F^{-1}, S_\bullet)$ is a CDG: (*i*) for $|F(X)| = |X| > p$, we know that R_X is bijective and we let $S_{F(X)} = R_X^{-1}$; (*ii*) for $|X| \le p$, we can construct an ad hoc $S_{F(X)}$ and prove its shift-invariance.

Notice that, ultimately, this result crucially relies on the compactness of $\mathcal{X}_{\Sigma, \Delta, \pi}$ which in turn relies on the boundedness of the degree $|\pi|$ and the finiteness of the internal states Σ and Δ.

6   Conclusion

Summary of Results. We have studied Reversible Causal Graph Dynamics, thereby extending Reversible Cellular Automata (RCA) results to time-varying, pointed graphs modulo. Pointed graphs modulo are arbitrary bounded-degree networks, with a pointed vertex serving as the origin, and modulo renaming of vertices. Some of these graphs have shift-equivalent vertices. We have shown that if a Causal Graph Dynamics (CGD) is invertible, then it preserves shift-equivalence classes. This in turn entails almost-vertex-preservingness, i.e. the conservation of each vertex for big enough graphs. Finally, we have shown that the inverse of a CGD is a CGD. In a companion paper, we build upon this result in order to port another classical result [7, 14, 15] from RCA theory to Reversible CGD, namely the fact that their evolution admits a block decomposition, i.e. F can be described as a circuit of finite depth of local reversible gates [4].

Future Work. Related to this block decomposition result, let us mention yet another classical result from RCA theory, namely that of the intrinsic universality of Partioned Cellular Automata [18]. An analogous result would greatly simplify the study of Reversible CGD—we leave this as an open problem. Here we have shown that invertible causal graph dynamics implies almost vertex-preservingness or, in other words, that beyond some finitary cases, information conservation implies conservation of the systems that support this information. Still, this cannot forbid that some 'dark matter' which was there at all times, could now be made 'visible'. We plan to follow this idea in a subsequent work. Finally, we also wish to explore the quantum regime of these models, as similar results where given for Quantum Cellular Automata over fixed graphs [3]. Such results would be of interest to theoretical physics, in the sense of discrete time versions of [17].

Acknowledgements. This work has been funded by the ANR-12-BS02-007-01 TAR-MAC grant, the ANR-10-JCJC-0208 CausaQ grant, and the John Templeton Foundation, grant ID 15619. The authors acknowledge enlightening discussions with Bruno Martin and Emmanuel Jeandel. This work has been partially done when PA was delegated at Inria Nancy Grand Est, in the project team Carte.

A   Proofs of Sections 4 and 5

A.1   Proofs of Section 4

Lemma 1 (Shift-equivalence classes isometry). *Let $X \in \mathcal{X}_{\Sigma,\Delta,\pi}$ be a graph. If $C_1 \subseteq V(X)$ and $C_2 \subseteq V(X)$ are two shift-equivalence classes of X, then $|C_1| = |C_2|$.*

Proof. Consider two shift-equivalent and distinct vertices u and v in X. Consider a path w. The vertices $u.w$ and $v.w$ are shift-equivalent and distinct. More generally, if we have n shift-equivalent and distinct vertices $v_1, ..., v_n$, any vertex $u = v_1.w$ will be shift-equivalent to $v_2.w, ..., v_n.w$ and distinct from all of them, hence the equivalence classes are all of the same size.   □

Lemma 2 (Invertible CGD preserves shift-equivalence classes). *Let $(F, R_\bullet)$ be a shift-invariant dynamics over $\mathcal{X}_{\Sigma,\Delta,\pi}$, such that F is a bijection. Then for any X and any $u, v \in X$, $u \approx v$ if and only if $R_X(u) \approx R_X(v)$.*

Proof. $u \approx v$ expresses $X_u = X_v$, which by bijectivity of F is equivalent to $F(X_u) = F(X_v)$ and hence $F(X)_{R_X(u)} = F(X)_{R_X(v)}$. This in turn is expressed by $R_X(u) \approx R_X(v)$.   □

Lemma 3 (Properties of primal extensions). *Any primal extension $^\square X$ is asymmetric.*

Proof. As $^\square X$ has a prime number of vertices, by Lemma 1, its has either one single equivalence class of maximal size or only trivial equivalence classes. As the primal extension adds at least two vertices and that these vertices have different degree (1 for the last vertex on the line, and 2 for its only neighbor), $^\square X$ contains at least two non equivalent vertices, hence the first result.   □

Theorem 1 (Invertible implies almost-vertex-preserving). *Let $(F, R_\bullet)$ be a CGD over $\mathcal{X}_{\Sigma,\Delta,\pi}$, such that F is a bijection. Then there exists a bound p, such that for any graph X, if $|X| > p$ then R_X is bijective.*

Proof. When $|\pi| \leq 1$, $\mathcal{X}_{\Sigma,\Delta,\pi}$ is finite so the theorem is trivial. So we assume in the rest of the proof that $|\pi| > 1$.

[Finite graphs] First we prove the result for any finite graph. By contradiction, assume that there exists a sequence of finite graphs $(X(n))_{n \in \mathbb{N}}$ such that $|X(n)|$ diverges and such that for all n, $R_{X(n)}$ is not bijective. As this sequence is infinite, we have that one of the two following cases is verified an infinite number of n:

- $R_{X(n)}$ is not surjective,
- $R_{X(n)}$ is not injective.

- [$R_{X(n)}$ not surjective]. There exists a vertex $v' \notin \operatorname{im} R_{X(n)}$. Without loss of generality, we can assume that $|v'| < b$ where b is the bound from the boundedness property of F. We will now consider a particular primal extension of $F(X(n))$, $^\square F(X(n))$, where the chosen vertex in $F(X(n))$ is the furthest away from the pointed vertex ε. Indeed, if $F(X(n))$ is large enough, a vertex lying at maximal distance of ε in $F(X(n))$ either has a free port or is part of a cycle, and thus is a valid vertex to perform the primal extension. Indeed, if this vertex has no free port, then any of its edge can be removed without splitting the graph, as it would contradict its maximality – therefore it is in a cycle. Now, consider the graph $Y(n) = F^{-1}(^\square F(X(n)))$. Using uniform continuity of F^{-1} and $R_\bullet$, and the fact that $|X(n)|$ is as big as we want, we have that there exists an index n and a radius r such that $Y(n)^r = X(n)^r$ and $R^b_{Y(n)^r} = R^b_{X(n)^r}$. As $F(Y(n))$ is asymmetric by construction, $v' \in \operatorname{im} R^b_{Y(n)^r}$ which contradicts $v' \notin \operatorname{im} R_{X(n)}$.

- [$R_{X(n)}$ not injective]. There exist two vertices $u, v \in X(n)$ such that $R_{X(n)}(u) = R_{X(n)}(v)$ and $u \neq v$. Without loss of generality, we can assume that $u = \varepsilon$ as F is shift-invariant. According to Lemma 2, we have that $\varepsilon \approx v$. Moreover, using the uniform continuity of $R_\bullet$, we have that, as $R_{X(n)}(v) = R_{X(n)}(\varepsilon) = \varepsilon$, there exists a radius l, which does not depend on n, such that $|v| < l$. Let us consider a primal extension of $X(n)$, $^\square X(n)$, where the primal extension has been performed at maximal distance from ε, by the same argument as in the previous •. In this graph, ε and v are not shift-equivalent and thus, $R_{^\square X(n)}(\varepsilon) \neq R_{^\square X(n)}(v)$. By continuity of $R_\bullet$, we have that there exists a radius $r > l$ such that $R^0_{^\square X(n)^r} = R^0_{X(n)^r}$ for a large enough n, hence $R^0_{^\square X(n)^r}(v) = R^0_{X(n)^r}(v) = \varepsilon$, which contradicts $R_{^\square X(n)}(\varepsilon) \neq R_{^\square X(n)}(v)$.

[Infinite graphs] Now we show that the result on finite graphs can be extended to infinite graphs, proving that for any infinite graph R_X is bijective:

- [R_X injective]. By contradiction. Take X infinite such that there is $u \neq v$ and $R_X(u) = R_X(v)$. Without loss of generality we can take $u = \varepsilon$, i.e. $v \neq \varepsilon$ and $R_X(v) = \varepsilon$. By continuity of $R_\bullet$, there exists a radius r, which we can take larger than $|v|$ and p, such that $R_X = R_{X^r}$. Then $R_{X^r}(v) = R_X(v) = \varepsilon$, thus R_{X^r} is not injective in spite of X^r being finite and larger than p, leading to a contradiction.

• [R_X surjective]. By contradiction. Take X infinite such that there is v' in $F(X)$ and $v' \notin \operatorname{im} R_X$. By boundedness, there exists $u' \in F(X)$ such that u' lies at distance less than b of v'. Using shift-invariance, we can assume without loss of generality that $u' = \varepsilon$, hence, $|v'| < b$. By continuity of $R_\bullet$, there exists a radius r, which we can take larger than p, such that the images of R_X and R_{X^r} coincide over the disk of radius b. Then, $v' \notin \operatorname{im} R_X$ implies $v' \notin \operatorname{im} R_{X^r}$, thus R_{X^r} is not surjective in spite of X^r being finite and larger than p, leading to a contradiction.

A.2   Proofs of Section 5

Lemma 4. *If $(F, R_\bullet)$ is an invertible, shift-invariant dynamics such that for all X, R_X is a bijection, then $(F^{-1}, S_\bullet)$ is a shift-invariant dynamics, with $S_Y = (R_{F^{-1}(Y)})^{-1}$.*

Proof. Consider Y and $u'.v' \in Y$. Take X and $u.v \in X$ such that $F(X) = Y$, $R_X(u) = u'$ and $R_X(u.v) = u'.v'$. We have: $F^{-1}(Y_{u'}) = F^{-1}(F(X)_{R_X(u)}) = F^{-1}(F(X_u)) = X_{(R_X)^{-1}(u')} = F^{-1}(Y)_{S_Y(u')}$. Moreover, take $v \in X_u$ such that $R_X(u.v) = R_X(u).R_{X_u}(v) = u'.v'$. We have: $S_Y(u'.v') = (R_X)^{-1}(R_X(u.v)) = u.v = (R_X)^{-1}(u').(R_{X_u})^{-1}(v') = S_Y(u').S_{Y_{u'}}(v')$. □

Theorem 2 (Invertible implies reversible). *If $(F, R_\bullet)$ is an invertible CGD, then $(F, R_\bullet)$ is reversible.*

Proof. Continuity of F^{-1} is directly given by the continuity of F together with the compactness of $\mathfrak{X}_{\Sigma,\Delta,\pi}$. Its boundedness derives either from the bijectivity of R_X for $|X| > p$ or from the finiteness of X when $|X| > p$.

We must construct $S_\bullet$. For $|F(X)| = |X| > p$, we know that R_X is bijective and we let $S_{F(X)} = R_X^{-1}$. For $|X| \leq p$, we will proceed in two steps. First, we will construct an appropriate $S_{F(X)}$ for X. Second, we will make consistent choices for $S_{F(X)_{u'}}$ so that $S_\bullet$ is shift invariant.

We write $\tilde{u}$ for the shift-equivalence class of u in X. For all $v' \in F(X)$, we make the arbitrary choice $S_{F(X)}(\tilde{v'}) = v$, where v is such that its image $R_X(v)$ is shift equivalent to v' in $F(X)$, i.e. $R_X(v) \approx v'$. For this X, we have enforced $\approx$-compatibility. Then we make consistent choices for $S_{F(X)_{u'}}$. This is obtained by demanding that $S_{F(X)_{u'}}(\widetilde{u'.v'}) = \tilde{u}.v$. Indeed, this accomplishes shift-invariance because $S_{F(X)_{u'}}(v') = S_{F(X)_{u'}}(\widetilde{u'.u'.v'}) = \varepsilon.v' = v'$ implying the equality: $S_{F(X)}(u'.v') = u.v = S_{F(X)}(u').S_{F(X)_{u'}}(v')$. Moreover, $S_{F(X)_{u'}}$ is itself shift-invariant because: $S_{F(X)_{u'.v'}}(w') = S_{F(X)_{u'.v'}}(\widetilde{u'.v'.u'.v'.w'}) = \overline{u.v}.u.v.w = w$, and $S_{F(X)_{u'}}(v') = v$ implying that $S_{F(X)_{u'}}(v'.w') = v.w = S_{F(X)_{u'}}(v').S_{F(X)_{u'.v'}}(w')$, and $\approx$-compatible because $v' \approx w'$ implies $S_{F(X)_{u'}}(v') = S_{F(X)_{u'}}(w')$, and thus $S_{F(X)_{u'}}(v') \approx S_{F(X)_{u'}}(w')$.

Continuity of the constructed $S_\bullet$ is due to the continuity of $R_\bullet$ and the finiteness of p.

Shift-invariance of $(F^{-1}, S_\bullet)$ follows from $\approx$-compatibility of $S_\bullet$ and shift-invariance of $(F, R_\bullet)$, because $F^{-1}(F(X)'_u) = X_v$ where v is such that $R_X(v) \approx u'$, hence $F^{-1}(F(X)'_u) = X_{S_{F(X)}(u')}$. □

References

1. Arrighi, P., Dowek, G.: Causal graph dynamics. In: Czumaj, A., Mehlhorn, K., Pitts, A., Wattenhofer, R. (eds.) ICALP 2012, Part II. LNCS, vol. 7392, pp. 54–66. Springer, Heidelberg (2012)

2. Arrighi, P., Martiel, S., Nesme, V., Cayley, G.: Graphs, cellular automata over them submitted (long version) (2013). Pre-print arXiv:1212.0027

3. Arrighi, P., Nesme, V., Werner, R.: Unitarity plus causality implies localizability. J. Comput. Syst. Sci. **77**, 372–378 (2010). QIP 2010 (long talk)

4. Arrighi, P., Martiel, S., Perdrix, S.: Block representation of reversible causal graph dynamics. In: Kosowski, A., Walukiewicz, I. (eds.) FCT 2015. LNCS, vol. 9210, pp. 351–363. Springer, Heidelberg (2015)

5. Boehm, P., Fonio, H.R., Habel, A.: Amalgamation of graph transformations: a synchronization mechanism. J. Comput. Syst. Sci. **34**(2–3), 377–408 (1987)

6. Danos, V., Laneve, C.: Formal molecular biology. Theoret. Comput. Sci. **325**(1), 69–110 (2004). Computational Systems Biology

7. Durand-Lose, J.O.: Representing reversible cellular automata with reversible block cellular automata. Discret. Math. Theoret. Comput. Sci. **145**, 154 (2001)

8. Ehrig, H., Lowe, M.: Parallel and distributed derivations in the single-pushout approach. Theoret. Comput. Sci. **109**(1–2), 123–143 (1993)

9. Ferrari, G.-L., Hirsch, D., Lanese, I., Montanari, U., Tuosto, E.: Synchronised hyperedge replacement as a model for service oriented computing. In: Boer, F.S., Bonsangue, M.M., Graf, S., Roever, W.-P. (eds.) FMCO 2005. LNCS, vol. 4111, pp. 22–43. Springer, Heidelberg (2006)

10. Gromov, M.: Endomorphisms of symbolic algebraic varieties. J. Eur. Math. Soc. **1**(2), 109–197 (1999)

11. Hasslacher, B., Meyer, D.A.: Modelling dynamical geometry with lattice gas automata. In: Expanded Version of a Talk Presented at the Seventh International Conference on the Discrete Simulation of Fluids Held at the University of Oxford, June 1998

12. Hedlund, G.A.: Endomorphisms and automorphisms of the shift dynamical system. Math. Syst. Theor. **3**, 320–375 (1969)

13. Kari, J.: Reversibility of 2D cellular automata is undecidable. In: Cellular Automata: Theory and Experiment, vol. 45, pp. 379–385. MIT Press (1991)

14. Kari, J.: Representation of reversible cellular automata with block permutations. Theor. Comput. Syst. **29**(1), 47–61 (1996)

15. Kari, J.: On the circuit depth of structurally reversible cellular automata. Fundamenta Informaticae **38**(1–2), 93–107 (1999)

16. Klales, A., Cianci, D., Needell, Z., Meyer, D.A., Love, P.J.: Lattice gas simulations of dynamical geometry in two dimensions. Phys. Rev. E. **82**(4), 046705 (2010)

17. Konopka, T., Markopoulou, F., Smolin, L.: Quantum graphity. Arxiv preprint arXiv:hep-th/0611197 (2006)

18. Morita, K.: Reversible simulation of one-dimensional irreversible cellular automata. Theoret. Comput. Sci. **148**(1), 157–163 (1995)

19. Sorkin, R.: Time-evolution problem in Regge calculus. Phys. Rev. D. **12**(2), 385–396 (1975)

20. Taentzer, G.: Parallel and distributed graph transformation: formal description and application to communication-based systems. Ph.D. thesis, Technische Universitat Berlin (1996)

21. Taentzer, G.: Parallel high-level replacement systems. Theoret. Comput. Sci. **186**(1–2), 43–81 (1997)
22. Tomita, K., Kurokawa, H., Murata, S.: Graph automata: natural expression of self-reproduction. Physica D: Nonlinear Phenom. **171**(4), 197–210 (2002)

Boosting Reversible Pushdown Machines
by Preprocessing

Holger Bock Axelsen[1], Martin Kutrib[2], Andreas Malcher[2(✉)],
and Matthias Wendlandt[2]

[1] Department of Computer Science, University of Copenhagen,
Universitetsparken 5, 2100 Copenhagen E, Denmark
funkstar@di.ku.dk
[2] Institut für Informatik, Universität Giessen, Arndtstr. 2, 35392 Giessen, Germany
{kutrib,malcher,matthias.wendlandt}@informatik.uni-giessen.de

Abstract. It is well known that reversible finite automata do not accept all regular languages and that reversible pushdown automata do not accept all deterministic context-free languages. It is of significant interest both from a practical and theoretical point of view to close these gaps. We here extend these reversible models by a preprocessing unit which is basically a reversible injective and length-preserving sequential transducer. It turns out that preprocessing the input using such weak devices increases the computational power of reversible deterministic finite automata to the acceptance of all regular languages, whereas for reversible pushdown automata the accepted family of languages lies strictly in between the reversible deterministic context-free languages and the real-time deterministic context-free languages. Moreover, it is shown that the computational power of both types of machines is not changed by allowing the preprocessing sequential transducer to work irreversibly. Finally, we examine the closure properties of the family of languages accepted by such machines.

1 Introduction

Recent years have seen a number of results exploring reversible computations from the viewpoint of automata theory. Of particular interest here is the separation (or coalescing) of various reversible and deterministic models of computation. This can be a subtle issue: even when a model of computation has a very clean separation of the reversible and deterministic variants (as is the case with e.g. finite automata [5,7]), a simple modification of the model may sometimes close this gap, even at no change in power to the deterministic variant. For example, allowing two-way head movement is sufficient to unify reversible and deterministic finite automata [4], but these still recognize only the regular languages. Conversely, even when the reversible and deterministic variants are of identical power (e.g. Turing machines under language recognition), we can sometimes still separate the model variants along more fine-grained measures. For example, between real-time and linear time, the reversible Turing machines

S. Devitt and I. Lanese (Eds.): RC 2016, LNCS 9720, pp. 89–104, 2016.
DOI: 10.1007/978-3-319-40578-0_6

are strictly weaker than the deterministic Turing machines [1]. Thus, studying such gaps and how to bridge them provides insight into the fundamental nature of computational reversibility, and our aim with the present paper is to contribute to this, specifically for finite and pushdown automata.

One approach to this type of problem is to show the existence of a hierarchy with respect to a particular complexity measure, and consider which kind of *internal* resource can be used to bridge the gap, usually resulting in trade-off results. We here take a somewhat orthogonal approach, and consider the use of an *external* resource, a computational preprocessing device: the input to be processed by the base reversible machine is allowed to first be processed by another (usually weaker, and reversible) machine. This kind of staged computation is quite common in computer science, e.g. compilers preprocess code by parsing, and subsequently perform code analysis and generation by stronger methods; input in web forms may be sanitized and subsequently processed, etc.

Here, for the base machines we consider reversible finite state machines, REV-FA, and reversible pushdown automata, REV-PDA, and boost these by preprocessing their inputs with reversible sequential transducers, yielding the T-REV-FAs and T-REV-PDAs models (Sect. 2). We show that these accept, respectively, the regular languages, and a class of languages strictly between reversible deterministic context-free languages and real-time deterministic context-free languages, and that this holds even when the preprocessing unit is allowed to be irreversible (Sect. 3). Finally, we consider the closure properties of these machines under a number of usual language operations (Sect. 4).

2   Preliminaries

We write Σ^* for the set of all finite words over the finite alphabet Σ. The empty word is denoted by λ, and we let $\Sigma^+ = \Sigma^* \setminus \{\lambda\}$. The set of words of length at most $m \geq 0$ is denoted by $\Sigma^{\leq m}$. The reversal of a word w is denoted by w^R, and for the length of w we write $|w|$. We use $\subseteq$ for inclusions and $\subset$ for strict inclusions.

A *deterministic finite automaton* (DFA) is a system $M = \langle Q, \Sigma, q_0, \delta, F \rangle$, where Q is the finite set of *internal states*, Σ is the finite set of *input symbols*, q_0 is the *initial state*, $F \subseteq Q$ is the set of *final states* and $\delta : Q \times \Sigma \to Q$ is the partial *transition function*. The *language accepted* by M is defined as $L(M) = \{w \in \Sigma^* \mid \delta(q_0, w) \in F\}$, where, as usual, δ is recursively extended to $\delta : Q \times \Sigma^* \to Q$. The *reverse* transition function of δ is $\delta^\leftarrow : Q \times \Sigma \to 2^Q$, where $\delta^\leftarrow(q, a) = \{p \in Q \mid \delta(p, a) = q\}$.

A state $r \in Q$ is said to be *irreversible* if there are two distinct states p and q in Q and a letter $a \in \Sigma$ such that $\delta(p, a) = r = \delta(q, a)$. A DFA is called *reversible* (a REV-FA), if it does not have any irreversible state. Then, the reverse transition function $\delta^\leftarrow$ of a REV-FA can be seen as a partial function $\delta^\leftarrow : Q \times \Sigma \to Q$.

We turn to the definition of reversible pushdown automata. General deterministic pushdown automata that are not allowed to perform λ-steps are weaker than deterministic pushdown automata that may move on λ input [3]. However, in [6] it has been shown that every reversible pushdown automaton can be simulated by a *real-time* reversible pushdown automaton, that is, without λ-steps. This real-time reversible machine can effectively be constructed from the given one. Moreover, the sequential transducers defined below are real-time devices as well. For this reason, and to simplify matters, we disallow λ-steps from the outset. A *real-time deterministic pushdown automaton* (DPDA$_\lambda$) is a system $M = \langle Q, \Sigma, \Gamma, F, q_0, \bot, \delta \rangle$, where Q is the finite set of *internal states*, Σ is the finite set of *input symbols*, Γ is the finite set of *pushdown symbols*, $F \subseteq Q$ is the set of *accepting states*, $q_0 \in Q$ is the *initial state*, $\bot \in \Gamma$ is a distinguished pushdown symbol called the *bottom-of-stack symbol*, which initially appears on the stack, and the partial *transition function* $\delta \colon Q \times \Sigma \times \Gamma \to Q \times \Gamma^*$.

A *configuration* of a pushdown automaton is a quadruple (u, q, v, γ), where q is the current state, $u \in \Sigma^*$ is the part of the input to the left of the input head, $v \in \Sigma^*$ the part of the input to the right of the input head, and $\gamma \in \Gamma^*$ is the current content of the pushdown store, with the leftmost symbol of γ being the top symbol. On input w the initial configuration is defined to be $(\lambda, q_0, w, \bot)$. For $p \in Q$, $a \in \Sigma$, $u, v \in \Sigma^*$, $\gamma \in \Gamma^*$, and $Z \in \Gamma$, let $(u, p, av, Z\gamma)$ be a configuration. Then its *successor configuration* is $(ua, q, v, \beta\gamma)$, where $\delta(p, a, Z) = (q, \beta)$. We write $(u, p, av, Z\gamma) \vdash (ua, q, v, \beta\gamma)$ in this case. The reflexive transitive closure of $\vdash$ is denoted by $\vdash^*$.

To simplify matters, we require that in any configuration the bottom-of-pushdown symbol appears exactly once at the bottom of the pushdown store, that is, it can never appear at some other position in the pushdown store nor can it be popped. Formally, we require that if $\delta(p, a, Z) = (q, \beta)$ then either $Z \neq \bot$ and β does not contain $\bot$, or $Z = \bot$ and β is $\beta'\bot$, where β' does not contain $\bot$. The *language accepted* by M with accepting states is

$$L(M) = \{\, w \in \Sigma^* \mid (\lambda, q_0, w, \bot) \vdash^* (w, q, \lambda, \gamma), \text{ for some } q \in F \text{ and } \gamma \in \Gamma^* \,\}.$$

Reversible pushdown automata have been introduced and studied in [6], where reversibility requires that any configuration must have at most one predecessor which, in addition, is computable by a DPDA$_\lambda$. For reverse computation steps the head of the input tape is always moved to the *left*. Therefore, the automaton rereads the input symbol which has been read in the preceding forward step. For reversible pushdown automata there must exist a *reverse transition function* $\delta^\leftarrow \colon Q \times \Sigma \times \Gamma \to Q \times \Gamma^*$ that maps a configuration to its *predecessor configuration*. For $q \in Q$, $a \in \Sigma$, $u, v \in \Sigma^*$, $Z \in \Gamma$, and $\beta, \gamma \in \Gamma^*$, let $(ua, q, v, Z\gamma)$ be a configuration. Then its *predecessor configuration* is $(u, p, av, \beta\gamma)$ if $\delta^\leftarrow(q, a, Z) = (p, \beta)$. We write $(ua, q, v, Z\gamma) \vdash^\leftarrow (u, p, av, \beta\gamma)$ in this case.

A DPDA$_\lambda$ $M = \langle Q, \Sigma, \Gamma, F, q_0, \bot, \delta \rangle$ is said to be *reversible* (a REV-PDA), if there exists a reverse transition function $\delta^\leftarrow$ inducing a relation $\vdash^\leftarrow$ from one configuration to the next, so that $(u, p, v, \gamma) \vdash^\leftarrow (u', p', v', \gamma')$ if and only if $(u', p', v', \gamma') \vdash (u, p, v, \gamma)$. So, for all configurations the unique predecessor can be reached by $\vdash^\leftarrow$, if the predecessor exists at all.

The following properties of reversible pushdown automata have been derived in [6]. In one reverse step the height of the pushdown store can be decreased by at most one. Therefore, in a forward step the height of the pushdown store may be increased by at most one, as well. Furthermore, when a forward step pops a symbol, this operation simply reveals the next-to-top symbol. Therefore, one has to take care that the original top-of-stack symbol remains unaltered in a forward step in which the height of the pushdown is increased: If $\delta(p, a, Z) = (q, \beta)$ and $|\beta| > 1$, then $\beta = YZ$ for some symbol $Y \in \Gamma$. So, for a REV-PDA there are only the following possibilities:

push: $\delta(p, a, Z) = (q, Z'Z) \implies \delta^{\leftarrow}(q, a, Z') = (p, \lambda)$

change top: $\delta(p, a, Z) = (q, Z') \implies \delta^{\leftarrow}(q, a, Z') = (p, Z)$

pop $(Z \neq \bot)$: $\delta(p, a, Z) = (q, \lambda) \implies$ for all $X \in \Gamma$: $\delta^{\leftarrow}(q, a, X) = (p, ZX)$

As mentioned before, we shall allow the input of reversible devices to be weakly preprocessed by *deterministic one-way sequential transducers* (DST) which are basically DFAs with the ability to output symbols. In general, the output of a DST is written on an initially empty output tape. Here, with an eye towards reversible computations we define a DST as a machine with a single tape from which the input is read and to which the output is written, such that the head moves from left to right over the tape and in every computation step rewrites the current tape square. To enable the latter feature the transducer has to be length-preserving.

Formally, a DST is a system $T = \langle Q, \Sigma, \Delta, q_0, \delta \rangle$, where Q is the set of *internal states*, Σ is the set of *input symbols*, Δ is the set of *output symbols*, q_0 is the initial state, and $\delta: Q \times \Sigma \to Q \times \Delta$ is the *transition function*. By $T(w) \in \Delta^*$ we denote the output computed by T on input $w \in \Sigma^*$. In the following, we will consider in particular *injective* DSTs (also known as injective Mealy machines).

For $p \in Q$, $a \in \Sigma$, $v \in \Sigma^*$, $w \in \Delta^*$ let (w, p, av) be a configuration, where p is the current state, $w \in \Delta^*$ is the already processed part of the input to the left of the input head, and $av \in \Sigma^*$ the still unread part of the input to the right of the input head. The *successor configuration* is (wz, q, v), if $\delta(p, a) = (q, z)$. As before, we write $(w, p, av) \vdash (wz, q, v)$ in this case.

A DST $T = \langle Q, \Sigma, \Delta, q_0, \delta \rangle$ is said to be *reversible* (a REV-DST), if there exists a *reverse transition function* $\delta^{\leftarrow}$ inducing a relation $\vdash^{\leftarrow}$ from one configuration to the next, so that $(w, p, v) \vdash^{\leftarrow} (w', p', v')$ if and only if $(w', p', v') \vdash (w, p, v)$. In that case, the reverse transition function $\delta^{\leftarrow}: Q \times \Delta \to Q \times \Sigma$ of a DST maps a configuration to its *predecessor configuration*.

In backward computation steps a REV-DST moves its head from right to left. Thus, the automaton reads the output symbol which was written in the preceding forward step and restores both the input symbol and the prior state of the automaton before the step.

Let M be a REV-FA and T be an injective REV-DST so that the output alphabet of T is the input alphabet of M. The pair (M, T) is called a *transducer reversible finite automaton* (a T-REV-FA) and the language accepted by (M, T) is defined as $L(M, T) = \{w \in \Sigma^* \mid T(w) \in L(M)\}$. If M is a

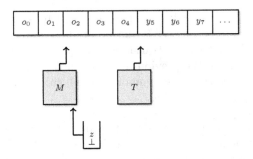

Fig. 1. A transducer reversible pushdown automata (M, T) consisting of a pushdown automaton M with input preprocessed by a sequential transducer T. Here, T has already read the input symbols y_0, y_1, y_2, y_3, and y_4 and has written corresponding output symbols o_0, o_1, o_2, o_3, and o_4, which in turn are input symbols for M, of which M has read o_0 and o_1.

REV-PDA the pair (M, T) is called a *transducer reversible pushdown automaton* (a T-REV-PDA). Such a pair is depicted in Fig. 1.

In the following, the family of all languages accepted by some device of type X is denoted by $\mathscr{L}(X)$. In order to clarify our notations we present some examples.

Example 1. The regular language $L = \{a^m b^n \mid m, n \geq 0\}$, which is not accepted by any REV-FA, is accepted by a T-REV-FA (M, T). The transducer $T = \langle Q, \Sigma, \Delta, q_0, \delta \rangle$ has two states $Q = \{q_0, q_1\}$. The output alphabet consists of four symbols $\Delta = \{a, b, \$, \nabla\}$. For every a, transducer T emits an a. When the first b appears, it emits a $\$$, and all subsequent b's are translated to b's. When the input is incorrectly formatted, that is, an a follows a b, transducer T emits the error symbol ∇, stays in its state, and continues its computation. The transition function is formally defined as follows.

REV-DST forward	REV-DST backward
$\delta(q_0, a) = (q_0, a)$	$\delta^{\leftarrow}(q_0, a) = (q_0, a)$
$\delta(q_0, b) = (q_1, \$)$	$\delta^{\leftarrow}(q_1, \$) = (q_0, b)$
$\delta(q_1, b) = (q_1, b)$	$\delta^{\leftarrow}(q_1, b) = (q_1, b)$
$\delta(q_1, a) = (q_1, \nabla)$	$\delta^{\leftarrow}(q_1, \nabla) = (q_1, a)$

The reversibility of T is immediately verified by inspecting the transition function. The output language $T(L)$ is $\{a^m \mid m \geq 0\} \cup \{a^m \$ b^{n-1} \mid m \geq 0, n \geq 1\}$ which is accepted by some reversible DFA M. Whenever the input does not belong to L, it is incorrectly formatted and T emits the error symbol ∇ on which M halts and rejects. So, M is reversible in these cases as well. ∎

Example 2. The language $L = \{a^n b^n \mid n \geq 0\}$, that is not accepted by any reversible pushdown automaton [6], is accepted by a T-REV-PDA. The transducer works in the same way as in the previous example. Therefore, we have

$T(L) = \{\lambda\} \cup \{a^n \$ b^{n-1} \mid n \geq 1\}$ which *is* accepted by some reversible deterministic pushdown automaton M. If the input does not belong to L but is otherwise correctly formatted, its translation is rejected by M without further modification. Finally, as in the previous example, if the input is incorrectly formatted then T emits the the error symbol $\triangledown$ on which M halts and rejects. So, M is reversible in these cases as well.   ∎

Example 3. Reversible pushdown automata can accept any regular language, even if the language is not accepted by any reversible DFA. The simple idea is to simulate a DFA whereby the history of the simulation is pushed. However, modifying the language $\{a^n b^n \mid n \geq 0\}$ so that there is always an arbitrary word from a given (irreversible) regular language, say $\{c^m d^l \mid m, l \geq 1\}$, in between the a's and b's yields a language that cannot be treated in this way. If the history has to be pushed while processing the infix, the number of a's cannot be compared with the number of b's.

Nevertheless, language $L = \{a^n c^m d^l b^n \mid l, m \geq 1, n \geq 0\}$ is accepted by a T-REV-PDA (M, T). The task of the transducer T is twofold. On the one hand, it checks the correct format of the input. When it detects a format error it emits an error symbol $\triangledown$ whose index is the rewritten symbol, stays in its state, and continues its computation. The other task of T is to rewrite the first occurrences of the symbols c, d, and b by their primed version (it does not change any subsequent occurrences of the symbols). In this way, T can work reversibly, and M can work reversibly by combining the techniques of Examples 1 and 2. ∎

3   Computational Capacity

In this section, we consider the computational capacity of T-REV-FAs and T-REV-PDAs. In the definition of both models it is required that the sequential transducers involved have to be reversible. A first result of this section is that this condition is not necessary since the computational capacity of both models does not change even if the transducers are irreversible. First, we show a technical lemma.

Lemma 4. *Let T be a DST with input alphabet Σ. A length-preserving homomorphism h and an injective REV-DST T' can effectively be constructed such that $T(w) = h(T'(w))$, for all $w \in \Sigma^*$.*

Proof. The idea of the proof is that T' basically simulates $T = \langle Q, \Sigma, \Delta, q_0, \delta \rangle$, but in every step it additionally outputs the information of which transition of T is currently simulated. Using this information will enable T' to work reversibly, that is, to recover its states and the original input symbols in the backward computation. Formally, we define $T' = \langle Q, \Sigma, \Delta', q_0, \delta' \rangle$ with $\Delta' = \Delta \times Q \times \Sigma$. For $q \in Q$ and $a \in \Sigma$, we define $\delta'(q, a) = (p, (o, q, a))$, if $\delta(q, a) = (p, o)$ for some $p \in Q$ and $o \in \Delta$.

The reverse transition function $\delta'^{\leftarrow}$ of T' is defined for $p, q \in Q$, $a \in \Sigma$, and $o \in \Delta$ as $\delta'^{\leftarrow}(p, (o, q, a)) = (q, a)$, if $\delta'(q, a) = (p, (o, q, a))$. Thus, $\delta'^{\leftarrow}(\delta'(q, a)) =$

(q, a) for all $q \in Q$ and $a \in \Sigma$. Hence, T' is a reversible DST. Moreover, T' computes an injective transduction since the input appears as third component in the output and T' is deterministic.

Finally, the homomorphism $h : \Delta \times Q \times \Sigma \to \Delta$ is defined as a projection to the first component, that is, $h(o, q, a) = o$ for all $o \in \Delta$, $q \in Q$, and $a \in \Sigma$. This definition implies that h is length-preserving. Moreover, we have $h(T'(w)) = T(w)$, for all $w \in \Sigma^*$. $\qquad\square$

The previous lemma can immediately be used to show that pairs of reversible DSTs and reversible DFAs accept the same family of languages as pairs of not necessarily reversible DSTs and reversible DFAs.

Theorem 5. *The family of languages accepted by T-REV-FAs is equal to the family of languages accepted by pairs of DSTs and REV-FAs.*

Proof. Let $T = \langle Q, \Sigma, \Delta, q_0, \delta \rangle$ be a DST and $M = \langle Q_M, \Delta, q_{0,M}, \delta_M, F_M \rangle$ be a REV-FA. First, Lemma 4 is applied to T which results in an injective REV-DST $T' = \langle Q, \Sigma, \Delta', q_0, \delta' \rangle$ and a length-preserving homomorphism h so that $T(w) = h(T'(w))$, for all $w \in \Sigma^*$. Now, we construct a DFA M' which basically simulates M. Formally, $M' = \langle Q_M, \Delta', q_{0,M}, \delta'_M, F_M \rangle$, where δ'_M is defined as $\delta'_M(p, a) = q$ if $\delta_M(p, h(a)) = q$, for $p, q \in Q_M$ and $a \in \Delta'$. Since M is reversible, M' is reversible as well. Moreover, a word $w \in \Sigma^*$ is accepted by (M, T) if and only if w is accepted by (M', T'). $\qquad\square$

The same idea can be applied to pairs of DSTs and reversible DPDAs.

Theorem 6. *The family of languages accepted by T-REV-PDAs is equal to the family of languages accepted by pairs of DSTs and REV-PDAs.*

Proof. The construction is similar to the construction in the proof of Theorem 5. First, for a given DST T an injective REV-DST T' with output alphabet Δ' and a length-preserving homomorphism h so that $T(w) = h(T'(w))$, for all $w \in \Sigma^*$, is constructed according to Lemma 4. Let $M = \langle Q_M, \Delta, \Gamma_M, F_M, q_{0,M}, \bot, \delta_M \rangle$ be a REV-PDA. Then, $M' = \langle Q_M, \Delta', \Gamma_M, F_M, q_{0,M}, \bot, \delta'_M \rangle$, is constructed, where $\delta'_M(p, a, Z) = (q, \gamma)$ if $\delta_M(p, h(a), Z) = (q, \gamma)$, for $p, q \in Q_M$, $a \in \Delta'$, $Z \in \Gamma_M$, and $\gamma \in \Gamma_M^*$. Again, M' is reversible and (M', T') is equivalent to (M, T). $\qquad\square$

By the last two theorems, for easier reasoning we can safely forgo the reversibility of the transducers, knowing that we can always recover it effectively.

It is known that the family of languages accepted by REV-FAs is a proper subset of the set of regular languages. For example, it is known that the regular language $\{ a^n b^m \mid n, m \geq 0 \}$ from Example 1 is not accepted by any REV-FA [5,7]. The next theorem shows that this gap can be closed by considering T-REV-FAs instead of REV-FAs.

Theorem 7. *The family of languages accepted by T-REV-FAs coincides with the family of regular languages.*

Proof. We have to show that every regular language R is accepted by some T-REV-FA. Let R be accepted by some DFA $M_R = \langle Q, \Sigma, q_0, \delta, F \rangle$. Then we construct a T-REV-FA (M, T) accepting R setting $T = \langle Q, \Sigma, Q \times Q \times \Sigma, q_0, \delta_T \rangle$, $M = \langle Q, Q \times Q \times \Sigma, q_0, \delta_M, F \rangle$, and $\delta_T(p, a) = (q, (q, p, a))$, if $\delta(p, a) = q$ for some $p, q \in Q$ and $a \in \Sigma$.

Next, automaton M simply moves from left to right, reading the current symbol, say (q, p, a), and entering the state q which is the state that M would be in at this tape square. Thus, we set $\delta_M(p, (q, p, a)) = q$. In this way, M and M_R are in the same state after reading their inputs. Since M has the same accepting states as M_R, we obtain that $L(M, T) = R$. Furthermore, M is reversible since M cannot have irreversible states due to the above definition of δ_M on input alphabet $Q \times Q \times \Sigma$. □

So, the following corollary settles the comparison between T-REV-FAs and REV-FAs (see also Fig. 2).

Corollary 8. *The family of languages accepted by T-REV-FAs strictly includes the family of languages accepted by REV-FAs.*

Next, we turn to explore the situation for pushdown automata. It is known from [6] that reversible pushdown automata are strictly stronger than (irreversible) finite automata and are strictly weaker than deterministic pushdown automata, even if the latter are restricted to work in real time. Here we refine the hierarchy by showing that the computational capacity of T-REV-PDAs lies properly in between the computational capacities of real-time deterministic pushdown automata and REV-PDAs. To this end, we consider the language

$$L_{mic} = \{ w\$w^R \mid w \in \{a, b\}^* \} \cup \{ w\$c^n \mid w \in \{a, b\}^* \text{and } |w| = n \}.$$

Lemma 9. *The language L_{mic} is not accepted by any T-REV-PDA.*

Proof. In contrast to the assertion, we assume that L_{mic} is accepted by the T-REV-PDA (M, T) with transducer $T = \langle Q_T, \Sigma, \Delta, q_{0,T}, \delta_T \rangle$ and REV-PDA $M = \langle Q_M, \Delta, \Gamma, F, q_{0,M}, \bot, \delta_M \rangle$. First, we consider the computation of (M, T) on input words of the form $w\$c^{|w|}$ in more detail. So, let $T(w\$c^{|w|}) = \tilde{w}\tilde{\$}\tilde{z}$, where $|\tilde{w}| = |w|$, $|\tilde{\$}| = 1$, and $|\tilde{z}| = |w|$.

The accepting computation of M has the form

$$(\lambda, q_{0,M}, \tilde{w}\tilde{\$}\tilde{z}, \bot) \vdash^* (\tilde{w}, q_1, \tilde{\$}\tilde{z}, \gamma_1) \vdash (\tilde{w}\tilde{\$}, q_2, \tilde{z}, \gamma_2)$$
$$\vdash^* (\tilde{w}\tilde{\$}x, q_3, y, \gamma_3) \vdash^* (\tilde{w}\tilde{\$}\tilde{z}, q_f, \lambda, \gamma_4)$$

where $xy = \tilde{z}$, $q_f \in F$, and γ_3 is the shortest pushdown content occurring in the computation *after* processing the input symbol $\tilde{\$}$. If the length $|\gamma_3|$ of the shortest pushdown content appears more than once *after* processing the input symbol $\tilde{\$}$, the first appearance is chosen. Since M is reversible and can push at most one symbol in every step, we have $0 \leq |\gamma_3| \leq |w| + 1$.

Moreover, all pushdown contents appearing in the sub-computation from configuration $(\tilde{w}\tilde{\$}, q_2, \tilde{z}, \gamma_2)$ up to but not including configuration $(\tilde{w}\tilde{\$}x, q_3, y, \gamma_3)$

are longer than γ_3 and, thus, γ_3 at the bottom of the pushdown is untouched in the sub-computation. This observation is used to split the input prefix $\tilde{w}\$$ uniquely into two parts, say, $uv = \tilde{w}\$$. The first part u is defined to be the longest prefix so that M has stored γ_3 in the pushdown after processing it. That is, $(\lambda, q_{0,M}, \tilde{w}\$\tilde{z}, \perp) \vdash^* (u, q, v\tilde{z}, \gamma_3)$ and in all subsequent configurations up to $(\tilde{w}\$, q_2, \tilde{z}, \gamma_2)$ the pushdown contents are of the form $\gamma\gamma_3$ with $\gamma \in \Gamma^+$.

Let $Z \in \Gamma$ be the topmost symbol of γ_3. Furthermore, let the transducer T be in state s after processing the input $T^{-1}(u)$ and, thus, after emitting u. Then u is said to be a (s, q, Z)-prefix, since it drives M into a configuration used to split the input and having state q and topmost pushdown symbol Z.

Similarly, v is said to be a (s, t, q, Z, p, i)-suffix, if the transducer T starts in state s and ends in state t when it emits v, and if vx drives M from a configuration with state q and topmost pushdown symbol Z into a configuration having the shortest pushdown content occurring in the computation after processing v, and having state p and topmost pushdown symbol Z. Here, x denotes the prefix of $\tilde{z}$ whose length is i.

In this way, every word $w \in \{a, b\}^*$ uniquely determines the splitting of $\tilde{w}\$$ into $u_w v_w$ as well as the number of symbols $i_w = |x|$ from the suffix $\tilde{z}$ that are processed by M until it reaches the configuration $(\tilde{w}\$x, q_3, y, \gamma_3)$.

Let P be the set of all prefixes u_w and S be the set of all suffixes obtained in this way by splitting $\tilde{w}\$$ for every word $w \in \{a, b\}^*$. For any triple $(s, q, Z) \in Q_T \times Q_M \times \Gamma$, the subset of P containing exactly all (s, q, Z)-prefixes is denoted by $P(s, q, Z)$. Similarly, we denote the subset of S containing exactly all (s, t, q, Z, p, i)-suffixes by $S(s, t, q, Z, p, i)$.

After these considerations, we continue to derive a contradiction to the assumption that L_{mic} is accepted by the T-REV-PDA (M, T).

First assume that there is some $(s, q, Z) \in Q_T \times Q_M \times \Gamma$ so that the set $P(s, q, Z)$ contains at least two prefixes, say u_{w_1} and u_{w_2} of different lengths. We consider the inputs $u_{w_1} v_{w_1} \tilde{z}$ and $u_{w_2} v_{w_1} \tilde{z}$, where $u_{w_1} v_{w_1} \tilde{z} = T(w_1 \$ c^{|w_1|})$ and, thus, $|\tilde{z}| = |w_1|$.

The accepting computation of M on $u_{w_1} v_{w_1} \tilde{z}$ is

$$(\lambda, q_{0,M}, u_{w_1} v_{w_1} \tilde{z}, \perp) \vdash^* (u_{w_1}, q, v_{w_1} \tilde{z}, Z\gamma)$$
$$\vdash^* (u_{w_1} v_{w_1} x, p, y, Z\gamma) \vdash^* (u_{w_1} v_{w_1} \tilde{z}, q_f, \lambda, \gamma' Z\gamma)$$

where v_{w_1} is a (s, t, q, Z, p, i)-suffix, $xy = \tilde{z}$, $|x| = i$, and $\gamma, \gamma' \in \Gamma^*$. However, the computation of M on $u_{w_2} v_{w_1} \tilde{z}$ is

$$(\lambda, q_{0,M}, u_{w_2} v_{w_1} \tilde{z}, \perp) \vdash^* (u_{w_2}, q, v_{w_1} \tilde{z}, Z\gamma'')$$
$$\vdash^* (u_{w_2} v_{w_1} x, p, y, Z\gamma'') \vdash^* (u_{w_2} v_{w_1} \tilde{z}, q_f, \lambda, \gamma' Z\gamma'')$$

where $\gamma'' \in \Gamma^*$. So, both words $u_{w_1} v_{w_1} \tilde{z}$ and $u_{w_2} v_{w_1} \tilde{z}$ are accepted by M. Therefore, $T^{-1}(u_{w_1} v_{w_1} \tilde{z}) \in L_{mic}$ is accepted by (M, T).

However, since u_{w_1} and u_{w_2} are both $P(s, q, Z)$-prefixes, the transducer T is in the same state s after emitting u_{w_1} and u_{w_2}. Let $w_1 \$ = \hat{u}_1 \hat{v}_1$ and $w_2 \$ = \hat{u}_2 \hat{v}_2$ with $|\hat{u}_1| = |u_{w_1}|$, $|\hat{v}_1| = |v_{w_1}|$, $|\hat{u}_2| = |u_{w_2}|$, and $|\hat{v}_2| = |v_{w_2}|$. Then on input

$\hat{u}_2\hat{v}_1 c^{|w_1|}$, transducer T emits $u_{w_2}v_{w_1}\tilde{z}$ which is accepted by M as well. This is a contradiction, since $|u_{w_2}v_{w_1}| \neq |u_{w_1}v_{w_1}|$, T is injective and length-preserving, and $|T^{-1}(u_{w_2}v_{w_1})| - 1$ does not match $|\tilde{z}|$, that is, the number of c's after the \$ in the original input.

We conclude that for all $(s, q, Z) \in Q_T \times Q_M \times \Gamma$ the set $P(s, q, Z)$ does not include two words of different lengths, thus, $P(s, q, Z)$ is finite. This implies that P is finite as well.

Next, we consider a prefix u_w, say from the set $P(s, q, Z)$, the matching suffix v_w, say from the set $S(s, t, q, Z, p, i)$, and a different suffix v' from the set $S(s, t, q, Z, p, i)$ as well, where $u_w v_w \tilde{z} = T(w\$c^{|w|})$ and, thus, $|\tilde{z}| = |w|$.

Since v_w and v' are both $S(s, t, q, Z, p, i)$-suffixes that match the $P(s, q, Z)$-prefix u_w, there is an input $w'\$c^{|w|}$ so that $T(w'\$c^{|w|}) = u_w v'\tilde{z}$.

The first part of the computation of M on $u_w v_w \tilde{z}$ is

$$(\lambda, q_{0,M}, u_w v_w \tilde{z}, \bot) \vdash^* (u_w, q, v_w \tilde{z}, Z\gamma) \vdash^* (u_w v_w x, p, y, Z\gamma)$$

where $xy = \tilde{z}$, $|x| = i$, and $\gamma \in \Gamma^*$. The first part of the computation of M on $u_w v'\tilde{z}$ is

$$(\lambda, q_{0,M}, u_w v'\tilde{z}, \bot) \vdash^* (u_w, q, v'\tilde{z}, Z\gamma) \vdash^* (u_w v' x, p, y, Z\gamma).$$

Since M is reversible, the reverse computations

$$(u_w v_w x, p, y, Z\gamma) \vdash^{\leftarrow*} (u_w v_w, p', \tilde{z}, \gamma' Z\gamma)$$

and

$$(u_w v' x, p, y, Z\gamma) \vdash^{\leftarrow*} (u_w v', p', \tilde{z}, \gamma' Z\gamma)$$

with some $p' \in Q_M$ and $\gamma' \in \Gamma^*$ reveal that the pushdown content after processing the sole \$ is the same in both forward computations. Since $w\$w^R$ belongs to L_{mic} and, thus, is accepted by (M, T), we conclude that $w'\$w^R$ is accepted as well, a contradiction. So, we obtain a contradiction to the assumption that L_{mic} is accepted by (M, T), provided that there is some set $S(s, t, q, Z, p, i)$ with at least two members.

Let k be the length of a longest word in the finite set P and choose some n large enough. There are 2^{n+k} many different words $w \in \{a, b\}^{n+k}$ and therefore at least 2^{n+k} many different words in the set $\{T(w) \mid w \in \{a, b\}^{n+k}\}$. After splitting all these words there are at least 2^n different suffixes. On the other hand, there are at most $|Q_T|^2 \cdot |Q_M|^2 \cdot |\Gamma| \cdot n \in O(n)$ many different suffix sets $S(s, t, q, Z, p, i)$. So, there is at least one of these sets with at least two members. $\qquad\square$

Theorem 10. *The family of languages accepted by real-time deterministic pushdown automata strictly includes the family of languages accepted by T-REV-PDAs.*

Proof. First, we have to argue that there is an inclusion between the language families at all. To this end, let (M, T) be a T-REV-PDA consisting of a DST $T = \langle Q_T, \Sigma, \Delta, q_{0,T}, \delta_T \rangle$ and a REV-PDA $M = \langle Q_M, \Delta, \Gamma, F_M, q_{0,M}, \bot, \delta_M \rangle$.

The idea of the construction of an equivalent real-time DPDA M' is to simulate the two computations of T and M in parallel. Automaton M' stores in its state set the current state of M as well as the current state of T. Furthermore, in each computation step M' first simulates T and then uses the output of T as input for the simulation of M. Formally, we define

$$M' = \langle Q_T \times Q_M, \Sigma, \Gamma, Q_T \times F_M, (q_{0,T}, q_{0,M}), \bot, \delta' \rangle$$

where $\delta'((p', p), a, Z) = ((q', q), \gamma)$, if $\delta_T(p', a) = (q', o)$ and $\delta_M(p, o, Z) = (q, \gamma)$, for some $p, q \in Q_M$, $p', q' \in Q_T$, $a \in \Sigma$, $o \in \Delta$, $Z \in \Gamma$, and $\gamma \in \Gamma^*$.

Second, the properness of the inclusion follows by the witness language L_{mic} discussed in Lemma 9, which is accepted by some real-time deterministic pushdown automaton, but not by any T-REV-PDA. □

In order to complete the placement of the family $\mathscr{L}$(T-REV-PDA) in the hierarchy of language families, the computational capacity of T-REV-PDA is shown to be strictly stronger than that of REV-PDA.

Theorem 11. *The family of languages accepted by T-REV-PDAs strictly includes the family of languages accepted by REV-PDAs.*

Proof. Every REV-PDA M can be considered as T-REV-PDA (M, T) where T is a one-state DST that realizes the identity map. Thus, $\mathscr{L}$(REV-PDA) is a subset of $\mathscr{L}$(T-REV-PDA). Example 2 shows that the language $L = \{ a^n b^n \mid n \geq 1 \}$ is accepted by some T-REV-PDA. On the other hand, it is shown in [6] that L is not accepted by any REV-PDA. □

In particular, we conclude that providing even weak preprocessing for reversible DFAs and REV-PDAs strictly increases their computational power. The inclusion structure of the language families accepted by devices in question is summarized in Fig. 2.

Finally, we turn to another aspect of the sequential transducers considered. Above we have shown that, in connection with our setting, we do not have to care about their reversibility since we always can get it by an effective construction. In the literature sequential transducers are often more generally defined than here. First, they normally possess two tapes where one tape is used to read the input and another, initially empty tape to write the output. Furthermore, a transducer is not necessarily length-preserving, that is, in each computation step it may append some word $w \in \Delta^*$ to the output tape. Formally, we define a general deterministic one-way sequential transducer as a system $T = \langle Q, \Sigma, \Delta, q_0, \delta \rangle$ where Q are the *internal states*, Σ are the *input symbols*, Δ are the *output symbols*, q_0 is the initial state, and $\delta \colon Q \times \Sigma \to Q \times \Delta^*$ is the *transition function*.

The next theorem shows that even a pair of a general sequential transducer and reversible deterministic pushdown automaton can be simulated by a T-REV-PDA. So, in principle, we do not have to care about the length-preservation either, since we always can get it by an effective construction.

Theorem 12. *The family of languages accepted by T-REV-PDAs is equal to the family of languages accepted by pairs of general DSTs and REV-PDAs.*

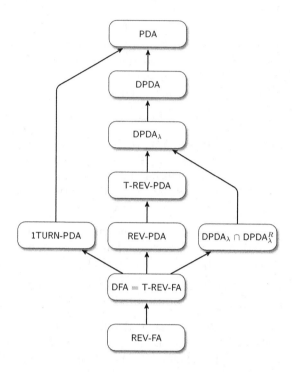

Fig. 2. Inclusion structure of language families accepted by devices in question. The arrows indicate strict inclusions. Classes not linked by a path are pairwise incomparable. 1TURN-PDA is the class of one-turn pushdown automata, which accept the linear context-free languages [2].

4   Closure Properties

By Theorem 7, the family of languages accepted by T-REV-FAs coincides with the family of regular languages. So, its closure properties are known. In this section, we complement these results by studying the closure properties of the family of languages accepted by T-REV-PDAs. We start with the Boolean operations.

Theorem 13. *The family of languages accepted by T-REV-PDAs is closed under complementation.*

Proof. Let (M, T) be a T-REV-PDA. We construct a T-REV-PDA accepting the complement $\overline{L(M, T)}$ of $L(M, T)$. The main idea of the construction is to leave the transducer T as it is and to interchange the accepting and the non-accepting states of the reversible pushdown automaton M. In the corresponding construction for deterministic pushdown automata (see, for example, [3]) one has to take care of λ-moves as well as of the problem that the pushdown automaton may reject its input by getting stuck without reading the input entirely.

The first problem does not occur for T-REV-PDA which by definition work in real time. To overcome the second problem we have to make sure that in every configuration a next move is defined. This can be realized with the usual construction of adding a non-accepting sink state which cannot be exited once entered. So, transitions undefined thus far are added, and all lead to the new sink state. To maintain reversibility, the pushdown automaton pushes the predecessor state of the sink state (using some marking) onto the pushdown store. Subsequently, in the sink state all symbols read are simply pushed.

In this way, in the backward computation the exact moment at which the sink state was entered can be identified and, thus, the sink state can be exited and the predecessor state restored. With M modified in this way, the final step is to construct another REV-PDA M' by interchanging accepting and non-accepting states. Then (M', T) is a T-REV-PDA so that $L(M', T) = L(M, T)$.   □

In the following, we exploit the fact that both languages

$$L_1 = \{ a^m b^m c^n \mid m, n \geq 1 \} \text{ and } L_2 = \{ a^m b^n c^n \mid m, n \geq 1 \}$$

are accepted by T-REV-PDAs. To this end, transducer T translates the input as $T(L_1) = \{ a^m \$ b^{m-1} \$ c^{n-1} \mid m, n \geq 1 \}$ and $T(L_2) = \{ a^m \$ b^{n-1} \$ c^{n-1} \mid m, n \geq 1 \}$. Both languages are straightforwardly accepted by REV-PDAs.

Theorem 14. *The family of languages accepted by T-REV-PDAs is neither closed under intersection nor under union.*

Proof. Assume that the family of languages accepted by T-REV-PDAs is closed under intersection. Then $L_1 \cap L_2 = \{ a^m b^m c^m \mid m \geq 1 \}$ is accepted by some T-REV-PDA. However, language $L_1 \cap L_2$ is not even context free, a contradiction to Theorem 10.

Since the family of languages accepted by T-REV-PDAs is closed under complementation by Theorem 13, the closure under union would imply the closure under intersection which is again a contradiction.   □

Despite the non-closure under union and intersection, $\mathscr{L}$(T-REV-PDA) is closed under union and intersection with regular languages, which is shown not to be true for REV-PDAs in [6].

Theorem 15. *The family of languages accepted by T-REV-PDAs is closed under union and intersection with regular languages.*

Proof. Let R be a regular language accepted by a deterministic finite automaton $M_R = \langle Q_R, \Sigma, q_{0,R}, \delta_R, F_R \rangle$, and (M, T) be a T-REV-PDA consisting of a DST $T = \langle Q_T, \Sigma, \Delta, q_{0,T}, \delta_T \rangle$ and a REV-PDA $M = \langle Q_M, \Delta, \Gamma, F_M, q_{0,M}, \bot, \delta_M \rangle$. According to the construction given in the proof of Theorem 13 we may assume that M is a REV-PDA that always reads its input entirely.

The basic idea for T-REV-PDAs (M', T') that accept $L(M, T) \cup R$ and $L(M, T) \cap R$ is that T' simulates T and M_R in parallel, and emits the simulated states as well as their predecessors, while M' simulates M and additionally stores the simulated state of M_R emitted by T' in its state. Formally, we define

$$T' = \langle Q_T \times Q_R, \Sigma, \Delta \times Q_R \times Q_R, (q_{0,T}, q_{0,R}), \delta_{T'} \rangle \text{ and}$$
$$M' = \langle Q_M \times Q_R, \Delta \times Q_R \times Q_R, \Gamma, F_{M'}, (q_{0,M}, q_{0,R}), \perp, \delta_{M'} \rangle.$$

The transition function $\delta_{T'}$ is defined as $\delta_{T'}((p, p'), a) = ((q, q'), (o, p', q'))$, if $\delta_T(p, a) = (q, o)$ and $\delta_R(p', a) = q'$, for $p, q \in Q_T$, $p', q' \in Q_R$, $a \in \Sigma$, and $o \in \Delta$. The transition function $\delta_{M'}$ is defined for all $p', q' \in Q_R$ as follows: $\delta_{M'}((p, p'), (a, p', q'), Z) = ((q, q'), \gamma)$, if $\delta_M(p, a, Z) = (q, \gamma)$ for $p, q \in Q_M$, $a \in \Delta$, $Z \in \Gamma$, and $\gamma \in \Gamma^*$. Then the reverse transition function $\delta_{M'}^-$ is defined for all $p', q' \in Q_R$ as follows: $\delta_{M'}^-((q, q'), (a, p', q'), Z) = ((p, p'), \gamma)$, if $\delta_M^-(q, a, Z) = (p, \gamma)$ for $p, q \in Q_M$, $a \in \Delta$, $Z \in \Gamma$, and $\gamma \in \Gamma^*$. With this definition it is ensured that a predecessor configuration can be computed since the correct state and stack contents of M are computed by δ_M^-, whereas the correct state of M_R is restored using the input symbol. Thus, M' is a REV-PDA.

To accept $L(M, T) \cup R$ we define $F_{M'} = (F_M \times Q_R) \cup (Q_M \times F_R)$ and to accept $L(M, T) \cap R$ we define $F_{M'} = F_M \times F_R$. Thus, we obtain that $L(M', T')$ is $L(M, T) \cup R$ respectively $L(M, T) \cap R$.   □

Theorem 16. *The family of languages accepted by T-REV-PDAs is closed under inverse homomorphism.*

Proof. Let (M, T) be a T-REV-PDA consisting of a DST over some alphabet Σ and a REV-PDA over some alphabet Δ. Furthermore, let $h : \Lambda^* \to \Sigma^*$ be a homomorphism. Our goal is to construct a T-REV-PDA (M, T') accepting language $h^{-1}(L(M, T)) = \{ w \in \Lambda^* \mid h(w) \in L(M, T) \}$.

The idea to construct DST T' from T and h is to simulate h on the current input symbol x and then T on input $h(x)$ in one step. On input $x \in \Lambda$, transducer T' emits $T(h(x))$.

So, we have a general transducer T' and the REV-PDA M such that (M, T') accepts the inverse homomorphic image of $L(M, T)$, since

$$L(M, T') = \{ w \in \Lambda^* \mid T'(w) \in L(M) \} = \{ w \in \Lambda^* \mid T(h(w)) \in L(M) \}$$
$$= \{ w \in \Lambda^* \mid h(w) \in L(M, T) \} = h^{-1}(L(M, T)).$$

Finally, Theorem 12 shows that $L(M, T') = h^{-1}(L(M, T))$ is accepted by some T-REV-PDA.   □

Finally, we turn to further non-closure results for which we exploit language $L_3 = \{ a^m b^n c^m \mid m, n \geq 1 \}$ which can be accepted by some T-REV-PDA in a similar way as the language $L_1 = \{ a^m b^m c^n \mid m, n \geq 1 \}$ from above. Here we consider $L_4 = \$L_1 \cup L_3$ which is a real-time deterministic context-free language that is accepted by a T-REV-PDA in a straightforward way.

Table 1. Closure properties of the language classes discussed.

	—	∪	∩	∪REG	∩REG	·	*	$h_{l.p.}$	h^{-1}	R
REG	Yes	Yes	Yes	Yes	Yes	Yes	Yes	Yes	Yes	Yes
$\mathscr{L}$(REV-PDA)	Yes	No	No	No	No	No	No	No	Yes	No
$\mathscr{L}$(T-REV-PDA)	Yes	No	No	Yes	Yes	No	No	No	Yes	No
DPDA$_\lambda$	Yes	No	No	Yes	Yes	No	No	No	Yes	No

Theorem 17. *The family of languages accepted by T-REV-PDAs is not closed under concatenation, iteration, length-preserving homomorphism, and reversal.*

Proof. The family of languages accepted by T-REV-PDA is closed under intersection with regular languages by Theorem 15. We consider the concatenation of the finite and, thus, regular language $\{\lambda, \$\}$ with L_4, which both belong to $\mathscr{L}$(T-REV-PDA), and intersect the result with the regular language $\$a^*b^*c^*$. In this way, we obtain $\$L_1 \cup \$L_3 = \{\, \$a^\ell b^m c^n \mid \ell, m, n \geq 1$ and $\ell = m$ or $\ell = n \,\}$ which is not a deterministic context-free language, since its complement is not even context free. This shows the non-closure under concatenation.

Similarly, the non-closure under iteration follows by $(\{\lambda, \$\} \cup L_4)^* \cap \$a^*b^*c^*$ which is again $\$L_1 \cup \$L_3$.

For the non-closure under length-preserving homomorphism we consider the length-preserving homomorphism h, where $h(\$) = h(a) = a$, $h(b) = b$, and $h(c) = c$. Then $h(L_4) = \{\, a^\ell b^m c^n \mid \ell, m, n \geq 1$ and $\ell + 1 = m$ or $\ell = n \,\}$ which is again not a deterministic context-free language.

Finally, $\mathscr{L}$(T-REV-PDA) is not closed under reversal, since L_4 is accepted by some T-REV-PDA, but L_4^R is not even deterministic context free. □

The closure properties derived in this section are summarized in Table 1 where also the closure properties of related language families are listed.

Acknowledgments. The authors acknowledge partial support from COST Action IC1405 *Reversible Computation*. H.B. Axelsen was supported by the Danish Council for Independent Research | Natural Sciences under the *Foundations of Reversible Computing* project, and by an IC1405 STSM (short-term scientific mission) grant.

References

1. Axelsen, H.B., Jakobi, S., Kutrib, M., Malcher, A.: A hierarchy of fast reversible turing machines. In: Krivine, J., Stefani, J.-B. (eds.) RC 2015. LNCS, vol. 9138, pp. 29–44. Springer, Switzerland (2015)
2. Ginsburg, S., Spanier, E.H.: Finite-turn pushdown automata. SIAM J. Control **4**, 423–434 (1966)
3. Harrison, M.A.: Introduction to Formal Language Theory. Addison-Wesley, Reading (1978)

4. Kondacs, A., Watrous, J.: On the power of quantum finite state automata. In: Proceeding of Foundations of Computer Science, pp. 66–75. IEEE (1997)
5. Kutrib, M.: Aspects of reversibility for classical automata. In: Calude, C.S., Freivalds, R., Kazuo, I. (eds.) Computing with New Resources. LNCS, vol. 8808, pp. 83–98. Springer, Heidelberg (2014)
6. Kutrib, M., Malcher, A.: Reversible pushdown automata. J. Comput. Syst. Sci. **78**, 1814–1827 (2012)
7. Pin, J.E.: On reversible automata. In: Simon, I. (ed.) Latin 1992. LNCS, vol. 583, pp. 401–416. Springer, Heidelberg (1992)

Reversible Computation vs. Reversibility in Petri Nets

Kamila Barylska[1], Maciej Koutny[2], Łukasz Mikulski[1(✉)],
and Marcin Piątkowski[1]

[1] Faculty of Mathematics and Computer Science,
Nicolaus Copernicus University, Chopina 12/18, Toruń, Poland
{kamila.barylska,lukasz.mikulski,marcin.piatkowski}@mat.umk.pl
[2] School of Computing Science, Newcastle University,
Newcastle upon Tyne NE1 7RU, UK
maciej.koutny@newcastle.ac.uk

Abstract. Petri nets are a general formal model of concurrent systems which supports both action-based and state-based modelling and reasoning. One of important behavioural properties investigated in the context of Petri nets has been reversibility, understood as the possibility of returning to the initial marking from any reachable net marking. Thus reversibility in Petri nets is a global property. Reversible computation, on the other hand, is typically a local mechanism using which a system can undo some of the executed actions. This paper is concerned with the modelling of reversible computation within Petri nets. A key idea behind the proposed construction is to add 'reverse' versions of selected transitions. Since such a modification can severely impact on the behavior of the system, it is crucial, in particular, to be able to determine whether the modified system has a similar set of states as the original one. We first prove that the problem of establishing whether the two nets have the same reachable markings is undecidable even in the restricted case discussed in this paper. We then show that the problem of checking whether the reachability sets of the two nets cover the same markings is decidable.

Keywords: Petri net · Reversibility · Reversible computation · Decidability

1 Introduction

Petri nets are a general formal model of concurrent systems which supports both action-based and state-based modelling and reasoning. One of important behavioural properties investigated in the context of Petri nets has been reversibility, understood as the possibility of returning to the initial marking (a global state) from any reachable marking. But it is not required that any specific transitions (global states) are used to bring the net back to the initial marking.

ⓒ Springer International Publishing Switzerland 2016
S. Devitt and I. Lanese (Eds.): RC 2016, LNCS 9720, pp. 105–118, 2016.
DOI: 10.1007/978-3-319-40578-0_7

Reversibility in Petri nets has been investigated for years, for example, in the context of enforcing controllability in discrete event systems [18,20,29]. Intuitively, it is a global property which is related to the existence of home states [5,16], i.e., those markings which can be reached from all forward reachable markings.

Unlike Petri net reversibility, reversible computation typically refers to a local mechanism using which a system can undo (the effect of) some of the already executed actions. Such an approach has been applied, in particular, to various kinds of process calculi and event structures (see, e.g., [2,7–9,19,21–23]). A category theory based rendering of reversible computation with an application to Petri nets has been proposed in [10].

1.1 Previous Work

A good deal of decision problems related to reversibility as well as home states and home spaces has been investigated over the past decades. These problems were usually considered within the domain of potentially infinite-state Place/Transition-net (PT-nets) and their subclasses, as most problems become trivial for finite-state net models. Typically, these problems are of one of two kinds.

In the case of the first kind of problems, one wants to establish whether a given marking (or a set of markings) satisfies a desirable property. For instance, the fundamental home state problem is concerned with establishing whether a given marking of a given PT-net is a home state. The problem was shown in [1] to be decidable, as well as its restricted version consisting in deciding whether the initial marking of a PT-net is a home state. Another example problem is that of establishing whether a linear set of markings is a home space of a given PT-net, and [11] demonstrated that such a problem is decidable. Problems of the second kind put the emphasis on the existence of a marking (or set of markings) satisfying a desirable property. For example, the fundamental home state existence problem, shown to be decidable in [4], is to establish whether there exists a home state for a given PT-net.

Although there are several positive decidability results related to reversibility, in general, the complexity of potential solutions appears to be high or difficult to establish. For example, the problem of the reversibility property is decidable but its complexity is still unknown [4,16] demonstrated that the problem of home state existence is at least as hard as the reachability problem [15]. This, rather pessimistic results, meant that the quest for effective algorithms, and indeed decidable problems, has for many years been carried out within special subclasses of PT-nets. Such subclasses are often defined by imposing restrictions on the structure of a net, or by assuming boundedness, with the resulting submodels of PT-nets being still relevant for a wide range of practical applications.

For example, it was shown in [6] that all live and bounded free-choice nets have home states, and the free-choice assumption cannot be changed to asymmetric choice. The home space problem is polynomial for live and bounded free-choice Petri nets [3,12], and they also were shown to have home states [28]. Other, often progressively less restricted, net classes were considered in [3,16,24,26,27].

1.2 Our Contribution

This paper is concerned with the modelling of reversible computation in Petri nets. A key idea is to add *reversed* versions of selected net transitions, each such reversed transition being obtained by simply changing the directions of adjacent arcs. The resulting reversible computations implement in a direct way what can be seen as the *undoing* of an executed action, and the simple form of such an undoing is possible thanks to the local nature of marking changes effected by net transitions.

Adding reversed transitions can greatly impact on the behavior of the system. It is therefore crucial to be able to determine whether the modified net has similar set of states as the original one. In this paper we present two key results. First, we prove that the problem of establishing whether the original net and that resulting from adding reverse transitions have the same reachable markings is undecidable even in the case of adding a single reverse. This is a strong result indicating that unless reversing of transitions is applied to restricted classes of Petri nets, such as bounded nets, controlling reversibility (so that the state space of a system does not grow) is too hard a task. We then turn to more relaxed requirement on the state space of the 'reversed' net by stipulating that what one requires is that the two nets 'cover' the same sets of markings. We then demonstrate that the problem of checking whether the reachability sets of the two nets are equivalent w.r.t. coverability is decidable.

It should be noted that focussing on coverability still has a significant application potential. For example, if all the markings covered by the original Petri net are safe on a given subset of places, then all the reachable markings of the 'reversed' net are guaranteed to be safe on this subset of places as well, provided that the nets cover the same sets of markings.

1.3 Organisation of This Paper

The paper is organised as follows. In Sect. 2, we recall some basic definitions concerning Petri nets and their behavioural properties. Section 3 contains examples motivating our work and facilitating the understanding of the proposed approach. In Sect. 4, we provide the proof of undecidability of the problem of establishing whether two given nets have the same sets of reachable markings. In the Sect. 5, we prove that the problem of checking whether the reachability sets of two nets cover the same markings is decidable. Section 6 concludes the paper.

2 Preliminaries

The set of non-negative integers is denoted by $\mathbb{N}$. The cardinality of a set X is denoted by $|X|$, and multisets over X are members of $\mathbb{N}^X$, i.e., mappings from

X to $\mathbb{N}$. If X is finite, then the multisets in $\mathbb{N}^X$ can be represented by vectors $\mathbb{N}^{|X|}$, assuming a fixed ordering of the elements of X.

The set of all multisets with componentwise addition and comparison $\leq$ is denoted by $\mathbb{N}^X$ (where $|X| \geq 1$). The componentwise subtraction is also defined if the result belongs to $\mathbb{N}^X$. One can extend the notion of $\mathbb{N}^X$ to ω-*multisets* $\mathbb{N}_\omega^X = (\mathbb{N} \cup \{\omega\})^X$, where $\omega = |\mathbb{N}|$, with the standard extensions of the addition, comparison and subtraction, assuming $\omega + n = \omega$, $\omega - n = \omega$, and $n < \omega$, for all $n \in \mathbb{N}$. The *left closures* of $y \in \mathbb{N}_\omega^X$ and $Y \subseteq \mathbb{N}_\omega^X$ are respectively defined by $\downarrow y = \{z \in \mathbb{N}_\omega^X \mid z \leq y\}$ and $\downarrow Y = \bigcup \{\downarrow y \mid y \in Y\}$. In a similar way we can define ω-vectors $\mathbb{N}_\omega^k$ as vector representations of ω-multisets.

Petri Nets

A *place/transition net* (p/t-net) is a tuple $N = (P, T, W^-, W^+, M_0)$, where:

- P and T are finite disjoint sets, of *places* and *transitions*, respectively;
- $W^-, W^+ : T \to \mathbb{N}^{|P|}$ are arc weight functions; and
- $M_0 \in \mathbb{N}^{|P|}$ is the *initial marking*.

Any multiset in $\mathbb{N}^P$ is a *marking* (global state) of N, and it will be represented by a vector in $\mathbb{N}^{|P|}$, after assuming some fixed ordering of the places in P. The following terminology applies to the case of ω-markings $\mathbb{N}_\omega^P$ as well.

Petri nets admit a natural graphical representation, with nodes representing places and transitions, and annotated arcs representing the weight function. Places are indicated by circles, and transitions by boxes. For each transition $t \in T$ and place $p \in P$, $W^-(t)(p)$ is the weight of the arc from p to t, and $W^+(t)(p)$ is the weight of the arc from t to p. Arcs with zero weights are not drawn at all, and arcs with unit weights are not annotated with 1. Markings are depicted by placing tokens inside the circles.

A transition $t \in T$ is *enabled* at a marking M of N whenever $W^-(t) \leq M$. We denote this by $M[t\rangle_N$, or simply $M[t\rangle$ if N is clear from the context. If t is enabled in M, then it can be *executed*. The execution changes the current marking M to the new marking $M' = M - W^-(t) + W^+(t)$. We denote this by $M[t\rangle_N M'$, or simply $M[t\rangle M'$ if N is clear from the context.

The notions of transition enabledness and execution extend, in the usual way, to strings of transitions (computations). The empty string ε is enabled at any marking and $M[\varepsilon\rangle M$, and a string $w = tw'$ is enabled at a marking M whenever $M[t\rangle M'$ and w' is enabled at M'; moreover, $M[w\rangle M''$, where $M'[w'\rangle M''$.

If $M[w\rangle M'$, for some $w \in T^*$, then M' is *reachable from* M, and the set of all markings reachable from M is denoted by $[M\rangle_N$, or simply $[M\rangle$ if N is clear from the context. The *reachability set* of N is the set $[M_0\rangle$ of all markings reachable from the initial marking, and the markings in $[M_0\rangle$ are called *reachable* in N.

A marking M of N is a *home state* if $M \in [M'\rangle$, for every marking $M' \in [M_0\rangle$, and N is *reversible* if M_0 is a home state.

A marking $M \in \mathbb{N}^P$ *coverable* in N if there exist a reachable marking $M' \in [M_0\rangle$ such that $M \leq M'$, and $\downarrow[M_0\rangle$ is the *coverable set* of N.

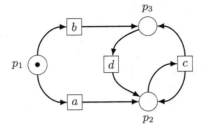

Fig. 1. A Petri net (see [25]) consisting of three places (p_1, p_2 and p_3) and four transitions (a, b, c, d).

A *reverse* of a transition $t \in T$ is a new transition $\overline{t}$ such that $W^-(\overline{t}) = W^+(t)$ and $W^+(\overline{t}) = W^-(t)$. To improve readability, we depict transitions of the original nets using solid lines, and the newly created reverses by dashed ones (see Fig. 2).

Reachability and Coverability Graphs

Reachability graphs represent precisely the reachability sets of nets, but can be infinite, while coverability graphs are always finite, but represent precisely the coverable sets rather than reachability sets (see, e.g., [15]).

The *reachability graph* of a p/t-net $N = (P, T, W^-, W^+, M_0)$ is a directed graph $RG = ([M_0\rangle, G, M_0)$, where $[M_0\rangle$ is the set of vertices, M_0 is the initial vertex and $G = \{(M, t, M') \mid M \in [M_0\rangle \wedge M[t\rangle M'\}$ is the set of labelled arcs. Thus, the vertices of the reachability graph are the reachable markings of N.

In the case of a coverability graph, it is convenient to present a constructive definition based on [17].

Algorithm Constructing a Coverability Graph

Let $N = (P, T, W^-, W^+, M_0)$ be a p/t-net. The vertices of the coverability graph constructed below are ω-vectors in $\mathbb{N}_\omega^{|P|}$.

Step 0. *Initial vertex*
   We take M_0 to be the initial vertex, and set it to blue (i.e., marked). GOTO Step 1.

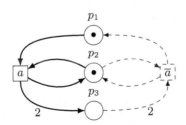

Fig. 2. A transition a and its reverse $\overline{a}$.

Step 1. *Generating new working vertices*

If there is no blue vertex then STOP. Otherwise, we take an arbitrary blue vertex M and draw from it all the arcs of the form (M, t, M'), for all $t \in T$ enabled at M (i.e., $W^-(t) \le M$) and $M' = M - W^-(t) + W^+(t)$. If M' is not yet a vertex we add it and set to yellow (i.e., working). After drawing all such arcs we set M to grey (i.e., processed). GOTO Step 2.

Step 2. *Coverability adjustment*

If there is no yellow vertex GOTO Step 1. Otherwise, we take an arbitrary yellow vertex M and check, for all the paths from M_0 to M, whether a vertex M' such that $M' \le M$ lies on the path and store all such vertices in $V(M)$. If $V(M) \ne \emptyset$ then every coordinate of the marking M greater than the corresponding coordinate of any marking $M' \in V(M)$ changes to ω. Finally, we set M to blue. GOTO Step 2.

The above construction always terminates, and the resulting labelled directed graph $CG = (\mathcal{M}, G^{cov}, M_0)$ is a *coverability graph* of N.

Coverability graphs are related to coverability sets (see, e.g., [13]), where a *coverability set* of N is $CS \subseteq \mathbb{N}_\omega^P$ such that the following hold:

CS1. CS covers the reachability set of N, i.e., $[M_0\rangle \subseteq \downarrow CS$; and

CS2. $[M_0\rangle$ tightly approximates all non-reachable vectors in CS, i.e., for every $M \in CS \setminus [M_0\rangle$, there is an infinite sequence of distinct markings $M_1, M_2, \cdots \in [M_0\rangle$ such that, for all $i \ge 1$:

$$M_i < M_{i+1} \quad and \quad M_{\omega/i} \le M_i \le M ,$$

where $M_{\omega/i} \in \mathbb{N}^P$ is obtained from M by replacing each ω by i.

Moreover, CS is *minimal* if no proper subset of CS is a coverability set of N (Fig. 3).

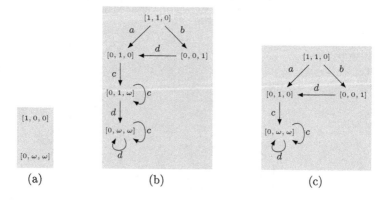

(a)   (b)   (c)

Fig. 3. The minimal coverability set (a) and two possible coverability graphs (b) and (c) of the net of Fig. 1. During the generation of the graph of (b), the vertex $[0, 1, 0]$ was chosen before $[0, 0, 1]$ in the algorithm described in Sect. 1, while in the case of (c), the vertex $[0, 0, 1]$ was chosen before $[0, 1, 0]$.

Proposition 1. *The set of vertices of the coverability graph CG constructed above is a finite coverability set of N.*

Remark 1. Referring to [13], there exists a unique <u>finite</u> minimal coverability set which can be used to represent the coverable set of N, usually smaller than the set of all vertices of the coverability graph. Note that although the reachability set of N is a coverability set included in $\mathbb{N}^P$, it contains the minimal coverability set if and only if it is finite. Whenever the set of reachable markings is infinite, a finite coverability set has to use true ω-markings.

3   Motivating Examples

A rather natural way of implementing the *undoing* of executed transitions is to introduce reverses of them, as shown in Fig. 2. In this section, we will discuss the impact of adding reverse transitions on net behaviour.

In Fig. 4, the solid lines depict a p/t-net together with its reachablility graph. Moreover, using the dashed lines, the diagram shows the reverse transition added to the original net, and the resulting enlargement of the original reachability graph. We observe that the original p/t-net was not reversible (it did not even have a home state), but the modified one is reversible and its set of reachable markings is the same as for the original net. Hence, in this case, reversing transitions 'improved' the overall net behaviour.

Figure 5 shows a p/t-net which has a home state $[0, 0, 1, 1]$. In this case, one only needs to add a reverse $\overline{b}$ of transition b to obtain a reversible net. Also, the set of reachable marking stays unchanged.

The first two examples demonstrated that adding reverse transitions can sometimes 'improve' the behaviour of the original net. In general, however,

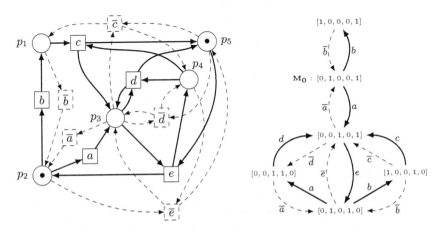

Fig. 4. A p/t-net with reverses for all transitions and its reachability graph. Reverse transitions yield reversibility.

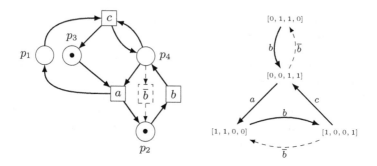

Fig. 5. A p/t-net with a single reverse transition and its reachability graph. Reverse transition yields reversibility.

adding reverse transition changes the reachability set and also allows computations based on the original transitions which were not enabled in the original net. This may happen even if we limit ourselves to reversing only one transition.

Figure 6 shows a p/t-net with a finite set of reachable markings for which adding only one reverse $\bar{c}$ changes the reachability set to an infinite one. Note that the execution of the reverse transition $\bar{c}$ is enabled *before* the first execution of c at $[0, 1, 1]$. As a consequence, this p/t-net would model a system in which some action can be undone before it has been done, which is contrary to our intuition behind reversing a computation.

Starting with a net possessing a home state does not help either, as Fig. 7 shows. The net has a home state $[0, 1, 0, 1, 1, 0]$, but, again, it is enough to add $\bar{a}$ to obtain a net with a bigger set of reachable markings.

The above examples suggest that it is not obvious when one can add reverses to a p/t-net without radically changing its behavior. We could also see that adding even one such transition may cause great changes in net behaviour. Thus, it is crucial to be able to decide whether a particular reverse can be added to a p/t-net without changing 'too much' its reachability set. To this end, we will

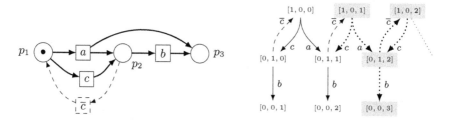

Fig. 6. A p/t-net with a single reverse transition and its reachability graph, where: the solid arcs denote arcs present in the reachability graph of the original net; the dashed arcs denote the introduced reverse of c enabled at markings reachable in the original net; and the dotted arcs represent transitions (or reverses) enabled only at markings (with gray background) which were not reachable in the original net.

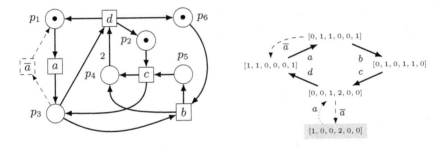

Fig. 7. A reversible p/t-net with a single reverse transition and its reachability graph. The marking with gray background is not reachable in the original net.

discuss the decidability of the following problems involving comparisons of the state spaces of two p/t-nets.

Marking equality with single transition: MEST
   Are the reachability sets of two given p/t-nets, where the second one is obtained from the first by adding a single transition, equal?

Marking equality with single transition reverse: MESTR
   Are the reachability sets of two given p/t-nets, where the second one is obtained from the first by adding a single transition reverse, equal?

Coverable set equality: CSE
   Are the coverable sets of two given p/t-nets equal?

By Theorem 7.5 of [14] MEST is undecidable. In the following section, we will prove that MESTR is undecidable. Next, we will argue that CSE is decidable.

4   Undecidability of MESTR

In this section, we will show that MESTR is undecidable. The key observation is formulated as the following result.

Proposition 2. *MEST is reducible to MESTR.*

Proof. Let $\mathbb{A} = (P, T_A, W_A^-, W_A^+, M_0)$ and $\mathbb{B} = (P, T_B, W_B^-, W_B^+, M_0)$ be two p/t-nets, with the same sets of places and initial marking, and such that $T_B = \{t' \mid t \in T_A\} \uplus \{a\}$, $W_A^-(t) = W_B^-(t')$ and $W_A^+(t) = W_B^+(t')$ for every $t \in T_A$. Note that $\mathbb{B}$ can be seen as a copy or mirror[1] of $\mathbb{A}$ with an additional transition a (however, the transition sets of $\mathbb{A}$ and $\mathbb{B}$ are disjoint).
   We will now describe how to construct two nets, $\mathbb{C}$ and $\mathbb{D}$, with the construction being illustrated in Fig. 8.

---

[1] The mirror of $t_1 t_2 \ldots t_k \in T_A^*$ is $t_1' t_2' \ldots t_k' \in T_B^*$, and vice versa.

The net $\mathbb{C} = (P_C, T_C, W_C^-, W_C^+, M_0^C)$ is such that $P_C = P \uplus \{A_R, B_R\}$ and $T_C = T_A \uplus T_B \uplus \{c, e\}$. Moreover,

$$M_0^C(p) = \begin{cases} M_0(p) & \text{if} \quad p \in P \\ 1 & \text{if} \quad p = A_R \\ 0 & \text{if} \quad p = B_R \end{cases}$$

and the weight functions are as follows:

$$W_C^-(t)(p) = \begin{cases} W_A^-(t)(p) & \text{if} \quad p \in P & \& \quad t \in T_A \\ W_B^-(t)(p) & \text{if} \quad p \in P & \& \quad t \in T_B \\ 1 & \text{if} \quad p = A_R & \& \quad t \in T_A \\ 0 & \text{if} \quad p = B_R & \& \quad t \in T_A \\ 1 & \text{if} \quad p = B_R & \& \quad t \in T_B \\ 0 & \text{if} \quad p = A_R & \& \quad t \in T_B \\ 1 & \text{if} \quad p = A_R & \& \quad t = c \\ 0 & \text{if} \quad p \neq A_R & \& \quad t = c \\ 1 & \text{if} \quad p = A_R & \& \quad t = e \\ 0 & \text{if} \quad p \neq A_R & \& \quad t = e \end{cases}$$

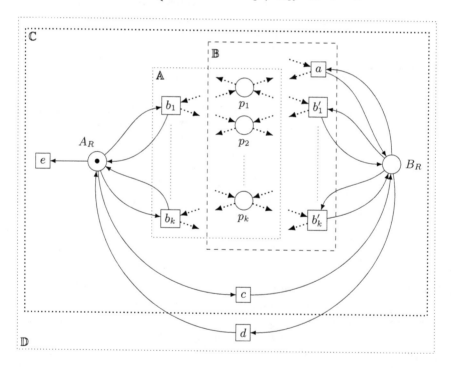

Fig. 8. The construction used in the proof of Proposition 2.

and

$$W_C^+(t)(p) = \begin{cases} W_A^+(t)(p) & \text{if } p \in P & \& \quad t \in T_A \\ W_B^+(t)(p) & \text{if } p \in P & \& \quad t \in T_B \\ 1 & \text{if } p = A_R & \& \quad t \in T_A \\ 0 & \text{if } p = B_R & \& \quad t \in T_A \\ 1 & \text{if } p = B_R & \& \quad t \in T_B \\ 0 & \text{if } p = A_R & \& \quad t \in T_B \\ 1 & \text{if } p = B_R & \& \quad t = c \\ 0 & \text{if } p \neq B_R & \& \quad t = c \\ 0 & \text{if } p \in P_C & \& \quad t = e \end{cases}$$

The net $\mathbb{D} = (P_C, T_D, W_D^-, W_D^+, M_0^C)$ is such that $T_D = T_C \uplus \{d\}$ and the weight functions are given by:

$$W_D^-(t)(p) = \begin{cases} W_C^-(t)(p) & \text{if } p \in P & \& \quad t \in T_C \\ 1 & \text{if } p = B_R & \& \quad t = d \\ 0 & \text{if } p \neq B_R & \& \quad t = d \end{cases}$$

and

$$W_D^+(t)(p) = \begin{cases} W_C^+(t)(p) & \text{if } p \in P & \& \quad t \in T_C \\ 1 & \text{if } p = A_R & \& \quad t = d \\ 0 & \text{if } p \neq A_R & \& \quad t = d \end{cases}$$

Note that in $\mathbb{D}$, transition d is the reverse of c.

In what follows, we denote a marking $M^C \in \mathbb{N}^{P_C}$ as $M_{\langle x,y \rangle}$, where $M \in \mathbb{N}^P$, $x, y \in \mathbb{N}$ and

$$M^C(p) = \begin{cases} M(p) & \text{if } p \in P \\ x & \text{if } p = A_R \\ y & \text{if } p = B_R \end{cases}$$

The net $\mathbb{C}$ works as follows. Before the first (and only) execution of c or e we can simulate the behaviour of $\mathbb{A}$ obtaining, as a result, a marking $M^C = M_{\langle 1,0 \rangle}$ such that M is any marking reachable in $\mathbb{A}$. Then there are two ways of continuing:

- After executing c we obtain $M_{\langle 0,1 \rangle}$ and may proceed with the simulation of $\mathbb{B}$. Note that we can reach the same marking by executing c followed by the mirror computation in the net $\mathbb{B}$. Hence every marking reachable by some computation containing c leads to a marking $M_{\langle 0,1 \rangle}$, where M is a marking reachable in $\mathbb{B}$.
- After firing e we obtain the dead marking $M_{\langle 0,0 \rangle}$.

As a result, the set of reachable markings of $\mathbb{C}$ is:

$$[M_0^C \rangle_C = \{M_{\langle 0,1 \rangle} \mid M \in [M_0 \rangle_B\} \cup \{M_{\langle 1,0 \rangle} \mid M \in [M_0 \rangle_A\} \\ \cup \{M_{\langle 0,0 \rangle} \mid M \in [M_0 \rangle_A\} \,.$$

The net $\mathbb{D}$ works similarly as $\mathbb{C}$. The only difference is a possible transfer of the control token from B_R to A_R using the transition d. This means that every execution in the net $\mathbb{D}$ is an alternation of executions in $\mathbb{A}$ and $\mathbb{B}$ (possibly followed by a single execution of e). As a result, from the point of view of reachable markings, we may focus only on the net $\mathbb{B}$ (starting every computation with c and ending it with d or de, if necessary). Hence, the set of reachable markings of $\mathbb{D}$ is:

$$[M_0^C\rangle_D = \{M_{\langle 0,1\rangle} \mid M \in [M_0\rangle_B\} \cup \{M_{\langle 1,0\rangle} \mid M \in [M_0\rangle_B\}$$
$$\cup \{M_{\langle 0,0\rangle} \mid M \in [M_0\rangle_B\} .$$

We therefore conclude that $[M_0\rangle_A = [M_0\rangle_B$ if and only if $[M_0^C\rangle_C = [M_0^C\rangle_D$, which means that MEST has been reduced to MESTR. $\square$

As a direct consequence of the above result and Theorem 7.5 of [14] we obtain

Theorem 1. *MESTR is undecidable.*

Thus verifying whether reversing a transition in a p/t-net does not change its reachability set is not a feasible problem. Clearly, for restricted classes of nets one may still look for decision procedures but, in the general case, one needs to relax the required correspondence between the state space of the original net and that resulting from reversing of some of its transitions.

5   Decidability of CSE

The construction of coverability graphs in [13] differs a bit from our approach, which is a deterministic version of Karp-Miller procedure [17]. Nevertheless, the set of labels of the coverability graph's nodes is the coverability set and so the unique minimal coverability set (see [13]) might be obtained from the set of labels of coverability graph's nodes by taking its maximal subset.

Theorem 2. *CSE is decidable.*

Proof. Let A and B be two p/t-nets with the initial markings M_0^A and M_0^B, respectively. We need to show that it is possible to effectively establish whether $\downarrow[M_0^A\rangle = \downarrow[M_0^B\rangle$. By Proposition 1, we can effectively compute finite coverability sets, CS_A and CS_B, of A and B, respectively. It then suffices to show that the following statements are equivalent:

(i) For every $M \in CS_A$, there is $M' \in CS_B$ such that $M \leq M'$.
(ii) $\downarrow[M_0^A\rangle \subseteq \downarrow[M_0^B\rangle$.

(i) $\Longrightarrow$ (ii) :
Suppose that $M \leq M'$ and $M' \in [M_0^A\rangle$. Then, by (CS1), there exists $M'' \in CS_A$ such that $M' \leq M''$. Thus, by (i), there exists $M''' \in CS_B$ such that $M'' \leq M'''$. If $M''' \in [M_0^B\rangle$, we get $M \in \downarrow[M_0^B\rangle$. Otherwise, by (CS2), there exists $M_i \in [M_0^B\rangle$ such that $M'' \leq M_i$. Hence, again, $M \in \downarrow[M_0^B\rangle$.

(ii) $\Longrightarrow$ (i) :
Suppose that $M \in CS_A$. If $M \in [M_0^A\rangle$ then, by (ii), there exists $M' \in [M_0^B\rangle$ such that $M \leq M'$. Hence, by (CS1), there exists $M'' \in CS_B$ such that $M' \leq M''$. Hence $M \leq M''$.

If $M \notin [M_0^A\rangle$ then, by (CS2), there exist distinct $M_1, M_2, \cdots \in [M_0^A\rangle$ such that, for all $i \geq 1$, $M_{\omega/i} \leq M_i \leq M_{i+1} \leq M$. Hence, by (ii), there exist (not necessarily distinct) $M_1', M_2', \cdots \in [M_0^B\rangle$ such that $M_{\omega/i} \leq M_i \leq M_i'$, for all $i \geq 1$. Moreover, by (CS1), there exist $M_1'', M_2'', \cdots \in CS_B$ such that $M_{\omega/i} \leq M_i' \leq M_i''$, for all $i \geq 1$. Since CS_B is finite, there exists $M' \in CS_B$ which occurs in the sequence $M_1'', M_2'', \ldots$ infinitely many times. This means that $M_{\omega/i} \leq M'$, for infinitely many i's, and so $M \leq M'$. $\qquad\square$

Thus, in practice, we can effectively check whether the introduction of reverse transitions changes the coverable set of a p/t-net.

6 Concluding Remarks

In this paper, we considered a very liberal way of reversing computation in Petri nets as it allows one to 'undo' a transition which has not yet been executed. Preventing such a behaviour would be straightforward by introducing a fresh empty 'buffer' place p_t between t and $\overline{t}$ (i.e., $W^+(t)(p_t) = W^-(\overline{t})(p_t) = 1$ $W^-(t)(p_t) = W^+(\overline{t})(p_t) = 0$). The two results we established in this paper carry over to the modified setting as in the net $\mathbb{D}$ used in the proof of Proposition 2, the executions of transitions c and d strictly alternate, starting with c.

Acknowledgements. We would like to thank the anonymous reviewers for their remarks which allowed us to improve the presentation of the paper. This work was supported by the EU COST Action IC1405, and by the Polish National Science Center (grant No. 2013/09/D/ST6/03928).

References

1. Araki, T., Kasami, T.: Decidable problems on the strong connectivity of Petri net reachability sets. Theoret. Comput. Sci. **4**(1), 99–119 (1977)
2. Berry, G., Boudol, G.: The chemical abstract machine. Theoret. Comput. Sci. **96**(1), 217–248 (1992)
3. Best, E., Desel, J., Esparza, J.: Traps characterize home states in free choice systems. Theoret. Comput. Sci. **101**, 161–176 (1992)
4. Best, E., Esparza, J.: Existence of home states in Petri nets is decidable. Inf. Process. Lett. **116**(6), 423–427 (2016)
5. Best, E., Schlachter, U.: Analysis of Petri nets and transition systems. In: Proceedings of 8th Interaction and Concurrency Experience (ICE 2015), EPTCS, vol. 189, pp. 53–67 (2015)
6. Best, E., Klaus, V.: Free choice systems have home states. Acta Informatica **21**, 89–100 (1984)
7. Cardelli, L., Laneve, C.: Reversible structures. In: Fages, F. (ed.) Proceedings of 9th International Computational Methods in Systems Biology (CMSB 2011), pp. 131–140. ACM (2011)
8. Danos, V., Krivine, J.: Reversible communicating systems. In: Gardner, P., Yoshida, N. (eds.) CONCUR 2004. LNCS, vol. 3170, pp. 292–307. Springer, Heidelberg (2004)

9. Danos, V., Krivine, J.: Transactions in RCCS. In: Abadi, M., de Alfaro, L. (eds.) CONCUR 2005. LNCS, vol. 3653, pp. 398–412. Springer, Heidelberg (2005)

10. Danos, V., Krivine, J., Sobocinski, P.: General reversibility. Electron. Notes Theoret. Comput. Sci. **175**(3), 75–86 (2007)

11. de Frutos Escrig, D., Johnen, C.: Decidability of home space property. Technical report 503, Laboratoire de Recherche en Informatique, Université de Paris-Sud (1989)

12. Desel, J., Esparza, J.: Reachability in cyclic extended free-choice systems. Theoret. Comput. Sci. **114**, 93–118 (1993)

13. Finkel, A.: The minimal coverability graph for Petri nets. In: Rozenberg, G. (ed.) Petri Nets 1993. LNCS, vol. 674, pp. 210–243. Springer, Heidelberg (1993)

14. Michael, H.: Decidability questions for Petri nets. Technical report TR-161, MIT Laboratory for Computer Science (1976)

15. Michael, H.: Petri net languages. Technical report TR 159, MIT Laboratory for Computer Science (1976)

16. Hujsa, T., Delosme, J.-M., Munier-Kordon, A.: On the reversibility of live equal-conflict Petri nets. In: Devillers, R., Valmari, A. (eds.) PETRI NETS 2015. LNCS, vol. 9115, pp. 234–253. Springer, Heidelberg (2015)

17. Karp, R., Miller, R.: Parallel program schemata. J. Comput. Syst. Sci. **3**, 147–195 (1969)

18. Kezić, D., Perić, N., Petrović, I.: An algorithm for deadlock prevention based on iterative siphon control of Petri net. Automatika **47**, 19–30 (2006)

19. Lanese, I., Mezzina, C.A., Stefani, J.-B.: Reversing higher-order Pi. In: Gastin, P., Laroussinie, F. (eds.) CONCUR 2010. LNCS, vol. 6269, pp. 478–493. Springer, Heidelberg (2010)

20. Özkan, H.A., Aybar, A.: A reversibility enforcement approach for Petri nets using invariants. WSEAS Trans. Syst. **7**, 672–681 (2008)

21. Phillips, I., Ulidowski, I.: Reversing algebraic process calculi. J. Log. Algebr. Program. **73**(1–2), 70–96 (2007)

22. Phillips, I., Ulidowski, I.: Reversibility and asymmetric conflict in event structures. J. Log. Algebr. Methods Program. **84**(6), 781–805 (2015)

23. Phillips, I., Ulidowski, I., Yuen, S.: A reversible process calculus and the modelling of the ERK signalling pathway. In: Glück, R., Yokoyama, T. (eds.) RC 2012. LNCS, vol. 7581, pp. 218–232. Springer, Heidelberg (2013)

24. Recalde, L., Teruel, E., Silva, M.: Modeling and analysis of sequential processes that cooperate through buffers. IEEE Trans. Robot. Autom. **14**(2), 267–277 (1998)

25. Reisig, W.: Petri Nets: An Introduction. EATCS Monographs on Theoretical Computer Science, vol. 4. Springer, Berlin (1985)

26. Teruel, E., Silva, M., Colom, J.M.: Choice-free Petri nets: a model for deterministic concurrent systems with bulk services and arrivals. IEEE Trans. Syst. Man Cybern. Part A **27**, 73–83 (1997)

27. Teruel, E., Silva, M.: Liveness and home states in equal conflict systems. PETRI NETS 1993. LNCS, vol. 691, pp. 415–432. Springer, Heidelberg (1993)

28. Vogler, W.: Live and bounded free choice nets have home states. Petri Net Newslett. **32**, 18–21 (1989)

29. Wang, P., Ding, Z., Chai, H.: An algorithm for generating home states of Petri nets. J. Comput. Inf. Syst. **12**(7), 4225–4232 (2011)

Programming Languages

Toward an Energy Efficient Language and Compiler for (Partially) Reversible Algorithms

Nirvan Tyagi$^{(\boxtimes)}$, Jayson Lynch$^{(\boxtimes)}$, and Erik D. Demaine$^{(\boxtimes)}$

MIT CSAIL, Cambridge, USA
{ntyagi,jaysonl,edemaine}@mit.edu

Abstract. We introduce a new programming language for expressing reversibility, Energy-Efficient Language (Eel), geared toward algorithm design and implementation. Eel is the first language to take advantage of a partially reversible computation model, where programs can be composed of both reversible and irreversible operations. In this model, irreversible operations cost *energy* for every bit of information created or destroyed. To handle programs of varying degrees of reversibility, Eel supports a log stack to automatically trade energy costs for space costs, and introduces many powerful control logic operators including protected conditional, general conditional, protected loops, and general loops. In this paper, we present the design and compiler for the three language levels of Eel along with an interpreter to simulate and annotate incurred energy costs of a program.

1 Introduction

Continued progress in technology has created a world where we are increasingly dependent on computers and computing power. Computer use is greatly increasing and thus becoming a significant energy expenditure for the world. It is estimated that computing consumes more than 3 % of the global electricity consumption [16], growing at a steady rate. Improved energy efficiency of computers translates to savings in money and environmental toll. Additionally, improved energy efficiency would lead to increased longevity of batteries or use of a smaller battery for the same lifespan. This applies most directly to portable devices such as laptops, mobile phones, and watches where battery size and life are of the utmost importance. Finally, improved energy efficiency would lead to faster CPUs. The main bottleneck in increasing clock speeds are cooling restraints. With decreased energy consumption, we can expect to be able to increase CPU speed by roughly the same factor with the same cooling. Given these many motivations, continued improvement of the energy efficiency of computation is an important research field.

Fundamental Limits to Efficiency. If computer energy efficiency continues to progress at a similar rate, we will expect to hit a fundamental limit based in physics and information theory known as Landauer's limit [8] within the next 15–60 years. Landauer gives a lower limit for the energy cost of losing one bit of information

© Springer International Publishing Switzerland 2016
S. Devitt and I. Lanese (Eds.): RC 2016, LNCS 9720, pp. 121–136, 2016.
DOI: 10.1007/978-3-319-40578-0_8

of $kT \ln 2$ units of energy where k is Boltzmann's constant and T is temperature. Our current computation systems depend on computing models that require the erasure of information; however, reversible computation, where the inputs can always be recovered from the outputs, gets around this limitation. In this paper, we consider a variant of the traditional reversible computation model we call *partially* reversible computation [6], allowing for both reversible and irreversible operations. Traditional models of computation include two main constraints in the asymptotic analysis of algorithms, time and space. However, with the introduction of partially reversible computation, a new natural metric emerges, which we call *energy*. In this model, from Landauer's principle, reversible computation is free, but creating or destroying bits of information costs energy. The energy cost of an operation is equal to each bit of information created or destroyed and comes from the change in information entropy from inputs to outputs.

Energy-efficient Language (Eel). We break down the results into two main parts. First, we present a new reversible programming language, Eel. Eel is composed of three language levels with the high-level based on Python and the low-level based on PISA [19,20]. Eel is the first programming language to take advantage of partially reversible computation. Past research on reversible programming languages has focused on computation which is performed fully reversibly. Eel allows operations to erase bits and incur energy cost. Eel also allows users to indicate operations for reversal and will automatically store the proper information in a log stack (separate from the stack). In addition, we introduce a number of high level control logic operators of varying degrees of reversibility. With the partial reversibility model, Eel brings the time, space, and energy tradeoffs to the forefront.

Second, we present a compiler and interpreter in Java for Eel. We describe the compilation techniques used between the Eel language levels to handle the high level control logic. We also describe the interpreter technique to simulate and annotate the energy costs of program execution. Since general purpose fully-reversible computers are still years away from development, an interpreter that simulates energy costs is valuable for algorithm development and implementation.

2   Previous Work

The study of reversible computation to circumvent Landauer's limit has been a broad area of research for a number of years, ranging from development of reversible hardware, analysis of reversible algorithmic theory, to development of reversible programming languages and computer architecture. The origins of the field can be traced back to Lecerf [10] and to Bennett [3]. Early theory results show that any algorithm can be made reversible with either quadratic space overhead [4] or with exponential time overhead [5,9]. However, it is unknown whether or not any given algorithm can be converted to a reversible version maintaining the same time and space constraints. Some models introduce an algorithmic complexity based on information erased during a computation [6,11] laying a foundation for partially reversible computing.

Past research on reversible programming languages has focused on fully reversible programming languages and architectures. The first high-level reversible programming languages developed were Janus and R [7,12,21]. We understand that there are a set of properties that must be held by all reversible languages [22], and that these properties are satisfied in Janus. Fully reversible computer architectures have been built. Pendulum [19,20], the first reversible architecture built, was introduced along with a reversible low-level instruction set, PISA, which is used as a basic reversible instruction set in many future works. An improved reversible architecture [2] compatible with PISA introduces a novel technique for handling branches, previously handled with traces, using space to keep track of program counter jumps. Most recently, this architecture has been further improved with the development of Bob [18] using a slightly modified version of PISA known as BobISA, providing more efficient branch handling and address calculation. The Eel low level language uses an instruction set based on PISA expanded to support irreversible operations.

There exist both a reversible self-interpreter for Janus [23] and a partial evaluator for Janus [13,14]. The main high level control logic operators in Janus for fully reversible logic, If-Then-Else-Fi and From-Do-Loop-Until, can be implemented in Eel, shown in Appendix. There also exist general techniques for compilation between reversible languages [1] and compilation of regular programs to reversible programs [15].

Although Eel is still in its early stages of development, it is designed to provide a unique perspective to reversible programming and, specifically, algorithm development. Where Janus is a powerful and mature language for fully reversible programming, the partial reversibility of Eel opens up a whole new set of options for developers. Eel brings forward the tradeoff for irreversible logic between energy cost and space cost in the log stack. Eel introduces new high level control logic operators that represent different options on the energy-space tradeoff spectrum. Additionally, Eel allows for partial reversals of the program for each code block, a useful feature to have for algorithm development. While this is also possible in Janus, it requires a nesting of function calls and uncalls. Overall, the aim of Eel is to provide a reversible language geared toward algorithm design and implementation in a partially reversible model.

3   Language Design

In this section we discuss some of the design decisions that went into the language. There is an overview of what operations are exposed in each of the three languages written. We also discuss how reversing computation is notated.

3.1   Logging and Unrolling

Eel supports partially reversible programs consisting both of logic blocks that will be reversed and logic blocks that will only be executed in the forward direction. In the high level, to denote a section of code to be reversed, it is placed inside of a `Log` statement to form a log block. The high level is organized into code blocks of varying levels of nesting. An `Unroll` statement indicates the reverse execution of pending log blocks within the block. All log blocks within a code block must be unrolled before exiting to the previous nesting level. This unroll method can be generalized to allow for a more complex unrolling order. See future works section for further discussion.

Some operations in a log block, such as assignments and branching, are not easily reversible. Eel handles these operations by automatically logging information (storing trace information) about the operation using auxilary space when executed in the forward direction. Upon reversal, the logged information is used to reverse the operation and is then zeroed out. The notion of using auxiliary space, or a "history" stack (we call *log stack*), to make irreversible computation reversible has been used in the past for irreversible operations such as memory overwrites and switch branching [17,24]. We extend this idea to support higher level control logic operators and see how different assumptions on control logic conditions change what information needs to be logged. A basic example of how the log stack is used for an irreversible assignment operation is in Fig. 1. The assignment operation is irreversible since the information previously stored at the memory location is overwritten. To make the assignment operation reversible, the previous value is stored in and retrieved from the log stack using `LPUSH` and `LPOP` operations. These operations increment and decrement the log pointer and maintain the memory location at the top of the log stack to be zero.

Eel automatically handles logging information for supported control logic operators and irreversible operations, but for more advanced functions additional information may need to be stored. Eel high level provides the `LogPush` command to push an item onto the log stack. `LogPush` can be used to make user-defined functions supported reversibly.

3.2   Language Levels

Eel is designed with three different levels exposing different levels of complexity. The high level language provides a Python-like syntax and common control operators for algorithm development. This is meant to seem familiar and to hide some

```
'High Level'                    'High Level'
Log:                            Log:
    x += 1                          x = 1
Unroll                          Unroll

'Low Level'                     'Low Level'
ADD(x,1)                        LPUSH(x)
SUB(x,1)   //Unroll starts      ADD(x,1)
                                SUB(x,1)   //Unroll starts
                                LPOP(x)
```

Fig. 1. Basic example of using log stack and not using log stack for reversal. `LPUSH` and `LPOP` perform the appropriate operation to the log stack and zero out the previous location.

of the difficulties of working in a partially reversible environment. The intermediate level is stripped down to a simpler set of commands and attempts to resemble working in transdichotomious RAM models of computation. By necessity it also exposes some fairly mechanical parts of execution such as the program and log stacks. It reduces the control logic to a series of jumps. This tries to compromise between readability, clear resource calculations, and expressive power. The low level gives a basic instruction set one might imagine for a semi-reversible computer based off of PISA. Here we have a small number of basic operations where the time, space, and energy costs of each line are clear.

High Level. The high level handles the partial reversibility of Eel with the `Log` and `Unroll` keywords. Placing operations inside of a `Log` block indicates to the compiler that these operations will be reversed. If there is an irreversible operation or control logic operator in a `Log` block, specific information is stored (logged) in the log stack. During an unroll, this information is used to properly reverse the operation and zeroed out.

Variables are not strongly typed and do not have explicit declaration. Instead variables are created the first time they are used. There are interesting questions concerning performance and ease-of-use with respect to typing in reversible programming languages; however, we have not yet been able to explore this substantially.

Basic control logic operators, such as conditionals and loops, are supported at the high level. However, different keywords are used to describe operators of different reversibility. For example, a *protected* conditional is completely reversible and does not require any space in the log, but requires assumptions on the usage of the condition variables. A *general* conditional, with no such assumptions, is not inherently reversible and requires a single bit of information to be stored in the log for reversibility. Table 1 summarizes the operators available at the high level and the space required in the log stack to be made reversible. The reversibility of these high level control logic operators is studied in more detail in a companion paper [6]. In an attempt to simplify the control logic, we note that the current protected operators in the high level provide less

Table 1. Summary of high level control keywords and the amount of space in the log stack required to make reversible if appearing in a log block.

Control Operator	Keyword	Log (bits)	Sec.
Protected Conditional	`PIf`(cond)	0	5.2
General Conditional	`If`(cond)	1	5.2
Protected For loop	`PFor`(init,cond,incr)	0	5.3
General For loop	`For`(init,cond,incr)	$\lceil \lg l \rceil$	5.3
General While loop	`While`(cond)	$\lceil \lg l \rceil$	5.3
Function call	`Def fxnName`(args)	0	5.4
Log Block	`Log`		3.1
Unroll	`Unroll`		3.1

expressiveness than other languages such as Janus. However, the intermediate language is fully expressive, and future iterations of the high level can include more complex operators built from the intermediate level. Figure 2 shows the grammar of the high level.

$\langle program \rangle$	$::= \langle b \rangle$	block
$\langle b \rangle$	$::= \langle s \rangle^*$	statement sequence
$\langle s \rangle$	$::= x \otimes= \langle e \rangle \mid x = \langle e \rangle$	assignment
	$\mid$ 'PIf'($\langle e \rangle$): $\langle b \rangle$ ('Else': $\langle b \rangle$)?	protected conditional
	$\mid$ 'If'($\langle e \rangle$): $\langle b \rangle$ ('Else': $\langle b \rangle$)?	general conditional
	$\mid$ 'PFor'($\langle s \rangle$, $\langle e \rangle$, $\langle s \rangle$): $\langle b \rangle$	protected for loop
	$\mid$ 'For'($\langle s \rangle$, $\langle e \rangle$, $\langle s \rangle$): $\langle b \rangle$	general for loop
	$\mid$ 'While'($\langle e \rangle$): $\langle b \rangle$	general while loop
	$\mid$ 'Def' $q(x, \ldots, x)$: $\langle b \rangle$	function definition
	$\mid$ $q(x, \ldots, x)$	function call
	$\mid$ 'Log': $\langle b \rangle$	log block
	$\mid$ 'Unroll'	unroll
$\langle e \rangle$	$::= c \mid x \mid \langle e \rangle \odot \langle e \rangle$	expression
$\langle \otimes \rangle$	$::= + \mid - \mid *$	operators
$\langle \odot \rangle$	$::= \otimes \mid / \mid \leq \mid \geq \mid \neq \mid ==$	

Fig. 2. Eel high level grammar, where $x \in$ Vars, $q \in$ FxnIds, $c \in$ IntConsts

Intermediate Level. The Eel intermediate language breaks down the high level control logic into jumps and labels. Jumps and labels are separated into two categories: *protected* jumps and *general* jumps. Protected jumps (PGoto, PGotoIf, PGotoIfN) are fully reversible and require no additional space in log stack. A protected conditional jump takes in a forward condition and a backward condition. It uses the assumption that the forward condition will always evaluate the same in the forward direction as the backwards condition in the reverse direction. General jumps (Goto, GotoIf, GotoIfN) do not require this assumption and log a bit in order to reverse. Both protected jumps and general jumps must be paired with a corresponding destination protected label or general label. Jumps and labels have a 1 : 1 correspondence.

One strength of the intermediate language lies in the flexibility and variety of the jump operations. Common control logic operators of the high level can be broken down to a simple combination of protected and general jumps. This also allows new operators for the high level to be easily defined in the intermediate language without needing to touch the low level assembly-like code. Figure 3 shows the grammar of the intermediate language.

Low Level. The low level language consists of basic assembly-level instructions that are assumed to be built into a reversible machine. Since Eel is designed for a partial reversibility model, a number of irreversible operations are also

$$
\begin{array}{llll}
\langle program \rangle & ::= & \langle b \rangle & \text{block} \\
\langle b \rangle & ::= & \langle s \rangle^* & \text{statement sequence} \\
\langle s \rangle & ::= & x \otimes = \langle e \rangle \mid x = \langle e \rangle & \text{assignment} \\
& & \mid \text{`PGoto'}(\, l \,) & \text{protected jump} \\
& & \mid \text{`PGotoIf'}(\, \langle e \rangle, \langle e \rangle, l \,) & \\
& & \mid \text{`PGotoIfN'}(\, \langle e \rangle, \langle e \rangle, l \,) & \\
& & \mid \text{`PLabel'}(\, l \,) & \\
& & \mid \text{`Goto'}(\, l \,) & \text{general jump} \\
& & \mid \text{`PGotoIf'}(\, \langle e \rangle, l \,) & \\
& & \mid \text{`PGotoIfN'}(\, \langle e \rangle, l \,) & \\
& & \mid \text{`Label'}(\, l \,) & \\
& & \mid \text{`Def'} \; q(x, \ldots, x) & \text{function definition} \\
& & \mid \text{`Call'} \; q(x, \ldots, x) & \text{function call} \\
& & \mid \text{`Log':} \; \langle b \rangle & \text{log block} \\
& & \mid \text{`Unroll'} & \text{unroll} \\
& & \mid \text{`LogPush'}(x) & \text{log stack modification} \\
\langle e \rangle & ::= & c \mid x \mid \langle e \rangle \odot \langle e \rangle & \text{expression} \\
\langle \otimes \rangle & ::= & + \mid - \mid * & \text{operators} \\
\langle \odot \rangle & ::= & \otimes \mid / \mid \leq \mid \geq \mid \neq \mid == & \\
\end{array}
$$

Fig. 3. Eel intermediate level grammar, where $x \in$ Vars, $l \in$ LabelIds, $q \in$ FxnIds, $c \in$ IntConsts

supported. Table 2 lists the operations available at the low level. Jump operations are completely reversible and require every Goto instruction to be paired with the corresponding Comefrom instruction (`GOTOIFN` with `CMFRMIFN`). The comefrom statement is necessary in instructing the machine on bookkeeping of the program counter during jumps.

The low level also introduces various "special" memory locations that are reserved for specific uses. These are the program counter (`pc`), log pointer (`lp`), and stack pointer (`sp`).

Table 2. Summary of low level operations.

Operation	Description	Irreversible Operations	
Reversible Operations		$\text{MOVE}(a, b)$	$a = b$
$\text{ADD}(a, b)$	$a + = b$	$\text{AND}(a, b)$	$a = a \land b$
$\text{SUB}(a, b)$	$a - = b$	$\text{OR}(a, b)$	$a = a \lor b$
$\text{MULT}(a, b)$	$a * = b$	**Jump Operations**	
$\text{NEG}(a)$	$a * = -1$	$\text{GOTO}(l)$	jump to l
$\text{SWAP}(a, b)$	values a and b swap	$\text{GOTOIF}(b, l)$	jump to l if b
$\text{LPUSH}(x)$	push x to log stack	$\text{GOTOIFN}(b, l)$	jump to l if not b
$\text{LPOP}(x)$	pop x from log stack	$\text{CMFRM}(l)$	comefrom l
$\text{PUSH}(x)$	push x to stack	$\text{CMFRMIF}(b, l)$	comefrom l if b
$\text{POP}(x)$	pop x from stack	$\text{CMFRMIFN}(b, l)$	comefrom l if not b

4   Correct Program Conventions

An Eel program is a code block of a sequence of statements. Statements consist of various operations and control logic which themselves can contain code blocks nested within. We model the statement execution flow of a code block as a series of forward blocks, log blocks, and unroll statements. Unroll statements trigger the reverse execution of all "un-reversed" log blocks in the code block executed prior to the statement. If there are no pending log blocks, the Unroll statement is skipped. Every log block must be unrolled before the end of the block (synonymous to putting an unroll statement at the end of every block).

Call the set of all forward blocks, log blocks, and unrolls in a code block, $\mathcal{B}$. Let $\mathcal{B} = \mathcal{R} \cup \mathcal{F} \cup \mathcal{U}$ be the union of three distinct sets $r \in \mathcal{R}$ of log blocks, $f \in \mathcal{F}$ of forward blocks, and $u \in \mathcal{U}$ of unrolls. Every element r has an element in $\mathcal{U}$ corresponding to the unroll that triggers the reverse execution of r, notated by u_r. Note that a single u can satisfy the reverse execution of many r. The set $\mathcal{B}$ has a strict universal ordering where for all $b_i, b_j \in \mathcal{B}$, $b_i \prec b_j$ if b_i occurs first in the Eel program.

Every block b can be modeled as taking an input set of variables $V(b)$, executing block code, and returning the same set of variables with potentially modified values. The input and output *values* of the variables are denoted $\mathcal{V}_{in}(b)$ and $\mathcal{V}_{out}(b)$. We also care about the subset of these variables that were modified, denoted by $V_{mod}(b)$. For guaranteed correct reversal of log block r, we desire that $\mathcal{V}_{out}(r) = \mathcal{V}_{in}(u_r)$. To receive this property, all forward blocks between r and u_r must not irreversibly modify any of the variables $V(r) = V(u_r)$.

$$\forall r \, \forall f \quad (r \prec f \prec u_r) \quad \rightarrow \quad \left(V(r) \cup V_{mod}(f) = \emptyset \right)$$

In addition to the variable modification among blocks, for a log block to be correctly reversed, control logic *within* the block must be correct. This means that the requirements for all protected conditionals and for loops are satisfied. In protected conditionals, the variables in the condition cannot be modified within the conditional. In protected for loops, the variable controlling the loop cannot be modified within the loop.

It is possible for users to purposefully break these rules and still create a program that compiles and executes as they wanted. However, this requires careful variable bookkeeping and falls outside the intended use cases of the language.

5   Control Logic Operators

Eel supports conditionals, loops, and function calls in the high level. These control logic operators are handled reversibly using the log stack. Since these operators are largely broken down in the intermediate level, we start by examining the reversibility of the jump operations. High level control operators are then built directly from intermediate jump operations, avoiding the low level. Examples are given using a log block followed by an unroll, but in general, the unroll statement need not directly follow the log block. The compilation of control logic outside of a log block is not shown here since it does not use the log stack and is compiled standardly. We note that the incorrect use of control logic and log blocks can result in an incorrect reversal and we examine this issue in the Correct Program Conventions section.

5.1 Jumps

The jump operations of the intermediate level are the building blocks for all of the high level control logic operators. The jump operations are divided into two main classes, protected jumps (fully reversible) and general jumps (require 1 logged bit). Because of their reversibility assumptions, these two classes are semantically different and are compiled differently.

Jumps are paired with labels of the same class (protected or general). In our design, we require a one-to-one pairing of jumps to labels. It is possible to support a many-to-one matching of jumps to labels, but additional information is required to be logged for reversal. Both classes support conditional jumps which use the suffixes If and IfN corresponding to jumping if the condition is non-zero or zero respectively.

In the low level, jumps can be performed by a reversible update to the program counter (pc). However, by allowing changes to the program counter, we can no longer assume every line was reached from the previous line by an increment to the pc. This creates an irreversible situation. To deal with this, every jump instruction is paired with a comefrom instruction. The Comefrom statement is used to properly handle the manipulation of the pc. Since the jump requires the manipulation of the pc, one might imagine this value being swapped or copied and manipulated. The comefrom statement performs the necessary cleaning of that value. This is necessary within the computer but not exposed at the assembly level, which is why the Comefrom simply appears to be a label or no-op.

Protected Jumps. Protected jumps are fully reversible and do not use any space in the log stack. A *protected* jump contains a "backward" condition which can be evaluated in the reverse direction to indicate whether the jump was executed in the forward direction.

Consider the protected conditional jump (PGotoIf). It takes the form:

PGotoIf(fwdcond, bwdcond, label). In the forward direction, if the forward condition is true, jump to label. Upon reaching the label location when reversing, if the backward condition is true, jump to original jump start location. This gives the requirement that the backward condition evaluates to true if and only if the forward condition evaluated to true for the proper code to be reversed. With this assumption, we can evaluate the backward condition to determine if the jump was executed in the forward direction without additional information stored in the log stack.

General Jumps. General jumps are used when the condition evaluated to decide the execution of the jump in the forward direction is not preserved and thus cannot be re-evaluated in the backward direction. In this case, we log a bit of information to the log stack to represent whether or not the jump was executed. A general jump takes the form: `GotoIf(cond, label)` where the jump to `label` is executed if `cond` is true.

In the forward direction, every time a label is reached, it was the result of either (1) increment from the line above or (2) the execution of a jump. In case (1), a 0-bit is logged, and in case (2), a 1-bit is logged. Therefore in the reverse direction, whenever a label is reached, the top bit of the log stack indicates whether to reverse the jump.

5.2   Conditional Statements

Eel high level distinguishes between two types of conditional statements, *protected* conditionals and *general* conditionals. In a protected conditional, the condition variables are not modified within the conditional statement.

Protected conditionals are implemented reversibly using protected jumps. If the condition variables are not modified within the conditional statement, the condition can be reevaluated after the execution of the conditional to see if the statement was executed. Thus, the condition can be used as both the forward condition and backward condition of the intermediate level protected jump. Note that this is a stronger assumption than the protected jump in the intermediate language which separates the forward and backward conditions. Figure 4 shows an example of an unsatisfied protected conditional.

The implementation of general conditionals is analogous to protected conditionals. Because the condition is subject to change in the conditional statement, the value of the condition is logged upon forward execution. This logged value is used in the backward direction to determine if the conditional statement was executed.

```
'High Level - Unsatisfied Protected Conditional'
Log:
  x = 1
  PIf(x):
    x -= 1
    [logic block]
Unroll
```

Fig. 4. Example of an unsatisfied protected conditional. When reversing the condition will be `x = 0` regardless of whether the conditional statement was executed.

5.3   For and While Loops

Eel high level distinguishes between two types of for loops, *protected* for loops and *general* for loops. Protected for loops use no space in log stack. General for loops require the number of loop iterations l to be logged using $\lg l$ bits in the log stack.

A protected for loop takes the form: PFor(init(x), cond(x), incr(x)). An initial value init(x), a terminating expression cond(x), and a reversible incrementation function incr(x). A protected for loop requires (1) the incrementation function incr(x) is the only modifier to x in the loop, and (2) the termination condition cond(x) is determined only by x and no other modified variables in the loop. With these assumptions, a protected for loop can be implemented fully reversibly. The protected for loop can be undone by reversing the incrementation function and unrolling each loop until x matches the initialization value. Protected jumps are used to implement the protected for loop with no space in log stack. Figure 5 shows the compilation of a protected for loop.

```
'Protected For Loop'
'High Level'
Log:
  PFor(init(x), cond(x), incr(x)):
      [loop logic block]
    [end logic block]
Unroll
```

```
'Intermediate Level'
Log:
  init(x)
  PLabel(start-label)    //checks if x == init
  PGotoIfEq(cond(x), cond(x), end-label) //ends if cond(x)
  [loop logic block]
  incr(x)                //increments x
  PGotoIfNeq(x != init, x != init, start-label) //loops
  PLabel(end-label)
  [end logic block]
Unroll
```

Fig. 5. The high to intermediate level compilation of a protected for loop.

A general for loop is of the form: For(init(), cond(), incr()). The general for loop keeps track of the number of loop iterations l in the forward direction. It does not rely on the initialization variable being protected, only that the loop terminates. However, if we use general jumps, a bit of information is stored per loop and l space in the log stack is required. Instead, we maintain and store a separate loop counter in the log stack using $\lg l$ bits. Protected jumps are then used with the general for loop condition in the forward direction and decrementation of the loop counter in the backward direction. Figure 6 shows the compilation of a general for loop. General while loops are handled in the same way as general for loops. The initialization variable and incrementation function are disregarded.

```
'General For Loop'
'High Level'
Log:
  For(init(), cond(), incr()):
      [loop logic block]
    [end logic block]
Unroll
```

```
'Intermediate Level'
Log:
  init()
  l = 0
  PLabel(start-label)
  PGotoIfEq(cond(), cond(), end-label) //ends loop if cond()
  [loop logic block]
  incr()                   //incrementation function
  l += 1                   //increment loop counter
  PGotoIfEq(l > 0, l > 0, start-label) //restarts loop
  PLabel(end-label)
  LPush(l)                 //push loop counter to log
  [end logic block]
Unroll
```

Fig. 6. The high to intermediate level compilation of a general for loop. The total number of loop iterations are counted and logged. Medium minus importance.

5.4 Function Calls

Reversible function calls are handled in a similar manner to normal ones. The function arguments and return pointer are pushed to the regular stack. The arguments are passed by reference, so changes to a variable effect it outside the scope of the function unless a local copy is made. Different from normal functions, for every reversible function in the high level, two versions of the function are created in the low level. One is the regular function used in the forward direction, while the other is the unrolled version used in the backward direction to reverse. Since the locations of these functions are known, protected jumps can be used to enter and exit. Thus, functions require no additional space in the log stack than what is needed for the function logic itself. Eel functions use a pointer passing parameter model taking in and modifying parameter memory locations. Figure 7 shows the compilation of a function call.

6 Energy Simulation

Since we can't actually run our code on a semi-reversible computer, we add additional annotation to estimate the energy cost of our programs. We find this useful in two directions. First, comparing our results against theoretical predictions of the energy cost and scaling of algorithms allows us to check for inefficiencies in the compiler. Second, if our code only uses well examined transformation we

```
'Function Call'                     'Intermediate Level'
'High Level'                        Def FXN(x):
Def FXN(x):                             [fxn logic block]
    [fxn logic block]

                                    Log:
Log:                                    [logic block 1]
    [logic block 1]                 Call FXN(x)
    FXN(x)                              [logic block 2]
    [logic block 2]                 Unroll
Unroll
```

```
'Low Level'
//Def FXN(x):                       //FXN-start
CMFRM(mem[sp-1])                    //where fxn was called from
ADD(x, mem[sp-2])                   //pulls input from stack
[fxn logic block]
GOTO(mem[sp-1])                     //returns to program
                                    //FXN-end
//Def RFXN(x):                      //RFXN-start
CMFRM(mem[sp-1])                    //where fxn was called from
ADD(x, mem[sp-2])                   //pulls input from stack
[reverse fxn logic block]
GOTO(mem[sp-1])                     //returns to program
                                    //RFXN-end

[logic block 1]
PUSH(x)
PUSH(A)
GOTO(FXN-start)                     //jump to fxn
CMFRM(FXN-end)                      //A
POP(A)
POP(x)
[logic block 2]
[reverse of logic block 2]         //Unroll starts
PUSH(x)
PUSH(B)
GOTO(RFXN-start)                    //jump to reverse fxn
CMFRM(RFXN-end)                     //B
POP(B)
POP(x)
[reverse of logic block 1]
```

Fig. 7. The full compilation of a function call. The low level shows two versions of the function for the forward direction and the backward direction.

can use an implementation of an algorithm as a check against the analysis of its time, space, and energy complexity.

The energy costs for an operation are defined by the change in entropy or information across the inputs to the outputs. In particular, we follow the model used in [6] where one calculates $\log\left(\frac{I}{O}\right)$ Where I is the size of the input space of the function and O is the size of the output space of the function. This means the energy cost only depends on the instructions being called, not on the values being passed into that function. For example, this would mean an irreversible AND of two bits would always be charged 1 unit of energy, even though an output of 0 would tell us that both inputs had to be 0. The appropriateness of this model either in an exact, or average case setting will depend on details of the computer architecture.

In high level programming languages, energy costs are hard to calculate since they are masked by high level control logic and complex expressions. One of the reasons Eel is designed to have multiple levels of compilation is to reveal these energy costs in the lower levels. The simplest way to calculate energy costs is in the low level language. Here the input and output spaces are small and the energy cost can be calculated on a line by line basis. Each instruction modifies only one input and since we have a restricted instruction set, each instruction's energy cost is individually evaluated. At the low level, instructions are batched into two different energy costs, 0 and w, where w is the word size.

After calculating energy cost per line at the level, the compiler can backtrack to the intermediate and high level language and annotate each line with the costs incurred by the corresponding generated low/intermediate lines. The simulation takes the same time and space requirements of running the actual program. The annotation takes the form, (E, L), representing the energy cost and space in log stack cost respectively. Logic in log blocks will incur no energy cost and instead may incur log stack cost. Conversely, logic not in log blocks will not incur any log stack cost, but may incur energy cost.

7   Conclusion and Future Work

Eel is a new reversible programming language that supports a partially reversible model. The key contributions of this project are as follows:

1. Development of Eel (language + compiler) and description of three language levels.
2. Introduction of the log stack as a way to make design decisions between energy cost and space cost.
3. Introduction of new high-level control logic and compilation techniques for protected conditional, general conditional, protected loops, and general loops.
4. Development of an interpreter for energy simulation and annotation.

Eel is intended to be a prototype for what partially-reversible languages may look like in the future, and to serve as a platform for the development of partially-reversible algorithms. A programming language allows us to be precise about the computations being done and serves as a platform to help verify theoretical results about partial reversibility. Because many usual programming assumptions do not hold in this model, working with Eel can help build new intuition. With the goal of algorithm development in mind, Eel has included annotation of estimated time, space, and energy costs of programs. Through the development of the Eel language and compiler, we have built a strong foundation upon which future research and development of reversible algorithms can be conducted. Once a few more important features are added, the ability to actually run algorithms and count the resource usage of a program will give a powerful tool for checking algorithmic results.

Several further features are necessary to achieve these goals of being a tool for algorithmic design and a prototype language for a future computing environment. First, the implementation of standard data structures are necessary for many algorithms. Many of the results for efficient data structures [6] in the partially reversible model are themselves not obvious and their implementation would also be a good confirmation of those results. Second, we would like to implement some of the memory management and garbage collection algorithms which have been developed. Third, only a simple version of log and unroll was implemented, which does not contain as much expressive power as we might want. Currently, the language only allows unrolling log blocks in order, but especially in data structures, we would like to be able to unroll code in dynamic orders. This extension could be implemented with multiple log stacks, or a more complicated data structure underlying the log and unroll system. Fourth, some of the transformations performed by the compiler lack optimization, and thus may make an algorithm seem less efficient than anticipated. A final practical direction is to consider hybrid programming models which mix standard irreversible computation with reversible core subroutines, for use in a future hybrid architecture combining traditional CPUs with a reversible accelerator or co-processor.

Acknowledgements. We thank Geronimo Mirano for useful discussion in differentiating and developing our language levels. We also thank Maria L. Messick and Licheng Rao for help in early programming of the Eel compiler.

References

1. Axelsen, H.B.: Clean translation of an imperative reversible programming language. In: Knoop, J. (ed.) CC 2011 and ETAPS 2011. LNCS, vol. 6601, pp. 144–163. Springer, Heidelberg (2011)
2. Axelsen, H.B., Glück, R., Yokoyama, T.: Reversible machine code and its abstract processor architecture. In: Diekert, V., Volkov, M.V., Voronkov, A. (eds.) CSR 2007. LNCS, vol. 4649, pp. 56–69. Springer, Heidelberg (2007)
3. Bennett, C.H.: Logical reversibility of computation. Maxwell Demon. Entropy Inf. Comput. 197–204 (1973). http://liinwww.ira.uka.de/cgi-bin/bibshow?e=Njtd0jcnkse/fyqboefe%7d2789553&r=bibtex&mode=intra
4. Charles, H.: Bennett. time/space trade-offs for reversible computation. SIAM J. Comput. **18**(4), 766–776 (1989)
5. Buhrman, H., Tromp, J., Vitányi, P.M.B.: Time and space bounds for reversible simulation. In: Orejas, F., Spirakis, P.G., van Leeuwen, J. (eds.) ICALP 2001. LNCS, vol. 2076, p. 1017. Springer, Heidelberg (2001)
6. Demaine, E.D., Lynch, J., Mirano, G.J., Tyagi, N.: Energy-efficient algorithms. In: Proceedings of 2016 ACM Conference on Innovations in Theoretical Computer Science, pp. 321–332. ACM (2016)

7. Frank, M.P., Knight, Jr. T.F.: Reversibility for efficient computing. Ph.D. thesis, Department of Electrical Engineering and Computer Science, Massachusetts Institute of Technology (1999)
8. Landauer, R.: Irreversibility and heat generation in the computing process. IBM J. Res. Dev. **5**(3), 183–191 (1961)
9. Lange, K.-J., McKenzie, P., Tapp, A.: Reversible space equals deterministic space. J. Comput. Syst. Sci. **60**(2), 354–367 (2000)
10. Lecerf, Y.: Logique mathematique-machines de turing reversibles-recursive insolubilite en nsigman de lequation u= thetanu, ou theta est un isomorphisme de codes. Comptes rendus hebdomadaires des séances de l'Académie des sciences **257**(18), 2597 (1963)
11. Li, M., Vitanyi, P.: Reversible simulation of irreversible computation. In: Proceedings of 11th Annual IEEE Conference on Computational Complexity, pp. 301–306. IEEE (1996)
12. Lutz, C., Derby, H.: Janus: a time-reversible language. Caltech Class Project (1982)
13. Mogensen, T.Æ.: Partial evaluation of Janus Part 2: assertions and procedures. In: Clarke, E., Virbitskaite, I., Voronkov, A. (eds.) PSI 2011. LNCS, vol. 7162, pp. 289–301. Springer, Heidelberg (2012)
14. Mogensen, T.Æ., Partial evaluation of the reversible language Janus. In: Proceedings of 20th ACM SIGPLAN Workshop on Partial Evaluation and Program Manipulation, pp. 23–32. ACM (2011)
15. Perumalla, K., Fujimoto, R.: Source code transformations for efficient reversibility. Coll. Comput. Georgia Inst. Technol. (1999). https://smartech.gatech.edu/handle/1853/6621
16. Somavat, P., Namboodiri, V., et al.: Energy consumption of personal computing including portable communication devices. J. Green Eng. **1**(4), 447–475 (2011)
17. Stoddart, B., Lynas, R., Zeyda, F.: A virtual machine for supporting reversible probabilistic guarded command languages. Electron. Notes Theoret. Comput. Sci. **253**(6), 33–56 (2010)
18. Thomsen, M.K., Axelsen, H.B., Glück, R.: A reversible processor architecture and its reversible logic design. In: Vos, A., Wille, R. (eds.) RC 2011. LNCS, vol. 7165, pp. 30–42. Springer, Heidelberg (2012)
19. Vieri, C., Ammer, M.J., Frank, M., Margolus, N., Knight, T.: A fully reversible asymptotically zero energy microprocessor. In: Power Driven Microarchitecture Workshop, pp. 138–142. Citeseer (1998)
20. Vieri, C.J.: Reversible computer engineering and architecture. Ph.D. thesis, Massachusetts Institute of Technology (1999)
21. Yokoyama, T.: Reversible computation and reversible programming languages. Electron. Notes Theoret. Comput. Sci. **253**(6), 71–81 (2010)
22. Yokoyama, T., Axelsen, H.B., Glück, R.: Principles of a reversible programming language. In: Proceedings of 5th Conference on Computing Frontiers, pp. 43–54. ACM (2008)
23. Yokoyama, T., Glück, R.: A reversible programming language and its invertible self-interpreter. In: Proceedings of 2007 ACM SIGPLAN Symposium on Partial Evaluation and Semantics-based Program Manipulation, pp. 144–153. ACM (2007)
24. Zuliani, P.: Logical reversibility. IBM J. Res. Dev. **45**(6), 807–818 (2001)

Mixing Hardware and Software Reversibility for Speculative Parallel Discrete Event Simulation

Davide Cingolani$^{(\boxtimes)}$, Mauro Ianni, Alessandro Pellegrini,
and Francesco Quaglia

DIAG - Sapienza, University of Rome, Rome, Italy
{cingolani,mianni,pellegrini,quaglia}@dis.uniroma1.it

Abstract. Speculative parallel discrete event simulation requires a support for reversing processed events, also called state recovery, when causal inconsistencies are revealed. In this article we present an approach where state recovery relies on a mix of hardware- and software-based techniques. We exploit the Hardware Transactional Memory (HTM) support, as offered by Intel Haswell CPUs, to process events as in-memory transactions, which are possibly committed only after their causal consistency is verified. At the same time, we exploit an innovative software-based reversibility technique, fully relying on transparent software instrumentation targeting x86/ELF objects, which enables undoing side effects by events with no actual backward re-computation. Each thread within our speculative processing engine dynamically (on a per-event basis) selects which recovery mode to rely on (hardware vs software) depending on varying runtime dynamics. The latter are captured by a lightweight analytic model indicating to what extent the HTM support (not paying any instrumentation cost) is efficient, and after what level of events' parallelism it starts degrading its performance, e.g., due to excessive data conflicts while manipulating causality meta-data within HTM-based transactions. We released our implementation as open source software and provide experimental results for an assessment of its effectiveness.

1 Introduction

The move of Discrete Event Simulation (DES) onto parallel architectures has been historically based on the Parallel DES (PDES) paradigm [7]. In this kind of simulation, as well as in the traditional DES paradigm, the evolution of the system is described in terms of *timestamped discrete events*, which are impulsive—they happen at a specific simulation time instant, the timestamp of the event, and have no duration. Parallelism is achieved in PDES by partitioning the simulation model into several distinct entities, called *simulation objects* or *logical processes* (LPs). Each LP is associated with a private simulation state—the whole simulation state is the union of these private states—and the execution of an impulsive simulation event at any LP produces a state transition on the state of the LP itself. The privateness of the LPs' simulation states implies that information exchange across different LPs is only supported via the exchange of events, which can be generated (in any number) during the execution of other events.

S. Devitt and I. Lanese (Eds.): RC 2016, LNCS 9720, pp. 137–152, 2016.
DOI: 10.1007/978-3-319-40578-0_9

PDES speculative execution [10] allows processing events with no previous assurance of their causal consistency. This means that an event destined to some LP can be dispatched for execution with no guarantee at all regarding the fact that no other event with a higher priority, say lower timestamp, will be ever received by that same LP in the future. Such events, referred to as *straggler events*, are the a-posteriori materialization of a timestamp-order violation, also referred to as *causal violation*. Such violations require some state recovery (reversibility) support for undoing the side effects on the LPs' states which are associated with inconsistent processing of events.

In literature, the reversibility support has been traditionally based on pure software implementations exploiting either checkpointing techniques (see, e.g., [15,16]) or reverse computing ones (see, e.g., [2]). A few other approaches have been based on off-loading the checkpoint task to off-the-shelf or unconventional hardware [9,18]. More recently, the Hardware Transactional Memory (HTM) support offered by modern processors, such as the Intel Haswell, has been taken into consideration in order to enable the speculative execution of events as in-memory transactions [19], making them automatically recoverable with low overhead thanks to the reliance on the hardware transactional cache.

In this article we present a speculative PDES engine, oriented to multi-core machines, which exploits hardware-based and software-based reversibility in a synergistic manner. In particular, we enable each concurrent worker thread operating within the engine to dynamically select the best-suited reversibility support among two: (1) one relying on HTM facilities inspired to [19] and (2) another relying on software-based reversibility, in the form of *undo code blocks* [3]. The dynamic selection is based on the consideration that not every speculatively-executed event is *valuable* in the same manner when run as an HTM-based transaction due to several reasons. A first one deals with the fact that the final commit of the transaction needs to check/update causality meta-data, hence the higher the degree of concurrency while accessing these meta-data, the higher the likelihood of yielding to data conflicts that lead to the abort of the HTM-based transactions. Also, causality meta-data are updated according to the progress of the commit horizon of the PDES run, as determined along time by the commit of the event with the lowest timestamp. Hence speculatively-processed events with HTM support that are further ahead of the commit horizon will need to find causality meta-data reflecting more updates upon trying to commit, which again leads to an abort if these updates were not yet issued by the commitment of events with higher priority, say lower timestamps. Finally, the HTM support is limited to transactions whose read/write set fits (with no capacity conflict by other cores of the same CPU) the transactional hardware cache. Hence for models with events that (or execution phases where the events) have large data sets the likelihood of successfully committing the corresponding HTM-based transactions may be (significantly) reduced.

We overcome these drawbacks in our speculative PDES engine by dynamically enabling any worker thread to process an event not as an HTM-based transaction (just to reduce the likelihood of running non-valuable transactions), but rather via a modified version of the original event-handler code. This version is transparently instrumented in order to generate (at runtime) the minimal set of machine instructions (the so called undo code block) which allows reversing any memory side effect. In the instrumentation process we target x86/ELF objects. The possibility to commit events run with software reversibility is no longer bound to the possibility to commit an HTM-based transaction. This leads to the scenario where the engine is able to improve fruitful usage of computing resources due to the possibility to exploit the HTM support in the most valuable manner, while jointly relying on a bit more costly software-based reversibility when the valence of hardware-based reversibility would be impaired.

The coexistence of HTM and software-based reversibility (with concurrent threads relying on one or the other at a given time instant) needs solutions in order to avoid that the two techniques interfere with each other. Specifically, valuable HTM-based work should not be interfered by the one relying on software-based reversibility. For the case of concurrent speculatively processed events bound to the same LP (hence operating within the same local state) this is achieved by introducing a prioritization mechanism that leads an HTM-processed event to gain higher priority with respect to the events processed with the software reversibility support. So the latter will never concurrently access (any portion of) the overall data set—say the LP state as a whole—possibly targeted by the HTM-based transaction, hence not leading to its abort. On the other hand, we still enable inter-LP concurrency, thus enabling the so called weak-causality model [17], by not preventing multiple HTM-based transactions to successfully operate on disjoint data sets within the LP state. Also, given that in our software reversibility scheme we avoid the usage of checkpoints (in fact the undo code block is not a log of data), we avoid at all the typically large usage of memory by checkpointing (only partially resolved by incremental checkpointing schemes) hence further reducing the (potential) problems related to limited cache capacity issues of the HTM support and conflicting cache accesses by the threads.

Our engine has been released as open source software[1], and we also provide some experimental data for an assessment of its effectiveness when running the Phold PDES benchmark [8] on an Intel Haswell processor, with HTM support, equipped with 4 physical cores.

The remainder of this article is structured as follows. In Sect. 2 we discuss related work. In Sect. 3 we present the methodology standing behind hardware- and software-reversibility based execution of PDES models, and we describe the design principles characterizing our mixed simulation engine architecture. Section 4 presents an experimental assessment of our proposal.

2 Related Work

The state restore operation is of fundamental importance in speculative PDES, and has therefore been extensively studied in the literature. Two main incarnations of state restore schemes have been proposed, one based on *state*

---

[1] https://github.com/HPDCS/htmPDES/tree/reverse.

checkpoint and reload, and one based on *reverse computing*. The former flavour is based on the possibility for the simulation engine to know what are the memory buffers that keep each LP's simulation state, which are copied into a separate buffer—called the *simulation snapshot*—at a given point of the execution. In this way, undoing a chain of wrongly-computed events (namely, state updates) boils down to selecting a simulation snapshot which is still consistent (i.e., it was taken at a simulation time smaller than the straggler's one). This snapshot is then copied onto the LP live state image, thus undoing the effects of causal-inconsistent events. This approach is both memory- and computationally-intensive, and might lead to poor simulation performance, since if no causal inconsistency is detected at all, resources are spent for taking unnecessary snapshots. To this end, several proposals have addressed the possibility to take state snapshots less frequently (see, e.g., [16]) or in an incremental way (see, e.g., [21]) or combining the two schemes (see, e.g., [15,20]). Other solutions rely on hardware support to offload from the CPU the memory copy for taking the checkpoint. Specifically, the work in [18] proposed to exploit programmable DMA engines to perform the copy, while [9] presents the design of a so called rollback-chip, a hardware facility that automatically saves old versions of state variables upon their updates. Both these approaches reduce the CPU-time for checkpointing tasks but do not directly cope with memory usage.

Reverse computing is based on the notion of *reverse events*. A reverse event $\bar{e}$ associated with a forward event e is such that if the execution of e produces the state transition $e(S) \rightarrow S'$, the execution of $\bar{e}$ on S' produces the inverse transition $\bar{e}(S') \rightarrow S$. Such reverse events could be implemented manually [2] or via compiler-assisted approaches [12]. Although reverse computation is much less memory-greedy than checkpointing, the main issue with this approach lies in the *rollback length*, namely the number of events which must be undone upon a state restore operation. In particular, the total cost of a rollback operation is directly proportional to the number of undone events and their granularity, as reverse events re-process (although in a reversed fashion) all the steps of a forward event, even if some of them are not directly related to state updates.

The more recent proposal in [3] has tackled the state restore operation via software reversibility through the adoption of *undo code blocks*. The goal of this approach is to reduce the time-complexity of the rollback operation, making the reversibility of events independent of the forward execution's granularity. This is done by relying on static binary instrumentation, targeting x86/ELF objects, where the simulation model's code is scanned searching for all machine-level instructions which entail a memory update. These instructions are transparently augmented with an ad-hoc routine which computes the target address of the memory write just before it takes place, so that the original value is directly packed into an on-the-fly assembled machine instruction whose execution restores it. All these runtime generated assembly instructions are stored into an undo code block which, when executed, undoes all the effects of the execution of a forward event on the simulation state. This solution finds a good balance between incremental checkpointing—no actual meta-data are required to restore a previous state—and reverse computing—the execution cost to undo events is no longer dependent on the complexity of forward events. Nevertheless, if an event is unlikely to be undone due to a rollback operation, the cost of tracing memory updates and generating the undo code block is paid unnecessarily.

Another recent proposal [19] exploits HTM facilities offered by modern Intel Haswell CPUs to allow running simulation events within transactions. An ad-hoc routine determines whether the execution of an event is safe or not, by checking compact shared meta-data keeping track of the simulation time associated with the events that are being run by the concurrent threads. The event associated with the smallest timestamp is considered safe, and it is therefore the only event which is executed outside of a transaction. By using this scheme, all the events which are transactionally executed are automatically aborted if a conflict on the same data structures is detected. At the end of a transaction, the safety of the just-executed event is evaluated again, and in case the event has become safe, it is then committed. In the negative case, the transaction is immediately aborted and (possibly) restarted, because the access to the shared meta-data makes it doomed if the event is not safe yet—in fact, another thread will eventually update the content of the meta-data, to indicate that the execution of a safe event has been completed. A dynamic throttling strategy is used to increase the likelihood of committing a transaction, by delaying the time instant at which the shared meta-data are accessed.

Our work differs from previously published ones since none of the aforementioned proposals makes use of a combination of hardware and software reversibility for state restore operations. Particularly, we use the results in [3, 19] as baselines for building a mixed hardware/software recoverability support that takes the advantages of the two different techniques As pointed out in the introduction, we dynamically resort to undo code blocks (thus paying the cost of running an instrumented code version) only in case valuable speculative work cannot be carried out (by a thread at some point in time) via the reliance on HTM. Thus we pay the overhead of software-based reversibility only when HTM-based reversibility does not pay off (or is inviable due to, e.g., transactional cache capacity limitations).

3   The Simulation Engine

3.1   Basics

We target a baseline speculative PDES engine structure that is independent of the actual reversibility support, whose schematization is provided in Fig. 1. In compliance with traditional PDES, the engine supports the partitioning of the simulation model into n distinct LPs, each one associated with a unique ID in the range $[0, n-1]$. Each LP is associated with a private simulation state (although possibly scattered on dynamic memory) and with one or more event handlers representing the code blocks in charge of processing the simulation events and generating state updates, as well as of (possibly) producing new events to be injected in the system. The delivery of a simulation event to the correct handler is demanded from the underlying simulation kernel, which is also

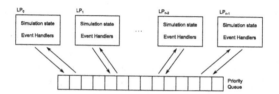

Fig. 1. Basic engine organization

in charge of guaranteing consistency of a shared event pool that keeps all the already scheduled events, as well as causal consistency of the updates occurring on the LPs' states. Concerning the event pool, we rely on a shared lock-protected calendar queue [1]. Multiple concurrent worker threads can extract events from the event pool and can concurrently dispatch the execution of the corresponding LPs by activating some event handler as a callback function.

3.2 Simulation Horizons and Value of Speculative Work

In speculative PDES, we can always identify a point on the simulation time axis which is the *commit horizon*—commonly referred to as Global Virtual Time (GVT). This is the simulation time instant that distinguishes between events which might be undone (e.g., due to some causality violation) and events which will never be undone. This time instant can be logically identified by considering that any simulation event e executed at simulation time T can only generate some new event e' associated with timestamp $T' \geq T$. In fact, violating this assumption would imply that an event in the future might affect the past, which is clearly a non-meaningful condition for any real-world process/phenomenon. Therefore, to identify the commit horizon, it is sufficient to identify the event with the smallest timestamp among all the events which are currently scheduled at (or have just been processed by) any LP in the system. Such timestamp corresponds to the commit horizon. In fact, no event still to be executed might produce a causal inconsistency involving the LP in charge of the execution of the commit-horizon event[2].

With our target engine organization, the commit horizon is associated with the oldest event that is currently being executed (or has just been executed) at any worker thread. Therefore, keeping track of the commit horizon boils down to registering, for each worker thread, the timestamp of the event e currently being executed, by replacing the value only after a new event is fetched for processing from the event pool, so that any new event possibly produced by e has its timestamp already reflected into the event pool. The commit horizon can be computed as the minimum among the registered values.

At any time, the commit-horizon event can be considered as a *safe* (namely, causally consistent) one, and therefore does not require any reversibility

---

[2] Simultaneous events do not violate this assumption. Nevertheless, if not properly handled by some tie-breaking function [11,13], they could give rise to livelocks in the speculative execution.

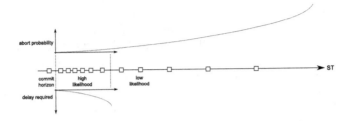

Fig. 2. Three logical regions on the simulation time (ST) axis, with varying density of pending events—those still to be processed, which will possibly generate new ones

mechanism for its execution. Let us now discuss about the likelihood of safety of other events to be processed, which stand ahead of the commit horizon. Empirical evidence and statistical considerations based on common distributions for the timestamp increment driving the generation of events in simulation models (see, e.g., [5,6]) have shown that event patterns are, at any time, characterized by greater density of events, say locality of activities, in the near future of the actual GVT. This situation is depicted in Fig. 2. Also, such locality tends to move along the time axis just based on the advancement of the commit horizon. The implication is that the risk of materialization of causal inconsistencies when speculatively processing one event that is ahead of the commit horizon is somehow linked to its distance from such horizon. This is also linked to the notion of lookahead of DES models, a quantity expressing the minimal timestamp increment we can experience for a given model when processing whichever event that originates new events to be injected in the system. Larger lookahead leads to produce new events in the far future, hence those getting closer to the current commit horizon become automatically safe.

By this consideration, the speculative processing of events that are closer to the commit horizon looks more valuable in terms of avoidance of causality inconsistencies. Hence in our approach we enable the processing of these events as HTM-based transactions, say via the more efficient (lower overhead) recoverability support. We also note that running events that are close to the commit horizon as HTM-based transactions will also lead to a faster advancement of this horizon, as compared to what we would expect if running them via software-based reversibility, since this would lead to longer processing times due to the overhead for producing the undo code blocks. However, an HTM-based transaction can commit only after events standing in the past have already been committed and the corresponding worker threads have already updated their entries in the meta-data array keeping their current timestamp. So, in order to increase the likelihood of committing the HTM-based transactional execution of some event, this transaction typically needs to include a busy-loop delay enabling a waiting phase just before checking whether the meta-data were updated[3].

---

[3] Other kind of delays, such as operating system sleeps, are unfeasible since any user/kernel transition will lead an HTM-based transaction to abort deterministically on current HTM-equipped processors.

Checking the meta-data at some wrong point in time will in its turn lead to the impossibility to recheck these data fruitfully in the future, since the updates occurring between the two checks will lead to a data conflict and to the abort of the checking transaction. In Fig. 2 we show how such a delay should be selected somehow proportionally to the distance (in terms of event count) of the event processed via HTM support from the commit horizon. Overall, for events that are further ahead from the commit horizon, the delay could not pay off, hence a more profitable approach to speculatively processing them is to run them outside of HTM-based transactions, still with reversibility guarantees achieved via software.

The problem of determining what is the threshold distance from the commit horizon beyond which the HTM support does not pay off is clearly also related to the interference between concurrent HTM-based transactions when using the underlying hardware resources. In fact, if we experience a scenario where two concurrent transactions both require large transactional cache storage for executing the corresponding dispatched events, and the cache is shared across the cores, then even if an event would ideally reveal as causally consistent upon attempting to finalize the transactions, it would anyhow be doomed to abort due to cache capacity conflicts. A similar cache capacity-due abort may even be experienced in case of single HTM-based transaction instance, just depending on the transaction data set, which might exceed the cache capacity.

To cope with the runtime adaptive selection of the threshold value, we rely on a hill climbing scheme based on the following parameters, easily measurable at runtime across successive wall-clock-time windows:

- T_{HTM}, the total processing time spent across all the worker threads while processing events (either committed or aborted) via HTM support;
- $COMMIT_{HTM}$, the total number of committed events whose speculative execution has been based on the HTM support;
- T_{soft}, the total processing time spent across all the worker threads while processing events (either committed or aborted) that are made recoverable via the software-based support (here we include the time spent for instrumentation code used to generate undo code blocks, plus the time for running the undo code blocks in case the events are eventually undone);
- $COMMIT_{soft}$, the total number of committed events whose execution has been based on the software support for recoverability.

By the above quantities, we compute the so called work-value ratio (WVR) for both HTM-based and software-based recoverability just like:

$$WVR_{HTM} = \frac{T_{HTM}}{COMMIT_{HTM}} \qquad WVR_{soft} = \frac{T_{soft}}{COMMIT_{soft}} \qquad (1)$$

which expresses the average amount of CPU time required for performing useful work (namely, for processing an event that is not undone) with the two different recoverability supports. Then, the threshold value THR determining the commit horizon distance (evaluated as event count) beyond which we consider it more convenient to process the event via software-based reversibility, rather than HTM-based one, is increased or decreased depending on whether the relation $WVR_{HTM} \leq WVR_{soft}$ is verified (as computed on the basis of statistics, on the baseline parameters listed above, collected in the last observation window). In order to avoid stalling in local minima (e.g. due to the avoidance of runtime samples for any of the above listed parameters), we intentionally perturb THR by ± 1 within the hill climbing scheme if its value reaches either zero or the number of threads currently running in the PDES platform.

3.3 Engine Architecture

As mentioned, our engine allows the coexistence of hardware-based and software-based reversibility facilities. While introducing hardware-based reversibility facilities is somehow easy—it can be done using the primitives TRANSACTION_START, TRANSACTION_END, and TRANSACTION_ABORT to drive event processing—software-based reversibility requires a bit more care, especially when targeting full transparency to the application-level developer. To cope with this issue, we rely on *static binary instrumentation*. In particular, we exploit the Hijacker [14] open-source customizable static binary instrumentation tool. Using this tool, we are able (before the final linking stage of the application-level simulation model) to identify any memory writing instruction (either a simple mov or more complex ones, like cmove or movs instructions) and to place just before each memory-update instruction a call to a reverse_generator module which reads the current value of the target memory location so as to generate the reverse instruction able to undo the corresponding side effect according to the proposal in [3]. The sequence of reversing instructions for a same event forms the undo code block of the event. Clearly, the instrumented and the non-instrumented versions of the application modules also need to coexist (since the non-instrumented version is the one to be run in case of HTM-based reversibility). Such coexistence has been achieved by using a multi-coding scheme when rewriting the ELF of the program at instrumentation time, and by identifying the entry points to the two versions of code (instrumented and not) within the same executable using function pointers exposed to the PDES engine.

In our implementation the reversing instructions associated with an event (those forming the undo code block of the event) are organized into a *reverse window*, which is used as a stack of negative instructions that can be invoked via a call. Correct execution of an undo code block is ensured by the presence of a ret instruction at the end of the reverse window. Also, if the forward execution of an event updates multiple times the same memory location, only the first instruction updating that location should be associated with the generation of an inverse instruction, since the following updates would be anyhow undone by the first inverse instruction. We therefore employ a fast hashmap to keep track of destination addresses within a forward event. Whenever reverse_generator is activated, this hashmap is queried to determine whether the destination address was already involved in a negative instruction generation.

Algorithm 1. Shared Lock Acquisition/Release

```
 1: int lock_vector[n]
 2: double timestamp[n]                              ▷ To avoid priority inversion
 3: int thread_id[n]                                 ▷ To avoid priority inversion
 4: procedure LOCK_LP(e, LP, mode, locking)
 5:     acquired ← false
 6:     do
 7:        if mode = EXCLUSIVE then
 8:          if CAS(-1, 0, lock_vector[LP]) then
 9:            acquired ← true
10:        else
11:            old_lock ← lock_vector[LP]
12:            if old_lock ≥ 0 then
13:              if CAS(old_lock + 1, old_lock, lock_vector[LP]) then
14:                 acquired ← true
15:          if ¬acquired then
16:            atomically {
17:              if timestamp[LP] ¿ T(e) ∨ ( timestamp[LP] = T(e)∧ thread_id[LP] > tid) then
18:                 timestamp[LP] ← T(e)
19:                 thread_id[LP] ← thread_id
20:            }
21:     while ¬acquired ∧ locking
22:     return acquired
23: procedure UNLOCK_LP(LP)
24:     if lock_vector[LP] = −1 then
25:        lock_vector[LP] ← 0
26:     else
27:        do
28:            old_lock ← lock_vector[LP]
29:        while ¬ CAS(old_lock − 1, old_lock, lock_vector[LP])
```

As mentioned before, to ensure consistency and minimize the effects of data contention on HTM-based execution of events, we must ensure that at no time two different worker threads can execute both software-reversible and hardware-reversible events at once, which target the same LP state. In fact, if this would happen, we might incur the risk of having less valuable work to invalidate more valuable one (since the HTM-based transaction would be aborted if its data set would overlap the write set of the event executed via software-based reversibility). Also, we cannot allow two (or more) events run via software-based reversibility to simultaneously target the same LP state. In fact, these events would not be regulated by any transactional execution scheme[4]. To this end, we rely on a synchronization mechanism similar in spirit to an atomic shared read/write lock [4]. Whenever a worker thread extracts an event from the shared event pool, it first determines whether the event should be executed using hardware-based or software-based reversibility according to the policy introduced in Sect. 3.2. If the selected execution mode is HTM-based, the worker thread tries to acquire the lock on the target LP in a non-exclusive way, which fails (i.e., requires spinning) in case any other worker thread already took it in an exclusive way. On the other hand, if the selected execution mode is based on software reversibility, the worker thread tries to acquire the lock in an exclusive way, yet this operation requires spinning if at least one worker thread has non-exclusively taken the

---

[4] The undo code blocks guarantee reversibility of memory updates limited to events executing the updates on the LP state in isolation, which complies with classical PDES where each LP is an intrinsically sequential entity.

lock. Nevertheless, this approach might lead to some priority inversion, among the threads which are running more valuable events via the HTM support and threads which are running less valuable events via software-based reversibility. To avoid this, we use a *locking* flag to instruct the algorithm to avoid spinning if it was not possible, for any reason, to acquire the lock—namely, setting *locking* to false transforms the lock into a trylock. If the lock is not taken, two additional values in two arrays are updated atomically: `timestamp` and `thread_id`, which are exploited on a per-LP basis. In particular, the worker thread registers the timestamp it has an event to process at, and its thread id. The latter value is only used to create a total order among threads in case simultaneous events are present, to avoid possible deadlock conditions. These values are periodically inspected by other worker threads (upon a safety check for the current processed event, which fails), so as to determine whether some higher priority event is waiting. In that case, if the work carried out is not likely to be committed shortly, thanks to the reversibility supports it gets squashed, so that higher priority is given immediately to events with a smaller timestamp. Algorithm 1 shows the lock management pseudo-code, which relies on the Compare and Swap (CAS) read-modify-write primitive to increase/decrease the value of a shared per-LP counter. The value -1 for the counter means that the lock is exclusively taken, while the value 0 indicates that no thread is running an event bound to the LP. A positive value is a reference counter indicating how many worker threads are concurrently executing events bound to the LP via hardware-based reversibility.

We can now discuss the organization of the main loop of threads within our speculative PDES engine, whose pseudo-code is shown in Algorithm 2. Essentially, it is made up by three different execution paths, each one associated with one of the different execution modes. Initially, a call to a FETCH() procedure allows to extract from the shared event pool the event with the smallest timestamp. Then, a statistical approximation of the number of events which are expected to fall before the currently fetched event (since others may still be processed or might be produced as a result of the processing) is computed as:

$$\frac{T(e) - commit\_horizon}{average\_timestamp\_increment} \tag{2}$$

where $average\_timestamp\_increment$ is computed[5] as $\frac{commit\_horizon}{total\_committed\_events}$. This value, together with the threshold THR (see Sect. 3.2), is used to determine whether a certain event might be more valuable or not, thus requiring either HTM-support or software-based reversibility (line 12). Additionally, if an event is executed exploiting HTM, this value drives as well the selection of a delay before checking again the safety of the corresponding transaction (namely,

---

[5] For non-stationary models, where the distribution of the timestamp increment between successive events can change over time in non-negligible way, this same statistic could be simply rejuvenated periodically, by discarding non-recent events commitments and subtracting from *commit_horizon* the upper limit of the discarded simulation time portion.

Algorithm 2. Main Loop

```
 1: procedure MAINLOOP
 2:     new_events = ∅                              ▷ Set of events generated during the execution of an event
 3:     while ¬endSimulation do
 4:         e ← FETCH( )
 5:         if e = NULL then
 6:             goto 3
 7:         events_before ← ───────────────────────           ▷ Safe execution: on the commit horizon
 8:         if SAFE( ) then                         ▷ Safe execution: on the commit horizon
 9:             LOCK_LP((e, LP(e), NON_EXCLUSIVE, true))
10:             new_events ← PROCESSEVENT(e)
11:             UNLOCK_LP(LP(e))
12:         else if events_before ≤ THR then        ▷ HTM-based execution: high likelihood region
13:             if ¬ LOCK_LP((e, LP(e), NON_EXCLUSIVE, false)) then
14:                 goto 7
15:             BEGINTRANSACTION( )
16:             new_events ← PROCESSEVENT(e)
17:             THROTTLE(events_before)
18:             if SAFE( ) then
19:                 COMMITTRANSACTION( )
20:                 UNLOCK_LP(LP(e))
21:             else
22:                 ABORTTRANSACTION( )
23:                 UNLOCK_LP(LP(e))
24:                 goto 7
25:         else                                    ▷ Software-reversible execution: low likelihood region
26:             if ¬ LOCK_LP((e, LP(e), EXCLUSIVE, false)) then
27:                 goto 7
28:             SETUPUNDOCODEBLOCK( )
29:             new_events ← PROCESSEVENT_REVERSIBLE(e)
30:             while ¬ SAFE( ) do
31:                 if timestamp[LP] ¡ T(e) ∨ ( timestamp[LP] = T(e)∧ thread_id[LP] < tid) then
32:                     UNLOCK_LP(LP(e))
33:                     UNDOEVENT(e)
34:                     new_events = ∅
35:                     goto 7
36:         FLUSH(e, new_events)
37:         atomically {
38:             if thread_id[LP] = tid then
39:                 timestamp[LP] ← ∞
40:                 thread_id[LP] ← ∞
41:         }
```

The equation at line 7:

$$events\_before \leftarrow \frac{T(e) - commit\_horizon}{average\_timestamp\_increment}$$

whether the timestamp of the event has in the meanwhile become the commit horizon), so as to avoid making it doomed with a high likelihood (line 17).

In case of a safe execution, i.e. the execution of the event on the commit horizon (lines 8–11), we take a non-exclusive lock, which is used to inform any other thread that the destination LP is currently processing an event. This avoids that any other worker thread starts processing an event via software-based reversibility at the same LP while we are processing in safe mode. Moreover, we configure the lock to spin because the worker thread in charge of executing this event has the highest priority and any other competing thread will try to give it permission to continue execution as fast as possible.

For a transactional execution (lines 12–24), we use the trylock version of the per-LP lock. If we fail to acquire the lock, the execution resumes from line 7, meaning that we check again whether the extracted event has become safe or not, in the meanwhile. Otherwise, as already explained before, we start executing the event within an HTM-based transaction, introducing an artificial delay—via the THROTTLE(*events_before*) call—which is proportional to the estimated number of events in between the commit horizon and the currently executed event. If the transaction becomes doomed (lines 21–24) the execution restarts from line 7, so as to check whether the just-aborted event has become safe.

The case of execution via software reversibility (lines 25–35) is a bit different. In fact, first we have to take an exclusive lock—in a trylock fashion, for the same consideration related to the HTM-based execution—and we have to setup the undo code block, by allocating a reverse window buffer. At the end of the execution of the event, similarly to the HTM-based case, we have to wait for the event to become safe. Nevertheless, since this execution entails taking an exclusive lock, we continuously check whether some other thread is registered at the same LP with a higher priority (line 31). This situation might arise due to another event, executed at any other worker thread, generating a new event to the same LP with a timestamp smaller than the one of the event currently processed via software-based reversibility. Failing to make this specific check could either hamper liveness (a thread waits its event to be the commit horizon, which cannot happen) or correctness (events are committed out of order). Line 31, paired with lines 15–20 of Algorithm 1, is able to ensure both correctness and liveness.

Whenever an event is executed, and then committed thanks to safety assurance, in whichever execution mode, we first place into the calendar queue any possible new event generated (line 36), and we then unregister the thread from the `timestamp` and `thread_id` vectors which are used to avoid priority inversion (lines 37–41). For the implementations of FETCH(), FLUSH(), and SAFE(), we refer the reader to [19].

4   Experimental Results

We tested our proposal with the Phold benchmark [8]. We included 1024 LPs in the simulation model, each one scheduling events for itself or for the others. Specifically, upon processing an event, the probability to schedule a new event destined to another LP has been set to 0.2, which is representative of scenarios with non-minimal interactions across the simulated parts. Also, the initial population of events has been set to 1 event per LP, while the timestamp increment determining the actual timestamp of newly scheduled events has been set to follow the exponential distribution with mean value equal to one simulation time unit. The model lookahead has been set to a minimal value computed as the 0.5 % of the average timestamp increment. Further, the overall simulation is partitioned into 4 phases where the LPs exhibit alternate behaviors in terms of updates of their states. Phases 1 and 3 are write-mild since each event only updates the classical counter of processed events and a few other statistical values within the LP state. Contrariwise, phases 2 and 4 are write-intensive, since event processing also updates an array of counters' values, still embedded with the LP state, by performing 500 updates on the array entries. Overall, the different phases mimic varying locality and memory access profiles. A classical busy-loop characterizing Phold event processing steps is also added which is set to generate an average event granularity of about 25 microseconds. In this experiment, we compared the performance of our hardware- and software-based mixed approach to both pure hardware-based reversibility (as proposed in [19]) and pure software-based one exclusively relying on undo code blocks (this is achieved by preventing any thread to exploit the HTM support in our engine). We did not compare with the performance achievable by some last generation traditional speculative PDES platform just because the data reported in [19] have shown that event granularity values of a few (tens of) microseconds do not allow this type of platforms to provide significative speedup values (due to the fact that they are based on explicit partitioning of the workload across the threads, and on explicit message passing for event cross-scheduling, thus resulting more adequate for larger grain simulation models). Overall, we assessed our proposal with a workload configuration just requiring alternative forms of speculative parallelization (like the one we propose), as compared to the classical ones.

We have run this benchmark by varying the number of employed threads from 1 to the maximum number of physical CPU-cores in the underlying machine with HTM support, which is equipped with two Intel Haswell 3.5 GHz processors, 24 GB of RAM and runs Linux—kernel 3.2[6]. For the case of single-thread runs, the execution time values are those achieved by simply running the application code on top of a calendar queue scheduler.

In Fig. 3 we report the observed execution time values while varying the number of threads (each reported value resulting as the average over 5 different samples). The data show how our mixed HW/SW approach outperforms both the others, with a maximum gain of up to 10 % vs the pure HW approach and of 30 % vs the pure SW approach (achieved when running with 4 threads). Such a gain by the mixed approach is clearly related to the fact that write-intensive phases lead the pure SW approach to become more intrusive, because of costly generation of larger undo code blocks, which does not pay-off compared to the reliance on pure HTM-based reversibility. On the other hand, the pure HW approach does not allow the maximization of the usefulness of the carried out speculative work for larger thread counts. In fact, the slope of the execution time curve for the pure HW approach becomes slightly worse than the one of the pure SW approach when moving from 3 to 4 threads. Our mixed approach is able to get the best of the two by just avoiding excessive aborts of HTM-based transactions when relying on larger thread counts, also reducing the cost of undo code blocks' generation thanks to a fraction of events executed with HTM support. The data reported in Fig. 4 show how the pure HW approach suffers from thrashing when increasing the thread count, while the pure SW approach has minimal incidence of events undo. The mixed approach avoids the thrashing

---

[6] The hyper-threading support offered by the processors has been excluded just to avoid cross-thread interferences—due to conflicting hyper-threads' accesses to hardware resources—which might alter the reliability of our analysis.

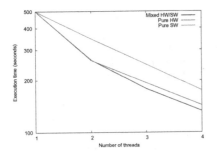

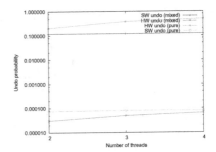

Fig. 3. Execution time - log scale on the y-axis

Fig. 4. Undo probability for HW and SW speculatively processed events

phenomenon just like the pure SW approach does, but has less overhead since executes a portion of the events via the HTM support.

5   Conclusions

We have presented a speculative PDES engine where reversibility of causal inconsistent events is based on a mix of hardware and software facilities. The hardware part relies on the HTM support offered by modern processors, particularly the Intel Haswell, while software reversibility is based on transparent instrumentation and on the dynamic generation of blocks of code able to undo memory side effects. We have shown via an experimental study with a classical benchmark how the proposed mixed approach can overcome the drawbacks of both the two baseline ones, in terms of delivered performance by the simulation engine.

References

1. Brown, R.: Calendar queues: a fast O(1) priority queue implementation for the simulation event set problem. Commun. ACM **31**(10), 1220–1227 (1988)
2. Carothers, C.D., Perumalla, K.S., Fujimoto, R.M.: Efficient optimistic parallel simulations using reverse computation. ACM Trans. Model. Comput. Simul. **9**(3), 224–253 (1999)
3. Cingolani, D., Pellegrini, A., Quaglia, F.: Transparently mixing undo logs and software reversibility for state recovery in optimistic PDES. In: Proceedings of the ACM SIGSIM Conference on Principles of Advanced Discrete Simulation, pp. 211–222 (2015)
4. Dice, D., Shavit, N.: TLRW: return of the read-write lock. In: Proceedings of the 22nd Annual ACM Symposium on Parallel Algorithms and Architectures, pp. 284–293 (2010)
5. Ferscha, A.: Probabilistic adaptive direct optimism control in time warp. In: Proceedings of the 9th Workshop on Parallel and Distributed Simulation, pp. 120–129 (1995)
6. Ferscha, A., Luthi, J.: Estimating rollback overhead for optimism control in time warp. In: Proceedings of the 28th Annual Simulation Symposium, pp. 2–12 (1995)

7. Fujimoto, R.M.: Parallel discrete event simulation. Commun. ACM **33**, 19–28 (1989)
8. Fujimoto, R.M.: Performance of time warp under synthetic workloads. In: Proceedings of the Multiconference on Distributed Simulation, pp. 23–28 (1990)
9. Fujimoto, R.M., Tsai, J.J., Gopalakrishnan, G.: Design and evaluation of the rollback chip: special purpose hardware for time warp. IEEE Trans. Comput. **41**(1), 68–82 (1992)
10. Jefferson, D.R.: Virtual time. ACM Trans. Program. Lang. Syst. **7**(3), 404–425 (1985)
11. Jha, V., Bagrodia, R.: Simultaneous events and lookahead in simulation protocols. ACM Trans. Model. Comput. Simul. **10**(3), 241–267 (2000)
12. LaPre, J.M., Gonsiorowski, E.J., Carothers, C.D.: LORAIN: a step closer to the PDES 'Holy Grail'. In: Proceedings of the ACM SIGSIM Conference on Principles of Advanced Discrete Simulation, pp. 3–14 (2014)
13. Mehl, H.: A deterministic tie-breaking scheme for sequential and distributed simulation. In: Proceedings of the Workshop on Parallel and Distributed Simulation (1992)
14. Pellegrini, A.: Hijacker: efficient static software instrumentation with applications in high performance computing. In: Proceedings of the International Conference on High Performance Computing and Simulation, pp. 650–655 (2013)
15. Pellegrini, A., Vitali, R., Quaglia, F., Pellegrini, A., Quaglia, F.: Autonomic state management for optimistic simulation platforms. IEEE Trans. Parallel Distrib. Syst. **26**(6), 1560–1569 (2015)
16. Preiss, B.R., Loucks, W.M., MacIntyre, D.: Effects of the checkpoint interval on time and space in time warp. ACM Trans. Model. Comput. Simul. **4**(3), 223–253 (1994)
17. Quaglia, F., Baldoni, R.: Exploiting intra-object dependencies in parallel simulation. Inf. Process. Lett. **70**(3), 119–125 (1999)
18. Quaglia, F., Santoro, A.: Non-blocking checkpointing for optimistic parallel simulation: description and an implementation. IEEE Trans. Parallel Distrib. Syst. **14**(6), 593–610 (2003)
19. Santini, E., Ianni, M., Pellegrini, A., Quaglia, F.: HTM based speculative parallel discrete event simulation of very fine grain models. In: Proceedings of the 22nd International Conference on High Performance Computing, pp. 145–154 (2015)
20. Soliman, H.M., Elmaghraby, A.S.: An analytical model for hybrid checkpointing in time warp distributed simulation. IEEE Trans. Parallel Distrib. Syst. **9**(10), 947–951 (1998)
21. West, D., Panesar, K.: Automatic incremental state saving. In: Proceedings of the 10th Workshop on Parallel and Distributed Simulation, pp. 78–85 (1996)

Elements of a Reversible
Object-Oriented Language
Work-in-Progress Report

Ulrik Pagh Schultz[1]($\boxtimes$) and Holger Bock Axelsen[2]

[1] University of Southern Denmark, Odense, Denmark
ups@mmmi.sdu.dk
[2] University of Copenhagen, Copenhagen, Denmark
funkstar@di.ku.dk

Abstract. This paper presents initial ideas for the design and implementation of a reversible object-oriented language based on extending Janus with object-oriented concepts such as classes that encapsulate behavior and state, inheritance, virtual dispatching, as well as constructors. We show that virtual dispatching is a reversible decision mechanism easily translatable to a standard reversible programming model such as Janus, and we argue that reversible management of state can be accomplished using reversible constructors. The language is implemented in terms of translation to standard Janus programs.

1 Introduction

Extant reversible programming languages such as Janus [7], Theseus [3] and RFUN [8] have been developed with a focus on providing features (such as control flow operators) that enables the programmer to understand how execution is performed reversibly. However, unlike most modern programming languages, this is usually *not* paired with other programmer-friendly abstractions. This has unfortunate consequences, in particular that reversible programmers have to build implicit data types out of the given primitives when dealing with complex data, leading to longer, less readable, and more error-prone reversible code.

From recent advances in compiler technology for reversible programming languages we know that it is possible to reversibly and efficiently represent and manipulate complex data objects in the heap [2,6], opening the door for associated advances in reversible language design. Here, we consider *reversible object-orientation*. Object-oriented programming uses classes as a means to providing higher-level structures that encapsulate behavior and state. We show how a number of object-oriented concepts (encapsulation, inheritance, and virtual methods) can be captured reversibly by extending the Janus language with support for

The authors acknowledge partial support from COST Action IC1405 *Reversible Computation*. H.B. Axelsen was supported by the Danish Council for Independent Research | Natural Sciences under the *Foundations of Reversible Computing* project.

© Springer International Publishing Switzerland 2016
S. Devitt and I. Lanese (Eds.): RC 2016, LNCS 9720, pp. 153–159, 2016.
DOI: 10.1007/978-3-319-40578-0_10

such features, and describe them by translation to ordinary Janus programs. These concepts have been implemented in a prototype language named Joule (a homonym of JOOL, Janus Object-Oriented Language), which will be used throughout this paper to illustrate our ideas. This paper presents initial concepts in the design of the Joule language, serving as a report on the work in progress to provide a useful, reversible object-oriented programming language.

2   Reversible Object-Oriented Programming

Similarly to mainstream object-oriented languages such as C++ and Java, we propose to extend Janus with a static inheritance mechanism encapsulating state and behavior, and a corresponding virtual dispatching mechanism that dynamically decides which method implementation to invoke based on the runtime type of the receiver object. We hypothesize that such a language will allow programs to be written at a higher level of abstraction without introducing complications due to memory management.

Object-oriented polymorphism is implemented using inheritance, where operations are expressed in terms of an abstract interface implemented by subclasses. Polymorphism allows different implementations to be composed and then selected at runtime depending on the specific class of each object. Since objects do not change their class at runtime in our proposed language, the decision of which method to invoke at runtime will be reversible: invoking and "uninvoking" a specific method on a given object will always select the same method.

Regarding memory management, some object-oriented languages have been conceived with limited-memory systems in mind, and today they are routinely used to implement embedded systems. For example, the Beta language (an early derivative of Simula-67, the first object-oriented language) included static object allocation as a design criterion [4], to enable it to function on memory-constrained systems with static and stack allocation. Today, the C++ language is commonly used as a systems programming language: the combination of object-oriented system decomposition and a disciplined approach to manual memory management often offers significant advantages compared to, e.g., C.

3   Encapsulation and Construction

We now describe how classes are used as an encapsulation mechanism in Joule, our proposed syntax for reversible method invocation, and how we propose to deal with the issue of reversibly constructing objects.

3.1   Encapsulation

Object-oriented classes should not be considered as a module mechanism, but classes have nonetheless been proven as a practical mechanism for providing the encapsulation and abstraction required for, e.g., abstract datatypes [5]. Taking

```
class Point {
  int x; int y; // private fields, zero-initialized
  Point(int x, int y) { // constructor, runs after allocation
    this.x += x; this.y += y; // 'this.x' is a field, 'x' a parameter
  }
  procedure add_to_x(int x) { this.x += x; }
  procedure add_to_y(int y) { this.y += y; }
}
```

Fig. 1. Joule implementation of a basic point class

inspiration from mainstream languages, we can allow classes to define fields and methods that can operate on the data stored in these fields. The data is initialized using a constructor and uninitialized by uncalling the constructor.

As a concrete example, we define a class `Point` that encapsulates two values, x and y coordinates, and provides operations to manipulate these values (see Fig. 1). The fields x and y can only be manipulated using the provided methods (we consider all fields private). The fields are initialized upon object initialization using the constructor. Note that the initial value of any field is assumed to be zero (or null for a reference type). Joule objects can be considered as records that contain a mix of runtime type information, integers, and object references (the specific Janus-based implementation will be discussed later, in Sect. 5).

The class `Point` can be instantiated and methods can be invoked (called) using the standard "." operator for accessing an object. To support uncalling method (uninvoking), we adopt "!" as an inverse operator.

```
local Point p = Point.new(5,8); // construct
p.add_to_x(2); // p.x==7
p!add_to_y(3); // p.y==5
```

Note the slightly nonstandard syntax `C.new(...)` for creating an object and invoking the constructor, which in Java would have been written `new C(...)`. Calling and uncalling methods works similar to calling and uncalling procedures in Janus. Nevertheless, the introduction of a class hierarchy will require a run-time decision to select which implementation to use, as discussed in the next section.

3.2 Construction and Unconstruction

To properly dispose of a locally allocated object we must restore the value of the fields to their initial blank values from before the constructor was invoked.[1] To

---

[1] We here follow the memory model of Janus, where variables can be dynamically allocated on the call stack using a `local` declaration that initializes the variable to a given value, but must symmetrically by deallocated using a `delocal` declaration that must provide the final value of the variable, resetting the memory and providing an initializer for the variable when running the program in reverse.

this end, we propose to uncall the constructor using arguments that return the corresponding fields to zero (or null for references). The locally allocated variable p of type Point now representing the point $(7, 5)$ can for example be disposed using delocal Point!new(7,5) p; The "!" operator is used here to denote running the constructor in reverse with the given arguments, unconstructing the object.

```
class Counter {
    int limit; // stop incrementing this.count when limit is reached
    int value; // updated when calling 'count'
    Counter(int limit) { this.limit += limit; }
    procedure count(int flag) {
        if(this.value<this.limit) { this.value += 1; }
        else { flag += 1; } fi(flag==0);
    }
    procedure finalize(int uncount) { this.value -= uncount; }
}
```

Fig. 2. Joule implementation of counting up to a limit

In general objects may contain state that evolves over time and that is not initialized using constructor parameters. As an example, consider the class Counter shown in Fig. 2. The field limit is initialized upon construction, but the field value evolves over time: as long as its value is less than limit it is increased by one when the method value is called (the parameter flag is used to signal when the limit has been reached). Uncalling the constructor would not serve to return the field value to a zero state. Here we could adopt the notion of a destructor to reset the remaining state, but as an alternative we adopt a simple programming pattern where a method (by convention named finalize) is used to bring the object back to a state where it can be unconstructed by running the constructor in reverse:

```
local Counter c = Counter.new(3); // construct
local int flag = 0;
c.count(flag); c.count(flag);
c.finalize(2);                     // reset c.value to 0
delocal flag == 0;
delocal Counter!new(3) c;          // unconstruct
```

The method finalize serves to "unfinalize" the object, bringing it into a state where the constructor can be run backwards to reset the memory. In the concrete example the finalization method takes an argument, but the finalization could also have written with the assumption that the counter is in a specific state (e.g., limit reached), in which case no argument would have been needed.

We speculate that the question of how to unconstruct objects will be a key challenge in reversible object-oriented programming, but that a notion of *reversible design patterns* may provide useful programming abstractions. For example, objects created by a factory design pattern could then be unconstructed by a hypothetical *unfactory* pattern derived from the original factory pattern. This issue is however left for future work.

3.3   Object References

Most object-oriented programs rely on the ability for objects to refer to each other, which raises the question of how to reversibly store references to other objects in a field. We adopt the simple approach that references only can be stored into null references, which is done using the := operator:

```
local Point p = Point.new(1,7); local Point q = null;
q := p;                   // essentially q += p;
q.add_to_x(2);            // p.x==3
delocal q == p;           // removes local variable
delocal Point!new(3,7) p; // unconstructs object
```

Reverse execution of the := operator is done by subtracting the provided reference from the reference being operated on, producing a null reference.

4   Inheritance and Virtual Calls

Inheritance often serves the dual purpose of creating a subtype hierarchy and implementation reuse, and for simplicity we follow this approach here. Although concepts of reverse inheritance have been proposed [1], we see inheritance and the subtype hierarchy as a means to model the information on which the methods operate. Thus, we believe that inheritance works the same in non-reversible and reversible languages, although as noted earlier the immutability of type information in an object is particularly advantageous for reversible computing since it ensures that virtual calls are a reversible mechanism.

Our proposed syntax for calling and uncalling methods has already been introduced, and straightforwardly generalizes to invocation of virtual methods. As a concrete example, consider the Joule program shown in Fig. 3. The classes Add, Sub and Twice all extend the common (abstract) superclass Op. The class Twice takes a given operator as an argument, and applies it twice whenever the app method is called (note the use of the reversible := null-reference assignment operator). These classes can be used as follows:

```
abstract class Op { abstract procedure app(int var, int x); }
class Add extends Op { procedure app(int var, int x) { var += x; } }
class Sub extends Op { procedure app(int var, int x) { var -= x; } }
class Twice extends Op {
  Op p;
  Twice(Op p) { this.p := p; } // := only on null references
  procedure app(int var, int x) {
    local Op p = this.p; // copy of reference, fewer indirections
    p.app(var,x); p.app(var,x); // Polymorphic call site
    delocal p == this.p;
  }
}
```

Fig. 3. Joule program implementing a hierarchy of reversible operators

```
local Op a = Add.new(); local Op b = Sub.new();
local Op aa = Twice.new(a); local Op bb = Twice.new(b);
local int v = 0; aa.app(v,4); bb!app(v,1); delocal v == 10;
delocal Twice!new(b) bb; delocal Twice!new(a) aa;
delocal Sub!new() b; delocal Add!new() a;
```

Here, the calls p.app inside the method app in class Twice execute different methods, depending on the type of the Op object stored in the field p.

5 Implementation

Joule has been implemented by translation to Janus, and all the examples provided in this paper have been automatically compiled using our prototype Joule compiler.[2] Objects are currently represented as arrays of integers: the first element is a compile-time constant determining the class of the object, the remaining elements represent the fields of the object. Objects are allocated in a heap represented as a two-dimensional array, thus object references are simply indices into this array. The dimensions of the array are currently determined manually, and memory management is currently manual and completely unsafe, meaning objects could be deallocated in the wrong order leading to undefined behavior (e.g., an object could be overwritten by user data).

Virtual calls are implemented using standard dispatcher functions, e.g., for a given virtual method m a Janus procedure dispatch_m is generated that uses nested if-then-else-fi statements to select the specific method implementation to call depending on the type of the receiver object (the value of the first element of the array representing the receiver object). Uncalling a method is simply done by uncalling the corresponding dispatcher procedure. This implementation approach is simple and supports compile-time modularity (e.g., classes can be written independently) but rules out runtime modularity (e.g., dynamic class loading). Since reversible computing normally operates under a closed-world hypothesis, this restriction is considered appropriate for the time being.

References

1. Chirila, C.B., Crescenzo, P., Lahire, P.: Reverse inheritance: improving class library reuse in Eiffel. In: Langages et Modeles a Objets (2007)
2. Hansen, J.S.K.: Translation of a reversible functional programming language. Master's thesis, Department of Computer Science, University of Copenhagen (2014)
3. James, R.P., Sabry, A.: Theseus: a high level language for reversible computing, work-in-progress report at RC (2014). http://www.cs.indiana.edu/~sabry/papers/theseus.pdf
4. Kristensen, B.B., Madsen, O.L., Møller-Pedersen, B.: The when, why and why not of the beta programming language. In: Proceedings of the Third ACM SIGPLAN Conference on History of Programming Languages, pp. 10-1–10-57. HOPL III, NY, USA (2007). http://doi.acm.org/10.1145/1238844.1238854

---

[2] Source code for compiler, examples, and generated Janus programs are available at https://github.com/joule-lang/joule/tree/master/doc/papers/rc16.

5. Meyer, B.: Object-Oriented Software Construction, vol. 2. Prentice Hall, New York (1988)
6. Mogensen, T.: Garbage collection for reversible functional languages. In: Krivine, J., Stefani, J.B. (eds.) RC 2015. LNCS, vol. 9138, pp. 79–94. Springer, Heidelberg (2015)
7. Yokoyama, T., Axelsen, H.B., Glück, R.: Principles of a reversible programming language. In: Proceedings of Computing Frontiers, pp. 43–54. ACM (2008)
8. Yokoyama, T., Axelsen, H.B., Glück, R.: Towards a reversible functional language. In: De Vos, A., Wille, R. (eds.) RC 2011. LNCS, vol. 7165, pp. 14–29. Springer, Heidelberg (2012)

Initial Ideas for Automatic Design and Verification of Control Logic in Reversible HDLs

Work in Progress Report

Robert Wille[1,2]([✉]), Oliver Keszocze[2,3], Lars Othmer[3],
Michael Kirkedal Thomsen[4], and Rolf Drechsler[2,3]

[1] Institute for Integrated Circuits, Johannes Kepler University, Linz, Austria
robert.wille@jku.at
[2] Cyber-Physical Systems, DFKI GmbH, Bremen, Germany
{keszocze,lothmer,drechsler}@informatik.uni-bremen.de
[3] Institute of Computer Science, University of Bremen, Bremen, Germany
[4] Department of Computer Science, University of Copenhagen,
Copenhagen, Denmark
shapper@diku.dk

Abstract. In imperative reversible languages the commonly used conditional statements must, in addition to the established *if*-condition for forward computation, be extended with an additional *fi*-condition for backward computation. Unfortunately, deriving correct and consistent *fi*-conditions is often not obvious. Moreover, implementations exist which may not be realized with a reversible control flow at all. In this work, we propose automatic methods for descriptions in the reversible HDL SyReC that can generate the required *fi*-conditions and check whether a reversible control flow indeed can be realized. The envisioned solution utilizes *predicate transformer semantics* based on *Hoare logic*. The presented ideas constitute the first steps towards automatic methods for these important designs steps in the domain of reversible circuit design.

1 Introduction

In order to guarantee reversibility of the descriptions of reversible HDLs (such as SyReC [1]), a reversible control flow has to be implemented. For example, conditional statements do not only require an *if*-condition (in order to decide which of the *then*- or the *else*-block is to be executed next), but also a so-called *fi*-condition (for the same reason, if the computation is conducted in reverse direction). This was first introduced in Janus where it is called an assertion [2].

Moreover, HDL descriptions do occur from which it is not possible to realize a reversible control flow at all. Hence, designers of reversible circuits and systems are not only faced with the problem of properly describing a reversible control flow, but also the uncertainty whether such a control flow even is possible. Section 2 describes and illustrates these issues in more detail.

© Springer International Publishing Switzerland 2016
S. Devitt and I. Lanese (Eds.): RC 2016, LNCS 9720, pp. 160–166, 2016.
DOI: 10.1007/978-3-319-40578-0_11

In this work, we propose the ideas to tackle these two problems. A methodology is envisioned that applies symbolic simulation in order to automatically generate a representation of all system states that originated from the execution of a conditional statement. From that, the respectively desired *fi*-condition can be derived. Moreover, the symbolic simulation (together with some solving engines) can also be utilized to check whether a given HDL description allows for a fully reversible control flow at all; in other words, whether the control flow of the description is total. As a result, some manual and time-consuming tasks for the design of reversible circuits and systems could be automated.

2 Control Logic in Reversible HDLs

Relying on reversible assignments, a reversible data flow is ensured. However, in a similar fashion the control flow has to be made reversible. This is clearly manifested in conditional statements. Here, in contrast to non-reversible languages, it has to be guaranteed that the correct block (either, the *then*-block or the *else*-block) is executed when performing the computations in reverse direction. To this end, an additional *fi*-condition has to be provided for each conditional statement. If computations are performed in forward direction, the *fi*-condition can be applied as an assertion. If computations are performed in reverse direction, the *fi*-condition decides whether the *then*-block or the *else*-block is supposed to be executed next and the *if*-condition can be used as the end-assertion. The following example illustrates the idea.

Example 1. Consider the following two conditional statements:

```
if (b = 5) then
   x += y // executed if b = 5
else
   x -= y // executed if b != 5
fi (b = 5);
```

```
if ((x % 2) = 1) then
   x += 3;
else
   x += 1;
   y += c;
fi (((x - 3) % 2) = 1)
```

The first one does not modify any of the signals of the conditional expression (signal *b* in this case). Hence, the *if*- and the *fi*-condition are identical. In contrast, the *then*-block of the second conditional statement modifies the value of signal *x* which is used in the conditional expression. Hence, a suitable *fi*-condition different from the *if*-condition has to be provided in order to ensure correct execution semantics in both directions.

The examples above are very simple, but in general it is not obvious to derive a correct *fi*-condition. In particular when more complex or even nested conditional statements have to be considered, the generation of a correct control logic for a reversible circuit becomes a hard and error-prone task, which has been conducted manually thus far.

Besides that, another problem poses an obstacle to the correct generation of control logic for reversible circuits. Statements in the *then/else*-blocks could prevent the generation of a fully reversible control logic; in other words, the *if*-conditions together with two statements might not implement a total and injective (bijective) function. Then, only *fi*-conditions that satisfy parts of the range can be derived. The following example illustrates the problem.

Example 2. Consider the following conditional statement:

```
if (x = y) then
  x += 1
else
  y += 2
fi ( (x - 1) = y );
```

This statement works for most of the possible assignments of x, y in both directions. However, a problem occurs if e.g. $x = 4$ and $y = 1$ are considered. In forward direction, this would not satisfy the *if*-condition and, hence, would trigger the execution of the *else*-block (leading to $x = 4$ and $y = 3$). This assignment however would satisfy the *fi*-condition, i.e., if executed in reverse direction, the *then*-block would reversibly be executed (leading to $x = 3$ and $y = 3$). In other words, the two input states $(x, y) = (4, 1)$ and $(x, y) = (3, 3)$ both map to the output state $(4, 3)$ – a clear violation of the reversible computing paradigm.

Cases like this are called *partially reversible control statements* in the following, as they now implement a partial reversible function. Often the conditional statements become partial reversible only because of a very small set of possible signal assignments (with $k \in \mathbb{N}$) which both lead to the *fi*-condition being satisfied. , so detecting such signals becomes even harder than generating the *fi*-condition. Again, no automatic support is available to the designers thus far.

Overall, this leads to two major challenges to be addressed when designing control logic in HDL-based synthesis of reversible circuits, namely (1) how to efficiently generate a correct *fi*-condition for a given control statement and (2) how to efficiently check whether a control statement is partially or fully reversible.

3   Envisioned Solution

In this section, we envision a methodology that relies on the symbolic simulation of a given HDL description to automatically address the challenges discussed above. Specifically, we utilize *predicate transformer semantics* that is based on *Hoare logic* [3]. In the following, we first describe how these semantics can be applied for *fi*-generation. Afterwards, we describe the utilization in order to automatically check for partial reversibility.

3.1   Generation of *fi*-Conditions

The *if*-condition of a conditional statement is a symbolic description of all system states which are supposed to enter the *then*-block. In a similar fashion, the *fi*-condition is a symbolic description of the system states which originated from executing the *then*-block. Hence, in order to automatically derive a *fi*-condition, it is sufficient to perform a symbolic simulation. To this end, Hoare logic can be utilized. More formally, for a given *if*-condition B and a *then*-block composed of statements S_{then}, the desired *fi*-condition is equivalent to the strongest post-condition $sp(S_{\text{then}}, B)$.

However, in order to become applicable for the purposes considered here, some additional adjustments and assumptions have to be employed. In order to describe those properly, we first assume the notation of a reversible conditional statement to be

$$S_{\text{if}} := \textbf{if} \, (B) \, \textbf{then} \, S_{\text{then}} \, \textbf{else} \, S_{\text{else}} \, \textbf{fi} \, (), \tag{1}$$

where S_{if}, B, S_{then}, and S_{else} denote the entire conditional statement, the *if*-condition, the statements of the *then*-block, and the statements of the *else*-block, respectively. Note that the *fi*-condition is intentionally left empty as it is about to be generated. Furthermore, we assume that S_{then} and S_{else} are fully reversible (sequences of) statements which, however, may be empty (i.e. $S_{\text{then}} = \text{skip}$ or $S_{\text{else}} = \text{skip}$ is possible). Finally, we firstly assume that there are no nested if-statements.

The overall procedure for *fi*-generation is given in Algorithm 1. Initially, it is assumed that all system states are allowed to execute the statements; hence the pre-condition P is set to *true* (line 1). Afterwards, all statements of the HDL description are traversed (line 2). If the currently considered statement S is *not* a conditional statement, P is updated accordingly using Hoare rules for skip or assignment (line 4). The rule for statement sequencing is implicitly employed by iteratively updating the condition P. Otherwise, the Hoare rule for a conditional is applied which splits the determination of the post-condition into two steps (lines 6/7), leading to a post-condition P_{then} obtained for the *then*-block and a post-condition P_{else} obtained for the *else*-block. The disjunction of both yields the updated description for P (line 8). Moreover, the post-condition P_{then} additionally yields the *fi*-condition for the currently considered if-statement and can accordingly be updated (line 9).

Using Algorithm 1, *fi*-conditions can automatically be generated for many HDL descriptions. However, problems remain when nested if-statements occur. Then, two further issues have to be dealt with:

1. *Inner if-statements would be skipped*
   This is because an entire conditional statement S_{if} is always considered to be a single statement $S \in HDL$ as defined in Eq. 1. Hence, strictly following Algorithm 1 would indeed generate a *fi*-condition for S_{if} but, afterwards, move on with the next statement $S' \in HDL$ – leaving possible further if-statements within S_{then} and S_{else} unconsidered.
2. *Inner if-statements are subject to restricted system states*
   In order to correctly determine the strongest post-condition and, hence, the *fi*-condition, P is constantly updated in Algorithm 1. However, if a *fi*-condition for an inner if-statement is to be generated, the *if*-conditions of the respective outer if-statements have to be additionally employed. This is not yet incorporated in Algorithm 1.

Algorithm 1: Generation of *fi*-conditions

Data: Reversible HDL description HDL given as a list of statements S
Result: Reversible HDL description with *fi*-conditions

1 $P \leftarrow true$
2 **foreach** $S \in HDL$ **do**
3   **if** S *is* not *an if-statement* **then**
4          $P \leftarrow sp(S, P)$
5   **else**
6          $P_{\text{then}} \leftarrow sp(S_{\text{then}}, P \wedge B)$
7          $P_{\text{else}} \leftarrow sp(S_{\text{else}}, P \wedge \neg B)$
8          $P \leftarrow P_{\text{then}} \vee P_{\text{else}}$
9   add P_{then} as *fi*-condition to S

Obviously, the first issue can easily be handled by modifying Algorithm 1 such that not only top level statements are traversed, but also all statements within the respective *then*- and *else*-blocks. Dealing with the second issue, however, requires a more elaborated adjustment and is left for future work.

Algorithm 2: *fi*-generation for nested if-statements

Data: If-statement S_{if}, pre-condition P valid before S_{if}
Result: Returns post-condition of provided if-statement; recursively adds valid
      fi-conditions to all if-statements visited in the process (including itself)

/* Initialize block conditions   */
1 $P_{\text{then}} \leftarrow P \wedge B$
2 $P_{\text{else}} \leftarrow P \wedge \neg B$
/* Iterate over statements   */
3 **foreach** $S \in S_{\text{then}}$ **do**
4   **if** S *is if-statement* **then**
5          $P_{\text{then}} \leftarrow$ result of Algorithm 2 with S and P_{then}
6   attach P_{then} as *fi*-condition to S
7   **else**
8          $P_{\text{then}} \leftarrow sp(S, P_{\text{then}})$

9 **foreach** $S \in S_{\text{else}}$ **do**
10   **if** S *is if-statement* **then**
11         $P_{\text{else}} \leftarrow$ result of Algorithm 2 with S and P_{else}
12   attach P_{else} as *fi*-condition to S
13   **else**
14         $P_{else} \leftarrow sp(S, P_{\text{else}})$

15 **return** $P_{\text{then}} \vee P_{\text{else}}$

3.2 Check for Partial Reversibility

As discussed in Sect. 2, checking whether a given reversible HDL description indeed is fully reversible remains the second challenge designers have to address when creating control logic for reversible circuits and systems. A (sequence of) statements S is partially reversible, if there exist two different input states whose execution of S yields the same output state. Since assignment statements are by definition fully reversible, they can never be the reason for a partial reversible HDL description. In contrast, conditional statements allow for the execution of two different sequences of statements (the *then*-block and the *else*-block) and, hence, may indeed transform two different input states to the same output states (as illustrated in Example 2).

In order to check that, the method for *fi*-generation as introduced above can be re-used and accordingly extended. More precisely, recall that a (generated) post-condition $sp(S_{\text{then}}, P \wedge B)$ is a symbolic representation of all system states that originate from the execution of all statements in the *then*-block. Accordingly, a (generated) post-condition $sp(S_{\text{else}}, P \wedge \neg B)$ is a symbolic representation of all system states that originate from the execution of all statements in the *else*-block. Hence, if there exists an output state which originated from two different input states, the conjunction

$$sp(S_{\text{then}}, P \wedge B) \wedge sp(S_{\text{else}}, P \wedge \neg B) \tag{2}$$

must evaluate to true.

This constitutes a typical *satisfiability problem* (SAT, cf. [4]): If an assignment to all variables of an HDL description exists which satisfies Eq. 2, a system state showing the partial reversibility can be derived. If it has been shown that no such assignment exists, the HDL description has been proven to be fully reversible. In order to conduct those checks, various powerful solving engines (so called *SAT solvers*) have been proposed in the past and can be utilized for this purpose. To this end, Eq. 2 has to be converted into a proper format and, afterwards, simply passed to a SAT solver. Note that checking for partial reversibility has also been addressed in [5] for Boolean functions where a similar scheme is applied.

4 Conclusions

In this work, we considered the generation of control logic in HDL descriptions following the reversible computing paradigm. Here, obstacles occur since (1) corresponding descriptions may not necessarily be reversible and (2) conditional statements in reversible logic require a *fi*-condition in addition to the established *if*-condition. Both issues resulted in new design tasks which have been addressed manually thus far. We envisioned a solution which applies symbolic simulation as well as solvers for satisfiability problems in order to automatically tackle these tasks. In future work, we aim for addressing the open issues stated above and implementing the proposed ideas. Afterwards, an evaluation of the applicability of the resulting solutions will be conducted. If successful, important tasks for the design of reversible circuits and systems eventually got automated – the resulting methods will be an important part of future design tools.

Acknowledgments. This work has partially been supported by the EU COST Action IC1405.

References

1. Wille, R., Schönborn, E., Soeken, M., Drechsler, R.: SyReC: a hardware description language for the specification and synthesis of reversible circuits. Integr. VLSI J. **53**, 39–53 (2016)
2. Yokoyama, T., Axelsen, H.B., Glück, R.: Principles of a reversible programming language. In: Proceedings of 5th Conference on Computing Frontiers (CF 2008), pp. 43–54. ACM (2008)
3. Hoare, C.A.R.: An axiomatic basis for computer programming. Commun. ACM **12**(10), 576–580 (1969)
4. Biere, A., Biere, A., Heule, M., van Maaren, H., Walsh, T.: Handbook of Satisfiability. IOS Press, Amsterdam (2009)
5. Wille, R., Lye, A., Niemann, P.: Checking reversibility of Boolean functions. In: Conference on Reversible Computation (2016)

Quantum Computing

Design and Fabrication of CSWAP Gate Based on Nano-Electromechanical Systems

Mert Yüksel[1], Selçuk Oğuz Erbil[1], Atakan B. Arı[1],
and M. Selim Hanay[1,2(✉)]

[1] Department of Mechanical Engineering,
Bilkent University, Bilkent, Ankara 06800, Turkey
selimhanay@bilkent.edu.tr
[2] National Nanotechnology Research Center (UNAM),
Bilkent University, Bilkent, Ankara 06800, Turkey

Abstract. In order to reduce undesired heat dissipation, reversible logic offers a promising solution where the erasure of information can be avoided to overcome the Landauer limit. Among the reversible logic gates, Fredkin (CSWAP) gate can be used to compute any Boolean function in a reversible manner. To realize reversible computation gates, Nano-electromechanical Systems (NEMS) offer a viable platform, since NEMS can be produced *en masse* using microfabrication technology and controlled electronically at high-speeds. In this work-in-progress paper, design and fabrication of a NEMS-based implementation of a CSWAP gate is presented. In the design, the binary information is stored by the buckling direction of nanomechanical beams and CSWAP operation is accomplished through a mechanism which can selectively allow/block the forces from input stages to the output stages. The gate design is realized by fabricating NEMS devices on a Silicon-on-Insulator substrate.

Keywords: Reversible logic · CSWAP gate · NEMS · Buckling · Nanomechanical computation

1 Introduction

Transistor-based irreversible computation is the most commonly used paradigm for information processing which has shown a significant improvement in last few decades, especially with the adoption of complementary metal-oxide semiconductor (CMOS) transistor technology. However, further development of irreversible computing is limited by the inability to reduce heat dissipation. Landauer demonstrated that one-bit erasure of information can only be achieved with at least $k_B T ln2$, where k_B is the Boltzmann's constant and T is the operating temperature, amount of heat dissipation to the environment during the irreversible logic operation [1], which was experimentally demonstrated in 2012 [2]. Since then, reversible computation has been receiving great attention with its ability to lower heat dissipation. It was shown that reversible logic can also be used for information processing [3].

Development of reversible logic gates is considered as a basis of the reversible computation as proposed by CSWAP (Fredkin), Toffoli, Feynman, and others. CSWAP

© Springer International Publishing Switzerland 2016
S. Devitt and I. Lanese (Eds.): RC 2016, LNCS 9720, pp. 169–174, 2016.
DOI: 10.1007/978-3-319-40578-0_12

gate is one of the universal reversible logic gates, meaning that all Boolean operations can be performed with a system that consists of only CSWAP gates. Mechanical implementations of logic gates were proposed before [4–6]; however, the design proposed here has higher integration density and does not require external signal generators to drive resonance motion; as a result, the cost and complexity of the proposed system is expected to be lower. Developments in NEMS technology, which allows the fabrication of mechanical systems working at high speeds [7] and at high temperatures [8], enable the realization of reversible logic gates, such as the CSWAP gate architecture presented here.

In this work-in progress paper, NEMS based implementation of CSWAP gate design is introduced and working principle of the proposed system is discussed. Proposed design is computation-wise reversible. A basic fabrication process of the architecture is also demonstrated.

2 Information Storage via Buckling

In this work, we propose to store information in NEMS devices by using the buckling of beam structures [9]. Here, each beam represents one-bit information where the buckling direction (left or right) corresponds to logic 0 or logic 1. Figure 1 demonstrates how one-bit information can be registered on NEMS structures via buckling. The beams are designed as pinned and anchored at one end. The other end, where a compressive force is applied, is free to move axially and restrained from any transverse movement in order to observe longitudinal buckling. The beam is sandwiched by two electrodes (A1/B1) which apply a preloading force to the beam in order to determine buckling direction when the voltage is applied. For instance, if 5 V is applied to the electrode on the right, an electrostatic attraction force develops which preloads the beam to the right-hand side. After the beam is directed by the electrodes, a compressive force is applied via electrostatic actuation. Upon the exertion of the compressive force, the beam buckles to the direction determined by the preloading force. In order to buckle the beam, the compressive force must exceed the critical value which is determined by:

$$F_{critical} = \frac{\pi^2 EI}{L^2} \tag{1}$$

where E is Young's Modulus, L is the length of the beam and I is the moment of inertia [10].

Threshold for the compressive force to induce buckling is calculated to be 22.5 μN for a typical device with 2μm length, 150 nm width and 250 nm thickness. This force can be produced by an electrostatic comb drive composed of capacitive gates with 350 nm gaps as demonstrated in Fig. 1. The critical voltage applied to comb drive is calculated by:

$$V_{critical} = \sqrt{\frac{2dF_{critical}}{\epsilon N t}} \tag{2}$$

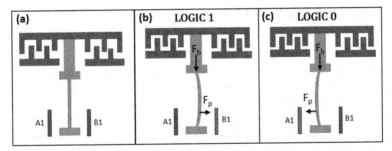

Fig. 1. Demonstration of one-bit information storage: (a) Off-state. Nano-mechanical beam is shown in gray, electrodes used to preload the data are shown in blue and the comb-drive to induce buckling is shown in green. (b) On-State Logic 1: A voltage is applied to B1 gate to first preload the beam (exerting F_p), then the beam is buckled to the right by the application of buckling force F_b. (c) On-State Logic 0: A1 gate first preloads the beam, which is then buckled to the left. (Color figure online)

where ϵ is electric permittivity, N is number of fingers, t is thickness of a finger and d is gap spacing between fingers of the comb drive [11].

Different dimensions for the beam can be considered to optimize N and $V_{critical}$. It is more convenient to have fewer fingers for comb drive for simplicity of the design. Also, having a low critical voltage is desired to decrease the power consumption. For different lengths (L) of the beam, $N - V_{critical}$ relation is shown in Fig. 2. It can be observed that for the longer lengths of the beams, it is easier to reach $F_{critical}$ with lower $V_{critical}$. Although $V_{critical}$ levels are relatively higher than voltage values commonly used in digital circuits, these voltage levels can be achieved with low power using DC-to-DC voltage converters. More importantly, triggering voltage will only be used to initiate buckling process – the actual data to be written can still be applied at the standard logic voltages such as 5.0 V or 3.3 V. In this regard, triggering voltage is similar to the clock signals of conventional digital circuits: each stage of the logic gates computes the output when a triggering voltage compresses the set of beams in turn.

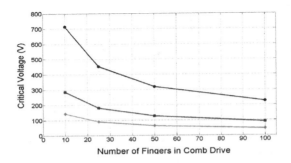

Fig. 2. Number of fingers (N) vs. critical voltage ($V_{critical}$) for beams with different lengths. Top green curve is for 2 μm, blue curve is for 5 μm and bored curve is for 10 μm long beams. (Color figure online)

3 NEMS Based CSWAP Gate

3.1 Design

Principle of the CSWAP gate is to swap the inputs when the controller bit is set (logic high), and to rehash the inputs when the controller bit is reset (logic low). In this design, inputs are applied to the gate by preloading the beams to the logic 1 or 0 states. The displacement of the input beams, after they buckle, leads to compression or tension of the spring-like structures linking inputs to outputs (Fig. 3). Through these links, the input beams exert either a push or pull force, depending on their logic state, to preload the output beams. Each output beam is connected to both input beams and the equivalent preloading force determines the eventual state of the output beam.

The symmetry of the force transmission between input beams to output beams is broken by the controller beam, C. Controller beam (C) disrupts a direct transmission of one of the input forces (A or B), by locating one of its arm to the gap found on the connecting beam. When C is logic 0, the connection between A and BO, and B and AO are disrupted, therefore the preloading will favor A for A0, and B for BO respectively, which will map the outputs in the way of A to A0 and B to B0. On the other hand, when C is logic 1, the connection between A and AO, and B and BO are disrupted by controller, consequently outputs AO and BO will swap the inputs and read B and A respectively. Thus, CSWAP gate architecture is mechanically achieved as demonstrated in Fig. 3. The required processing area for one CSWAP gate is approximately 150 μm^2 which includes the part of the comb drive transmitting buckling force. This area translates into an integration density of 200,000 gates per cm^2.

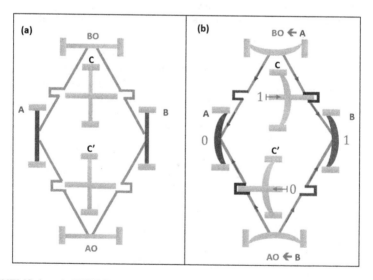

Fig. 3. NEMS based CSWAP gate (a) CSWAP architecture (b) example demonstration of CSWAP operation. Inputs are taken as A = 0, B = 1, C = 1. Outputs; AO = B = 1, BO = A = 1, C' = 1. Forces transmitted by the input stages through the springs are either blocked or uninterrupted depending on the controller bit.

3.2   Nano-Fabrication

A proof-of-principle fabrication process has been implemented using dices of a commercially available Silicon on Insulator (SOI) wafer which has a composition of: 250 nm thick p-doped Silicon on top of 3 μm buried oxide (BOX) with a 650 μm silicon base substrate. After the standard cleaning procedure, Electron-beam lithography was performed using PMMA bilayer as resist. Following the patterning, a 60 nm thick layer of SiO_2 dry etch mask was deposited via E-Beam evaporation. The sample was left in an acetone bath for lift-off overnight. For the next step, the top Silicon layer is anisotropically etched with an Inductively Coupled Plasma device, using Cl_2 plasma, until the BOX layer. Then the patterned Silicon structures were suspended by wet etching the BOX layer using a 1:7 Buffered Oxide Etch solution. Since the SiO_2 dry etch mask was also removed during the wet etching step, there was no need for an extra mask removal step (Fig. 4).

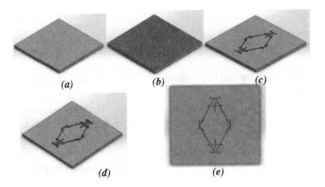

Fig. 4. Fabrication Process Flow: (a) SOI Chip, (b) after EBL and SiO_2 deposition, (c) after lift-off process, (d) after ICP etching of Si layer, (e) topside view of the system

For future progress, Au electrodes and comb drive will be fabricated on the sample respectively. Electrodes will be patterned by EBL. Following that step, a layer Au will be deposited by a Physical Thermal Deposition device and the sample will be left for lift-off. After the fabrication of the electrodes, comb drives will be fabricated using similar steps (Fig. 5).

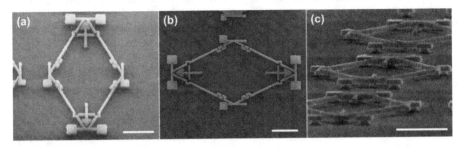

Fig. 5. SEM images of the fabricated proof-of-principle device from different perspectives. The scale bars are 3 μm in each image.

4   Conclusion

In this work-in-progress paper, logically-reversible CSWAP gates are designed using NEMS technology. One-bit data can be stored on a nano-mechanical beam depending on its direction of buckling. Basic calculations are presented for forces and voltages necessary to induce buckling in nanoscale beams. A basic nano-fabrication process is demonstrated to implement the CSWAP gate. By further integrating structures to trigger buckling process, information processing will be demonstrated in the future. With its large integration density and high speeds, NEMS technology is a promising platform to implement reversible logic operations.

Acknowledgements. This work was funded by The Scientific and Technological Research Council of Turkey (TÜBİTAK) with project number 115E833. We acknowledge support from European Cooperation in Science and Technology (COST) under Action IC1405.

References

1. Landauer, R.: Irreversibility and heat generation in the computing process. IBM J. Res. Dev. **5**, 183–191 (1961)
2. Berut, A., Arakelyan, A., Petrosyan, A., Ciliberto, S., Dillenschneider, R., Lutz, E.: Experimental verification of Landauer's principle linking information and thermodynamics. Nature **483**, 187–189 (2012)
3. Bennet, C.H.: Logical reversibility of computation. IBM J. Res. Dev. **17**(6), 525–532 (1973)
4. Sharma, A., Ram, W.S., Amarnath, C.: Mechanical logic devices and circuits. NaCoMM **9**, 235–239 (2009)
5. Wenzler, J.S., Dunn, T., Toffoli, T., Mohanty, P.: A nanomechanical Fredkin gate. Nano Lett. **14**(1), 89–93 (2013)
6. Mahboob, I., Mounaix, M., Nishiguchi, K., Fujiwara, A., Yamaguchi, H.: A multimode electromechanical parametric resonator array. Sci. Rep. 4 (2014). Article no. 4448
7. Huang, X.M.H., Zorman, C.A., Mehregany, M., Roukes, M.L.: Nanodevice motion at microwave frequencies. Nature **421**, 496–496 (2003)
8. Lee, T.H.: Electromechanical computing at 500 °C using silicon carbide. Science **329** (5997), 1316–1318 (2010)
9. Merkle, R.C.: Two types of mechanical reversible logic. Nanotechnology **4**(2), 114 (1993)
10. Hopcroft, M.A.: What is the Young's modulus of silicon. IEEE J. Microelectromech. Syst. **19**, 229–238 (2010)
11. Legtenberg, R., Groeneveld, A.W., Elwenspoek, M.: Comb-drive actuators for large displacements. J. Micromech. Microeng. **6**, 320–329 (1996). IOPscience

Design of p-Valued Deutsch Quantum Gates with Multiple Control Signals and Mixed Polarity

Claudio Moraga$^{(\boxtimes)}$

Chair Informatics 1, TU Dortmund University, 44227 Dortmund, Germany
claudio.moraga@tu-dortmund.de

Abstract. This paper presents a detailed study of the realization of p–valued Deutsch quantum gates with $n > 2$ controlling signals, both under conjunctive and disjunctive control, and including zero or mixed polarity of the controlling signals. It is shown that the realization complexity is in $O(p^{n-1})$. The realization comprises only Muthukrishnan-Stroud elementary quantum gates.

Keywords: p-valued Deutsch gate · Multi-control · Mixed polarity · Quantum computing

1 Introduction

Deutsch introduced in 1989 [3] a universal (binary) quantum gate that may be seen as a generalization of the earlier reversible Toffoli gate [8]. In the quantum world, the work on systems with p "levels" is possible and can in principle offer a trade-off between complexity of realization and computing capability of elementary circuits. (See e.g. the introduction of [6]).

The development of p-valued quantum gates and circuits was strongly influenced by the work of Muthukrishnan and Stroud [6], who introduced a model for a multi-level quantum system and proved that any unitary operations on any number of p-level systems can be decomposed into elementary controlled gates working on just two "qupits" [1] at a time. The elementary gates being active iff the control qupit is in the state $|p-1\rangle$, otherwise being inhibited and behaving as an identity. Furthermore, the authors reported experimental realization of controlled gates based on the linear ion trap model. In what follows, p will be a prime, with $p > 2$, taking advantage of additions modulo p and the fact that both p and p^k are odd.

A design of a p-levels Deutsch gate with **two** control qupits was briefly presented in [1]; revisited and given an extended functionality in [4, 5]. It was shown that the Deutsch gate may be realized with $2p + 1$ MS auxiliary gates. Notice that if $p = 2$, $2p + 1 = 5$, and this value equals that of [2].

Work leading to this paper was partially supported by the EU COST-Action IC-1405 on Reversible Computation – Extending Horizons of Computing.

S. Devitt and I. Lanese (Eds.): RC 2016, LNCS 9720, pp. 175–180, 2016.
DOI: 10.1007/978-3-319-40578-0_13

2 Realization of a *p*-Valued Deutsch Quantum Gate with Three Controlling Qupits

In analogy to [2], a Deutsch quantum gate with **three** controlling qupits will be decomposed in a cascade of simple Muthukrishnan-Stroud (MS) gates, each controlled by a different qupit, followed by a cascade of Deutsch gates controlled by two qupits –(which, as shown in [5] may also be realized using only MS gates)– closing with a gate with "pseudo-three" control qupits. It is fairly clear that a closing gate taking directly all three control qupits would make the gate scheme "recursive". This is why a controlled-controlled-X^1 was used to drive the last gate on the target line, this sub-structure, however, repeated $p - 1$ times. The proposed realization is shown in Fig. 1.

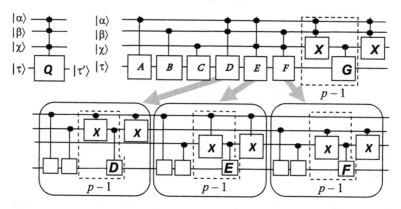

Fig. 1. Realization of a Deutsch quantum gate with three control qupits. Top: High level scheme. Bottom: Detailed realization of the double-controlled auxiliary gates.

For the analysis of behaviour of the Deutsch gate, the following notational simplifications will be adopted:

- The gate A will be merged with the MS gates controlled by $|\alpha\rangle$ inside the explicit realizations of D and E, respectively, to build a gate A.
- The gate B will be merged with the MS gates controlled by $|\beta\rangle$ inside the explicit realizations of D and F, respectively, to build a gate B.
- The gate C will be merged with the MS gates controlled by $|\chi\rangle$ inside the explicit realizations of E and F, respectively, to build a gate C.
- The controlled gates inside the blocks of the realization of D, E, and F, will be called D, E, and F, respectively.

Table 1 summarizes the behaviour specification of the MS-gates building the Deutsch gate. In the table $q = p - 1$, and $|\omega\rangle$ represents any state different from $|p-1\rangle$. The column

---

[1] X represents a Muthukrishnan-Stroud (MS) gate realizing a p-valued Pauli matrix shifting by 1 (modulo p) the state of its input qupit when its controlling qupits are in the state $|p - 1\rangle$.

labeled **and** specifies the behavior of the Deutsch gate with conjunctive control (*all* controlling qupits must be in state $|p-1\rangle$ to activate the Deutsch gate), meanwhile the column labeled **or**, shows the specification with disjunctive control (*at least one* controlling qupit must be in state $|p-1\rangle$). The solution of the corresponding seven variables systems of equations is given in details in [5]. The results are presented in Table 2.

Table 1. Abstract level behavior of the Deutsch gate of Fig. 1

	$\|\alpha\rangle$	$\|\beta\rangle$	$\|\chi\rangle$	A	B	C	D	E	F	G	and	or
0	$\|\omega\rangle$	$\|\omega\rangle$	$\|\omega\rangle$	I	I	I	I^q	I^q	I^q	I^q	I	I
1	$\|\omega\rangle$	$\|\omega\rangle$	$\|p-1\rangle$	I	I	C	I^q	E^q	F^q	G^q	I	Q
2	$\|\omega\rangle$	$\|p-1\rangle$	$\|\omega\rangle$	I	B	I	D^q	I^q	F	I^q	I	Q
3	$\|p-1\rangle$	$\|\omega\rangle$	$\|\omega\rangle$	A	I	I	D	E	I^q	I^q	I	Q
4	$\|\omega\rangle$	$\|p-1\rangle$	$\|p-1\rangle$	I	B	C	D^q	E^q	I^q	G^q	I	Q
5	$\|p-1\rangle$	$\|\omega\rangle$	$\|p-1\rangle$	A	I	C	D	I^q	F^q	G^q	I	Q
6	$\|p-1\rangle$	$\|p-1\rangle$	$\|\omega\rangle$	A	B	I	I^q	E	F	G	I	Q
7	$\|p-1\rangle$	$\|p-1\rangle$	$\|p-1\rangle$	A	B	C	I^q	I^q	I^q	I^q	Q	Q

As shown in Table 2, it is fairly obvious that in the case of conjunctive control, the identity blocks E and F may be deleted. As shown in [5], the Deutsch gate with conjunctive control requires $2p^2 + 4p + 1$ MS gates, meanwhile the Deutsch gate with disjunctive control needs $2p^2 + 8p - 1$ MS gates. In summary the realization complexity of the gate is in $O(p^2)$.

With respect to the required roots of Q it should be recalled that any non-singular matrix has a p-th root [9]. A p-th root of Q may easily be calculated in Matlab or Scilab with the statement **expm[(1/p)*logm(Q)]**. Since Q by definition is unitary, and unitary matrices form a multiplicative group, then all integer powers of Q are also unitary. Moreover in [4] it was shown that the p-th root of Q is also unitary. Therefore the quantum realizability of all required MS gates is secured.

Table 2. Specification of the auxiliary target gates for the realization of a Deutsch gate with three controlling qupits

A	B	C	D	E	F	G
Conjunctive control						
$\sqrt[p^2]{Q}$	$\sqrt[p^2]{Q^{p-1}}$	$\sqrt[p]{Q^{p-1}}$	$\sqrt[p^2]{Q^{-1}}$	I	I	$\sqrt[p]{Q^{-1}}$
Disjunctive control						
$\sqrt[p^2]{Q^{(p-1)^2}}$	$\sqrt[p^2]{Q^{p-1}}$	$\sqrt[p]{Q}$	$\sqrt[p^2]{Q^{p-1}}$	$\sqrt[p]{Q}$	$\sqrt[p]{Q}$	$\sqrt[p]{Q^{-1}}$

3 Introducing Mixed Polarity

The concept of "mixed polarity" applied to Toffoli gates was possibly introduced in [7] for the binary case, to indicate which controlling qupits are effective in state $|1\rangle$, and which are effective in state $|0\rangle$. In the circuit representation, "white dots" were used to indicate that a $|0\rangle$ qupit would (contribute to) activate the gate. For the p–valued domain, in the context of Muthukrishnan-Stroud gates, the controlling state $|p - 1\rangle$ is the activating one and all others –($|\omega\rangle$ states)– are inhibiting states. A polarity will make of an $|\omega\rangle$ state, an activating state. In the circuit representation not a white dot, but a "white diamond" will be used to indicate that *any* non-$|p - 1\rangle$ state will (contribute to) activate the corresponding gate. This is illustrated in Fig. 2.

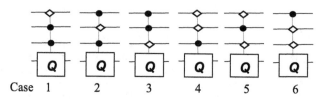

Fig. 2. Deutsch gates with three controlling qupits and mixed polarity

The behaviour of the Deutsch gate for the 6 cases presented in Fig. 2, under conjunctive control, and the specification of the component MS-gates may be found in [5].

With respect to disjunctive control with mixed polarity, the following two cases have been considered:

Case 7: A gate is active iff *any two* control qupits are in state $|p - 1\rangle$ and the state of the remaining control qupit is $|\omega\rangle$. Otherwise the gate is inhibited and behaves as the identity. (This represents the disjunctive union of Case 1 *or* Case 2 *or* Case 3).

Case 8: A gate is active iff *any* control qupit is in state $|p - 1\rangle$ and the states of the remaining two control qupits are $|\omega\rangle$. Otherwise the gate is inhibited and behaves as the identity. (This represents the disjunctive union of Case 4 *or* Case 5 *or* Case 6).

The behaviour of the Deutsch gate for the above two cases and the specification of the component MS-gates may be found in [5].

4   On the Complexity of Realization for Any Number of Control Qupits

In [2], for the realization of (binary) Toffoli gates with n control signals, the gates on the target line were controlled by signals following a Grey code (without the word 00... 0), leading to a realization with minimal cost. Notice that one selector word is (11...1) producing a linear combination of all control signals.

In the case of p–valued Deutsch quantum gates with three control qupits, for the realization of the gate, as mentioned in Sect. 2, an increasing "pseudo Hamming weight" was considered, where the pseudo Hamming weight corresponds to the number of qupits that directly control a given sub-circuit or gate on the target line. It is clear that it would not be possible to take all three control qupits to directly –(conjunctively)– drive one of the MS auxiliary gates on the target line, because that would make the realization proposal recursive. Instead, two control qupits were used to control a Pauli X-gate which would shift by $1 \bmod p$ the state of the third control qupit, which would then drive a G-gate on the target line. This scheme is repeated $p - 1$ times, as in the realization of the Deutsch gate with two control qupits [5]. Since the controlled-controlled-X has a realization complexity of $2p + 1$ MS gates, but will be repeated $p - 1$ times, this leads to a realization complexity in $O(p^2)$. Inductively reasoning allows to see that for any n controlling qupits, a realization with a block containing $(p - 1) X$ gates controlled by $(n - 1)$ qupits will be needed; where each one of them may be realized by a sub-block containing $(p - 1) X$ gates controlled by $(n - 2)$ qupits. This will continue until reaching sub-blocks with $(p - 1) X$ gates controlled by $(n - (n - 1))$ qupits, i.e. MS gates. This leads to a final realization complexity in $O(p^{n-1})$, where this represents the number of single controlled elementary gates needed for the realization. This, at the same time, illustrates the Muthukrishnan-Stroud realizability of the p-valued Deutsch quantum gates.

5 Conclusions

The proposed scheme for the realization of p-valued Deutsch quantum gates with two control qupits may be extended to the realization of gates with n control qupits using only Muthukrishnan-Stroud elementary quantum gates on two qupits. Both conjunctive and disjunctive control under different polarities were shown to be possible. Let a "Toffoli-set" comprise all p–valued Deutsch quantum gates such that Q is self-inverse (i.e., besides being unitary, Q is Hermitian). In the case of gates from this Toffoli-set, strong simplifications are possible, since $Q^{eben} = I$ and $Q^{odd} = Q$. Notice that from the last follows that an odd root of Q also equals Q. Moreover, since p is a prime and $p > 2$, both p and p^k, $k \in \mathbb{N}$, are odd. Therefore, e.g., $\sqrt[p^2]{Q^{3p+2}} = Q$.

Finally, the proposed realization scales with n with a complexity in $O(p^{n-1})$.

References

1. Aharonov, D., Ben-Or, M.: Fault-tolerant quantum computation with constant error rate. SIAM J. Comput. **38**(4), 1207–1282 (2008)
2. Barenco, A., Bennett, C.H., Cleve, R., Di Vincenzo, D.P., Margolus, N., Shor, P., Sleator, T., Smolin, J.A., Weinfurter, H.: Elementary gates for quantum computation. Phys. Rev. A **52**, 3457–3467 (1995)
3. Deutsch, D.: Quantum computational networks. Proc. Roy. Soc. Lond. A **425**, 73–90 (1989)
4. Moraga, C.: Aspects of reversible and quantum computing in a p-valued domain. IEEE JETCAS **6**(1) (2016, in press). doi:10.1109/JETCAS.2016.2528658
5. Moraga, C.: Realization of p-valued Deutsch quantum gates under multi-control and mixed polarity. Research report 851, Faculty of Computer Science, TU Dortmund University. ISSN 0933-6192 (2016)
6. Muthukrishnan, A., Stroud, C.R.: Multilevalued logic gates for quantum computation. Phys. Rev. A **62**, 052309 (2000)

Using πDDs for Nearest Neighbor Optimization of Quantum Circuits

Robert Wille[1,2]([✉]), Nils Quetschlich[3], Yuma Inoue[4], Norihito Yasuda[4], and Shin-ichi Minato[4]

[1] Institute for Integrated Circuits, Johannes Kepler University Linz, Linz, Austria
robert.wille@jku.at
[2] Cyber-Physical Systems, DFKI GmbH, Bremen, Germany
[3] University of Bremen, 28359 Bremen, Germany
nquet@informatik.uni-bremen.de
[4] Hokkaido University, Sapporo, Japan
{yuma,yasuda,minato}@ist.hokudai.ac.jp

Abstract. Recent accomplishments in the development of quantum circuits motivated research in Computer-Aided Design for quantum circuits. Here, how to consider physical constraints in general and so-called nearest neighbor constraints in particular is an objective of recent developments. Re-ordering the given qubits in a circuit provides thereby a common strategy in order to reduce the corresponding costs. But since this leads to a significant complexity, existing solutions either worked towards a single order only (and, hence, exclude better options) or suffer from high runtimes when considering all possible options. In this work, we provide an alternative which utilizes so-called πDDs for this purpose. They allow for the efficient representation and manipulation of sets of permutations and, hence, provide the ideal data-structure for the considered problem. Experimental evaluations confirm that, by utilizing πDDs, optimal or almost optimal results can be generated in a fraction of the time needed by exact solutions.

1 Introduction

Quantum computation [1] exploits quantum mechanical phenomena such as superposition, entanglement, etc. and utilizes qubits rather than conventional bits for computation. This allows for solving many practically relevant problems much faster than with conventional circuits. Prominent examples include problems such as factorization (for which Shor's algorithm [2] has been proposed) or database search (for which Groover's iteration [3] has been proposed). While first corresponding quantum circuits have been developed by hand, the design of more complex quantum functionality will require automatic methods – motivating the research in *Computer-Aided Design* (CAD) for quantum circuits. Since each quantum computation is inherently reversible, methods for the design of reversible circuits are frequently utilized for this purpose.

This led to the development of first CAD methods e.g. for the synthesis of reversible circuits [4–12], the corresponding mapping to quantum circuits [13–16], or design schemes which directly address quantum circuit synthesis [17–21]. Besides that, physical constraints and how to already consider them during the

© Springer International Publishing Switzerland 2016
S. Devitt and I. Lanese (Eds.): RC 2016, LNCS 9720, pp. 181–196, 2016.
DOI: 10.1007/978-3-319-40578-0_14

design phase has received increasing attention. In particular, the satisfaction of so-called nearest neighbor constraints was an objective of recent developments. Here, the interaction distance between the involved qubits is limited and it is required that computations are performed between adjacent, i.e. nearest neighbor, qubits only. Corresponding CAD-methods addressing this restriction have been proposed e.g. in [22–27].

In this work, we consider the *global reordering scheme* as employed in [22, 26, 27] whose main idea is to determine a qubit order which – applied through the entire circuit – yields the smallest nearest neighbor costs. This often provides the basis for further optimization steps and, hence, constitutes an important part of nearest neighbor optimization. However, since determining the best possible qubit order requires the consideration of $n!$ possible permutations (where n is the number of qubits), existing solutions either

- apply a heuristic which aims for generating a single, dedicated permutation only which, in many cases, is far from optimal or
- apply an exact approach which guarantees an optimal solution but suffers from the underlying complexity.

Motivated by this, we are considering the research question how to optimize heuristic global reordering in order to generate nearly-optimal results while, at the same time, remaining efficient. To this end, we propose the utilization of *Permutation Decision Diagrams* (πDDs, [28]) – a data-structure for the efficient representation and manipulation of sets of permutations. Using πDDs it is possible to consider all permutations at once in an efficient fashion and to subsequently reduce them with respect to the nearest neighbor constraints. This provides an ideal compromise between the existing solutions which directly worked towards a single permutation only and, hence, likely excluded better options or had to deal with an inefficient handling of the complexity. Experimental evaluations confirm the benefits of the proposed approach: In all cases, optimal or almost optimal results are generated in a fraction of the runtime needed for the exact approach.

The remainder of this work is structured as follows: Sect. 2 reviews the background on quantum circuits and nearest neighbor optimization, while Sect. 3 reviews the corresponding optimization methods. These sections build the motivation of the proposed approach whose general idea is afterwards presented in Sect. 4. Then, details on the solution are presented in Sect. 5. Finally, experimental results are reported and discussed in Sect. 6 and the paper is concluded in Sect. 7.

2   Background

In order to keep the paper self-contained, this section briefly reviews the quantum circuit model usually applied in electronic design automation and provides the background on nearest neighbor optimization.

2.1   Quantum Circuits

In contrast to conventional computation, *quantum computation* [1] works on qubits instead of bits. A *qubit* is a two level quantum system, described by a two dimensional complex Hilbert space. The two orthogonal quantum states $|0\rangle$ $\equiv \left(\begin{smallmatrix}1\\0\end{smallmatrix}\right)$ and $|1\rangle \equiv \left(\begin{smallmatrix}0\\1\end{smallmatrix}\right)$ are used to represent the Boolean values 0 and 1. Any state of a qubit may be written as $|x\rangle = \alpha |0\rangle + \beta |1\rangle$, where the amplitudes α and β are complex numbers with $|\alpha|^2 + |\beta|^2 = 1$.

Operations on n-qubits states are performed through multiplication of appropriate $2^n \times 2^n$ unitary matrices. Thus, each quantum computation is inherently reversible but manipulates qubits rather than pure logic values. At the end of the computation, a qubit can be measured. Then, depending on the current state of the qubit, either a 0 (with probability of $|\alpha|^2$) or a 1 (with probability of $|\beta|^2$) returns. After the measurement, the state of the qubit is destroyed.

Quantum computations are usually represented by *quantum circuits*. Here, the respective qubits are denoted by solid *circuit lines*. Operations are represented by *quantum gates*. Table 1 lists common quantum gates together with the corresponding unitary matrices describing their operation. In order to perform operations on more than one qubit, *controlled quantum gates* are applied. These gates are composed of a *target line* $|t\rangle$ and a control line $|c\rangle$ and realize the unitary operation represented by the matrix

$$M = \begin{pmatrix} 1 & 0 & 0 & 0 \\ 0 & 1 & 0 & 0 \\ 0 & 0 & & \\ 0 & 0 & & U \end{pmatrix}$$

where U denotes the operation applied to the target line. In the remainder of this work, we use the following formal notation:

Definition 1. *A quantum circuit is denoted by the cascade $G = g_1 g_2 \ldots g_{|G|}$ (in figures drawn from left to right), where $|G|$ denotes the total number of gates. The number of qubits and, thus, the number of circuit lines is denoted by n. The costs of a quantum circuit (also denoted as* quantum cost*) are defined by the number $|G|$ of gates.*

Table 1. Quantum gates

Hadamard-Gate	Pauli-Y-Gate
$\boxed{H}$ $\frac{1}{\sqrt{2}}\begin{pmatrix}1 & 1 \\ 1 & -1\end{pmatrix}$	$\boxed{Y}$ $\begin{pmatrix}0 & -i \\ i & 0\end{pmatrix}$
Pauli-X-Gate	**Pauli-Z-Gate**
$\boxed{X}$ $\begin{pmatrix}0 & 1 \\ 1 & 0\end{pmatrix}$	$\boxed{Z}$ $\begin{pmatrix}1 & 0 \\ 0 & -1\end{pmatrix}$
V-Gate	**S-Gate**
$\boxed{V}$ $\frac{1+i}{2}\begin{pmatrix}1 & -i \\ -i & 1\end{pmatrix}$	$\boxed{}$ $\begin{pmatrix}1 & 0 \\ 0 & e^{\frac{i\pi}{2}}\end{pmatrix}$
W-Gate	**T-Gate**
$\boxed{}$ $\frac{1}{2}\begin{pmatrix}1+\sqrt{i} & 1-\sqrt{i} \\ 1-\sqrt{i} & 1+\sqrt{i}\end{pmatrix}$	$\boxed{}$ $\begin{pmatrix}1 & 0 \\ 0 & e^{\frac{i\pi}{4}}\end{pmatrix}$

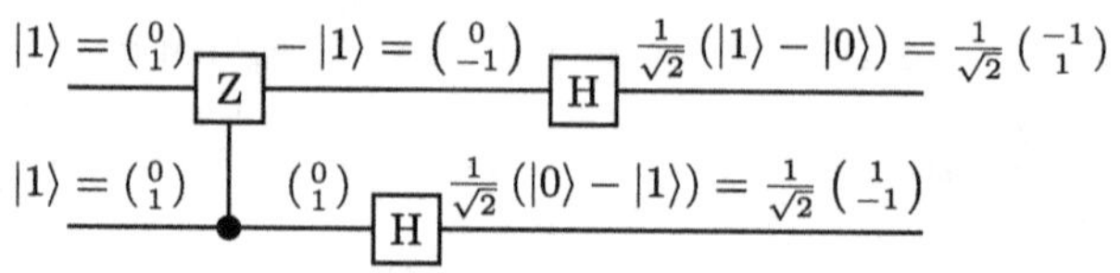

Fig. 1. Quantum circuit

Example 1. Figure 1 shows a quantum circuit composed of $n = 2$ circuit lines and $|G| = 3$ gates. This circuit gets $|11\rangle$ as input and transforms the qubits as indicated at the circuit signals.

In the following, we do not focus on the dedicated functionality of a quantum circuit, but on the structure and whether it satisfies nearest neighbor constraints (as reviewed next). To this end, we omit unary quantum gates (as they are irrelevant for nearest neighbor optimization) and generically denote quantum gates using the notation ●—U.

2.2 Nearest Neighbor Optimization

In the recent years, researchers proposed several physical realizations for quantum circuits. This led to a better understanding of their physical limitations and constraints, e.g. with respect to the interaction distance, decoherence time, or scaling (see e.g. [29–31]). Besides that, so-called *nearest neighbor constraints* have to be satisfied for many quantum circuit architectures. This particularly holds for technologies based on proposals for ion traps [32–34], nitrogen-vacancy centers in diamonds [35,36], quantum dots emitting linear cluster states linked by linear optics [37], laser manipulated quantum dots in a cavity [38], and superconducting qubits [39,40]. Here, nearest neighbor constraints limit the interaction distance between gate qubits and require that computations are performed between adjacent, i.e. nearest neighbor, qubits only.

In order to formalize this restriction for electronic design automation, a corresponding metric representing the costs of a quantum circuit to become nearest neighbor compliant has been introduced in [22]. There, the authors defined the *Nearest Neighbor Cost* as follows.

Definition 2. *Assume a 2-qubit quantum gate $g(c,t)$ with a control at the line c and a target at line t where c and t are numerical indices holding $0 \leq c, t < n$. Then, the Nearest Neighbor Cost (NNC) for g is calculated using the distance between the target and the control line. More precisely,*

$$NNC(g) = |c - t| - 1.$$

As a result, a single control gate g is termed nearest neighbor compliant *if* $NNC(g) = 0$. *1-qubit gates are assumed to have NNC of 0. The resulting NNC for a complete quantum circuit is defined by the sum of the NNC of its gates:*

$$NNC(G) = \sum_{g \in G} NNC(g).$$

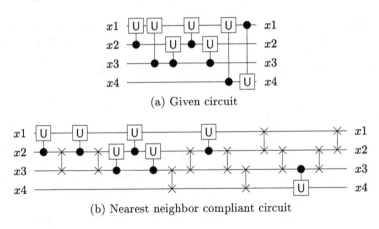

(a) Given circuit

(b) Nearest neighbor compliant circuit

Fig. 2. Establishing nearest neighbor compliance

A quantum circuit G is termed nearest neighbor compliant *if* $NNC(G) = 0$, *i.e.
if all quantum gates are 1-qubit gates or adjacent 2-qubit gates.*

Example 2. Consider the circuit G depicted in Fig. 2(a). Gates are denoted by $G = g_1 \ldots g_7$ from the left to the right. As can be seen, gates g_2, g_6, as well as g_7 are non-adjacent and have nearest neighbor costs of $NNC(g_2) = 1$, $NNC(g_6) = 2$, as well as $NNC(g_7) = 2$, respectively. Hence, the entire circuit has nearest neighbor costs of $NNC(G) = 5$.

A naive way to make an arbitrarily given quantum circuit nearest neighbor compliant is to modify it by additional SWAP gates.

Definition 3. *A* SWAP gate *is a quantum gate* $g(q_i, q_j)$ *including two qubits* q_i, q_j *and maps* $(q_0, \ldots, q_i, q_j, \ldots, q_{n-1})$ *to* $(q_0, \ldots, q_j, q_i, \ldots, q_{n-1})$. *That is, a SWAP gate realizes the exchange of two quantum values (in figures drawn using two connected × symbols).*

These SWAP gates allow for making all control lines and target lines adjacent and, by this, help to satisfy the nearest neighbor constraint. More precisely, a cascade of adjacent SWAP gates can be inserted in front of each gate g with non-adjacent circuit lines in order to shift the control line of g towards the target line, or vice versa, until they are adjacent. Afterwards, SWAP gates are inserted to restore the original ordering of circuit lines.

Example 3. Consider again the circuit depicted in Fig. 2(a). In order to make this circuit nearest neighbor compliant, SWAP gates in front and after all these gates are inserted as shown in Fig. 2(b).

3   Motivation

Adding SWAP gates in a naive fashion as reviewed in the previous section is a simple way of transforming any given quantum circuit into a nearest neighbor compliant version (in fact, this can be conducted in linear time with respect to the number of gates). But the insertion of SWAP gates obviously increases the quantum cost: For each non-adjacent gate, $2 \cdot (|t - c| - 1)$ SWAP gates are additionally inserted to the circuit. In order to minimize these additional costs, researchers investigated how to reduce the number of SWAP gate insertions in order to make a given quantum circuit nearest neighbor compliant.

A broad variety of different approaches has been presented for this purpose – including solutions relying on templates [22], local and global reordering strategies [22], dedicated data-structures [23–25], etc. Also exact approaches, i.e. solutions guaranteeing the minimal number of SWAP gate insertions, have been proposed [26,27]. The work published in [27] provides a good overview. All these approaches particularly focus on how to properly reorder the qubits in the circuit so that the respective interaction distance (and, hence, the number of required SWAP gates) is reduced.

In this work, we consider *global reordering schemes*, where the main objective is to determine a qubit order which – applied through the entire circuit – yields the smallest nearest neighbor costs. Results obtained from global reordering often provide the basis for further optimization steps and, hence, constitute an important part of nearest neighbor optimization. Unfortunately, determining the best qubit order requires the explicit checking of all possible qubit permutations. For a circuit with n qubits, this yields $n!$ possible combinations – a significant complexity. Two complementary solutions to deal with this complexity represent the current state-of-the-art:

The first one is a heuristic solution proposed in [22]. Here, a good permutation is determined by calculating the *contribution* of each circuit line of a given quantum circuit G. Therefore, for each 2-qubit gate g of G with control line at position c and target line at position t, the NNC value (see Definition 2) is calculated. Afterwards, this value is added to variables imp_c and imp_t which are used to store the "impacts" of the circuit lines c and t on the total NNC, respectively. More precisely, the impact imp_i of the ith circuit line ($0 \leq i < n$) is calculated by

$$imp_i = \sum_{g(c,t) \in G \ | \ c=i \ \vee \ t=i} NNC(g).$$

Using these impacts, the algorithm selects the circuit line with the greatest value and permutes it with the middle circuit line. If the selected line already is the middle line, the one with the next greatest impact is selected. This whole procedure is repeated until no further improvements are achieved.

The second one is an exact solution proposed in [26,27], which determines the best possible permutation. To this end, the underlying design problem is formulated as an *optimal linear arrangement problem* which, in turn, is formulated as an instance of *pseudo-Boolean Optimization* (PBO, see e.g. [41]). By utilizing corresponding solving engines, the resulting PBO problem is solved.

Example 4. Consider again the circuit depicted in Fig. 2(a). Applying the heuristic of [22], the resulting impacts of the circuits lines are $imp_{x1} = 5$, $imp_{x2} = 0$, $imp_{x3} = 1$, and $imp_{x4} = 4$, respectively. Permuting the line order such that the lines with high impact are located in the middle (descending towards the outer lines) results in the circuit depicted in Fig. 3(a). Compared to the naive method (see result depicted in Fig. 2(b)), this reduces the number of required SWAP gates from 10 to 4. However, significantly further reductions can be achieved

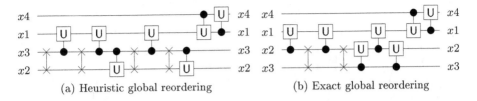

(a) Heuristic global reordering   (b) Exact global reordering

Fig. 3. Global reordering (applied to the circuit from Fig. 2(a))

if the best permutation is determined (using the exact solution from [26,27]). Then, a circuit as shown in Fig. 3(b) results which reduces the required number of SWAP gates by another 50 % to 2.

Overall, it can be concluded that the heuristic solution provides a very efficient way of further reducing the number of SWAP gates compared to the naive method. But the obtained results are still far from optimal. In contrast, exact methods guarantee minimality with respect to the number of additionally required SWAP gates, but suffer from the significant complexity (and, hence, the resulting run-time and scalability issues). Motivated by this, we are considering the research question how to optimize heuristic global reordering in order to generate nearly-optimal results while, at the same time, remaining scalable to larger quantum circuits.

4   General Idea

Obviously, considering more permutations – ideally all $n!$ possible ones – will allow for the determination of a qubit order that is better than the one determined by the heuristic solution reviewed above. But then, the question remains how to deal with the corresponding complexity? In this work, we are proposing a scheme which utilizes the compact representation of *Permutation Decision Diagrams* (πDDs) for this purpose. In this section, we first review the basics of πDDs. Afterwards, we describe the general idea of utilizing this data-structure and illustrate its potential by means of an example.

4.1   Permutation Decision Diagrams (πDDs)

A πDD is a graph which represents a set of permutations and is based on transposition decomposition [28]. Compared to other representation relying on arrays, πDDs can represent sets of permutations more compactly. Besides that, πDDs are also capable of efficiently conducting operations on the represented sets of permutations. Before introducing the structure of πDDs in detail, we describe the decomposition of a permutation called *transposition decomposition*.

Let $\pi = \pi_1 \ldots \pi_n$ be a permutation of length n. Then, π can be considered as a numerical sequence satisfying $\pi_i \in \{1 \ldots, n\}$ for $1 \leq i \leq n$ and $\pi_i \neq \pi_j$ for $1 \leq i < j \leq n$. A *transposition* $\tau_{i,j}$ is a swap between two elements π_i and π_j. Any permutation of length n can be uniquely decomposed into a sequence of at most $n - 1$ transpositions by conducting the following two steps:

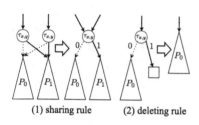

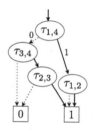

Fig. 4. Two reduction rules of πDDs   **Fig. 5.** A πDD repr. $\{2431, 4231, 1423\}$

1. Prepare the initial permutation $1 \ldots n$.
2. For each k running from n to 1, move π_k to the k-th position by applying a transposition.

Example 5. Consider a permutation $\pi = 2431$ to be decomposed. First, we start with the initial permutation 1234 and set $k = n = 4$. Since $\pi_k = 1$, we swap the first element and the fourth element ($\tau_{1,4}$) and obtain 4231. The third element 3 is at the same position as given by π, i.e. no transposition is needed for $k = 3$. Finally, since $\pi_2 = 4$ is at the first position of 4231, we swap the first element and the second element ($\tau_{1,2}$) and obtain $2431 = \pi$. By this, the given permutation $\pi = 2431$ is uniquely decomposed into a transposition sequence $\tau_{1,4}\tau_{1,2}$.

Following this transposition decomposition, a πDD is defined as follows:

Definition 4. *A πDD is a rooted and directed graph consisting of five types of components: internal nodes, 0-edges, 1-edges, the 0-sink, and the 1-sink. Figure 5 shows an example of a πDD. Each internal node is labeled with a transposition, and has exactly two out-going edges: a 0-edge and a 1-edge. Each path from a root to the 1-sink corresponds to a permutation held by the πDD as follows: if a 1-edge originates from a node with label $\tau_{x,y}$, the decomposition of the permutation contains $\tau_{x,y}$, while a 0-edge means that the decomposition does not contain $\tau_{x,y}$.*

In order to make a πDD compact and canonical, we apply the following two rules called reduction rules (as illustrated in Fig. 4):

– sharing rule: share all nodes which have the same labels and child nodes.
– deleting rule: delete all nodes whose 1-edge points to the 0-sink.

Example 6. Consider the three permutations $\{2431, 4231, 1423\}$. The transposition decomposition easily shows that all these permutations can be realized by the transpositions $\tau_{1,4}\tau_{1,2}$, $\tau_{1,4}$, and $\tau_{3,4}\tau_{2,3}$. Hence, all of them can be represented by the πDD as shown in Fig. 5.

Although the number of πDD nodes is exponential in the length of permutations in the worst case, in many practical cases, it demonstrates a high compression ratio. For example, Fig. 6 shows an example of an exponentially compact πDD; it represents a set of 2^5 permutations with only 5 internal nodes.

A notable feature of the πDD is that it supports efficient restriction operations that make a πDD representing a restricted subset from the original πDD.

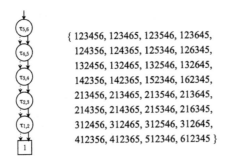

$$\{ 123456, 123465, 123546, 123645,$$
$$124356, 124365, 125346, 126345,$$
$$132456, 132465, 132546, 132645,$$
$$142356, 142365, 152346, 162345,$$
$$213456, 213465, 213546, 213645,$$
$$214356, 214365, 215346, 216345,$$
$$312456, 312465, 312546, 312645,$$
$$412356, 412365, 512346, 612345 \}$$

Fig. 6. A πDD with 5 nodes representing 2^5 permutations

An instance of restriction used in the following section is an adjacent restriction; it makes a πDD that only contains permutations such that two elements a and b must be adjacent in the permutation.

Since πDD operations are implemented as recursive procedures on a graph, the computation time of πDD operations depends on the number of πDD nodes, not on the cardinality of the set represented by a πDD. Hence, if a πDD is highly compressed and has a small number of nodes, manipulation on a set of permutations can be efficient.

4.2   Proposed Exploitation of πDDs

The concept of πDDs allows one to efficiently represent all $n!$ possible qubit permutations at once. Based on that, the general idea of the proposed nearest neighbor optimization is to iteratively reduce this set of permutations to a subset including *efficient* permutations only. "Efficiency" is thereby defined by the number of SWAP gates that would be required in order to make a given quantum circuit – whose qubits are aligned according to these permutations – nearest neighbor compliant. Hence, permutations are removed which would clearly yield a quantum circuit with high NNC. In the following, the general idea is sketched by means of an example.

Example 7. For the quantum circuit from Fig. 2(a), a qubit order is to be determined. To this end, all $4! = 24$ possible qubit permutations are considered at the beginning. Those are efficiently represented by the πDD depicted in Fig. 7(a). Now, permutations shall be excluded which are clearly not efficient. Obviously, the interactions between qubits x_1 and x_4 dominates in the circuit from Fig. 2(a). Accordingly, we are removing all permutations in which these two qubits are *not* adjacent. This can easily be employed using πDDs and, eventually, yields to a total of 12 remaining permutations represented by the structure shown in Fig. 7(b).

In a similar fashion, further permutations can be removed. This can be continued until either

– all permutations are excluded, i.e. an empty set results, or
– no further restrictions are left to be considered.

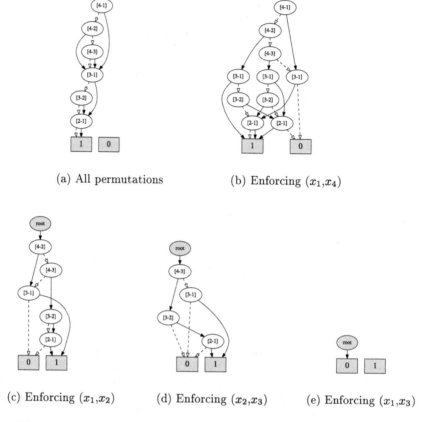

(a) All permutations   (b) Enforcing (x_1, x_4)

(c) Enforcing (x_1, x_2) (d) Enforcing (x_2, x_3) (e) Enforcing (x_1, x_3)

Fig. 7. Reducing the considered permutations using a πDD representation

In the first case, restrictions have to be loosened again – even if this would yield a quantum circuit which is not nearest neighbor compliant. After all, the representations is satisfying as many of the restrictions as possible. In the second case, no further actions are needed. From the resulting subset, the permutation leading to the lowest NNC is chosen and used in order to realize the circuit. Again, the example illustrates the issue.

Example 8. Using the subset represented by the πDD shown in Fig. 7(b), another restriction is employed, namely that qubits x_1 and x_2 shall be adjacent (this is motivated by the fact that there are 2 gates in which these two qubits interact). Applying this restriction yields the πDD shown in Fig. 7(c). Because of the same reason, x_2 and x_3 are enforced to be adjacent in the next step (yielding the πDD shown in Fig. 7(d)). Finally, x_1 and x_3 is enforced to be adjacent. However, the last restriction yields a πDD representing the empty set (see Fig. 7(e)). Because of that, this restriction is waived (i.e. we backtrack to the πDD shown in Fig. 7(d)). As no further restrictions are left (all qubit interactions of the original circuit from Fig. 2(a) have been considered), the best permutation regarding its

NNC can be calculated and taken from the resulting πDD (shown in Fig. 7(d)). This eventually yields the circuit already shown in Fig. 3(b), i.e. the proposed approach determined a permutation requiring a minimal number of SWAP gates.

Following this scheme aims for keeping permutations that satisfy certain restrictions, while excluding those which are identified as non-efficient (motivated by the interactions of qubits in the circuit). This is a clear improvement compared to the previously proposed heuristic which directly worked towards a single permutation only and, hence, likely excluded better options. The increased complexity caused by considering and manipulating (sub)sets of permutations is tackled through the efficient representation provided by the πDDs. However, the order in which restrictions are applied (and, hence, permutations are excluded) still has an effect on the determined result. The next section deals with how the proposed solution handles this ordering problem.

5   Applying Restrictions to the πDDs

As illustrated in the example from above, the interactions between the qubits provide crucial information on the nearest neighbor compliance of a given permutation. Accordingly, this information builds the basis for deciding what permutations are removed from further consideration. This section describes how this information is obtained, represented and, eventually, applied to the πDD.

5.1   Obtaining and Weighting Restrictions

In order to store information on the interaction of the qubits (and, eventually, derive restrictions from it), a pre-process is conducted which traverses the entire circuit G. For each gate $g \in G$, the corresponding interaction between the involved qubits is determined and stored. This way, an adjacency matrix is built representing what and how many interactions between qubits are conducted. More formally:

Definition 5. *For a given quantum circuit G with n qubits, an* adjacency matrix *A of size $n \times n$ represents the number of interactions between all qubits. Each entry $a_{i,j} \in A$ contains the number of interactions between the qubits x_i and x_j and between the qubits x_j and x_i. Since no qubit interacts with itself, all entries a_{ii} are left empty. Furthermore, since A is symmetric, only half of the entries has to be considered.*

Example 9. Consider the quantum circuit from Fig. 8(a). The corresponding adjacency matrix is shown in Fig. 8(b).

From this representation, the restrictions to be applied to the πDDs can easily be derived. Each interaction between the qubits x_i and x_j motivate to restrict the set of considered permutation to only those in which x_i and x_j are adjacent. Moreover, the adjacency matrix can be used to assign a weight to each restriction. For example, if the qubits x_i and x_j interact more frequently than the qubits x_k and x_l, then the restriction of having (x_i,x_j) adjacent should be prioritized to the restriction of having (x_k,x_l) adjacent.

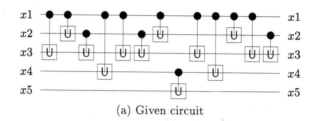

(a) Given circuit

	x_1 x_2 x_3 x_4 x_5
x_1	- 3 4 2 0
x_2	- - 3 0 0
x_3	- - - 0 0
x_4	- - - - 1
x_5	- - - - -

(b) Derived adjacency matrix

Restr.	Involved qubits	Weight
R1	(x_1,x_3)	4
R2	(x_1,x_2)	3
R3	(x_2,x_3)	3
R4	(x_1,x_4)	2
R5	(x_4,x_5)	1

(c) Derived restrictions

Fig. 8. Obtaining and weighting restrictions from a given circuit

Example 10. From the adjacency matrix shown in Fig. 8(b), restrictions and their weights as shown in Fig. 8(c) are derived.

5.2 Applying Resulting Restrictions to the πDD

In an ideal scenario, all restrictions derived above should be applied to the πDD. Then, a subset of permutations would remain in which all qubits that have interactions with each other are adjacent (eventually leading to a nearest neighbor compliant quantum circuit). However, in most of the cases this would yield an empty subset of permutations. Hence, a procedure is required deciding which restrictions are applied and which are not.

The weight which is assigned to each restriction provides an obvious metric for this purpose. But still, options exists how this metric is utilized. The following two possible schemes could be applied:

- In a *greedy* scheme, all restrictions are applied in the order of their weight. That is, the restriction with the highest weight is considered first; afterwards, the restriction with the second highest weight; and so on. This way, stronger restrictions are clearly preferred over weaker restrictions. However, there might be cases in which the application of several restrictions with a relatively small weight outperforms the application of a single restriction with a higher weight.
- This motivates the consideration of an *advanced* scheme which works as follows: First, a threshold e is defined stating the maximum number of restrictions which shall be considered together. Then, *all* possible combinations of the e restrictions with the highest weight are considered (including all e restrictions solely as well as all possible supersets of them). The combination of restrictions which can be applied to the πDD without causing an empty set of permutations and, additionally, satisfies the highest weight is eventually chosen. Afterwards, all remaining restrictions are applied following the greedy scheme.

The two schemes are illustrated by the following example:

Example 11. Consider again the quantum circuit from Fig. 8(a) and the obtained restrictions as shown in Fig. 8(c). Following the greedy scheme would suggest an application of R1, followed by R2, R3, R4, and R5. This eventually results in a set of permutations whose best one would lead to a circuit requiring 10 SWAP gates.

In contrast, the advance scheme would consider all combinations of the $e = 4$ restrictions with the highest weight, i.e. {R1}, {R2}, {R3}, {R4}, {R1,R2}, {R1,R3}, {R1,R4}, {R2,R3}, {R2,R4}, {R3,R4}, {R1,R2,R3}, etc. This way it can be observed that {R1,R2} can be applied together but not {R1,R2,R3}. Since the combination {R1,R3,R4} (i.e. without R2) yields a higher weight than all other non-empty combinations, this set of restrictions is applied to the πDD. Eventually, this results in a quantum circuit requiring 6 SWAP gates.

6   Experimental Evaluation

The solution proposed in the previous sections has been implemented on top of the πDD-package introduced in [28]. Based on this implementation, the performance of the proposed solution has been evaluated using benchmark quantum circuits taken from *RevLib* [42]. Afterwards, the obtained results have been compared to results obtained by the previously proposed solutions reviewed in Sect. 3. This section summarizes and discusses the obtained results. All evaluations have been conducted on an Intel i3-4030U machine with 1.9 GHz and 4 GB of memory.

Table 2 summarizes the obtained results. The first columns provide the name of the considered benchmarks as well as its respective number of lines (n) and gates ($|G|$). Afterwards, the number of required SWAP gates are reported if the naive method (reviewed in Sect. 2.2), the heuristic and exact method (reviewed in Sect. 3), as well as the proposed method (introduced in Sects. 4 and 5 and following the advanced scheme) are applied. In the case of the exact method as well as the proposed method, the required runtime (in CPU seconds) is additionally provided (both, the naive and heuristic approach where able to determine all results in negligible time, i.e. in less than a second). Finally, the last columns provide a comparison of the results obtained by the proposed approach to the respective numbers from the naive, heuristic, and exact approaches.

The results clearly confirm that the proposed approach fulfills the promises discussed in Sect. 3. By considering sets of permutations (rather than constructing a single one only), significantly better results compared to the previously proposed heuristic can be obtained. Improvements of more than 66 % in the best case are reported. Moreover, the proposed solution is capable of generating optimal or almost optimal results (see comparison of the proposed approach to the exact solution). This quality is achieved by requiring only a fraction of the runtime needed for the exact approach thus far. That is, πDDs as utilized in this work allow for determining results of optimal or almost optimal quality while, at the same time, they handle the underlying complexity in an efficient fashion.

Table 2. Experimental evaluation

Benchmark	n	$\|G\|$	Previously proposed solutions				Prop. solution		Comparison (wrt. number of SWAP gates)		
			Naive	Heuristic	Exact						
			SWAPs	SWAPs	SWAPs	Time	SWAPs	Time	to naive	to heuristic	to exact
3_17_13	3	13	6	6	4	0.1	6	0.1	1.00	1.00	1.50
decod24-v3_46	4	9	18	8	4	0.1	4	0.1	0.22	0.50	1.00
hwb4_52	4	23	28	18	18	0.1	18	0.1	0.64	1.00	1.00
4gt11_84	5	7	14	6	2	0.1	2	0.1	0.14	0.33	1.00
4gt13-v1_93	5	16	52	20	6	0.1	8	0.1	0.15	0.40	1.33
4mod5-v1_23	5	24	50	30	30	0.1	30	0.1	0.60	1.00	1.00
hwb5_55	5	106	230	146	114	0.1	120	0.1	0.52	0.82	1.05
hwb6_58	6	146	358	316	290	0.1	294	0.2	0.82	0.93	1.01
rd32-v0_67	4	8	10	4	4	1.1	4	0.1	0.40	1.00	1.00
rd53_135	7	78	264	194	136	1.8	136	0.3	0.52	0.70	1.00
ham7_104	7	87	204	162	140	1.9	140	0.3	0.69	0.86	1.00
urf2_152	8	25150	90676	83152	71280	22.0	73932	0.4	0.82	0.89	1.04
urf1_149	9	57770	245604	200804	179832	231.3	203836	0.6	0.83	1.02	1.13
urf5_158	9	51380	229568	206288	176284	247.0	179348	0.6	0.78	0.87	1.02
rd73_140	10	76	238	190	150	1579.4	178	0.9	0.75	0.94	1.19
sys6-v0_144	10	62	192	116	114	1586.4	118	0.8	0.61	1.02	1.04
Shor3	10	2076	6710	6710	4802	1846.2	4802	0.8	0.72	0.72	1.00
sym9_148	10	4452	16848	13656	10984	2415.1	12128	0.7	0.72	0.89	1.10
urf3_155	10	132340	663156	491356	453368	3023.6	458476	0.9	0.69	0.93	1.01
4_49_17	4	30	42	32			32	0.1	0.76	1.00	
4gt10-v1_81	5	36	82	74			32	0.1	0.39	0.43	
4gt5_75	5	22	40	40			22	0.1	0.55	0.55	
4mod7-v0_95	5	40	72	68			44	0.1	0.61	0.65	
aj-e11_165	5	59	118	70			52	0.1	0.44	0.74	
alu-v4_36	5	31	70	70			34	0.1	0.49	0.49	
4gt12-v1_89	6	52	172	76			52	0.1	0.30	0.68	
4gt4-v0_80	6	43	66	58			44	0.1	0.67	0.76	
mod5adder_128	6	81	188	148			120	0.2	0.64	0.81	
mod8-10_177	6	108	218	166			156	0.1	0.72	0.94	
hwb7_62	8	2659	8824	7876			7596	0.4	0.86	0.96	
hwb8_118	9	16608	57378	51998			50184	0.6	0.87	0.97	
hwb9_123	10	20405	84630	78266			74086	0.8	0.88	0.95	
cycle10_2_110	12	1212	5272	5272			4500	1.6	0.85	0.85	
plus63mod4096_163	13	29019	155668	144752			144752	1.9	0.93	1.00	
0410184_169	14	82	48	68			48	13.0	1.00	0.71	
plus127mod8192_162	14	65455	376734	362986			349236	14.6	0.93	0.96	
plus63mod8192_164	14	37101	211276	182856			178122	5.6	0.84	0.97	
ham15_108	15	458	3108	2772			1438	2.5	0.46	0.52	
rd84_142	15	112	468	424			348	4.7	0.74	0.82	
urf6_160	15	53700	478068	427344			257604	10.0	0.54	0.60	
cnt3-5_180	16	125	400	400			356	63.9	0.89	0.89	

n: Number of lines $\|G\|$: Number of gates   Time: Runtime in CPU seconds
SWAPs: Number of SWAP gates required when applying the naive method (reviewed in Section 2.2), the heuristic
and exact method (reviewed in Section 3), as well as the proposed method (introduced in Sections 4 and 5)
No runtime is provided for the naive and the heuristic method (since all results were obtained in negligible time)

7   Conclusions

In this work, we considered nearest neighbor optimization of quantum circuits
using πDDs. Since πDDs allow for an efficient representation and manipulation
of sets of permutations, they allow for considering all possible permutations at
once and an subsequent reduction of them with respect to the nearest neighbor constraints. This way, an ideal compromise between existing solutions is
provided. Experimental evaluations confirmed the efficiency and quality of the
obtained results.

Acknowledgments. This work has partially been supported by the EU COST Action
IC1405, the JST ERATO Minato Project, as well as JSPS KAKENHI 15H05711 and
15J01665.

References

1. Nielsen, M., Chuang, I.: Quantum Computation and Quantum Information. Cambridge Univ. Press, Cambridge (2000)
2. Shor, P.W.: Algorithms for quantum computation: discrete logarithms and factoring. In: Foundations of Computer Science, pp. 124–134 (1994)
3. Grover, L.K.: A fast quantum mechanical algorithm for database search. In: Theory of Computing, pp. 212–219 (1996)
4. Gupta, P., Agrawal, A., Jha, N.K.: An algorithm for synthesis of reversible logic circuits. IEEE Trans. CAD **25**(11), 2317–2330 (2006)
5. Maslov, D., Dueck, G.W., Miller, D.M.: Techniques for the synthesis of reversible Toffoli networks. ACM Trans. Des. Autom. Electron. Syst. **12**(4), 1–20 (2007)
6. Saeedi, M., Sedighi, M., Zamani, M.S.: A novel synthesis algorithm for reversible circuits. In: International Conference on CAD, pp. 65–68 (2007)
7. Wille, R., Große, D., Dueck, G., Drechsler, R.: Reversible logic synthesis with output permutation. In: VLSI Design, pp. 189–194 (2009)
8. Große, D., Wille, R., Dueck, G.W., Drechsler, R.: Exact multiple control Toffoli network synthesis with SAT techniques. IEEE Trans. CAD **28**(5), 703–715 (2009)
9. Wille, R., Drechsler, R.: BDD-based synthesis of reversible logic for large functions. In: Design Automation Conference, pp. 270–275 (2009)
10. Saeedi, M., Sedighi, M., Zamani, M.S.: A library-based synthesis methodology for reversible logic. Microelectron. J. **41**(4), 185–194 (2010)
11. Saeedi, M., Zamani, M.S., Sedighi, M., Sasanian, Z.: Reversible circuit synthesis using a cycle-based approach. J. Emerg. Technol. Comput. Syst. **6**(4), 1–26 (2010)
12. Soeken, M., Wille, R., Hilken, C., Przigoda, N., Drechsler, R.: Synthesis of reversible circuits with minimal lines for large functions. In: ASP Design Automation Conference, pp. 85–92 (2012)
13. Barenco, A., Bennett, C.H., Cleve, R., DiVinchenzo, D., Margolus, N., Shor, P., Sleator, T., Smolin, J., Weinfurter, H.: Elementary gates for quantum computation. Am. Phys. Soc. **52**, 3457–3467 (1995)
14. Miller, D.M., Wille, R., Sasanian, Z.: Elementary quantum gate realizations for multiple-control Toffoli gates. In: International Symposium on Multi-valued Logic, pp. 288–293 (2011)
15. Sasanian, Z., Wille, R., Miller, D.M.: Realizing reversible circuits using a new class of quantum gates. In: Design Automation Conference, pp. 36–41 (2012)
16. Wille, R., Soeken, M., Otterstedt, C., Drechsler, R.: Improving the mapping of reversible circuits to quantum circuits using multiple target lines. In: ASP Design Automation Conference, pp. 85–92 (2013)
17. Shende, V.V., Bullock, S.S., Markov, I.L.: Synthesis of quantum-logic circuits. IEEE Trans. CAD **25**(6), 1000–1010 (2006)
18. Hung, W., Song, X., Yang, G., Yang, J., Perkowski, M.: Optimal synthesis of multiple output Boolean functions using a set of quantum gates by symbolic reachability analysis. IEEE Trans. CAD **25**(9), 1652–1663 (2006)
19. Große, D., Wille, R., Dueck, G.W., Drechsler, R.: Exact synthesis of elementary quantum gate circuits. Multiple-Valued Logic Soft Comput. **15**(4), 270–275 (2009)
20. Saeedi, M., Arabzadeh, M., Zamani, M.S., Sedighi, M.: Block-based quantum-logic synthesis. Quant. Inf. Comput. **11**(3&4), 262–277 (2011)
21. Niemann, P., Wille, R., Drechsler, R.: Efficient synthesis of quantum circuits implementing Clifford group operations. In: ASP Design Automation Conference, pp. 483–488 (2014)
22. Saeedi, M., Wille, R., Drechsler, R.: Synthesis of quantum circuits for linear nearest neighbor architectures. Quant. Inf. Proc. **10**(3), 355–377 (2011)
23. Khan, M.H.: Cost reduction in nearest neighbour based synthesis of quantum Boolean circuits. Eng. Lett. **16**(1), 1–5 (2008)

24. Hirata, Y., Nakanishi, M., Yamashita, S., Nakashima, Y.: An efficient method to convert arbitrary quantum circuits to ones on a linear nearest neighbor architecture. In: Conference on Quantum, Nano and Micro Technologies, pp. 26–33 (2009)

25. Shafaei, A., Saeedi, M., Pedram, M.: Optimization of quantum circuits for interaction distance in linear nearest neighbor architectures. In: Design Automation Conference, pp. 41–46 (2013)

26. Wille, R., Lye, A., Drechsler, R.: Optimal SWAP gate insertion for nearest neighbor quantum circuits. In: ASP Design Automation Conference, pp. 489–494 (2014)

27. Wille, R., Lye, A., Drechsler, R.: Exact reordering of circuit lines for nearest neighbor quantum architectures. IEEE Trans. CAD $33(12)$, 1818–1831 (2014)

28. Minato, S.: πDD: a new decision diagram for efficient problem solving in permutation space. In: Conference on Theory and Applications of Satisfiability Testing, pp. 90–104 (2011)

29. Fowler, A.G., Devitt, S.J., Hollenberg, L.C.L.: Implementation of Shor's algorithm on a linear nearest neighbour qubit array. Quant. Inf. Comput. 4, 237–245 (2004)

30. Meter, R.V., Oskin, M.: Architectural implications of quantum computing technologies. J. Emerg. Technol. Comput. Syst. $2(1)$, 31–63 (2006)

31. Ross, M., Oskin, M.: Quantum computing. Comm. ACM $51(7)$, 12–13 (2008)

32. Amini, J.M., Uys, H., Wesenberg, J.H., Seidelin, S., Britton, J., Bollinger, J.J., Leibfried, D., Ospelkaus, C., VanDevender, A.P., Wineland, D.J.: Toward scalable ion traps for quantum information processing. New J. Phys. $12(3)$, 033031 (2010)

33. Kumph, M., Brownnutt, M., Blatt, R.: Two-dimensional arrays of radio-frequency ion traps with addressable interactions. New J. Phys. $13(7)$, 073043 (2011)

34. Nickerson, N.H., Li, Y., Benjamin, S.C.: Topological quantum computing with a very noisy network and local error rates approaching one percent. Nat. Commun. 4, 1756 (2013)

35. Devitt, S.J., Fowler, A.G., Stephens, A.M., Greentree, A.D., Hollenberg, L.C.L., Munro, W.J., Nemoto, K.: Architectural design for a topological cluster state quantum computer. New J. Phys. $11(8)$, 083032 (2009)

36. Yao, N.Y., Gong, Z.X., Laumann, C.R., Bennett, S.D., Duan, L.M., Lukin, M.D., Jiang, L., Gorshkov, A.V.: Quantum logic between remote quantum registers. Phys. Rev. A 87, 022306 (2013)

37. Herrera-Martí, D.A., Fowler, A.G., Jennings, D., Rudolph, T.: Photonic implementation for the topological cluster-state quantum computer. Phys. Rev. A 82, 032332 (2010)

38. Jones, N.C., Van Meter, R., Fowler, A.G., McMahon, P.L., Kim, J., Ladd, T.D., Yamamoto, Y.: Layered architecture for quantum computing. Phys. Rev. X 2, 031007 (2012)

39. Ohliger, M., Eisert, J.: Efficient measurement-based quantum computing with continuous-variable systems. Phys. Rev. A 85, 062318 (2012)

40. DiVincenzo, D.P., Solgun, F.: Multi-qubit parity measurement in circuit quantum electrodynamics. New J. Phys. $15(7)$, 075001 (2013)

41. Gebser, M., Kaufmann, B., Neumann, A., Schaub, T.: Conflict-driven answer set solving. In: International Joint Conference on Artificial Intelligence, pp. 386–392 (2007)

42. Wille, R., Große, D., Teuber, L., Dueck, G.W., Drechsler, R.: RevLib: an online resource for reversible functions and reversible circuits. In: International Symposium Multi-valued Logic, pp. 220–225 (2008). RevLib is available at http://www.revlib.org

Quantum Programming

Circular CNOT Circuits: Definition, Analysis and Application to Fault-Tolerant Quantum Circuits

Alexandru Paler[(✉)]

Facultatea de Matematică şi Informatică, Universitatea Transilvania,
Braşov, Romania
alexandrupaler@gmail.com

Abstract. The work proposes an extension of the quantum circuit formalism where qubits (wires) are circular instead of linear. The left-to-right interpretation of a quantum circuit is replaced by a circular representation which allows to select the starting point and the direction in which gates are executed. The representation supports all the circuits obtained after computing cyclic permutations of an initial quantum gate list. Two circuits, where one has a gate list which is a cyclic permutation of the other, will implement different functions. The main question appears in the context of scalable quantum computing, where multiple subcircuits are used for the construction of a larger fault-tolerant one: can the same circular representation be used by multiple subcircuits? The circular circuits defined and analysed in this work consist only of CNOT gates. These are sufficient for constructing computationally universal, fault-tolerant circuits formed entirely of qubit initialisation, CNOT gates and qubit measurements. The main result of modelling circular CNOT circuits is that a derived Boolean representation allows to define a set of equations for X and Z stabiliser transformations. Through a well defined set of steps it is possible to reduce the initial equations to a set of stabiliser transformations given a series of cuts through the circular circuit.

Keywords: Quantum circuits · Fault-tolerant quantum circuits · ICM

1   Motivation

The quantum circuit formalism is a generally accepted representation of quantum information processing. It is mainly inspired by the classical circuit representation, where input information is transformed through the application of gate sequences into output information. The main differences between classical and quantum circuits are that the latter have an equal number of inputs and outputs, do not accept FANIN or FANOUT and the quantum gates represent reversible transformations required by the unitarity of quantum mechanics, unlike classical gates (e.g. the classical AND gate) which are not reversible.

A quantum circuit is specified as a gate sequence containing gates from an universal gate set, and in the context of practical quantum computing this set

© Springer International Publishing Switzerland 2016
S. Devitt and I. Lanese (Eds.): RC 2016, LNCS 9720, pp. 199–212, 2016.
DOI: 10.1007/978-3-319-40578-0_15

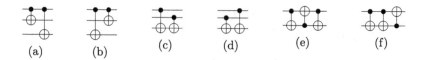

Fig. 1. CNOT circuits: (a–d) CNOT commutativity rules; (e) the SWAP circuit; (f) a cyclic permutation of the SWAP circuit.

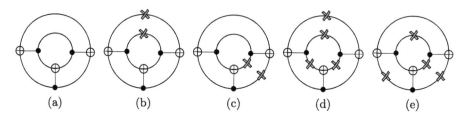

Fig. 2. Cutting a circular CNOT circuit results in ICM circuits: (a) the initial circular SWAP circuit; (b) radial cut for the linear SWAP circuit; (c) radial cut for the linear CNOT circuit; (d) cuts for the teleported CNOT circuit; (Fig. 3a) (e) cuts for the selective destination teleportation circuit (Fig. 3b).

is $\{CNOT, T, P, V\}$. T and P are $\pi/4$ and $\pi/2$ rotations around the Z-axis and V is the $\pi/2$ rotation around the X-axis of the Bloch sphere [6]. These gates are sufficient for approximating any quantum computation with arbitrary precision, and are preferred because they have known fault-tolerant implementations used within error corrected quantum computing architectures [2]. The gate sequence introduces a temporal ordering of information processing, although this ordering is not entirely strict because some gates can commute (Fig. 1).

Universal fault-tolerant quantum circuits can be represented as ICM circuits which are formed entirely of qubit (I)nitialisations, (C)NOT gates and qubit (M)easurements [7]. The circuits include only CNOT gates, because rotational gates are implemented by teleportation mechanisms [6,7] and rotations are achieved by initialising certain qubits in specific ancillary states. The computational universality of ICM circuits is based on the choice of the qubit initialisation and measurement basis: the Y and the A basis can be chosen in addition to the X and Z basis [2]. Therefore, ICM circuit qubits can be initialised into $|0\rangle$, $|+\rangle$, $|Y\rangle = |0\rangle + i|1\rangle$ and $|A\rangle = |0\rangle + e^{\pi/4}|1\rangle$, and can be measured in the X, Y, Z, A basis [3]. The $|Y\rangle$ and $|A\rangle$ states are required for implementing the T (Fig. 5b), P (Fig. 5c) and V (Fig. 5d) gate.

Multiple circuits share the same CNOT gates circuit structure resulting after not considering the initialisations and measurements of an arbitrary ICM circuit. This is illustrated by the example of the SWAP circuit (Fig. 1e). The circuit has two qubit lines and three CNOT gates. Consider that, without being offered any definition, the circular representation from Fig. 2a results after joining the inputs and the outputs. The initial SWAP circuit can be reconstructed after making a *cut* on each of the circular qubits, so that there is no case where two CNOTs have the same control or target. However, if the cuts are made as indicated in

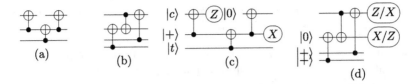

Fig. 3. Circuits after cutting the circular SWAP circuit: (a) as in Fig. 2d; (b) as in Fig. 2e. The ICM versions of the previous two CNOT structures is obtained after choosing appropriate qubit initialisation and measurements basis: (c) remote CNOT circuit; (d) selective destination teleportation, where the measurement of the two upper qubits dictates on which qubit (third or fourth) the first qubit is to be teleported. In general, the $|0\rangle$ state can be replaced with an arbitrary state.

Fig. 2c, the result will be a circuit that implements a single CNOT, because the other two cancel out (Fig. 1f).

The circular representation of the SWAP can be cut in different ways, and the resulting circuits will have different functionality. The circuit from Fig. 3a is obtained by executing the cuts from Fig. 2d. Furthermore, if the cyclic permutation of SWAP is cut according to Fig. 2e, the resulting circuit will be the one from Fig. 3b. By augmenting both resulting circuits with specific qubit initialisation and measurement bases, these have practical functional interpretations: Fig. 3a depicts a remote CNOT (Fig. 3c), and Fig. 3b implements the selective destination teleportation circuit [4] (Fig. 3d).

2 Circular CNOT Circuits

A circular CNOT circuit was presented in the previous section without any definition or discussing its properties. In the following paragraphs definitions will be introduced and explained. It should be noted that the notion of treating a circuit in a circular fashion is the basis for the approach to template matching [5], where templates are considered cyclic gate sequences. In contrast, the circuits presented in this paper have circular wires that can be cut. This leads to a set of implementable fault-tolerant quantum circuits requiring different amount of qubits.

Definition 1. *A circular CNOT circuit has circular qubit wires and consists entirely of CNOT gates, thus it has no inputs or outputs.*

The circular CNOT circuits proposed herein are not able to process information because of to their lack of inputs and outputs, but can be transformed into linear quantum circuits by cutting the circular wires. Quantum circuit reversibility is captured by the circular wire representation, and the temporal ordering of the gates is dictated by the direction in which the wires are traversed. Therefore, after cutting the wires, depending on the direction chosen, some wire end points are the inputs and others represent outputs.

Definition 2. *A cut is an interruption of a circular qubit wire that generates two end points associated to an input or an output.*

A set of cuts is *correct* if it does not lead to CNOTs intersecting themselves in the resulting circuit. It can be shown that at least one *radial cut* across all the wires is necessary for generating a valid quantum circuit: each cut introduces two end points; if two cuts generate end points which are not co-linear on the same radius then, after choosing any traversal direction, at least one CNOT will have one of its control/target after an input and right before an output.

Definition 3. *A linear quantum circuit is the result of performing two operations: (1) cut correctly at least once each circular wire of a circular CNOT circuit; (2) chose a direction in which to traverse the CNOTs (clockwise, counterclockwise).*

3   Boolean Model of Circular CNOT Circuits

Classical circuits can be modelled using Boolean formula, and this section shows that circular CNOT circuits have a Boolean representation, too. This is not surprising as the CNOT gate is a reversible gate. However, the Boolean model uses the fact that the CNOT gate is a stabiliser gate [1,6] whose transformations have a Boolean representation. An exact definition of the introduced Boolean variables is offered only after discussing the effect of the cuts on the circular representation.

3.1   Stabiliser Transformations

The Pauli matrices I, X, Y, Z play a central role in the definition of quantum circuits. In the following the discussion will focus on X and Z, because $Y = iXZ$ and I is the 2×2 identity matrix. The matrices can be decomposed into ± 1 eigenvalues with corresponding eigenvectors. The eigenvectors of Z are $|0\rangle$ and $|1\rangle$, and the ones of X are $|+\rangle = \frac{1}{\sqrt{2}}(|0\rangle + |1\rangle)$ and $|-\rangle = \frac{1}{\sqrt{2}}(|0\rangle - |1\rangle)$. The states $|0\rangle$ and $|+\rangle$ are $+1$ eigenvectors, and $|1\rangle, |-\rangle$ are -1 eigenvectors respectively.

$$I = \begin{pmatrix} 1 & 0 \\ 0 & 1 \end{pmatrix} \quad Y = \begin{pmatrix} 0 & -i \\ i & 0 \end{pmatrix} \quad X = \begin{pmatrix} 0 & 1 \\ 1 & 0 \end{pmatrix} \quad Z = \begin{pmatrix} 1 & 0 \\ 0 & -1 \end{pmatrix}$$

An operator M, consisting of N tensor products of Pauli operators, stabilises the N-qubit state $|q\rangle$, if $|q\rangle$ is a $+1$ eigenvector of M. Therefore, for example, X stabilises $|+\rangle$ and $-Z$ stabilises $|1\rangle$. The matrix I stabilises any state. The action of certain quantum gates (Clifford gates), which includes CNOT, can be formulated entirely in terms of stabiliser transformations. The following equations illustrate how the input states of a CNOT ($_c$ denotes the control and $_t$ the target) are transformed. For example, Eq. 1, shows that if the control qubit is stabilised by X (is in the $|+\rangle$ state), after the CNOT both the control and the

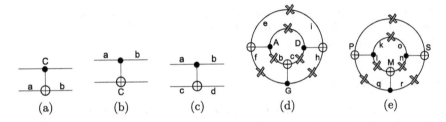

Fig. 4. Boolean variables assigned to wire segments for: (a) CNOT X transformations; (b) CNOT Z transformations; (c) CNOT combined X and Z transformations (Sect. 3.5); (d) SWAP X transformations; (e) SWAP Z transformations.

target are stabilised by X. The set of four stabiliser transformations below are a complete description of the function of a CNOT.

$$X_c I_t \rightarrow X_c X_t \tag{1}$$
$$I_c X_t \rightarrow I_c X_t \tag{2}$$
$$Z_c I_t \rightarrow Z_c I_t \tag{3}$$
$$I_c Z_t \rightarrow Z_c Z_t \tag{4}$$

3.2 A Single CNOT

The functionality of a CNOT gate can be modelled by two Boolean expressions of the form Eq. 5, because the transformations are of two types: X and Z. In general, a wire segment is delimited by cut points or CNOT symbols ($\bullet$ or $\oplus$). In particular, Boolean variables denoted with small letters stand for variables representing wire segments ending at one of the symbols $\oplus$ or $\bullet$, and capitalised variables represent a wire segment running over one the CNOT symbols. To be more precise, in Fig. 4a a and b represent the wire segments having the target symbol $\oplus$ as an end point, and C is the variable for the entire control wire. In Fig. 4b a and b represent the segments having $\bullet$ as an end point, and C the entire target wire (contains $\oplus$).

$$C(a, b, C) = a \oplus b \oplus \neg C \tag{5}$$

The following example shows how Eq. 5 works and how to interpret the truth values of the variables. A definition of variables is offered in Sect. 3.3. If the control input of the CNOT is stabilised by Z, then $a \leftarrow true$ is replaced in Eq. 5 so that Eq. 6 results. The expression will be *true* only if one of the variables is true; either $C = true$ or $b = true$. The first case corresponds to the result of multiplying Eqs. 3 and 4 ($Z_c Z_t \rightarrow I_c Z_t$), and the latter to Eq. 3. Thus, a *true* variable signals that a corresponding wire segment is stabilised, and a *false* variable indicates the stabiliser I (not stabilised). The possible stabiliser transformations of a CNOT are represented by each of the four clauses of the disjunctive normal form of Eq. 5.

$$C(true, b, C) = true \oplus b \oplus \neg C = C \oplus b \tag{6}$$

Expression 6 is a valid example of X stabiliser transformations, too: if the target input (variable a) is stabilised by X, then $C = true$ corresponds to $X_c X_t \rightarrow X_c I_t$, and $b = true$ to Eq. 2.

3.3 Modelling Cuts

The CNOT gate discussion did not consider a circular representation because stabiliser transformations are functioning only in proper linear quantum circuits. This section introduces the Boolean modelling of cuts by the example of a circular single CNOT circuit (Fig. 1f). The only possible radial cut will result into two end points per wire: $c_{1,2}$ for the control wire, and $t_{1,2}$ for the target. Considering Fig. 4a, the variable C is the segment spanned between c_1 and c_2, a the segment between t_1 and $\oplus$, and b the segment between $\oplus$ and t_2.

A linear quantum circuit is the result of a radial cut. In a circular representation with multiple CNOTs, this will generate two segment types: (1) segments delimited by a cut end point and a CNOT; (2) segments delimited by two distinct CNOTs. The first segment type represents wires reaching inputs or outputs, and the second type are circuit internal wires. However, the radial cut can be followed by additional cuts which affect only second type segments. Considering that a variable s represented any of these segments and that, after a cut, the resulting subsegments are called r and t, Eq. 7 captures the Boolean behaviour before the cut: the Boolean variables are equivalent (the segments are joined), both can be either $true$ or false.

$$\mathcal{J}(r, t) = \neg r \oplus t \tag{7}$$

Cuts are modelled by not enforcing the subsegments to be equivalent, thus by not using expressions like Eq. 7. As a result, in the absence of cuts, segments delimited by two CNOTs are not considered independently, but as the result of joining the two subsegments generated after a potential cut. This observation leads to the Boolean variables interpretation (in the light of Sect. 3.2).

Definition 4. *A Boolean variable represents a wire segment delimited by at least one cut end point.*

Definition 5. *The truth value of a Boolean variable indicates if the qubit represented by the segment is stabilised or not.*

3.4 Modelling an Entire Circular Circuit

The Boolean model of an entire circular circuit includes, as mentioned in Sect. 3.2, two Boolean expressions ($\mathcal{B}_x$ and $\mathcal{B}_z$): one capturing X and the other Z stabiliser transformations. The expressions are built as *conjunctions of clauses* (Eqs. 5 and 7) formed after all the possible cut points were determined and the corresponding Boolean variables defined. The SWAP circular circuit is used once more as an example. Figure 4d, e depict all the possible cuts, the resulting segments and the necessary variables for forming $\mathcal{B}_x$ and $\mathcal{B}_z$.

$$\mathcal{B}_x = \mathcal{C}(A, e, f)\mathcal{C}(G, b, c)\mathcal{C}(D, h, i)$$
$$\mathcal{J}(A, D)\mathcal{J}(A, b)\mathcal{J}(c, D)\mathcal{J}(e, i)\mathcal{J}(f, G)\mathcal{J}(G, h) \tag{8}$$
$$\mathcal{B}_z = \mathcal{C}(P, k, l)\mathcal{C}(M, q, r)\mathcal{C}(S, n, o)$$
$$\mathcal{J}(k, o)\mathcal{J}(l, M)\mathcal{J}(M, n)\mathcal{J}(P, S)\mathcal{J}(P, q)\mathcal{J}(r, S) \tag{9}$$

Equations 8 and 9 model the circular SWAP, where no cuts were made. In order to generate a functioning SWAP circuit, the necessary radial cut will remove the clauses $\mathcal{J}(A, D)$ and $\mathcal{J}(e, i)$ from $\mathcal{B}_x$, and the clauses $\mathcal{J}(k, o)$ and $\mathcal{J}(P, S)$ from $\mathcal{B}_z$. The Boolean expressions resulting after the removals will represent the circuit in Fig. 1e.

In order to generate the circular permutation of the SWAP and to obtain the circuit that implements a single CNOT (Fig. 1f) the radial cut could remove $\mathcal{J}(c, D)$ and $\mathcal{J}(G, h)$ from $\mathcal{B}_x$, and $\mathcal{J}(M, n)$ and $\mathcal{J}(r, S)$ from $\mathcal{B}_z$. The teleported CNOT circuit (Fig. 3a) is the result of performing the cuts $\mathcal{J}(A, D)$; $\mathcal{J}(e, i)$; $\mathcal{J}(A, b)$; $\mathcal{J}(c, D)$ in $\mathcal{B}_x$, and the cuts $\mathcal{J}(k, o)$; $\mathcal{J}(P, S)$; $\mathcal{J}(l, M)$; $\mathcal{J}(M, n)$ in $\mathcal{B}_z$. Finally, the selective destination teleportation circuit (Fig. 3b) is obtained by cutting $\mathcal{J}(c, D)$; $\mathcal{J}(G, h)$; $\mathcal{J}(A, D)$; $\mathcal{J}(f, G)$ in $\mathcal{B}_x$ and $\mathcal{J}(M, n)$; $\mathcal{J}(r, S)$; $\mathcal{J}(k, o)$; $\mathcal{J}(P, q)$ in $\mathcal{B}_z$.

3.5   Discussion

Boolean models of circular CNOT circuits include two expressions, and this structure was chosen because each expression is equivalent to a linear equations system: each clause is a linear equation (XOR is a linear function). The equivalence between the Boolean model and a stabiliser table obtained after simulating a stabiliser circuit can be observed, too. Stabiliser table operations are performed as if the table were a linear equations system (e.g. Gaussian elimination is used for determining individual qubit measurement results) [1]. A second argument for the chosen structure was that in a CNOT circuit the X and the Z stabilisers transformations do not interact one with another. This would have not been the case if, for example, Hadamard ($H = PVP$) gates were included in the circuit. The Hadamard transforms the input X stabiliser into Z, and vice versa. Similarly, if the circular circuits had included CPHASE gates, X and Z would have been referenced in the same stabiliser transformations.

The manner in which cuts and Boolean variables were defined could have been simplified if a single Boolean expression per CNOT had modelled both the X and Z stabiliser transformations. In this situation, a wire segment is determined by exactly one cut point and a CNOT element ($\bullet$ or $\oplus$). Each wire segment has a Boolean variable attached, and for a single CNOT circuit the segments and the variables are similar to Fig. 4c, and Eq. 10 models all the stabiliser transformations.

$$F(a, b, c, d) = x\mathcal{C}(a, c, d)(a \oplus \neg b) \oplus (\neg x)\mathcal{C}(c, a, b)(c \oplus \neg d) \tag{10}$$

The previous expression references the function defined in Eq. 5 and introduces two additional variables x and z. If one would like to compute the X transformation of a CNOT the x variable needs to be set to true, and for the Z transformation the variable has to be *false*. The complete Boolean model of a circular CNOT circuit results after conjugating for all the CNOTs the corresponding expressions of form Eq. 10. The Boolean model of the cuts will remain the same.

Irrespective of the used model (with a single or two Boolean expressions), the temporal ordering of the gates is not relevant. The traversal direction of the gates is not important when trying to determine a stabiliser transformation computed by the modelled circuit. The CNOT gate is reversible, its Boolean model captures its reversibility. If a variable is set to *true* and the truth value of another variable has to be computed, the direction of the stabiliser transformations (equivalent to gate traversal order) is dictated by the modelled Boolean constraints.

It can be also noted that the Boolean expressions capture the CNOT commutativity inside the circuit (Fig. 1). This is due to how the segments were defined: in $\mathcal{B}_x$ the capitalised variables represent segments containing the •, and in $\mathcal{B}_z$ the capitalised variables stand for segments containing ⊕. For neighbouring CNOTs having the control ($\mathcal{B}_x$) or the target ($\mathcal{B}_z$) on the same qubit, the capitalised variables need to be interchanged in order to commute the gates. Variables of joined (uncut) segments can be interchanged due to Eq. 7, which is the Boolean equivalence relation between two variables.

4   ICM Circuits Are Instances of Circular CNOT Circuits

There are two strategies for constructing a quantum circuit from a circular representation. The first is to make a single radial cut, and the second is to make additional single cuts following a radial cut. A radial cut generates an ICM circuit having an equal number of wires to the circular representation, while each additional single cut introduces an additional qubit (wire) in the circuit. This is observed after comparing Fig. 2a, b. Consequently, circuits obtained after radial cuts have indeed cyclic permuted gate lists. The second construction strategy, however, does not preserve the number of wires from the circular representation, and the resulting gate lists are cyclic permutations only in the sense of the CNOT ordering and direction (the affected qubits are not identical).

The position of the cuts dictates the chosen gate list permutation of the resulting ICM circuit, but the circuit will not implement any function until its qubits are configured. Configuration is the process of selecting qubit initialisation and measurement basis. In general, a quantum circuit includes both input/output and ancillae qubits (have predetermined initialisation and measurement basis). In particular, for ICM circuits the basis determine either the rotational gate being implemented or supplemental decisions required during information processing. An example for the latter situation offers the selective destination teleportation circuit which acts like a multiplexer: the third or the fourth qubit outputs the state of one the first qubit depending on the measurement basis of these first two qubits (Fig. 3d). Non-ancillae qubits take the states

$$|\varphi\rangle \oplus Z \quad |\varphi\rangle \oplus Z \quad |\varphi\rangle \oplus Z \quad |Y\rangle \oplus -V|\varphi\rangle \quad |0\rangle \oplus \quad |0\rangle \oplus Z$$
$$|+\rangle \bullet |\varphi\rangle \quad |A\rangle \bullet -T|\varphi\rangle \quad |Y\rangle \bullet -P|\varphi\rangle \quad |\varphi\rangle \bullet X \quad |+\rangle \bullet \quad |\varphi\rangle \bullet$$
$$\text{(a)} \qquad\qquad \text{(b)} \qquad\qquad \text{(c)} \qquad\qquad \text{(d)} \qquad\qquad \text{(e)} \qquad \text{(f)}$$

Fig. 5. The ICM circuits have the same CNOT gate structure, but different qubit initialisation and measurements: (a) information teleportation circuit; (b) teleported implementation of the T gate; (c) teleported implementation of the P gate; (d) teleported implementation of the V gate; (e) construction of a Bell pair; (f) measurement of the Z operator. The qubits marked with $|\varphi\rangle$ are input/output, and all the others are ancillae. All the circuits will have the same circular CNOT circuit representation, thus the same Boolean model.

supplied to the circuit (inputs) or are used for reading out states after circuit execution (outputs). Each end point introduced after a cut will represent either an ancilla or an input/output qubit. Thus, the construction of ICM circuits from circular CNOT circuits requires three steps: (1) correctly cut and choose traversal direction of the circular circuit; (2) select which end points belong to ancillae and which not; (3) choose the initialisation and measurement basis of the ancillae. The example of the circular SWAP circuit in the previous Section illustrates these steps.

There are two abstraction levels, conforming to the previously listed steps, necessary for highlighting circular CNOT circuit capabilities. The *first level* is represented by circuits having the same CNOT structure but different initialisation/measurement basis (e.g. Fig. 5). At this level all the circuits implement the same underlying stabiliser transformations, because the CNOTs are arranged identically. The *second level* is the circular CNOT representation and its Boolean model, which abstracts all the circuits that have the same set of gates, but arranged as cyclic permutations. In contrast to the first level, at the second level the abstracted circuits do not implement the same stabiliser transformations, because their gates are arranged differently (once more compare Fig. 1e, f). As a result, constructing an ICM circuit from a circular representation is equivalent to selecting an ICM circuit instance from the set of abstracted circuits. It is straightforward to compute the circuit's stabiliser transformations using the Boolean expressions resulting after the cuts.

The main advantage of circular CNOT circuits is that they abstract a large set of ICM circuits, and by this their Boolean model is the abstraction of multiple related possible stabiliser transformations. Each different cut choice in the circular representation has the potential to result in a different ICM circuit structure with correspondingly different stabiliser transformations. It is beneficial to have the possibility to generate/select a specific set of stabiliser transformations which are required for a particular quantum computation, because scalable error corrected quantum circuits are equivalent to ICM circuits. Although including only CNOTs, their computational universality is given by the appropriate initialisation and measurement basis, and it is advantageous to derive sets of related quantum circuits and understand their structure.

As a conclusion, a circular CNOT circuit can be formed as a generalisation for any fault-tolerant error corrected circuit.

5 Example: The ICM Toffoli Gate

Reversible circuits make extensive use of the Toffoli gate because it is classically universal (can simulate the classical AND, OR and NOT gates). Quantum computing architectures, especially large-scale error corrected ones, do not support the direct application of this gate. Therefore, the Toffoli gate needs to be firstly decomposed into a sequence of architecture specific gates. The decomposition into T and Hadamard gates, and the ICM implementation of the Toffoli gate are presented in Figs. 6 and 7.

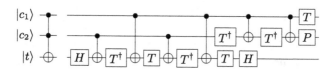

Fig. 6. Toffoli gate using CNOT, T ($T^\dagger$), P and Hadamard gates [6].

The previous sections discussed the construction of ICM circuits from the circular representation, but this section will backtrack the steps from ICM to circular CNOT circuit (Fig. 8). Firstly, for the ICM Toffoli gate implementation, the (I)nitialisations and the (M)easurement components are removed (backtrack second and third steps from Sect. 4). Secondly, all qubits operated by a single CNOT are uncut (joined). At this stage circuits like Fig. 3a are backtracked to a structure like Fig. 1e. Thirdly, all the remaining wire end points are looped, such that a circular structure finally emerges. The circular CNOT circuit of the ICM Toffoli is depicted in Fig. 8. Algorithm 1 summarises the circular CNOT construction using pseudo code. The algorithm assumes that circuit inputs are on the right and outputs on the left and that each CNOT is applied at a specific time t. The construction starts with the bottom most qubit. For the current qubit to be processed, the algorithm searches for the first CNOT gate that is applied on it (e.g. at time min), and selects the closest upper qubit which is not affected by a CNOT applied at time $\geq min$. The current and the closest upper wire are joined.

Comparing Figs. 6 and 8 against Fig. 7 shows that the circular representation uses less wires than the ICM equivalent (9 vs. 45), and increases the number of wires of the non-ICM decomposition by a factor of three (9 vs. 3). The cause of this is that single CNOT operated qubits are uncut. The circular representation shows that potential future ICM circuit optimisation techniques should consider *qubit reuse* techniques.

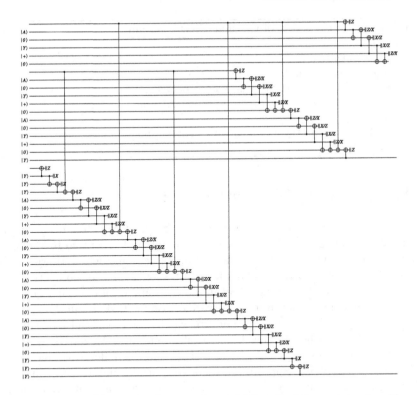

Fig. 7. The ICM Toffoli gate implementation. Additional qubits are introduced because each of the T and Hadamard gates from Fig. 6 is implemented using the teleported rotational gates from Fig. 5b–d and with the use of measurement-controlled teleportation subcircuits (e.g. Fig. 3d). The configurable measurement basis (Z/X and X/Z) are an ICM mechanism for controlling the information flow in the circuit.

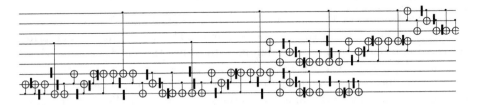

Fig. 8. The circular circuit of the ICM Toffoli decomposition. The circular representation is obtained after joining the left and right wire end points. The linear representation simplifies the visualisation. The cuts necessary to reconstruct the ICM equivalent circuit (Fig. 7) are depicted with black horizontal bars.

Algorithm 1. Construction of Circular CNOT Circuit

Require: *icm* an ICM circuit
1: $nrq \leftarrow icm.qubits$
2: **for all** $qub \in [nrq, 1]$ **do**
3:    *min* time of left-most (first) • or $\oplus$ on wire qub
4:    $pqub$ first wire so that: 1) $pqub < nrq$, and 2) $pqub$ is not used by any CNOT with time $\geq min$
5:    Join left end point of qub (input) with right end point of $pqub$ (output)
6: **end for**

6   Applications of Circular CNOT Circuits

The stabiliser transformations supported by a circular CNOT circuit are representative for an entire set of ICM circuits. The number of generated ICM circuits is a function of the number of cuts allowed on the circular wires. However, the number of equivalent generated circuits is not known for the moment. Future work on circular CNOT circuits will evaluate the number of equivalent circuits, but also on using these for the test and verification of ICM circuits.

The circular CNOT circuit representation can be used to model single missing gate faults (SMGF) when testing ICM quantum circuits. An SMGF is defined as a missing gate from the ideal gate list of the circuit under test. Such faults are detected by applying appropriate tests (initialising qubits according to a pattern) at circuit inputs and reading out the computed states at circuit output [9]. Methods for determining appropriate tests were investigated for example in [8,9]. Because ICM circuit gate lists include only CNOTs, a CNOT SMGF is equivalent to having a control *stuck at* $|0\rangle$; thus, the target is never affected. Considering a set of cuts that generate the tested circuit, the fault is modelled by introducing at most two additional cuts around the control of the CNOT, so that an ancilla qubit results (similar to Fig. 3a). The ancilla will have its state stuck at $|0\rangle$.

The verification of ICM circuits is a problem encountered in the context of fault-tolerant quantum computations. Large scale circuits need to be error corrected in order to achieve a certain fault-tolerance threshold, and one of the most promising error correction techniques is based on topological properties of the encoded information [3]. In that particular computational model information is encoded as strands and braids are the implementation of CNOT gates, thus the resulting circuits have an ICM interpretation. The information strands can be arbitrarily deformed as long as the braiding structure is left unchanged and, furthermore, circuit inputs and outputs can be placed anywhere on a strand. The placement is not guaranteed to make any computational sense, but it does not invalidate the strands (encoded qubit states) or the braids (CNOTs). The main issue with such error corrected circuits is that their ICM interpretation is a function of input/output location: the same circuit description in terms of strands and braids can be interpreted as different ICM circuit. It can be seen (e.g. Fig. 9) that input/output placement on strands is similar to cutting a circular

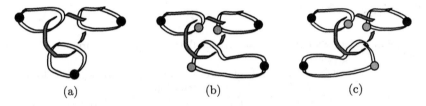

Fig. 9. Four qubits are encoded as strands and braided. The figures contain three braids (CNOTs), as the grey strand is braided with the three white strands. The black points denote potential input/output locations. The grey points represent additionally included input/outputs. The strands can be arbitrarily deformed, so that (b) and (c) have a CNOT structure equivalent to (a). The figures (b) and (c) assume that there is a horizontal temporal axis, and that inputs are on the left while outputs on the right side. The functionality of the ICM equivalent circuits depends on the initialisation and measurement basis chosen for the qubits.

representation. For this reason, the proposed circular representation is a valuable tool for verifying topologically error corrected ICM circuits: which cuts need to be made, and which traversal direction is required for the resulting ICM circuit to support a given set of stabiliser transformations? The support guarantees that the structure of the circuit (number of qubits and CNOT gate list) is correct, and that if the circuit were configured with corresponding qubit initialisations and measurements, a correct sequence of teleported rotational gates (T,P,V) and CNOTs would be implemented.

7   Conclusion

This work introduced circular CNOT circuits and their Boolean model. Two Boolean expressions are capturing all the possible stabiliser transformations supported by the circular circuits, one for X stabiliser transformations and another for Z transformations. Circular circuits can be transformed into fault-tolerant error corrected quantum circuits after performing a well defined set of cuts. The resulting circuits are the basis of ICM circuits, which are required for universal scalable fault-tolerant quantum computing. ICM circuits consist entirely of qubit initialisations, CNOTs (because all the single qubit quantum gates are implemented by teleportation) and qubit measurements. ICM circuits originating from the same circular CNOT circuit will have gate lists which are cyclic permutations of one another. Having modelled all the stabiliser mappings supported by a circular circuit, it is straightforward to infer the stabiliser transformations of a particular ICM instance.

Applications of circular CNOT circuits were enumerated in conjunction with their ICM transformation and showcase new possibilities for the design of quantum circuits. Future work will detail circular CNOT circuit based methods for optimisation, SMGF testing and verification of ICM circuits.

References

1. Aaronson, S., Gottesman, D.: Improved simulation of stabilizer circuits. Phys. Rev. A **70**(5), 052328 (2004)
2. Bravyi, S., Kitaev, A.: Universal quantum computation with ideal Clifford gates and noisy ancillas. Phys. Rev. A **71**(2), 022316 (2005)
3. Fowler, A.G., Mariantoni, M., Martinis, J.M., Cleland, A.N.: Surface codes, towards practical large-scale quantum computation. Phys. Rev. A **86**, 032324 (2012)
4. Fowler, A.G.: Time-optimal quantum computation (2012). arXiv arXiv:1210.4626
5. Maslov, D., Dueck, G.W., Michael Miller, D.: Simplification of Toffoli networks via templates. In: Proceedings 16th Symposium on Integrated Circuits and Systems Design, SBCCI 2003, pp. 53–58. IEEE (2003)
6. Nielsen, M.A., Chuang, I.L.: Quantum Computation and Quantum Information. Cambridge University Press, Cambridge (2010)
7. Paler, A., Polian, I., Nemoto, K., Devitt, S.J.: A fully fault-tolerant representation of quantum circuits. In: Krivine, J., Stefani, J.-B. (eds.) RC 2015. LNCS, vol. 9138, pp. 139–154. Springer, Heidelberg (2015)
8. Patel, K.N., Hayes, J.P., Markov, I.L.: Fault testing for reversible circuits. IEEE Trans. Comput. Aided Des. Integr. Circuits Syst. **23**(8), 1220–1230 (2004)
9. Polian, I., Fiehn, T., Becker, B., Hayes, J.P.: A family of logical fault models for reversible circuits. In: Proceedings of the 14th Asian Test Symposium 2005, pp. 422–427. IEEE (2005)

Towards Quantum Programs Verification: From Quipper Circuits to QPMC

Linda Anticoli[1]([✉]), Carla Piazza[1], Leonardo Taglialegne[1], and Paolo Zuliani[2]

[1] Department of Mathematics, Computer Science and Physics, University of Udine,
Udine, Italy
anticoli.linda@spes.uniud.it, carla.piazza@uniud.it
[2] School of Computing Science, Newcastle University, Newcastle upon Tyne, UK
paolo.zuliani@ncl.ac.uk

Abstract. We present a translation from the quantum programming language Quipper to the QPMC model checker, with the main aim of verifying Quipper programs. We implemented and tested our translation on several quantum algorithms, including Grover's quantum search.

Keywords: Quantum languages · Quantum circuits · Model checking

1 Introduction

The specification of algorithms in human readable form and their translation into machine executable code is one of the main goals of high-level programming languages. Quantum algorithms and protocols are usually described by quantum circuits (i.e., circuits involving quantum states and quantum logic gates). Even if such circuits have a simple mathematical description they can be very difficult to realise in practice without a deep knowledge of the essential features of the physical phenomena under consideration. The above reasons justify the need for tools that permit to abstract from a low-level description of quantum algorithms and protocols, thereby allowing people who know very little of quantum physics to program a quantum device.

The introduction of high-level formalisms allows to define and automatically verify formal properties of algorithms abstracting away from low-level physical details. Formal verification techniques such as *model checking* allow to test temporal properties of a system evaluating all possible cases. In the context of quantum computation, the possibility of verifying quantum protocols is very important. In particular, protocols for quantum cryptography, that are deeply investigated at the moment hoping for future applications in the secure transmission of information, require certification of correctness.

Although both the quantum computation and verification fields are quite new, we found two interesting tools: the functional language Quipper [8] and the model checking system QPMC [1], which we decided to use as a starting point

This work has been partially supported by the GNCS group of INdAM.

© Springer International Publishing Switzerland 2016
S. Devitt and I. Lanese (Eds.): RC 2016, LNCS 9720, pp. 213–219, 2016.
DOI: 10.1007/978-3-319-40578-0_16

for the development of a framework providing both a high-level programming style and formal verification tools.

The paper is organized as follows. In Sect. 2 we recall some basic quantum notations and briefly introduce Quipper and QPMC. In Sect. 3 we define an abstract algorithm for translating Quipper circuits into QPMC models. In Sect. 4 we describe our implementation of the translation algorithm together with some experimental results. Section 5 ends the paper.

2   Preliminaries

Quantum systems are represented through complex Hilbert spaces. There are two possible formalisms based on Hilbert spaces for quantum systems: the *state vector* formalism and the *density matrix* one. In the state vector formalism, used by Quipper, the state of a system is completely described by a normalized vector while evolutions are unitary operators. In the density matrix formalism, used by QPMC, the state of a system is a density matrix, while evolutions are superoperators. See [7] for more details.

Quipper is an embedded functional programming language within Haskell for quantum computation [4] based on the Knill's QRAM model [5] of quantum computation. Quipper is above all a circuit description language, for this reason it uses the state vector formalism and its main purpose is to make circuit implementation easier providing high level operations for circuit manipulation. This is encapsulated in a Haskell monad called `Circ`, where a sequence of unitary and measurement gates can be applied to qubits and bits. Quipper allows to generate a graphical representation and to simulate through three different simulators a circuit written in the monad.

QPMC is a model checker for quantum programs and protocols based on the density matrix formalism available in both web-based and off-line version at http://iscasmc.ios.ac.cn/too/qmc. It takes in input programs written in an extension of the guarded command language PRISM [6] that permits the specification of types `vector`, `matrix`, and `superoperator`.

The semantics of a QPMC program is given in terms of *superoperator weighted Markov chain*, which is a Markov chain in which the state space is taken classical, while all quantum effects are encoded in the superoperators labelling the transitions (see, e.g., [1,2]). Let $\mathcal{S}^{\mathcal{I}}(\mathcal{H})$ be the set of trace-nonincreasing superoperators over a complex Hilbert space $\mathcal{H}$. Given a density matrix ρ representing the state of a system, $\mathcal{E} \in \mathcal{S}^{\mathcal{I}}(\mathcal{H})$ implies that $tr(\mathcal{E}(\rho)) \in [0, 1]$. Hence, it is natural to regard the set $\mathcal{S}^{\mathcal{I}}(\mathcal{H})$ as the quantum correspondent of the domain of traditional probabilities [1]. A quantum Markov chain is a discrete time Markov chain, where classical probabilities are replaced with quantum probabilities.

Definition 1 (Quantum Markov Chain [1,2]). *A superoperator weighted Markov chain, also referred to as quantum Markov chain (herein QMC) over a Hilbert space $\mathcal{H}$ is a tuple (S, Q, AP, L), where:*

– *S is a countable (finite) set of classical states;*

- $Q : S \times S \to \mathcal{S}^{\mathcal{I}}(\mathcal{H})$ is called the transition matrix where for each $s \in S$, the superoperator $\sum_{t \in S} Q(s, t)$ is trace-preserving;
- AP is a finite set of atomic propositions and $L : S \to 2^{AP}$ is a labelling function.

The properties to be verified over QMC are expressed using the quantum computation tree logic (QCTL), a temporal logic for reasoning about evolution of quantum systems introduced in [2] that is a natural extension of PCTL. For instance, the quantum operator formula $\mathbb{Q}_{\sim\epsilon}[F]$ is a more general case of the PCTL probabilistic operator $\mathbb{P}_{\sim_i}[F]$ and it expresses a constraint on the probability that the paths from a certain state satisfy the formula F. QPMC also provides a function $qeval((Q =?)[F], \rho)$ to compute the density operator obtained applying the resultant superoperator on a given density operator ρ.

3   From Circuits to Quantum Markov Chains

We define a mapping from Quipper to QPMC programs at the semantic level, i.e., we consider a quantum circuit generated by Quipper and we define a correspondent QMC having an *equivalent* behavior.

We assume the reader to be familiar with the classical notions of graphs and boolean circuits. Given a node v of a directed graph we use the notation $In(v)$ ($Out(v)$) to denote the number of edges incoming (outcoming, respectively) in v. A quantum circuit is an extension of a boolean circuit in which operation gates are labeled with unitary operators. When a unitary operator is applied to k qubits it is necessary to know in which order the qubits are used for this reason each edge of a quantum circuit has two integer labels.

Definition 2 (Quantum Circuit). *A Quantum Circuit is a directed acyclic graph (herein DAG)* $C = (V, E)$ *whose nodes are of types* Qubit (Q), Unitary (U), Measurement (M) *and* Termination (T) *and are such that:*

1. *Q gates: each node v of type* Qubit *is an input node;*
2. *U gates: each node v of type* Unitary *is labelled with an integer $dim(v)$ and a square unitary matrix $U(v)$ of complex numbers of dimension $2^{dim(v)}$. Moreover, it holds that $In(v) = Out(v) = dim(v)$;*
3. *M gates: each node v of type* Measurement *is an output node;*
4. *T gates: each node v of type* Termination *is an output node;*
5. *Edges: each edge $e \in E$ is labelled with two integers $\mathcal{S}(e)$ and $\mathcal{T}(e)$ such that:*

```
deutsch :: (Qubit, Qubit) -> Circ Bit
deutsch (q1, q2) = do
    hadamard q1
    hadamard q2
    qnot_at q2 'controlled' q1
    hadamard q1
    measure q1
```

Fig. 1. Deutsch circuit in Quipper.

– *for all $u \in V$ the set $\mathcal{T}(\cdot)$ of its ingoing edges is $\{1, \ldots, In(u)\}$;*
– *for all $u \in V$ the set $\mathcal{S}(\cdot)$ of its outgoing edges is $\{1, \ldots, Out(u)\}$.*

A Quantum Circuit with k nodes of type Qubit *is said to have* size k.

Example 1. Let us consider the following Quipper implementation of Deutsch's algorithm.

Quipper graphically represents the circuit as shown in Fig. 1.

Our definition enriches the above representation with labels denoting the order in which the qubits are used, as depicted in Fig. 2.

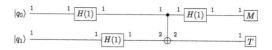

Fig. 2. Deutsch circuit with labels.

A Quantum Circuit of size k is said to be in *Normal Form* if each *Unitary* node v in the circuit has $dim(v) = k$.

Definition 3 (Strong Normal Form). *A Quantum Circuit C of size k is said to be in* Strong Normal Form *(herein SNF) if C is in Normal Form, for each edge $e \in E$ between two Unitary nodes $\mathcal{S}(e) = \mathcal{T}(e)$ holds and the first $h \leq k$ edges outgoing the last Unitary node enter into Measurement nodes.*

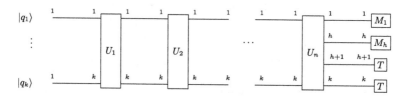

Fig. 3. Example of a circuit in strong normal form

A circuit C in SNF is completely specified by the tuple $(k, [U_i, \ldots, U_n], h)$ where k is the size of C, $U_1, \ldots, U_n$ are the Unitary operators in the order they occur in C, and h is the number of Measurement nodes.

In circuits the order of the labels on the edges is not preserved. On the contrary, SNF circuits require a precise ordering of the input and output edges. In order to match this requirement, SWAP operators have to be added.

Two quantum circuits are equivalent if, for any k-tuple of initial values of the qubits, the values of the qubits before measurements/terminations are the same. Moreover, to be equivalent two circuits need to give the same outputs with the same probabilities. Formally, let C be a Quantum Circuit of size k we denote by $Sem(C)$ the pair of functions $(F(C), M(C))$ where:

- $F(C) : \mathcal{H}^k \longrightarrow \mathcal{H}^k$ is the function which maps k qubits to the value they have just before the Measurement and Termination nodes;
- $M(C) : \mathcal{H}^k \times \{0,1\}^h \longrightarrow [0,1]$ is such that $M(C)(|\psi\rangle, (b_1, \ldots, b_h))$ is the probability of getting output $(b_1, \ldots, b_h) \in \{0,1\}^h$ on input $|\psi\rangle$.

Given two Quantum Circuits C_1 and C_2 of size k, C_1 and C_2 are equivalent, denoted by $C_1 \approx C_2$ if and only if $Sem(C_1) = Sem(C_2)$.

Lemma 1. *Every Quantum Circuit is equivalent to a SNF one.*

We are ready to define the QMC associated to a circuit in SNF. Intuitively, the states of the QMC correspond to the edges of the circuit, while the edges of the QMC connect subsequent states. Moreover, states without outgoing edges are added in the QMC to represent all the possible outputs of the circuit.

Definition 4 (QMC Associated to a Circuit). *Let C be a Quantum Circuit in SNF of size k with n Unitary nodes $\{U_1, \ldots, U_n\}$ and h Measurement nodes, the QMC Q_C associated to C is defined as follows:*

- *the k-tuple of edges of C entering U_i is associated to the state s_i in Q_C;*
- *the k-tuple of edges outgoing from U_n is associated to the state s_{n+1};*
- *in Q_C there are 2^h states $t_0, t_1, \ldots, t_{2^h-1}$;*
- *for each $i \in \{1, \ldots, n\}$ there is an edge from s_i to s_{i+1} is labelled with the superoperator $\mathcal{E}_{U_i}$ associated to U_i;*
- *for each $i \in \{0, \ldots, 2^h - 1\}$ there is an edge from s_{n+1} to t_i labelled with the superoperator $\widetilde{M}_i = M_i^h \otimes I^{k-h}$, where I^{k-h} is the identity matrix of size 2^{k-h} and M_i^h is a matrix of size 2^h having 1 in the $i+1$-th position and all 0's in the remaining.*

In Fig. 4 we can see the QMC associated to the circuit of Fig. 3.

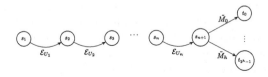

Fig. 4. QMC associated to the circuit of Fig. 3.

Lemma 2. *Given C in SNF we can always build the QMC Q_C associated to C and it holds that:*

1. *$\forall |\tau\rangle \in \mathcal{H}, \forall i \in \{1, \ldots, n\}, U_i|\tau\rangle = |\psi\rangle$ iff $\mathcal{E}_{U_i}|\tau\rangle\langle\tau|\mathcal{E}_{U_i}^\dagger = |\psi\rangle\langle\psi|$*
2. *$\forall |\tau\rangle \in \mathcal{H}$ if $F(C)(|\tau\rangle) = |\psi\rangle$ and $M(C)(|\tau\rangle, \{b_1, \ldots, b_h\}) = p$, with $m = bin(b_1 \ldots b_h)$ (i.e., the natural with binary expansion $b_1 \ldots b_h$) then: $p = tr(\widetilde{M}_m|\psi\rangle\langle\psi|\widetilde{M}_m^\dagger)$, and $\widetilde{M}_m|\psi\rangle\langle\psi|\widetilde{M}_m^\dagger = |b_1, \ldots, b_h \ldots\rangle\langle b_1, \ldots, b_h \ldots|$*

As a consequence of the above lemma any Temporal Logic coherently defined on both formalisms can be equivalently model checked either on the circuit or on its associated QMC.

4 Implementation and Experiments

The results described in the previous sections allow us to define an algorithm that maps a quantum circuit into an *equivalent* QMC. In particular, Algorithm Translate performs the following steps: it transforms a normal form circuit into a SNF circuit (see Lemma 1) and a SNF circuit into its corresponding QMC (see Lemma 2). Hence, given a quantum circuit C the output of Translate(C) is a QMC equivalent to C in the sense of Lemma 2.

The computational complexity of Translate(C) depends on the number n of Unitary nodes occurring in C and on its size k: Translate(C) generates a QMC having $O(n * k^2)$ internal nodes.

Our implementation of Translate(C) is available at https://github.com/miniBill/entangle. It exploits the `Transformer` module of Quipper –a library providing functions for defining general purpose transformations on low-level circuits– and works at data structure level.

We tested our translation tool with our Quipper implementation of *Grover's search algorithm* [7]. We implemented it on a search space of dimension 4.

Exploiting our implementation we automatically generate the code for QPMC. We tested the formulas to evaluate the density matrix associated to each terminal state and the results are coherent with expectations.

5 Conclusions

We proposed a framework that performs a translation from Quipper to QPMC. The main idea is to use this framework to create a tool that allows, on the one hand, the description of quantum algorithms and protocols in an high-level programming language, and on the other hand their formal verification. We implemented and tested our translator on some common quantum algorithms and the final results validated our expectations. We are working on enrichment and optimization of our framework in order to match the requirement of validating complex algorithms and protocols, e.g., the ones involving also a classical control outside the `Circ` monad. Another direction of research we are interested in concerns model checking techniques that efficiently deal with special circuits [3].

References

1. Feng, Y., Hahn, E.M., Turrini, A., Zhang, L.: QPMC: a model checker for quantum programs and protocols. In: Björner, N., Boer, F. (eds.) FM 2015. LNCS, vol. 9109, pp. 265–272. Springer, Heidelberg (2015)
2. Feng, Y., Yu, N., Ying, M.: Model checking quantum Markov chains. J. Comput. Syst. Sci. **79**, 1181–1198 (2013)
3. Gay, S., Nagarajan, R., Papanikolaou, N.: Probabilistic model-checking of quantum protocols. In: Proceedings of the 2nd International Workshop on Developments in Computational Models (2006)
4. Green, A.S., Lumsdaine, P.L., Ross, N.J., Selinger, P., Valiron, B.: Quipper: a scalable quantum programming language. SIGPLAN Not. **48**(6), 333–342 (2013)

5. Knill, E.: Conventions for Quantum Pseudocode. Technical report, Los Alamos National Laboratory (1996)
6. Kwiatkowska, M., Norman, G., Parker, D.: PRISM 4.0: verification of probabilistic real-time systems. In: Qadeer, S., Gopalakrishnan, G. (eds.) CAV 2011. LNCS, vol. 6806, pp. 585–591. Springer, Heidelberg (2011)
7. Nielsen, M.A., Chuang, I.L.: Quantum Computation and Quantum Information. Cambridge University Press, Cambridge (2011)
8. Smith, J.M., Ross, N.J., Selinger, P., Valiron, B.: Quipper: concrete resource estimation in quantum algorithms. In: Workshop on Quantitative Aspects of Programming Languages and Systems, QApPL, Grenoble (2014). arxiv:1412.0625

Circuit Theory

Application of Permutation Group Theory in Reversible Logic Synthesis

Dmitry V. Zakablukov[✉]

Department of Information Security, Bauman Moscow State Technical University,
Moscow, Russian Federation
dmitriy.zakablukov@gmail.com

Abstract. The paper discusses various applications of permutation group theory in the synthesis of reversible logic circuits consisting of Toffoli gates with negative control lines. An asymptotically optimal synthesis algorithm for circuits consisting of gates from the NCT library is described. An algorithm for gate complexity reduction, based on equivalent replacements of gates compositions, is introduced. A new approach for combining a group-theory-based synthesis algorithm with a Reed–Muller-spectra-based synthesis algorithm is described. Experimental results are presented to show that the proposed synthesis techniques allow a reduction in input lines count, gate complexity or quantum cost of reversible circuits for various benchmark functions.

Keywords: Reversible logic · Synthesis · Permutation group theory

1 Introduction

Reversible logic circuits have been studied in many recent papers [1,10,12,14, 18]. On the one hand, the interest in these circuits is caused by the theoretically possible reduction of energy consumption in digital devices due to the reversibility of all computations [4]. On the other hand, all quantum computations are necessarily reversible. Hence, with the help of a reversible circuit, one can model a quantum circuit.

One important research area is the development of new efficient and fast synthesis algorithms, which can produce a reversible circuit with low gate complexity and depth. However, for the purpose of a comparison between different synthesis algorithms, we should first choose a library of gates, from which a synthesized circuit will consist. One such gate library is one that includes NOT (inversion gate), CNOT (Feynman gate) and C^2NOT (Toffoli gate). We will refer to it as the NCT library. Another popular gate library is the GT library, which includes generalized Toffoli gates with positive and negative control input lines. Both libraries are functionally complete in terms of the ability to construct a reversible circuit that implements a desired even permutation from the alternating group $A(\mathbb{B}^n)$ without using additional inputs. An odd permutation from the symmetric group $S(\mathbb{B}_2^n)$ can always be realized in a reversible circuit without additional inputs in the GT, but not in the NCT library.

© Springer International Publishing Switzerland 2016
S. Devitt and I. Lanese (Eds.): RC 2016, LNCS 9720, pp. 223–238, 2016.
DOI: 10.1007/978-3-319-40578-0_17

For many proposed synthesis algorithms, an upper bound for the gate complexity of a reversible circuit in the worst case is proved. Though it was proved that the worst case requires $\Omega(n2^n / \log n)$ gates from the NCT library [15], almost all these bounds are of the form $O(n2^n)$ in the NCT library [9].

Recently, the first asymptotically optimal in NCT library synthesis algorithm was introduced with the gate complexity $L(\mathfrak{S}) \lesssim 3n2^{n+4} / \log_2 n$ of a reversible circuit in the worst case [18]. In Sect. 2, we briefly describe this cycle-based algorithm. Section 3 contains descriptions of the replacement rules from [17] and of a "moving and replacing" algorithm for reducing the gate complexity of a reversible circuit in NCT and GT libraries with the help of these rules. In Sect. 4, we discuss various approaches of reducing the gate complexity during the synthesis process. In Sect. 5, we introduce a novel technique for combining a cycle-based synthesis algorithm with a Reed–Muller-spectra-based one. Experimental results of benchmark functions synthesis are presented in Sect. 6; all new circuits were obtained with the help of our open source software *ReversibleLogic-Generator* [19] that implements all synthesis techniques described in this paper. All results we present here (except Sect. 2 and the first part of Sect. 3) are new.

We use the following notation for a generalized Toffoli gate with negative control input lines.

Definition 1. *A generalized Toffoli gate* $TOF(I; J; t) = TOF(i_1, \cdots, i_r; j_1, \cdots, j_s; t)$ *is a reversible gate, which defines a transformation* $f_{I;J;t} \colon \mathbb{B}^n \to \mathbb{B}^n$ *as follows:*

$$f_{I;J;t}(\langle x_1, \cdots, x_n \rangle) = \langle x_1, \cdots, x_t \oplus x_{i_1} \wedge \cdots \wedge x_{i_r} \wedge \bar{x}_{j_1} \wedge \cdots \wedge \bar{x}_{j_s}, \cdots, x_n \rangle,$$

where $I = \{ i_1, \cdots, i_r \}$ *is a set of indices of positive control input lines,* $J = \{ j_1, \cdots, j_s \}$ *is a set of indices of negative control input lines, and* t *is an index of a controlled output line,* $I \cap J = \emptyset$, $t \notin I \cup J$.

In the case of the absence of negative control input lines, a generalized Toffoli gate will be referenced as $TOF(I; t)$, and in the case when a generalized Toffoli gate has no control input lines at all, it will be referenced as $TOF(t)$. In other words, $TOF(t) = TOF(\emptyset; \emptyset; t)$ and $TOF(I; t) = TOF(I; \emptyset; t)$. Using this notation, we can refer to a NOT gate as $TOF(a)$, to a CNOT gate as $TOF(b; a)$ and to a C^2NOT gate as $TOF(b, c; a)$.

2   Asymptotically Optimal Synthesis Algorithm

In [18] a cycle-based synthesis algorithm that can produce a reversible circuit with the asymptotically optimal in NCT library gate complexity for any even permutation on the set $\mathbb{B}^n$, was described. It is the first and currently (as far as we know) the only asymptotically optimal non-search synthesis algorithm for the NCT library. Our software [19] is based on it, so we are going to briefly describe the essence of the algorithm.

Let's consider an even permutation $h \in A(\mathbb{B}^n)$. The main idea is a decomposition of h into a product of transpositions in such a way that all of them can be grouped by K independent transpositions[1]:

$$h = G_1 \circ G_2 \circ \cdots \circ G_t \circ h' ,$$

where $G_i = (\mathbf{x}_{i,1}, \mathbf{y}_{i,1}) \circ \cdots \circ (\mathbf{x}_{i,K}, \mathbf{y}_{i,K})$ is an i-th group of K independent transpositions, $\mathbf{x}_{i,j}, \mathbf{y}_{i,j} \in \mathbb{B}^n$ and h' is a residual permutation.

Using vectors of a group G_i, we construct a matrix A_i as follows:

$$A_i = \begin{bmatrix} \mathbf{x}_{i,1} \ \mathbf{y}_{i,1} \ \cdots \ \mathbf{x}_{i,K} \ \mathbf{y}_{i,K} \end{bmatrix}^T .$$

The matrix A_i is a $2K \times n$ binary matrix. If $2^{2K} < n$, then some columns in it are equal to one another. These duplicated columns can be zeroed-out in the matrix, using CNOT gates, with the help of conjugation; this results in a new matrix $A_i^{(1)}$.

Note that the matrix A_i defines a permutation $\pi_i \in S(\mathbb{B}^n)$ and every gate e from the NCT library defines a permutation $h_e \in S(\mathbb{B}^n)$, for which $h_e^{-1} = h_e$. Therefore, a conjugation of a permutation π by a permutation h_e, denoted as $\pi^{h_e} = h_e^{-1} \circ \pi \circ h_e$, corresponds to attaching the gate e to the front and back of a current sub-circuit. For example, if the first two columns in the matrix A_i are equal, we can zero-out the second column with the help of two $TOF(1; 2)$ gates.

Next, we fix all pairwise distinct nonzero columns $\{ c_{j_1}, \cdots, c_{j_d} \}$ in the matrix $A_i^{(1)}$ and choose an index of a controlled output t from the set $\{ j_1, \cdots, j_d \}$. After that we transform the matrix $A_i^{(1)}$ to the canonical form $A_i^{(2)}$ with the help of conjugation, where an l-th row, l is odd, differs from the $(l + 1)$-th row only in t-th element.

And finally, we transform the matrix $A_i^{(2)}$ to the final form $A_i^{(3)}$ with the help of $TOF(j)$ gates, where $j \notin \{ j_1, \cdots, j_d \}$. In [18] it was proved that the matrix $A_i^{(3)}$ can be realized by the single gate $TOF(\{ 1, \cdots, n \} \setminus \{ j_1, \cdots, j_d \}; t)$. The gate can be represented as a composition of C^2NOT gates if $K > 1$ (the number of independent transpositions in a group G_i).

A synthesized reversible circuit $\mathfrak{S}$, produced by the algorithm, has the gate complexity $L(\mathfrak{S}) \lesssim 3n2^{n+4} / \log_2 n$, if $K = O(\log_2 n - \log_2 \log_2 n - \log_2 \phi(n))$, where $\phi(n) < n / \log_2 n$ is an arbitrarily slowly growing function, and the gate complexity $L(\mathfrak{S}) \lesssim 6n2^n$, if $K = 2$. These results were proved in [18].

In our software [19], we can change the parameter K to achieve the best synthesis result in a particular case. But in practice, when the number of input lines in a circuit is large, it is almost always the best option to use $K = \lceil \log_2 n \rceil$ during the synthesis process.

The time complexity of the synthesis algorithm is $T(A) = O(n2^n / \log_2 n)$ in the worst case.

---

[1] Hereinafter a multiplication of permutations is left-associative: $(f \circ g)(x) = g(f(x))$.

3   Generalized Replacement Rules for Gate Compositions

One of the most widely used gate complexity reduction techniques is an applying gate compositions templates to a reversible circuit. For example, such templates were considered in [9]. This approach involves storing templates and finding them in a circuit. But we can interchange some adjacent gates of NCT and GT libraries in a reversible circuit without changing the resulting transformation, defined by the circuit. We call such gates *independent*.

In [5] the necessary and sufficient conditions for the independence of two $TOF(I_j; t_j)$ gates were proved. However, for the gates from the GT library we can supplement these conditions.

Lemma 1. *Gates $TOF(I_1; J_1; t_1)$ and $TOF(I_2; J_2; t_2)$ are independent iff at least one of the following condition holds (see Fig. 1):*

1. $t_1 \notin I_2 \cup J_2$ and $t_2 \notin I_1 \cup J_1$ (in particular, $t_1 = t_2$);
2. $I_1 \cap J_2 \neq \emptyset$ or $I_2 \cap J_1 \neq \emptyset$.

Proof of the Lemma 1 was partly given in [17]. Even though the first condition of gate independence was already known before [5] (see Fig. 1a and b), the second one cannot be derived from it (see Fig. 1c).

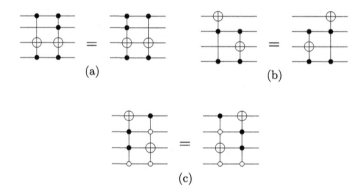

(a)   (b)

(c)

Fig. 1. Examples of independent gates: (a)–(b) NCT library specific; (c) GT library specific.

In [2] rule-based optimization techniques based on Karnaugh maps for the optimization of sub-circuits with common targets were described. The main disadvantage of this approach is the restricted scalability for circuits with the large number of input lines. On the other hand, the advantage of using negative control Toffoli gates for the simplification of reversible circuits and reducing their quantum cost was shown by the authors.

In [17] we proposed generalized replacement rules for the case of an arbitrary number of input lines. Moreover, we were able to obtain a new rule for interchanging two gates with changing the polarity of a control line for one of these gates (see the last rule in Table 4). Our replacement rules are essentially templates of small length. But the advantage of using them is in changing the set of negative control input lines in a gate. This makes it possible to obtain independent gates instead of dependent ones in some cases, interchange or move them in a reversible circuit to new places and apply other replacement rules. "Moving and replacing" algorithm will be described later.

A similar approach was used in [11], though replacement rules in that paper differ from ours.

Let's consider a composition of two dependent gates $e_1 * e_2$. Let h_{e_1} and h_{e_2} be permutations defined by them respectively. If we want to obtain an equal composition $\mathfrak{S}_1 * e_1 = e_1 * e_2$, then the circuit $\mathfrak{S}_1$ must implement the permutation $h_1 = h_{e_2}^{h_{e_1}}$. And if we want to obtain an equal composition $e_2 * \mathfrak{S}_2 = e_1 * e_2$, then the circuit $\mathfrak{S}_2$ must implement the permutation $h_2 = h_{e_1}^{h_{e_2}}$.

All our replacement rules can be classified as follow:

1. Representing a gate from the GT library as a composition of gates from the NCT library.
2. Merging two gates into one.
3. Reducing the negative control lines number.
4. Interchanging two dependent gates.

For the sake of clarity, we will organize the detailed description of our rules in the form of Tables 1, 2, 3 and 4, one for each rule "class". The left column of the tables contains a gate composition before applying replacement rule, and the right column contains the result of the replacement. For every rule a picture goes first (for understanding the concept of a rule), then, a text description of the rule, and finally, a condition for applying the rule.

Now we can describe the "moving and replacing" algorithm implemented in our software [19], which may reduce the gate complexity of a circuit.

Let a reversible circuit $\mathfrak{S}$ be a composition of l gates from the GT library: $\mathfrak{S} = \overset{l}{\underset{i=1}{*}} e_i$. If a gate composition $e_i * e_j$ satisfies the condition of a replacement, where $i < j$, and there is such an index s, $i \leq s < j$, that gates e_i and e_k are independent for every $i < k \leq s$, and gates e_j and e_k are independent for every $s < k < j$, then the gates e_i and e_j can be removed from the circuit and a result of the replacement for $e_i * e_j$ can be inserted between gates e_s and e_{s+1}.

So, the "moving and replacing" algorithm first searches a pair of gates, the composition of which satisfies the condition of a replacement. After that the algorithm checks if they can be moved to each other, using Lemma 1. If yes, it implements a replacement as described above. In the case, when the gate complexity is not reduced after replacement, but there are new gates in a circuit, the algorithm continues to work, until the gate complexity is reduced or there are no new gates.

The time complexity of the proposed "moving and replacing" algorithm $T(A) \geq R \cdot l^2$, where R is the number of replacement rules, l is the gate complexity of an original circuit. It is almost the same as the time complexity of any template based optimization algorithm. At the same time, our "moving and replacing" algorithm seems to be more flexible than a template-based approach,

Table 1. Representing a gate from the GT library as a composition of gates from the NCT library.

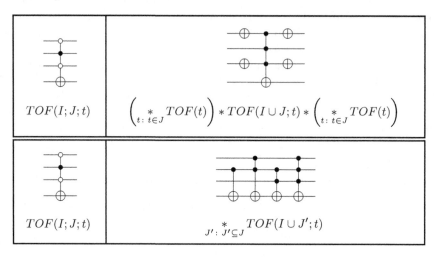

because proposed replacement rules do not depend on the number of inputs in a reversible circuit, therefore there is no need to store a large number of templates and search them in a library.

4   Boolean Hypercube Search

Let's consider the following permutation:

$$h =(\langle 1,0,0,0,0\rangle, \langle 1,0,1,0,1\rangle)\circ$$
$$\circ(\langle 1,0,0,0,1\rangle, \langle 1,0,1,0,0\rangle)\circ$$
$$\circ(\langle 1,0,0,1,0\rangle, \langle 1,0,1,1,1\rangle)\circ$$
$$\circ(\langle 1,0,0,1,1\rangle, \langle 1,0,1,1,0\rangle) .$$

As we can see, vectors in every transposition of permutation h presented above differ only in the 3rd and 5th coordinates. There are four transpositions total. Hence, a set of all vectors in these transpositions represents a Boolean 3-cube $\mathbb{B}^{5,1,2}_{1,0}$ contained in a Boolean 5-cube $\mathbb{B}^5$. This 3-cube can also be denoted as $\langle 1,0,*,*,*\rangle$. Therefore, the permutation h can be implemented by a composition of gates $TOF(1;2;3) * TOF(1;2;5)$.

Let's assume we can represent a permutation $h \in A(\mathbb{B}^n)$ as a product of transpositions in such a way that a set of all vectors of first k transpositions in this product represents a Boolean $(1 + \log_2 k)$-cube. In the case, when we use only our cycle-based approach for the synthesis, we have to divide these k transpositions into groups and synthesize them separately. This approach can lead to significant gate complexity of a produced reversible circuit. On the other hand, any Boolean hypercube contained in $\mathbb{B}^n$ can be implemented by a composition of no more than n generalized Toffoli gates $TOF(I;J;t)$.

Table 2. Merging two gates into one.

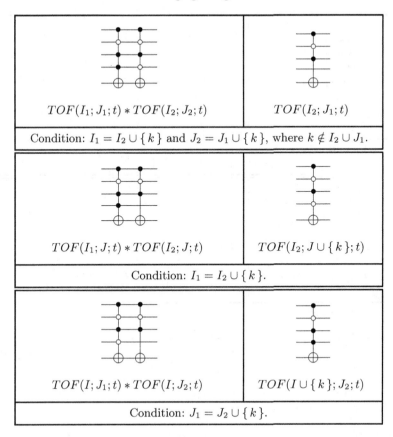

$TOF(I_1; J_1; t) * TOF(I_2; J_2; t)$	$TOF(I_2; J_1; t)$
Condition: $I_1 = I_2 \cup \{k\}$ and $J_2 = J_1 \cup \{k\}$, where $k \notin I_2 \cup J_1$.	
$TOF(I_1; J; t) * TOF(I_2; J; t)$	$TOF(I_2; J \cup \{k\}; t)$
Condition: $I_1 = I_2 \cup \{k\}$.	
$TOF(I; J_1; t) * TOF(I; J_2; t)$	$TOF(I \cup \{k\}; J_2; t)$
Condition: $J_1 = J_2 \cup \{k\}$.	

For example, a transformation $f(\langle x_1, x_2, \cdots, x_n \rangle) = \langle x_1, x_2 \oplus x_1, x_3, \ldots, x_n \rangle$ can be implemented by a reversible circuit, produced by our main synthesis algorithm, with the gate complexity $O(n2^n)$, and it can be implemented by a single gate $TOF(1; 2)$, because there is a Boolean 1-cube $\langle 1, *, \cdots, * \rangle$.

It is obvious that searching a Boolean hypercube can take a significant amount of time and can be inefficient for large functions. But this approach makes it possible to obtain better synthesis results in some cases.

4.1 Effective Disjoints of Cycles

To find a larger Boolean hypercube, we should somehow effectively represent a permutation h as a product of specific transpositions. Let's consider a permutation $h = (a, b, c, e, f, g)$, where the Hamming distances $d(a, e) = d(b, g) = d(c, f) = \Delta$ and the Hamming distance for any other two elements of h is not equal to Δ. We have the two possible representations of h as a product of cycles:

Table 3. Reducing the negative control lines number.

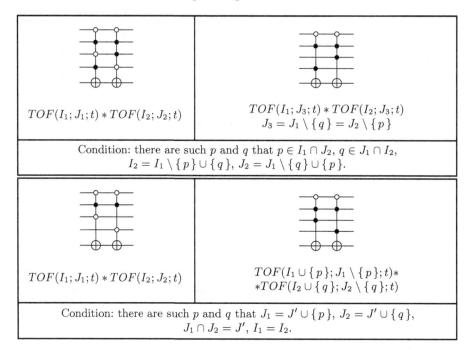

$TOF(I_1; J_1; t) * TOF(I_2; J_2; t)$	$TOF(I_1; J_3; t) * TOF(I_2; J_3; t)$ $J_3 = J_1 \setminus \{q\} = J_2 \setminus \{p\}$
Condition: there are such p and q that $p \in I_1 \cap J_2$, $q \in J_1 \cap I_2$, $I_2 = I_1 \setminus \{p\} \cup \{q\}$, $J_2 = J_1 \setminus \{q\} \cup \{p\}$.	
$TOF(I_1; J_1; t) * TOF(I_2; J_2; t)$	$TOF(I_1 \cup \{p\}; J_1 \setminus \{p\}; t)*$ $*TOF(I_2 \cup \{q\}; J_2 \setminus \{q\}; t)$
Condition: there are such p and q that $J_1 = J' \cup \{p\}$, $J_2 = J' \cup \{q\}$, $J_1 \cap J_2 = J'$, $I_1 = I_2$.	

1. $h = (a, e) \circ (a, f, g) \circ (e, b, c)$.
2. $h = (b, g) \circ (c, f) \circ (a, b) \circ (c, g) \circ (e, f)$.

We can see that in the first case only the cycle (a, e) has the two elements with the Hamming distance equal to Δ. But in the second case there are two cycles (b, g) and (c, f) that have the two elements with the Hamming distance equal to Δ. Therefore, we can assume that the set $\{b, g, c, f\}$ may contain a larger Boolean hypercube, compared to the set $\{a, e\}$, and we will call the second representation of h an *effective disjoint of cycles*.

There is a simple linear algorithm for an effective disjoint of cycles of a permutation for a given Hamming distance Δ. In the first pass, the algorithm searches all pairs of elements in a cycle with the Hamming distance equal to Δ. In the second pass, the algorithm calculates for a found pair p how many other pairs would be broken, if we disjoint the cycle by the pair p. In the third pass, the algorithm chooses a pair p, for which the number of broken pairs is minimal. And finally, the algorithm disjoints the cycle by the chosen pair. After that we don't have to repeat all steps for obtained cycles, because we can simply remove broken pairs and use previous results for further disjoints.

For our example above, we have the three pairs with the Hamming distance equal to Δ: (a, e), (b, g) and (c, f). If we choose the pair (a, e), it would break two pairs (b, g) and (c, f). And if we choose either (b, g) or (c, f), they would break

Table 4. Interchanging two dependent gates.

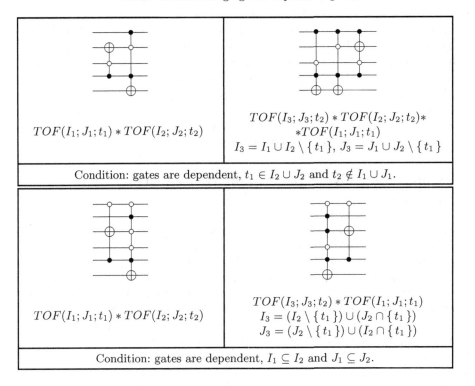

$TOF(I_1; J_1; t_1) * TOF(I_2; J_2; t_2)$	$TOF(I_3; J_3; t_2) * TOF(I_2; J_2; t_2)*$ $*TOF(I_1; J_1; t_1)$ $I_3 = I_1 \cup I_2 \setminus \{t_1\},\ J_3 = J_1 \cup J_2 \setminus \{t_1\}$
Condition: gates are dependent, $t_1 \in I_2 \cup J_2$ and $t_2 \notin I_1 \cup J_1$.	
$TOF(I_1; J_1; t_1) * TOF(I_2; J_2; t_2)$	$TOF(I_3; J_3; t_2) * TOF(I_1; J_1; t_1)$ $I_3 = (I_2 \setminus \{t_1\}) \cup (J_2 \cap \{t_1\})$ $J_3 = (J_2 \setminus \{t_1\}) \cup (I_2 \cap \{t_1\})$
Condition: gates are dependent, $I_1 \subseteq I_2$ and $J_1 \subseteq J_2$.	

only the pair (a, e). Hence, an effective disjoint will be for the pair (b, g) or (c, f). It is not difficult to show that the proposed algorithm for an effective disjoint of cycles doesn't depend on the order of elements in a cycle. The disjoint result will be the same for the permutation $h = (a, b, c, e, f, g)$ and for the permutation $h' = (c, e, f, g, a, b)$.

The time complexity of a single disjoint operation for a cycle of length l is no more than $O(l \log_2 l)$.

4.2   Left and Right Multiplication

Until now we used a left multiplication for a cycle disjoint. But we can also use a right multiplication. E. g., a cycle (a, b, c) can be represented in two ways for the transposition (a, b):

1. Left multiplication: $(a, b, c) = (a, b) \circ (a, c)$.
2. Right multiplication: $(a, b, c) = (b, c) \circ (a, b)$.

We can see that the results of the multiplications are different. This difference can lead to significantly different synthesis results.

There is no way to find out on an i-th step of our basic synthesis algorithm, whether the left or right multiplication would be the best in the end. The only thing we can do is to make both left and right multiplications on an i-th step and choose the one which leads to the greater permutation reduction and to the lower gate complexity of a current reversible circuit. This approach doubles the synthesis time, but it also leads to better reversible circuits in some cases.

And finally, another area for optimizations is the constructing of a bijective transformation for a given non-bijective one. We believe that in terms of reversible logic synthesis the best result can be achieved, when this bijective transformation has minimal Hamming distances between inputs and outputs.

5   Combining Cycle-Based and RM-spectra Based Algorithms

In [13] a hybrid framework was proposed, which combines a cycle-based and a RM-spectra based algorithms. Unfortunately, this combination is only the choice of a better reversible circuit synthesized by one or another algorithm.

We propose a new approach for combining a cycle-based and a RM-spectra based algorithms. In [9] a RM-spectra based synthesis algorithm was described. For a reversible specification $f\colon \mathbb{B}^n \to \mathbb{B}^n$ the algorithm successively transforms the truth table T_n to the truth table that corresponds to the identity transformation. This is done by changing an i-th row in T_n, for which $T_n[i] \neq i$, to the form $T_n[i] = i$ for every $i = 0, \cdots, (2^n - 1)$. Every row $j < i$ is not changed after a transformation of an i-th row: $T_n[j] = j$.

Our combining approach allows us to modify the truth table T_n in such a way that for the first row i, for which $T_n[i] \neq i$, $T_n[j] = j$, $j < i$, each row $k \leq i$ in a modified truth table T_n' will be equal to itself: $T_n'[k] = k$.

On an i-th step of the RM-spectra based synthesis algorithm from [9] a reversible circuit $\mathfrak{S}$ which we synthesize is of the form:

$$\mathfrak{S} = \mathfrak{S}_l * \mathfrak{S}_{T_n} * \mathfrak{S}_r \,,$$

where sub-circuits $\mathfrak{S}_l$ and $\mathfrak{S}_r$ were constructed on the previous steps and a circuit $\mathfrak{S}_{T_n}$ is unknown, it implements a transformation described by the truth table T_n, for which $T_n[j] = j$, $j < i$, $T_n[i] \neq i$. The original RM-spectra based synthesis algorithm appends gates to the $\mathfrak{S}_l$ or $\mathfrak{S}_r$ after modifying the i-th row in T_n.

Let h, h_l, h_t, h_r be the permutations, defined by the circuits $\mathfrak{S}$, $\mathfrak{S}_l$, $\mathfrak{S}_{T_n}$ and $\mathfrak{S}_r$ respectively. This implies that

$$h = h_l \circ h_t \circ h_r \,.$$

Let's assume $T_n[i] = k$ and $T_n[l] = i$, where $k, l > i$. We can state that

$$h = h_l \circ h_t' \circ (i, k) \circ h_r = h_l \circ h_t' \circ h_r \circ (i, k)^{h_r} \,,$$
$$h = h_l \circ (i, l) \circ h_t' \circ h_r = (i, l)^{h_l^{-1}} \circ h_l \circ h_t' \circ h_r \,,$$

where a permutation h'_t is defined by the truth table T'_n, $T'_n[j] = j$ for every $j \leq i$.

From this it follows that we can "push" one transposition (i, k) or (i, l) from the permutation h_t to the right or to the left, conjugate it by the permutation h_r or h_l^{-1} respectively and "skip" the transformation of the i-th row in the truth table T_n by the original RM-spectra based synthesis algorithm. After that we can move to the next row and repeat this process.

After a RM-spectra based synthesis algorithm finishes its work, we can use a cycle-based synthesis algorithm to synthesize pushed transpositions. There are several approaches to decide, whether an i-th row is pushed or not and where it will be pushed (left or right). For example, we can push an i-th row only when the Hamming weight of i is greater or equal to a predefined threshold w. It is equivalent to processing all monomials of degree $d < w$ in a Reed–Muller polynomial with a RM-spectra based synthesis algorithm. All other monomials will be processed by a cycle-based synthesis algorithm.

We realized the proposed combining approach in our software [19] with the ability to choose a "push policy" and a weight threshold. This allowed us to find a reversible circuit implementing **rd53** function with 7 inputs and with the gate complexity equal to 11 in the GT library (see Fig. 2). The weight threshold was equal to one during the synthesis process.

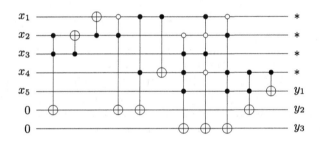

Fig. 2. Realization of **rd53** function in a reversible circuit with 7 inputs and 11 gates in the GT library.

6   Experimental Results

We developed an open source software *ReversibleLogicGenerator* [19], which implements the basic cycle-based synthesis algorithm from [18] and all the gate complexity reduction techniques, described in this paper. Using our software, we conducted a series of experiments on reversible benchmark functions synthesis. The results are presented in Tables 5, 6 and 7. The synthesis time in the worst case was a matter of seconds.

We were able to obtain more than 40 new reversible circuits, which have less input count, less gate complexity or less quantum cost compared to existing circuits. All specifications for benchmark functions and their names were taken from the *Reversible Logic Synthesis Benchmarks Page* [7] and from the *RevLib*

Table 5. Benchmark functions synthesis (new circuits with less input count).

Function	New circuits				Existing circuits			
	lines$_{min}$	GC	QC	T-count	lines$_{min}$	GC	QC	T-count
gf2^3mult	7	73	740	632				
gf2^3mult	7	79	712	632	9	11	47	63
gf2^3mult	7	145	704	654				
gf2^4mult	9	415	47649	10838*	12	19	83	112
gf2^4mult	9	1834	5914	5156				
nth_prime9_inc	9	3942	19313	15234	10	7522	17975	14193
rd73	9	296	43421	8765*	10	20	64	98
rd73	9	835	4069	3521				
rd84	11	679	359384	25364*	15	28	98	147
rd84	11	2560	12397	8772*				

*An ancillary line is required

site [16]. We use the following conventions in the tables: *lines* is the number of inputs in a reversible circuit $\mathfrak{S}$, GC is the gate complexity $L(\mathfrak{S})$ of this circuit and QC is its quantum cost $W(\mathfrak{S})$; T-count is the number of T gates in a decomposition of the circuit into Clifford$+T$ gates.

The quantum cost of obtained circuits was calculated with the help of the software *RCViewer+* [3]. Its calculation is based on the paper [6], according to which a generalized Toffoli gate with negative control lines may have the same quantum cost as the corresponding generalized Toffoli gate without negative control lines. Also we included the T-count cost measure for all circuits in the tables (cost calculation was based on the paper [8]). Despite the fact that this cost measure is very popular for fault-tolerant circuits in the literature, it is not universal in the case of limited ancillary lines availability. According to [8], there is a circuit of Toffoli gates that cannot be implemented, using Clifford$+T$ gates, without an ancillary line. We marked such T-count metrics by the asterisk symbol in the tables.

Tables 5, 6 and 7 contain results for obtained reversible circuits with less input count (column lines$_{min}$), less gate complexity (column GC$_{min}$) and less quantum cost (column QC$_{min}$) compared to existing circuits respectively. Since we compare our circuits only with circuits consisting of gates from NCT and GT libraries and since the NCT library is a part of the GT library, such comparison made by us is correct.

We have not included circuits with more than 12 inputs in the tables just because of the limited format of the paper. One can easily synthesize such circuits with the help of our software.

With the help of developed software we were able to find a reversible circuit with 7 input lines and with 11 gates from the GT library for one of the most

Table 6. Benchmark functions synthesis (new circuits with less gate complexity).

Function	New circuits				Existing circuits			
	lines	GC_{min}	QC	T-count	lines	GC_{min}	QC	T-count
2of5	6	**9**	268	191[*]	6	**15**	107	119
2of5	6	**10**	118	135				
2of5	7	**11**	32	42	7	**12**	32	49
3_17	3	**4**	14	14	3	**6**	12	14
3_17	3	**5**	13	14				
4b15g_2	4	**12**	57	55[*]	4	**15**	31	35
4b15g_4	4	**12**	49	45[*]	4	**15**	35	31[*]
4b15g_4	4	**14**	47	45[*]				
4b15g_5	4	**14**	72	54[*]	4	**15**	29	42
4mod5	5	**4**	13	14	5	**5**	7	7
5mod5	6	**7**	429	294[*]	6	**8**	84	70[*]
6sym	7	**14**	1308	628[*]	7	**36**	777	741
6sym	7	**15**	825	624[*]				
9sym	10	**73**	61928	7004[*]	10	**129**	6941	5484[*]
9sym	10	**74**	31819	6788[*]				
ham7	7	**19**	77	85	7	**25**	49	42
hwb12	12	**42095**	134316	98482	12	**55998**	198928	134131
nth_prime7_inc	7	**427**	10970	5403[*]	7	**1427**	3172	2837
nth_prime7_inc	7	**474**	10879	5403[*]				
nth_prime7_inc	7	**824**	2269	1906				
nth_prime8_inc	8	**977**	10218	7359[*]	8	**3346**	7618	5985
nth_prime8_inc	8	**1683**	6330	5213				
nth_prime9_inc	10	**2234**	22181	17292	10	**7522**	17975	14193
nth_prime10_inc	11	**5207**	50152	38261	11	**16626**	40299	30315
nth_prime11_inc	12	**11765**	124408	92937	12	**35335**	95431	68255
rd53	7	**11**	96	100	7	**12**	120	124

[*]An ancillary line is required

popular benchmark functions **rd53** (see Fig. 2). This circuit and all other circuits described in the tables above can be freely downloaded in TFC and REAL formats from the cite [19] as well as *ReversibleLogicGenerator* software itself.

Table 7. Benchmark functions synthesis (new circuits with less quantum cost).

Function	New circuits				Existing circuits			
	lines	GC	QC_{min}	T-count	lines	GC	QC_{min}	T-count
2of5	7	12	**31**	42	7	12	**32**	49
6sym	7	41	**206**	184	7	36	**777**	741
9sym	10	347	**1975**	1680	10	210	**4368**	4368
hwb7	7	603	**1728**	1400	7	331	**2611**	2245[*]
hwb8	8	1594	**4852**	3748	8	2710	**6940**	5201
hwb9	9	3999	**12278**	10220	9	6563	**16173**	12150
hwb10	10	8247	**26084**	20368	10	12288	**35618**	25939
hwb11	11	21432	**69138**	52922	11	32261	**90745**	63430
hwb12	12	42095	**134316**	98482	12	55998	**198928**	134131
nth_prime7_inc	7	824	**2269**	1906	7	1427	**3172**	2837
nth_prime8_inc	8	1683	**6330**	5213	8	3346	**7618**	5985
rd53	7	12	**82**	92				
rd53	7	12	**95**	100	7	12	**120**	**124**
rd53	7	11	**96**	100				

[*]An ancillary line is required

7 Conclusion

A reversible circuit with n inputs necessarily defines a permutation from the symmetric group $S(\mathbb{B}^n)$. Permutations that correspond to all the gates NOT, CNOT and C^2NOT generate the alternating group $A(\mathbb{B}^n)$ if $n > 3$, and permutations that correspond to all the gates C^kNOT, $1 \leq k \leq n$ generate the symmetric group. This implies that we can use the permutation group theory to successfully synthesize a reversible circuit for a given reversible specification.

In the paper, we briefly described the first asymptotically optimal in NCT library synthesis algorithm, based on the permutation group theory, which makes it possible to obtain a reversible circuit without additional inputs. We also suggested the "moving and replacing" algorithm for gate complexity reduction for circuits consisting of the gates from the GT library; the algorithm is based on equivalent replacements of gate compositions and on conditions of independence for the gates with negative control lines.

We described some gate complexity reduction techniques that use the permutation group theory. Among them are the search of a Boolean hypercube and an effective cycle disjoint. We presented experimental results for benchmark functions synthesis, which include more than 40 reversible circuits consisting of gates from the GT library, obtained with the help of developed open source software that implements all described techniques.

We believe that the permutation group theory may allow us to obtain better reversible circuits for all benchmark functions, and we hope that this paper will motivate other researchers to improve our results.

Acknowledgments. The reported study was partially supported by RFBR, research project No. 16-01-00196 A.

References

1. Abdessaied, N., Wille, R., Soeken, M., Drechsler, R.: Reducing the depth of quantum circuits using additional circuit lines. In: Dueck, G.W., Miller, D.M. (eds.) RC 2013. LNCS, vol. 7948, pp. 221–233. Springer, Heidelberg (2013). http://dx.doi.org/10.1007/978-3-642-38986-3_18

2. Arabzadeh, M., Saeedi, M., Zamani, M.S.: Rule-based optimization of reversible circuits. In: 2010 15th Asia and South Pacific Design Automation Conference (ASP-DAC), pp. 849–854 (2010). http://dx.org/10.1109/ASPDAC.2010.5419684

3. Arabzadeh, M., Saeedi, M.: RCViewer+ — a viewer/analyzer for reversible and quantum circuits (2013). http://ceit.aut.ac.ir/QDA/RCV.htm

4. Bennett, C.H.: Logical reversibility of computation. IBM J. Res. Dev. **17**(6), 525–532 (1973). http://dx.org/10.1147/rd.176.0525

5. Iwama, K., Kambayashi, Y., Yamashita, S.: Transformation rules for designing CNOT-based quantum circuits. In: Proceedings of 39th Annual Design Automation Conference (DAC 2002), NY, USA, pp. 419–424 (2002). http://dx.org/10.1145/513918.514026

6. Maslov, D., Dueck, G.W., Miller, D.M., Negrevergne, C.: Quantum circuit simplification and level compaction. IEEE Trans. Comput.-Aided Des. **27**(3), 436–444 (2008). http://dx.org/10.1109/TCAD.2007.911334

7. Maslov, D.A.: Reversible logic synthesis benchmarks page (2011). http://webhome.cs.uvic.ca/~dmaslov/

8. Maslov, D.A.: On the advantages of using relative phase Toffolis with an application to multiple control Toffoli optimization. CoRR abs/1508.03273 (2016). http://arxiv.org/abs/1508.03273

9. Maslov, D.A., Dueck, G.W., Miller, D.M.: Techniques for the synthesis of reversible Toffoli networks. ACM Trans. Des. Autom. Electron. Syst. **12**(4), 42 (2007). http://dx.org/10.1145/1278349.1278355

10. Miller, D.M., Wille, R., Drechsler, R.: Reducing reversible circuit cost by adding lines. In: Proceedings of 40th IEEE International Symposium on Multiple-Valued Logic (ISMVL 2010), pp. 217–222 (2010). http://dx.org/10.1109/ISMVL.2010.48

11. Rahman, M.Z., Rice, J.E.: Templates for positive and negative control Toffoli networks. In: Yamashita, S., Minato, S. (eds.) RC 2014. LNCS, vol. 8507, pp. 125–136. Springer, Heidelberg (2014). http://dx.doi.org/10.1007/978-3-319-08494-7_10

12. Saeedi, M., Markov, I.L.: Synthesis and optimization of reversible circuits — a survey. ACM Comput. Surv. **45**(2), 21:1–21:34 (2013). http://dx.org/10.1145/2431211.2431220

13. Saeedi, M., Zamani, M.S., Sedighi, M., Sasanian, Z.: Reversible circuit synthesis using a cycle-based approach. ACM J. Emerg. Technol. Comput. Syst. **6**(4), 13:1–13:26 (2010). http://dx.org/10.1145/1877745.1877747

14. Schaeffer, B., Perkowski, M.A.: A cost minimization approach to synthesis of linear reversible circuits. CoRR abs/1407.0070 (2014). http://arxiv.org/abs/1407.0070

15. Shende, V.V., Prasad, A.K., Markov, I.L., Hayes, J.P.: Synthesis of reversible logic circuits. IEEE Trans. Comput.-Aided Des. **22**(6), 710–722 (2003). http://dx.org/10.1109/TCAD.2003.811448

16. Wille, R., Große, D., Teuber, L., Dueck, G.W., Drechsler, R.: RevLib: an online resource for reversible functions and reversible circuits. In: Proceedings of 38th IEEE International Symposium on Multiple-Valued Logic (ISMVL 2008), pp. 220–225 (2008). http://www.revlib.org

17. Zakablukov, D.V.: Reduction of the reversible circuits gate complexity without using the equivalent replacement tables for the gate compositions. BMSTU J. Sci. Educ. **3**, 275–289 (2014). (in Russian), http://dx.org/10.7463/0314.0699195

18. Zakablukov, D.V.: On asymptotic gate complexity and depth of reversible circuits without additional memory. CoRR abs/1504.06876 (2015). http://arxiv.org/abs/1504.06876

19. Zakablukov, D.V.: ReversibleLogicGenerator Software (2015). https://github.com/dmitry-zakablukov/ReversibleLogicGenerator

Strongly Universal Reversible Gate Sets

Tim Boykett[1,2], Jarkko Kari[3(✉)], and Ville Salo[3,4]

[1] Institute for Algebra, Johannes Kepler University, Linz, Austria
[2] Time's Up Research, Linz, Austria
[3] Department of Mathematics and Statistics, University of Turku, Turku, Finland
jkari@utu.fi
[4] Center for Mathematical Modeling, University of Chile, Santiago, Chile

Abstract. It is well-known that the Toffoli gate and the negation gate together yield a universal gate set, in the sense that every permutation of $\{0,1\}^n$ can be implemented as a composition of these gates. Since every bit operation that does not use all of the bits performs an even permutation, we need to use at least one auxiliary bit to perform every permutation, and it is known that one bit is indeed enough. Without auxiliary bits, all even permutations can be implemented. We generalize these results to non-binary logic: For any finite set A, a finite gate set can generate all even permutations of A^n for all n, without any auxiliary symbols. This directly implies the previously published result that a finite gate set can generate all permutations of A^n when the cardinality of A is odd, and that one auxiliary symbol is necessary and sufficient to obtain all permutations when the cardinality of A is even. We also consider the conservative case, that is, those permutations of A^n that preserve the weight of the input word. The weight is the vector that records how many times each symbol occurs in the word. It turns out that no finite conservative gate set can, for all n, implement all conservative even permutations of A^n without auxiliary bits. But we provide a finite gate set that can implement all those conservative permutations that are even within each weight class of A^n.

1 Introduction

The study of reversible and conservative binary gates was pioneered in the 1970s and 1980s by Toffoli and Fredkin [3,8]. Recently, Aaronson et al. [1] described all binary gate sets closed under the use of auxiliary bits, as a prelude to their eventual goal of classifying these gate sets in the quantum case. It has been noted that ternary gates have similar, yet distinct properties [10].

In this article, we consider the problem of finitely-generatedness of various families of reversible logic gates without using auxiliary bits. In the case of a binary alphabet, it is known that the whole set of gates is not finitely generated,

The authors would like to acknowledge the contribution of the COST Action IC1405. This work was partially funded by Austrian national research agency FWF research grants P24077 and P24285, and by FONDECYT research grant 3150552.

S. Devitt and I. Lanese (Eds.): RC 2016, LNCS 9720, pp. 239–254, 2016.
DOI: 10.1007/978-3-319-40578-0_18

but the family of gates that perform an even permutation of $\{0,1\}^n$ is $[1,5,9]$. In [10], it is shown that for the ternary alphabet, the whole set of reversible gates is finitely generated. In [4] the result is announced for all odd alphabets, with a proof attributed to personal communication, which has recently been published as [6]. Another proof of this fact can be found in [2]. In this paper, we look at gate sets with arbitrary finite alphabets, and prove the natural generalization: the whole set of gates is finitely generated if and only if the alphabet is odd, and in the case of an even alphabet, the even permutations are finitely generated.

In [9], it is proved that in the binary case the conservative gates, gates that preserve the numbers of symbols in the input (that is, its weight), are not finitely generated, even with the use of 'borrowed bits', bits that may have any initial value but must return to their original value in the end. On the other hand, it is shown that with bits whose initial value is known (and suitably chosen), all permutations can be performed. We prove for all alphabets that the gates that perform an even permutation in every weight class are finitely generated, but the whole class of permutations is far from being finitely generated (which implies in particular the result of [9]).

Our methods are rather general, and the proofs both in the conservative case and the general case follow the same structure. The negative aspect of these methods is that our universal gates are not the usual ones, and for example in the conservative case, one needs a bit of work (or computer time) to construct our universal gate family from the Fredkin gate.

We start by introducing our terminology, taking advantage of the concepts of clone theory [7] applied to bijections as developed in [2], leading to what we call *reversible clones* or *revclones*, and *reversible iterative algebras* or *revitals*. We note in passing that one can also use category-theoretic terminology to discuss the same concepts, and this is the approach taken in [4,5]. In this terminology, what we call revitals are strict symmetric monoidal groupoids in the category where objects are sets of the form A^n and the horizontal composition rule is given by Cartesian product. A formal difference is that unlike morphism composition in a category, our composition operation is total.

We generalize the idea of the Toffoli gate and Fredkin gate to what we call 'controlled permutations' and prove a general induction lemma showing that if we can add a single new control wire to a controlled permutation, we can add any number of control wires. We then show two combinatorial results about permutation groups that allow us to simplify arguments about revitals. This allows us to describe generating sets for various revclones and revitals of interest, with the indication that these results will be useful for more general revital analysis, as undertaken for instance in [1]. While theoretical considerations show that finite generating sets do not exist in some cases, in other cases explicit computational searches are able to provide small generating sets.

2   Background

Let A be a finite set. We write S_A or $\mathrm{Sym}(A)$ for the group of permutations or bijections of A, S_n for $Sym(\{1,\ldots,n\})$ and $\mathrm{Alt}(A)$ for the group of even permutations of A, $A_n = Alt(\{1, \ldots, n\})$. We will compose functions from left to right. Let $B_n(A) = \{f : A^n \to A^n \mid f \text{ a bijection}\} = \text{Sym}(A^n)$ be the group of n-ary bijections on A^n, and let $B(A) = \cup_{n \in \mathbb{N}} B_n(A)$ be the collection of all bijections on powers of A. We will call them *gates*. We denote by $\langle X \rangle$ the group generated by $X \subseteq B_n(A)$, a subgroup of $B_n(A)$.

Each $\alpha \in S_n$ defines a *wire permutation* $\pi_\alpha \in B_n(A)$ that permutes the coordinates of its input according to α:

$$\pi_\alpha(x_1, \ldots, x_n) = (x_{\alpha^{-1}(1)}, \ldots, x_{\alpha^{-1}(n)}).$$

The wire permutation $id_n = \pi_{()}$ corresponding to the identity permutation $() \in S_n$ is the n-ary identity map. Conjugating $f \in B_n(A)$ with a wire permutation $\pi_\alpha \in B_n(A)$ gives $\pi_\alpha \circ f \circ \pi_\alpha^{-1}$, which we call a *rewiring* of f. Rewirings of f correspond to applying f on arbitrarily ordered input wires.

Any $f \in B_\ell(A)$ can be applied on A^n for $n > \ell$ by applying it on selected ℓ coordinates while leaving the other $n - \ell$ coordinates unchanged. Using the clone theory derived terminology in [2] we first define, for any $f \in B_n(A)$ and $g \in B_m(A)$, the *parallel application* $f \oplus g \in B_{n+m}(A)$ by

$$(f \oplus g)(x_1, \ldots x_{n+m}) = (f_1(x_1, \ldots, x_n), \ldots, f_n(x_1, \ldots, x_n),$$
$$g_1(x_{n+1}, \ldots, x_{n+m}), \ldots, g_m(x_{n+1}, \ldots, x_{n+m})).$$

Then the *extensions* of $f \in B_\ell(A)$ on A^n are the rewirings of $f \oplus id_{n-\ell}$.

Let $P \subseteq B(A)$. We denote by $\lceil P \rceil \subseteq B(A)$ the set of gates that can be obtained from the identity id_1 and the elements of P by compositions of gates of equal arity and by extensions of gates of arities ℓ on A^n, for $n \geq \ell$. Clearly $P \mapsto \lceil P \rceil$ is a closure operator. Sets $P \subseteq B(A)$ such that $P = \lceil P \rceil$ are called *revitals*. We say that P *generates* revital C if $C = \lceil P \rceil$. We say that revital C is *finitely generated* if there exists a finite set P that generates it.

To relate the concepts to clone theory, one defines the generalized compositions of permutations of arbitrary arities as follows: Let $f \in B_n(A)$ and $g \in B_m(A)$. For $k \leq \min(m, n)$, let $f \circ_k g \in B_{n+m-k}(A)$ be defined by

$$f \circ_k g = (g_1(f_1(x_1, \ldots, x_n), \ldots, f_k(x_1, \ldots, x_n), x_{n+1}, \ldots, x_{n+m-k}), \ldots,$$
$$g_m(f_1(x_1, \ldots, x_n), \ldots, f_k(x_1, \ldots, x_n), x_{n+1}, \ldots, x_{n+m-k}),$$
$$f_{k+1}(x_1, \ldots, x_n), \ldots, f_n(x_1, \ldots, x_n))$$

If $n = m = k$ this is the usual composition $f \circ g$. We call $(B(A); \{\oplus, \circ, \pi_\alpha \mid \exists n \in \mathbb{N} : \alpha \in S_n\})$ the *full reversible clone on A* and any subalgebra a reversible clone on A, or simply a *revclone*.[1] Every revclone is a revital and, in fact, revclones are precisely the revitals that contain all wire permutations π_α or, equivalently, the revitals that contain the wire permutation $\pi_{(1\ 2)} \in B_2(A)$ that swaps two

---

[1] In this paper, we are more concerned with the set of functions in a revital or revclone, rather than the particular signatures chosen, and thus have chosen this revclone signature due to its (apparent) simplicity – in clone theory, finite signatures are preferred, see [2] for such a revclone signature.

wires. Note that $\lceil \pi_{(1\,2)} \rceil$ is exactly the set of wire permutations. It follows that if P generates C as a revclone, then $P' = P \cup \{\pi_{(1\,2)}\}$ generates it as a revital, so there is no difference in the finitely-generatedness of a revclone when we consider it as a revital instead of a revclone.

We sometimes refer to general elements of $B_n(A)$ as *word permutations* to distinguish them from the wire permutations. In particular, by a wire swap we mean a function $f : A^2 \to A^2$ with $f(a, b) = (b, a)$ for all $a, b \in A$ (or an extension of such a function), while a word swap refers to a permutation $(u\,v) \in B_n(A)$ that swaps two individual words of the same length. Of course, a wire swap is a composition of word swaps, but the converse is not true. Similarly, and more generally, we talk about *wire and word rotations*. A *symbol permutation* is a permutation of A.

We are interested in finding out if some naturally arising revitals are finitely generated. First of all, we have the *full revital $B(A)$* and the *alternating revital* $Even(A) = \bigcup_n \mathrm{Alt}(A^n)$ that contains all even permutations.

We also consider permutations that conserve the letters in their inputs. For any $n \in \mathbb{N}$, define $w_n : A^n \to \mathbb{N}^A$, such that for all $x \in A^n$, $a \in A$, $w_n(x)(a)$ the number of occurences of a in x. We say $w_n(u)$ is the *weight* of the word u. A mapping $f \in B_n(A)$ is *conservative* if for all $x \in A^n$, $w_n(f(x)) = w_n(x)$, we let $Cons_n(A) \subseteq B_n(A)$ be the set of conservative maps of arity n. Then $Cons(A) = \bigcup_{n \in \mathbb{N}} Cons_n(A)$ is the *conservative revital*. We also consider the set of conservative permutations that perform an even permutation on each weight class, denoted by $ECons(A)$, called the *alternating conservative revital*.

A wire swap α, on A^n, has parity $\frac{|A|(|A|-1)}{2}|A|^{n-2}$. When $n = 2$, this is even only when $|A| \equiv 0$ or $|A| \equiv 1 \pmod 4$. It follows that $Even(A)$ is a revclone only when $|A| \equiv 0$ or $|A| \equiv 1 \pmod 4$. The revital $ECons(A)$ is never a revclone because swaps are odd permutations on the words with a single symbol different from the others.

Furthermore, for any $k \in \mathbb{N}$, we can define the mappings that are *conservative modulo k* by replacing $\mathbb{N}$ with $\mathbb{Z}_k$ in the above definition. We will write $Mod_k(A)$ for these maps.

Using the terminology in [9], we say that gate $f \oplus id_k \in B_{n+k}(A)$ computes $f \in B_n(A)$ using k *borrowed* bits. The borrowed bits are auxiliary symbols in the computation of f that can have arbitrary initial values, and at the end these values must be restored unaltered. Regardless of the initial values of the borrowed bits, the permutation f is computed on the other n inputs. We have cases where borrowed bits help (Corollary 7) and cases where they don't (Theorem 4).

A *hypergraph* is a set V of vertices and a set E of edges, $E \subseteq \mathcal{P}(V)$. A *$k$-hypergraph* is a hypergraph where every edge has the same size, k. A 2-hypergraph is a standard (undirected) graph. A *path* is a series of vertives $(v_1, \ldots, v_n)$ such that for each pair (v_i, v_{i+1}) there is an edge $e_i \in E$ such that $\{v_i, v_{i+1}\} \subseteq e_i$. Two vertices $a, b \in V$ are *connected* if there is a path $(v_1, \ldots, v_n)$ with $v_1 = a$ and $v_n = b$. The relation of being connected is an equivalence relation and induces a partition of the vertices into *connected components*.

If H is a 3-hypergraph, write $Graph(H)$ for the underlying graph of H: $V(Graph(H)) = V(H)$ and $(a,b) \in E(Graph(H)) \iff \exists c : (a,b,c) \in E(H)$. Note that by our definition, the connected components of a 3-hypergraph H are precisely the connected components of $Graph(H)$.

3   Induction Lemma

In this section, we introduce the concept of controlled gate, a generalisation of the Toffoli and Fredkin gates. With this definition, we are able to formulate a useful induction lemma. This lemma formalizes the following idea. If we can build an $(n+1)$-ary controlled gate in a certain class from gates of arity n, then by replacing each n-ary gate with its $(n+1)$-ary extension, we have a "spare" control line from each $n+1$ gate, which can then be attached to an extra control input to get an $(n+2)$-ary gate.

Definition 1. *Let $k \in \mathbb{N}$ and $P \subseteq B_\ell(A)$. For $w \in A^k$ and $p \in P$, define the function $f_{w,p} : A^{k+\ell} \to A^{k+\ell}$ by*

$$f_{w,p}(uv) = \begin{cases} uv & \text{if } u \neq w \\ up(v) & \text{if } u = w \end{cases}$$

where $u \in A^k$, $v \in A^\ell$. The functions $f_{w,p}$, and more generally their rewirings $\pi_\alpha \circ f_{w,p} \circ \pi_\alpha^{-1}$ for $\alpha \in S_{k+\ell}$, are called k-controlled P-permutations, and we denote this set of functions by $CP(k,P) \subseteq B_{k+\ell}(A)$. We refer to $CP(P) = \bigcup_k CP(k,P)$ as controlled P-permutations.

When P is a named family of permutations, such as the family of all swaps in S_A, we usually talk about 'k-controlled swaps' instead of 'controlled swap permutations'. These will be word swaps rather than wire swaps. The Toffoli gate is a (particular) 2-controlled symbol permutation, while the Fredkin gate is a (particular) 1-controlled wire swap. Note that the 'k' in 'k-controlled' refers to the fact that the number of controlling wires is k. Of course, sometimes we want to talk about also the particular word w in $f_{w,p}(uv)$. To avoid ambiguity, we say such $f_{w,p}(uv)$ is w-*word controlled permutation*. In particular, the Toffoli gate is the 11-word controlled symbol permutation, while the Fredkin gate is a 1-word controlled wire swap.

The following lemma formalizes the idea of adding new common control wires to all gates in a circuit.

Lemma 1. *Let $k, h, \ell \in \mathbb{N}$, $P \subseteq B_\ell(A)$ and $Q \subseteq B_n(A)$. If $CP(h,Q) \subseteq \lceil CP(k,P) \rceil$, then $CP(h+m,Q) \subseteq \lceil CP(k+m,P) \rceil$ for all $m \in \mathbb{N}$.*

Proof. Consider an arbitrary $f \in CP(h+m,Q)$. Let $uv \in A^{h+m}$ be its control word where $u \in A^m$ and $v \in A^h$, and let $p \in Q$ be its permutation. By the hypothesis, $f_{v,p}$ can be implemented by maps in $CP(k,P)$. In all their control words, add the additional input u. This implements f as a composition of maps in $CP(k+m,P)$, as required.   □

The main importance of the lemma comes from the following corollary:

Lemma 2 (Induction Lemma). *Let* $P \subseteq B_\ell(A)$ *be such that* $CP(k+1, P) \subseteq \lceil CP(k, P) \rceil$ *for some* $k \in \mathbb{N}$. *Then* $\lceil CP(m, P) \rceil \subseteq \lceil CP(n, P) \rceil$ *for all* $m \geq n \geq k$.

Proof. We apply Lemma 1, setting $Q = P$ and $h = k + 1$. We obtain that $CP(k + m + 1, P) \subseteq \lceil CP(k + m, P) \rceil$ for all $m \in \mathbb{N}$. As $\lceil \cdot \rceil$ is a closure operator we have that $\lceil CP(k + m + 1, P) \rceil \subseteq \lceil CP(k + m, P) \rceil$ for all $m \in \mathbb{N}$. Hence

$$\lceil CP(k, P) \rceil \supseteq \lceil CP(k + 1, P) \rceil \supseteq \lceil CP(k + 2, P) \rceil \supseteq \dots$$

which clearly implies the claimed result. $\qquad\square$

By the previous lemma, in order to show that a revital C is finitely generated, it is sufficient to find some $P \subseteq B_\ell(A)$ such that

(i) $\langle CP(m, P) \rangle = C \cap B_{m+\ell}(A)$ for all large enough m, and
(ii) $CP(k + 1, P) \subseteq \lceil CP(k, P) \rceil$ for some k.

Indeed, if $n \geq k$ is such that (i) holds for all $m \geq n$ then,

$$C \cap B_{m+\ell}(A) = \langle CP(m, P) \rangle \subseteq \lceil CP(m, P) \rceil \subseteq \lceil CP(n, P) \rceil,$$

where the last inclusion follows from (ii) and the Induction lemma. Note that by (i) we also have $CP(n, P) \subseteq C$. So the finite subset $CP(n, P)$ of C generates all but finitely many elements of C.

Condition (i) motivates the following definition.

Definition 2. *Let* C *be a revital. We say that a set of permutations* $P \subseteq B_\ell(A)$ *is* n-control-universal *for* C *if* $\langle CP(n - \ell, P) \rangle = C \cap B_n(A)$. *More generally, a set* $P \subseteq B(A)$ *that may contain gates of different arities, is* n-control-universal *for* C *if*

$$\left\langle \bigcup_\ell \bigcup_{f \in B_\ell(A) \cap P} CP(n - \ell, P) \right\rangle = C \cap B_n(A).$$

If P *is* n-control-universal *for all large enough* n, *we say it is* control-universal *for* C.

In the next two sections we find gate sets that are control-universal for revitals of interest.

4   Some Combinatorial Group Theory

In this section, we prove some basic results that the symmetric group is generated by any 'connected' family of swaps, and the alternating group by any 'connected' family of 3-cycles. Similar results are folklore in combinatorial group theory, but we include full proofs for completeness' sake.

Let H be a graph with nodes $V(H)$ and edges $E(H)$. The *swap group* $SG(H)$ is the group $G \leq \text{Sym}(V(H))$ generated by swaps $(a\ b)$ with $(a, b) \in E(H)$.

Lemma 3. *Let H be a graph with connected components $H_1, \ldots, H_k$. Then*

$$SG(H) = \mathrm{Sym}(V(H_1)) \times \cdots \times \mathrm{Sym}(V(H_k))$$

Proof. All of the swaps act in one of the components and there are no relations between them. Thus, the swap group will be the direct product of some permutation groups of the connected components. We only need to show that in each connected component H_i, we can realize any permutation. Since swaps generate the symmetric group, it is enough to show that if $a, b \in V(H_i)$ then the swap $(a\ b)$ is in $SG(H)$. For this, let $a = a_0, a_1, a_2, \ldots, a_\ell = b$ be a path from a to b. Then

$$(a, b) = (a_1\ a_2) \cdots (a_{\ell-3}\ a_{\ell-2})(a_{\ell-2}\ a_{\ell-1})(a_\ell\ a_{\ell-1}) \cdots (a_3\ a_2)(a_2\ a_1).$$

$\square$

Let H be a 3-hypergraph with nodes $V(H)$ and undirected edges $E(H)$. The *cycling group* $CG(H)$ of H is the group $G \le \mathrm{Sym}(V(H))$ generated by cycles $(a\ b\ c)$ where $(a, b, c) \in E(H)$.

The following observation allows us to take any element of the alternating group given two 3-hyperedges that intersect in one or two places.

Lemma 4.
$$A_4 = \langle (1\ 2\ 3), (2\ 3\ 4) \rangle,$$
$$A_5 = \langle (1\ 2\ 3), (3\ 4\ 5) \rangle.$$

Lemma 5. *Let H be a hypergraph, and let the connected components of H be $H_1, \ldots, H_k$. Then*

$$CG(H) = \mathrm{Alt}(V(H_1)) \times \mathrm{Alt}(V(H_2)) \times \cdots \times \mathrm{Alt}(V(H_k)).$$

Proof. We prove the claim by induction on the number of hyperedges. If there are no hyperedges, then $CG(H) = \{\mathrm{id}(V(H))\}$, as required. Now, suppose that the claim holds for a hypergraph H' and H is obtained from H' by adding a new hyperedge (a, b, c). If none of a, b, c are part of a hyperedge of H' or are fully contained in a connected component of $Graph(H')$, then the claim is trivial, as either we add a new connected component and by definition add its alternating group $\mathrm{Alt}_3 \cong \langle (a, b, c) \rangle$ to $CG(H)$, or we do not modify the connected components at all.

Every permutation on the right side of the equality we want to prove decomposes into even permutations in the components. In components that do not intersect $\{a, b, c\}$, we can implement this permutation by assumption. We thus only have to show that a pair of swaps $(x\ y)(u\ v)$ can be implemented. If $x, y, u, v \in \{a, b, c\}$, the permutation is in $CG(H)$ by definition. Since $(x\ y)(u\ v) = (x\ y)(a\ b)^2 (u\ v)$ it is enough to implement the permutation $(a\ b)(u\ v)$.

Now, we have two cases (up to reordering variables). Either $u \in \{a, b, c\}$ and $v \notin \{a, b, c\}$ or $\{u, v\} \cap \{a, b, c\} = \emptyset$. By analysing cases, the claim reduces to the Alt_5 or the Alt_4 situation of the previous lemma. $\square$

5 Control-Universality

As corollaries of the previous section, we will now find control-universal families of gates for our revitals of interest: the full revital $B(A) = \bigcup_n \text{Sym}(A^n)$, the conservative revital $Cons(A)$, the alternating revital $Even(A) = \bigcup_n \text{Alt}(A^n)$ and the alternating conservative revital $ECons(A)$. Corollaries 1, 2, 3 and 4 below provide control-universal gate sets for these revitals.

(a) **The full revital $B(A)$.** Define the graph $G_{A,n}^{(1)}$ that has nodes A^n and edges (u, v) where the Hamming distance between u and v is one.

Lemma 6. *The graph $G_{A,n}^{(1)}$ is connected.*

Let $P_1 = \{(a\ b) \mid a, b \in A\} \subseteq B_1(A)$, the set of symbol swaps. The swap group of $G_{A,n}^{(1)}$ is then $\langle CP(n-1, P_1)\rangle$ so, by Lemma 3, we have the following:

Corollary 1. *For all n, P_1 is n-control-universal for the revital $B(A)$.*

(b) **The conservative revital $Cons(A)$.** Define the graph $G_{A,n}^{(2)}$ that has nodes A^n and edges $(uabv, ubav)$ for all $a, b \in A$ and words u, v with $|u| + |v| = n - 2$.

Lemma 7. *The connected components of $G_{A,n}^{(2)}$ are the weight classes.*

Corollary 2. *Let $P_2 = \{(ab\ ba) \mid a, b \in A\} \subseteq B_2(A)$. Then P_2 is n-control-universal for the conservative revital $Cons(A)$, for all $n \geq 1$.*

The classical Fredkin gate that operates on $\{0, 1\}^3$ is a 1-controlled P_2-permutation. However, note that in the case of a larger alphabet the controlled P_2-permutations only swap a specific pair of symbols, not just the arbitrary contents of two cells.

We can extend this result to $Mod_k(A)$ by considering the graph as above with added edges (ua^k, ub^k) for all $a, b \in A$ and $u \in A^*$ with $|u| = n - k$. Then the set of permutations $P_2 \cup \{(a^k\ b^k) \mid a, b \in A\} \subseteq B_2(A) \cup B_k(A)$ is n-control-universal for $Mod_k(A)$ for large enough n.

(c) **The alternating revital $Even(A)$.** Define the 3-hypergraph $G_{A,n}^{(3)}$ that has nodes A^n and hyperedges $(uabv, uacv, udbv)$ where $a, b, c, d \in A$, $a \neq d$ and $b \neq c$, that is, all triples of words of which two are at Hamming distance 2 and others at distance 1, and the symbol differences are in consecutive positions.

Lemma 8. *If $n \geq 2$, then $G_{A,n}^{(3)}$ is connected. If $n = 1$, then $G_{A,n}^{(3)}$ is discrete.*

Corollary 3. *Let $P_3 = \{(ab\ ac\ db) \mid a, b, c, d \in A\} \subseteq B_2(A)$. Then P_3 is n-control-universal for the alternating revital $Even(A)$, for all $n \geq 2$.*

(d) **The alternating conservative revital $ECons(A)$.** Define the 3-hypergraph $G_{A,n}^{(4)}$ that has nodes A^n and hyperedges $(uabcv, ubcav, ucabv)$ where a, b, c are single symbols, that is, all (word) rotations that rotate three consecutive symbols.

Lemma 9. *If $n > |A|$, then the connected components of $G_{A,n}^{(4)}$ are the weight classes.*

Proof. When $n > |A|$ and two words x and y are in the same weight class then there is an even permutation $\alpha \in S_n$ such that $y = \pi_\alpha(x)$. This is because x contains some letter twice, say in positions i and j, so that $\pi_{(i\ j)}(x) = x$ for the odd permutation $(i\ j) \in S_n$. The even permutation α is a composition of 3-cycles of the type $(k\ k{+}1\ k{+}2)$. (To see this, apply Lemma 5 on the 3-hypergraph with the vertex set $\{1,\dots,n\}$ and hyperedges $(k, k+1, k+2)$ for $1 \le k \le n-2$.) But then also π_α is a composition of wire swaps of the type $\pi_{(k\ k{+}1\ k{+}2)}$. Clearly, for all $u \in A^n$, words u and $\pi_{(k\ k{+}1\ k{+}2)}(u)$ belong to the same hyperedge of $G_{A,n}^{(4)}$ so we conclude that x and $y = \pi_\alpha(x)$ are in the same connected component. □

We note that if $n \le |A|$, then there are weight classes where each symbol occurs at most once. These classes split into two connected components depending on the parity of the ordering of the letters.

Corollary 4. *Let $P_4 = \{(abc\ bca\ cab) \mid a,b,c \in A\} \subseteq B_3(A)$. Then P_4 is n-control-universal for the alternating conservative revital $ECons(A)$, for all $n > |A|$.*

6   Finite Generating Sets of Gates

In order to apply the Induction Lemma we first observe that 2-controlled 3-word-cycles in any five element set can obtained from 1-controlled 3-word-cycles.

Lemma 10. *Let $X \subseteq A^n$ contain at least five elements, and let*

$$P = \{(x\ y\ z) \mid x,y,z \in X \text{ all distinct}\} \subseteq B_n(A)$$

contain all 3-word-cycles in X. Then $CP(2,P) \subseteq \lceil CP(1,P) \rceil$.

Proof. Let $x,y,z \in X$ be pairwise different, and pick $s,t \in X$ so that x,y,z,s,t are five distinct elements of X. Let $p_1 = (s\ t)(x\ y)$ and $p_2 = (s\ t)(y\ z)$. Then p_1 and p_2 consist of two disjoint word swaps, so they are both involutions. Moreover, $(x\ y\ z) = p_1 p_2 p_1 p_2$. Further, we have that

$$p_1 = (s\ t\ x)(x\ s\ y), \text{ and}$$
$$p_2 = (s\ t\ y)(y\ s\ z).$$

Let $a,b \in A$ be arbitrary and consider the 2-controlled P-permutation $f = f_{ab,(x\ y\ z)} \in B_{2+n}(A)$ determined by the control word ab and the 3-word-cycle $(x\ y\ z)$. Then $f = g \circ g$ where

$$g = f_{a*,p_1} \circ f_{*b,p_2} = f_{a*,(s\ t\ x)} \circ f_{a*,(x\ s\ y)} \circ f_{*b,(s\ t\ y)} \circ f_{*b,(y\ s\ z)}$$

is a composition of four 1-controlled P-permutations, where the star symbol indicates the control symbol not used by the gate. See Fig. 1 for an illustration.

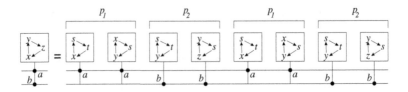

Fig. 1. A decomposition of the ab-controlled 3-word-cycle $(x\ y\ z)$ into a composition of eight 1-controlled 3-word-cycles.

To verify that indeed $f = g \circ g$, consider an input $w = a'b'u$ where $a', b' \in A$ and $u \in A^n$. If $a' \neq a$ then $g(w) = f_{*b,p_2}(w)$, so that $g \circ g(w) = w = f(w)$ since p_2 is an involution. Analogously, if $b' \neq b$ then $g \circ g(w) = w = f(w)$, because p_1 is an involution. Suppose then that $a' = a$ and $b' = b$. We have $g \circ g(w) = ab((p_1 p_2 p_1 p_2)(u)) = f(w)$. We conclude that $f \in \lceil CP(1, P) \rceil$, and because f was an arbitrary element of $CP(2, P)$, up to reordering the input and output symbols, the claim $CP(2, P) \subseteq \lceil CP(1, P) \rceil$ follows.   □

Corollary 5. *Let $X \subseteq A^n, P \subseteq B_n(A)$ be as in Lemma 10. Then $\lceil CP(m, P) \rceil \subseteq \lceil CP(1, P) \rceil$ for all $m \geq 1$.*

Proof. Apply Lemma 2 with $k = 1$.   □

6.1   The Alternating and Full Revitals

Assuming that $|A| > 1$, the set $X = A^3$ contains at least five elements. For $P = \{(x\ y\ z) \mid x, y, z \in A^3$ all distinct$\} \subseteq B_3(A)$ we then have, by Corollary 5, that $\lceil CP(m, P) \rceil \subseteq \lceil CP(1, P) \rceil$ for all $m \geq 1$.

Recall that $P_3 = \{(ab\ ac\ db) \mid a, b, c, d \in A\} \subseteq B_2(A)$ is n-control-universal for the alternating revital $Even(A)$, for $n \geq 2$ (Corollary 3). Clearly $CP(1, P_3) \subseteq P \subseteq \lceil CP(0, P) \rceil$, so by Lemma 1, for any $m \geq 1$,

$$CP(m + 1, P_3) \subseteq \lceil CP(m, P) \rceil \subseteq \lceil CP(1, P) \rceil.$$

Hence $Even(A) \cap B_{m+3}(A) = \langle CP(m + 1, P_3) \rangle \subseteq \lceil CP(1, P) \rceil$. We conclude that $\lceil CP(1, P) \rceil$ contains all permutations of $Even(A)$ except the ones in $B_1(A), B_2(A)$ and $B_3(A)$. We have proved the following theorem.

Theorem 1. *The alternating revital $Even(A)$ is finitely generated. Even permutations of A^4 generate all even permutations of A^n for all $n \geq 4$.*

Corollary 6 [2,6]. *Let $|A|$ be odd. Then the full revital $B(A)$ is finitely generated. The permutations of A^4 generate all permutations of A^n for all $n \geq 4$.*

Proof. Let $|A| > 1$ be odd. Let P be the set of all permutations of A^4, and let $n \geq 4$. By Theorem 1, the closure $\lceil P \rceil$ contains all even permutations of A^n. The set P also contains an odd permutation f, say the word swap $(0000\ 1000)$.

Consider $\pi = f \oplus id_{n-4} \in B_n(A)$ that applies the swap f on the first four input symbols and keeps the others unchanged. This π is an odd permutation because it consists of $|A|^{m-4}$ disjoint swaps and $|A|$ is odd. Because $\lceil P \rceil \cap B_n(A)$ contains all even permutations of A^n and an odd one, it contains all permutations. $\square$

Recall that if a circuit implements the permutation $f \oplus id_k \in B_{n+k}(A)$, we say it implements $f \in B_n(A)$ using k borrowed bits.

Corollary 7. *The revital $B(A)$ is finitely generated using at most one borrowed bit.*

Proof. For $|A|$ odd the claim follows from Corollary 6. When A is even then the permutations $f \oplus id$ with one borrowed bit are all even, so the claim follows from Theorem 1. $\square$

6.2 The Alternating Conservative Revital

Assuming $|A| > 1$, every non-trivial weight class of A^5 contains at least five elements. (The trivial weight-classes are the singletons $\{a^5\}$ for $a \in A$.) For every non-trivial weight class X we set $P_X = \{(x\ y\ z) \mid x, y, z \in X\} \subseteq B_5(A)$ for the 3-word-cycles in X. By Corollary 5 we know that $\lceil CP(m, P_X) \rceil \subseteq \lceil CP(1, P_X) \rceil$ for all $m \geq 1$. Let P be the union of P_X over all non-trivial weight classes X. Then, because $\lceil \cdot \rceil$ is a closure operator, also $\lceil CP(m, P) \rceil \subseteq \lceil CP(1, P) \rceil$ for all $m \geq 1$.

By Corollary 4, the set $P_4 = \{(abc\ bca\ cab) \mid a, b, c \in A\} \subseteq B_3(A)$ is n-control-universal for the alternating conservative revital $ECons(A)$, for all $n > |A|$.

Let $m \in \mathbb{N}$ be such that $m \geq 1$ and $m + 5 > |A|$. Because $CP(2, P_4) \subseteq P \subseteq \lceil CP(0, P) \rceil$, by Lemma 1 we have

$$CP(m + 2, P_4) \subseteq \lceil CP(m, P) \rceil \subseteq \lceil CP(1, P) \rceil.$$

Hence $ECons(A) \cap B_{m+5}(A) = \langle CP(m + 2, P_4) \rangle \subseteq \lceil CP(1, P) \rceil$. We conclude that $\lceil CP(1, P) \rceil$ contains all permutations of $ECons(A)$ except possibly the ones in $B_k(A)$ for $k \leq 5$ and for $k \leq |A|$. This proves the following theorem.

Theorem 2. *The alternating conservative revital $ECons(A)$ is finitely generated. A gate set generates the whole $ECons(A)$ if it generates, for all $n \leq 6$ and all $n \leq |A|$, the conservative permutations of A^n that are even on all weight classes.* $\square$

7 Non-finitely Generated Revitals

It is well known that the full revital is not finitely generated over even alphabets. The reason is that any permutation $f \in B_n(A)$ can only compute even permutations on A^m for $m > n$.

Theorem 3 [8]. *For even $|A|$, the full revital $B(A)$ is not finitely generated.*

By another parity argument we can also show that the conservative revital $Cons(A)$ is not finitely generated on any non-trivial alphabet, not even if infinitely many borrowed bits are available. This generalizes a result in [9] on binary alphabets. Our proof is based on the same parity sequences as the one in [9], where these sequences are computed concretely for generalized Fredkin gates. However, our observation only relies on the (necessarily) low rank of a finitely-generated group of such parity sequences, and the particular conserved quantity is not as important.

Let $n \in \mathbb{N}$, and let W be the family of the weight classes of A^n. For any $f \in Cons(A) \cap B_n(A)$ and any weight class $c \in W$, the restriction $f|_c$ of f on the weight class c is a permutation of c. Let $\phi(f)_c \in \mathbb{Z}_2$ be its parity. Clearly, $\phi(f \circ g)_c = \phi(f)_c + \phi(g)_c$ modulo two, so ϕ defines a group homomorphism from $Cons(A) \cap B_n(A)$ to the additive abelian group $(\mathbb{Z}_2)^W$. The image $\phi(f)$ that records all $\phi(f)_c$ for all $c \in W$ is the *parity sequence* of f. Because each element of the commutative group $(\mathbb{Z}_2)^W$ is an involution, it follows that the subgroup generated by any k elements has cardinality at most 2^k.

Consider then a function $f \in Cons(A) \cap B_\ell(A)$ for $\ell \leq n$. Its application $f_n = f \oplus id_{n-\ell} \in B_n(A)$ on length n inputs is conservative, so it has the associated parity sequence $\phi(f')$, which we denote by $\phi_n(f)$. Note that any conjugate gfg^{-1} of f by a wire permutation g has the same parity sequence, so the parity sequence does not depend on which input wires we apply f on.

Let $f^{(1)}, f^{(2)}, \ldots, f^{(m)} \in Cons(A)$ be a finite generator set, and let us denote by $C \subseteq Cons(A)$ the revital they generate. Let $n \geq 2$ be larger than the arity of any $f^{(i)}$. Then $C \cap B_n(A)$ is the group generated by the applications $f_n^{(1)}, f_n^{(2)}, \ldots, f_n^{(m)}$ of the generators on length n inputs, up to conjugation by wire permutations. We conclude that there are at most 2^m different parity sequences on $C \cap B_n(A)$, for all sufficiently large n. We have proved the following lemma.

Lemma 11. *Let C be a finitely generated subrevital of $Cons(A)$. Then there exists a constant N such that, for all n, the elements of $C \cap B_n(A)$ have at most N different parity sequences.*

Now we can prove the following negative result. Not only does it state that no finite gate set generates the conservative revital, but even that there necessarily remain conservative permutations that cannot be obtained using any number of borrowed bits.

Theorem 4. *Let $|A| > 1$. The conservative revital $Cons(A)$ is not finitely generated. In fact, if $C \subseteq Cons(A)$ is finitely generated then there exists $f \in Cons(A)$ such that $f \oplus id_k \notin C$ for all $k = 0, 1, 2, \ldots$.*

Proof. Let $0, 1 \in A$ be distinct. Let C be a finitely generated subrevital of $Cons(A)$, and let N be the constant from Lemma 11 for C. Let us fix $n \geq N + 2$. For each $i = 1, 2, \ldots, N + 1$, consider the non-trivial weight classes c_i containing the words of A^n with i letters 1 and $n - i$ letters 0. For each i, let f_i be the

the permutation $f_i \in Cons(A) \cap B_n(A)$ that swaps two elements of c_i, keeping all other elements of A^n unchanged. This f_i is odd on c_i and even on all other weight classes, so all f_i have different parity sequences. We conclude that some f_i is not in C.

For the second, stronger claim, we continue by considering an arbitrary $k \in \mathbb{N}$. For $i = 1, 2, \ldots, N + 1$, let $c_i^{(k)}$ be the parity class of A^{n+k} containing the words with i letters 1 and $n + k - i$ letters 0. Note that $f_i^{(k)} = f_i \oplus id_k$ is odd on $c_i^{(k)}$ and even on all $c_j^{(k)}$ with $j < i$. This means that the parity sequences of $f_1^{(k)}, f_2^{(k)}, \ldots, f_{N+1}^{(k)}$ are all different, hence some $f_i^{(k)}$ is not in C. But then, for some $i \in \{1, 2, \ldots, N + 1\}$, there are infinitely many $k \in \mathbb{N}$ with the property that $f_i^{(k)} = f_i \oplus id_k$ is not in C. This means that $f_i \oplus id_k \notin C$ for *any* $k \in \mathbb{N}$ as $f_i \oplus id_k \in C$ implies that $f_i \oplus id_\ell \in C$ for all $\ell > k$. The permutation $f = f_i$ has the claimed property. □

The theorem generalizes directly to revitals defined by a certain type of conserved quantities, at least when borrowed bits are not used.

Definition 3. *Let $|A| > 1$ and let $\sim$ be a sequence of equivalence relations, so that for all n, $\sim_n$ is an equivalence relation on A^n. If $u \sim_n v \implies ua \sim_{n+1} va$ then we say $\sim$ is compatible, and if $u \sim_n v \implies \pi(u) \sim_n \pi(v)$ for all wire permutations π, then we say $\sim$ is permutable. We say $\sim$ is a generalized conserved quantity if it is both compatible and permutable. If for all $m \in \mathbb{N}$, there exists n such that $\sim_n$ has at least m equivalence classes with more than one word, we say $\sim$ is infinite-dimensional.*

Say that $f \in B_n(A)$ is $\sim$-preserving if $f(u) \sim_{|u|} u$ for all $u \in \bigcup_n A^n$, and write $C_\sim$ for the set of all $\sim$-preserving permutations.

Theorem 5. *If $\sim$ is a generalized conserved quantity, then $C_\sim$ is a revital. If $\sim$ is infinite-dimensional, then $C_\sim$ is not finitely generated.*

The theorem shows, for example, that the revital of functions in $B(\{0, 1, 2\})$ that preserve the number of zeroes, and preserve the number of ones modulo k, is not finitely generated.

8   Concrete Generating Families

We have found finite generating sets for revitals in the general and the conservative case. Our generating sets are of the form 'all controlled 3-word cycles that are in the family', and the reader may wonder whether there are more natural gate families that generate these classes. Of course, by our results, there is an algorithm for checking whether a particular set of gates is a set of generators, and in this section we give some examples.

First, we observe that $CP(2, P_1)$ (that is, 2-controlled symbol swaps) generate all permutations of A^3 and all even permutations of A^n for all $n \geq 4$. Indeed, by Corollary 1 they generate $B_3(A)$, and by Fig. 2 they generate $CP(2, P_3)$

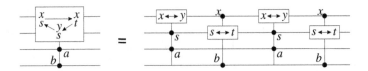

Fig. 2. A decomposition of the ab-controlled 3-cycle $(xs\ xt\ ys)$ into a composition of four 2-controlled swaps.

(the 2-controlled 3-cycles of length-two words). These in turn, by Corollary 3, generate all even permutations of A^4 which is enough by Theorem 1 to get all even permutations on A^n for $n \geq 4$.

It is easy to see that $CP(2, P_1)$ in turn is generated by all symbol swaps and the w-word-controlled symbol swaps for a single $w \in A^2$. In particular in the case of binary alphabets, we obtain that the alternating revital is generated by the Toffoli gate and the negation gate, which was also proved in [9].

In the conservative binary case, the Fredkin gate is known to be universal (in the sense of auxiliary bits, see [9]). The Fredkin gate is, due to the binary alphabet, both the unique 1-word-controlled wire swap and the unique nontrivial conservative 1-word-controlled word swap. The natural generalizations would be to show that in general the 1-controlled wire swaps or conservative word swaps generate the alternating conservative revital. We do not prove this, but do show how the universality of the Fredkin gate follows from our results and a bit of computer search.

The following shows that the 00-word-controlled rotation is generated by the 0-word-controlled rotation.

Lemma 12. *The 00-word-controlled (resp. 01-word-controlled) three-wire rotation can be implemented with nine (resp. eight) 0-word-controlled three-wire rotations but can not be implemented with eight (resp. seven).*

Proof. A computer search shows that eight and seven gates do not suffice. We show how to compose the 00-word-controlled rotation out of nine 0-word-controlled rotations.

Let $A = \{0, 1\}$ and $R \in B_3(A)$ be the rotation $R = \pi_{(1\,2\,3)}$. Write $\rho_{a,b,c,d}(f)$ for f applied to cells a, b, c, d in that order.

$$f_{00,R} = \rho_{1,0,2,3}(f_{0,R}) \circ \rho_{3,1,4,2}(f_{0,R}) \circ \rho_{1,0,2,4}(f_{0,R})\circ$$
$$\rho_{3,0,1,2}(f_{0,R}) \circ \rho_{0,1,3,4}(f_{0,R}) \circ \rho_{1,2,3,4}(f_{0,R})\circ$$
$$\rho_{0,1,4,3}(f_{0,R}) \circ \rho_{1,0,2,3}(f_{0,R}) \circ \rho_{3,0,2,4}(f_{0,R})$$

See Fig. 3 for the diagrams of both these.   □

A similar brute force search also shows the following.

Lemma 13. *The word cycle (0001 0010 0100) can be built from six 0-word-controlled three-wire rotations (but no less). The same is true for (0011 0110 0101).*

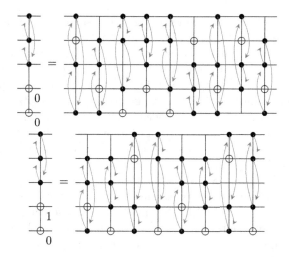

Fig. 3. 00-controlled and 01-controlled rotations built from 0-controlled rotations. These are controlled by the two bottommost wires, the rotation rotates the wires in order $2 \rightarrow 3 \rightarrow 4 \rightarrow 2$, where the bottommost wire is the 0th. The diagram is read from left to right, in each column we perform a 0-controlled rotation. The large circle indicates the control wire, the dots are the rotated wires, the arrows indicate rotation.

Let $\pi_1 = (001\ 010\ 100)$ and $\pi_2 = (011\ 110\ 101)$. Note that $\pi_1 \circ \pi_2$ is the three-wire rotation. Then, by Lemma 12 and Lemma 2, 1-control $(\pi_1 \circ \pi_2)$-permutations generate k-controlled $(\pi_1 \circ \pi_2)$-permutations for all k. By Lemma 13, 1-controlled $(\pi_1 \circ \pi_2)$-permutations generate 1-controlled $\{\pi_1, \pi_2\}$-permutations, and then by Lemma 1, k-controlled $(\pi_1 \circ \pi_2)$-permutations generate k-controlled $\{\pi_1, \pi_2\}$-permutations. Putting these together and combining with Corollary 4, we have:

Theorem 6. *Let* $A = \{0, 1\}$. *Then the alternating conservative revital* $ECons(A)$ *is generated by the controlled wire rotation*

$$f(a, b, c, d) = \begin{cases} (a, c, d, b) & \text{if } a = 0 \\ (a, b, c, d) & \text{otherwise} \end{cases}$$

and the even conservative permutations of A^3.

Clearly $f(a, b, c, d)$ is generated by 1-controlled wire swaps. It follows that the Fredkin gate together with the (unconditional) wire swap generates all even conservative permutations of $\{0, 1\}^n$ for $n \geq 4$.

9   Conclusion

We have precisely determined the revital generated by a finite set of generators on an even order alphabet and show that on an odd alphabet, a finite collection of mappings generates the whole revital. The first result confirms a conjecture in [2] and the second gives a simpler proof of the same result from that paper. Moreover, we have shown that the alternating conservative revital is finitely generated on all alphabets, but the conservative revital is never finitely generated.

The methods are rather general: We have developed an induction result (Lemma 2) for finding generating sets for revitals of controlled permutations, allowing us to determine finite generating sets for some revitals with uniform methods. We also prove the nonexistence of a finite generating family for conserved gates with a general method in Theorem 5, when borrowed bits are not used. We only need particular properties of the weight function in the proof of Theorem 4, where it is shown that the (usual) conservative revital is not finitely generated even when borrowed bits are allowed.

In [1] the full list of reversible gate families in the binary case is listed, when the use of auxiliary bits is allowed. This includes the conservative revital, various modular revitals and nonaffine revitals. As we do not allow the use of auxiliary bits, we are not limited to these revitals; still, it is an interesting question which of them are finitely generated in our strict sense.

While this paper develops strong techniques for showing finitely generatedness and non-finitely generatedness of revitals, our generating sets are rather abstract, not corresponding very well to known generating sets. It would be of value to replace the constructions found in Sect. 8 by more understandable constructions, in order to find more concrete generating sets in the case of general alphabets for conservative gates.

References

1. Aaronson, S., Grier, D., Schaeffer, L.: The classification of reversible bit operations. Electron. Colloq. Comput. Complex. (66) (2015)
2. Boykett, T.: Closed systems of invertible maps (2015). http://arxiv.org/abs/1512. 06813, submitted
3. Fredkin, E., Toffoli, T.: Conservative logic. Int. J. Theor. Phys. **21**(3), 219–253 (1982). http://dx.doi.org/10.1007/BF01857727
4. LaFont, Y.: Towards an algebraic theory of boolean circuits. J. Pure Appl. Algebra **184**, 257–310 (2003)
5. Musset, J.: Générateurs et relations pour les circuits booléens réversibles. Technical report 97-32, Institut de Mathématiques de Luminy (1997). http://iml.univ-mrs. fr/editions/
6. Selinger, P.: Reversible k-ary logic circuits are finitely generated for odd k, April 2016. http://arxiv.org/abs/1604.01646
7. Szendrei, Á.: Clones in universal algebra, Séminaire de Mathématiques Supérieures [Seminar on Higher Mathematics], vol. 99. Presses de l'Université de Montréal, Montreal (1986)
8. Toffoli, T.: Reversible computing. Technical report MIT/LCS/TM-151, MIT (1980)
9. Xu, S.: Reversible Logic Synthesis with Minimal Usage of Ancilla Bits. Master's thesis, MIT, June 2015. http://arxiv.org/pdf/1506.03777.pdf
10. Yang, G., Song, X., Perkowski, M., Wu, J.: Realizing ternary quantum switching networks without ancilla bits. J. Phys. A **38**(44), 9689–9697 (2005). http://dx.doi.org/10.1088/0305-4470/38/44/006

Enumeration of Reversible Functions and Its Application to Circuit Complexity

Mathias Soeken[1](✉), Nabila Abdessaied[2], and Giovanni De Micheli[1]

[1] Integrated Systems Laboratory, EPFL, Lausanne, Switzerland
mathias.soeken@epfl.ch
[2] Cyber-Physical Systems, DFKI GmbH, Bremen, Germany

Abstract. We review combinational results to enumerate and classify reversible functions and investigate the application to circuit complexity. In particularly, we consider the effect of negating and permuting input and output variables and the effect of applying linear and affine transformations to inputs and outputs. We apply the results to reversible circuits and prove that minimum circuit realizations of functions in the same equivalence class differ at most in a linear number of gates in presence of negation and permutation and at most in a quadratic number of gates in presence of linear and affine transformations.

Keywords: Reversible function · Equivalence class · Permutation group · Reversible circuit complexity

1 Introduction

In 1959, Nicolaas Govert de Bruijn has generalized George Pólya's theorem [14] for counting the number of equivalence classes that result from partitioning the set of all functions $f : D \to R$ under the consideration of permutation groups G and H acting on domain D and range R, respectively [4]. Two functions f_1 and f_2 are considered equivalent if there exists permutations $\pi \in G$ and $\sigma \in H$ such that $f_1(x) = \sigma f_2(\pi x)$ for all $x \in D$. The computation involves the groups' cycle index polynomials. Driven by the work of C.S. Lorens [12], Michael A. Harrison has investigated the effect of negation and permutation (using cycle indices derived by Ashenhurst [2] and Slepian [16]) and the effect of linear and affine transformations for Boolean functions [11]. As special cases he also considered the application of all these groups to reversible functions [8,11]. Primenko [15] applied an alternative method to count the number of equivalence classes, but considered different permutation groups in his work.

In this paper, we review the above mentioned work. Afterwards, we and compute and apply the combinational results to reversible circuits and circuit complexity. We relate the investigated permutation groups to classes of reversible gates. Furthermore, we show that the size difference of reversible circuits

© Springer International Publishing Switzerland 2016
S. Devitt and I. Lanese (Eds.): RC 2016, LNCS 9720, pp. 255–270, 2016.
DOI: 10.1007/978-3-319-40578-0_19

composed of mixed-polarity multiple-controlled Toffoli (MPMCT) gates for functions of the same equivalence class is (i) linearly bounded when applying negations and permutation of inputs and outputs and (ii) quadratically bounded when applying linear and affine transformations to inputs and outputs.

For reversible functions with 2 and 3 variables, we explicitly enumerate all equivalence classes and their circuit realizations which allows us to derive correlations and find conjectures. It is unclear whether the classification helps to find a class of *difficult* reversible functions, i.e., functions which have reversible circuits of worst-case or almost worst-case size. Thomas G. Draper [5] has conducted a similar study. He uses complementary techniques to classify Boolean functions into the same classes and uses his results to introduce a new notion of complexity. This notion allows to measure a circuit's complexity in terms of "rounds of nonlinearity" instead of counting gates.

The paper is organized as follows. Section 2 introduces necessary notation and definitions. Section 3 reviews how to compute the number of equivalence classes in reversible functions when applying permutation groups to inputs and outputs. Section 4 applies the results to circuit complexity of reversible circuits and Sect. 5 to Boolean functions. Section 6 concludes the paper.

2   Preliminaries

This section introduces background on permutation groups and reversible functions and circuits.

2.1   Permutation Groups

We assume that the reader is familiar with the basics of permutation groups, i.e., subgroups of the symmetric group S_n over the elements $\{0, \ldots, n-1\}$. Including 0 in the set is unconventional but simplifies forthcoming computations. In the following, we introduce integer partitions and borrow the notation of [1].

Definition 1 (Integer Partition). *An* integer partition *of a natural number* n *is a sequence of natural numbers* $\lambda = (\lambda_1, \lambda_2, \ldots, \lambda_k)$ *such that*

$$\lambda_1 \leqslant \lambda_2 \leqslant \cdots \leqslant \lambda_k \qquad and \qquad \lambda_1 + \lambda_2 + \cdots + \lambda_k = n. \qquad (1)$$

We call the λ_i *the parts of* λ *and write* $\lambda \vdash n$ *to say that* λ *is an integer partition of* n. *Sometimes it is useful to directly refer to the counts of a part. If* $\lambda = (\lambda_1, \lambda_2, \ldots, \lambda_k) \vdash n$, *we write*

$$\lambda = (1^{f_1} 2^{f_2} \ldots n^{f_n}), \qquad (2)$$

where

$$f_i = |\{1 \leqslant j \leqslant k \mid \lambda_j = i\}| \qquad for\, 1 \leqslant i \leqslant n, \qquad (3)$$

i.e., exactly f_i of the λ_j are equal to i. Also, we define

$$z_\lambda = \prod_{i=1}^{n} i^{f_i} f_i!. \tag{4}$$

Example 1. All integer partitions of $n = 4$ are

$$(1,1,1,1) \qquad (1,1,2) \qquad (1,3) \qquad (2,2) \qquad (4).$$

For $\lambda = (1,1,2)$ we have $f_1 = 2$, $f_2 = 1$, $f_3 = 0$, and $f_4 = 0$. Note that $\sum_{i=1}^{n} if_i = n$.

Definition 2 (Permutation Type). *Let $\pi \in S_n$ be a permutation. Then its type* type$(\pi) \vdash n$ *is an integer partition where each element corresponds to the length of one cycle in the cyclic representation of π.*

Example 2. Let $\pi = (0,1)(2)(3,7,4)(5,6) \in S_8$. Then type$(\pi) = (1,2,2,3)$.

Theorem 1 (e.g., [1]). *For each $\lambda \vdash n$, the number of permutations $\pi \in S_n$ with* type$(\pi) = \lambda$ *is $\frac{n!}{z_\lambda}$.* □

Definition 3 (Cycle Index Polynomial). *Let $G \subseteq S_n$ be a permutation group and*

$$g(\lambda) = |\{\pi \in G \mid \text{type}(\pi) = \lambda\}| \tag{5}$$

be the number of permutations in G that have type $\lambda \vdash n$. The cycle index polynomial of G is

$$Z_G(x_1,\ldots,x_n) = \frac{1}{|G|} \sum_{\lambda \vdash n} g(\lambda) x_1^{f_1} x_2^{f_2} \cdots x_n^{f_n}. \tag{6}$$

For each $\lambda \vdash n$ we implicitly assume that $\lambda = (1^{f_1} 2^{f_2} \ldots n^{f_n})$ as introduced in (2). We use the f_i in the same manner in the remainder of this paper.

Example 3. Let $G_1 = \{\pi_e\} \subset S_n$ where π_e is the identity permutation. Then

$$Z_{G_1} = x_1^n,$$

since G contains a single permutation of type $\lambda = (1,1,\ldots,1)$ and $f_1 = n$.

Let $G_2 = \{(0)(1)(2)(3), (0,1)(2,3), (0,2)(1,3), (0,3)(1,2)\}$. Then

$$Z_{G_2} = \tfrac{1}{4}\left(x_1^4 + 3x_2^2\right),$$

since G contains four permutations, one of type $\lambda = (1,1,1,1)$ with $f_1 = 4$ and three of type $\lambda = (2,2)$ with $f_2 = 2$.

Let $G_3 = S_n$. Then

$$Z_{G_3} = \frac{1}{n!} \sum_{\lambda \vdash n} \frac{n!}{z_\lambda} x_1^{f_1} x_2^{f_2} \cdots x_n^{f_n},$$

because there are $n!$ permutations out of which $\frac{n!}{z_\lambda}$ have type λ (see Theorem 1).

Harrison reformulated De Bruijn's enumeration theorem [4] for the special case of reversible functions, and it is restated here.

Theorem 2 (De Bruijn [4], Harrison [8]). *The number of classes of reversible functions of n variables with a group G acting on the domain and a group H acting on the range is*

$$Z_G\left(\frac{\partial}{\partial z_1}, \frac{\partial}{\partial z_2}, \cdots, \frac{\partial}{\partial z_k}\right) Z_H(1 + z_1, 1 + 2z_2, \ldots, 1 + sz_s) \tag{7}$$

evaluated at $z_1 = z_2 = \cdots = z_s = 0$ where $s \leqslant 2^n$.

Harrison introduces the notation of a *product of variables* to ease writing the complex cycle index polynomials (see also Sect. 3.2).

Definition 4 (Product of Variables [10]). *Let $x_1^{i_1} \cdots x_r^{i_r}$ and $x_1^{j_1} \cdots x_s^{j_s}$ be two products of variables. The product of these terms, written '$\times$', is defined as*

$$\prod_{p,q}(x_p^{i_p} \times x_q^{j_q}) \tag{8}$$

where

$$x_p^{i_p} \times x_q^{i_q} = x_{\text{lcm}(p,q)}^{i_p j_q \gcd(p,q)}$$

and gcd and lcm are the greatest common divisor and least common multiple, respectively.

2.2   Reversible Functions and Circuits

Let $\mathbb{B} = \{0,1\}$ denote the *Boolean values*. We refer to functions $f: \mathbb{B}^n \to \mathbb{B}^m$ as *Boolean multiple-output functions* with n inputs and m outputs. We define $x^0 = \bar{x}$ and $x^1 = x$.

Definition 5 (Reversible Function). *A function $f: \mathbb{B}^n \to \mathbb{B}^n$ is called reversible if f is bijective, i.e., if each input pattern uniquely maps to an output pattern, and vice versa. Otherwise, it is called irreversible.*

Each reversible function $f: \mathbb{B}^n \to \mathbb{B}^n$ corresponds to a permutation $\pi_f \in S_{2^n}$ by letting

$$f(x_0, \ldots, x_{n-1}) = (y_0, \ldots, y_{n-1}) \quad \text{if and only if} \quad \pi(x) = y, \tag{9}$$

where $x = (x_0 x_1 \ldots x_{n-1})_2$ and $y = (y_0 y_1 \ldots y_{n-1})_2$ are the binary expansions of x and y. Reversible functions over n variables are realized by reversible circuits consisting of least n lines with gates from library of reversible gates. In this work, we consider the library of mixed-polarity multiple control Toffoli gates [18].

(a) Full adder   (b) SWAP gate

Fig. 1. Reversible circuits.

Definition 6 (MPMCT Gate). *Let* $X = \{x_1, \ldots, x_n\}$ *be a set of variables. A mixed-polarity multiple-control Toffoli (MPMCT) gate* $\mathrm{T}(C, t)$ *has control lines* $C = \{x_{j_1}^{p_1}, x_{j_2}^{p_2}, \ldots, x_{j_k}^{p_k}\}$ *and a target line* $t \in X$ *with* $\{t, \bar{t}\} \notin C$. *The gate maps* $t \mapsto t \oplus (x_{j_1}^{p_1} \wedge x_{j_2}^{p_2} \wedge \cdots \wedge x_{j_k}^{p_k})$. *Values on remaining lines are passed through unaltered. A positive literal in* C *is referred to as* positive control line *and a negative literal as* negative control line. *A gate* $\mathrm{T}(\{x_i\}, t)$ *is called a CNOT gate, and a gate* $\mathrm{T}(\{\}, t)$ *is called a NOT gate.*

Example 4. Figure 1a shows a reversible circuit that realizes a full adder. The annotated values demonstrate the intermediate values of the gates for a given input assignment. The control lines are either denoted by solid black circles to indicate positive controls, or white circles to indicate negative controls. The target line is denoted by '$\oplus$'. Figure 1b depicts a SWAP gate for two variables and its realization using CNOT gates. In total three gates are required. The SWAP gate is not part of the MPMCT gate library.

3 Reversible Function Classification

In this section we review the main results from [8,11]. These works derive the number of classes after applying different permutation groups, which are subgroups of S_{2^n}, to the domain and range of reversible Boolean functions over n variables. The considered permutation groups are the group of *complementations* $\mathcal{C}_n$, the group of *permutations* $\mathcal{S}_n$, the group of *complementations and permutations* $\mathcal{G}_n$, the group of *linear transformations* $\mathcal{L}_n$, and the group of *affine transformations* $\mathcal{A}_n$. We slightly simplified the notation of the groups compared to the original papers for the sake of readability. We provide detailed definitions of all groups in the remainder of this section; a summary of the groups is given in Table 1.

3.1 Permutation Groups

The aim of the following definitions is to describe a constructive approach on how to derive the permutations that are contained in the considered groups. This is orthogonal to the algebraic approach used in [8,11] in which the groups are expressed in terms of other algebraic structures.

Table 1. The permutation groups that are considered in this paper to act on the inputs and outputs of reversible functions over n variables. The table shows its notation, order, corresponding gate library, as well as the reference in which the cycle index polynomial has been derived.

Group	Notation	Order	Gates	Cycle index
Complementations	$\mathcal{C}_n$	2^n	NOT	[2]
Permutations	$\mathcal{S}_n$	$n!$	SWAP	[10]
Compl. and perm	$\mathcal{G}_n$	$n!2^n$	SWAP, NOT	[10]
Linear transf.	$\mathcal{L}_n$	$2^{n(n-1)/2}\prod_{i=1}^{n}(2^i-1)$	CNOT	[11]
Affine transf.	$\mathcal{A}_n$	$2^{n(n+1)/2}\prod_{i=1}^{n}(2^i-1)$	CNOT, NOT	[11]

Definition 7. *The group of all 2^n complementations of n variables is*

$$\mathcal{C}_n = \bigcup_{0 \leqslant b < 2^n} \pi_b, \tag{10}$$

where $\pi_b \in \mathcal{S}_{2^n}$ is a permutation such that $\pi_b(j) = j \oplus b$ for all $0 \leqslant j < 2^n$ and $j \oplus b$ refers to the bit-wise exclusive OR (addition modulo 2) on the binary expansions of j and b.

Example 5. The group $G_2 = \{(0)(1)(2)(3), (0,1)(2,3), (0,2)(1,3), (0,3)(1,2)\}$ in Example 3 is $\mathcal{C}_2$.

The group $\mathcal{C}_n$ contains all permutations that are described by all reversible circuits on n lines that only contain NOT gates.

Definition 8. *The group of all $n!$ permutations of n variables is*

$$\mathcal{S}_n = \bigcup_{\sigma \in S_n} \pi_\sigma, \tag{11}$$

where $\pi_\sigma \in \mathcal{S}_{2^n}$ is a permutation such that $\pi_\sigma(j) = (j_{\sigma 0}j_{\sigma 1}\ldots j_{\sigma(n-1)})_2$ and $j = (j_0j_1\ldots j_{n-1})_2$ is the binary expansion of j.

Example 6. We have $\mathcal{S}_2 = \{\pi_e, (1,2)\}$ and

$$\mathcal{S}_3 = \{\pi_3, (1,2)(5,6), (2,4)(3,5), (1,2,4)(3,6,5), (1,4)(3,6), (1,4,2)(3,5,6)\}.$$

The group $\mathcal{S}_n$ contains all permutations that are described by all reversible circuits on n lines that only contain SWAP gates.

Definition 9. *The group of all complementations and permutations is the combination of $\mathcal{C}_n$ and $\mathcal{S}_n$ and is denoted*

$$\mathcal{G}_n = \mathcal{C}_n \rtimes \mathcal{S}_n, \tag{12}$$

where '$\rtimes$' is the semi-direct product.

Example 7. We have

$$\mathcal{G}_2 = \{\pi_e, (0,3), (1,2), (0,1)(2,3), (0,2)(1,3), (0,3)(1,2), (0,1,3,2), (0,2,3,1)\}.$$

The notion of the semi-direct product is transferred to the circuit analogy of the group: The group $\mathcal{G}_n$ contains all permutations that are described by all reversible circuits on n lines that only contain SWAP and NOT gates.

Definition 10. *The group of all* linear *transformations on n variables is*

$$\mathcal{L}_n = \bigcup_{\substack{A \in \mathbb{B}^{n \times n} \\ \det(A) \neq 0}} \pi_A \tag{13}$$

where $\pi_A \in S_{2^n}$ is a permutation such that

$$\pi_A(j) = k \quad \text{if, and only if} \quad A(j_0, j_1, \ldots, j_{n-1})^T = (k_0, k_1, \ldots, k_{n-1})^T,$$

where $j = (j_0 j_1 \ldots j_{n-1})_2$ and $k = (k_0 k_1 \ldots k_{n-1})_2$ are the binary expansions of j and k. Note that all arithmetic operations in $\det(A)$ are modulo 2.

Example 8. We have

$$\mathcal{L}_2 = \{\pi_e, (1,2), (2,3), (1,3), (1,2,3), (1,3,2)\}.$$

The group $\mathcal{L}_n$ contains all permutations that are described by all reversible circuits on n lines that only contain CNOT gates that have a positive control line.

Definition 11. *The group of all* affine *transformations on n variables is*

$$\mathcal{A}_n = \mathcal{C}_n \rtimes \mathcal{L}_n. \tag{14}$$

Example 9. We have $\mathcal{A}_1 = S_2$ and $\mathcal{A}_2 = S_4$. However, note that $\mathcal{A}_3 \neq S_8$, as for example permutation $(6,7) \in S_8$ which corresponds to the Toffoli gate $T(\{x_1, x_2\}, x_3)$ is not contained in $\mathcal{A}_3$.

The group $\mathcal{L}_n$ contains all permutations that are described by all reversible circuits on n lines that only contain CNOT gates and NOT gates.

3.2   Cycle Index Polynomials

In order to derive the number of equivalence classes using Theorem 2, one must derive the cycle index polynomial of the considered group. These are not simple to derive and we only give the general idea on how to derive them. References to detailed proofs are listed in the last column of Table 1. The simplest one is $Z_{\mathcal{C}_n}$:

$$Z_{\mathcal{C}_n} = \frac{1}{2^n} \left(x_1^{2^n} + (2^n - 1) x_2^{2^{n-1}} \right) \tag{15}$$

The group C_n contains of the identity (corresponds to no NOT gate on any line) and $2^n - 1$ permutations that consists of 2^{n-1} transpositions, i.e., cycles of size 2 [2] (corresponds to all configuration where there is at least one NOT gate on a line).

Example 10. We give an example on how Theorem 2 can be applied to

$$Z_{C_2} = \frac{1}{4}\left(x_1^4 + 3x_2^2\right)$$

in order to derive the number of equivalence classes of reversible functions over 2 variables with complementation acting on inputs and outputs. We need to compute

$$Z_{C_2}\left(\frac{\partial}{\partial z_1}, \frac{\partial}{\partial z_2}\right) Z_{C_2}(1 + z_1, 1 + 2z_2)$$

evaluated at $z_1 = z_2 = 0$. The first factor in the product evaluates to

$$Z_{C_2}\left(\frac{\partial}{\partial z_1}, \frac{\partial}{\partial z_2}\right) = \frac{1}{4}\left(\frac{\partial^4}{\partial z_1^4} + 3\frac{\partial^2}{\partial z_2^2}\right)$$

and the second product evaluates to

$$Z_{C_2}(1 + z_1, 1 + 2z_2) = \frac{1}{4}((1 + z_1)^4 + 3(1 + 2z_2)^2).$$

The first factor is a sum containing partial derivatives and the second factor is a sum containing polynomials. The effect of the distributive law when multiplying the two factors is to combine all partial derivatives with all polynomials:

$$\frac{1}{16}\left(\frac{\partial^4}{\partial z_1^4}(1 + z_1)^4 + \frac{\partial^4}{\partial z_1^4}3(1 + 2z_2)^2 + 3\frac{\partial^2}{\partial z_2^2}(1 + z_1)^4 + 3\frac{\partial^2}{\partial z_2^2}3(1 + 2z_2)^2\right)$$

The second and the third term vanish and one gets $\frac{1}{16} \cdot 24 \cdot 3 \cdot 24 = 6$.

In [8], a lemma describes the effect of applying the resulting partial derivatives to the resulting polynomials in general. This allows to obtain a closed form solution for some cycle index polynomials. For example, applying Theorem 2 to Z_{C_n} simplifies to

$$\frac{1}{2^{2n}}\left(2^n! + (2^n - 1)^2(2^{n-1})!2^{2^{n-1}}\right). \tag{16}$$

Key to derive the cycle index polynomial for S_n is to notice that π_σ in (11) is a homomorphism from S_n to S_{2^n} [10]. From this, one can derive that for two permutations $\sigma_1, \sigma_2 \in S_n$ with type(σ_1) = type(σ_2) one also has type(π_{σ_1}) = type(π_{σ_2}). Investigating in detail how a k-cycle in σ translates to π_σ yields

$$Z_{S_n} = \frac{1}{n!}\sum_{\lambda \vdash n}\frac{n!}{z_\lambda}\prod_{i_1 | 1}\cdots\prod_{i_n | n}x_{\mathrm{lcm}(i_1,\ldots,i_n)}^{g(f_1,i_1)\cdots g(f_n,i_n)\gcd(i_1,\ldots,i_n)} \tag{17}$$

where

$$g(f_k, i_k) = \frac{1}{i_k} \sum_{d|i_k} 2^{f_k d} \mu \left(\frac{i_k}{d} \right) \tag{18}$$

where μ is the Möbius function.

A technique in [7] shows how to derive the cycle index polynomial for a permutation group $G = G_1 \rtimes G_2$ from its constituent groups. Applied to $\mathcal{G}_n = \mathcal{C}_n \rtimes \mathcal{S}_n$, this yields [8]:

$$Z_{\mathcal{G}_n} = \frac{1}{n!2^n} \sum_{\lambda \vdash n} \frac{n!2^n}{\prod_{i=1}^{n} f_i!(2i)^{f_i}} \times \prod_{i=1}^{n} \left(\prod_{d|i} x_d^{e(d)} + \prod_{\substack{d|2i \\ d \nmid i}} x_d^{g(d)} \right)^{\times f_i} \tag{19}$$

with

$$e(k) = \frac{1}{k} \sum_{d|k} 2^d \mu \left(\frac{k}{d} \right) \quad \text{and} \quad g(2k) = \frac{1}{2k} \sum_{\substack{d|2k \\ d \nmid k}} 2^{d/2} \mu \left(\frac{2k}{d} \right). \tag{20}$$

Based on the properties of irreducible polynomials of $\mathbb{Z}_2[x]$ and the technique described in [7], in [11] the cycle index polynomials for $\mathcal{L}_n$ and $\mathcal{A}_n$ are derived. Since their description is quite involved and requires a lot of additional definitions, the reader is referred to [11] for all details.

The number of equivalence classes that result from applying the described five permutation groups both to the inputs and outputs of n-variable reversible functions is given in Table 2 for $n \leq 4$. In the remainder, we refer to two reversible functions f and g as NN-equivalent, if they are in the same equivalence class when the group $\mathcal{C}_n$ acts on both inputs and outputs. We use the abbreviations PP-, NPNP-, LL-, and AA-equivalent for the groups $\mathcal{S}_n$, $\mathcal{G}_n$, $\mathcal{L}_n$, and $\mathcal{A}_n$, respectively.

Table 2. Number of equivalence classes when applying a permutation group to the inputs and outputs of all reversible functions over n variables.

n	$\mathcal{C}_n$ (NN)	$\mathcal{S}_n$ (PP)	$\mathcal{G}_n$ (NPNP)	$\mathcal{L}_n$ (LL)	$\mathcal{A}_n$ (AA)
1	1	2	1	2	1
2	6	7	2	2	1
3	924	1 172	52	10	4
4	81 738 720 000	36 325 278 240	142 090 700	52 246	302

4   Application to Reversible Circuits

In this section we discuss how to apply the above introduced classification to reversible circuits. We study the relation of optimal circuit realizations for functions in the same equivalence class. Optimality refers to the minimal number of required Toffoli gates in an MPMCT circuit.

Theorem 3. *Let f and g be two NPNP-equivalent reversible functions over n variables. Then the size difference of two optimal circuits for f and g is at most $3(n-1)$ gates.*

Proof. Let F be an optimal circuit for f. Since f and g are NPNP-equivalent, there exists two permutations $\pi, \sigma \in S_n$ and two bit-vectors $p, q \in \mathbb{B}^n$ such that

$$g_j(x_1, \ldots, x_n) = f_{\sigma j}^{q_j}\left(x_{\pi 1}^{p_1}, \ldots, x_{\pi n}^{p_n}\right)$$

for all $1 \leqslant j \leqslant n$. A circuit for g can therefore be obtained from F by extending it with circuits for the permutations and negations:

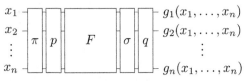

Since each permutation in S_n can be decomposed into $n-1$ transpositions, the circuits for π and σ consist each of at most $n-1$ SWAP gates. The circuits for p and q consist each of at most n NOT gates.

First, we move the circuit for p to the right of F by switching the polarities of the controls on lines i if $p_i = 1$ [17], leading to an updated circuit F' of the same size. Using the identities

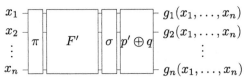

$$\tag{21}$$

we can then pass the NOT gates to the back of the circuit, which changes p into p':

$$
\begin{array}{c}
x_1 \\
x_2 \\
\vdots \\
x_n
\end{array}
\;\boxed{\pi}\;\boxed{F'}\;\boxed{\sigma}\;\boxed{p' \oplus q}\;
\begin{array}{c}
g_1(x_1, \ldots, x_n) \\
g_2(x_1, \ldots, x_n) \\
\vdots \\
g_n(x_1, \ldots, x_n)
\end{array}
$$

The circuit that realizes $p' \oplus q$ requires at most n NOT gates. A generalization of the identities in (21) is

$$
\begin{array}{c}
\times \; \boxed{A} \\
\times \; \boxed{B}
\end{array}
=
\begin{array}{c}
\boxed{B} \; \times \\
\boxed{A} \; \times
\end{array}
$$

in which A and B are either an empty line, a control line, or a target line. This identity allows to move all SWAP gates in π over F' by updating the gates accordingly, resulting in a circuit F'' still of the same size as F:

$$
\begin{array}{c}
x_1 \\
x_2 \\
\vdots \\
x_n
\end{array}
\;\boxed{F''}\;\boxed{\pi \circ \sigma}\;\boxed{p' \oplus q}\;
\begin{array}{c}
g_1(x_1, \ldots, x_n) \\
g_2(x_1, \ldots, x_n) \\
\vdots \\
g_n(x_1, \ldots, x_n)
\end{array}
$$

The permutation $\pi \circ \sigma$ is still an element of S_n and hence can be realized using $(n-1)$ SWAP gates which are $3(n-1)$ CNOT gates.

The identity

allows to absorb NOT gates from $p \oplus q$ into CNOT gates from $\pi \circ \sigma$. The worst case requires all $(n-1)$ SWAP gates, since a SWAP gate need at least 3 CNOT gates [19]. In other words, in the worst case, there cannot be a line that is not part of a CNOT gate but contains a NOT gate.   □

Conjecture 1. Let $\sigma \in S_n$. Any circuit that realizes π_σ requires at least $3(n-1)$ gates.

A proof to Conjecture 1 would make the upper bound of Theorem 3 a tight bound. We leave the proof to this conjecture for future work, but show experimental evidences for the validity later in this section and show that the conjecture is valid for $n = 2$ and $n = 3$.

Theorem 4. *Let f and g be two LL-equivalent reversible functions over n variables. Then the size difference of two optimal circuits for f and g is at most $2n^2$ gates.*

Proof. We apply the same technique as in Theorem 3 and construct a circuit for g from a minimal circuit for f by extending it with two circuits in the front and in the back that realize linear reversible functions. The result follows from the property that any linear reversible function over n variables can be realized with at most n^2 CNOT gates [3]. Since CNOT gates cannot easily be moved through a circuit without changing the size of the circuit, improving the bound as in the proof for Theorem 3 is not obvious.   □

Table 3. Equivalence classes for all 2-variable reversible functions in NPNP-, LL-, and AA-classification.

Representative	Size	Min	Max		Representative	Size	Min	Max
$[0, 1, 2, 3]$	8	0	3		$[0, 1, 2, 3]$	6	0	3
$[0, 3, 2, 1]$	16	1	2		$[2, 3, 0, 1]$	18	1	3
2	24				2	24		

| (a) NPNP-equivalence | (b) LL-equivalence |

Representative	Size	Min	Max
$[0, 1, 2, 3]$	24	0	3
1	24		

(c) AA-equivalence

Table 4. Number of equivalence classes of Boolean functions when applying a permutation group to the domain.

Representative	Size	Min	Max
$[0,1,2,3,4,5,6,7]$	48	0	6
$[0,1,6,7,4,5,2,3]$	288	1	5
$[0,1,2,7,4,5,6,3]$	576	1	5
$[0,1,7,6,5,4,2,3]$	288	2	5
$[0,5,6,3,4,1,2,7]$	144	2	4
$[0,3,6,5,4,7,2,1]$	288	2	5
$[0,1,7,6,4,5,3,2]$	144	2	5
$[0,1,6,5,4,7,2,3]$	576	2	5
$[0,1,7,6,4,5,2,3]$	1152	2	5
$[0,1,2,5,6,7,4,3]$	576	2	5
$[0,1,2,5,4,7,6,3]$	2304	2	6
$[0,1,2,7,6,5,4,3]$	1152	2	5
$[0,3,5,6,7,4,2,1]$	144	3	4
$[0,1,3,6,5,4,2,7]$	576	3	5
$[0,1,5,6,7,4,2,3]$	576	3	4
$[0,3,7,5,4,6,2,1]$	576	3	5
$[0,1,2,5,4,3,6,7]$	288	3	5
$[0,1,7,5,4,6,3,2]$	288	3	6
$[0,1,7,5,4,6,2,3]$	1152	3	5
$[0,1,6,5,4,7,3,2]$	1152	3	5
$[0,5,3,6,4,1,2,7]$	576	3	5
$[0,3,5,6,4,7,2,1]$	576	3	4
$[0,1,5,6,4,7,2,3]$	1152	3	5
$[0,1,2,4,7,6,5,3]$	576	3	5
$[0,1,2,5,7,6,4,3]$	1152	3	5
$[0,1,3,5,6,7,4,2]$	1152	3	5
$[0,1,3,5,4,6,7,2]$	1152	3	5
$[0,1,2,5,4,6,7,3]$	2304	3	6
$[0,5,2,1,4,7,6,3]$	288	3	5
$[0,1,3,5,4,7,6,2]$	1152	3	6
$[0,1,2,4,5,7,6,3]$	2304	3	6
$[1,0,2,5,4,7,6,3]$	2304	3	6
$[0,1,2,6,7,5,4,3]$	1152	3	6
$[1,0,2,7,6,5,4,3]$	384	3	6
$[0,1,3,4,7,6,2,5]$	288	4	5
$[0,1,3,6,7,4,2,5]$	1152	4	5
$[0,1,5,2,3,4,6,7]$	288	4	5
$[0,1,5,7,6,4,3,2]$	288	4	5
$[0,7,3,1,4,6,2,5]$	576	4	5
$[0,1,2,4,5,3,7,6]$	576	4	5
$[0,1,2,5,4,3,7,6]$	576	4	6
$[0,1,3,5,4,2,6,7]$	576	4	6
$[0,5,3,1,4,6,2,7]$	576	4	6
$[0,1,3,5,4,6,2,7]$	1152	4	6
$[0,5,6,1,4,3,7,2]$	576	4	5
$[0,5,1,6,4,3,2,7]$	576	4	5
$[0,1,5,2,4,3,6,7]$	576	4	6
$[0,5,2,1,3,6,4,7]$	1152	4	5
$[0,1,2,5,4,6,3,7]$	384	4	6
$[0,5,2,1,4,6,7,3]$	1152	4	6
$[0,1,2,5,6,4,7,3]$	1152	4	6
$[0,5,3,1,6,4,2,7]$	192	5	6
52	40320		

(a) NPNP-equivalence

Representative	Size	Min	Max
$[0,1,2,3,4,5,6,7]$	168	0	6
$[4,5,6,7,0,1,2,3]$	1176	1	6
$[0,1,2,7,4,5,6,3]$	1176	1	6
$[4,1,2,3,0,5,6,7]$	1176	1	6
$[4,7,6,5,0,1,2,3]$	7056	2	6
$[0,1,2,5,4,7,6,3]$	2352	2	6
$[2,1,0,7,4,5,6,3]$	7056	2	6
$[4,6,7,5,0,1,2,3]$	9408	3	6
$[0,1,2,5,4,6,7,3]$	1344	3	6
$[1,0,2,5,4,7,6,3]$	9408	3	6
10	40320		

(b) LL-equivalence

Representative	Size	Min	Max
$[0,1,2,3,4,5,6,7]$	1344	0	6
$[0,1,2,7,4,5,6,3]$	9408	1	6
$[0,1,2,5,4,7,6,3]$	18816	2	6
$[0,1,2,5,4,6,7,3]$	10752	3	6
4	40320		

(c) AA-equivalence

Corollary 1. *Let f and g be two AA-equivalent reversible functions over n variables. Then the size difference of two optimal circuits for f and g is at most $2n^2$ gates.*

Proof. This follows from applying the NOT absorption argument used in the proof to Theorem 3 to the result of Theorem 4. □

Evaluation. We computed all optimal reversible circuits for reversible functions of 2 and 3 variables and classified them with respect to NPNP-, LL-, and AA-equivalence. Tables 3 and 4 list the results of the evaluation. Each row refers to one equivalence class identified by its representative, which is chosen to be the lexicographically smallest permutation. For each class, the tables mention the size of the equivalence class (*Size*), the size of the smallest optimal reversible circuit in the class (*Min*), and the size of the largest optimal reversible circuit in the class (*Max*). Equivalence classes are sorted first by the size of the smallest circuit and in case of a tie by the size of the largest circuit. The bottom row lists the number of classes and the number of reversible functions.

The experimental results give evidence for the validity of Conjecture 1. The equivalence class π_e for NPNP-classification has Min $= 0$ and Max $= 3$ for $n = 2$ and Min $= 0$ and Max $= 6$ for $n = 3$, i.e., the difference is $3(n - 1)$. Among the largest circuits in the equivalence class are the permutations $\pi_{(0,1)} \in \mathcal{S}_2$ and $\pi_{(0,1)(1,2)} \in \mathcal{S}_3$, which are those permutations with the maximum number of transpositions:

It is hard to derive from the results a class of *difficult* functions, i.e., where almost each function requires the maximum number of gates in its optimal circuit realization. For NPNP-equivalence of 3-variable functions, there are 4, 30, and 18 classes for which Max is 4, 5, and 6. For LL- and AA-equivalence each equivalence class contains at least one difficult function (however, a regular pattern of the values for Min can be observed). As a result, without results for reversible functions with more than 3 variables, it is not possible to derive any conclusions.

Already Lorens [13] listed all equivalence classes of 3-variable reversible functions under these permutation groups. He devised a further classification based on properties of the inverse permutations of the equivalence classes' representatives. However, no correspondence to reversible circuits is given.

We provide the details of this evaluation including one minimal MPMCT circuit for each function in each equivalence class (for each considered permutation group) on msoeken.github.io/revclass.html. We expect that several interesting correlations and conjectures can be found in this data set. The web page also contains the programs that produced the enumeration results. By integrating them with the techniques described by Golubitsky [6], one may be able to obtain the classification results for 4-variable reversible functions.

5   Application to Boolean Functions

Harrison has also investigated the effect of the groups $\mathcal{C}_n$, $\mathcal{S}_n$, $\mathcal{G}_n$, $\mathcal{L}_n$, and $\mathcal{A}_n$ when being applied to the domain of Boolean functions $f : \mathbb{B}^n \to \mathbb{B}$. The results can be found in [10, 11]. All these groups are subgroups of S_{2^n} which is isomorphic to the set of all reversible functions over n variables (see Eq. (9)). In this section, we investigate the effect of the group S_{2^n} when applied to the domain of Boolean functions. This corresponds to a reversible transformation of the input variables, which can, e.g., be realized using a reversible circuit.

We apply Pólya's theorem [14] to compute the number of equivalence classes with respect to S_{2^n} by assigning 2 to all variables in the cycle index polynomial:

$$Z_{S_{2^n}}(2, \ldots, 2) = \sum_{\lambda \vdash 2^n} \frac{1}{z_\lambda} 2^{f_1 + \cdots + f_{2^n}} \tag{22}$$

(cf. Example 3). The number of equivalence classes when additionally considering output negation is [9]

$$\frac{1}{2} \left(Z_{S_{2^n}}(2, \ldots, 2) + Z_{S_{2^n}}(0, 2, 0, 2, \ldots, 0, 2) \right). \tag{23}$$

Tables 5 and 6 show all numbers for n up to 6.

Conjecture 2. Let us denote the results of Eqs. (22) and (23) with a_n and b_n. Then the numbers in the tables lead us to conjecture that $a_n = 2^n + 1$ and $b_n = a_{n-1}$. We have not found these equations nor their derivations in the literature, but assume that such identities have already been proven.

Table 5. Number of equivalence classes of Boolean functions when applying a permutation group to the domain.

n	$\mathcal{C}_n$ [10]	$\mathcal{S}_n$ [10]	$\mathcal{G}_n$ [10]	$\mathcal{L}_n$ [11]	$\mathcal{A}_n$ [11]	S_{2^n}
1	3	4	3	4	3	3
2	7	12	6	8	5	5
3	46	80	22	20	10	9
4	4 336	3 984	402	92	32	17
5	134 281 216	37 333 248	1 228 158	2 744	382	33
6	288 230 380 379 570 176	25 626 412 338 274 304	400 507 806 843 728	950 998 216	15 768 919	65

Table 6. Number of equivalence classes of Boolean functions when applying a permutation group to the domain and output complementation.

n	$\mathcal{C}_n$ [9]	$\mathcal{S}_n$ [9]	$\mathcal{G}_n$ [9]	$\mathcal{L}_n$ [11]	$\mathcal{A}_n$ [11]	S_{2^n}
1	2	2	2	2	2	2
2	5	6	4	4	3	3
3	30	40	14	10	6	5
4	2 288	1 992	222	46	18	9
5	67 172 352	18 666 624	616 126	1 372	206	17
6	144 115 192 303 714 304	12 813 206 169 137 152	200 253 952 527 184	475 999 108	7 888 299	33

6 Conclusions

We have reviewed the research on classification of reversible Boolean functions and applied the results to reversible circuit complexity. Our main result is that the size difference of optimal circuit realizations for two NPNP-equivalent functions is at most linear and that the size difference of optimal circuit realizations for two LL- or AA-equivalent functions is at most quadratic. We have exhaustively classified all reversible functions with 2 and 3 variables. The results can help to discover further properties of reversible functions and circuits. In future work we further investigate the two conjectures in this paper.

Acknowledgments. This research was supported by H2020-ERC-2014-ADG 669354 CyberCare and by the European COST Action IC 1405 'Reversible Computation'.

References

1. Andrews, G.E.: The Theory of Partitions. Cambridge University Press, Cambridge (1984)
2. Ashenhurst, R.L.: The application of counting techniques. In: Proceedings of the ACM National Meeting, pp. 293–305 (1952)
3. Beth, T., Rötteler, M.: Quantum algorithms: applicable algebra and quantum physics. In: Springer Tracts in Modern Physics, vol. 173, pp. 96–150 (2001)
4. De Bruijn, N.G.: Generalization of Pólya's fundamental theorem in enumerative combinational analysis. Konikl. Nederl. Akademie Van Wetenschappen A **52**(2), 59–69 (1959)
5. Draper, T.G.: Nonlinear complexity of Boolean permutations. Ph.D. thesis, University of Maryland (2009)
6. Golubitsky, O., Maslov, D.: A study of optimal 4-bit reversible toffoli circuits and their synthesis. IEEE Trans. Comput. **61**(9), 1341–1353 (2012)
7. Harrison, M.A.: Combinational problems in Boolean algebras and applications to the theory of switching. Ph.D. thesis, University of Michigan (1963)
8. Harrison, M.A.: The number of classes of invertible Boolean functions. J. ACM **10**(1), 25–28 (1963)
9. Harrison, M.A.: The number of equivalence classes of Boolean functions under groups containing negation. IEEE Trans. Electron. Comput. **12**, 559–561 (1963)
10. Harrison, M.A.: The number of transitivity sets of Boolean functions. J. Soc. Appl. Ind. Math. **11**, 806–828 (1963)
11. Harrison, M.A.: On the classification of Boolean functions by the general linear and affine groups. J. Soc. Appl. Ind. Math. **12**, 285–299 (1964)
12. Lorens, C.S.: Invertible Boolean functions. Technical report 21, Space-General Corporation, El Monte, California, Research Memorandum (1962)
13. Lorens, C.S.: Invertible Boolean functions. IEEE Trans. Electron. Comput. **13**, 529–541 (1964)
14. Pólya, G.: Kombinatorische Anzahlbestimmungen für Gruppen, Graphen und Chemische Verbindungen. Acta Math. **68**, 145–253 (1937)
15. Primenko, É.A.: Equivalence classes of invertible Boolean functions. Cybernetics **20**(6), 771–776 (1984)

16. Slepian, D.: On the number of symmetry types of Boolean functions of n variables. Can. J. Math. **5**, 185–193 (1953)
17. Soeken, M., Thomsen, M.K.: White dots do matter: rewriting reversible logic circuits. In: International Conference on Reversible Computation, pp. 196–208 (2013)
18. Toffoli, T.: Reversible computing. In: de Bakker, J.W., van Leeuwen, J. (eds.) ICALP 1980. LNCS, vol. 85, pp. 632–644. Springer, Heidelberg (1980)
19. Vatan, F., Williams, C.: Optimal quantum circuits for general two-qubit gates. Phys. Rev. A **69**, 032315-1–032315-5 (2004)

A Finite Alternation Result for Reversible Boolean Circuits

Peter Selinger[⊠]

Dalhousie University, Halifax, Canada
selinger@mathstat.dal.ca

Abstract. We say that a reversible boolean function on n bits has *alternation depth* d if it can be written as the sequential composition of d reversible boolean functions, each of which acts only on the top $n-1$ bits or on the bottom $n-1$ bits. We show that every reversible boolean function of $n \geqslant 4$ bits has alternation depth 9.

1 Introduction

A reversible boolean function on n bits is a permutation of $\{0,1\}^n$. It is well-known that the NOT, controlled NOT, and Toffoli gates form a universal gate set for reversible boolean functions [1,2,4]. More precisely, these gates generate (via the operations of composition and cartesian product, and together with the identity functions) all reversible boolean functions on n bits, when $n \leqslant 3$, and all even reversible boolean functions on n bits, when $n \geqslant 4$. A particular representation of a reversible boolean function as a composition of cartesian products of generators and identity functions is called a *reversible circuit*. The problem of finding a (preferably short) circuit to implement a given reversible function is called the *synthesis problem* [3].

When working with reversible boolean functions and circuits, it is not typically possible to reason inductively; we cannot usually reduce a problem about circuits on n bits to a problem about circuits on $n-1$ bits. In this paper, we prove a theorem that may, in some cases, make such inductive reasoning possible: we prove that when $n \geqslant 4$, every even reversible function on n bits can be decomposed into at most 9 reversible functions on $n-1$ bits:

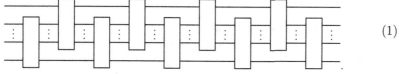

$$(1)$$

It is of course not remarkable that n-bit circuits can be decomposed into $(n-1)$-bit circuits: after all, we already know that they can be decomposed into 3-bit circuits, namely gates. What is perhaps remarkable is that the bound 9 is independent of n.

There are some potential applications of such a result — although admittedly, they may not be very practical. As a first application, one may obtain an

© Springer International Publishing Switzerland 2016
S. Devitt and I. Lanese (Eds.): RC 2016, LNCS 9720, pp. 271–285, 2016.
DOI: 10.1007/978-3-319-40578-0_20

alternative proof of universality, by turning any universal gate set on n bits into a universal gate set on $n + 1$ bits, provided that $n \geqslant 3$. This also yields a new method for circuit synthesis: given a good procedure for synthesizing n-bit circuits, we obtain a procedure for synthesizing $(n + 1)$-bit circuits that is at most 9 times worse. By applying this idea recursively, we obtain circuits of size $O(9^n)$ for any reversible function on n bits. This is worse than what can be obtained by other methods. However, it may be possible to improve this procedure further, for example by noting that the 9 subcircuits need not be completely general; they can be chosen to be of particular forms, which may be easier to synthesize recursively.

Another potential application is the presentation of (even) reversible boolean functions by generators and relations. While the NOT, CNOT, and Toffoli gates are a well-known set of generators, to the author's knowledge, no complete set of relations for these generators is known. For any given n, the group of n-bit reversible functions is a finite group, so finding a complete set of relations for any fixed n is a finite (although very large) problem. However, it is not trivial to find a set of relations that works for all n; at present, it is not even known whether the theory is finitely axiomatizable. If we had a procedure for rewriting every circuit into one of the form (1), then we could obtain a complete set of relations for n-bit circuits by considering (a) a complete set of relations for $(n - 1)$-bit circuits, (b) the relations required to do the rewriting, and (c) any relations required to prove equalities between circuits of the form (1). In particular, if it could be shown that a finite set of relations are sufficient for (b) and (c), a finite equational presentation of reversible boolean functions could be derived.

2   Statement of the Main Result

We write $S(X)$ for the group of permutations of a finite set X. For $f \in S(X)$ and $g \in S(Y)$, let $f \times g \in S(X \times Y)$ be the permutation defined componentwise by $(f \times g)(x, y) = (f(x), g(y))$. We also write $\mathrm{id}_X \in S(X)$ for the identity permutation on X. Recall that a permutation is *even* if it can be written as a product of an even number of 2-cycles.

Let $2 = \{0, 1\}$ be the set of booleans, which we identify with the binary digits 0 and 1. By abuse of notation, we also write $2 = \mathrm{id}_2$ for the identity permutation on the set 2.

Definition. Let A be a finite set, and let $\sigma \in S(2 \times A \times 2)$ be a permutation. We say that σ has *alternation depth* d if it can be written as a product of d factors $\sigma = \sigma_1 \sigma_2 \cdots \sigma_d$, where each factor σ_i is either of the form $f \times 2$ for some $f \in S(2 \times A)$ or of the form $2 \times g$ for some $g \in S(A \times 2)$.

The purpose of this paper is to prove the following theorem:

Theorem 2.1. *Let A be a finite set of 3 or more elements. Then every even permutation $\sigma \in S(2 \times A \times 2)$ has alternation depth 9.*

In circuit notation, Theorem 2.1 can be understood as stating that every reversible boolean function on the set $2 \times A \times 2$ can be expressed as a circuit in the following form:

x

a 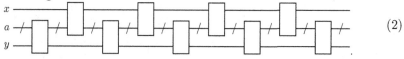 (2)

y

Here, the lines labelled x and y each represent a bit, and the line labelled a represents an element of the set A. The case of boolean circuits arises as the special case where the cardinality of A is a power of 2.

Remark 2.2. The evenness of σ is a necessary condition for Theorem 2.1, because all permutations of the forms $f \times 2$ and $2 \times g$ are even, and therefore only even permutations can have an alternation depth.

Our proof of Theorem 2.1 is in two parts. In Sect. 3, we will show that every even permutation of a certain form $g + h$ has alternation depth 5. In Sect. 4, we will show that every even permutation can be decomposed into a permutation of alternation depth 4 and a permutation of the form $g + h$. Together, these results imply Theorem 2.1.

3   First Construction: Balanced Permutations

3.1   Preliminaries

We fix some terminology. The *support* of a permutation $\sigma \in S(X)$ is the set supp $\sigma = \{x \in X \mid \sigma(x) \neq x\}$. Two permutations $\sigma, \tau \in S(X)$ are *disjoint* if supp $\sigma \cap$ supp $\tau = \emptyset$. In this case, σ and τ commute: $\sigma\tau = \tau\sigma$. We also call $\sigma\tau$ a *disjoint product* in this case. Recall the cycle notation for permutations: for $k > 1$, we write $(a_1\ a_2\ \ldots\ a_k)$ for the permutation with support $\{a_1, \ldots, a_k\}$ defined by $a_1 \mapsto a_2$, $a_2 \mapsto a_3$, $\ldots$, $a_{k-1} \mapsto a_k$ and $a_k \mapsto a_1$. Such a permutation is also called a k-*cycle*. Every permutation can be uniquely decomposed (up to the order of the factors) into a product of disjoint cycles. A k-cycle is even if and only if k is odd.

Two permutations $\sigma, \sigma' \in S(X)$ are *similar*, in symbols $\sigma \sim \sigma'$, if there exists τ such that $\sigma' = \tau^{-1}\sigma\tau$. It is easy to see that σ, σ' are similar if and only if their cycle decompositions contain an equal number of k-cycles for every k.

If $g, h \in S(X)$ are permutations on some finite set X, we define their *disjoint sum* $g + h \in S(2 \times X)$ as

$$(g + h)(0, x) = (0, g(x)) \quad \text{and} \quad (g + h)(1, x) = (1, h(x)).$$

We note the following properties:

$$g + g = 2 \times g, \tag{3}$$
$$(g + h) \times 2 = g \times 2 + h \times 2, \tag{4}$$
$$(g + h)(g' + h') = gg' + hh'. \tag{5}$$

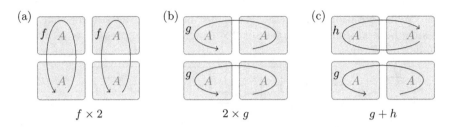

Fig. 1. Visualizing permutations of $2 \times A \times 2$

Property (3) also helps explain our choice of writing "2" for the identity permutation in $S(2)$.

Although it will not be strictly necessary for the proofs that follow (which are combinatorial), it may sometimes be helpful to visualize sets of the form $2 \times A \times 2$, and permutations thereon, as follows. We visualize the set $2 \times A$ as two copies of A stacked vertically, with elements of the form $(0, a)$ and $(1, a)$ belonging to the lower and upper copy, respectively. Similarly, we visualize the set $A \times 2$ as two copies of A side by side, with elements of the form $(a, 0)$ and $(a, 1)$ belonging to the left and right copy, respectively. In the same vein, we visualize the set $2 \times A \times 2$ as four copies of A arranged in two rows and columns. The effect of a permutations of the form $f \times 2$ is to apply f separately to the left and right column, as shown in Fig. 1(a). Similarly, the effect of $2 \times g$ is to apply g separately to the top and bottom rows, and the effect of $g + h$ is to apply g to the bottom row and h to the top row, as shown in Fig. 1(b) and (c).

3.2 Decomposition into Balanced Permutations

Definition. A permutation σ is *balanced* if the number of k-cycles in its cycle decomposition is even for all $k \geqslant 2$. Moreover, σ is *nearly balanced* if the number of k-cycles in its cycle decomposition is even for all $k \geqslant 3$.

For example, the permutation $(1\ 2)(3\ 4)(5\ 6\ 7)(8\ 9\ 10)$ is balanced, the permutation $(1\ 2)(3\ 4\ 5)(8\ 9\ 10)$ is nearly balanced, and $(1\ 2)(3\ 4)(5\ 6\ 7)$ is neither balanced nor nearly balanced.

Remark 3.1. The disjoint product of any number of (nearly) balanced permutations is (nearly) balanced. Moreover, a nearly balanced permutation is balanced if and only if it is even.

The purpose of this subsection is to prove that every even permutation on a set of 5 or more elements can be decomposed into a product of two balanced permutations. This will be Proposition 3.8 below. The proof requires a sequence of lemmas.

Lemma 3.2. *Let σ be a k-cycle, where $k \geqslant 2$ and $k \neq 3$. Then there exists a balanced permutation ρ and a nearly balanced permutation τ such that $\sigma = \tau\rho$. Moreover, $\operatorname{supp} \tau \cup \operatorname{supp} \rho \subseteq \operatorname{supp} \sigma$.*

Proof. Let $\sigma = (a_1\ a_2\ \ldots\ a_k)$. If $k = 2t$ is even, let

$$\rho = (a_1\ a_2\ \ldots\ a_t)(a_{t+1}\ a_{t+2}\ \ldots\ a_{2t}),$$
$$\tau = (a_1\ a_{t+1}).$$

If $k = 2t + 1$ is odd (and therefore, by assumption, $t \geqslant 2$), let

$$\rho = (a_1\ a_2\ \ldots\ a_t)(a_{t+1}\ a_{t+3}\ a_{t+4}\ \ldots\ a_{2t+1}),$$
$$\tau = (a_1\ a_{t+1})(a_{t+2}\ a_{t+3}).$$

In both cases, the conclusion of the lemma is satisfied.

Lemma 3.3. *Let σ be the disjoint product of a 3-cycle and a k-cycle, where $k \geqslant 2$. Then there exists a balanced permutation ρ and a nearly balanced permutation τ such that $\sigma = \tau\rho$. Moreover, $\operatorname{supp} \tau \cup \operatorname{supp} \rho \subseteq \operatorname{supp} \sigma$.*

Proof. Let $\sigma = (b_1\ b_2\ b_3)(a_1\ a_2\ \ldots\ a_k)$. If $k = 2$, let

$$\rho = (b_1\ b_2)(a_1\ a_2),$$
$$\tau = (b_1\ b_3).$$

If $k = 3$, let

$$\rho = (b_1\ b_2)(a_1\ a_2),$$
$$\tau = (b_1\ b_3)(a_1\ a_3),$$

If $k = 4$, let

$$\rho = (b_1\ b_2\ b_3)(a_1\ a_2\ a_3),$$
$$\tau = (a_1\ a_4).$$

If $k = 2t + 1$ is odd, with $t \geqslant 2$, let

$$\rho = (b_1\ b_2\ b_3)(a_t\ a_{t+1}\ a_{2t+1}),$$
$$\tau = (a_1\ a_2\ \ldots\ a_t)(a_{t+2}\ a_{t+3}\ \ldots\ a_{2t+1}).$$

If $k = 2t$ is even, with $t \geqslant 3$, let

$$\rho = (a_3\ a_4\ \ldots\ a_t\ a_{2t})(a_{t+1}\ a_{t+2}\ \ldots\ a_{2t-1}),$$
$$\tau = (b_1\ b_2\ b_3)(a_1\ a_2\ a_3)(a_{t+1}\ a_{2t}).$$

In all cases, the conclusion of the lemma is satisfied.

Lemma 3.4. *Let σ be a disjoint product of two or more 3-cycles. Then there exist balanced permutations ρ, τ such that $\sigma = \tau\rho$. Moreover, $\operatorname{supp} \tau \cup \operatorname{supp} \rho \subseteq \operatorname{supp} \sigma$.*

Proof. By assumption, σ factors as $\sigma = \gamma_1\gamma_2\cdots\gamma_\ell$, where $\gamma_1,\ldots,\gamma_\ell$ are pairwise disjoint 3-cycles and $\ell \geqslant 2$. Note that γ_i^2 is also a 3-cycle, and $\gamma_i^4 = \gamma_i$, for all i.

If ℓ is even, let $\rho = \tau = \gamma_1^2\gamma_2^2\cdots\gamma_\ell^2$. If ℓ is odd, let $\rho = \gamma_1\gamma_2^2\gamma_3^2\cdots\gamma_{\ell-1}^2$ and $\tau = \gamma_2^2\gamma_3^2\cdots\gamma_{\ell-1}^2\gamma_\ell$. In both cases, the conclusion of the lemma is satisfied.

Lemma 3.5. *Let σ be an even permutation, other than a 3-cycle. Then σ can be written as $\sigma = \tau\rho$, where ρ, τ are balanced.*

Proof. By considering the cycle decomposition of σ, it is easy to see that σ can be factored into disjoint factors such that each factor satisfies the premise of one of Lemmas 3.2, 3.3, or 3.4. Let $\sigma = \sigma_1 \cdots \sigma_\ell$ be such a factorization. Using the lemmas, each σ_i can be written as $\sigma_i = \tau_i\rho_i$, where ρ_i is balanced and τ_i is nearly balanced. Moreover, since the support of each ρ_i and τ_i is contained in that of σ_i, the ρ_i are pairwise disjoint, the τ_i are pairwise disjoint, and $\rho_i\tau_j = \tau_j\rho_i$ whenever $i \neq j$. Let $\rho = \rho_1 \cdots \rho_\ell$ and $\tau = \tau_1 \cdots \tau_\ell$. Then we have $\sigma = \tau\rho$. Moreover, by Remark 3.1, ρ is balanced and τ is nearly balanced. Finally, since σ and ρ are even permutations, so is τ, and it follows, again by Remark 3.1, that τ is balanced. ∎

Lemma 3.6. *Let σ be a 3-cycle in $S(X)$, where $|X| \geqslant 5$. Then there exist balanced permutations ρ, τ such that $\sigma = \tau\rho$.*

Proof. Let $\sigma = (a_1\ a_2\ a_3)$. Since $|X| \geqslant 5$, there exist elements a_4, a_5 of X that are different from each other and from $a_1, \ldots, a_3$. Let

$$\rho = (a_1\ a_2)(a_4\ a_5),$$
$$\tau = (a_1\ a_3)(a_4\ a_5).$$

Then the conclusion of the lemma is satisfied. ∎

Remark 3.7. Unlike the situation in Lemmas 3.2–3.5, it is not possible to choose ρ and τ in Lemma 3.6 so that their support is contained in that of σ. An easy case distinction shows that Lemma 3.6 is false when $|X| \leqslant 4$.

Proposition 3.8. *Let σ be an even permutation in $S(X)$, where $|X| \geqslant 5$. Then there exist balanced permutations ρ, τ such that $\sigma = \tau\rho$.*

Proof. By Lemma 3.6 if σ is a 3-cycle, and by Lemma 3.5 otherwise. ∎

3.3   Alternation Depth of Permutations of the Form $g + h$

We now come to the main result of Sect. 3, which is that every even permutation of the form $g + h$ has alternation depth 5.

Proposition 3.9. *Let A be a finite set of 3 or more elements, and let $g, h \in S(A \times 2)$ be permutations such that $\sigma = g + h$ is even. Then σ has alternation depth 5.*

The proof requires two lemmas.

Lemma 3.10. *Let $\tau \in S(A \times 2)$ be a balanced permutation. Then there exist permutations $g \in S(A \times 2)$ and $h \in S(A)$ such that*

$$\tau = g^{-1}(h \times 2)g.$$

Proof. For all $k \geqslant 2$, let y_k be the number of k-cycles in the cycle decomposition of τ. Since the cycles are disjoint, we have $\sum_k k y_k \leqslant 2|A|$. Since τ is balanced, all y_k are even. We can therefore find a permutation $h \in S(A)$ whose number of k-cycles is exactly $y_k/2$, for all k. Since $h \times 2$ and τ have, by construction, the same number of k-cycles for all k, we have $h \times 2 \sim \tau$. By definition of similarity, it follows that there exists some g with $\tau = g^{-1}(h \times 2)g$, as claimed.

Lemma 3.11. *Let* $\tau \in S(A \times 2)$ *be a balanced permutation, and let* $\sigma = \mathrm{id}_{A \times 2} + \tau \in S(2 \times A \times 2)$. *Then there exist permutations* $g \in S(A \times 2)$ *and* $f \in S(2 \times A)$ *such that*

$$\sigma = (2 \times g^{-1})(f \times 2)(2 \times g).$$

Proof. By Lemma 3.10, we can find $g \in S(A \times 2)$ and $h \in S(A)$ such that $\tau = g^{-1}(h \times 2)g$. Let $f = \mathrm{id}_A + h \in S(2 \times A)$. Then

$$\begin{aligned}
&(2 \times g^{-1})(f \times 2)(2 \times g) \\
&= (2 \times g^{-1})((\mathrm{id}_A + h) \times 2)(2 \times g) \\
&= (g^{-1} + g^{-1})(\mathrm{id}_A \times 2 + h \times 2)(g + g) \\
&= (g^{-1}\,\mathrm{id}_{A \times 2}\,g) + (g^{-1}(h \times 2)g) \\
&= \mathrm{id}_{A \times 2} + \tau \\
&= \sigma.
\end{aligned}$$

Here, in addition to the defining properties of f, g, h, and σ, we have also used (3) and (4) in the second step and (5) in the third step.

Proof (Proof of Proposition 3.9). Let $\tau = hg^{-1} \in S(A \times 2)$, and note that τ is even. By Proposition 3.8, there exist balanced permutations $\tau_1, \tau_2 \in S(A \times 2)$ such that $\tau = \tau_2\tau_1$. By Lemma 3.11, there exist $g_1, g_2 \in S(A \times 2)$ and $f_1, f_2 \in S(2 \times A)$ such that $\mathrm{id}_{A \times 2} + \tau_i = (2 \times g_i^{-1})(f_i \times 2)(2 \times g_i)$, for $i = 1, 2$. Then we have:

$$\begin{aligned}
\sigma &= g + h \\
&= \mathrm{id}_{A \times 2}g + \tau g \\
&= (\mathrm{id}_{A \times 2} + \tau)(g + g) \\
&= (\mathrm{id}_{A \times 2} + \tau_2\tau_1)(2 \times g) \\
&= (\mathrm{id}_{A \times 2} + \tau_2)(\mathrm{id}_{A \times 2} + \tau_1)(2 \times g) \\
&= (2 \times g_2^{-1})(f_2 \times 2)(2 \times g_2)(2 \times g_1^{-1})(f_1 \times 2)(2 \times g_1)(2 \times g) \\
&= (2 \times g_2^{-1})(f_2 \times 2)(2 \times g_2g_1^{-1})(f_1 \times 2)(2 \times g_1g),
\end{aligned}$$

which is of alternation depth 5 as desired.

4   Second Construction: Colorings

4.1   Colorings

As before, let $2 = \{0, 1\}$. If X is any finite set, a *coloring* of X is a map $c : X \to 2$. Here, we think of the binary digits 0 and 1 as *colors*, i.e., $x \in X$ has color $c(x)$.

We say that the coloring c is *fair* if there is an equal number of elements of each color, i.e., $|c^{-1}\{0\}| = |c^{-1}\{1\}|$.

The group $S(X)$ acts in a natural way on the colorings of X as follows: we define $\sigma \bullet c = c'$, where $c'(x) = c(\sigma^{-1}(x))$. Note that $(\sigma\tau) \bullet c = \sigma \bullet (\tau \bullet c)$. Also, $\sigma \bullet c$ is fair if and only if c is fair.

On a set of the form $2 \times X$, the *standard coloring* is the one given by $c_{\mathrm{st}}(0, x) = 0$ and $c_{\mathrm{st}}(1, x) = 1$, for all x.

Remark 4.1. The standard coloring is fair. Conversely, if c is a fair coloring of $2 \times X$, there exists a permutation $f \in S(2 \times X)$ such that $f \bullet c = c_{\mathrm{st}}$.

The following lemma relates colorings to permutations of the form $g + h$ considered in the previous section.

Lemma 4.2. *A permutation $\sigma \in S(2 \times X)$ is of the form $\sigma = g + h$, for some $g, h \in S(X)$, if and only if $\sigma \bullet c_{\mathrm{st}} = c_{\mathrm{st}}$.*

Proof. This is elementary. We have $\sigma \bullet c_{\mathrm{st}} = c_{\mathrm{st}}$ if and only if for all x, $\sigma(0, x)$ is of the form $(0, y)$, and $\sigma(1, x)$ is of the form $(1, z)$. By setting $g(x) = y$ and $h(x) = z$, this is equivalent to σ being of the form $g + h$.

We are now ready to state the main result of Sect. 4, which is that every fair coloring of $2 \times A \times 2$ can be converted to the standard coloring by the action of a permutation of alternation depth 4.

Proposition 4.3. *Let A be a finite set of 3 or more elements, and let c be a fair coloring of $2 \times A \times 2$. Then there exists a permutation $\sigma \in S(2 \times A \times 2)$ such that $\sigma \bullet c = c_{\mathrm{st}}$ and σ has alternation depth 4.*

The proof of Proposition 4.3 will take up the remainder of Sect. 4.

4.2   Visualizing Colorings

Colorings on $2 \times A \times 2$ can be visualized in the same row-and-column format we used in Fig. 1. An example of a coloring, where $A = \{p, q, r\}$, is shown in Fig. 2(a). The figure indicates, for example, that $c(1, p, 0) = 0$, $c(1, q, 0) = 1$, and so on. When the names of the elements of A are not important, we omit them. Additionally, we sometimes represent the colors 0 and 1 by black and white squares, respectively, as in Fig. 2(b).

(a)
$$\begin{array}{ccc|ccc} p & q & r & p & q & r \\ \hline 0 & 1 & 1 & 1 & 1 & 1 \\ 0 & 0 & 0 & 1 & 0 & 0 \end{array}$$

(b)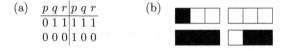

Fig. 2. Visualizing colorings of $2 \times A \times 2$

4.3   Color Pairs

We begin by characterizing when two colorings c, c' of $2 \times X$ are related by the action of a permutation of the form $2 \times g$ for $g \in S(X)$. This is the case if and only if c and c' have the same *color pair distribution*.

Definition. Let X be a set, and consider a coloring c of $2 \times X$. We define a function $c^* : X \to 2 \times 2$ by $c^*(x) = (c(0, x), c(1, x))$. We call $c^*(x)$ the *color pair* of x.

Informally, a color pair corresponds to a single column of digits in Fig. 2(a). We note that the action of permutations $g \in S(X)$ respects color pairs in the following sense: let $c' = (2 \times g) \bullet c$. Then

$$c'^*(g(x)) = (c'(0, g(x)), c'(1, g(x))) = (c(0, x), c(1, x)) = c^*(x). \qquad (6)$$

In particular, the action of $2 \times g$ on colorings does not change the *number* of elements of X with each color pair. Conversely, whenever two colorings c, c' have this property, then they are related by the action of $2 \times g$, for some g. The following definition helps us state this more precisely.

Definition. Let X be a set, and c a coloring of $2 \times X$. For any $i, j \in 2$, define $N_c(i, j) \subseteq X$ to be the set of elements with color pair (i, j), i.e.,

$$N_c(i, j) = \{x \in X \mid c^*(x) = (i, j)\}.$$

Note that X is the disjoint union of the $N_c(i, j)$, for $i, j \in 2$. Let $n_c(i, j) = |N_c(i, j)|$ be the number of elements with color pair (i, j). Then the *color pair distribution* of c is the 4-tuple

$$(n_c(0, 0), n_c(0, 1), n_c(1, 0), n_c(1, 1)).$$

For example, the coloring from Fig. 2 has color pair distribution $(1, 4, 0, 1)$, because the color pair $(0, 0)$ occurs once, the color pair $(0, 1)$ occurs four times, and so on. The following lemma is then obvious.

Lemma 4.4. *Let c, c' be colorings of $2 \times X$. Then c, c' have the same color pair distribution if and only if there exists a permutation $g \in S(X)$ such that $c' = (2 \times g) \bullet c$.*   □

4.4   Color Standardization

Definition. Let A be a set, and let c be a coloring of $2 \times A \times 2$. We say that c is

- *standard* if $c = c_{\mathrm{st}}$, i.e., if $c^*(a, 0) = c^*(a, 1) = (0, 1)$ for all $a \in A$;
- *symmetric* if $c^*(a, 0) = c^*(a, 1)$ for all $a \in A$;
- *regular* if each color pair occurs an even number of times, i.e., if $n_c(0, 0)$, $n_c(0, 1)$, $n_c(1, 0)$, and $n_c(1, 1)$ are even;

- *nearly standard* if $c^*(a,0) = c^*(a,1) = (0,1)$ for almost all $a \in A$, except that there is at most one $a_1 \in A$ such that $c^*(a_1,0) = (0,0)$ and $c^*(a_1,1) = (1,1)$, and at most one $a_2 \in A$ such that $c^*(a_2,0) = (0,1)$ and $c^*(a_2,1) = (1,0)$;
- *nearly symmetric* if $c^*(a,0) = c^*(a,1)$ for almost all $a \in A$, except that there is at most one $a_1 \in A$ such that $c^*(a_1,0) = (0,0)$ and $c^*(a_1,1) = (1,1)$, and at most one $a_2 \in A$ such that $c^*(a_2,0) = (0,1)$ and $c^*(a_2,1) = (1,0)$.

An example of each of these properties is shown in Fig. 3. Our strategy for proving Proposition 4.3 is to use the action of permutations of the forms $2 \times g$ and $f \times 2$ to successively improve the properties of a coloring until it is standard. This procedure is also outlined in Fig. 3, along with the number of the lemma that will be used in each step. The remainder of this section is devoted to the statements and proofs of these lemmas, culminating in the proof of Proposition 4.3 in Sect. 4.5.

Lemma 4.5. *Let c be a symmetric fair coloring of $2 \times A \times 2$. Then there exists $f \in S(2 \times A)$ such that $(f \times 2) \bullet c$ is standard.*

Proof. Since c is symmetric, we have $c(i,a,0) = c(i,a,1)$ for all $(i,a) \in 2 \times A$; write $p(i,a) = c(i,a,0)$. Since c is fair, $p : 2 \times A \to 2$ is also fair. By Remark 4.1, there exists a permutation $f \in S(2 \times A)$ such that $f \bullet p$ is the standard coloring of $2 \times A$. It follows that $(f \times 2) \bullet c$ is the standard coloring of $2 \times A \times 2$.

Lemma 4.6. *Let c be a regular coloring of $2 \times A \times 2$. Then there exists $g \in S(A \times 2)$ such that $(2 \times g) \bullet c$ is symmetric.*

Proof. Since c is regular, we can find integers p, q, r, s such that $n_c(0,0) = 2p$, $n_c(1,1) = 2q$, $n_c(0,1) = 2r$, and $n_c(1,0) = 2s$. Note that $n_c(0,0) + n_c(0,1) +$

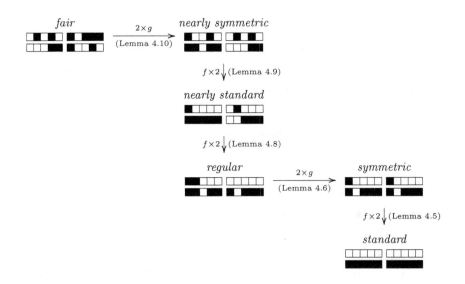

Fig. 3. Standardizing a fair permutation

$n_c(1,0) + n_c(1,1) = 2|A|$, and therefore $p + q + r + s = |A|$. Write A as a disjoint union of sets $P \cup Q \cup R \cup S$, where $|P| = p$, $|Q| = q$, $|R| = r$, and $|S| = s$. Define a coloring c' by

$$
\begin{aligned}
c'^*(a,0) &= c'^*(a,1) = (0,0), \text{ if } a \in P, \\
c'^*(a,0) &= c'^*(a,1) = (1,1), \text{ if } a \in Q, \\
c'^*(a,0) &= c'^*(a,1) = (0,1), \text{ if } a \in R, \\
c'^*(a,0) &= c'^*(a,1) = (1,0), \text{ if } a \in S.
\end{aligned}
$$

Then by construction, c' is symmetric and has the same color pair distribution as c. Hence by Lemma 4.4, there exists $g \in S(A \times 2)$ such that $c' = (2 \times g) \bullet c$, which was to be shown.

Lemma 4.7. *Suppose* $|A| = 3$ *and* c *is a nearly standard coloring of* $2 \times A \times 2$. *Then there exists* $f \in S(2 \times A)$ *such that* $(f \times 2) \bullet c$ *is regular.*

Proof. Write A as the disjoint union $A_1 \cup A_2 \cup A_3$, where $c^*(a_1, 0) = (0,0)$ and $c^*(a_1, 1) = (1,1)$ for all $a_1 \in A_1$, $c^*(a_2, 0) = (0,1)$ and $c^*(a_2, 1) = (1,0)$ for all $a_2 \in A_2$, and $c^*(a,0) = c^*(a,1) = (0,1)$ for all $a \in A_3$. By the definition of nearly standard, we know that A_1 and A_2 have at most one element each. Since we assumed $|A| = 3$, this leaves us with four cases.

- Case 1. Assume $|A_1| = |A_2| = 0$. Say $A_3 = \{p, q, r\}$. Since $c^*(a,0) = c^*(a,1) = (0,1)$ for all $a \in A$, c is the following coloring (using the notation of Sect. 4.2):

$$
\begin{array}{ccc|ccc}
p & q & r & p & q & r \\
\hline
1 & 1 & 1 & 1 & 1 & 1 \\
0 & 0 & 0 & 0 & 0 & 0.
\end{array}
$$

Since c is already regular (in fact, standard), we can take f to be the identity permutation.

- Case 2. Assume $|A_1| = 1$ and $|A_2| = 0$. Say $A_1 = \{a_1\}$ and $A_3 = \{p, q\}$. Then c is the coloring

$$
\begin{array}{ccc|ccc}
a_1 & p & q & a_1 & p & q \\
\hline
0 & 1 & 1 & 1 & 1 & 1 \\
0 & 0 & 0 & 1 & 0 & 0.
\end{array}
$$

Define $f : 2 \times A \to 2 \times A$ by $f(0, a_1) = (1, p)$, $f(1, p) = (0, q)$, $f(0, q) = (0, a_1)$, and the identity elsewhere. Then $(f \times 2) \bullet c$ is the coloring

$$
\begin{array}{ccc|ccc}
a_1 & p & q & a_1 & p & q \\
\hline
0 & 0 & 1 & 1 & 1 & 1 \\
0 & 0 & 1 & 0 & 0 & 1.
\end{array}
$$

- Case 3. Assume $|A_1| = 0$ and $|A_2| = 1$. Say $A_2 = \{a_2\}$ and $A_3 = \{p, q\}$. Then c is the coloring

$$
\begin{array}{ccc|ccc}
a_2 & p & q & a_2 & p & q \\
\hline
1 & 1 & 1 & 0 & 1 & 1 \\
0 & 0 & 0 & 1 & 0 & 0.
\end{array}
$$

Define $f : 2 \times A \to 2 \times A$ by $f(0, a_2) = (1, p)$, $f(1, p) = (0, q)$, $f(0, q) = (0, a_2)$, and the identity elsewhere. Then $(f \times 2) \bullet c$ is the coloring

$$
\begin{array}{ccc|ccc}
a_2 & p & q & a_2 & p & q \\
\hline
1 & 0 & 1 & 0 & 1 & 1 \\
0 & 0 & 1 & 0 & 0 & 1.
\end{array}
$$

– Case 4. Assume $|A_1| = |A_2| = 1$. Say $A_1 = \{a_1\}$, $A_2 = \{a_2\}$, and $A_3 = \{p\}$. Then c is the coloring

$$
\begin{array}{ccc|ccc}
a_1 & a_2 & p & a_1 & a_2 & p \\
\hline
0 & 1 & 1 & 1 & 0 & 1 \\
0 & 0 & 0 & 1 & 1 & 0.
\end{array}
$$

Define $f : 2 \times A \to 2 \times A$ by $f(0, a_1) = (1, a_2)$, $f(1, a_2) = (0, p)$, $f(0, p) = (0, a_1)$, and the identity elsewhere. Then $(f \times 2) \bullet c$ is the coloring

$$
\begin{array}{ccc|ccc}
a_1 & a_2 & p & a_1 & a_2 & p \\
\hline
0 & 0 & 1 & 1 & 1 & 1 \\
0 & 0 & 1 & 0 & 1 & 0.
\end{array}
$$

In all four cases, $(f \times 2) \bullet c$ is regular, as desired.

Lemma 4.8. *Suppose $|A| \geqslant 3$ and c is a nearly standard coloring of $2 \times A \times 2$. Then there exists $f \in S(2 \times A)$ such that $(f \times 2) \bullet c$ is regular.*

Proof. The only difference to Lemma 4.7 is that A may have more than 3 elements. However, by the definition of nearly standard, c is already standard (hence regular) on the excess elements. Therefore, we can ignore all but 3 elements of A and proceed as in Lemma 4.7.

Lemma 4.9. *Let c be a nearly symmetric fair coloring of $2 \times A \times 2$. Then there exists $f \in S(2 \times A)$ such that $(f \times 2) \bullet c$ is nearly standard.*

Proof. Let $A' = \{a \in A \mid c^*(a, 0) = c^*(a, 1)\}$, and let c' be the coloring of $2 \times A' \times 2$ obtained by restricting c to the domain $2 \times A' \times 2$. Then c' is symmetric. By definition of "nearly symmetric", there exists at most two elements $a_1, a_2 \in A \setminus A'$; moreover, the element a_1, if any, satisfies $c^*(a_1, 0) = (0, 0)$ and $c^*(a_1, 1) = (1, 1)$ and the element a_2, if any, satisfies $c^*(a_2, 0) = (0, 1)$ and $c^*(a_2, 1) = (1, 0)$. By assumption, c is fair. Since c restricted to $2 \times (A \setminus A') \times 2$ is evidently fair as well, it follows that c' is also fair. We will choose the permutation f so that its support does not touch the elements a_1 and a_2; it therefore suffices to find some permutation $f' \in S(2 \times A')$ such that $(f' \times 2) \bullet c'$ is standard. But such an f' exists by Lemma 4.5.

Lemma 4.10. *Let c be a fair coloring of $2 \times A \times 2$. Then there exists $g \in S(A \times 2)$ such that $(2 \times g) \bullet c$ is nearly symmetric.*

Proof. The proof is very similar to that of Lemma 4.6. Consider the color pair distribution $(n_c(0,0), n_c(0,1), n_c(1,0), n_c(1,1))$ of the given coloring c, and note that

$$n_c(0,0) + n_c(0,1) + n_c(1,0) + n_c(1,1) = 2|A|. \tag{7}$$

Because c is fair, we must have $n_c(0,0) = n_c(1,1)$, and in particular, $n_c(0,0)$ and $n_c(1,1)$ have the same parity (even or odd). From (7), it follows that $n_c(0,1)$ and $n_c(1,0)$ have the same parity. Therefore, there exist natural numbers p, q, r, s, t, u, with $t, u \in \{0,1\}$, such that

$$n_c(0,0) = 2p + t, \quad n_c(1,1) = 2q + t, \quad n_c(0,1) = 2r + u, \quad n_c(1,0) = 2s + u.$$

(As a matter of fact, $p = q$, but we will not make further use of this fact). From (7), we have that $p + q + r + s + t + u = |A|$. Write A as a disjoint union $P \cup Q \cup R \cup S \cup T \cup U$, where $|P| = p$, $|Q| = q$, $|R| = r$, $|S| = s$, $|T| = t$, and $|U| = u$. Define a coloring c' by

$$
\begin{aligned}
c'^*(a,0) = c'^*(a,1) &= (0,0), & \text{if } a \in P, \\
c'^*(a,0) = c'^*(a,1) &= (1,1), & \text{if } a \in Q, \\
c'^*(a,0) = c'^*(a,1) &= (0,1), & \text{if } a \in R, \\
c'^*(a,0) = c'^*(a,1) &= (1,0), & \text{if } a \in S, \\
c'^*(a,0) = (0,0) \quad \text{and} \quad c'^*(a,1) &= (1,1), \text{if } a \in T, \\
c'^*(a,0) = (0,1) \quad \text{and} \quad c'^*(a,1) &= (1,0), \text{if } a \in U.
\end{aligned}
$$

By construction, c' has the same color pair distribution as c. Hence by Lemma 4.4, there exists $g \in S(A \times 2)$ such that $c' = (2 \times g) \bullet c$. On the other hand, by construction, c' is nearly symmetric (with a_1 being the unique element of T, if any, and a_2 being the unique element of U, if any).

4.5 Proof of Proposition 4.3

Proposition 4.3 is now an easy consequence of Lemmas 4.5–4.10. Figure 3 contains a proof "without words". For readers who prefer a proof "with words", we give it here:

Assume $|A| \geqslant 3$ and let c be a fair coloring of $2 \times A \times 2$. By Lemma 4.10, there exists $g_1 \in S(A \times 2)$ such that $c_1 = (2 \times g_1) \bullet c$ is nearly symmetric. By Lemma 4.9, there exists $f_2 \in S(2 \times A)$ such that $c_2 = (f_2 \times 2) \bullet c_1$ is nearly standard. By Lemma 4.8, there exists $g_3 \in S(A \times 2)$ such that $c_3 = (2 \times g_3) \bullet c_2$ is regular. By Lemma 4.6, there exists $g_4 \in S(A \times 2)$ such that $c_4 = (2 \times g_4) \bullet c_3$ is symmetric. By Lemma 4.5, there exists $f_5 \in S(2 \times A)$ such that $c_5 = (f_5 \times 2) \bullet c_4$ is standard. Let

$$
\begin{aligned}
\sigma &= (f_5 \times 2)(2 \times g_4)(2 \times g_3)(f_2 \times 2)(2 \times g_1) \\
&= (f_5 \times 2)(2 \times g_4 g_3)(f_2 \times 2)(2 \times g_1).
\end{aligned}
$$

Then $\sigma \bullet c = c_{\text{st}}$, and σ has alternation depth 4, as claimed. $\qquad \square$

5 Proof of the Main Theorem

Our main result, Theorem 2.1, follows from Propositions 3.9 and 4.3. Specifically, let $\sigma \in S(2 \times A \times 2)$ be an even permutation, and let $c = \sigma^{-1} \bullet c_{\mathrm{st}}$. By Proposition 4.3, we can find $\tau \in S(2 \times A \times 2)$ of alternation depth 4 such that $\tau \bullet c = c_{\mathrm{st}}$. Note that τ is even by Remark 2.2. Let $\rho = \sigma\tau^{-1}$. Then ρ is also even, and $\rho \bullet c_{\mathrm{st}} = \sigma \bullet (\tau^{-1} \bullet c_{\mathrm{st}}) = \sigma \bullet c = c_{\mathrm{st}}$. Therefore, by Lemma 4.2, ρ is of the form $g + h$, for $g, h \in S(A \times 2)$. By Proposition 3.9, ρ has alternation depth 5, and it follows that $\sigma = \rho\tau$ has alternation depth 9, as claimed.   □

6 Conclusion and Further Work

We showed that every even permutation of $2 \times A \times 2$ has alternation depth 9. The bound 9 is probably not tight. The constructions of Sects. 3 and 4 have many degrees of freedom, making it plausible that a tighter bound on alternation depth can be found.

The best lower bound for alternation depth known to the author is 5. An exhaustive search shows that for $A = \{a, b, c\}$, a 3-cycle with support $\{0\} \times A \times \{0\}$ cannot be written with alternation depth 4. Of course, this particular permutation can be realized with alternation depth 5 by Proposition 3.9.

It is reasonable to conjecture that there is nothing special about the number 2 in Theorem 2.1. Specifically, if N and M are finite sets, I conjecture that there exists a finite bound on the alternation depth of all permutations $\sigma \in S(N \times A \times M)$ (or all even permutations, when N and M are even), for large enough A, independently of the size of A.

The reader may have noticed that in our definition of alternation depth, in the factors of the form $f \times 2$ and $2 \times g$, we did not require the permutations f and g to be even. However, if the construction is to be used recursively (as required, for example, by some potential applications mentioned in the introduction), each f and g must be even. We say that $\sigma \in S(2 \times A \times 2)$ has *even alternation depth* d if it can be written as a product of d factors of the forms $f \times 2$ or $2 \times g$, where each such $f \in S(2 \times A)$ and $g \in S(A \times 2)$ is an even permutation. Then an analogue of Theorem 2.1 holds for even alternation depth. A very inefficient proof is the following: first, it is easy to find some odd permutation $g \in S(A \times 2)$ and even permutations $f_1, f_3, f_5 \in S(2 \times A)$ and $g_2, g_4 \in S(A \times 2)$ such that $(2 \times g) = (f_1 \times 2)(2 \times g_2)(f_3 \times 2)(2 \times g_4)(f_5 \times 2)$. Using this, every permutation of alternation depth d can be rewritten as a permutation of even alternation depth at most $5d + 1$. Naturally, this naive proof yields a bound on even alternation depth that is not very tight, namely, $d = 5 \cdot 9 + 1 = 46$. With a more careful argument, it can be shown that the even alternation depth is in fact bounded by 13, and I expect that it is bounded by 9 or less. But the details of this are left for future work.

References

1. De Vos, A., Raa, B., Storme, L.: Generating the group of reversible logic gates. J. Phys. A **35**(33), 7063 (2002)
2. Musset, J.: Générateurs et relations pour les circuits booléens réversibles. Technical report 97–32, Institut de Mathématiques de Luminy (1997). http://iml.univ-mrs.fr/editions/
3. Saeedi, M., Markov, I.L.: Synthesis and optimization of reversible circuits – a survey. ACM Comput. Surv. **45**(2), 34 p. (2013). arXiv:1110.2574
4. Toffoli, T.: Reversible computing. In: de Bakker, J., van Leeuwen, J. (eds.) Automata, Languages and Programming. LNCS, vol. 85, pp. 632–644. Springer, Heidelberg (1980). Abridged version of Technical Memo MIT/LCS/TM-151, MIT Lab. for Comput. Sci. (1980)

Syntheses

Generating Reversible Circuits from Higher-Order Functional Programs

Benoît Valiron$^{(\boxtimes)}$

LRI, CentraleSupélec, Université Paris Saclay,
Bâtiment 650, 91405 Orsay Cedex, France
benoit.valiron@lri.fr

Abstract. Boolean reversible circuits are boolean circuits made of reversible elementary gates. Despite their constrained form, they can simulate any boolean function. The synthesis and validation of a reversible circuit simulating a given function is a difficult problem. In 1973, Bennett proposed to generate reversible circuits from traces of execution of Turing machines. In this paper, we propose a novel presentation of this approach, adapted to higher-order programs. Starting with a PCF-like language, we use a monadic representation of the trace of execution to turn a regular boolean program into a circuit-generating code. We show that a circuit traced out of a program computes the same boolean function as the original program. This technique has been successfully applied to generate large oracles with the quantum programming language Quipper.

1 Introduction

Reversible circuits are linear, boolean circuits with no loops, whose elementary gates are reversible. In quantum computation, reversible circuits are mostly used as oracle: the *description* of the problem to solve. Usually, this description is given as a classical, conventional algorithm: the graph to explore [17], the matrix coefficients to process [13], *etc.* These algorithms use arbitrarily complex structures, and if some are rather simple, for example [28], others are quite complicated and make use of analytic functions [13], memory registers [2] (which thus have to be simulated), *etc.*

This paper is concerned with the design of reversible circuits as *operational semantics* of a higher-order purely functional programming language. The language is expressive enough to encode most algorithms: it features recursion, pairs, booleans and lists, and it can easily be extended with additional structures if needed. This operational semantics can be understood as the *compilation* of a program into a reversible circuit.

Compiling a program into a reversible circuit is fundamentally different from compiling on a regular back-end: there is no notion of "loop", no real control flow, and all branches will be explored during the execution. In essence, a reversible circuit is the *trace* of all possible executions of a given program. Constructing a reversible circuit out of the trace of execution of a program is what Bennett [3]

© Springer International Publishing Switzerland 2016
S. Devitt and I. Lanese (Eds.): RC 2016, LNCS 9720, pp. 289–306, 2016.
DOI: 10.1007/978-3-319-40578-0_21

proposed in 1973, using Turing machines. In this paper, we refer to it as Landauer embeddings [16].

In this paper, we build up on this idea of circuit-as-trace-of-program and formalize it into an operational semantics for our higher-order language. This semantics is given externally as an abstract machine, and internally, as a *monadic interpretation*.

The strength of our approach to circuit synthesis is to be able to reason on a regular program independently from the constraints of the circuit construction. The approach we follow is similar to what is done in Geometry of synthesis [9] for hardware synthesis, but since the back-end we aim at is way simpler, we can devise a very natural and compact monadic operational semantics.

Contribution. The main contribution of this paper is a monadic presentation of Landauer embeddings [16] in the context of higher-order programs. Its main strength is its parametricity: a program really represents a *family* of circuits, parametrized on the size of the input. Furthermore, we demonstrate a compositional monadic procedure for generating a reversible circuit out of a regular, purely functional program. The generated circuit is then provably computing the same thing as the original program. This can be used to internalize the generation of a reversible circuit out of a functional program. It has been implemented in Quipper [23] and used for building complex quantum oracles.

Related Works. From the description of a conventional function it is always possible to design a reversible circuit computing the function out of its truth table or properties thereof and several methods have been designed to generate compact circuits (see e.g. [7,12,18,24,25,35]). However, if these techniques allow one to write reversible functions with arbitrary truth tables [34], they do not usually scale well as the size of the input grows.

Synthesis of reversible circuits can be seen as a small branch of the vast area of hardware synthesis. In general, hardware synthesis can be structural (description of the structure of the circuit) or behavioral (description of algorithm to encode). Functional programming languages have been used for both. On the more structural side one finds Lava [6], BlueSpec [20], functional netlists [22], *etc.* On the behavioral side we have the Geometry of Synthesis [9], Esterel [4], ForSyDe [26], *etc.* Two more recent contributions sitting in between structural and behavioral approaches are worth mentioning. First, the imperative, *reversible* synthesis language SyRec [36], specialized for reversible circuits. Then, Thomsen's proposal [33], allowing to represent a circuit in a functional manner, highlighting the behavior of the circuit out of its structure.

On the logic side, the geometry of interaction [10] is a methodology that can be used to turn functional programs into reversible computation [1,9,32]: it is based on the idea of turning a typing derivation into a reversible automaton.

There have also been attempts to design reversible abstract machines and to compile regular programs into reversible computation. For example, a reversible version of the SEMCD machine has been designed [15]. More recently, the compiler REVS [21] aims at compiling conventional computation into reversible circuits.

Monadic semantics for representing circuits is something relatively common, specially among the DSL community: Lava [6], Quipper [11], Fe-Si [5], *etc.* Other approaches use more sophisticated constructions, with type systems based on arrows [14] in order to capture reversibility.

In the present work, the language is circuit-agnostic, and the interest of the method lies more in the fact that the monadic semantics to build reversible circuits is completely *implicit* and only added at circuit-generation time, following the approach in [31], rather than in the choice of the language. Compared to [14], our approach is also parametric in the sense that a program does not describe one fixed-size circuit but a family of circuits, parametrized by the size of the input.

Plan of the Paper. Section 2 presents the definition of reversible circuits and how to perform computation with them. Section 3 describes a PCF-like lambda-calculus and proposes two operational semantics: one as a simple beta-reduction and one using an abstract machine and a partial evaluation procedure generating a circuit. Section 4 describes the call-by-value reduction strategy and explains how to internalize the abstract-machine within the language using a monad. Section 5 discusses the use of this technique in the context of the generation of quantum oracles. Finally, Sect. 5 concludes and proposes some future investigations.

2   Reversible Circuits

A reversible boolean circuit consists in a set of *open wires* and *elementary gates* attached onto the wires. Schematically, a reversible boolean circuit is of the form shown on the right. To each gate is associated a boolean operation, supposed to be reversible. In this circuit example, G is a one-bit operation (for example a not-gate, flipping a bit) while F is a two-bit operation. In each wire, a bit "flows" from left to right. All the bits go at the same pace. When a gate is met, the corresponding operation is applied on the wires attached to the gate. Since the gates are reversible, the overall circuit is reversible by making the bits flow backward.

Choice of Elementary Gates. Many gates have been considered in the literature [24]. In this paper, we will consider multi-controlled-not gates. A not gate, represented by $-\oplus-$ is flipping the value of the wire on which it is attached. The operator **not** stands for the bit-flip operation. Given a gate F acting on n wires, a controlled-F is a gate acting on $n + 1$ wires. The control can be positive or negative, represented respectively as shown on the right. In both cases, the 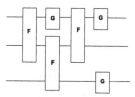 top wire is not modified. On the bottom wires, the gate F is applied if x is true for the positive control, and false for the negative control. Otherwise, no gate is applied: the values $\vec{y}$ flow unchanged through the gate. A positively-controlled not gate will be denoted CNOT.

A reversible circuit runs a computation on some query: some input wires correspond to the query, and some output wires correspond to the answer. The auxiliary input wires that are not part of the query are initially fed with the boolean "false" (also written 0).

Computing with Reversible Circuits. As described by Landauer [16] and Bennett [3], a conventional, classical algorithm computing a boolean function $f : \mathtt{bit}^n \to \mathtt{bit}^m$ can be mechanically transformed into a reversible circuit sending the triplet $(x, \vec{0}, \vec{0})$ to $(x, \mathrm{trace}, f(x))$, as in Fig. 1a. Its input wires are not modified by the circuit, and the trace of all intermediate results are kept in garbage wires.

Because of their particular structure, two Landauer embeddings T_g and T_h can be composed to give a Landauer embedding of the composition $h \circ g$. Figure 1b shows the process: the wires of the output of T_g are fed to the input of T_h, and the output of the global circuit is the one of T_h. The garbage wires now contain all the ones of T_g and T_h.

(a) Landauer embedding of f.

(b) Composing two Landauer embeddings.

Fig. 1. Landauer embeddings.

Note that it is easy to build elementary Landauer embeddings for negation and conjunction: the former is a negatively-controlled not while the latter is a positively doubly-controlled not. Any boolean function can then be computed with Landauer embeddings.

3   Reversible Circuits as Trace of Programs

In this section, we present an implementation of Landauer embeddings to the context of a higher-order functional programming language, and show how it can be understood through an abstract machine.

3.1   Simple Formalization of Reversible Circuits

A reversible circuit has a very simple structure. As a linear sequence of elementary gates, it can be represented as a simple list of gates.

Definition 1. A *reversible gate* G is a term $\mathtt{N}(i \cdot b_1^{j_1} \ldots b_n^{j_n})$ where $i, j_1, \ldots, j_n$ are natural numbers such that for all k, $i \neq j_k$, and where $b_1, \ldots, b_n$ are booleans. If the list of $b_k^{j_k}$ is empty, we simply write $\mathtt{N}(i)$ in place of $\mathtt{N}(i \cdot)$. The *wires* of the gate $\mathtt{N}(i \cdot b_1^{j_1} \ldots b_n^{j_n})$ is the set of natural numbers $\{i, j_1, \ldots, j_n\}$. The wire i is called *active* and the j_k's are called the *control wires*. Given a list C of gates, the union of the sets of wires of the elements of C is written $Wires(C)$. Finally, the boolean values True and False flowing in the wires are respectively represented with tt and ff throughout the paper.

Definition 2. A *reversible boolean circuit* is a triplet (I, C, O) where C is a list of reversible gates and where I and O are sets of wires. The list C is the *raw circuit*, I is the set of *inputs wires* and O the set of *outputs wires*. We also call $Wires(C) \setminus I$ the *auxiliary wires* and $Wires(C) \setminus O$ the *garbage wires*.

Executing a reversible circuit on a given tuple of booleans computes as follows.

Definition 3. Consider a circuit (I, C, O) and a family of bits $(x_i)_{i \in I}$. A *valuation* for the circuit is an indexed family $v = (v_j)_{j \in Wires(C) \cup I \cup O}$ of booleans. The *execution of a gate* $N(i \cdot b_1^{j_1} \ldots b_n^{j_n})$ *on the valuation* v is the valuation w such that for all $l \neq i$, $w_l = v_l$ and $w_i = v_i$ xor $\wedge_{k=1}^n (v_{j_k}$ xor b_k xor tt$)$ if $n \geq 1$ and $w_i = not(v_i)$ otherwise. The execution of the circuit (I, C, O) with input $(x_i)_{i \in I}$ is the succession of the following operations: (1) Initialization of a valuation v such that for all $k \in I$, $v_k = x_k$, and for all the other values of k, v_k is false. (2) Execution of every gate in C on v, *in reverse order*. (3) The execution of the circuit returns the sub-family $(v_k)_{k \in O}$.

3.2 A PCF-like Language with Lists of Booleans

In this section, we present the functional language **PCF**^{list} that we use to describe the regular computations that we eventually want to perform with a reversible circuit. The language is simply-typed and it features booleans, pairs and lists.

$$
\begin{aligned}
M, N \ ::=\ & x \mid \lambda x.M \mid MN \mid \langle M, N \rangle \mid \pi_1(M) \mid \pi_2(M) \mid \text{skip} \mid M;N \mid \text{tt} \mid \text{ff} \mid \\
& \text{if } M \text{ then } N \text{ else } P \mid \text{and} \mid \text{xor} \mid \text{not} \mid \text{inj}_1(M) \mid \text{inj}_2(M) \mid \\
& \text{match } P \text{ with } (x \mapsto M \mid y \mapsto N) \mid \text{split}^A \mid Y(M) \mid \text{Err}, \\
A, B \ ::=\ & \text{bit} \mid A \oplus B \mid A \times B \mid 1 \mid A \to B \mid [A].
\end{aligned}
$$

The language comes equipped with the typing rules of Table 1. There are several things to note. First, the construct if‑then‑else can only output *first-order types*. A first order type is a type from the grammar $A^0, B^0 ::= \text{bit} \mid A^0 \times B^0 \mid [A^0]$. Despite the fact that one can encode them with the test construct, for convenience we add the basic boolean combinators not, xor and and. There are no constructors for lists, but instead there is a coercion from $1 \oplus (A \times [A])$ to $[A]$; the term split turns a list-type into a additive type. There is a special-purpose term Err that will be used in particular in Sect. 3.4 as an error-spawning construct. The boolean values True and False are respectively represented with tt and ff. skip is the unit term and $M;N$ is used as the destructor of the unit. Finally, Y is a fixpoint operator. As we shall eventually work with a call-by-value reduction strategy, we only consider fixpoints defining functions.

Table 1. Typing rules of $\mathbf{PCF}^{\text{list}}$.

$$\overline{\Delta, x:A \vdash x:A} \quad \overline{\Delta \vdash \texttt{tt}:\texttt{bit}} \quad \overline{\Delta \vdash \texttt{ff}:\texttt{bit}} \quad \overline{\Delta \vdash \texttt{skip}:1} \quad \overline{\Delta \vdash \texttt{Err}:A}$$

$$\overline{\Delta \vdash \texttt{not}:\texttt{bit} \to \texttt{bit}} \quad \overline{\Delta \vdash \texttt{and}:\texttt{bit} \times \texttt{bit} \to \texttt{bit}} \quad \overline{\Delta \vdash \texttt{xor}:\texttt{bit} \times \texttt{bit} \to \texttt{bit}}$$

$$\overline{\Delta \vdash \texttt{split}:[A] \to 1 \oplus (A \times [A])}$$

$$\frac{\Delta, x:A \vdash M:B}{\Delta \vdash \lambda x.M:A \to B} \quad \frac{\Delta \vdash M:A_1 \times A_2}{\Delta \vdash \pi_i(M):A_i} \quad \frac{\Delta \vdash M:A_i}{\Delta \vdash \texttt{inj}_i(M):A_1 \oplus A_2}$$

$$\frac{\Delta \vdash M:A \to B \quad \Delta \vdash N:A}{\Delta \vdash MN:B} \quad \frac{\Delta \vdash M:A \quad \Delta \vdash N:B}{\Delta \vdash \langle M,N \rangle:A \times B} \quad \frac{\Delta \vdash M:1 \quad \Delta \vdash N:B}{\Delta \vdash M;N:B}$$

$$\frac{\Delta \vdash P:A \oplus B \quad \Delta, x:A \vdash M:C \quad \Delta, y:B \vdash N:C}{\Delta \vdash \texttt{match } P \texttt{ with } (x^A \mapsto M | y^B \mapsto N):C} \quad \frac{\Delta \vdash M:1 \oplus (A \times [A])}{\Delta \vdash M:[A]}$$

$$\frac{\Delta \vdash M:A \to A}{\Delta \vdash Y(M):A} \quad \frac{\Delta \vdash P:\texttt{bit} \quad \Delta \vdash M:C \quad \Delta \vdash N:C \quad \text{the type } C \text{ is first-order}}{\Delta \vdash \texttt{if } P \texttt{ then } M \texttt{ else } N:C}$$

Notation 4. We write $\texttt{nil}$ for $\texttt{inj}_1(\texttt{skip})$ and $M :: N$ in place of $\texttt{inj}_2(M \times N)$. We also write $[M_1, \ldots M_n]$ for $M_1 :: \ldots :: M_n :: \texttt{nil}$. We also write general products $\langle M_1, \ldots, M_n \rangle$ as $\langle M_1, \langle \ldots M_n \ldots \rangle \rangle$. Projections π_i for $i \leq n$ extends naturally to n-ary products. We write $\texttt{letrec } f\,x = M \texttt{ in } N$ for the term $(\lambda f.N)(Y(\lambda f.\lambda x.M))$.

Remark 5. The typing rule of the $\texttt{if-then-else}$ construct imposes a first-order condition on the branches of the test. This will be clarified in Remark 19. For now, let us just note that this constraint can be lifted with some syntactic sugar: if M and N are of type $A_1 \to \ldots \to A_n$, where A_n is first-order, then a "higher-order" test $\texttt{if } P \texttt{ then } M \texttt{ else } N$ can be defined using the native, first-order test by an η-expansion with the lambda-abstraction $\lambda x_1 \ldots x_n.\texttt{if } P \texttt{ then } M x_1 \ldots x_n \texttt{ else } N x_1 \ldots x_n$.

3.3 Small-Step Semantics

We equip the language $\mathbf{PCF}^{\text{list}}$ with the smallest rewrite-system closed under subterm reduction, satisfying the rewrite rules of Table 2, and satisfying the obvious rules regarding $\texttt{not}$, $\texttt{and}$ and $\texttt{xor}$: for example, $\texttt{not tt} \to \texttt{ff}$ and $\texttt{not ff} \to \texttt{tt}$. Note that the term $\texttt{Err}$ does not reduce. This is on purpose: it represents an error that one cannot catch with the type system; in particular it will be used in Sect. 3.4. The usual safety properties are satisfied, modulo the error-spawning term $\texttt{Err}$.

Table 2. Small-step semantics for $\mathbf{PCF}^{\text{list}}$: reduction rules, acting on subterms.

$$(\lambda x.M)N \to M[N/x] \qquad \pi_i \langle M_1, M_2 \rangle \to M_i \quad \texttt{skip};M \to M$$

$$\texttt{if tt then } M \texttt{ else } N \to M \qquad \texttt{if ff then } M \texttt{ else } N \to N \quad \texttt{split } M \to M$$

$$\texttt{match inj}_i(P) \texttt{ with } (x_1 \mapsto M_1 | x_2 \mapsto M_2) \to M_i[P/x_i] \quad Y(M) \to M(Y(M))$$

Definition 6. A value is a term V defined by the grammar $\lambda x.M \mid \langle U_1, U_2 \rangle \mid \text{inj}_i(U) \mid c$, where c is a constant term: skip, tt, ff.

Theorem 7 (Safety). *Type preservation and progress are verified: (1) If $\Delta \vdash M : A$, then for all N such that $M \to N$ we also have $\Delta \vdash N : A$.   (2) If M is a closed term of type A then either M is a value, or M contains the term* Err, *or M reduces.*   □

In summary, the language is well-behaved. It is also reasonably expressive, in the sense that most of the computations that one could want to perform on lists of bits can be described, as shown in Example 9.

Convention 8. When defining a large piece of code, we will be using a Haskell-like notation. So instead of defining a closed function as a lambda-term on a typing judgment, we shall be using the notation

```
function : type_of_the_function
function arg1 arg2 ... = body_of_the_function
```

Also, we shall use the convenient notation *let* $x = M$ *in* N for $(\lambda x.N)M$ and the notation *let* $\langle x, y \rangle = M$ *in* N for *let* $z = M$ *in let* $x = \pi_1(z)$ *in let* $y = \pi_1(z)$ *in* N. Similarly, we allow multiple variables for recursive functions, and we use pattern-matching for lists and general products in the same manner.

Example 9 (List Combinators). The usual list combinators can be defined. Here we give the definition of foldl: $(A \to B \to A) \to A \to [B] \to A$. The other ones (such as map, zip...) are written similarly.

```
foldl f a l = letrec g z l' = match (split l') with
                      nil  ↦ z
                    | ⟨h,t⟩ ↦ g (f z h) t
              in g a l
```

Example 10 (Ripple-Carry Adder). One can easily encode a bit-adder: it takes a carry and two bits to add, and it replies with the answer and the carry to forward.

```
bit_adder : bit → bit → bit → (bit × bit)
bit_adder carry x y =
    let majority a b c = if (xor a b) then c else a in
    let z = xor (xor carry x) y in
    let carry' = majority carry x y in ⟨carry', z⟩
```

Encoding integers as lists of bits, low-bit first, one can use the bit-adder to write a complete adder in a ripple-carry manner, amenable to a simple folding. We use an implementation similar to the one done in [23].

```
adder_aux : (bit × [bit]) → (bit × bit) → (bit × [bit])
adder_aux ⟨w, cs⟩ ⟨a, b⟩ = let ⟨w', c'⟩ = bit_adder w a b in ⟨w', c'::cs⟩

adder : [bit] → [bit] → [bit]
adder x y = π₂ (foldl adder_aux ⟨ff, nil⟩ (zip y x))
```

3.4   Reversible Circuits from Operational Semantics

We consider the language $\mathbf{PCF}^{\mathrm{list}}$ as a *specification language* for boolean reversible circuits in the following sense: A term of type $x_1 : \mathtt{bit}, \ldots, x_n : \mathtt{bit} \vdash M : \mathtt{bit}^m$ computes a boolean function $f_M : \mathtt{bit}^n \to \mathtt{bit}^m$.

In this section, we propose an operational semantics for the language $\mathbf{PCF}^{\mathrm{list}}$ generating Landauer embeddings, as described in Sect. 2. The circuit is produced during the execution of an abstract machine and partial evaluation of terms. Essentially, a term reduces as usual, except for the term constructs handling the type $\mathtt{bit}$, for which we only record the operations to be performed. Formally, the definitions are as follows.

Definition 11. A *circuit-generating abstract machine* is a tuple consisting of (1) a typing judgment $p_1 : \mathtt{bit}, \ldots, p_{n+k} : \mathtt{bit} \vdash M : \mathtt{bit}^m$;   (2) a partial circuit $RC := (\{1, \ldots, n\}, C)$ where C is a list of gates;   (3) a one-to-one linking function mapping the free variables p_i of M to the wires $Wires(C) \cup \{1, \ldots, n\}$.

Intuitively, $\{1, \ldots, n\}$ is the set of input wires. The set of output wires is not yet computed: we only get it when M is a value. If G is a gate, we write $G :: (I, C)$ for the partial circuit $(I, G :: C)$. Given a judgment $p_1 : \mathtt{bit}, \ldots, p_n : \mathtt{bit} \vdash M : \mathtt{bit}^m$, the empty machine is $(M, (\{1, \ldots, n\}, \{\}), \{p_i \mapsto i \mid i = 1 \ldots n\})$ and is denoted with $EmptyAM(M)$. The size of the domain of a linking function L is written $\sharp(L)$.

By abuse of notation, we shall write abstract machine with terms, and not typing judgements. It is assumed that all terms are well-typed according to the definition.

Definition 12. Given a linking function L, a *first-order extension of L* consists of a term of shape $M ::= p_i \mid \langle M_1, \ldots M_n \rangle \mid [M_1, \ldots M_n]$, where the p_i's are in the domain of L. We say that two first-order extensions of L have *the same shape* provided that they are both products with the same size or lists with the same size such as their components have pairwise the same shape.

The set of circuit-generating abstract machines is equipped with a rewrite-system $(\to_{am})$ defined using a notion of *beta-context*, that is, a term with a hole, as follows.

$$C[-] ::= [-] \mid \lambda x.C[-] \mid (C[-])N \mid M(C[-]) \mid \langle C[-], N \rangle \mid \langle M, C[-] \rangle \mid$$
$$\pi_1(C[-]) \mid \pi_2(C[-]) \mid C[-];N \mid M;C[-] \mid \mathtt{if}\ C[-]\ \mathtt{then}\ N\ \mathtt{else}\ P \mid$$
$$\mathtt{if}\ M\ \mathtt{then}\ C[-]\ \mathtt{else}\ P \mid \mathtt{if}\ M\ \mathtt{then}\ N\ \mathtt{else}\ C[-] \mid \mathtt{inj}_1(C[-]) \mid \mathtt{inj}_2(C[-]) \mid$$
$$\mathtt{match}\ C[-]\ \mathtt{with}\ (x \mapsto M|y \mapsto N) \mid \mathtt{match}\ P\ \mathtt{with}\ (x \mapsto C[-]|y \mapsto N) \mid$$
$$\mathtt{match}\ P\ \mathtt{with}\ (x \mapsto M|y \mapsto C[-]) \mid Y(C[-]).$$

The constructor $[-]$ is the *hole* of the context. Given a context $C[-]$ and a term M, we define $C[M]$ as the variable-capturing substitution of the hole $[-]$ by M.

The rewrite rules can then be split in two sets. The first set concerns all the term constructs unrelated to the type $\mathtt{bit}$. In these cases, the state of the abstract machine is not modified, only the term is rewritten. The rules, presented

Table 3. Rewrite rules for circuit-generating abstract-machine: generic rules.

$$(C[(\lambda x.M)N],RC,L) \to_{am} (C[M[N/x]],RC,L) \quad (C[\pi_i\langle M_1,M_2\rangle],RC,L) \to_{am} (C[M_i],RC,L)$$

$$(C[\texttt{skip};M],RC,L) \to_{am} (C[M],RC,L) \qquad (C[\texttt{split } M],RC,L) \to_{am} (C[M],RC,L)$$

$$(C[\texttt{match inj}_i(P) \texttt{ with } (x_1 \mapsto M_1|x_2 \mapsto M_2)],RC,L) \to_{am} (C[M_i[P/x_i]],RC,L)$$

$$(C[Y(M)],RC,L) \to_{am} (C[M(Y(M))],RC,L)$$

Table 4. Rewrite rules for circuit-generating abstract-machines: rules for booleans

$$(C[\texttt{ff}],RC,L) \to_{am} (C[p_{i_0}],RC,L') \quad (C[\texttt{tt}],RC,L) \to_{am} (C[p_{i_0}],(\texttt{N}(i_0)) :: RC,L')$$

$$(C[\texttt{not } p_i],RC,L) \to_{am} (C[p_{i_0}],\texttt{N}(i_0 \cdot \texttt{ff}^i) :: RC,L')$$

$$(C[\texttt{and } p_i \, p_j],RC,L) \to_{am} (C[p_{i_0}],\texttt{N}(i_0 \cdot \texttt{tt}^i\texttt{tt}^j) :: RC,L')$$

$$(C[\texttt{xor } p_i \, p_j],RC,L) \to_{am} (C[p_{i_0}],\texttt{N}(i_0 \cdot (i,\texttt{tt})) :: \texttt{N}(i_0 \cdot \texttt{tt}^j) :: RC,L')$$

$$(C[\texttt{if } p_i \texttt{ then } V \texttt{ else } W],RC,L) \to_{am} \begin{cases} (C[U],RC',L'') & V \text{ and } W \text{ of the same shape} \\ C[\texttt{Err}] & \text{otherwise} \end{cases}$$

in Table 3, are the same as for the small-step semantics of Table 2: apart from the two rules concerning if-then-else, all the others are the same.

The second set of rules concerns the terms dealing with the type bit, and can be seen as partial-evaluation rules: we only record in the circuit the operations that would need to be done. The rules are shown in Table 4. The linking function L' is $L \cup \{p_{i_0} \mapsto i_0\}$, where i_0 is a new wire. The variable p_{i_0} is assumed to be fresh. For the case of the if-then-else, we assume V and W are first-order extensions of L with the same shape. The term U is a first-order extension of L with the same shape as V and W containing only (pairwise-distinct) free variables and mapping to new distinct garbage wires. L'' is L updated with this new data. Suppose that V contains the variables $v_1, \ldots v_k$, that W contains the variables $w_1, \ldots w_k$ and that U contains the variables $u_1, \ldots u_k$. Then RC' is RC with the following additional series of gates: $\texttt{N}(u_j \cdot \texttt{tt}^{p_i}\texttt{tt}^{v_i}))$ and $\texttt{N}(u_j \cdot \texttt{ff}^{p_i}\texttt{tt}^{w_i})$.

Remark 13. Note that the set I is never modified by the rules

Safety properties hold for this new semantics, in the sense that the only error uncaught by the type system is the term Err that might be spawned.

Theorem 14 (Type Preservation). *If* $p_1 : \texttt{bit}, \ldots, p_{\sharp(L)} : \texttt{bit} \vdash M : \texttt{bit}^m$, *if* (M,RC,L) *is an abstract machine and if* $(M,RC,L) \to_{am} (N,RC',L')$, *then we have the judgement* $p_1 : \texttt{bit}, \ldots, p_{\sharp(L')} : \texttt{bit} \vdash N : \texttt{bit}^m$. □

Theorem 15 (Progress). *If* $p_1 : \texttt{bit}, \ldots, p_{\sharp(L)} : \texttt{bit} \vdash M : \texttt{bit}^m$ *is valid and if* (M,RC,L) *is an abstract machine then either* M *is a value, or* M *contains* Err, *or* (M,RC,L) *reduces through* $(\to_{am})$. □

3.5 Simulations

The abstract machine M generates a circuit computing the same function as the small-step reduction of M in the following sense.

Definition 16. Let $(M, (I, C), L)$ be an abstract machine. We write $C(M, (I, C), L)$ for the circuit defined as $(I, C, \text{Range}(L))$. Let $(v_k)_{k \in \text{Range}(L)}$ be the execution of the circuit $C(M, (I, C), L)$ on the valuation $\vec{u} = (u_i)_{i \in I}$. We define $T(M, (I, C), L)(\vec{u})$ as the term M where each free variable x has been replaced with $v_{L(x)}$.

Intuitively, if (M, RC, L) is seen as a term where some boolean operations have been delayed in RC, then $T(M, RC, L)$ corresponds to the term resulting from the evaluation of the delayed operations.

Theorem 17. *Consider a judgment* $x_1 : \texttt{bit}, \dots, x_n : \texttt{bit} \vdash M : \texttt{bit}^m$ *and suppose that* $EmptyAM(M) \to_{am}^* (\langle p_{i_1}, \dots p_{i_k} \rangle, (I, C), L)$. *Then* $k = m$, *and provided that* $\vec{u} = (b_i)_{i \in I}$, *the term* $T(\langle p_{i_1}, \dots p_{i_k} \rangle, (I, C), L)(\vec{u})$ *is equal to* $\langle c_1, \dots c_m \rangle$ *if and only if the term* let $\langle x_1, \dots x_n \rangle = \langle b_1, \dots b_n \rangle$ in M *reduces to* $\langle c_1, \dots c_m \rangle$.

The proof is done using an invariant on a single step of the rewriting of abstract machines, stated as follows.

Lemma 18. *Consider a judgment* $x_1 : \texttt{bit}, \dots, x_n : \texttt{bit} \vdash M : \texttt{bit}^m$ *and suppose that* $(M, (I, C), L) \to_{am} (N, (I, C'), L')$. *Let* $\vec{u} = (u_i)_{i \in I}$ *be a valuation. Then either the term* $T(M, (I, C), L)(\vec{u})$ *is equal to* $T(N, (I, C'), L')(\vec{u})$ *if the rewrite corresponds to the elimination of a boolean* $\texttt{tt}$ *or* $\texttt{ff}$, *or* $T(M, (I, C), L)(\vec{u}) \to T(N, (I, C'), L')(\vec{u})$, *or* N *contains the error term* $\texttt{Err}$. $\square$

Proof of Theorem 17. If $EmptyAM(M) \to_{am}^* (\langle p_{i_1}, \dots p_{i_k} \rangle, (I, C), L)$, then there is a sequence of intermediate rewrite steps where none of the terms involved is the term $\texttt{Err}$. From Lemma 18, one concludes that for all valuations $\vec{u}$ on I, $T(EmptyAM(M))(\vec{u}) \to^* T(\langle p_{i_1}, \dots p_{i_k} \rangle, (I, C), L)(\vec{u})$. Choosing $\vec{u} = (b_i)_{i \in I}$, $T(EmptyAM(M))(\vec{u})$ is the term M where each free variable p_{i_j} has been substituted with its corresponding boolean b_{i_j}. Similarly, $T(\langle p_{i_1}, \dots p_{i_k} \rangle, (I, C), L)$ is equal to the value $\langle b_{i_1}, \dots b_{i_k} \rangle$. We can conclude the proof by remarking that the term let $\langle x_1, \dots x_n \rangle = \langle b_1, \dots b_n \rangle$ in M reduces to M where each of the free variables p_{i_j} have been substituted with b_{i_j}, that is, the term $T(EmptyAM(M))(\vec{u})$. $\square$

One would have also hoped to have a simulation result in the other direction, stating that if a (closed) term $M : \texttt{bit}^m$ reduces to a tuple of booleans, then $EmptyAM(M)$ generates a circuit computing the same tuple. Unfortunately this is not the case, and the reason is the particular status of the type $\texttt{bit}$ and the way the $\texttt{if-then-else}$ behaves.

Remark 19. Let us re-visit the first-order constraint of the $\texttt{if-then-else}$ discussed in Remark 5 in the light of this operational semantics. Here, this test behaves as a regular boolean operator acting on three arguments: they need to be all reduced to values before continuing. This test is "internal" to the circuit: both branches are evaluated during a run of the program. Because it is "internal", the type of the branches have to be "representable": thus the constraint on first-order. This test does not control the execution of the program: its characteristic only appears at circuit-evaluation time.

With this operational semantics, it is also interesting to note that there are two kinds of booleans: the "internal" type bit, and the "external" type defined e.g. as bool = $1 \oplus 1$. If the former does not control the flow, the latter does with the match constructor. And unlike if-then-else, match does not have type constraints on its branches.

The term Err can be explained in the light of this discussion. Thanks to the condition on the shape of the output branches of the test, it is used to enforce the fact that bit cannot be coerced to a bool. Indeed, consider the term if b then nil else [tt]: using a match against the result of the test, it would allow one to use the bit b for controlling the shape of the rest of the circuit. As there is not such construct for reversible circuits, it therefore has to be forbidden: it is not possible to control the flow of execution of the program through the type bit. And the fact that a well-typed term can produce an error is simply saying that the type-system is not "strong enough" to capture such a problem. It is very much related to the fact that the zip operator on lists cannot be "safely" typed without dependent types.

4   Internalizing the Abstract Machine

Instead of defining an external operational semantics as we did in Sect. 3.4, one can internalize the definition of circuits in the language $\mathbf{PCF}^{\mathrm{list}}$. Given a program, provided that one chooses a reduction strategy, one can simulate the abstract-machine semantics inside $\mathbf{PCF}^{\mathrm{list}}$ using a generic *monadic lifting*, close to what was proposed in [31].

4.1   Monadic Lifting

Before going ahead with the full abstract-machine semantics, we present the monadic lifting of $\mathbf{PCF}^{\mathrm{list}}$ for a monadic function-type. It is the transposition of Haskell's monads to our language $\mathbf{PCF}^{\mathrm{list}}$. The main characteristic of the reversible abstract-machine is to change the operational behavior of the type bit: the terms tt, ff, the inline bit-combinators and the term construct if - then - else do not reduce as regular lambda-terms. Instead, they trigger a side-effect, which can be simulated within a monad.

Definition 20. A *monad* is a function-type $\mathcal{M}(-)$ together with two terms $\mathrm{return}^A_{\mathcal{M}} : A \to \mathcal{M}(A)$ and $\mathrm{app}^{A,B}_{\mathcal{M}} : \mathcal{M}(A) \to (A \to \mathcal{M}(B)) \to \mathcal{M}(B)$. A *reversible-circuit monad* is a monad together with a type wire and the terms $\mathrm{mtt}_{\mathcal{M}}, \mathrm{mff}_{\mathcal{M}} : \mathcal{M}(\mathrm{wire})$, $\mathrm{mif}^A_{\mathcal{M}} : \mathrm{wire} \to \mathcal{M}(A) \to \mathcal{M}(A) \to \mathcal{M}(A)$, and $\mathrm{mnot}^A_{\mathcal{M}} : \mathcal{M}(\mathrm{wire} \to \mathcal{M}(\mathrm{wire}))$, and finally $\mathrm{mand}^A_{\mathcal{M}}, \mathrm{mxor}^A_{\mathcal{M}} : \mathcal{M}(\mathrm{wire} \times \mathrm{wire} \to \mathcal{M}(\mathrm{wire}))$.

Definition 21. Given a reversible-circuit monad $\mathcal{M}$, we inductively define the $\mathcal{M}$-*monadic lifting of a type* A, written $Lift_{\mathcal{M}}(A)$. We omit the index $\mathcal{M}$ for legibility.

$$Lift(\texttt{bit}) = \texttt{wire}, \qquad\qquad\qquad Lift(1) = 1,$$
$$Lift(A \to B) = Lift(A) \to \mathcal{M}(Lift(B)), \quad Lift(A \times B) = Lift(A) \times Lift(B),$$
$$Lift(A \oplus B) = Lift(A) \oplus Lift(B), \qquad\qquad Lift([A]) = [Lift(A)].$$

The $\mathcal{M}$-*monadic lifting of a term* M, denoted with $Lift_{\mathcal{M}}(M)$, is defined as follows. First, we set $Lift(\texttt{tt}) = \texttt{mtt}$, $Lift(\texttt{ff}) = \texttt{mff}$, $Lift(\texttt{and}) = \texttt{mand}$, $Lift(\texttt{xor}) = \texttt{mxor}$ and $Lift(\texttt{not}) = \texttt{mnot}$. Then

$$Lift(x) = \texttt{return } x, \quad Lift(\texttt{skip}) = \texttt{return skip},$$
$$Lift(\lambda x.M) = \texttt{return } \lambda \texttt{x}.Lift(M), \quad Lift(\texttt{split}) = \texttt{return } \lambda \texttt{x}.\texttt{return } (\texttt{split x}),$$
$$Lift(MN) = \texttt{app } Lift(M) \ \lambda \texttt{x}.\texttt{app } Lift(N) \ \lambda \texttt{y}.\texttt{xy},$$
$$Lift(\langle M, N\rangle) = \texttt{app } Lift(M) \ \lambda \texttt{x}.\texttt{app } Lift(N) \ \lambda \texttt{y}.\texttt{return } \langle x, y\rangle,$$
$$Lift(\pi_i(M)) = \texttt{app } Lift(M) \ \lambda \texttt{x}.\texttt{return } \pi_i(x),$$
$$Lift(\texttt{inj}_i(M)) = \texttt{app } Lift(M) \ \lambda \texttt{x}.\texttt{return inj}_i(x),$$
$$Lift(M;N) = \texttt{app } Lift(M) \ \lambda \texttt{x}.\texttt{app } Lift(N) \ \lambda \texttt{y}.\texttt{return } x;y,$$
$$Lift(\texttt{match } P \texttt{ with } (z_1 \mapsto M | z_2 \mapsto N)) =$$
$$\texttt{app } Lift(P) \ \lambda \texttt{x}.\texttt{match } x \texttt{ with } (z_1 \mapsto Lift(M) | z_2 \mapsto Lift(N)),$$
$$Lift(Y(M)) = \texttt{app } Lift(M) \ \lambda \texttt{f}.\texttt{return } (Y(\lambda y.\lambda z.\texttt{app } (y \texttt{ skip}) \ f))\texttt{skip}$$
$$Lift(\texttt{if } P \texttt{ then } M \texttt{ else } N) = \texttt{app } Lift(P) \ \lambda \texttt{x}.((\texttt{mif } x) \ Lift(M)) \ Lift(N)$$

Remark 22. Note that in this definition of the lifting, we followed a call-by-value approach: the argument $N : \mathcal{M}(A)$ of a function $M : A \to \mathcal{M}(B)$ is first reduced to a value before being fed to the function. This will be discussed in Sect. 4.3.

The fact that a monad is equipped with $\texttt{mtt}$, $\texttt{mff}$, $\texttt{mxor}$, $\texttt{mand}$, $\texttt{mnot}$ and $\texttt{mif}$ is not a guarantee that the lifting will behave as expected. One has to choose the right monad for it. It is the topic of Sect. 4.2. However, in general this monadic-lifting operation preserves types (proof by induction on the typing derivation).

Theorem 23. *Provided that* $x_1 : A_1, \ldots, x_n : A_n \vdash M : B$ *is valid, so is the judgment* $x_1 : Lift_{\mathcal{M}}(A_1), \ldots, x_n : Lift_{\mathcal{M}}(A_n) \vdash Lift_{\mathcal{M}}(M) : \mathcal{M}(Lift_{\mathcal{M}}(B))$. □

4.2 Reversible Circuits from Monadic Lifting

All the structure of the abstract machine can be encoded in the language **PCF^{list}**. A wire is a natural number. A simple way to represent them is with the type $\texttt{wire} := [1]$. The number 0 is the empty list while the successor of n is $(\texttt{skip} :: n)$. A gate is then $\texttt{gate} := \texttt{wire} \times [\texttt{wire} \times \texttt{bit}]$. A raw circuit is $[\texttt{gate}]$.

We now come to the abstract machine. In the formalization of Sect. 3.4, we were using a state with a circuit and a linking function. In this internal representation, the linking function is not needed anymore: the computation directly acts on wires. However, the piece of information that is still needed is the next fresh value. The state is encapsulated in $\texttt{state} := [\texttt{gate}] \times \texttt{wire}$. Finally, given a type A, we write $\texttt{circ}(A)$ for the type $\texttt{state} \to (\texttt{state} \times A)$: this is a computation generating a reversible circuit.

The type operator $\texttt{circ}(-)$ can be equipped with the structure of a reversible-circuit monad, as follows. First, it is obviously a state-monad, making the two first constructs automatic: $\texttt{return} := \lambda x.\lambda s.(s, x)$ and $\texttt{app} := \lambda x f.\lambda s.\textit{let } \langle s', a \rangle = x\, s \textit{ in } (f\, a)\, s'$. The others are largely relying on the fact that $\textbf{PCF}^{\text{list}}$ is expressive enough to emulate what was done in Sect. 3.4. Provided that $\textbf{S}$ stands for the successor function, we can $\texttt{mff}$ as the lambda-term $\lambda s.\textit{let } \langle c, w \rangle = s \textit{ in } \langle\langle c, \textbf{S}\, w \rangle, w \rangle$ and $\texttt{mtt}$ as the lambda-term $\lambda s.\textit{let } \langle c, w \rangle = s \textit{ in } \langle\langle\langle w, \texttt{nil}\rangle::c, \textbf{S}\, w \rangle, w \rangle$. Note how the definition reflects the reduction rules corresponding to $\texttt{tt}$ and $\texttt{ff}$ in Table 4: in the case of $\texttt{ff}$, the returned wire is the next fresh one, and the state is updated by increasing the "next-fresh" value by one unit. In the case of $\texttt{tt}$, on top of this we add a not-gate to the list of gates in order to flip the value of the returned wire. The definitions of $\texttt{mnot}$, $\texttt{mand}$ and $\texttt{mxor}$ are similar. For $\texttt{mif}$, one capitalizes on the fact that we know the structure of the branches of the test, as they are of first-order types. One can then define a zip-operator $A^0 \times A^0 \to A^0$ for each first-order type A^0.

4.3 Call-by-Value Reduction Strategy

As was mentioned in Remark 22, the monadic lifting intuitively follows a call-by-value approach. It can be formalized by developing a call-by-value reduction strategy for circuit-abstract machines. Such a definition follows the one of the reduction proposed in Sect. 3.4: we first design a notion of *call-by-value evaluation context* $E[-]$ characterizing the call-by-value redex that can be reduced. We then define the reduction: the generic rules of Table 3 are turned into their call-by-value version in the standard way. For example, we require that $(E[(\lambda x.M)V], RC, L) \to_{cbv} (E[M[V/x]], RC, L)$ happens only when V is a value. The rule requiring care is the rule for the fixpoint Y: we ask that $(E[Y(\lambda x.M)], RC, L) \to_{cbv} (E[M[Y(\lambda x.M)/x]], RC, L)$, for the term not to loop. Finally, the rules of Table 4 are similar, replacing $C[-]$ with $E[-]$.

In the light of this reduction strategy and of the monadic lifting of the previous section, one can now formalize what was mentioned in Remark 22. First, one can turn an abstract machine into a lifted term.

Definition 24. Let $x_1 : \texttt{bit}, \ldots, x_{n+k} : \texttt{bit} \vdash M : B$ and let $(M, (C, I), L)$ be an abstract machine where $I = \{1 \ldots n\}$. Then we define $\textit{Lift}(M, (C, I), L)$ as the term

$$\left(\textit{Lift}(M)[\overline{L(x_{n+1})}/x_{n+1} \ldots \overline{L(x_{n+k})}/x_{n+k}] \right) \langle \overline{C}, \textbf{S}\, \overline{\max(\textit{Range}(L))} \rangle,$$

where $\overline{C}$ is the representation of C as a term of type $[\texttt{gate}] \times \texttt{wire}$, and where $\overline{n}$ with n an integer is the representation of n as a term of type $[1]$.

Then, provided that $\simeq_\beta$ stands for the reflexive, symmetric and transitive closure of the beta-reduction on terms and choosing M and $(M, (C, I), L)$ as in Definition 24:

Theorem 25. *Suppose that* $(M, RC, L) \rightarrow_{cbv} (M', RC', L')$. *Then* Lift$(M, RC, L)$ *is beta-equivalent to* Lift(M', RC', L').   □

Provided that the beta-reduction is confluent, this essentially says that the abstract-machine semantics can be simulated with the monadic lifting.

Corollary 26. *If* $\vdash M : \mathtt{bit}^m$ *and* $EmptyAM(M) \rightarrow_{cbv} (\langle x_1, \ldots x_m \rangle, (C, I), L)$, *then the term* $\pi_1(Lift(M))$ *is beta-equivalent to* $\overline{C}$, *where* $\overline{C}$ *is the representation of* C *as a term, as described in* Definition 24.   □

5   Discussion

In this section, we present the main use for this tool: the design of oracles of quantum algorithms in the language Quipper [11]. We then discuss the optimality of the method.

Synthesis of Quantum Oracles. A rapid explanation is needed here: In quantum computation, one does not deal with classical bits but with the so-called *quantum bits*. At the logical level, a quantum algorithm consists of one or several *quantum circuits*, that is, reversible circuits with quantum bits flowing in the wires.

Quantum algorithms are used to solve classical problems. For example: factoring an integer [28], finding an element in a unordered list [19], finding the solution of a system of linear equations [13], finding a triangle in a graph [17], *etc.* In all of these algorithms, the description of the problem is a completely non-reversible function $f : \mathtt{bit}^n \rightarrow \mathtt{bit}^m$ and it has to be encoded as a reversible circuit computing the function $\bar{f} : \mathtt{bit}^n \times \mathtt{bit}^m \rightarrow \mathtt{bit}^n \times \mathtt{bit}^m$ sending (x, y) to $(x, y \mathtt{\,xor\,} f(x))$, possibly with some auxiliary wires set back to 0.

A canonical way to produce such a circuit is with a *Bennett embedding*. The procedure is shown on the right. First the Landauer embedding T_f of f is applied. Then the output of the circuit is xor'd onto the y input wires, and finally the inverse of T_f is applied. In particular, all the auxiliary wires are back to the value 0 at the end of the computation.

The method we propose in this paper offers a procedure for generating the main ingredient of this construction: the Landauer embedding. One just has to encode the problem in the language **PCF**^{list} (or extension thereof), possibly test and verify the program, and generate a corresponding reversible circuit through the monadic lifting. Theorems 17 and 26 guarantee that the monadic lifting of the program will give a circuit computing the same function as the original program.

This algorithm was implemented within the language Quipper, and used for non-trivial oracles [11,23]. Note that Quipper is not the only possible back-end for this generic monadic lifting: nothing forbids us to write a back-end in, say, Lava [6].

Example 27. The first example of code we saw (Example 10) computes an adder. One can run this code to generate a reversible adder: Fig. 2 shows the circuit generated when fed with 4-bits integers. One can see 4 blocks of pairs of similar shapes.

Example 28. In the oracle for the QLSA algorithm [13,27], one has to solve a system of differential equations coming from some physics problem using finite elements method. The bottom line is that it involves analytic functions such as sine and atan2.

Using fixed-point real numbers on 64 bits, we wrote a sine function using a Taylor expansion approximation. In total, we get a reversible circuit of 7,344,140 multi-controlled gates (with positive and negative controls). The function atan2 was defined using the CORDIC method. The generated circuit contains 34,599,531 multi-controlled gates. These two functions can be found in Quipper's distribution [23].

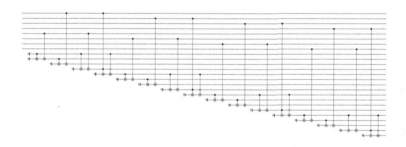

Fig. 2. Reversible adder for 4-bit integers.

Efficiency of the Monadic Lifting. The monadic lifting proposed in this paper generates circuits that are efficient in the sense that the size of a generated circuit is linear in the number of steps it takes to evaluate the corresponding program. This means that any program running in polynomial time upon the size of its input generates a polynomial-sized circuit. Without any modification or optimization whatsoever, the technique is therefore able to generate an "efficient" circuit for an arbitrary, conventional algorithm. This is how the circuit for the function sine cited in Example 28 was generated: first, a conventional implementation was written and tested. When ready the lifting was performed, generating a circuit.

Towards a Complete Compiler. Compared to other reversible compilers [21], the approach taken in this paper considers the construction of the circuit as a process that can be completely automatized: the stance is that it should be possible to take a classical, functional program with conventional inductive datatypes and let the compiler turn it into a reversible circuit without having to interfer (or only marginally). We do not claim to have a final answer: we only aim at proposing a research path towards such a goal.

A first step towards a more complete compiler for **PCF**[list] would involve optimization passes on the generated circuits. Indeed, as can be inferred from a quick analysis of Fig. 2, if monadic lifting generates efficient circuits it does not produces particularly lean circuits. There is a rich literature on optimization of reversible circuits [18, 24, 29, 30]. If all of these works are relevant for reducing the size of the circuits we get, we can more specifically capitalize on the particular shapes we obtain from the monadic semantics. If the reduction of a lambda-term into a reversible circuit is so verbose, it is partly due to the fact that garbage wires are created for every single intermediate result. It is possible to characterize a few optimization rules stemming from the circuit generation. And indeed, by applying these optimization schemes on the reversible adder of Fig. 2, one gets the circuit presented in Fig. 3. One can now clearly see the carry-ripple structure, and it is in fact very close to known reversible ripple-carry adders (see e.g. [8]). These optimizations were implemented in Quipper: applied on larger circuits such as the ones of Example 28, we get in general a size reduction by a factor of 10.

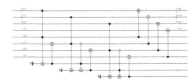

Fig. 3. Reversible adder for 4-bit integers, optimized.Reversible adder for 4-bit integers, optimized.

Confronting these specific optimizations against the original code of the program suggests that these could be designed at the level of code, therefore automatically generating leaner circuits up front. This opens the door to the design of specific type systems and code manipulations in a future full compiler.

Conclusion and Future Work. In this paper, we presented a simple and scalable mechanism to turn a higher-order program acting on booleans into into a family of reversible circuits using a monadic semantics. The main feature of this encoding is that an automatically-generated circuit is guaranteed to perform the same computation as the original program. The classical description we used is a small PCF-like language, but it is clear from the presentation that another choice of language can be made. In particular, an interesting question is whether it is possible to use a language with a stronger type system for proving properties of the encoded functions.

A second avenue of research is the question of the parallelization of the generated circuits. The circuits we produce are so far completely linear. Following the approach in [9], using parallel higher-order language might allow one to get parallel reversible circuits, therefore generating circuits with smaller depths.

Finally, the last avenue for research is the design of generic compiler with a dedicated type-system, code optimizations and back-end, specific circuit optimizations.

References

1. Abramsky, S.: A structural approach to reversible computation. Theor. Comput. Sci. **347**(3), 441–464 (2005)
2. Ambainis, A., Childs, A.M., et al.: Any AND-OR formula of size n can be evaluated in time $n^{\frac{1}{2}+o(1)}$ on a quantum computer. SIAM J. Comput. **39**, 2513–2530 (2010)
3. Bennett, C.H.: Logical reversibility of computation. IBM J. Res. Dev. **17**, 525–532 (1973)
4. Berry, G.: The foundations of esterel. In: Proof, Language, and Interaction, Essays in Honour of Robin Milner. MIT Press, Cambridge (2000)
5. Braibant, T., Chlipala, A.: Formal verification of hardware synthesis. In: Sharygina, N., Veith, H. (eds.) CAV 2013. LNCS, vol. 8044, pp. 213–228. Springer, Heidelberg (2013)
6. Claessen, K.: Embedded languages for describing and verifying hardware. Ph.D. thesis, Chalmers University of Technology and Göteborg University (2001)
7. Fazel, K., Thornton, M.A., Rice, J.E.: ESOP-based Toffoli gate cascade generation. In: Proceedings of PacRim, pp. 206–209 (2007)
8. Feynman, R.P.: Quantum mechanical computers. Optics News **11**, 11–20 (1985)
9. Ghica, D.R.: Geometry of synthesis. In: Proceedings of POPL, pp. 363–375 (2007)
10. Girard, J.-Y.: Towards a geometry of interaction. Contemp. Math. **92**, 69–108 (1989)
11. Green, A.S., Lumsdaine, P.L., et al.: Quipper: a scalable quantum programming language. In: Proceedings of PLDI, pp. 333–342 (2013)
12. Gupta, P., Agrawal, A., Jha, N.K.: An algorithm for synthesis of reversible logic circuits. IEEE Trans. CAD Int. Circ. Syst. **25**(11), 2317–2330 (2006)
13. Harrow, A.W., Hassidim, A., Lloyd, S.: Quantum algorithm for linear systems of equations. Phys. Rev. Lett. **103**(15), 150–502 (2009)
14. James, R.P., Sabry, A.: Information effects. In: Proceedings of POPL, pp. 73–84 (2012)
15. Kluge, W.: A reversible SE(M)CD machine. IFL'99. LNCS, vol. 1868, pp. 95–113. Springer, Heidelberg (1999)
16. Laundauer, R.: Irreversibility and heat generation in the computing process. IBM J. Res. Dev. **5**, 261–269 (1961)
17. Magniez, F., Santha, M., Szegedy, M.: Quantum algorithms for the triangle problem. SIAM J. Comput. **37**(2), 413–424 (2007)
18. Maslov, D., Dueck, G W., Miller, D.M.: Fredkin/Toffoli templates for reversible logic synthesis. In: Proceedings of ICCAD, pp. 256–261 (2003)
19. Nielsen, M.A., Chuang, I.L.: Quantum Computation and Quantum Information. Cambridge Univ. Press, Cambridge (2002)
20. Nikhil, R.S.: Bluespec: a general-purpose approach to high-level synthesis based on parallel atomic transactions. In: Coussy, P., Morawiec, A. (eds.) High-Level Synthesis, pp. 129–146. Springer, Heidelberg (2008)
21. Parent, A., Roetteler, M., Svore, K.M.: Reversible circuit compilation with space constraints. arXiv:1510.00377 (2015)

22. Park, S., Kim, J., Im, H.: Functional netlists. In: Proceedings of ICFP, pp. 353–366 (2008)
23. Quipper. http://www.mathstat.dal.ca/~selinger/quipper/
24. Saeedi, M., Markov, I.L.: Synthesis and optimization of reversible circuits - a survey. ACM Comput. Surv. **45**(2), 21:1–21:34 (2013)
25. Sanaee, Y., Saeedi, M., Zamani, M.S.:Shared-PPRM: a memory-efficient representation for boolean reversiblefunctions. In: Proceedings of ISVLSI, pp. 471–474 (2008)
26. Sander, I.: System modeling and design refinement in ForSyDe. Ph.D. thesis, Royal Institute of Technology, Stockholm, Sweden (2003)
27. Scherer, A., Valiron, B., et al.: Resource analysis of the quantum linear system algorithm. arxiv:1505.06552 (2015)
28. Shor, P.: Algorithms for quantum computation: discrete logarithm and factoring. In: Proceedings of FOCS (1994)
29. Soeken, M., Frehse, S., Wille, R., Drechsler, R.: RevKit: an open source toolkit for the design of reversible circuits. In: De Vos, A., Wille, R. (eds.) RC 2011. LNCS, vol. 7165, pp. 64–76. Springer, Heidelberg (2012)
30. Green, A.S., Lumsdaine, P.L.F., Ross, N.J., Selinger, P., Valiron, B.: White dots *do* matter: rewriting reversible logic circuits. In: Dueck, G.W., Miller, D.M. (eds.) RC 2013. LNCS, vol. 7948, pp. 196–208. Springer, Heidelberg (2013)
31. Swamy, N., Guts, N., et al.: Lightweight monadic programming in ML. In: Proceedings of ICFP, pp. 15–27 (2011)
32. Terui, K.: Proof nets and boolean circuits. In: Proceedings of LICS, pp. 182–191 (2004)
33. Thomsen, M.K.: A functional language for describing reversible logic. In: Proceedings of FDL, pp. 135–142 (2012)
34. Wille, R., Große, D., et al.: RevLib: an online resource for reversible functions and reversible circuits. In: International Symposium on Multi-valued Logic, pp. 220–225 (2008)
35. Wille, R., Le, H.M., Dueck, G.W., Grosse, D.: Quantified synthesis of reversible logic. In: Proceedings of DATE, pp. 1015–1020 (2008)
36. Wille, R., Offermann, S., Drechsler, R.:SyReC: a programming language for synthesis of reversible circuits. In: Forum on Specification Design Languages, pp. 1–6 (2010)

A Fast Symbolic Transformation Based Algorithm for Reversible Logic Synthesis

Mathias Soeken[1](✉), Gerhard W. Dueck[2], and D. Michael Miller[3]

[1] Integrated Systems Laboratory, EPFL, Lausanne, Switzerland
mathias.soeken@epfl.ch
[2] University of New Brunswick, Fredericton, NB, Canada
[3] University of Victoria, Victoria, BC, Canada

Abstract. We present a more concise formulation of the transformation based synthesis approach for reversible logic synthesis, which is one of the most prominent explicit ancilla-free synthesis approaches. Based on this formulation we devise a symbolic variant of the approach that allows one to find a circuit in shorter time using less memory for the function representation. We present both a BDD based and a SAT based implementation of the symbolic variant. Experimental results show that both approaches are significantly faster than the state-of-the-art method. We were able to find ancilla-free circuit realizations for large optimally embedded reversible functions for the first time.

Keywords: Reversible circuit synthesis · Symbolic methods · Binary decision diagrams · Boolean satisfiability

1 Introduction

The most important application areas of reversible logic are quantum computing and low power design. Due to the requirement of reversibility, only n-input and n-output Boolean functions that represent permutations can be considered. One of the most important problems to solve is *synthesis*, which is the problem of finding a circuit that realizes a given reversible function $f : \mathbb{B}^n \to \mathbb{B}^n$.

Due to the reversibility, a reversible circuit cannot have fanout. Therefore, it is composed as a cascade of reversible gates. The circuit has $r \geq n$ circuit lines. If $r = n$, i.e., no additional ancilla line is required to realize f, the synthesis is called ancilla-free. So far, almost all presented ancilla-free synthesis approaches (e.g., [4,7,9]) use an explicit representation of f, e.g., as a truth table or a permutation, which grows exponentially with n. Consequently, the approaches are not applicable to large reversible functions. Recently, two ancilla-free synthesis approaches [14,15] have been presented that work on a symbolic representation of f (using decision diagrams) and therefore overcome the limitation and are applicable to much larger functions.

In this paper, we present a symbolic ancilla-free synthesis approach based on the most prominent explicit ancilla-free synthesis approach, called transformation based synthesis [9]. We reformulate the algorithm in a more concise way

© Springer International Publishing Switzerland 2016
S. Devitt and I. Lanese (Eds.): RC 2016, LNCS 9720, pp. 307–321, 2016.
DOI: 10.1007/978-3-319-40578-0_22

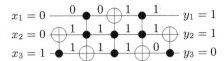

$$x_1 = 0 \quad \xrightarrow{\quad 0 \quad} \bullet \quad \xrightarrow{\quad 0 \quad} \oplus \quad \xrightarrow{\quad 1 \quad} \bullet \quad \xrightarrow{\quad 1 \quad} \quad y_1 = 1$$

Fig. 1. Example reversible circuit with sample simulation

and derive properties which we exploit in the symbolic variant. In addition to
a binary decision diagram (BDD) based implementation that follows principles
from [15] and [14], we also present an implementation based on Boolean satisfiability (SAT) of the symbolic synthesis approach for the first time. So far
Boolean satisfiability was only used for minimal circuit synthesis [6,20], which is
only applicable to very small functions. Due to the symbolic description of the
algorithm, it can be performed using fewer computation steps and using lower
memory requirements for the representation of f. An experimental evaluation
shows that the SAT based implementation outperforms the BDD based approach
and both approaches outperform the previously presented symbolic approaches
significantly.

The contributions of the paper can be summarized as follows: (1) a more
concise formulation for the transformation based synthesis approach presented
in [9], (2) a generic symbolic variant of the algorithm, and (3) two implementations, one based on BDDs and one based on SAT. With these contributions we
were able to find ancilla-free circuit realizations for several benchmarks for the
first time (including reversible functions with 68 variables). All these contributions make our approach particularly interesting for hierarchical reversible logic
synthesis to ensure local optimal results with respect to the number of ancilla
lines.

2   Preliminaries

A reversible function is a Boolean multi-output function $f : \mathbb{B}^n \to \mathbb{B}^n$ that
is bijective, i.e., every possible input pattern corresponds to a unique output
pattern. Let X be a set of lines identified as $\{1, \ldots, n\}$. In this work, we consider
the family of multiple-controlled Toffoli gates. A Toffoli gate, denoted $T(C, t)$,
inverts a target line $t \in X$ if, and only if, the value of each control line in
$C \subseteq X \setminus \{t\}$ is 1. All other lines remain unchanged. If $|C| = 0$ or if $|C| = 1$, we
refer to the gate as a NOT gate or a CNOT gate, respectively. As an example,
the gate $T(\{1, 2\}, 3)$ inverts the value of line 3 if, and only if, the first two lines
are set to 1. We use the customary notation of solid circles to denote control
lines and the '$\oplus$' symbol to denote the target line. Figure 1 shows an example
circuit using this notation with a simulation of the assignment $001 \mapsto 110$.

The assignment of a variable x_i in a Boolean function $f(x_1, \ldots, x_n)$ is referred
to as the *co-factor* of f with respect to x_i. If x_i is assigned 1, the co-factor is
called positive and denoted f_{x_i}. Otherwise, it is called negative and denoted
$f_{\bar{x}_i}$. Existential quantification of a variable in a Boolean function, also called

smoothing, is defined as $\exists x_i f = f_{\bar{x}_i} \vee f_{x_i}$. The effect is that all occurrences of x_i and $\bar{x}_i$ are removed from an expression representing f.

Let $f(x_1, \ldots, x_n) = (y_1, \ldots, y_m)$ be a multiple-output function, where each output is specified by a Boolean function $y_i = f_i(x_1, \ldots, x_n)$. Then the *characteristic function* of f is

$$F(x_1, \ldots, x_n, y_1, \ldots, y_m) = \bigwedge_{i=1}^{m} \left(\bar{y}_i \oplus f_i(x_1, \ldots, x_n) \right). \tag{1}$$

Note that $\bar{a} \oplus b = \overline{a \oplus b}$ is the XNOR operation.

Due to space limitations we refer the reader to the relevant literature for binary decision diagrams (e.g., [3]) and Boolean satisfiability (e.g., [2]).

3   Truth Table Based Algorithm

The transformation based synthesis algorithm [9] is one of the first and most popular ancilla-free synthesis algorithms for reversible functions. It works on the truth table representation of a reversible function $f : \mathbb{B}^n \to \mathbb{B}^n$. In each step, f is updated by applying a gate $g = T(C, t)$:

$$f \leftarrow f \circ g \tag{2}$$

This step is repeated until f is the identity function and at completion the composition of all collected gates $g_1, \ldots, g_k$ realizes the original f.

The gates are selected such that they *transform* output patterns to input patterns in an assignment $x \mapsto y$ with $x = x_1 \ldots x_n$ and $y = y_1 \ldots y_n$. The step in (2) is repeatedly applied to transform y in order to match x. Each gate will change one bit position y_i that differs from x_i in an order that first 0's are changed to 1's and then 1's are changed to 0's. Let $X_p = \{i \mid x_i = p\}$ and $Y_p = \{i \mid y_i = p\}$ partition the bits in x and y according to their polarities. The sets $X_1 \cap Y_0$ and $X_0 \cap Y_1$ characterize the bit positions in which x and y differ. Inserting the gate sequence

$$\bigcirc_{i \in X_1 \cap Y_0} T(Y_1, i) \circ \bigcirc_{i \in X_0 \cap Y_1} T(X_1, i) \tag{3}$$

in reverse order to the front end of the circuit will transform the output pattern such that it matches the input pattern. Here, '$\bigcirc$' denotes the accumulation symbol for functional decomposition. Besides transforming y to match x, the gates also transform other output patterns in the truth table. However, the following essential property holds. All output patterns $y' \neq y$ such that $y' \leq x$ are not affected by any gate in (3). This property was first observed in [1]. Hence, applying this transformation to all input/output assignments $x^{(i)} \mapsto y^{(i)}$ for $1 \leq i \leq 2^n$ will result in the identity function if the input patterns $x^{(i)}$ are ordered such that

$$x^{(i)} \neq x^{(j)} \text{ for all } i \neq j \text{ and } x^{(i)} \not\leq x^{(j)} \text{ for all } i > j, \tag{4}$$

$x_1x_2x_3$	$y_1y_2y_3$						$X_1 \cap Y_0$	$X_0 \cap Y_1$
000	111	<u>000</u>	000	000	000	000	$\emptyset$	$\{1,2,3\}$
001	000	111	<u>001</u>	001	001	001	$\emptyset$	$\{1,2\}$
010	110	001	111	<u>010</u>	010	010	$\emptyset$	$\{1,3\}$
011	100	011	101	101	<u>011</u>	011	$\{2\}$	$\{1\}$
100	010	101	011	110	100	100		
101	001	110	110	011	111	<u>101</u>	$\emptyset$	$\{2\}$
110	011	100	100	100	110	110		
111	101	010	010	111	101	111		

Fig. 2. Example application of the transformation based synthesis method. The synthesis five input/output assignments whose values after gate application are underlined. The two rightmost columns show the values of the sets $X_1 \cap Y_0$ and $X_0 \cap Y_1$ in each of these steps.

where '$\leq$' refers to bitwise comparison. Ordering the input patterns with respect to their integer representation, i.e., $0\ldots00, 0\ldots01, \ldots, 1\ldots11$ satisfies (4). The following algorithm formalizes the synthesis approach using this order.

Algorithm T. (*Transformation based synthesis*). Given an n-variable reversible function f, this algorithm computes a reversible circuit C that realizes f by transforming output patterns in numerical order of their corresponding input patterns.

T1. [Initialize.] Let C be empty and set $x \leftarrow 0$.
T2. [Prepend gates.] Compute X_0, X_1, Y_0, and Y_1 for x and $y = f(x)$. Set

$$f \leftarrow f \circ \bigcirc_{i \in X_1 \cap Y_0} T(Y_1, i) \circ \bigcirc_{i \in X_0 \cap Y_1} T(X_1, i) \tag{5}$$

according to (3) and prepend the gates in reverse order to C.
T3. [Terminate?] If $x = 2^n - 1$, terminate. Otherwise, set $x \leftarrow x + 1$ and return to step 2.

The function f is updated in (5) by adjusting all output patterns in f that match the control lines of the gates. An example application of the algorithm using this order is given in Fig. 2 that results in the reversible circuit

The time complexity of Algorithm T is exponential in the number of variables for all functions f since x is incremented by 1 in step 3 until all 2^n input patterns have been considered. One can check whether $f(x) \neq x$ before computing X_0, X_1, Y_0, and Y_1. However, the gain in efficiency is negligible. The problem is that there is no way to skip a whole sequence of assignments and *jump* to the next one that requires adjustment. In Sect. 5, we will present a symbolic variant of Algorithm T that allows such jumps, enabling a linear time complexity for certain classes of functions in the best case.

Since gates are appended to the front end of the circuit at each step, the algorithm is referred to as backward-directed transformation based synthesis. The algorithm can also be applied in the forward direction by adjusting input patterns to match their output patterns. For this purpose, gates

$$\bigcirc_{i \in X_0 \cap Y_1} T(X_1, i) \circ \bigcirc_{i \in X_1 \cap Y_0} T(Y_1, i) \tag{6}$$

are appended to the back end of the circuit at each step and the output patterns $y^{(i)}$ are ordered with respect to the constraints that are obtained by replacing x with y in (4). The two approaches can be combined into a bidirectional approach by fixing a valid order of patterns $z^{(1)}, \ldots, z^{(2^n)}$ and at each step i either inserting gates according to (3) in the backward direction to adjust the assignment $z^{(i)} \mapsto f(z^{(i)})$ or inserting gates according to (6) in the forward direction to adjust the assignment $f^{-1}(z^{(i)}) \mapsto z^{(i)}$. A good heuristic for choosing the direction is to select the assignment with the smaller Hamming distance, which directly corresponds to the number of gates. The circuits for the function in Fig. 2 obtained by applying the algorithm in the forward direction and bidirectional are

respectively. In the case of a tie for the Hamming distance in the bidirectional approach, backward direction was chosen.

The two circuits obtained from the unidirectional approaches each consist of 10 gates, whereas using the bidirectional algorithm a circuit consisting of 8 gates can be obtained. An optimal realization for the function using Tofolli gates with positive control lines requires 7 gates.

It is worth noting that the Toffoli gates in (3) to change 0's to 1's have the same set of control lines Y_1 and the Toffoli gates to change 1's to 0's have the same set of control lines X_1. This fact can be emphasized and the representation can be made more concise when allowing Toffoli gates to have multiple targets by passing a set of lines instead of a line as the second parameter for 'T':

$$T(Y_1, Y_0 \cap X_1) \circ T(X_1, X_0 \cap Y_1) \tag{7}$$

4   Symbolic Representation of Reversible Functions

We make use of binary decision diagrams to symbolically manipulate and evaluate a reversible function $f : \mathbb{B}^n \to \mathbb{B}^n$. When representing f using a BDD over n variables and n start vertices, the reversibility of f is not explicitly represented. Such a BDD representation corresponds to considering each column of the truth table representation of f individually. Instead, we use the BDD representation for the characteristic function of f (see [14,15]), which in the remainder of the paper is denoted F. Each one-path in the BDD of F represents one input/output assignments in f.

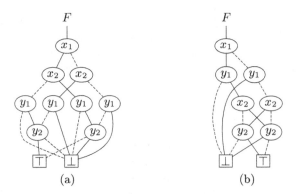

Fig. 3. BDDs for F in (8) using (a) the natural and (b) the interleaved variable order

As an example consider the CNOT gate $T(\{1\}, 2)$ over 2 variables. Its characteristic function is

$$F(x_1, x_2, y_1, y_2) = (\bar{y}_1 \oplus x_1)(\bar{y}_2 \oplus x_2 \oplus x_1)$$
$$= \bar{x}_1 \bar{x}_2 \bar{y}_1 \bar{y}_2 \vee \bar{x}_1 x_2 \bar{y}_1 y_2 \vee x_1 \bar{x}_2 y_1 y_2 \vee x_1 x_2 y_1 \bar{y}_2. \tag{8}$$

The first expression emphasizes the functional behavior of the gate, i.e., $y_1 = x_1$ and $y_2 = x_2 \oplus x_1$, whereas the second expression lists all input/output assignments explicitly.

The order of the variables in the BDD of a characteristic function F for a reversible function f is crucial. If inputs are evaluated before outputs, e.g., in their natural order $x_1 < \cdots < x_n < y_1 < \cdots < y_n$, the size of F will always be exponential. After all inputs have been evaluated each output pattern must be represented by a node (y_1), and there are 2^n different output patterns. The same effect can be observed if all outputs are evaluated before inputs due to the function reversibility. However, if we interleave the inputs with the outputs, e.g., $x_1 < y_1 < \cdots < x_n < y_n$, compact representations are possible [16]. Figure 3 shows the BDDs for F in (8) both in the natural and the interleaved order. Solid and dashed lines refer to high and low edges, respectively.

The symbolic representation of the reversible function f by the characteristic function F allows several operations that can be implemented efficiently using BDDs. The most important one is functional composition which is reduced to multiplication of the permutation matrices represented by the respective BDDs. Let $f_1(x_1, \ldots, x_n) = (z_1, \ldots, z_n)$ and $f_2(z_1, \ldots, z_n) = (y_1, \ldots, y_n)$ be two reversible functions and F_1 and F_2 their characteristic functions. Also, let $h = f_1 \circ f_2$ be the composition of f_1 and f_2. Then

$$H = \exists z (F_1 \wedge F_2) \tag{9}$$

is the characteristic function of h (see, e.g., [18]). We demonstrate how this operation works illustrated on the disjunctive normal forms that are represented by the BDDs. Note that existential quantification can be implemented using Bryant's APPLY algorithm [3] in the conventional manner. Let

$$F_1 = \bar{x}_1\bar{x}_2\bar{z}_1\bar{z}_2 \vee \bar{x}_1x_2\bar{z}_1z_2 \vee x_1\bar{x}_2z_1z_2 \vee x_1x_2z_1\bar{z}_2$$

and

$$F_2 = \bar{z}_1\bar{z}_2y_1\bar{y}_2 \vee \bar{z}_1z_2y_1y_2 \vee z_1\bar{z}_2\bar{y}_1\bar{y}_2 \vee z_1z_2\bar{y}_1y_2$$

be the characteristic functions of the CNOT gate $T(\{1\}, 2)$ and the NOT gate $T(\{\}, 1)$, respectively. The operation $F_1 \wedge F_2$ pairs up those minterms for which the polarities of z_1 and z_2 are equal; all other combinations evaluate to false and therefore vanish from the expression, i.e.,

$$F_1 \wedge F_2 = \bar{x}_1\bar{x}_2\bar{z}_1\bar{z}_2y_1\bar{y}_2 \vee \bar{x}_1x_2\bar{z}_1z_2y_1y_2 \vee x_1\bar{x}_2z_1z_2\bar{y}_1y_2 \vee x_1x_2z_1\bar{z}_2\bar{y}_1\bar{y}_2,$$

and existentially quantifying over z_1 and z_2 removes these *gluing variables* from the expression:

$$\exists z_1 \exists z_2 (F_1 \wedge F_2) = \bar{x}_1\bar{x}_2y_1\bar{y}_2 \vee \bar{x}_1x_2y_1y_2 \vee x_1\bar{x}_2\bar{y}_1y_2 \vee x_1x_2\bar{y}_1\bar{y}_2.$$

If the variable names don't match, one can also use existential quantification to locally rename them. To rename a function $F(x, y)$ to $F(x, z)$, denoted $F_{y \to z}$, one computes

$$\exists y \left(F \wedge \bigwedge_{i=1}^{n} \bar{y}_i \oplus z_i \right). \tag{10}$$

5 Symbolic Algorithm

The truth table based variant of the transformation based algorithm visits all 2^n assignments. It is not possible to only visit the assignments that need adjustment, i.e., for which the output pattern differs from the input pattern. In this section we discuss a symbolic variant of the algorithm. Besides a symbolic representation of the function, which can decrease the space requirements, a major difference of the symbolic variant is the order in which the assignments are visited. The truth table based variant of the algorithm, Algorithm T, visits all assignments in numerical order of the input patterns. For example, if $n = 4$, the order is

$$
\begin{aligned}
&0000, 0001, 0010, 0011, 0100, 0101, 0110, 0111, \\
&1000, 1001, 1010, 1011, 1100, 1101, 1110, 1111.
\end{aligned}
\tag{11}
$$

Ordering the input patterns according to their Hamming weight, i.e., the number of ones, is also valid. The symbolic variant of the transformation based algorithm makes use of this property. For $n = 4$, the order is

$$
0000, \quad
\begin{matrix}
 & 0011, & & \\
0001, & 0101, & 0111, & \\
0010, & 0110, & 1011, & \\
0100, & 1001, & 1101, & 1111 \\
1000, & 1010, & 1110 & \\
 & 1100, & &
\end{matrix}
\tag{12}
$$

where the order of patterns within a set of patterns of the same Hamming weight can be arbitrary. The key difference in the symbolic variant is that it iterates through these sets (of which there are $n + 1$, i.e., linearly many) instead of iterating through all patterns individually (of which there are 2^n, i.e., exponentially many). For each set the algorithm extracts assignments (in a possibly arbitrary order) that are not matched yet and disregards those that are already matched. The constraint (4) ensures that the inserted gates do not affect any other assignment within the current set or previously considered sets.

For an n-variable reversible function f, we can symbolically represent all input patterns x with Hamming weight k such that $f(x) \neq x$ with the expression

$$F(x, y) \wedge S_{=k}(x) \wedge D(x, y) \tag{13}$$

where F is the characteristic function of f, $x = x_1, \ldots, x_n$, and $y = y_1, \ldots, y_n$.

The symmetric function

$$S_{=k}(x) = [x_1 + \cdots + x_n = k] \tag{14}$$

restricts the assignments to those that have input patterns of Hamming weight k. The function

$$D(x, y) = \bigvee_{i=1}^{n} x_i \oplus y_i \tag{15}$$

further restricts the assignments such that the input patterns and output patterns differ in at least one bit. These are all requirements to describe the symbolic transformation based algorithm.

Algorithm S. (*Symbolic transformation based synthesis*). Given the characteristic function F to an n-variable reversible function f, this algorithm finds a circuit C that realizes f. In this algorithm, f and F always refer to the same function in different representations.

S1. [Initialize.] Let C be empty and set $k \leftarrow 0$.
S2. [Terminate?] If $k = n + 1$, terminate.
S3. [Increment k.] If $F \wedge S_{=k} \wedge D = \bot$, set $k \leftarrow k + 1$ and go to step 2.
S4. [Extract assignment and prepend gates.] Extract $x \mapsto y$ by picking any minterm from $F \wedge S_{=k} \wedge D$ and compute X_0, X_1, Y_0, and Y_1. Set

$$f \leftarrow f \circ \bigcirc_{i \in X_1 \cap Y_0} T(Y_1, i) \circ \bigcirc_{i \in X_0 \cap Y_1} T(X_1, i) \tag{16}$$

and prepend the gates in reverse order to C. Return to step 3.

The linear runtime complexity is readily verified by inspecting step 2. The possible exponential complexity comes with step 4 as it is executed $\binom{n}{k}$ times in the worst case for each $k \in \{0, \ldots, n\}$ and therefore $\sum_{i=0}^{n} \binom{n}{k} = 2^n$ times in total.

In the following, two implementations of Algorithm S are described. The first uses BDDs while the second uses SAT. There are two parts in the algorithm that require individual attention depending on the underlying technique: (i) solving $F \wedge S_{=k} \wedge D$ in step 3, extracting a solution in step 4 in case of the expression being satisfiable, and (ii) updating F in step 4 according to (16).

5.1 BDD Based Implementation

Solving $F \wedge S_{=k} \wedge D$ is done in a straightforward way by checking whether its BDD is not equal to $\boxed{\perp}$. If that is the case, a satisfying solution can be extracted by picking any path from the start vertex to $\boxed{\top}$. Every such path visits all variables and therefore represents a minterm. This is true because each path in F already represents a minterm and $S_{=k}$ and D only restrict F further.

The BDD of F is updated by composing it with a BDD that represents the characteristic function of a gate from the right. In order to execute fewer BDD operations we make use of the fact that the gates in (16) can be expressed as two multiple-target gates as described in (7). The characteristic function of a multiple-target gate $T(C, T)$ is

$$G = \bigwedge_{i \in T} \left(\bar{y}_i \oplus x_i \oplus \bigwedge_{j \in C} x_j \right) \wedge \bigwedge_{i \in \overline{T}} (\bar{y}_i \oplus x_i) \tag{17}$$

where $\overline{T} = \{1, \ldots, n\} \setminus T$. The gate can then be multiplied to F by computing $F \leftarrow \exists z \, (F_{y \to z} \wedge G_{x \to z})$ as described in (10).

5.2 SAT Based Implementation

For the SAT based implementation a satisfiability check is performed on the formula $F \wedge S_{=k} \wedge D$. For this purpose, the formula needs to be represented in conjunctive normal form. The characteristic function F is initially represented as a BDD as in the BDD based implementation. Each node $\widehat{x_i}$ with children h and l represents the function $f_v = x_i \, ? \, h : l$ and is translated to

$$(\bar{x}_i \vee \bar{h} \vee f_v)(\bar{x}_i \vee h \vee \bar{f}_v)(x_i \vee \bar{l} \vee f_v)(x_i \vee l \vee \bar{f}_v). \tag{18}$$

Similar clauses are added for each node $\widehat{y_i}$. To enforce only valid input/output assignments the variable representing the start vertex f_{v_0} is added as a unit clause.[1] The subexpression $S_{=k}$ is called a *cardinality constraint* and several ways to encode such constraints as clauses have been proposed. One such encoding has been proposed in [11], which is also used in this implementation. Finally, the formula D can be translated using the Tseytin encoding for representing gates as clauses. Some of the clauses can be saved by making use of blocked clause elimination [8,10].

The tricky part in Algorithm S is updating F in step 4. As the aim is to avoid BDD operations, we cannot just compute a new F by multiplying it with the gates that are computed from the extracted assignment. Instead, we extend the SAT formula by further constraints that represent the gates, and—since gates update the output patterns of f—compute new outputs y_i. Let $T(C, T)$

---

[1] We also tried to write F to an AIG, perform circuit optimization, and obtain the CNF from the optimized AIG, however, no improvement in runtime could be observed, although the number of clauses can be decreased this way.

be a multiple-target gate that is added in step 4. For each $i \in T$ we add a new variable y_i' and clauses for the constraint

$$G = \bigwedge_{i \in T} \left(\bar{y}_i' \oplus y_i \oplus \bigwedge_{j \in C} y_j \right) \tag{19}$$

using the Tseytin encoding. In this manner all created gates can be encoded and are added to the subsequent SAT calls, i.e., one updates F by setting $F \leftarrow F \wedge G_1 \wedge G_2$ where G_1 and G_2 are the two encoded multiple-target gates added in step 4. It is important to take care of the updated output variables which occur in D, see (15), and each G, see (19). For this purpose, we first introduce a set of variables $\tilde{y}_1, \dots, \tilde{y}_n$ initially set to $\tilde{y}_i \leftarrow y_i$ for $i \leq 1 \leq n$. Then, we replace y_i by $\tilde{y}_i$ and y_j by $\tilde{y}_j$ in Eqs. (15) and (19). Finally, we update $\tilde{y}_i \leftarrow y_i'$ for each $i \in T$ in each added multiple-target gate $\mathrm{T}(C, T)$.

In order to speed up the solving process, we have implemented the SAT based approach in an incremental manner. Constraints for $S_{=k}$ and D are added using activation literals to the solver whenever updated versions are required and enforced by assuming the respective activation literals in the SAT calls (see, e.g., [5]).

5.3   Runtime Behavior

A thorough experimental evaluation is given in the next section. In order to understand the differences of the BDD based and the incremental SAT based implementations of the transformation based synthesis approaches better, this section presents the results of a simple runtime evaluation experiment.

For each assignment, we recorded the runtime it took to obtain and apply the assignment (i.e., performing steps 3 and 4 in Algorithm S) as well as the size of F at that moment. In the case of the BDD implementation, the size of F is the number of nodes in the BDD, and in the case of the SAT implementation, the size of F is the number of clauses in the SAT instance. Four selected benchmarks, namely *dk27*, *alu3*, *x2*, and *dk17* serve as representatives. Other benchmarks show similar effects.

The results of the experimental evaluation are provided in the plots in Fig. 4. The x-axis shows the number of adjusted assignments, i.e., how often step 4 has been applied, the marks (left y-axis) show the required runtime in seconds to obtain and apply each assignment and the solid line (right y-axis) shows the current size of F. The four plots on the left hand side show the results for the BDD based implementation. It can be seen that the runtime to obtain and adjust an assignment correlates with the size of F. Also, the size of F is initially small, increases very quickly and then decreases towards the size of the identity function. All considered benchmark functions show this same effect; only four of them are depicted here as representatives. The effect may be explainable as follows: It is well-known that BDDs have an exponential size in the average case [19] when considering random Boolean functions, but often show reasonable space requirements for the very small subset of "nonrandom functions" that are

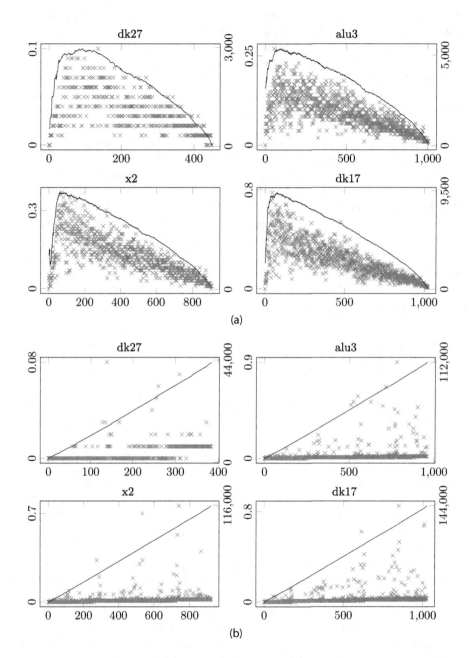

Fig. 4. Runtime behavior of (a) the BDD based and (b) the SAT based approach. The
x-axis shows the number of assignments, the left y-axis (marks) shows the runtime to
solve each assignment in seconds, the right y-axis (line) shows the size of the BDD
(nodes) or SAT instance (clauses)

often considered in realistic applications. The characteristic function that is input to Algorithm S is not random, and neither is the identity characteristic function which is obtained after the last step. However, applying the Toffoli gates in the course of the algorithm can depart this nonrandom space.

A completely different behavior is observed for the SAT based implementation, shown in the plots on the right hand side. The size of F increases linearly due to the addition of clauses for $S_{=k}$, D, and the gates. The runtime does not correlate with the size, although larger runtimes are only observed once the SAT instance has many clauses—yet many assignments can be obtained and adjusted in a very short time even when the number of clauses is large.

This experiment demonstrates that the SAT based approach in general is advantageous compared to the BDD based approach: (i) the size of F cannot explode, since it increases linearly, and (ii) the runtimes are not overly affected by the size of F. An improved encoding of the SAT instance therefore has a significant effect on the overall solution time. Also note that the size of F, both for BDDs and SAT, does not impact the size of the resulting reversible circuit, but only the number of assignments that need to be adjusted.

6   Experimental Evaluation

We have implemented both symbolic transformation based synthesis approaches in C++ on top of RevKit [13] in the command '*tbs*'.[2] We have compared the approach to the state-of-the-art symbolic ancilla-free synthesis approach presented in [14] that is based on functional decomposition (DBS). It was shown that the DBS approach is faster than the approach presented in [15]. Benchmarks were taken from *www.revlib.org* as PLA files and optimally embedded using the approach presented in [16] which returns a BDD of the characteristic function. The experimental results are shown in Table 1. Besides the benchmark function, their number of inputs and outputs are listed together with the minimum number of lines after optimum embedding. The columns list the number of gates and the runtime in seconds (with a timeout of one hour, referred to as TO) required for each synthesis approach. For both transformation based synthesis approaches, also the number of adjusted assignments, i.e., how often step 4 is executed in Algorithm S, is reported.

Our main concern in this work is scalability and the possibility to obtain a circuit with a minimum number of lines. Therefore, we compare the approaches with respect to runtime. Other metrics such as gate count and quantum cost can be improved using post optimization approaches. The SAT based variant outperforms the BDD based approach, in particular for *alu1*, *apex4*, and *ex5p*. Both approaches outperform the decomposition based synthesis approach; that algorithm did not terminate for the majority of the benchmarks within the one hour timeout. In very few cases (see *parity* and *urf6*) the DBS approach was able to find a solution in which both TBS approaches did not find a solution.

---

[2] The code can be downloaded at https://www.github.com/msoeken/cirkit. Check the file `addons/cirkit-addon-reversible/demo.cs` for a usage demonstration.

Table 1. Experimental results

Function	I / O	lines	DBS [14]		TBS (BDD)			TBS (SAT)		
			gates	time	assignments	gates	time	assignments	gates	time
add6	12 / 7	13	10989	997.58	4088	26479	867.21	4053	26731	837.76
alu1	12 / 8	18		TO	4012	35655	2488.80	4036	35664	414.12
alu2	10 / 6	14		TO	1021	6691	54.21	1006	6471	19.15
alu3	10 / 8	14		TO	1004	6785	65.38	959	6297	19.05
apex4	9 / 19	26		TO	452	3946	80.38	452	4007	6.76
apla	10 / 12	22		TO	1021	10351	349.09	1022	10234	28.90
cm152a	11 / 1	11	2660	21.35	2030	10644	138.68	2019	10434	84.68
cm85a	11 / 3	13	9489	836.93	1890	12324	186.89	1706	11305	62.37
dk17	10 / 11	19		TO	1023	9169	180.13	1024	8955	22.64
dk27	9 / 9	15		TO	449	2730	10.52	383	2391	1.41
ex1010	10 / 10	18		TO	1023	8874	161.13	1024	8719	21.02
ex5p	8 / 63	68		TO	253	3067	301.32	251	2943	4.83
parity	16 / 1	16	44	31.31			TO			TO
sym10	10 / 1	11	2409	36.60	1017	5445	27.07	1011	5574	16.24
urf4	11 / 11	11	2641	25.48	2027	10651	132.63	2029	10574	90.88
urf6	15 / 15	15	2164	7.00			TO			TO
x2	10 / 7	16		TO	905	7012	86.26	918	6946	14.85

When both DBS and TBS find a circuit, DBS shows a comparable performance and is sometimes even faster. Particularly, the reported gate costs for the circuits obtained by DBS is significantly lower compared to the circuits obtained from TBS. This effect is also observed when comparing the truth-table based implementations of these two algorithms. One reason for this improvement may be the ability of DBS to support mixed-polarity control lines, which cannot easily be utilized in transformation-based synthesis.

We have not compared our approach with heuristic hierarchical approaches that allow the use of additional lines. Such approaches are typically faster and can be applied to larger functions—however, with the disadvantage of adding a possibly large number of additional lines. For some functions, particularly arithmetic components, hand-crafted synthesis results exist that lead to significantly better results (see, e.g., [17])—however, we intend to have a general purpose algorithm that is not tailored to a specific function type.

7   Conclusions

In this paper we have presented a symbolic variant of the transformation-based synthesis approach for reversible logic. The approach allows the realization of large reversible functions without additional ancilla lines. It exploits a property considering the ordering in which assignments need to be considered for adjustment. Both a BDD and a SAT based implementation of the symbolic synthesis algorithm have been presented. So far, SAT has not been used for the synthesis of large reversible functions. An experimental evaluation shows that it significantly outperforms the state-of-the-art ancilla-free symbolic synthesis approaches regarding runtime. For some benchmarks, ancilla-free realizations have were found for the first time. In future work, we want to integrate further optimizations that have been proposed for the truth-table variant of the algorithm, such as bidirectional adjustment and the consideration of a larger gate library [12].

Acknowledgments. This research was supported by H2020-ERC-2014-ADG 669354 CyberCare and by the European COST Action IC 1405 'Reversible Computation'.

References

1. Alhagi, N., Hawash, M., Perkowski, M.A.: Synthesis of reversible circuits with no ancilla bits for large reversible functions specified with bit equations. In: ISMVL, pp. 39–45 (2010)
2. Biere, A., Heule, M., van Maaren, H., Walsh, T. (eds.): Handbook of Satisfiability, Frontiers in Artificial Intelligence and Applications, vol. 185. IOS Press, Amsterdam (2009)
3. Bryant, R.E.: Graph-based algorithms for Boolean function manipulation. IEEE-TC **35**(8), 677–691 (1986)
4. De Vos, A., Rentergem, Y.: Young subgroups for reversible computers. Adv. Math. Commun. **2**(2), 183–200 (2008)

5. Eén, N., Mishchenko, A., Amla, N.: A single-instance incremental SAT formulation of proof- and counterexample-based abstraction. In: FMCAD, pp. 181–188 (2010)
6. Große, D., Wille, R., Dueck, G.W., Drechsler, R.: Exact multiple-control Toffoli network synthesis with SAT techniques. TCAD **28**(5), 703–715 (2009)
7. Gupta, P., Agrawal, A., Jha, N.K.: An algorithm for synthesis of reversible logic circuits. TCAD **25**(11), 2317–2330 (2006)
8. Järvisalo, M., Biere, A., Heule, M.: Blocked clause elimination. In: Esparza, J., Majumdar, R. (eds.) TACAS 2010. LNCS, vol. 6015, pp. 129–144. Springer, Heidelberg (2010)
9. Miller, D.M., Maslov, D., Dueck, G.W.: A transformation based algorithm for reversible logic synthesis. In: DAC, pp. 318–323 (2003)
10. Plaisted, D.A., Greenbaum, S.: A structure-preserving clause form translation. JSC **2**(3), 293–394 (1986)
11. Sinz, C.: Towards an optimal CNF encoding of boolean cardinality constraints. In: CP, pp. 827–831 (2005)
12. Soeken, M., Chattopadhyay, A.: Fredkin-enabled transformation-based reversible logic synthesis. In: ISMVL, pp. 60–65 (2015)
13. Soeken, M., Frehse, S., Wille, R., Drechsler, R.: RevKit: a toolkit for reversible circuit design. Multiple-Valued Logic Soft Comput. **18**(1), 55–65 (2012)
14. Soeken, M., Tague, L., Dueck, G.W., Drechsler, R.: Ancilla-free synthesis of large reversible functions using binary decision diagrams. JSC **73**, 1–26 (2016)
15. Soeken, M., Wille, R., Hilken, C., Przigoda, N., Drechsler, R.: Synthesis of reversible circuits with minimal lines for large functions. In: ASP-DAC, pp. 85–92 (2012)
16. Soeken, M., Wille, R., Keszocze, O., Miller, D.M., Drechsler, R.: Embedding of large Boolean functions for reversible logic. JETC (2015). arXiv:1408.3586
17. Takahashi, Y., Tani, S., Kunihiro, N.: Quantum addition circuits and unbounded fan-out. Quantum Inf. Comput. **10**(9&10), 872–890 (2010)
18. Touati, H.J., Savoj, H., Lin, B., Brayton, R.K., Sangiovanni-Vincentelli, A.L.: Implicit state enumeration of finite state machines using BDDs. In: ICCAD, pp. 130–133 (1990)
19. Wegener, I.: The size of reduced OBDDs and optimal read-once branching programs for almost all Boolean functions. IEEE Trans. Comput. **43**(11), 1262–1269 (1994)
20. Wille, R., Große, D., Dueck, G.W., Drechsler, R.: Reversible logic synthesis with output permutation. In: VLSI Design, pp. 189–194 (2009)

Checking Reversibility of Boolean Functions

Robert Wille[1,2]([✉]), Aaron Lye[3], and Philipp Niemann[3]

[1] Institute for Integrated Circuits, Johannes Kepler University,
4040 Linz, Austria
`robert.wille@jku.at`
[2] Cyber-Physical Systems, DFKI GmbH, 28359 Bremen, Germany
[3] Institute of Computer Science, University of Bremen,
28359 Bremen, Germany
`{lye,pniemann}@informatik.uni-bremen.de`

Abstract. Following the reversible computation paradigm is essential in the design of many emerging technologies such as quantum computation or dedicated low power concepts. The design of corresponding circuits and systems heavily relies on information about whether the function to be realized is indeed reversible. In particular in hierarchical synthesis approaches where a given function is decomposed into sub-functions, this is often not obvious. In this paper, we prove that checking reversibility of Boolean functions is indeed coNP-complete. Besides that, we propose two complementary approaches which, despite the complexity, can tackle this problem in an efficient fashion. An experimental evaluation shows the feasibility of the approaches.

1 Introduction

Reversible circuits realize an alternative computation paradigm which, in contrast to conventional circuits, employs n-input n-output functions that map each possible input vector to a *unique* output vector. In other words, bijections are realized. This provides an essential characteristic for many emerging technologies such as

- quantum computation [15], which allows for solving many practical relevant problems (e.g. factorization [18] or database search [11]) exponentially faster and relies on quantum operations that are inherently reversible or
- certain aspects in low-power design motivated by the fact that reversible computation is information loss-less and, hence, the absence of information loss (at least theoretically) helps avoiding energy dissipation during computations[1].

Besides that, superconducting quantum interference devices [16], nanoelectromechanical systems [12,13], adiabatic circuits [2], and many further technologies utilize this computation paradigm. Even for conventional design tasks, useful

---

[1] Initial experiments verifying the underlying link between information-loss and thermodynamics have been reported in [3].

© Springer International Publishing Switzerland 2016
S. Devitt and I. Lanese (Eds.): RC 2016, LNCS 9720, pp. 322–337, 2016.
DOI: 10.1007/978-3-319-40578-0_23

applications have been proposed recently, e.g. for the design of efficient on-chip interconnect codings [28].

Because of this steadily increasing interest, also the design of reversible circuits and systems is gaining interest. Here, the inherent reversibility constitutes a major obstacle. In order to not violate the paradigm, each reversible function has to be realized by a sequence or cascade of (atomic) reversible operations or gates, respectively. To this end, established gate libraries (see e.g. [24]) or assembly-like software instructions (see e.g. [23]) have been introduced in the past. But how to realize (complex) reversible functionality in terms of these atomic operations remains a major problem.

To this end, complementary approaches have been introduced in the past. One set of solutions requires a fully reversible function as input (e.g. [10,14,17, 20]). As frequently also irreversible functionality is to be realized, a pre-synthesis process called *embedding* is conducted before (see e.g. [21,27]). As an alternative, hierarchical solutions e.g. based on decision diagrams or two-level representations have been proposed e.g. in [25] or [8], respectively. Here, large functionality is decomposed into smaller sub-functions from which the respectively desired atomic representations can be derived.

However, both directions suffer from the fact that it is often not known whether the respectively considered (sub-)function is indeed reversible. In fact, this causes that approaches such as proposed e.g. in [10,14,17,20] are usually applicable to rather small functions only, while solutions e.g. proposed in [8,25] yield designs of very large costs (this is discussed in more detail later in Sect. 3). As a consequence, the non-availability of solutions for efficiently checking the reversibility of a given function constitutes a major obstacle in the design of reversible circuit and systems[2].

In this work, we are addressing this problem. We first consider the underlying problem from a theoretical perspective showing that checking reversibility for a given function is coNP-complete. Afterwards, we provide efficient solutions which tackle this problem despite the proven complexity. More precisely, two complementary approaches are proposed: one utilizing the efficient function manipulation capabilities provided by decision diagrams and another which exploits the deductive power of solving engines for Boolean satisfiability.

In an experimental evaluation we demonstrate the applicability of the proposed approaches. While both complementary strategies can efficiently handle the problem, also differences between them are unveiled. Overall, the solution based on satisfiability solvers is capable of checking the reversibility of functions in negligible run-time even for some of the largest function considered in the design of reversible circuits and systems thus far.

The remainder of this work is structured as follows: The next section provides preliminaries, i.e. definitions of the different function representations utilized

---

[2] Note that this problem has been recognized in other works concerning embedding (e.g. [21]) and synthesis (e.g. [19]). But, thus far, the issue has only been addressed peripherally and without a theoretical consideration, explicit algorithms, or an experimental evaluation.

in this work. Section 3 discusses the importance of checking for reversibility and, hence, provides the motivation of this work. Afterwards, the complexity of the considered problem is considered in Sect. 4 before the two complementary approaches are introduced in Sects. 5 and 6. Results of the experimental evaluation are summarized in Sect. 7. Section 8 concludes this paper.

2   Preliminaries

Logic computations can be defined as functions over Boolean variables. More precisely:

Definition 1. *A Boolean function is a mapping* $f \colon \mathbb{B}^n \to \mathbb{B}$ *with* $n \in \mathbb{N}$. *A function* f *is defined over its* primary input *variables* $X = \{x_1, x_2, \ldots, x_n\}$ *and, hence, is also denoted by* $f(x_1, x_2, \ldots, x_n)$. *The concrete mapping may be described in terms of Boolean algebra with expressions formed over the variables from* X *and operations like* $\wedge$ *(AND),* $\vee$ *(OR), or* $\bar{}$ *(NOT).*

A multi-output Boolean function *is a mapping* $f \colon \mathbb{B}^n \to \mathbb{B}^m$ *with* $n, m \in \mathbb{N}$. *More precisely, it is a system of Boolean functions* $f_i(x_1, x_2, \ldots, x_n)$. *The respective functions* f_i *(*$1 \leq i \leq m$*) are also denoted as* primary outputs.

The set of all *Boolean functions with* n *inputs and* m *outputs is denoted by* $\mathcal{B}_{n,m} = \{f \mid f \colon \mathbb{B}^n \to \mathbb{B}^m\}$.

In this work, we consider the design of circuits and systems realizing reversible functions. Reversible functions are a subset of multi-output functions and are defined as follows:

Definition 2. *A* multi-output function *$f \colon \mathbb{B}^n \to \mathbb{B}^m$ is* reversible *iff* f *is a* bijection.

In other words, its number of inputs is equal to the number of outputs, i.e. $f \in \mathcal{B}_{n,n}$, and it performs a permutation of the set of input patterns. A function that is not reversible is termed *irreversible*.

Besides the representation in Boolean algebra, (reversible) functions can also be represented in terms of set relations.

Definition 3. *A function* $f \colon \mathbb{B}^n \to \mathbb{B}^m$ *is by definition a relation* $F \subset \mathbb{B}^n \times \mathbb{B}^m$ *of all possible input patterns to the set of possible output patterns. For a reversible function, this relation additionally inherits the property that each input pattern is related to exactly one output pattern, i.e.* $\forall y \in \mathbb{B}^m : |\{x \in \mathbb{B}^n \mid (x,y) \in F\}| = 1$. *The composition of two set relations* F *and* G *(i.e. two functions* f *and* g*) is defined by* $(G \circ F) \subset \mathbb{B}^n \times \mathbb{B}^k$ *so that*

$$G \circ F = \{(x,y) \mid \exists z \in \mathbb{B}^m : (x,z) \in F \wedge (z,y) \in G\}.$$

Finally, the input/output mapping of a (reversible) function can also be represented in terms of a characteristic function.

Definition 4. *The* characteristic function *for a Boolean relation* F *is defined as* $\chi_F \colon \mathbb{B}^n \times \mathbb{B}^m \to \mathbb{B}$ *where* $\chi_F(x,y) = 1$ *if and only if* $(x,y) \in F$.

3   Motivation

Although never explicitly considered thus far, knowing whether a given function is reversible is an important information in the design of reversible circuits and systems. This section briefly reviews the current state-of-the-art synthesis approaches and discusses why the non-availability of corresponding checking methods constitutes a major obstacle in the development of design methods for reversible circuits and systems.

3.1   Obstacles to the Embedding Process

Not surprisingly, many design methods for reversible circuits (e.g. those proposed in [10,14,17,20]) require a fully reversible function as input. As frequently also irreversible functionality is to be realized in reversible logic, a pre-synthesis process called *embedding* is conducted before (see e.g. [21,27]).

To this end, additional outputs (so-called *garbage outputs*) are added to the considered function $f \in \mathcal{B}_{n,m}$. More precisely, $\lceil \log_2(\mu(f)) \rceil$ additional outputs are required, whereby μ is the maximal number of times an output pattern is generated by f, i.e. $\mu(f) = \max_{y \in \mathbb{B}^m}(|\{x \mid y = f(x)\}|)$. In order to keep the number of inputs and outputs equal, this may also result in the addition of further inputs. That is, an irreversible function $f \colon \mathbb{B}^n \to \mathbb{B}^m$ is embedded into a function $f' \colon \mathbb{B}^{m+\lceil \log_2(\mu) \rceil} \to \mathbb{B}^{m+\lceil \log_2(\mu) \rceil}$. While f' is to be specified in a fully reversible fashion, the desired target functionality can be employed by setting the additionally added inputs to a constant value and recognizing only the non-garbage outputs. An example illustrates the idea.

Example 1. Consider the Boolean function $f \colon \mathbb{B}^2 \to \mathbb{B}^1$ with $f(x_1, x_2) = x_1 \wedge x_2$ to be synthesized as a reversible circuit. Obviously, f is irreversible. The maximal number of times an output pattern is generated by f is $\mu(f) = 3$ (namely 0 for the input patterns 00, 01, and 10). Hence, in order to realize f using a synthesis approach as e.g. proposed in [10,14,17,20], this function has to be embedded into a function $f' \colon \mathbb{B}^{2+1} \to \mathbb{B}^{1+2}$ with $\lceil \log_2(3) \rceil = 2$ additional outputs and $1 + \lceil \log_2(3) \rceil - 2 = 1$ additional input. The resulting function f' can be specified as

- $f'_1(x_1, x_2, x_3) = x_1$
- $f'_2(x_1, x_2, x_3) = x_2$
- $f'_3(x_1, x_2, x_3) = (x_1 \wedge x_2) \oplus x_3$.

This function is reversible (as can be checked by applying all $2^3 = 8$ possible input assignments) and realizes the target functionality f by setting x_3 to a constant zero value, i.e. $f = x_1 \wedge x_2 = (x_1 \wedge x_2) \oplus 0 = f'_3(x_1, x_2, 0)$.

However, generating an embedding as sketched above is an exponentially complex tasks: In order to determine μ, all 2^n output patterns generated by the inputs have to be inspected. Previous work tried to avoid this complexity by not aiming for a minimal result with respect to the number of additionally required outputs, but a heuristic one: In fact, since μ can never exceed 2^n, at most $\lceil \log_2(2^n) \rceil = n$ additional garbage outputs are required [27], i.e. *any* irreversible function can be embedded into a function $f' \colon \mathbb{B}^{n+m} \to \mathbb{B}^{m+n}$. But also here, the question remains how to specify the functionality of the newly added garbage outputs. Although heuristics assigning the additional outputs with a dedicated functionality as e.g. done in Example 1 are very promising, no solutions are available yet which guarantee that the resulting function f' is indeed reversible. As a consequence those heuristics did not become established and, hence, the design methods from [10,14,17,20] mostly remain applicable to small functions only.

3.2   Obstacles to the Synthesis Process

In order to overcome the problems sketched above, researchers considered alternative synthesis schemes (see e.g. [8,25]) relying on conventional decomposition methods (e.g. according to Shannon). Here, a given function f is decomposed with respect to an input variable x_i into two sub-functions $f_{x_i=0}$ and $f_{x_i=1}$ such that $f = (\overline{x}_i \wedge f_{x_i=0}) \vee (x_i \wedge f_{x_i=1})$ holds. The sub-functions are called co-factors of f and are obtained by assigning x_i to 0 and 1, respectively. The resulting co-factors are further decomposed until sub-functions result for which a building block is available. Plugging the resulting building blocks together eventually yields a circuit realizing the desired function. Because of this, no explicit embedding scheme is required, but the function is implicitly embedded.

In these approaches, information about the reversibility of the respectively considered (sub-)functions is essential to the quality of the resulting circuits. In fact, the decomposition almost always yields sub-functions which are not reversible anymore (even if the originally given function is). Hence, again garbage outputs and constant inputs are required in order to derive building blocks for them. Since this is conducted for each single sub-function (out of which a significant amount exists for a originally given function to be synthesized), this eventually leads to a significant amount of additional circuitry which is far beyond upper bounds (as evaluated by a corresponding study in [27]).

Being able to check whether a (sub-)function is reversible may offer the prospect of performing a decomposition such that not two arbitrary Boolean functions, but two *reversible* Boolean functions result. Since they can be realized with no additionally required outputs, significantly more compact circuits may be derived from that.

Either way, the non-availability of methods for checking the reversibility of a given function poses a major obstacle to the design of reversible circuits and systems. It prevents the application of (heuristic) embedding methods allowing to efficiently synthesize the desired function with dedicated approaches and it prevents the alternative, namely approaches based on decomposition, from generating compact circuits.

4   Theoretical Consideration

The previous section discussed why checking the reversibility of Boolean functions is of high importance. Now, we are considering the complexity of this problem. More precisely, the following decision problem is considered:

Definition 5. *Let $f \in \mathcal{B}_{n,n}$ be a Boolean function with n inputs and n outputs[3]. Moreover, let Rev_n denote the set of all reversible functions with n inputs and n outputs, i.e. $Rev_n = \{g \in \mathcal{B}_{n,n} \mid g \text{ is reversible}\}$. Then, REV is the decision problem asking whether $f \in Rev_n$.*

Note that the means of representing f is essential. For example, if f is given as a truth table, the check can be performed in linear time on the exponential input representation. In the following, we will consider the complexity with respect to the number of inputs/outputs. For this, we will prove the following:

Proposition 1. *REV is coNP-hard.*

The complexity of *REV* is shown by a reduction from the embedding problem which has been investigated in [21]. Using the notation of [21], let $f \in \mathcal{B}_{n,m}$, let $\mu(f) = max\{|f^{-1}(\{y\})| \mid y \in \mathbb{B}^m\}$ denote the number of occurrences of the most frequent output pattern, and let $l(f) = \lceil log_2\mu(f) \rceil$ denote the minimal number of additional variables required to embed f. Then, it was shown that:

Lemma 1 (Proposition 4.3 in [21]). *For each fixed $l \geq 0$, it is coNP-hard to decide for a given $f \in \mathcal{B}_{n,m}$ whether $l(f) = l$.*

In order to apply this in our context, we have to consider the case $l = 0$ for $m = n$. Then, we immediately obtain the following:

Corollary 1. *Let $f \in \mathcal{B}_{n,n}$ $(n \geq 1)$. It is coNP-hard to decide whether $l(f) = 0$.*

Proof. (adapted from [21]) The basic idea to proof this corollary is to provide a polynomial time many-one reduction from the validity problem for propositional formulas. This problem asks whether a propositional formula is a tautology and itself is known to be coNP-complete [6]. To this end, for a fixed propositional formula ϕ over the variables $\{x_1, \ldots, x_n\}$, we compute the function $f = (f_1, \ldots, f_n) \in \mathcal{B}_{n,n}$ by defining the component functions f_i by means of the propositional formulas

$$f_i(x_1, \ldots, x_n) := x_i \wedge \phi(x_1, \ldots, x_n) \wedge \phi(0, \ldots, 0).$$

Clearly, this computation can be performed in polynomial time. Now, as we have the equivalence

$$\begin{aligned} l(f) = 0 &\iff \lceil log_2\mu(f) \rceil = 0 \\ &\iff max\{|f^{-1}(\{y\})| \mid y \in \mathbb{B}^n\} = 1 \\ &\iff f \text{ is injective,} \end{aligned}$$

---

[3] Since functions $f\colon \mathbb{B}^n \to \mathbb{B}^m$ with $n \neq m$ are not reversible by definition, we are assuming an equal number n of inputs and outputs in the following.

it remains to show that the original formula ϕ is valid if and only if f is injective. Now, if ϕ is valid, we have $f_i = x_i$ and f turns out to be the identity function on $\mathbb{B}^n$ which is indeed injective. On the other hand, if ϕ is not valid there is an assignment $\tilde{x} = \{\tilde{x}_1, \ldots, \tilde{x}_n\}$ such that $\phi(\tilde{x}) = 0$. For the case $\tilde{x} = \{0, \ldots, 0\}$, all f_i are contradictions by construction and f always evaluates to 0^n. For the other case, $\tilde{x} \neq \{0, \ldots, 0\}$, we obtain $f(\tilde{x}) = 0^n = f(0, \ldots, 0)$. In both cases, f is not injective which proves the corollary.   □

As we have seen in the proof, $l(f) = 0$ is equivalent to the injectivity of f. Moreover, as f has the same (finite) domain and codomain $\mathbb{B}^n$, injectivity is equivalent to bijectivity and, thus, reversibility. Consequently, we obtain the following corollary from which Proposition 1 can be implied immediately:

Corollary 2. *Let $f \in \mathcal{B}_{n,n}(n \geq 1)$. It is coNP-hard to decide whether $f \in Rev_n$.*

Note that, in order to show coNP-completeness, a counterexample for reversibility is only polynomially sized (two inputs that provide the same output) and can also be checked in polynomial time (by evaluating the function for the two inputs). This inheritance in coNP together with the coNP-hardness proves, in fact, the coNP-completeness of REV.

Knowing the complexity of the considered problem, in the remainder of this work, we focus on how to solve it as efficient as possible. To this end, two complementary approaches are introduced and discussed.

5   Checking for Reversibility Using Decision Diagrams

Graph-based representation and manipulation of (Boolean) functions became very popular in computer-aided design after the initial work on *Binary Decision Diagrams* (BDDs) by Bryant [5]. Graph-based representations of Boolean functions have – besides others – two major advantages: (1) they describe the entire function in a compact manner and (2) they allow for efficiently applying logical manipulations (e.g. computing $f \wedge g$). Accordingly, they can be utilized for the problem considered in this work. In this section, a corresponding solution based on BDDs is introduced. To this end, we first sketch the general idea before details about the implementation are provided.

5.1   General Idea

While BDDs allow for an efficient representation of Boolean functions, the characteristic of reversibility cannot directly be derived from them. Consequently, our aim is to use the various possibilities for (efficient) function manipulation in order to transform a given function $f \in \mathcal{B}_{n,n}$ in such a way that its (non)-reversibility becomes clearly evident.

To this end, we exploit the fact that the composition of a reversible function with its inverse yields the identity function. Hence, the general idea of the proposed approach is to

1. determine the inverse function f^{-1} and, afterwards,
2. check whether the composition of f and f^{-1} is equivalent to the identity mapping, i.e.

$$f^{-1} \circ f = \mathrm{id}_{\mathbb{B}^n} \; .$$

If the check for identity holds, the considered function is reversible. Otherwise, it can be concluded that the considered function is not reversible.

However, while checking equivalence of two functions using their BDD representation is straight-forward, there are two main issues of this procedure that are non-trivial:

(1) how to create the inverse of f (especially: what if f is irreversible?) and
(2) how to perform the composition?

These issues will be addressed in the following.

5.2   Generating the Inverse Function

Unfortunately, an inverse *function* can only be constructed if the original function is reversible. To overcome this and to develop a procedure that can also be applied to irreversible functions, we consider the graph of the function, i.e. the underlying set relation, and perform the reversibility check at the level of relations (cf. Definition 3 from Sect. 2). Here, an inverse can easily be created by swapping the first and the second component of each pair.

Example 2. Consider the function $f \in \mathbb{B}_{2,2}$ shown in Fig. 1(a). The corresponding set relation $F \subset \mathbb{B}^2 \times \mathbb{B}^2$ is shown in Fig. 1(b) in terms of a complete list of related pairs. The inverse relation F^{-1} which is obtained by swapping the first and second component of each pair is shown in Fig. 1(c). Apparently, the composition $F^{-1} \circ F$ (as shown in Fig. 1(d)) is clearly different from the identity relation (as shown in Fig. 1(e)), since the pattern 10 is not only related to itself, but also to 11. Consequently, f is not reversible.

However, set relations are – in contrast to BDDs – not a very efficient representation of a function. But the same concept can similarly be applied to characteristic functions (cf. Definition 4 from Sect. 2) and, hence function representations for which BDDs are applicable.

x_1 x_2	f_1 f_2				
				$(00, 00)$	
				$(01, 01)$	
0 0	0 1	$(00, 01)$	$(01, 00)$	$(10, 10)$	$(00, 00)$
0 1	1 0	$(01, 10)$	$(10, 01)$	$(10, 11)$	$(01, 01)$
1 0	1 1	$(10, 11)$	$(11, 10)$	$(11, 10)$	$(10, 10)$
1 1	1 1	$(11, 11)$	$(11, 11)$	$(11, 11)$	$(11, 11)$
(a) f		(b) F	(c) F^{-1}	(d) $F^{-1} \circ F$	(e) id

Fig. 1. Set relations of Boolean functions

	Inputs			
	00	01	10	11
Outputs 00	0	0	0	0
01	1	0	0	0
10	0	1	0	0
11	0	0	1	1

(a) M_F

	Inputs			
	00	01	10	11
Outputs 00	0	1	0	0
01	0	0	1	0
10	0	0	0	1
11	0	0	0	1

(b) $M_{F^{-1}}$

Fig. 2. Matrix representations of characteristic functions.

Example 3. The characteristic function of a relation F, χ_F can be represented by a matrix M_F with entries $m_{ij} = \chi_F(i,j)$, i.e. the columns denote the possible input patterns and the rows denote the possible output patterns. Thus, a matrix entry is 1 if and only if the corresponding input pattern is related to the corresponding output pattern. The corresponding matrices for the relations from Fig. 1(b) and (c) are shown in Fig. 2(a) and (b), respectively. Note that the matrix for the inverse relation can be obtained by transposing the matrix M_F, i.e. $M_{F^{-1}} = M_F^T$.

Now, given χ_F, the representation for $\chi_{F^{-1}}$ can be obtained from the one for χ_F by simply swapping input and output variables and re-labelling the corresponding nodes. However, a multi-output Boolean function $f = (f_1, \ldots, f_n)$ is usually not given in terms of its characteristic function, but rather by a set (forest) of individual BDDs describing the component functions. Consequently, we have to compute χ_F as a pre-processing step in the first place. This is done by first computing the characteristic functions for the components $\chi_{F_i} = f_i \odot y_i$ (where $\odot$ denotes the XNOR-operation) and then combining these to $\chi_F = \chi_{F_1} \wedge \ldots \wedge \chi_{F_n}$.

5.3   Computing the Composition

Given the characteristic functions, χ_F and $\chi_{F^{-1}}$, we have to compute $\chi_{F^{-1} \circ F}$. In order to conduct this, we recall that the corresponding set relation is given by $F^{-1} \circ F = \{(x,y) \mid \exists z : (x,z) \in F \wedge (z,y) \in F^{-1}\}$. Returning to the level of characteristic functions, this translates to

$$\chi_{F^{-1} \circ F}(x,y) = \exists z : \chi_F(x,z) \wedge \chi_{F^{-1}}(z,y)$$

In order to construct this function, we use an (established) logic operation called *existential quantification*.

Definition 6. *Given $f \in \mathcal{B}_{n,m}$ over variables $x_1, \ldots, x_n$, we define the (Boolean) function $(\exists x_i : f) \in \mathcal{B}_{n-1,m}$ by $(\exists x_i : f) := f_{x_i=0} \vee f_{x_i=1}$, where $f_{x_i=0}$ and $f_{x_i=1}$ denote the co-factors of f restricted to the respective value of x_i. That means $(\exists x_i : f)$ evaluates to true for an input assignment $(x_1, \ldots, x_{i-1}, x_{i+1}, \ldots, x_n)$ if and only if x_i can be chosen such that $f(x_1, \ldots, x_{i-1}, x_i, x_{i+1}, \ldots, x_n) = 1$.*

This operation can be employed for our purpose of composing χ_F and $\chi_{F^{-1}}$ as follows: we define a (Boolean) helper function

$$H(x, y, z) = \chi_F(x, z) \wedge \chi_{F^{-1}}(z, y)$$

and can then obtain $\chi_{F^{-1} \circ F}$ by existentially quantifying z:

$$\chi_{F^{-1} \circ F} = (\exists z : H).$$

After this, the characteristic function for the identity function $id_{\mathbb{B}^n}$ has to be created. This can easily be done by constructing a BDD representing the function $\chi_{id} = x_1 \odot y_1 \wedge \ldots \wedge x_n \odot y_n$ (again, note that $\odot$ denotes the XNOR-operation). This states that $\chi_{id}(x, y) = 1$ if and only if $x = y$.

Finally, the resulting BDD representing $\chi_{F^{-1} \circ F}$ and the BDD representing χ_{id} have to be checked for equivalence. After constructing both BDDs this test can be performed in constant time. If both are equivalent, the considered function f is reversible. Otherwise, it has been shown that f is irreversible.

Another way to employ existential quantification for checking reversibility, as sketched in [19], is to quantify over all input variables of the characteristic function, i.e. to compute $\exists x : \chi_F$, which yields the disjunction of all output patterns. The resulting function is a tautology if and only if f is surjective/reversible. However, as existential quantification is the most expensive BDD operation used in the proposed flow, this alternative approach will not perform significantly different.

6 Checking for Reversibility Using Satisfiability Solvers

As an alternative to the BDD-based approach, we additionally propose a complementary solution to the problem considered in this work which is based on search methods. More precisely, solvers for the *Boolean satisfiability problem* (SAT problem) are utilized. In this section, we again sketch the general idea first before details on the implementation are provided.

6.1 General Idea

The SAT problem itself is simple to describe: For a given Boolean formula Φ, the SAT problem is about determining an assignment α to the variables of Φ such that $\Phi(\alpha)$ evaluates to true or to prove that no such assignment exists.

In the past years, tremendous improvements have been achieved in the development of corresponding solving engines (so-called SAT solvers). Instead of simply traversing the complete space of assignments, powerful techniques such as intelligent decision heuristics, conflict based learning schemes, and efficient implication methods e.g. through *Boolean Constraint Propagation* (BCP) are applied (see e.g. [7,9]). These techniques led to effective search procedures which can handle instances composed of thousands of variables and constraints. Furthermore, the SAT problem has been proven to be NP-complete [6], i.e. every problem in NP can be reduced in polynomial time to the SAT problem.

However, checking whether a given Boolean function is reversible does not obviously look like a satisfiability problem at a first glance: A certain property (namely unique output patterns) has to be checked *for all* possible input patterns. But this problem can easily be reformulated to a SAT problem: Instead of checking the uniqueness of all output patterns, we can negate the problem formulation and ask whether two input patterns *exist* which yield the same output pattern. This is a classical satisfiability problem.

Note that, by using this formulation, we are not considering the *REV*-problem (cf. Definition 5 in Sect. 4) anymore, but its negation (denoted by *NOTREV* in the following). Since *REV* is in coNP, the complementary problem *NOTREV* is in NP and, hence, can be solved as a SAT problem[4]. More formally, the following problem is left to be solved: Let $f \in \mathcal{B}_{n,n}$. Then, the SAT solver is asked for two patterns x, y, $x \neq y$ such that $f(x) = f(y)$ holds.

6.2   Implementation

In order to implement the proposed idea, the question "Do two input assignments $x, y \in \mathbb{B}^n$ exist so that $f(x) = f(y)$?" has to be formulated in terms of a SAT instance Φ which can be handled by corresponding solvers. Often, satisfiability solvers require the respectively given function Φ for which an assignment has to be determined in *Conjunctive Normal Form*, in *bit-vector logic*, or similar. In order to generate this formulation, the following steps have to be performed:

- *Introduce (SAT-)variables which symbolically represent all possible assignments:* A symbolic formulation for all possible assignments that have to be checked has to be created. In the problem considered here, this is accomplished by introducing a new free (Boolean) variable for each primary input, primary output, and internal signal of the considered function f. Since two different assignments are to be determined, all these variables have to be created twice (in the following distinguished between x-variables and y-variables). Figure 3(a) exemplary provides the respectively needed variables for checking the function $f = (a \wedge b) \oplus c$.
- *Introduce constraints in order to allow for valid solutions only:* Obviously, just passing the newly created variables to a solving engine does not lead to any useful result – without further constraints, the solver would just generate arbitrary assignments. Hence, in another step, constraints must be added which restrict the solving engine to determining *valid* solutions only. In the scenario considered here, this particularly includes constraints ensuring a valid input-output mapping of the considered function, i.e. depending on the representation of f, the internal signals and, by this, the primary outputs are restricted.

---

[4] A similar idea has been employed for equivalence checking in the domain of verification (see e.g. [1,4]). In our context, instead of two different functions, the same function is considered twice and, instead of applying the same pattern on both functions, we apply different patterns.

$$\begin{array}{c|cccccc} f & = & (a & \wedge & b) & \oplus & c \\ \hline \Phi_1 & x_6 & x_1 & x_4 & x_2 & x_5 & x_3 \\ \Phi_2 & y_6 & y_1 & y_4 & y_2 & y_5 & y_3 \end{array}$$

(a) Variables

$$\Phi_1 = ((x_4 = (x_1 \wedge x_2)) \wedge (x_5 = (x_4 \oplus x_3)) \wedge (x_6 = x_5))$$
$$\Phi_2 = ((y_4 = (y_1 \wedge y_2)) \wedge (y_5 = (y_4 \oplus y_3)) \wedge (y_6 = y_5))$$

(b) Constraints

$$\Phi_{obj} = ((x_1 \neq y_1) \vee (x_2 \neq y_2) \vee (x_3 \neq x_3)) \wedge (x_6 = y_6)$$

(c) Objective

Fig. 3. SAT formulation

This has to be done for both "copies" eventually leading to a sub-instance Φ_1 and a sub-instance Φ_2. This is illustrated in Fig. 3(b) for the function from above.

- *Employ the objective*: With the formulation thus far, a symbolic representation of the evaluation of the given function f for two arbitrary assignments is available. Finally, constraints have to be employed which enforce the considered objective. For the problem considered here, this includes constraints enforcing that both inputs are not equal, while their primary outputs must be equal (leading to a sub-instance Φ_{obj}). This is illustrated in Fig. 3(c) for the function from above.

Passing the conjunction of all sub-instances, i.e. $\Phi = \Phi_1 \wedge \Phi_2 \wedge \Phi_{obj}$, to a SAT solver, a satisfying assignment of the SAT variables is derived if indeed two input assignments exist for which f yields the same output. Then, these input assignments can be obtained from the solution determined by the SAT solver and serve as a witness for the non-reversibility. If in contrast the SAT solver proved that no satisfying assignment for the considered instance exists, it can be concluded that the function is reversible.

7 Experimental Evaluation

The approaches presented above provide non-trivial solutions to the coNP-complete problem of checking whether a given Boolean function is reversible. In order to evaluate how they eventually cope with the underlying complexity (as discussed in Sect. 4), both approaches have been implemented and thoroughly evaluated. In this section, we summarize and discuss the results of these evaluations.

7.1 Setup

The BDD-based approach from Sect. 5 and the SAT-based approach from Sect. 6 have been implemented in C/C++. To this end, *CUDD* [22] and *MiniSAT* [7] have been utilized as existing libraries for BDD construction and satisfiability solvers, respectively.

As benchmarks we considered functions from *RevLib* [26] and the well-known *LG-Synth* package. Since most of the functions are not reversible (particularly for large functions; see also the discussion of the obstacles for the design of these functions in Sect. 3), some irreversible functions have been made reversible using the implicit embedding from the BDD-based synthesis as proposed in [25]. More precisely, the originally given (irreversible) functions have been synthesized and, afterwards, functional descriptions have been derived from the resulting circuits using a restricted set of input/output mappings (ignoring constant inputs and garbage outputs). This way, a variety of reversible as well as irreversible functions of different sizes became available for evaluation.

Finally, all resulting functions have been processed with the implemented solutions. All experiments have been conducted on a 3 GHz Dual Opteron 2222 with 32 GB of main memory.

7.2   Results and Discussion

A selection of the obtained results are summarized in Table 1. The first columns provide the name of the respectively considered benchmarks (*Benchmark*), its number of inputs/outputs (n), as well as the desired information of whether it

Table 1. Experimental evaluation

Benchmark	n	REV?	BDD-based		SAT-based		
			Nodes	Time (s)	Vars	Clses	Time (s)
9sym	27	✓	16304	0.51	9731	8269	<0.01
9sym	9	✗	961	<0.01	353	545	<0.01
cordic	52	✓	31948	2.23	27601	20993	0.08
cordic	23	✗	2849	<0.01	879	1281	<0.01
revsyn_9sym	27	✓	233020	12.97	1929	1931	<0.01
revsyn_cordic	52	✓	$> 10^8$	>3600	1941	1573	<0.01
revsyn_xor5	6	✓	214	<0.01	161	109	<0.01
xor5	6	✓	178	<0.01	161	109	<0.01
xor5	5	✗	214	<0.01	123	185	<0.01
add64_184	193	✓	12606	0.53	7403	11171	0.02
add64_184	129	✗	$> 10^8$	>3600	4693	6743	0.01
bw	87	✓	$> 10^8$	>3600	13345	9417	0.03
bw	28	✗	12480	16.23	3143	3493	<0.01
dk17_224	21	✓	7544	0.08	1449	2077	<0.01
in0_235	26	✓	26246	1.15	6427	10019	<0.01
in0_235	15	✗	361	<0.01	299	271	<0.01

is reversible or not (denoted by ✓and ✗, respectively, in column *REV?*). Afterwards, the results obtained by the proposed approaches are summarized. Since both always provided the correct result on whether the function is reversible, only performance values are listed: For the BDD-based approach, the maximum number of nodes required to represent the (characteristic) function (*Nodes*) is given, while, for the SAT-based approach, the number of variables (*Vars*) and clauses (*Clses*) required to formulate the corresponding satisfiability problem is given. For both approaches additionally the required run-time (*Time*, in CPU seconds) is provided.

The results clearly show that both approaches are successful in efficiently solving the considered problem. Considering the coNP-hardness of the task, functions composed of more than 100 variables (constituting one of the largest functions currently considered in the design of reversible circuits and systems) can be handled quite efficiently.

Comparing both (complementary) solutions against each other, it is obvious that the SAT-based approach performs significantly better than the BDD-based approach. This can be explained by the "memory explosion" of the BDD representation. In fact, BDDs are known for their efficient representation of Boolean functions, but eventually require exponential space in the worst case. In the scenario considered here, this worst case is often approached because characteristic functions are considered. Building these often requires the BDD package to fold up the entire functionality before reductions e.g. due to sharing can be exploited. This obviously harms the efficiency of the approach.

In contrast, the SAT-based approach can handle the respective search space in a more efficient fashion. Even for larger functions, always negligible run-time is required. Hence, the SAT-based solution clearly constitutes itself as a very efficient solution for checking the reversibility of a given function.

8   Conclusions

In this work, we considered how to check whether a given function is reversible. Although never explicitly considered thus far, the absence of corresponding solutions constitutes a major obstacle in the design of reversible circuits and systems. We proved that the underlying problem is coNP-complete and proposed two complementary approaches addressing it – one based on decision diagrams and another exploiting satisfiability solvers. The experimental evaluation showed that, despite the complexity, both solutions can handle the problem. In fact, the SAT-based solution is even capable of solving the task in negligible run-time even for some of the largest functions considered in the design of reversible circuits and systems thus far.

Acknowledgments. This work has partially been supported by the EU COST Action IC1405.

References

1. Amarú, L., Gaillardon, P.E., Wille, R., De Micheli, G.: Exploiting inherent characteristics of reversible circuits for faster combinational equivalence checking. In: Design, Automation and Test in Europe (2016, to appear)
2. Athas, W., Svensson, L.: Reversible logic issues in adiabatic CMOS. In: Proceedings of Workshop on Physics and Computation PhysComp 1994, pp. 111–118 (1994)
3. Berut, A., Arakelyan, A., Petrosyan, A., Ciliberto, S., Dillenschneider, R., Lutz, E.: Experimental verification of Landauer's principle linking information and thermodynamics. Nature **483**, 187–189 (2012)
4. Brand, D.: Verification of large synthesized designs. In: International Conference on CAD, pp. 534–537 (1993)
5. Bryant, R.E.: Graph-based algorithms for Boolean function manipulation. IEEE Trans. Comp. **35**(8), 677–691 (1986)
6. Cook, S.: The complexity of theorem-proving procedures. In: Symposium on Theory of Computing, pp. 151–158. ACM (1971). http://doi.acm.org/10.1145/800157.805047
7. Eén, N., Sörensson, N.: An extensible SAT-solver. In: Giunchiglia, E., Tacchella, A. (eds.) SAT 2003. LNCS, vol. 2919, pp. 502–518. Springer, Heidelberg (2004)
8. Fazel, K., Thornton, M., Rice, J.: ESOP-based Toffoli gate cascade generation. In: IEEE Pacific Rim Conference on Communications, Computers and Signal Processing (PacRim 2007), pp. 206–209. IEEE (2007)
9. Gebser, M., Kaufmann, B., Neumann, A., Schaub, T.: Conflict-driven answer set solving. In: International Joint Conference on Artificial Intelligence, pp. 386–392 (2007)
10. Große, D., Wille, R., Dueck, G.W., Drechsler, R.: Exact multiple control Toffoli network synthesis with SAT techniques. IEEE Trans. CAD **28**(5), 703–715 (2009)
11. Grover, L.K.: A fast quantum mechanical algorithm for database search. In: Theory of Computing, pp. 212–219 (1996)
12. Houri, S., Valentian, A., Fanet, H.: Comparing CMOS-based and NEMS-based adiabatic logic circuits. In: Dueck, G.W., Miller, D.M. (eds.) RC 2013. LNCS, vol. 7948, pp. 36–45. Springer, Heidelberg (2013)
13. Merkle, R.C.: Reversible electronic logic using switches. Nanotechnology **4**(1), 21–40 (1993)
14. Miller, D.M., Maslov, D., Dueck, G.W.: A transformation based algorithm for reversible logic synthesis. In: Design Automation Confernce, pp. 318–323 (2003)
15. Nielsen, M., Chuang, I.: Quantum Computation and Quantum Information. Cambridge University Press, Cambridge (2000)
16. Ren, J., Semenov, V., Polyakov, Y., Averin, D., Tsai, J.S.: Progress towards reversible computing with nSQUID arrays. IEEE Trans. Appl. Supercond. **19**(3), 961–967 (2009)
17. Saeedi, M., Zamani, M.S., Sedighi, M., Sasanian, Z.: Synthesis of reversible circuit using cycle-based approach. J. Emerg. Technol. Comput. Syst. **6**(4), 1–26 (2010)
18. Shor, P.W.: Algorithms for quantum computation: discrete logarithms and factoring. Foundations of Computer Science, pp. 124–134 (1994)
19. Soeken, M., Tague, L., Dueck, G.W., Drechsler, R.: Ancilla-free synthesis of large reversible functions using binary decision diagrams. J. Symb. Comput. **73**, 41: 1–41: 26 (2016). http://dx.doi.org/10.1016/j.jsc.2015.03.002
20. Soeken, M., Wille, R., Hilken, C., Przigoda, N., Drechsler, R.: Synthesis of reversible circuits with minimal lines for large functions. In: ASP Design Automation Conference, pp. 85–92 (2012)

21. Soeken, M., Wille, R., Keszocze, O., Miller, D.M., Drechsler, R.: Embedding of large Boolean functions for reversible logic. J. Emerg. Technol. Comput. Syst. **12**(4), 1–26 (2015). http://doi.acm.org/10.1145/2786982

22. Somenzi, F.: Efficient manipulation of decision diagrams. Softw. Tools Technol. Transf. **3**(2), 171–181 (2001)

23. Thomsen, M.K.: Describing and optimising reversible logic using a functional language. In: Gill, A., Hage, J. (eds.) IFL 2011. LNCS, vol. 7257, pp. 148–163. Springer, Heidelberg (2012)

24. Toffoli, T.: Reversible computing. In: de Bakker, W., van Leeuwen, J. (eds.) Automata, Languages and Programming. LNCS, vol. 85, pp. 632–644. Springer, Heidelberg (1980)

25. Wille, R., Drechsler, R.: BDD-based synthesis of reversible logic for large functions. In: Design Automation Conference, pp. 270–275 (2009)

26. Wille, R., Große, D., Teuber, L., Dueck, G.W., Drechsler, R.: RevLib: an online resource for reversible functions and reversible circuits. In: International Symposyum on Multi-Valued Logic, pp. 220–225 (2008). http://www.revlib.org

27. Wille, R., Keszöcze, O., Drechsler, R.: Determining the minimal number of lines for large reversible circuits. In: Design, Automation and Test in Europe, pp. 1204–1207. IEEE (2011)

28. Wille, R., Drechsler, R., Osewold, C., Garcia-Ortiz, A.: Automatic design of low-power encoders using reversible circuit synthesis. In: Design, Automation and Test in Europe, pp. 1036–1041. IEEE (2012)

Author Index

Printed in the United States
By Bookmasters